PENGUIN REFERENCE

The Penguin Dictionary of English Idioms

Daphne Gulland was born in 1953. She was educated at Fidelis Grammar School in London. In 1975 she graduated with Honours in English and German at Bedford College, University of London. For many years she has been engaged in research into the origins of the most common idioms in the language, breaking new ground with her system of categorization for *The Penguin Dictionary of English Idioms*. She is married with four children. Her hobbies are gardening, walking, reading and history.

David Hinds-Howell was born in 1916. He was educated at Marlborough College, and obtained a Master of Arts degree in philosophy, politics and economics at Oxford University in 1938. After practising as a barrister, he had a long and distinguished career as director of the Hillcrest School of English (1952–81) and as a teacher of English at advanced and intermediate level. He died in 1995.

save my bacon   save my trouble.

out to lunch

The Penguin Dictionary of

English Idioms

Daphne M. Gulland
David Hinds-Howell

SECOND EDITION

PENGUIN BOOKS

PENGUIN BOOKS

Published by the Penguin Group
Penguin Books Ltd, 80 Strand, London WC2R 0RL, England
Penguin Putnam Inc., 375 Hudson Street, New York, New York 10014, USA
Penguin Books Australia Ltd, 250 Camberwell Road, Camberwell, Victoria 3124, Australia
Penguin Books Canada Ltd, 10 Alcorn Avenue, Toronto, Ontario, Canada M4V 3B2
Penguin Books India (P) Ltd, 11, Community Centre, Panchsheel Park, New Delhi – 110 017, India
Penguin Books (NZ) Ltd, Cnr Rosedale and Airborne Roads, Albany, Auckland, New Zealand
Penguin Books (South Africa) (Pty) Ltd, 24 Sturdee Avenue, Rosebank 2196, South Africa

Penguin Books Ltd, Registered Offices: 80 Strand, London WC2R 0RL, England

www.penguin.com

First published 1986
Reprinted with revisions and an additional category 1994
Second edition 2001
Reprinted with amended index 2002
3

Copyright © Daphne M. Gulland and David Hinds-Howell, 1986, 1994
Second edition © Daphne M. Gulland, 2001
All rights reserved

The moral right of the authors has been asserted

Set in ITC Stone
Typeset by Rowland Phototypesetting Ltd, Bury St Edmunds, Suffolk
Printed in England by Clays Ltd, St Ives plc

The Penguin Dictionary of English Idioms will be of absorbing interest to foreign and native speakers of English alike. Its aims are twofold: to provide a wide selection of the most commonly used idiomatic phrases in the English language; and, with the help of copious examples taken from real life, to offer guidance on the most effective way to use them.

The English language is rich in idioms, and though it is possible to converse correctly in non-idiomatic English, students with only a superficial knowledge of English idioms will find themselves at a serious disadvantage in their reading, and even more so when they take part in discussions and debates. Finding idioms in a general dictionary is a slow and laborious task, so it is hoped that this dictionary of idioms will provide assistance in a practical and interesting way.

What then is an idiom? We would define an idiom as a combination of words with a special meaning that cannot be inferred from its separate parts. The examples that follow will help to make the matter clear:

1. 'John couldn't say boo to a goose!' On the face of it, this is a very strange thing to say. Of course it is quite possible to say boo to a goose, but who would want to do such a thing? However, the statement has an idiomatic meaning, namely that John is so timid that he wouldn't dare to make even the mildest protest, however badly he was treated. Clearly, it is impossible to deduce this meaning from the separate words in the sentence above. In other words, the meaning of the whole is different from the parts. The sentence then has two meanings – a literal meaning which means very little, and a metaphorical one which is the idiom.
2. 'Shall we go Dutch?' Unlike the first example, this one has no literal meaning at all, only an idiomatic one: 'I suggest that you pay for your meal, and I'll pay for mine?' Again, it is impossible to infer the meaning of the idiom from the separate words in the question.

Every idiom belongs either to the first group or to the second as described above.

Traditionally, dictionaries of idioms present idiomatic expressions in alphabetical order; but we believe that the aims we have set ourselves can be achieved more efficiently by categorizing idioms, i.e. by grouping them round a limited number of key-words and putting them in the appropriate categories. For example, the first category, Colours (see the list of Categories on page ix), contains 13 different colours: red, blue, green, yellow, white, white and black, black, brown, grey, purple, pink, golden and silver. Each of these colours (key-words) is used to make up an idiom or idioms in the form of an entry that may contain variations (e.g. 'red-letter moment' under 'red-letter day'). The key-word 'red', for instance, is included in 15 idioms (or entries), as in 'to paint the town red', 'a red rag to a bull', 'to see red', and so on. All the 'red' idioms make up a group. 'Colours' itself, the name of the category, makes up a group of 19 idioms, as in 'to see someone in his true colours', 'with flying colours', and so on. The total number of groups make up the complete category with altogether 170 idioms. The same principle applies to the remaining 33 categories.

Categorizing idioms in this way has a number of important advantages over the alphabetical system. First, idioms that include the same key-word will be concentrated in greater numbers than is possible with the alphabetical system. For instance, there are 34 idioms in the 'dog' group, 86 idioms in the 'hand' and 49 in the 'heart' groups. With idioms concentrated in such large numbers, the reader is in a position to make a systematic study of all the idioms in a given group, and to compare and distinguish them in a way that would not be possible were they scattered over a whole dictionary. Secondly, categorizing makes it possible to introduce idioms in a coherent, logical order instead of the arbitrary, inconsequential order of the alphabet; and this makes for more interesting reading for students who like to browse through a dictionary. Finally, the use of categories will enable students to complete their study of a selected category with the minimum of effort, since all the items in which they are interested have already been assembled for them. Students are, of course, free to start wherever they wish. As they proceed through this *Dictionary*, category by category, they will find their knowledge of idioms growing until finally they have acquired a mastery of the subject.

How to Use the Index

We have provided an Index of idioms at the back of the *Dictionary*. The order of the idioms in the Index is strictly alphabetical. When you look an idiom up in the Index, look for it first under the noun, if there is one. If there are two or more nouns, look for the idiom under the first noun. If there are no nouns, then look for it under the first verb; if there is no verb, then under the first adjective.

Please note that if the idiom has two nouns standing next to each other, it will be indexed under both nouns, even if the first noun is a possessive, e.g. 'the lion's share' will be indexed under both 'lion's', and 'share'. Also note that idioms are not indexed under pronouns, e.g. 'one', 'someone', 'anyone', 'oneself', 'himself', etc., or the verbs 'to be' or 'to have'.

Every idiom has a reference consisting of two numbers divided by a stroke, e.g. **000/ 0**. The first number of the pair, **000**, refers to the page on which the idiom you are looking for appears; the second number, **0**, refers to the actual idiom: 'to be too big for one's boots'. Here are some more idioms for you to look up, followed by the correct answers which you can check for yourself:

1. 'to sail against the wind'. There is one noun in this idiom, namely 'wind', so it will appear under 'wind' with the reference number **204/7**.
2. 'to pull the rug from under one's feet'. There are two nouns in this idiom, so it will be indexed under the first noun of the two, 'rug', with the reference number **167/13**.
3. 'to read the riot act'. In this idiom there are two nouns, 'riot' and 'act', that stand next to each other. The idiom can therefore be found in the Index under either of them. The reference number for this idiom is **277/11**.
4. 'at arm's length'. There are two nouns in this phrase, one next to the other, so this idiom can be found in the Index under 'arm's' (a possessive) or 'length', with the reference number **95/19**.
5. 'to do someone proud'. There is no noun here, but there is the verb 'to do', so this idiom will appear under 'do' in the Index with the reference number **123/13**.
6. 'fair, fat and forty'. As this phrase contains no noun or verb, it will appear under an adjective.

There are, however, three adjectives, so, according to our rule, the phrase will appear under the first adjective, 'fair', with the reference number **261/19**.

7. 'nobody's poodle'. 'Nobody' is a pronoun (which we have excluded) so the idiom will appear under 'poodle' which has the reference number **54/10**.

A number of variations on the idioms are listed in the Index; these appear immediately under the appropriate entry in the text. The only variations excluded from the Index are those examples of usage listed after a 'frequent usage' heading within an entry.

When an idiom bears a close relation to one in a different category, it is given a cross-reference at the end of the note and readers can follow this up, if they wish, for further information. Apart from this, no cross-references are used and, once readers have obtained the reference number of the idiom they are looking for from the Index, they can be sure of finding the idiom required without being referred to other parts of the *Dictionary*.

I have updated this second edition by adding some 2,000 new idioms and leaving out those which are no longer frequently used. I hope you will continue to enjoy learning and using these idioms.

Daphne Gulland
2001

1. *Colours* **1**
Colours **1**; Red **2**; Blue **3**; Green **4**; Yellow **5**; White **5**; White and Black **6**; Black **7**; Brown **8**; Grey **8**; Purple **9**; Pink **9**; Golden **9**; Silver **10**.

2. *Elements* **11**
Element **11**; Air **11**; Space **12**; Water **12**; Tide **13**; Wave **13**; Ebb **13**; Flow **14**; Drift **14**; Flood **14**; Fire **14**; Flame **15**; Smoke **15**; Soot **15**; Earth **16**; Rift, Abyss, Edge **16**; Cliff, Rocks **16**; Ground **17**; Dirt, Muck, Dust **17**; Mud, Bog **18**; Lead **18**; Iron **18**; Flint, Granite **18**.

3. *Weather* **19**
Weather **19**; Rain **19**; Snow **20**; Ice **20**; Cold **20**; Cool **20**; Chill **21**; Shivers **21**; Fog **21**; Ray **21**; Hot **21**; Heat **21**; Rainbow **21**; Cloud **21**; Squalls **22**; Wind, Whirlwind **22**; Storm **23**; Thunder **24**; Lightning **24**; Blitz **24**; Sky **24**; Horizon **24**; Sun, Sunny **24**; Moon, Moonlight **24**; Star, Meteor **25**; Shade, Shadow **25**; Light **25**; Dark **26**.

4. *Time* **27**
Time **27**; Year **29**; Season **30**; The Seasons: Spring, Summer, Autumn **30**; Months: April, May **30**; Days of the Week: Monday, Friday, Sunday **30**; Day **30**; Daylight **32**; Yesterday **32**; Night **32**; Morning **32**; Hour **32**; Moment **33**; Second **33**; Age **33**; Date **34**; Clock **34**; By-gones **34**.

5. *Life and Death* **35**
Life **35**; Live, Living **36**; Existence **37**; Death **37**; Die **38**; Dead **39**; Grave, Graveyard **39**; Shroud, Pall **40**; Ghost **40**; Spirit **40**; Fortune **40**; Fate **41**; Miracle **41**; Holy Grail **41**; Halo **41**; Mantra **41**; Idol **41**; Icon **42**; Heaven, Nirvana **42**; God **42**; Angel **43**; Soul **43**; Charm **43**; Doom **43**; Damned **43**; Disaster **43**; Dire Straits **44**; Sin **44**; Hell **44**; Devil **44**; Demon **45**.

6. *Trees and Plants* **46**
Flowers **46**; Rose **46**; Other Flowers and Plants **46**; The Garden **47**; Thorn **47**; The Farm **47**; Hay **48**; Straw **48**; Cud, Seed, Grain **48**; Grass, Reeds, Weeds **48**; Roots **49**; Trees **49**; Bush, Hedge **50**; Wood **50**; Log, Branch **50**; Stick **51**; Leaf **51**; Rot **51**.

7. *Animals* 52

Animal **52**; Creature **52**; Beast **52**; Pet **52**; Dog **52**; Poodle, Spaniel **54**; Pup **54**; Tail **54**; Cat **55**; Kitten **56**; Pussy **56**; Horse **56**; Mare, Ass, Mule, Donkey **57**; Cow, Bull, Calf **58**; Sheep, Lamb **58**; Goat **59**; Pig, Guinea-pig **59**; Sow, Swine, Hog **59**; Mouse **60**; Rat, Lemming, Squirrel **60**; Rabbit, Hare **60**; Fox, Wolf **61**; Hyena **61**; Stag, Doe **61**; Beaver, Badger, Ferret, Weasel **61**; Opossum **62**; Hedgehog, Mole **62**; Bat **62**; Chameleon **62**; Frog **62**; Snake **62**; Turtle **62**; Whale **63**; Dragon, Lizard **63**; Crocodile **63**; Rhinoceros, Elephant **63**; Camel **63**; Kangaroo **63**; Monkey, Ape **64**; Lynx, Leopard **64**; Lion **64**; Tiger **64**; Bear **65**.

8. *Birds* 66

Bird **66**; Feather, Hackles, Wing **67**; Nest, Roost **67**; Robin, Lark **67**; Jay, Magpie, Cuckoo **68**; Crow **68**; Pigeon, Dove **68**; Hen **68**; Cock **68**; Chicken **69**; Duck **69**; Goose, Swan **70**; Turkey **70**; Stormy Petrel, Coot, Albatross **70**; Kingfisher **71**; Parrot, Canary **71**; Peacock, Phoenix, Dodo **71**; Owl **71**; Hawk, Eagle **71**; Vulture **72**; Ostrich **72**.

9. *Fish* 73

Fish **73**; Mackerel **74**; Herring **74**; Eel **74**; Sardines **74**; Fry **74**; Caviare **74**; Oyster **74**; Whelk **75**; Clam **75**; Limpet **75**; Crab **75**; Shark **75**.

10. *Insects* 76

Worm **76**; Spider **76**; Fly **76**; Grasshopper, Butterfly, Moth **77**; Bee, Drone, Wasp **77**; Bug **78**; Flea, Nit, Leech **78**; Stick Insect **78**; Snail **78**; Cricket **78**; Locust **78**; Pest **79**; Feelers **79**.

11. *Body* 80

Body **80**; Figure **80**; Head **80**; Hair **83**; Face **84**; Eye **86**; Eyelid **88**; Eyebrow **88**; Nose **88**; Ear **89**; Mouth **90**; Jaw **91**; Whisker **91**; Lip **91**; Tooth **92**; Teeth **92**; Tongue **93**; Throat **93**; Cheek **94**; Chin **94**; Neck **94**; Shoulder **95**; Arm **95**; Elbow **96**; Wrist **96**; Hand **96**; Palm **100**; Fist **101**; Thumb **101**; Finger **101**; Quick **102**; Knuckle **102**; Chest **103**; Breast **103**; Bosom **103**; Belly **103**; Navel **103**; Lap **103**; Back **103**; Spine **104**; Bottom **104**; Leg **105**; Knee **105**; Foot **105**; Feet **106**; Heel **108**; Toe **108**; Brain **108**; Nerve **109**; Vein **110**; Flesh **110**; Skin **110**; Bone **111**; Skeleton **112**; Breath **112**; Marrow **112**; Sinew **112**; Limb **112**; Muscle **113**; Blood **113**; Heart **114**; Stomach **116**; Gall **117**; Bile **117**; Spleen **117**; Gut **117**; Liver **117**.

12. *Mind* 118

Mind **118**; Mental **120**; Think **120**; Wits **120**; Sense, Senses **120**; Touch, Sight **121**; Reason **121**; Conscience **122**; Moral, Err, Fault **122**; Blame, Lie **122**; Character **122**; Purpose, Desire, Willing, Will **122**; Wise, Wiser **123**; Courage, Bold, Virtue **123**; Kindness, Kindly, Generous **123**; Proud, Pride **123**; Cruel, Mercies, Pity **124**; Grace **124**; Patience, Faith, Charity **124**; Happy, Humour, Laugh **124**; Bored, Sleep **125**; Fancy, Dream, Nightmare **125**; Love **126**; Kiss **126**; Hate, Fury, Rage **126**; Row, Annoyance **127**; Shouting **127**; Shame, Crying, Doubt **127**; Fear, Afraid, Scare, Horror **127**; Nervousness, Breakdown **128**; Sorrow, Grief, Misery, Tears **128**; Suffer, Woe, Throes **129**; Ill-will, Ill at Ease **129**; Dumps, Damper **129**; Joy, Hope **129**; Feel, Feelings **130**.

33. *Music and the Theatre* **315**

34. *Word and Words* **323**

Colours

1. **to see someone in his true colours** – to understand someone's true character, often for the first time. 'As soon as he made a fuss about returning her money, I saw him in his true colours.'
    to show oneself in one's true colours – to reveal one's true nature. 'When he lost his temper, he showed himself in his true colours.'

2. **to give/lend colour to** – to make (an account, story, explanation, etc.) more credible or more plausible. 'The broken window on the ground floor lent colour to Mrs Brown's story that her house had been burgled.'

3. **to add a splash of colour to something** – to brighten up, enliven by contrast. 'Those yellow roses you planted there add a splash of colour to the brown fence.'

4. **with flying colours** – with great success, with distinction. 'We were all expecting him to fail, but he passed with flying colours.'

5. **to sail under false colours** – to assume a false identity in order to conceal one's true purpose.

6. **to paint in bright/dark colours** – to describe something in a flattering or unflattering way. 'My brother wanted us all to emigrate to America and painted his life there in the brightest colours.'

7. **to win one's colours** – to win recognition for one's achievements. 'The young minister won his colours with a brilliant defence of the government's policy.' Literally, to win a place in one's school or college team, which entitles one to wear the school or college colours. cf. **'to win one's spurs' 305/14**.

8. **to nail (one's) colours to the mast** – to make absolutely clear what one's views are in a very forthright manner. 'Now he has nailed his colours to the mast, he cannot change his mind.'

9. **to be called to the colours** – to be conscripted into the army.

10. **to look through rose-coloured/tinted spectacles** – to see things in a flattering or over-optimistic light. 'Anne always enjoys her visits because she sees everything through rose-coloured spectacles, but she would feel differently if she had to live there.'

11. **to be colourless** – to lack personality, to be uninteresting or nondescript. 'We talked for over half an hour together, but nothing that he said stands out in my memory. I'm afraid he's a dull, colourless man.'

12. **to be colourful** – to be vivid, full of life. Frequent usage: **a colourful character**; **to have a colourful past** – a rather scandalous past.

13. **to be off colour** – to be not quite at one's best, to feel queasy or slightly ill. 'She's a little off colour today; she was up very late last night and may have had a little too much to drink!'

14. **under colour of** – in the guise of, under the pretext of. 'Under colour of consulting the kidney specialist, the newspaper man wormed a lot of information out of him for the television programme.'

1. **local colour** – background information about a place or event.

2. **to have one's views coloured by** – to have one's ideas and opinions changed by external influences. 'Like everyone else, his views were coloured by his background and upbringing.'

3. **to see the colour of (someone's) money** – to take some money in advance before parting with one's goods or services.

4. **colour bar** – discrimination against black and coloured people in favour of the whites, legally, socially or economically.

5. **a highly coloured report** – a report that is exaggerated or biased.

Red

6. Similes with 'red': **as red as a tomato**; **as red as a turkey-cock; as red as a lobster; as red as a rose; as red as fire; blood-red; ruby-red**.

7. **to catch someone red-handed** – to catch someone in the act of committing a crime, usually a theft. 'Caught you red-handed! I saw you take the money out of the box.' The reference is to the blood still on the hands of the criminal after stabbing his victim to death. The phrase is used now for less serious crimes.

8. **red-blooded** – of passionate young men. 'When the stunningly beautiful pop singer dropped her boyfriend, thousands of red-blooded males wrote her love letters.' cf. **'blue blood / blue-blooded' 4/2**.

9. **to paint the town red** (of US origin) – to celebrate by running wild, drinking and making a commotion. 'Richard has passed his exam. We are going to paint the town red tonight, so don't be surprised if we come home very late.'

10. **like painting a dead man's face red** – to conceal the truth. 'Giving the impression that the disgraced minister doesn't want to make a come-back is like painting a dead man's face red.' A dead man's face is white because the heart is no longer pumping blood around the body. By painting his face red, he would be given the appearance of still being alive, thus concealing the truth.

11. **a red rag to a bull** – a source of violent anger to someone. 'Mention of animal experiments was like a red rag to a bull to the anti-vivisectionist.' The phrase originated in the belief that any red-coloured object will infuriate a bull.
    like a red rag to someone – has the same meaning. 'Property developers were like a red rag to the Prime Minister.'

12. **reds under the bed** – the reds are everywhere. An ironic allusion to the obsession some people have that there are reds (communists) everywhere, plotting violent revolution.

13. **red in tooth and claw** – a violent revolutionary who shows no mercy and makes no compromises. Originally used as a description of nature: 'Nature, red in tooth and claw' (Alfred Lord Tennyson, *In Memoriam*, Part LVI, Stanza 4).

14. **to see red** – to react with uncontrollable rage against an object of one's hatred. The object is usually a stereotype, e.g. civil servants, businessmen, Jews, blacks. 'The sight of demonstrators marching past his house made Stephen see red.' The idiom originated in the idea that red symbolizes both violent revolution and the colour of blood; however, it has shed its political motivation and is associated now with any person or thing that excites strong disapproval.

15. **red tape** – bureaucratic delay, excessive attention to rules and regulations, often resulting in injustice to the ordinary citizen. The 'red tape' is the red ribbon with which the civil servant ties his or her papers together. 'Many small shops are closing down as they cannot keep up with all the red tape.' Frequent usage: **to choke on red tape; to be swamped by red tape; try to untangle red tape; a mountain of red tape**.

16. **a red-letter day** – a day of special importance, e.g. a wedding, the celebration of a victory or the receiving of a great honour. The phrase originates in the custom of recording saints' days and holidays on cal-

endars in red ink. Also: **a red-letter moment**.

1. **the red-light district** – that part of the town which is given over to brothels and prostitution. The red light over the front door advertises the presence of prostitutes in the house.

2. **to see the red light** – to recognize approaching danger, the red light being a danger signal. 'When the doctor warned her patient that further drinking would damage his liver, the man saw the red light.' The phrase usually implies that the warning was heeded.

3. **to be shown the red card** – to be dismissed from one's job. 'The accountant was shown the red card for defrauding the company.' The phrase derives from football: a footballer is shown the red card by the referee for committing an offence after he has been warned and may be barred from playing for his side in future matches. cf. **'to be shown the yellow card'** 5/9.

4. **to be in the red** – to have an overdraft, to be in debt. 'Oh dear, I am overdrawn again. I hate being in the red.' The idiom originated in the banks' custom of showing the amount overdrawn in red type. Overdrafts are shown in black today. cf. **'to be in the black'** 8/2.

Blue

5. Similes with 'blue': **ice-blue** – a very pale blue; **indigo-blue**; **cornflower-blue**; **china-blue**; **sea-blue**; **violet-blue**; **cobalt-blue**; **postcard-blue** – meaning the blue sky on a sunny day.

6. **to blue one's money** – spend money wildly. 'Peter has blued all the money you gave him on gambling and drink.'

7. **to look/feel blue** – to look/feel depressed or discontented. 'Now my girlfriend has left me, things are looking blue.' Blue is associated with gloom and depression in such expressions as having the blues, feeling blue, a fit of the blues.

   winter blues – depression caused by lack of sunshine. 'I wish I could live in the south of Spain. Then I would never have

to suffer the winter blues.' **baby blues** – a mother's post-natal depression.

8. **once in a blue moon** – extremely rarely, only once in a life-time. 'What does it matter what your uncle thinks of you? He only visits you once in a blue moon.'

9. **to appear out of the blue** – to arrive unexpectedly, usually after a long absence. 'My brother suddenly appeared out of the blue yesterday. We hadn't seen him for years and had given him up for dead.'

   a bolt from the blue – some unexpected bad news. 'We had no idea that their marriage was breaking up. The news came like a bolt from the blue.' A bolt was originally an arrow from a cross-bow, and is probably derived from Latin *catapulta*. 'Out of the blue' meant out of a blue sky; hence a blow struck without warning.

10. **to make the air turn blue** – to give vent to one's rage by swearing violently. 'When the engineer heard that his plans had been rejected, he fairly made the air turn blue.'

11. **to shout/scream blue murder** – to protest most violently at an injustice. 'If you take away the baby's toy, he'll shout blue murder.'

12. **to talk, argue, complain, protest, etc., until you are blue in the face** – to make a huge but vain effort to win a person's agreement. 'You can argue with Harry until you are blue in the face, but you will never get him to change his mind.' 'Until you are blue in the face' means 'for ever'. cf. **'till the cows come home'** 58/4.

13. **blue riband/ribbon** – the blue riband was an accolade awarded to the ship that made the fastest crossing of the Atlantic. Riband and ribbon are etymologically the same word.

14. **a blue-stocking** – a woman who is more interested in learning and an academic career than in marriage and bringing up children. 'I don't want to go out with that blue stocking. She is only interested in books!' The phrase has a derogatory meaning and dates back to the 1750s, when Mrs Montagu gave parties for literary

reading and discussions instead of card-playing. These parties were also attended by men, who wore blue worsted stockings instead of black silk ones.

1. **a blue-collar worker** – a manual or factory worker who wears overalls. cf. '**a white-collar worker**' 6/16.

2. **blue blood / blue-blooded** – of the nobility or aristocracy. The phrase is of Spanish origin. cf. '**red-blooded**' 2/7.

3. **men/boys in blue** – the police, from the colour of their uniform.
   the thin blue line against crime – the image of a line of policemen standing together to fight crime.

4. **a blue-eyed boy** – a boy/young man who has been singled out for special favours by someone in authority. Derogatory, since it implies that he has won favour by flattery and tale-bearing. 'Roger is Smith's blue-eyed boy; he can do no wrong.'

5. **a true blue** – one whose loyalty can always be counted on.
   a true blue Conservative – a person who holds strong Conservative convictions.

6. **the blue-rinse brigade** – elderly Conservative women who give their white or grey hair a bluish tint.

7. **to be a blue / get one's blue** – to represent Oxford or Cambridge University at games or sports. Dark blue stands for Oxford, and light blue for Cambridge.

8. **a blueprint** – a detailed plan or drawing of a proposed development or idea. 'Often ministers are hesitant about publishing blueprints on controversial subjects.'

9. **to blue pencil** – to censor. 'Most of my report on the treatment of the political prisoners was blue pencilled by the authorities.'

10. **blue ice** – glacier-formed ice which is clean and compact. 'The explorer discovered a skeleton which had probably lain in the blue ice of the Arctic for five thousand years.'

11. **a blue film** – a pornographic film, so called after the brothels of pre-revolutionary China which were painted blue outside to advertise the presence of prostitutes within.
    a blue joke – an indecent joke.

12. **blue chips / shares in a blue-chip company** – shares considered reliable and safe (usually industrial shares); generally said of something renowned and reputable. 'Amanda's uncle invests solely in blue chips. No wonder he is so rich!' Also: **blue-chip clients**.

Green

13. **to be green** – to be inexperienced or untried, from which comes the phrase '**to be as green as grass**' – to be naïve, totally inexperienced in the ways of the world. 'You cannot expect Mary to do business with such people. She is only 18 and as green as grass.'

14. **to be green with envy** – to feel extremely envious. 'If you buy that car, you'll make your friends green with envy.' At one time, a greenish complexion was believed to indicate jealousy. Shakespeare expresses the same idea in *Othello*: 'Beware of jealousy, it is a green-eyed monster' (III, iii, 165).

15. **to have green fingers** – to be blessed with luck in the growing of plants and flowers. 'She has green fingers! Everything she plants turns out well.'

16. **a green old age** (literary) – an old age in which a person's mental and physical powers are still strong and vigorous. 'I hope she will live to a green old age.' cf. '**a ripe old age**' 33/12.

17. **to give the green light to** – to give permission to go ahead; to encourage or approve an enterprise. 'The boss has given us the green light. We can make a start on the project straight away.'

18. **the grass might be greener somewhere else** – it might be better to start life afresh in more favourable surroundings. 'Guess what! Melanie thinks the grass might be greener with her new boyfriend and has gone with him to Majorca!' Note the saying 'The grass is always greener on the other side of the fence' – some people are never satisfied; which-

ever choice is made, then the disregarded option would appear to have proved better.

1. **to go green** – to switch to a diet of mostly vegetables, fruit and pulses, eating organic food. Also to adopt a certain sort of lifestyle – walking and cycling instead of going for short journeys by car; creating a non-toxic home, using natural, biodegradable products, not wasting water, and sorting out one's rubbish very carefully for recycling bins. 'Since Laura's parents have gone green, their health has improved considerably.'

   a green home – a non-toxic home, in keeping with 'green' ideals. See *The Green Home* by Karen Christensen.

2. **a green religion** – Paganism, a religion concerned with ecological issues whose followers live in harmony with nature instead of dominating over it. See *Phoenix from the Flame* by Vivianne Crowley.

3. **green issues** – matters concerning the preservation of the countryside, ecology, combating pollution, conserving energy, effective recycling of rubbish, etc. ' "We respect green issues," the director said, "and therefore we shall build the supermarket in the town, far away from these endangered birds." '

4. **a greenfield site** – a piece of land to be developed for the first time. 'A group of protesters occupied the greenfield site to stop the builders moving in.' cf. **'a brownfield site'** 8/15.

5. **greenbelt** – a strip of undeveloped land surrounding towns and cities. It has been legally stipulated that the greenbelt cannot be developed. 'There is always the fear that property developers will be allowed to build on the greenbelt.'

6. **green-wash** – downplaying the danger of nuclear power by presenting it alongside environmentally friendly images. 'Look at that advertisement, Brenda. A nuclear power station surrounded by flowers and butterflies – that's green-wash for you!' cf. **'to white-wash'** 5/13.

7. **green cuisine** – a vegetarian diet. 'With his heart condition, it is better to switch him to a green cuisine.'

Yellow

8. **to be yellow** – to be cowardly. Yellow is the traditional symbol of cowardice. 'You don't want to fight, do you? You are yellow.' **'to be yellow-livered'** 117/9.

   to show a yellow streak – to show cowardice.

9. **to be shown the yellow card** – to receive a warning that disciplinary action will be taken if an offence is repeated. 'I was shown the yellow card by the manager for coming in late to work.' The phrase derives from football: a player is shown the yellow card by a referee for committing an offence. cf. **'to be shown the red card'** 3/3.

White

10. **whiter than white** – (1) very pure, law-abiding. ' "I promise you that I really am whiter than white," the politician said earnestly.' (2) too pure to be true, hypocritical.

    a whited sepulchre – innocent and pure in appearance, but dirty and corrupt within. An allusion by Jesus Christ to the hypocrisy of the Pharisees (Matthew XXIII, 27). Jesus meant that one should judge someone by his inner self, not by his outward appearance. (Tombs in biblical times were whitened to make them conspicuous.)

11. **lily white** – of great purity and delicacy.

12. **a white wedding** – a wedding in church, so called because the bride is dressed in white, the symbol of chastity.

13. **to white-wash** – to exonerate someone by ignoring the evidence against him or her. 'It's no good complaining to the Post Office about the telephone engineer. They will only white-wash him.' cf. **'green-wash'** 5/6.

14. **to bleed someone white** – to extort all of someone's money, to overcharge grossly for a service. 'Why do you let Thompson blackmail you like this? He has bled you white!'

15. **white noise** – a sound which consists of a large number of frequencies transmitted

simultaneously. 'He couldn't tune the radio properly. All he got was white noise.'

1. **white light** – a spiritual healing power which gives strength to the ill. 'The faith healer's white light helped to make many ill people well again.'

2. **a white lie** – a harmless or well-intentioned lie. This is generally not considered morally wrong because the motive is to spare the feelings of the person lied to. 'It is better to tell a white lie than to lose a friend.'

3. **as white as a sheet** – in a state of very great fear. 'Have you seen a ghost? Your face is as white as a sheet.'

4. **white heat** – the most intense energy, dynamic expansion. 'The white heat of the technological revolution.' '**white-hot**'.

5. **to show the white feather** – to act in a cowardly way. In the First World War, young women used to seek out men who were dressed in civilian clothes and place a white feather in their coats in order to humiliate them for not having enlisted.

6. **to hang out/show the white flag** – when approaching the enemy, you show the white flag to indicate (1) that you have come to negotiate a peace and your mission is a peaceful one (it is an unwritten law that the enemy will not fire at you) or (2) that you wish to surrender and have no desire to continue resistance.

7. **white slave traffic** – the selling of girls into prostitution. This is often effected by luring them abroad with promises of employment in night clubs and cabarets, and then cancelling their contracts or withholding their wages.

8. **white goods** – kitchen appliances such as fridges, cookers and washing machines; so called because they are usually white. cf. '**brown goods**' 8/16.

9. **a white elephant** – a very big and useless possession which costs a lot of money to maintain and may prove to be a source of financial ruin. 'You have bought yourself a white elephant: this house is far too isolated. No one will stay here and the upkeep will ruin you.' A king of Siam is said to have given white elephants to his enemies in order to ruin them.

10. **white horses** – white waves, so called because they appear to be galloping forward on to the shore like horses.

11. **white water** – foaming water coming down from mountains as rapids, and used by enthusiasts for canoeing and rafting. 'John isn't afraid of anything. He loves white-water rafting, bungee jumping and hang-gliding.'

12. **a white-knuckle ride** – a thrilling and daring ride on a roller-coaster in theme parks and funfairs. 'Hundreds of mostly young people were queuing up for the thrill of a white-knuckle ride.' Fear makes one hold on to the safety rail so tightly that one's knuckles turn white. cf. '**a stomach-churner**'; 116/21.

13. **a white Christmas** – a Christmas when snow has fallen and the countryside is white.

14. **white magic** – in modern Paganism, this is a gentle, natural magic which is believed to harness the power of good and which is used to help those in need.

15. **white witch** – a wise woman, someone who performs spells for healing and uses her knowledge of herbal and natural medicine to help people.

16. **a white-collar worker** – the professional or office worker who wears a shirt with a white collar. cf. '**a blue-collar worker**' 4/1.

White and Black

17. **white or black?** – with milk or without (in coffee).

18. **in black and white** – reduced to writing. Unless this has been done, some agreements are unenforceable in law. 'If you come to any agreement with him, be sure to get it in black and white; you can't trust him.'

19. **to see (everything) in black and white** – to characterize everything and everyone as either very good or very bad, without any intermediate qualities.

1. **to swear black is white** – to perjure oneself or swear any falsehood, no matter how glaring.

2. **two blacks don't make a white** – two wrongs don't make a right. 'Just because Haines has cheated you, that's no reason why you should cheat his daughter; two blacks don't make a white.'

Black

3. **black and blue** – very badly bruised. 'The muggers beat the old woman black and blue.'

4. **things are looking black** – the prospects are very bad.

5. **black looks** – angry or revengeful looks. 'I got some black looks from the shopkeeper when I cancelled my order.'

6. **to look on the black side** – to see everything in a pessimistic light, to have gloomy forebodings.
   to be in a black mood – to be very depressed. 'George has been in a black mood ever since he lost his job.'

7. **to blacken someone's character** – to make someone appear worse than he really is by exaggerating his faults. 'Since you have blackened Miles' character, I shall give him the opportunity of defending himself.'

8. **not as black as one is painted** – not as bad as others say. 'Freddy may be selfish, but he took his blind neighbour to the doctor every day last week. He's not as black as he is painted.'

9. **to be on the black list** – to be on a list of persons under suspicion, who have committed crimes, or incurred the disapproval of the authorities. cf. '**to blackball**' 8/9.

10. **black magic / black art** – Satanic or devilish practices.

11. **black mass** – a travesty of the Christian Mass celebrated by practitioners of black magic and members of a Satanic cult.

12. **the black sheep (of the family)** – a member of the family who has disgraced him- or herself, one whose name is generally not mentioned in the family circle.

13. **the Black Country** – the industrial Midlands of England, formerly discoloured by soot from its many open chimneys.

14. **a blackleg** – someone who continues to work during a strike in defiance of trade-union instructions; hence '**blackleg labour**', workers who refuse to come out when a strike has been called and who cross the picket lines to get to their work.

15. **a black eye** – an eye that is bruised and swollen as the result of a blow or a collision.

16. **a black-out** – (1) a sudden loss of consciousness. 'The accused told the judge that he couldn't remember what happened next because at that moment he had a black-out.' (2) concealing all source of light (in wartime). (3) total loss of electric power in a district.

17. **to go into a black hole** – (1) to disappear without trace. 'A bank manager has recently been taken to court for fraudulently using clients' money which seems to have gone into a black hole.' (2) to suffer from depression. 'Lesley really ought to see a doctor. She goes into a black hole at least once a week.' A black hole is formed in space where a massive star has collapsed, and where no matter or energy can escape from it.

18. **like the Black Hole of Calcutta** – very hot, crowded and uncomfortable. 'This restaurant is like the Black Hole of Calcutta. Let's get out of here and go somewhere cooler and less busy.'

19. **a black comedy** – a story or play in which the theme is sad or tragic, but the treatment is comic.

20. **a black joke** – something to be laughed at derisively. 'Some citizens fear that law and order have become a black joke.' cf. '**a sick joke**' 135/5.

21. **the black economy** – that part of a country's economy which is carried on without the knowledge of the authorities for the purpose of avoiding tax. 'Despite the efforts of the government, the black economy continues to grow.'

22. **to black (goods)** – to refuse to handle goods coming from a source which has

incurred the disapproval of the trade union responsible for their carriage. Such goods are said to be '**blacked**'.

1. **the black market** – illegal buying and selling of products that have been rationed by the government.

2. **to be in the black** – to be in credit. 'After making losses for the last six years, we are at last in the black.' cf. '**to be in the red**' 3/4.

3. **to be in someone's black books** – to have incurred the strong disapproval or enmity of someone. 'The boy was in the teacher's black books for having been disobedient.'

4. **as black as thunder** – in a rage or fury. 'When I stood up to him, his face went as black as thunder.'

5. **black gold** – oil. 'Nine million tonnes of black gold are extracted from the earth every day.'

6. **black ice** – a layer of ice on the road which is invisible and therefore very dangerous.

7. **a blackspot** – a section of road with a bad reputation for accidents, usually at corners or bends. Blackspots also refer to areas of the country with environmental or social problems, such as pollution, nuclear power stations or unemployment. 'That part of Britain is a real blackspot. Because of industrial pollution, a very high number of people fall ill and have to take time off work.' cf. '**a hot spot**' 21/9.

8. **to blackmail someone** – to obtain money by threats and extortion. 'A schoolboy was accused of blackmailing a teacher who had given him a list of exam questions and answers the day before his exam.' cf. '**hate mail**' 126/11.

9. **to blackball** – to vote against a person's election to an organization when admission has to be by unanimous vote of its members. A white ball is dropped into the ballot box to signify a member's acceptance of the candidate, and a black ball, his or her rejection. Also: **to operate a blackball policy**. cf. '**to be on the black list**' 7/9.

Brown

10. **to be as brown as a berry** – to be pleasantly tanned by the sun. 'The children are as brown as berries after three weeks at the seaside.' Also: **as brown as a walnut**; **chocolate-brown**.

11. **to be browned off** – to be bored, disgruntled. 'I am browned off with this place – there's nothing to do.'

12. **to brown-nose** (vulgar) – to fawn over someone in order to gain an advantage. 'It's infuriating! Those three girls are always brown-nosing the teacher and she gives them the best marks!' Note the noun is **a brown nose / brown-noser**.

13. **to be in a brown study** – to be in a reverie, a dreamy, distracted state of mind, unaware of one's surroundings.

14. **a brownie point** – an imaginary mark of approval for having done something commendable. 'The typist earned several brownie points by helping her boss translate a business letter into Spanish.' A Brownie, aged between seven and 10, is a member of the junior branch of the Girl Guides, founded in 1910 by General Baden-Powell and his sister. Their uniform used to be brown but since 1990 it has been yellow.

15. **a brownfield site** – land in or near cities occupied by redundant warehouses and factories. 'The local Green Party managed to persuade the town planners to use the brownfield site for a new housing estate, instead of destroying the wood.' cf. '**greenfield site**' 5/4.

16. **brown goods** – televisions, CD players and other audio equipment. Long ago it was the custom to encase television sets and radios in wood so as to fit in better with the rest of the furniture. cf. '**white goods**' 6/8.

Grey

17. **a grey-beard** – an old man. Often used in a derogatory sense. 'I don't want to spend my holiday with a lot of grey-beards!'

1. **to grow grey (in the service)** – to remain in one occupation (usually the army, navy or a government department) for most of one's working life.

2. **grey matter** – the brain. 'Alan hasn't got much in the way of grey matter, but intelligence isn't everything.' The phrase comes from the fact that the active part of the brain is coloured grey.

3. **a grey area** – an indeterminate area between two branches of learning, not covered by either, a kind of intellectual no man's land. 'Philosophy is the grey area between science and religion.'

4. **grey men** – an anonymous body of men who work behind the scenes of large institutions and organizations. 'Grey men' see to the smooth running of Buckingham Palace, as well as controlling rumours and gossip about the Royal Family.
cf. **'backroom boys' 285/15**; **'faceless men' 86/1**.

5. **grey suits** – political heavyweights who have the power to remove a party leader.

6. **grey power** – the 'power' wielded by prosperous elderly retired people who have enough money to be able to afford private medicine and holidays and to live a life without financial worry.

7. **the grey pound** – a reference to elderly men and women spending money on themselves after their children have left home. 'The grey pound is gaining in importance, and shops and stores are catering more for the elderly.'

8. **the grey market** – business conducted in shares or goods before they are traded officially.

9. **grey literature** – government papers published non-commercially for public reference.

Purple

10. Purple symbolized the monarchy and high rank in ancient Greece and Rome, the Roman emperors, consuls, magistrates and generals being dressed in purple robes. Hence there are a number of idioms derived from purple: (1) **to be born in/ to the purple** – to be born the child of a king. (2) **to marry into the purple** – to marry a king or prince. (3) **to be raised to the purple** – to be created a cardinal in the Roman Catholic Church.

11. **purple passages/patches/prose** – passages in a book written in a florid, ornate style, contrasting with the style of the rest of the work, such as is to be found in the writings of Gibbon, Macaulay, Pater, Burke and sometimes Churchill.

Pink

12. **to be tickled pink** – to be very much amused, to relish a comical situation. 'He was tickled pink at the idea of taking a month's holiday at the expense of his company.'

13. **the pink of perfection** – sheer perfection, perfect to the smallest detail. 'Her skating was marvellous – graceful, elegant and stylish – the pink of perfection!'

14. **in the pink of condition / in the pink** – at peak fitness, often used in reference to athletes, racehorses or greyhounds.

15. **a pink socialist** – one who is less extreme than a full-blooded socialist. Sometimes used in contrast to a 'conviction socialist', and has largely been replaced by New Labour.

16. **pink elephants** – frightening hallucinations experienced during withdrawal from alcohol, when the patient is suffering an attack of delirium tremens (DTs) and thinks that he sees pink elephants or other impossible objects in the room.

17. **the pink market** – goods manufactured especially to be sold to homosexual men and women.

18. **the pink economy** – money spent by homosexual consumers. 'Latest figures from *Stonewall* put the pink economy at the value of £95 billion.'

19. **the power of the pink pound** – the strong marketing potential of goods aimed especially at homosexual men and women.

20. **a pink-pounder** – a wealthy homosexual

who is willing to spend his or her money on pink market goods.

1. **a pinkish tinge** – someone with homosexual leanings. 'The author Daphne du Maurier had a pinkish tinge about her, but one can't prove anything as she died some years ago.'

Golden
(see also *Gold* and *Golden* in Chapter 31)

2. **a golden opportunity** – a wonderful opportunity that may never recur. Also: **a golden chance**.

3. **the Golden Rule** – a wise rule, the best rule. 'Never to let yourself be rushed into a decision you may afterwards regret is a golden rule.' The Golden Rule is found in Leviticus XIX, 34: 'do unto others as you would like them to do to you'.

4. **the golden hour** – the crucial time between an accident occurring and the surgery necessary to save a patient's life. cf. **'from pen to knife' 170/11**.

5. **a golden future** – one filled with happiness, success and riches.

6. **golden opinions** – the highest praise. 'Peter's first book won golden opinions from the critics.'

7. **a golden girl/boy** – a young woman or man idolized for an outstanding skill, usually in sport, or for her or his good looks. 'The golden girl of tennis held her trophy high up in the air and smiled triumphantly.'

8. **the Golden Age** – (1) the first of the four ages when men were happy and innocent, the other three being the Silver, Bronze and Iron. (2) the finest period in a country's history and literature. 'The 17th century was the Golden Age of France.'

9. **the golden mean** – moderation in all things, a principle advocated by the Epicureans, a philosophic sect in ancient Greece.

10. **a Golden Jubilee** – celebration of the 50th anniversary of an important event, such as the 50 years of Queen Victoria's reign in 1887.
    Golden Wedding – the 50th anniversary of the wedding day.

11. **London's golden acres** – the 300 acres of Mayfair, the wealthiest part of London.

Silver
(see also *Silver* in Chapter 31)

12. **a Silver Jubilee** – celebration of the 25th anniversary of an important event, such as the 25th year after the accession of George V, in 1935.
    Silver Wedding – the 25th anniversary of the wedding day.

13. **the silver screen** – the cinema. 'Valentino was one of the earliest stars of the silver screen.'

14. **a silver/silvery tongue** – eloquence, persuasiveness and charm.

15. **silver surfers** – elderly people who enjoy using the Internet. 'There's a computer course specially for silver surfers, Mr Carey. Shall we go there together?'

Element

1. **in one's element** – in the conditions best suited to a person's tastes or abilities, enjoying oneself enormously. 'The sergeant-major is in his element drilling the young recruits.'

2. **to brave the elements** – to defy very bad weather. Used facetiously to mean simply going out in the rain. 'Well, I suppose I had better brave the elements or I shall miss my train.'

Air

3. **to vanish/disappear into thin air** – to disappear completely without leaving any trace. 'We used to see a lot of our next-door neighbours, then one day, without any warning, they vanished into thin air.' cf. '**to disappear like water on sand'** 12/19.
   out of thin air – out of nothing at all. 'Where do you imagine I can find £500 – out of thin air? I'm not a magician!'

4. **you could cut the air/atmosphere with a knife** – to sense at once a state of nervous tension, resentment or suppressed anger. 'When I went into the dining-room, there was an uncomfortable silence; you could have cut the air with a knife.'

5. **to air one's views** – to express one's opinions very freely, often in inappropriate situations. 'When we visit Aunt Mary, I hope you won't air your views the way you did last time. You will only annoy her if you do.'

6. **to put on airs / give oneself airs** – to behave as if one were socially superior to other people. 'She had better not give herself airs when she comes to live with us. My wife won't like it.'

7. **airs and graces** – affected manners which are intended to impress other people. 'I have never met your sister before; does she always give herself such airs and graces?'

8. **airy-fairy** – lofty and impractical. 'Jean wouldn't have these airy-fairy ideas if she had to work for a living.'

9. **a breath of fresh air** – a welcome change which brings happiness. 'Fergie was like a breath of fresh air to Diana . . . but she was more than a breath of fresh air. She was the wind of change' (*Behind Palace Doors* by Nigel Dempster and Peter Evans, © Weidenfeld & Nicolson). cf. '**the wind of change'** 22/11.

10. **a fresh-air fiend** – a fanatical believer in the importance of fresh air to one's health. 'My father was a terrible fresh-air fiend. Whenever he came into a room, he would throw all the windows wide open.'

11. **hot air** – bombastic nonsense. 'Don't take any notice of Hammond's letters; they are nothing but hot air.'

12. **to clear the air** – to remove any previous misunderstanding by open and frank discussion. 'I'm so glad we've had this talk, Irene; it has really cleared the air.'

13. **to give public airing to something** – to raise a question publicly so that the facts may be fully disclosed and debated.

14. **on/off the air** – to broadcast / to cease broadcasting. 'The first time I went on the air, I thought I would be terribly nervous,

but when the time came I was perfectly all right.'

1. **castles in the air** – dreams or hopes that will never be realized. 'I am afraid that all Tom's schemes will come to nothing; they are just castles in the air.' cf. '**castles in Spain**' 211/3 and '**pie in the sky**' 179/16, which mean the same.

2. **to walk/dance on air** – to be in a state of exaltation. 'Since Simon and Lilian got engaged, they have been walking on air.'

3. **an air kiss / air-kissing** – a formal kiss blown close to someone's face without coming into contact with his/her cheek. 'Air kisses don't spread viruses like herpes and don't smudge lipstick.'

4. **to go up in the air** – to become furiously angry. 'My parents went up in the air when I told them that I wanted to move out into a flat.' cf. '**to fly off the handle**' 173/14.

5. **in the air** – of plans, undecided, uncertain. 'We haven't made up our minds yet where we are going to live; our plans are still in the air.'

6. **something in the air** – rumours that something important is going to happen. 'The clerks were whispering together in the office today; something is in the air.'

7. **as free as (the) air** – without any burden or obligation. 'Now that I have passed my exams, I feel as free as the air and can do whatever I like.'

8. **open-air planning** – a modern design of building using plenty of glass. 'The new European Parliament building in Strasburg has been built with open-air planning in mind.'

Space

9. **to invade one's space** – to disturb someone's privacy. 'With three brothers and two sisters living in our house, my space is always being invaded by one of them.'

Water

10. **to water down** – to soften (the language or tone), to dilute. 'You'll have to water down your article if you want me to pub-

lish it. At present the wording is far too strong.' Alcoholic drinks can be watered down by the addition of water.

11. **to be on the (water) wagon** – to abstain from alcohol, usually on doctor's orders. 'Thank you very much, but I'm on the wagon; I'll have an orangeade.'

12. **a watershed** – a decisive turning-point. 'The general elections in 1979 and 1983 were a watershed in Britain's post-war history.' The watershed is the line which separates waters flowing into different river basins or seas.

13. **water-tight** – irrefutable. The analogy is with water-tight clothing or water-tight shoes which protect the wearer from the water, just as a water-tight alibi protects the accused from conviction or a water-tight case admits of no doubt.

14. **to hold water** – to be valid, tenable; used with reference to theories, arguments or explanations; in fact anything that is open to debate. 'At first the prisoner's explanation seemed reasonable enough, but under cross-examination it didn't hold water.'

15. **to test the water/waters** – to find out in advance what the response will be to some intended action. 'Let's test the waters first before opening a new restaurant in this small town.' cf. '**to put out feelers**' 79/2.

16. **to chart unknown waters** – to explore where no one else has ventured before. 'My genius of a brother got a wonderful new job in computing and is spending hours charting unknown waters on the Internet.'

17. **to pour oil on troubled waters** – to resolve a quarrel by the exercise of tact and diplomacy. 'Mandy and Ned do nothing but quarrel. What a pity Uncle Tom isn't here to pour oil on troubled waters.'

18. **to pour cold water (on a scheme or idea)** – to find fault with, disparage. 'I wish Father weren't so negative; he pours cold water on all my ideas.' cf. '**to put a damper on**' 129/7.

19. **to disappear like water on sand** – to vanish without trace. 'If only we could

catch these pickpockets but they disappear like water on sand.' cf. '**to go up in smoke**' 15/13; '**to vanish/disappear into thin air**' 11/3.

1. **dull as ditchwater** – uninteresting, boring. 'The play we saw last night was as dull as ditchwater.'

2. **to pass water** – to urinate.

3. **to tread water** – to be inactive or static. 'You've done nothing but tread water for the last six months. Isn't it time you took a job?' Literally, to keep one's head above water in swimming by moving one's hands and feet up and down. cf. '**mark time**' 27/14.

4. **in hot water** – in serious trouble. 'Jack has had to change his address. He's in hot water with the police again!'

5. **in deep water** – in difficulties. 'We are in deep water; we may have to sell the house to pay our debts.'

6. **to make a hole in the water** – to commit suicide by drowning.

7. **of the first water** – of the finest quality. 'Rubinstein was a musician of the first water, absolutely superb.' The phrase is derived from the custom of valuing diamonds according to their 'waters'. The 'water' is the colour or lustre of the diamond.

8. **to turn on the waterworks** – to weep. 'Susan can turn on the waterworks whenever she wants to.'

Tide

9. **a tide of joy** – great happiness. 'When Harry proposed to Vanessa, a tide of joy swept over her.'

10. **a growing tide** – an increasing tendency. 'A spokesman for the government admitted that there was a growing tide of anti-euro sentiment.'

11. **to turn the (political) tide / the tide has turned** – to change the general trend for the better. 'The tide had turned at last for the politician. He gained a large majority of votes after three heartbreaking defeats.'

12. **to swim with the tide** – to do what the majority of people are doing or thinking, to offer no resistance. 'A successful politician must swim with the tide of public opinion and steer it to his way of thinking.' cf. '**to go with the flow**' 14/1.

Wave

13. **to be on the crest of a wave** – to have achieved great success for the time being. 'After Sally-Ann won the beauty contest, she was on the crest of a wave.'

14. **to be on the same wavelength** – to be in sympathy with someone, sharing the same interests. 'Peter was the perfect person for me to work with. We found ourselves on the same wavelength right from the start.' Note the opposite: **to be on a different wavelength**. The wavelength refers to the length of a radio wave, which may be found by moving the controls of a radio.

15. **a tidal wave of something** – a deluge, an overwhelming amount. 'If sexually explicit films and videos are not better controlled, a tidal wave of pornography could sweep the country.'

16. **a wave of controversy/crime** – a sudden outbreak of events or action. 'The expensive new art gallery specializing in extraordinary exhibits opened this week on a wave of controversy.'

17. **to make waves** – (1) to cause trouble, to make a bad situation worse. 'Thomas has more than enough to cope with. Why did you have to make waves so that things are even worse for him?' (2) to attract great attention, make an impression. 'The famous artist's latest exhibition is making waves and getting lots of publicity.'

18. **to send shockwaves through something** – unexpected bad news which shocks a particular community. 'When the general was exposed as a spy, it sent shockwaves through the army.'

Ebb

19. **to be at one's lowest ebb / at a low ebb** – (1) to be the least popular. 'Sometimes politicians appear to be at their

lowest ebb, but they can recover remarkably well.' (2) to be depressed and vulnerable. 'Do let Alison go to Italy – it will cheer her up. She's been at a low ebb for far too long.'

Flow

1. **to go with the flow** – to be at ease and not put up any resistance. 'I realize now that I was far too nervous, stressed and always in a hurry. My illness made me see it's far better to relax and just go with the flow.' cf. '**to swim with the tide**' 13/12.

Drift

2. **to get the drift** – to understand the meaning of something. 'You are giving me a lot of money, Dad. I get the drift – you want me to enter the family business instead of studying medicine!'

Flood

3. **before the Flood** – a facetious comment on anything that is old-fashioned or out of date. 'Karen's room badly needs redecorating; the wallpaper looks as if it was put up before the Flood.' 'Before the Flood' refers to before Noah and the Great Flood.

4. **to stem the flood/tide** – to stop the flow. 'The Home Secretary is trying hard to stem the flood of teenage pregnancies.'

5. **to be in floods of tears** – to cry uncontrollably. 'When the elderly widow found out that she had been swindled out of her fortune, she broke out into floods of tears.'

6. **to open the floodgates** – to start a rush, to lose control over something. 'If the government of the United States wins its case against the cigarette manufacturers, it will open the floodgates for other countries to do the same.'

Fire

7. **a fire-eater** – someone who is eager for a fight, who quarrels on the slightest pretext. 'What a fire-eater you are, Joe; you aren't happy unless you are fighting with someone, are you?' The reference is to the 'fire-eaters' at the circus.

8. **to go through fire and water** – to undergo any danger, for another's sake. 'You know I would go through fire and water, Elizabeth, to be with you.'

9. **fire away!** – say whatever you want to. 'I am ready to listen to you now. Fire away!'

10. **where's the fire?** – what's the hurry? where's the urgency? 'The train isn't due to leave for another five minutes, so where's the fire?'

11. **to fire off questions** – to ask questions very fast, one after the other. 'They were firing off questions at me from all sides.'

12. **to hang fire** (of plans, arrangements) – to be delayed, to make no progress. 'Our plans to emigrate are hanging fire, but we are determined to go just the same.' The allusion is to a gun which is slow in detonating.

13. **to be fired** – to be dismissed from one's work for various reasons. 'The cook was fired because his kitchen was so unhygienic.'

14. **to hire and fire** – being in the position to engage or dismiss someone. 'I do feel sorry for you, Pam. Your new employer is very ruthless and famous for hiring and firing.'

15. **to add fuel to the fire** – to aggravate someone's rage, to make someone still angrier. 'Philip added fuel to the fire by telling Jane that it was her own fault he had missed his date with her.' cf. '**to fan the flames**' 15/12.

16. **to fight fire with fire** – to defend oneself by fighting back in the same way as one's attacker. 'That was an exciting debate! Both politicians were fighting fire with fire.'

17. **to come under fire / to be in the firing line** – to be criticized for something. 'The government came under fire for wanting to release more greenfield land for building on.' 'Fire' here means 'gun fire'. Frequent usage: **to come under immediate fire**.

1. **friendly fire** – accidentally attacking your own side instead of the enemy. 'During the last war, 10 Americans lost their lives through friendly fire.'

2. **to catch fire** – to arouse interest, excitement. 'Roger's play was well written and very realistic, but somehow it failed to catch fire.'

3. **to have many/several/other irons in the fire** – to have more than one interest at the same time. 'Don't worry if we have to close the shop; I have other irons in the fire.'

4. **to play with fire** – to take a needless risk, often by meddling in other people's affairs. 'I wouldn't advise Kate what to do when she and her husband quarrel; you'll be playing with fire if you do.'

5. **as quick as fire / quick-fire** – very fast indeed, swift, rapid, animated.
   quick-fire gags/jokes/verses – following one another very quickly. 'It was a very lively, funny play, full of quick-fire verses and gags.' A quick-firer is a gun with a mechanism for firing shots in rapid succession.

6. **sure-fire / as sure as fire** – to be absolutely certain about something; unerring; reliable. ' "These silk scarves with the designer's name on them are sure-fire sellers," the boutique owner said contentedly.'

7. **to pull the chestnuts out of the fire** – to get someone out of a predicament, often at some risk to oneself. 'I don't see why I should pull the chestnuts out of the fire for Andrew. He has only got himself to blame for the difficulty he is in.'

8. **to spread like wild fire / like a bush fire/prairie fire** – to circulate very rapidly; said of scandal, gossip and news (particularly bad news). 'The news of the minister's offer to resign spread like wild fire, although he hadn't discussed it with his staff.' Wild fire was formerly used in war. It was a composition of highly inflammable materials which caught fire easily and was extremely difficult to extinguish. cf. '**to sweep across like a plague . . .**' 132/17.

9. **to trigger a firestorm** – to set off a huge reaction. 'A television presenter insisted that there was nothing special about being 50, which triggered a firestorm of telephone calls and letters.'

10. **to threaten/call down fire and brimstone** – to threaten dire penalties; generally in a humorous sense. 'Peter is threatening us with fire and brimstone if we don't pay him back the £10 he lent us by the end of the week.' Fire and brimstone is a biblical phrase, meaning the punishment in hell that awaits the sinner on his death.

Flame

11. **an old flame** – a former girl/boyfriend. 'Was that an old flame you were speaking to on the telephone? You seemed very pleased to hear her voice!'

12. **to fan the flames** – to worsen existing ill-feeling by one's words or actions. 'The thieves seem to have taken most of Marion's jewellery, but you are only fanning the flames by exaggerating its value.' cf. '**to add fuel to the fire**' 14/15.

Smoke

13. **to go up in smoke** – to vanish, to come to nothing. 'When Emily's father was made bankrupt, her plans to go to university went up in smoke.' Also: **to disappear in a puff of smoke**. cf. '**to disappear like water on sand**' 12/19.

14. **a smokescreen** – a way of concealing the truth, a ploy by which one can hide one's true intentions. 'The Fine Food delivery van was being used as a smokescreen for smuggling cigarettes into the country.' cf. '**in a smoke-filled room**' 162/14; '**smoke and mirrors**' 168/5.

Soot

15. **as easy as juggling with soot** – very difficult, almost impossible. 'Trying to find my brother in this crowded funfair will be as easy as juggling with soot.' cf. '**like gripping blancmange**' 179/1; '**like swimming through porridge**' 180/7.

Earth

1. **down-to-earth** – practical, sensible; concerned with facts, not theories. 'I am surprised that a down-to-earth character like Jim should suddenly start taking an interest in astrology.'

2. **to come down to earth** – to abandon one's dreams and take a realistic view of life. 'One of these days, Alan will have to come down to earth; no amount of theorizing will pay the bills.'
   to bring someone down to earth – to force someone to abandon his or her dreams and take a realistic view of life.

3. **who/what/why/how, etc., on earth** – whoever/whatever/whyever/however, etc. 'What on earth have you done to your face? Have you been in a fight?' The addition of 'on earth' to the interrogative is an emphatic way of asking a question and may express surprise or annoyance.

4. **to go to earth/ground** – to seek refuge in a hiding place. 'The film star eventually went to earth in a small, out-of-the-way cottage in Rottingdean.'
   to run someone to earth/ground – to discover someone in a hiding place after a lengthy search.
   These two phrases have been taken from hunting when the quarry 'goes to earth' or 'is run to earth'.

5. **to pay the earth for** – to pay a very large sum of money for something. 'You must have paid the earth for that designer outfit!'

6. **no earthly reason** – no reason at all. 'There's no earthly reason why you should always follow your brother's advice.' This phrase is often used to express mild irritation.

7. **not to have an earthly chance / an earthly** – to have no chance of success at all. 'Swimming the Channel? In weather like this, she won't have an earthly chance of breaking the record.'

8. **like nothing on earth** – ghastly, awful. The phrase can be used with the following verbs: look, feel, sound, taste and smell.

'You look like nothing on earth in that ridiculous outfit.'

9. **a scorched-earth policy** – in war, the destruction of everything that may prove useful to an advancing army. 'The enemy pursued a scorched-earth policy and the refugees found they had no homes to return to.'

10. **to move heaven and earth** – to do everything humanly possible to achieve one's aim. 'We have moved heaven and earth to get the squatters out of our house, but so far without success.'

Rift, Abyss, Edge

11. **to open up a rift** – a serious disagreement has occurred. 'The question over whether to take strike action or not has opened up a rift in the Party.'

12. **to heal the rift** – to mend a breakdown in a relationship; bring about peace. 'Amanda's daughter helped to heal the rift between her parents, and now they are living happily together again.'

13. **to look into the abyss** – to be near destruction or on the edge of bankruptcy. 'For small firms, the constant rise of bureaucracy can be like looking into the abyss.' Also: **an abyss of despair/loneliness/misery/ignorance**.

14. **to be driven/tipped over the edge** – particularly bad circumstances that make one think about committing suicide. 'Gail's anxiety about her final exams nearly tipped her over the edge. cf. '**to snap under pressure' 128/5**.

Cliff, Rocks

15. **a cliffhanger** – a suspenseful story which keeps one guessing throughout, and where the solution is not known until the very end. 'The last episode is on TV tonight, Olivia. I can hardly wait – it's a real cliffhanger!'

16. **to hit the rocks** – to come to an unexpected end. 'Against all expectations, the marriage hit the rocks after only a few months.'
    to head for the rocks – moving towards failure or disaster.

1. **on the rocks** – ice in an alcoholic drink. 'Waiter – one neat whisky and one whisky on the rocks, please.'

2. **to reach/hit rock bottom** – (1) to have sunk down to the lowest level, deteriorated completely. 'Morale in the police force has hit rock bottom.' (2) to be in absolute despair. 'Tommy had no home, no money and no one to care for him; he was at rock bottom.'

3. **rock solid** – absolutely dependable; indestructible. Often used with the following words: evidence, relationship, discipline; and with currency, such as '**rock-solid dollar**'. ' "We need rock-solid evidence that there is water on Mars," the scientist told reporters.' Note other similes with 'rock': **as steady as a rock/rock steady**; **to stand like a rock**; **as hard as a rock**.

4. **bedrock** – the principle on which to build. 'To make a good medical student you must have a bedrock of compassion.'

5. **between a rock and a hard place** – nothing to choose between two difficult situations. 'The teacher was caught between a rock and a hard place, trying to satisfy the demands of the headmistress and trying not to overstrain the children.'

Ground

6. **to hit the ground running** – to be ready to start at full speed, with efficiency and dynamism. 'The newly chosen minister hit the ground running by passing 10 badly needed laws within her first month in office.' Note a humorous variation with the opposite meaning: **to hit the ground hobbling**.

7. **to prepare the ground** – to get ready for. 'You gave your daughter a new car. Are you preparing the ground for her to join you in the business?'

8. **to be thin on the ground** – to be scarce, in short supply. ' "Real musical talent is thin on the ground in my class," the teacher sighed.'

9. **to get something off the ground** – to start a new venture. 'Once we get the new line in sandals off the ground, it will be a success in no time.'
   not to get something off the ground – to fail in a new venture.

10. **to stand/hold one's ground** – to stick to one's opinion, principles or idea; to remain adamant. 'In spite of all the opposition to holding a party without alcoholic drinks, Peter stood his ground.'

11. **to gain ground** – to make advances or progress; to become more powerful and influential. 'You had better work a bit harder, Mr Notts; the opposition is gaining ground.'

12. **to cover a lot of ground** – to advance well in certain subjects. 'We covered a lot of ground during our first year of history at university.'

13. **to run into the ground** – (1) to reach a position of defeat or exhaustion. 'My father could not cope any longer and let his factory run into the ground.' (2) to exhaust someone or something. 'Old Mr Higgins ran his car into the ground and decided to give up his job as a travelling salesman.'

14. **to break fresh/new ground** – to make innovative advances in certain areas. 'Scientists are breaking new ground by experimenting with a vaccine to prevent asthma.' Also: **a ground-breaking case/invention**.

15. **to stand on shaky/firm ground** – to be in a weak / strong position. 'He can't go to court on that evidence. He'll be standing on very shaky ground.'

16. **to fall on stony ground** – to be badly received. 'His idea of opening another shop in a different town fell on stony ground with his partner.'

17. **to suit one down to the ground** – to suit one perfectly. 'Going to Italy next Thursday will suit me down to the ground.'

Dirt, Muck, Dust

18. **to dig the dirt on someone** – to try and find something disreputable in someone's past which could be used against him or her. 'A politician who is aspiring

for high office has always got to be aware that someone will dig the dirt on him.'
Also: **to rake up the muck / muck-raking**. cf. **'to drag someone's name through the dirt/mud'** 220/19.

1. **once the dust has settled** – when the arguments are over. 'The Queen has been advised not to visit Australia till the dust has settled over the question of keeping the monarchy or becoming a republic.'

Mud, Bog

2. **a stick-in-the-mud** – someone without initiative who never takes a chance. 'My husband has been working as a clerk in that firm for the last 20 years. He has no ambition – he's a real stick-in-the-mud.'

3. **a mudslinger** – a person who slanders someone to ruin his or her reputation; hence a person who engages in **'mud-slinging'**. 'Before an election, political parties often stoop to mudslinging. Also: **to sling/fling mud at someone**.

4. **to be bogged down** – to be overwhelmed by an enormous amount of work. 'I can't meet you today, Sarah. I'm so bogged down with paperwork.'

Lead

5. **to swing the lead** – to find excuses for not working; to be workshy. 'The government is issuing new rules for young people, to stop them swinging the lead.'

Iron

6. **to pump/push/throw iron** – to use weights for bodybuilding. 'Matthew wants to look as muscular as Arnold Schwarzenegger. He's going to the gym to pump iron all evening.'

7. **to have a will of iron / an iron will** – to be resolute and determined. 'Mrs Hudson can never change her husband's mind. He has a will of iron.'
   to have an iron grip on something – a very firm hold.

8. **a cast-iron case** – an irrefutable case, one that cannot possibly be disproved. ' "There is no hope of seeing that criminal sentenced unless we can make a cast-iron case against him," the lawyer explained.'
   Also: **a cast-iron defence/guarantee/pledge**; **to have a cast-iron constitution** – to be in robust health. Cast iron is iron in a molten condition which is poured into a mould, where it is cooled and sets solid.

Flint, Granite

9. **to set one's face like flint/granite** – to refuse to change one's opinion, to be resolute and unyielding. 'On hearing about the arms theft, the commander's face was set like flint/granite.'
   flint-hearted – hard-hearted, unfeeling.

Weather

1. **a fair-weather friend** – a friend only for as long as things are going well.

2. **to be/feel under the weather** – to feel unwell, depressed or out of sorts. 'I'm afraid John was out celebrating last night and didn't get home till late, so he's feeling a bit under the weather this morning.'

3. **to make heavy weather of something** – to take excessive pains over a relatively simple task, to exaggerate its difficulties. 'He made terribly heavy weather of mending the puncture; it only took a few minutes when he finally did it.'

4. **to weather the storm** – to overcome a crisis, often financial. 'If we cut out all unnecessary expenses, we shall have a reasonable chance of weathering the storm.'

5. **to weather an ordeal** – to endure criticism or a bad experience. 'The head teacher asked to see me about my unfinished essay, and I got ready to weather the ordeal.'

6. **to keep a weather eye open** – originally a seaman's phrase, meaning to be watchful – now used generally, as well as on board ship.

7. **freak weather conditions** – abnormal weather for the time of year. 'The freak weather conditions of extreme heat caused high pollution levels that brought misery to asthma sufferers.'

8. **to change/spin like a weather-cock** – to be for ever changing one's mind, to be easily influenced. **to change/spin . . .** The idiom is usually followed by phrases with 'wind' such as: 'in the shifting winds of '; 'in a wind of change', etc. 'The bishop has spun like a weather-cock in the shifting winds of public opinion, trying to please both the traditional and modern members of the church.' The weather-cock moves round according to the prevailing wind, and like the wind is always changing direction.

9. **a weather-vane constituency** – a constituency where the voters are always changing their minds, sometimes voting more for one party and the next time more for another party. 'The rural town has suddenly become a weather-vane constituency, and both major parties stand an equal chance of winning.'

Rain

10. **to be/feel as right as rain** – to be perfectly well again. The phrase implies that the speaker has been ill, or met with some accident, from which he has completely recovered. Often used with the object of reassuring the inquirer. 'Ann has got over her flu. She's as right as rain now!'

11. **to rain cats and dogs** – to pour with rain. The raindrops are compared with cats and dogs fighting one another.
    to rain in buckets – this has the same meaning: it rains so hard that the raindrops feel as though water were being poured out of buckets.

12. **a rainy day** – bad times when it will be difficult to make a living. 'Here's £50 for a rainy day. If things go wrong, it may come in handy.'
    to put something by for a rainy day – to save money against the day one

is too old or ill to work, or has lost one's job.

1. **come rain or shine** – whatever happens. 'Come rain or shine, Caroline always visits her husband in hospital after her work.'

2. **a drop in the ocean** – only a tiny fraction of what is needed. 'We need £70,000 to clear our debts. I'm afraid the £5,000 Ted has offered us is only a drop in the ocean.' In this phrase, the 'drop' is a raindrop.

Snow

3. **pure as the driven snow** – absolutely pure in one's moral character and behaviour. 'How Mary has changed! When she was a teenager, she was as pure as the driven snow.' Driven snow that has been blown into heaps by the wind and which is still perfectly clean. Also: **virgin snow**.

4. **to be snowed under** – to be overwhelmed. 'Since we issued our latest prospectus, we have been snowed under with inquiries.'

5. **to snowball** – to accelerate. 'The number of complaints about waiting lists in hospitals always snowballs around Christmas.'

6. **the snowball system** – a system whereby one pays a person, for example, £100, and then finds two other people to pay one £100, thus doubling one's profit. These two other people repeat this action, hence the name 'snowball'. 'Max is very upset. He's just lost £20,000 on the snowball system and his lawyer can't help him.'

7. **a snowbird** – an elderly person who flees the colder climate of the North for the warmer and far pleasanter one of southern countries. 'Are the beds ready, Arantxa? Here come some more British snowbirds to stay in our hotel.'

Ice

8. **to cut no ice** – to make no impression at all, to fail to produce the desired effect. 'Peter's success at school and college cut no ice with the selection committee. They were not impressed with academic attainments but wanted a man with practical experience.' The idiom comes from the cutting of the ice with the edge of the skate.

9. **to skate on thin ice** – to introduce a subject about which someone is especially sensitive. 'You were skating on thin ice, weren't you, when you praised his brother's book. Didn't you know they have nothing to do with each other?'

10. **to break the ice** – to overcome someone's shyness or reserve, usually in a social setting. 'I didn't know how to break the ice with him. We were both shy and had nothing in common.'

11. **to put on ice** – to defer a project for the time being while preserving it for future use. 'I'm sorry, Alan, but we've had to put your plan on ice. We'll have another look at it in six months' time.'

12. **the tip of the iceberg** – evidence that a great deal more exists but remains hidden. 'The police have uncovered a bad case of corruption, but they believe it is only the tip of the iceberg.' Only a small part of the iceberg is visible, nine-tenths or so remaining hidden from view below the surface of the water.

Cold

13. **to be in a cold sweat** – to be extremely worried and distressed. 'When Toby's father discovered a poisonous spider in the garden, he was in a cold sweat wondering how many more there might be.'

Cool

14. **stay cool!** – don't lose control over yourself, stay calm! 'Stay cool, Jane! Your purse has been stolen, but you've still got that reserve money hidden in your shoe!'

15. **to lose one's cool** – to lose one's temper. 'When the waitress spilt the red wine over his shirt by mistake, James lost his cool and shouted at her.'

16. **to go cool on plans, policies, etc.** – to lose interest in, to become unenthusiastic about something. 'The prime minister

was beginning to go cool on the single currency.'

1. **cool, calm and collected** – in complete control of oneself, unemotional. 'Now, Marion, if you want this job announcing the news on TV, you'll have to appear very confident and look cool, calm and collected.'

2. **cool!** – an exclamation or adjective that is fashionable among the young and used to express their pleasure about or approval of something. 'Uncool' is used to express their displeasure or disapproval. Peer pressure defines what is 'cool' and what is 'uncool'. 'Most of the children described as "cool" the school menu of pizzas, chips, pasta, burgers and salads.'

Chill

3. **to cast a chill on/over** – to depress or sadden. 'The news of her daughter's illness cast a chill over the party, and we all sat about in gloomy silence.'

4. **to chill out** – to hang around, to pass the time by doing something together. Used by teenagers and young adults. 'Hi, Silvia and Bob! Let's get our skateboards and chill out under the railway bridge.'

Shivers

5. **to give one the shivers** – to embarrass. 'He is so uneducated; it gives me the shivers to see him showing off in front of the guests.'

Fog

6. **to be (all) in a fog** – to be confused, nonplussed. 'When I saw Jack this morning, he was all in a fog about what to do next.'

7. **to have not the foggiest (idea)** – to have not the least idea. This is sometimes abbreviated in colloquial language to 'not the foggiest'. 'I haven't the foggiest idea what you are talking about.' 'I haven't the foggiest either; I was only practising my French.'

Ray

8. **a ray of hope** – some grounds for hope. The negative form is often used – '**not a ray of hope**' – not the slightest hope. 'I am so sorry but the doctor didn't offer a ray of hope; it's very sad.'

Hot

9. **a hot spot** – (1) something which is very much in demand. 'The bus took the party of German students to all the tourist hot spots in London.' (2) a dancehall or night club frequented by teenagers. 'I know of a new hot spot in town. Let's go!' (3) an area where one may expect political or military trouble. 'I must warn you, Mr Jenkins, that you will have to visit many political hot spots if you wish to be a journalist here.' (4) an area where there is very high radioactivity. 'You may find radon hot spots in Devon, Cornwall and Wales.' cf. '**a blackspot**' **8/7**.

Heat

10. **to take the heat out of something** – to weaken the impact, reduce the tension in an argument or quarrel. 'Mr Nobbet took the heat out of his children's disagreement by threatening to cancel their holiday if they didn't make up.' Also: **a heated argument**.

Rainbow

11. **a rainbow coalition** – an alliance of minority groups. 'Our rainbow coalition still hasn't got enough votes to get into government. Perhaps we'll manage it next time?'

Cloud

12. **to cast a cloud over** – to sadden, to fill with gloom, to mar one's pleasure. 'The news of her father's illness cast a cloud over Mary's honeymoon.'

13. **to hang over someone like a cloud / like a dark/poison cloud** – a menacing presence. 'Mr Collins was swindling the Inland Revenue, but his fear of

being discovered hung over him like a cloud.'

1. **to be under a cloud** – to be the object of someone's suspicion. 'Gerald has been under a cloud at the office ever since the petty cash went missing.'

2. **to have a cloud lifted from over one** – to be cleared of suspicion, to end a period of depression, to be restored to favour. 'Now that the cloud over Richard has been lifted, he will be much happier at the office.'

3. **wait till the clouds roll by** – wait until the difficulties have eased. 'I am sure our difficulties are only temporary. We must wait until the clouds roll by.'

4. **on Cloud Nine** (US colloquialism) – very happy, joyful. 'Since her engagement to Peter, Joan has been on Cloud Nine.' Cloud Nine was originally Cloud Seven, which was probably derived from 'the seventh heaven'. cf. '**in (the) seventh heaven**' 260/12.

5. **to be / to have one's head in the clouds** – to be out of touch with reality. 'It's no good asking him what to do. He has his head in the clouds.'

6. **to live in Cloud-cuckoo-land** – to live in one's imagination in a world that bears no relation to reality. 'If you think Judy's scheme would ever work, then the two of you must be living in Cloud-cuckoo-land!' From Aristophanes' comedy *The Birds*, which depicts the building of an imaginary city in the air by the birds. cf. '**never-never land**' 212/7; '**to live in a dream world**' 125/13.

7. **a cloud no bigger than a man's hand** – a distant, insignificant threat, but one that may become dangerous in the course of time.

Squalls

8. **look out for squalls** – be on your guard against trouble. A nautical phrase, meaning a sudden gust of wind that may capsize your boat if you are not careful.

Wind, Whirlwind

9. **a fair wind** – favourable conditions (for a project or enterprise).
   to wish something or someone a fair wind – to wish something or someone success. 'The prime minister wished the new legislation against football hooliganism a fair wind.'

10. **to whistle in the wind** – to talk to someone without obtaining a sensible reply. 'You might just as well whistle in the wind as talk to Larry.' Also: **like whistling in the wind**; **to spit into the wind**.

11. **the wind of change** – a new outlook, a fresh point of view. The phrase was first used by Harold Macmillan in reference to political developments in Africa. cf. '**a breath of fresh air**' 11/9.

12. **to know which way the wind is blowing** – to foresee the general drift of events, to know in advance what is likely to happen, to make a correct prediction. A variant is '**wait and see which way the wind blows**' – to await developments before making up one's mind. 'I shall wait and see which way the wind is blowing before committing myself.' Much used in political comment.

13. **to sail close to the wind** – to verge on the improper or the illegal, to stop just short of breaking the social code. 'The comedian sailed close to the wind. Some women in the audience were looking distinctly uneasy.'

14. **to take the wind out of someone's sails** – to embarrass someone by forestalling him, anticipating his actions. 'Counsel for the accused was about to address the jury when he had the wind taken out of his sails by his client, who blurted out that he was guilty.' Literally, the phrase means to take the wind out of another ship's sails by sailing close to it on its windward side. cf. '**to cut the ground from under one's feet**' 107/13; '**to pull the rug from under one's feet**' 167/13.

15. **to get one's second wind** – to regain one's energy, to acquire fresh strength.

'After a bad start, Paul got his second wind and tried again.'

1. **in the teeth of the wind** – literally, moving against the wind, despite the wind, and hence figuratively against any opposition. The wind can be a strong hindrance to the progress of a sailing ship.

2. **in the wind's eye** – directly facing the wind.

3. **to put the wind up someone** – to alarm or frighten someone. 'You put the wind up me, telephoning at three in the morning. I thought that something terrible had happened.'
   to get the wind up – to become alarmed or frightened. 'We all got the wind up when the bride didn't arrive at the church. We thought she must have changed her mind, but she was only late.'

4. **to throw caution to the winds** – to take bold action without considering one's own safety.

5. **to get wind of** – to receive early warning of imminent events, often from a confidential source. 'We got wind of his resignation a week before it was announced in the newspapers.' This is on the analogy of an animal that scents danger in the wind.

6. **there is something in the wind** – something is about to happen; one suspects that something important is going to happen without knowing what. 'The clerks in the office have been exchanging knowing glances for the last week, and there's been a lot of whispering going on. Something is in the wind.'
   what's in the wind? – what's up? what's going on? The same idiom as above in the interrogative form.

7. **to raise the wind** – to obtain the necessary finance.

8. **a windfall** – an unexpected stroke of good luck, e.g. a legacy from a distant relative. The literal meaning is fruit blown from the tree to the ground which can be eaten without being picked.

9. **a windbag** – someone who is talkative but incapable of action.

10. **long-winded** – verbose, using several words when one would have done. Here are some examples taken from a memorandum of the British Tourist Authority on the teaching of English, BLE/1980: 'an integrated programme of studies' *instead of* 'a curriculum'; 'suitably graded groups for teaching purposes' – *instead of* 'classes'; 'teachers with appropriate training and relevant experience' *instead of* 'qualified teachers'; 'transfer of students between one group and another' *instead of* 'promotion'. cf. **'gobbledygook' 216/11**; **'plain English' 215/10.**

11. **to tilt at windmills** – to fight imaginary enemies, hence to squander one's energy uselessly. 'Why do you always attack the landlords, Jack? There are hardly any private landlords left in London. You are tilting at windmills.' From Cervantes' *Don Quixote*, in which an elderly knight attacked windmills, in the mistaken belief that they were giants who had imprisoned innocent girls.

12. **a whirlwind romance/courtship/ marriage** – falling in love, entering a relationship at great speed. 'Peter and Barbara married secretly in Bristol after a whirlwind holiday romance.'

Storm

13. **the calm before the storm** – a period of quiet before an upheaval or crisis.

14. **to take by storm** – to exert an irresistible fascination over something (a woman, city, country, etc.). 'Caruso took all America by storm.'

15. **to take the world by storm** – to have phenomenal success everywhere. 'The performance of the Irish tap-dancers was so unusual that they took the world by storm.'

16. **to ride the storm** – to confront a crisis resolutely. 'I refuse to resign; I shall ride the storm, no matter how long it lasts.'

17. **to bow before the storm** – to submit to public indignation and protest. 'There was such an outcry when the government put forward its proposals that it was forced to bow before the storm and withdraw them.'

1. **to provoke/cause a storm** – to cause an outburst of fury. 'The sports minister provoked a storm when he admitted that he did not think England had a chance of winning the World Cup.' Frequent usage: **a storm of controversy**.

2. **a storm in a tea-cup** – a violent agitation over a trifle. 'Father was furious with Geoff for doing the *Times* crossword puzzle before he came down to breakfast, but they were soon friends again. It was all a storm in a tea-cup.'

3. **a storm chaser** – someone who follows a tornado or 'twister'. 'There are plenty of storm chasers in America who enjoy the excitement and danger of the chase.'

Thunder

4. **to steal someone's thunder** – to divert attention from the person expecting it to oneself by adopting his or her methods. This happens when a minor actor overshadows the leading player, and receives the applause the other was expecting. 'Although Philip had only a minor role, he completely overshadowed the leading player and stole all his thunder.'

5. **blood and thunder** – violent, melodramatic. Almost always applied to plays and stories. 'There were at least six murders in that blood-and-thunder story.'

Lightning

6. **as quick/fast as lightning / like (greased) lightning / lightning-like** – with the speed of lightning; so fast that you barely have time to see it. 'I've never seen anyone move so fast. He ran like lightning across the field.' Also: **like a bolt/streak of lightning**; **lightning-fast**.

7. **a lightning strike** – a strike that is called without warning.

Blitz

8. **to blitz something / to launch a blitz** – to start an attack. 'All this paperwork is piling up in the office. Let's launch a blitz on it and sort it all out.'

9. **to blitz / blitzing** – a price-cut initiative by the supermarkets. 'Blitzing of many product ranges is greatly welcomed by the consumer.' *Blitz* is the German for 'lightning'.

Sky

10. **sky-high** – very high indeed, soaring. 'Don't drink any more coffee, Granny! You know it sends your blood pressure sky-high!'
    sky-high prices – extremely expensive. 'We can't afford to go abroad anymore. Not with these sky-high prices everywhere.'

11. **the sky's the limit** – with no limit. 'I've just inherited a fortune, so spend what you like! The sky's the limit!'

12. **eye/spy in the sky** – satellite surveillance. 'Eye-in-the-sky satellites make their way through the heavens day and night, photographing us and gathering information.' cf. **'pie in the sky' 179/16**.

Horizon

13. **to broaden one's horizons** – to increase one's knowledge or experience, usually by travelling abroad. 'We have sent our son to America to broaden his horizons.'

14. **to loom (large) on the horizon** – likely to happen in the near future, threatening to happen soon. ' "Trouble's looming on the horizon," the policeman muttered into his mobile phone. "A gang of skinheads is approaching." '

Sun, Sunny

15. **sunny side up** – a fried egg that has not been turned over, so that the yoke is showing. 'I don't want my egg sunny side up this time, Louisa. Please fry it well on both sides to kill any salmonella germs!'

Moon, Moonlight

16. **to be over the moon** – to be extremely happy. After having failed her driving test four times, Anna was over the moon

when she passed it at last.' Also used as a football cliché: 'The football manager was over the moon when his team scored the winning goal.'

1. **to live on the moon** – to be out of touch with everyday life. 'You haven't given me enough petrol money, Grandad. You must be living on the moon!'

2. **to do a moonlight / a moonlight flit** – to escape from one's responsibilities, usually at night and often involving change of lodgings to avoid paying rent. 'Who would have thought my lodger would do a moonlight flit! He seemed such a decent young man.'

3. **moonlighting** – to have an unauthorized job besides one's legal job or occupation, earning extra money without declaring it to the Inland Revenue. 'The decorator was caught moonlighting last night in the Soho dancing school.'

4. **like the dark side of the moon** – mysterious. ' "Do you know what's going on in that research laboratory, Philip?" "No, it's like the dark side of the moon." ' Whatever the position of the moon, it is always impossible to see one part of it from the earth, which remains permanently hidden from our sight.

Star, Meteor

5. **a rising star** – a small celebrity whose fame is spreading and becoming well known. 'Melanie MacInty is a rising star in the movie world. We are going to see a lot more of her.'

6. **a star-gazer** – a dreamer. 'Don't force Alex to learn accountancy. A star-gazer like him would be better off at art school.'

7. **to see stars** – to see spots of light after being hit on the head. 'Alan's father saw stars after banging his head on the door post.'

8. **stars in their eyes** – young people dreaming of fame and stardom. 'In a TV programme called *Stars in their Eyes* young performers hope to be discovered for a career in films or television.'

9. **a meteoric rise to fame, power, etc.** – a sudden spectacular success. 'The lead singer of The Sandshifters began his meteoric rise to fame in a small Bristol night club.'

Shade, Shadow

10. **to put someone in the shade** – to outdo someone with a better performance. 'However hard she tried at school, someone always put her in the shade.'

11. **to emerge from the shadows** – to come out into the open. 'After having worked in obscurity for many years, the scientist emerged from the shadows with a brilliant invention.'

12. **beyond/without a shadow of doubt** – to be absolutely sure. 'When Linda saw the burglar at the identity parade, she was able to point him out without a shadow of doubt.'

13. **to be afraid of one's own shadow** – to be afraid to meet people, to be shy and timid. 'It's no good inviting Pam to your party. She never goes anywhere; I do believe the poor girl is afraid of her own shadow.'

Light
(see also *Light* in Chapter 17)

14. **to cast/shed/throw light on something** – to make something clear, to explain. 'The recovery of the knife might shed some light on the murder mystery.'

15. **to show someone in his/her true light** – to let it be known what a person is really like. 'When Silvia needed her friend's help urgently, the girl refused and so showed herself in her true light.'

16. **to be a leading light** – someone who is well thought of in a certain area. 'Dr Barnard was a leading light in heart transplants in his day.'

17. **to come to light** – to be discovered, exposed, to come out into the open. 'If you hadn't told me, his criminal record would never have come to light.'

18. **light at the end of the tunnel** – a glimmer of hope is in sight. 'After all her operations and suffering, the new treatment

meant there was light at the end of the tunnel.'

Dark

1. **to be kept in the dark / to keep in the dark** – to be kept in ignorance, not to divulge a secret. 'If farmers are kept in the dark about the location of GM crop-sites, they will not know what is being grown in a neighbouring field.' cf. '**a cloak of secrecy**' 193/19; '**a wall of silence . . .**' 156/12.

Time

1. **high time** – the time has come when delay is no longer possible. 'It's high time you got ready or you will miss your train.'

2. **to have a rough time** – to be treated severely, to have a run of bad luck.

3. **to have the time of one's life** – to have a wonderfully happy time. 'James was dreading his military service but now he is in the army, he is having the time of his life.'

4. **an all-time high** – an occurrence of the highest number ever. 'Complaints about train delays have rocketed to an all-time high.'
   an all-time low – (1) an occurrence of the lowest number ever. 'Polling stations recorded an all-time low in the number of voters.' (2) the worst depression imaginable. 'Julia reached an all-time low when she found out about her husband's third affair.'

5. **a good-time girl** – a girl who lives for pleasure, a loose woman.

6. **to be born before/ahead of one's time** – to be born before people are in a position to appreciate one's true worth. Many important scientists and artists have died in obscurity.

7. **for the sake of old times / for old times' sake** – to honour past friendships, to do someone a favour. 'I've only got the afternoon between flights, but I had to see you for old times' sake.'

8. **time out of mind** – time immemorial, beyond human memory. 'Some are born to rule, and others are born to serve; so it has always been, time out of mind.'

9. **more times than I've had hot dinners** – more times than I can remember. 'I've shown tourists round the Houses of Parliament more times than I've had hot dinners.'

10. **behind the times** – out of date in one's ideas. 'Why, Grandfather, you haven't got a video. You *are* behind the times!'

11. **to take one's time** – to do something at one's own pace without hurrying. 'Our builder is taking his time, isn't he? He's been three days on that job already.'

12. **to fritter away one's time/energy/money** – to divide one's attention among a number of activities so that time, energy and money are wasted. 'If you hadn't frittered your time away on so many useless projects, you would have qualified by now.'

13. **to bide one's time** – to wait for the right moment to take one's revenge, or carry out a plan.

14. **to mark time** – to delay taking action until everyone else is ready; from the military command 'Mark time!' – to stamp the feet on the same spot without advancing. cf. '**to tread water**' 13/3.

15. **to have a rare time** – to have exceptional fun.

16. **time(s) without number** – many, many times. Often used to express impatience or annoyance. 'I have warned you time without number not to accept lifts from strangers.' Literally, so many times that they can no longer be counted.

17. **time is of the essence** – time is the most important consideration. A condition is sometimes made in a contract

that time shall be of the essence, meaning that the work must be completed by a definite date, otherwise the contract is cancelled.

1. **to be pushed/pressed for time** – to have little or no time to spare, to be in a hurry.

2. **time flies/slips by** – time goes by really quickly, much quicker than one realizes. 'Soon it will be autumn. How time flies!'

3. **time is running out** – there is little time left. 'We have only three shopping days left till Christmas. Time is running out.' Time is here compared with sand running through an hour-glass.

4. **no time to lose** – there is a great urgency. 'To save the child, he must be taken to hospital immediately. There is no time to lose!'

5. **to live on borrowed time** – to regard each year exceeding the normal life-span as not one's own but for temporary use only. 'Susan tried her best to be happy for her family's sake, knowing she was gravely ill and living on borrowed time.'

6. **(dead) on time** – absolutely punctual.

7. **in the nick of time** – at the very last moment, with no time to spare. 'I caught my aeroplane in the nick of time.'

8. **near her time** – approaching the moment when her baby will be born.

9. **to make up for lost time** – to work extra hard to compensate for time wasted.

10. **to take time off** – to absent oneself from work, often for a particular reason. 'I took time off this morning to visit my sister in hospital. I'll make it up this evening.'

11. **to have time on one's hands** – to have nothing to do, to be idle. 'Why don't you ask Tony round for a game? During the holidays he will have time on his hands.'
    time hangs heavy on one's hands – time passes far too slowly and one is bored.

12. **how time drags!** – how slowly the time passes! what a boring time we are having!

13. **to kill (the) time** – to do anything, however trivial, to pass the time and so avoid being bored. 'We had an hour's wait, so we played cards to kill the time.'

14. **empty time** – time without one's loved one, time between engagements, meetings, etc. 'The princess didn't know what to do with all the empty time she had in Los Angeles while her husband was fulfilling his engagements.' cf. '**an empty existence**' 37/14.

15. **to serve one's time** – to work for the prescribed number of years in a service (army, navy, civil service, etc.).

16. **to do time** – to serve a prison sentence.

17. **a race against time** – a rush to get a task finished within a given time.

18. **a time-server** – someone who adopts the principles of his or her superiors in order to gain advancement.

19. **a time-lag** – the interval between a cause and its effect. For example, there is always a time-lag between the printing of money by the government and the resulting rise in prices.

20. **a time slip** – this is when one experiences a different time for a little while. One sees people from a different century, wearing clothes belonging to a different period and speaking an older version of one's language. The classic example is of two Englishwomen, Eleanor Jourdain and Anne Moberly, who went to Versailles in 1901 and experienced a time slip there which took them back to a day in the late 18th century.

21. **to live in a time warp** – a feeling that one is living in a different dimension in time, either in the past or in the future. The time-warp theme has often been used with great success in films and novels. Sometimes people choose to live in a time warp in the past to escape the stress of modern life. There is a village in the north of England where a group of people are living in a time warp, dressing and behaving in the manner of 200 years ago.

22. **time-consuming** – requiring a great deal of time. 'It was time-consuming work, going through all the Jessops in the

telephone directory, but we tracked him down in the end.'

1. **a question/matter of time** – sooner or later. 'It's only a question (or matter) of time before you are caught!'

2. **in the fullness of time** – at the proper time, in the end. 'In the fullness of time, your contribution to physics will be recognized; have patience and do not despair.'

3. **in one's own good time** – whenever someone is ready, and not before. 'Don't hurry me! I shall join you in my own good time!'

4. **to have no time for** – to disapprove strongly of. 'I have no time for people who preach equality and then take their holidays in the Bahamas.'

5. **to make time** – to spare time, even when one is busy, for an additional duty. 'I know you have a lot to do, but you must make time for Henry. He's an old friend of yours.'

6. **prime time** – the peak period for radio and television, drawing the largest audience. 'The controversial documentary about the Royal Family beat every prime-time programme on Saturday night.'

7. **quality time** – a phrase used by people who work all day but have set aside a period of time to devote to their children or friends. ' "I am determined to spend more quality time with my children during the week," said the managing director.'

8. **to play for time** – to try to delay some undesirable action in the hope that conditions will meanwhile improve. 'They want their money at once, but if your uncle is coming back on Tuesday, I can play for time until then.'

9. **to be in the right place at the right time / wrong place at the wrong time** – fortunate or inopportune/unfortunate circumstances. 'Mr Williams was in the right place at the right time when he was able to drag the child out of the pond and save her life.' 'My son is completely innocent. He is only guilty of being in the wrong place at the wrong time and with the wrong people.' Also: **to be the wrong man/woman in the wrong place at the wrong time; to do the wrong thing for the wrong reasons at the wrong time; to hit the wrong note at the wrong time in the wrong way**.

10. **to march/move/keep up with the times** – to keep one's attitude and methods up to date. 'If we don't march with the times, our customers will go elsewhere.'

11. **to fall on hard times** – to experience a sudden deterioration in one's living conditions. 'Poor Mrs Wilcox has fallen on hard times since her husband ran away. She can't afford to heat her house any more.'

Year

12. **year in, year out** – repeatedly over a long period of time. The phrase is often used of fixed habits. 'Year in, year out, Mr Masters would make his way to his local pub on the stroke of one.'

13. **a gap year** – a year's interval. 'Robert planned to spend his gap year between school and university touring New Zealand and then working on a sheep farm in Australia.'

14. **from the year dot** – a date so long ago that one cannot imagine it. 'From the year dot, humankind has been wondering about its origins.'

15. **the man of the year** – the most talked-of man of the year, in a good sense, cf. **'the man of the day' 31/5**.

16. **to be light years away from someone** – to have nothing in common with someone, to hold views that cannot be reconciled with the other person's. The analogy is with the time light takes to travel, implying a vast distance.

17. **the lost years** – wasted years that can never be made up.

18. **years of discretion** – the age at which a boy or girl is old enough to make moral judgements.

Season

1. **in season** – at the right time, at an opportune time. 'Why can't we have peaches? They are in season, aren't they?'
   out of season – at the wrong time, during the close season when game may not be shot.

2. **a word in season** – a timely piece of advice.

3. **the silly season** – the time of the year when Parliament is in recess, and newspapers, having little news to report, start idle theoretical discussions in their columns.

The Seasons: Spring, Summer, Autumn

4. **to spring clean** – to clean and redecorate one's house, when the winter is over.

5. **an Indian summer** – a period of great happiness that comes late in a person's life. Literally, a late summer, a spell of warm sunshine in October. (Late summers are common in the West of the USA, which was mostly settled by Native Americans, or 'Red Indians', when this phrase was first used.)

6. **the autumn of one's life** – well into middle age, with the best years behind one.

Months: April, May

7. **to make an April fool of someone** – to play a joke on someone on the morning of 1 April.

8. **a may-day warning** – an international call for help, a signal transmitted by ships and aeroplanes warning of impending danger. 'May-day' has nothing to do with the month of May but is a corruption of the French international signal 'M'aider', meaning 'Help me'.

Days of the Week: Monday, Friday, Sunday

9. **that Monday morning feeling** – a feeling of depression when people have to return to work after the weekend holiday.

10. **Black Monday** – the first day of the school when lessons are resumed.

11. **Man Friday** – a faithful servant and companion. From Defoe's *Robinson Crusoe*.
    Girl Friday – a personal assistant in an office, the phrase having been coined from Man Friday.

12. **Dress Down Friday** – one day in the week when employees in an office may exchange their formal suits for very casual clothes, such as jeans and a T-shirt. This is based on the idea that you work better if you are comfortably dressed.

13. **not in a month of Sundays** – not for a long time, far longer than is necessary; usually said in an exasperated or impatient tone. 'That won't be ready in a month of Sundays.'

14. **one's Sunday best** – one's best clothes.

Day

15. **day in, day out** – day after day without any interruption.

16. **one of these (fine) days** – before long. The phrase is used in predicting some (unpleasant) event. 'One of these fine days you'll get run over if you don't take care.'

17. **an off day** – a day when one works badly. 'Pauline must have had an off day; her typing is full of mistakes.'

18. **it's not my day** – everything is going wrong for me today.
    just one of those days – a day when everything goes wrong; said in a tone of resignation.

19. **not to have all day** – not to have any more time to spare for somebody. 'I do wish you'd tell me exactly what you want – I haven't got all day.' Used to express the speaker's impatience or exasperation (impolite).

20. **late in the day** – too late. The expression is often used as a reproach: 'It's a bit late in the day for you to cancel the booking; I've made all the arrangements.'

21. **to call it a day** – (1) to stop working,

often said when the workers feel they have done enough for one day. (2) it can also mean that it would be better to put an end to an arrangement. 'I suggested to my partner that, since we didn't agree, we should call it a day.'

1. **it's early days yet** – it's too early to judge. 'Wait until you have got used to the work before you make up your mind. You've only been there a few days. It's early days yet.'

2. **that will be the day!** – used ironically to indicate a desirable event that will never occur. 'When Peter finishes his book, did you say? That'll be the day!'

3. **to make someone's day** – to delight someone, often in an unexpected way. 'Receiving a call from her daughter in Australia made Pamela's day.'

4. **at the end of the day** – ultimately, when the battle or campaign is over. 'At the end of the day, I am sure our policies will have been justified.'

5. **to be the man of the/his day** – to be the outstanding man of his time. cf. '**man of the year**' 29/15.

6. **to carry/win the day** – to triumph over one's adversary, to win the struggle.

7. **a field day** – a highly successful occasion when full advantage is taken of every opportunity, especially an opportunity to ridicule or punish an opponent. 'Your new book is full of mistakes; the critics will have a field day!' Originally a military term for allocating a special day to army exercises.

8. **to have had one's day** – to be past one's best.

9. **a hey-day** – the best days, the prime. 'The early 19th century was the hey-day of English romantic poetry.' 'Hey' may be a corruption of 'high'. cf. '**in the halcyon days**' 71/3, which has the same meaning.

10. **open as the day** – transparently honest, without subterfuge.

11. **a day's grace** – grace days are those allowed by law or by the creditor for the payment of a debt. Hence, an extra period of time allowed before being called to account. 'Grace' in this idiomatic sense may apply to a number of days or months, or even to a year.

12. **to fall on evil days** – to live in poverty after having enjoyed better times.

13. **in the cold light of day** – in a mood of sober realism, as opposed to one of uncritical enthusiasm (frequently used with reference to ideas and plans that have been put forward). 'We discussed my idea at dinner and my boss became terribly excited about it. However, in the cold light of day, he saw many objections to it.'

14. **a black day** – a day that has disastrous consequences. 'It was a black day for us when Harris joined the firm. He has done nothing but make trouble for us ever since.'

15. **a bad-hair day** – the effect of bad-looking hair on a woman's emotions and actions. 'Leave her alone, Sally. She's in a terrible mood. She must be having another bad-hair day!' cf. '**flyaway hair**' 84/3.

16. **the order of the day** – (1) the day's routine or programme. 'Swimming is the order of the day.' (2) it can also mean the way things are: 'Open prisons are the order of the day.'

17. **all in the day's work** – all part of one's normal duties. ' "I am so grateful to you for giving my little girl first aid." "That's quite all right; it's all in the day's work." '

18. **to name the day** – to fix the date for the wedding.

19. **early-closing day** – one afternoon in the week, usually Wednesday or Thursday, when the shops are closed.

20. **the daily grind** – the monotonous routine of everyday life.

21. **the day of reckoning** – the time when one is obliged to answer for one's misdeeds. 'There will be a day of reckoning for what you have done to me!' The phrase comes from the biblical Day of Judgement.

Daylight

1. **to see daylight** – to gain an insight into a problem. 'After months of work, we are beginning to see daylight.'

2. **daylight robbery** – a shameless swindle. 'Charging you £200 for that simple repair was daylight robbery.'

3. **to frighten/scare the living daylights out of someone** – to terrify someone almost to death, by threats and intimidation.

4. **to beat the living daylights out of someone** – to give someone a severe beating.

Yesterday

5. **not born yesterday** – old or wise enough not to be easily taken in. 'You won't fool me with that trick. I wasn't born yesterday.'

6. **yesterday's man** – a man, especially a politician, who must make way for someone younger and more dynamic. 'I would get on good terms with Jenkins, if I were you. Mr Lightburn is yesterday's man and will be retiring soon anyway.'

Night

7. **to burn the midnight oil** – to work late into the night.

8. **a fly-by-night operator** – someone who sets up business for only a short time in order to make a big profit, and then moves on.

9. **a one-night stand** – a sexual encounter which lasts only one night. 'The actress demanded money for her baby from a famous TV personality after claiming her daughter was conceived after a one-night stand.'

Morning

10. **morning breath** – bad breath (or halitosis), which is often worse after a night's sleep – hence the name.

Hour

11. **in the small hours of the morning** – in the early hours of the morning.

12. **at all hours** – at an unusual time, often used in a censorious manner. 'The neighbours have parties at all hours.'

13. **an unearthly hour** – unreasonably, absurdly early. 'Switch off that alarm clock at once! I don't want to get up at this unearthly hour!'

14. **a good hour** – at the very least one hour, probably more.

15. **happy hour** – a certain time of day, often early in the evening, when food and drinks are sold at reduced prices.

16. **a solid hour** – a full hour, often used when the time passes slowly. 'We waited for you a solid hour.'

17. **to while away an hour** – to spend an hour in a pleasant way. 'If you have time to spare, let's while away an hour just lying on the beach watching the waves.'

18. **to improve the shining hour** – to make oneself useful. Used humorously: 'You can improve the shining hour by cleaning the car, Tom.'

19. **the question of the hour** – currently the most debated question.

20. **in one's hour of need** – at a time when help is most urgently required. 'Yes, £100 will be most useful. Thank you for helping me in my hour of need.'

21. **the rush hour** – the time of day when people travelling to and from their work are crowding the buses and trains.

22. **flexi hours / to work flexitime** – adaptable working hours which suit one's circumstances, e.g. starting early and leaving early, or starting late and leaving late. The agreed total of working hours must be adhered to.

23. **a long-hours culture** – the self-employed and managers who work between 50 and 70 hours a week in order to further their careers.

Moment

1. **on the spur of the moment** – on a sudden impulse, without premeditation.

2. **in the heat of the moment** – at a moment when one's anger has been aroused. 'In the heat of the moment I suppose I might attack an armed burglar, but never in cold blood.'

3. **the man of the moment** – one who enjoys public acclaim, but only for a short time.

4. **in an unguarded moment** – in an indiscreet moment. 'In an unguarded moment Alison told me she had been convicted of shop-lifting many years ago.'

5. **to have its moments** – to be good, exciting, interesting, but only occasionally. 'The cruise was disappointing although it had its moments. I shall always remember our day in Madeira.'

6. **the moment of truth** – the moment of crisis when one learns the truth about oneself. 'I have often wondered how I would react if I saw a girl in the street being attacked by a gang of hooligans. For me, that would be the moment of truth.'

7. **the psychological moment** – the most propitious time, the best time to seize an opportunity. 'He was on the point of proposing to Karen when the telephone rang. The psychological moment had passed.'

Second

8. **to be struck by the ohnosecond** – the sudden shocked realization that one has made a mistake or forgotten something. 'At passport control I was suddenly struck by the ohnosecond – I had left my passport on the kitchen table.'

Age

9. **to come of age** – to attain the legal age of manhood/womanhood.

10. **the age of consent** – the age when a girl or homosexual boy may lawfully consent to have sexual intercourse. The age of consent in Britain is currently 16 for a girl

and 18 for a homosexual boy. Below that age, her or his consent, even if freely given, is deemed to be unreal, and the man is guilty of the crime of rape.

11. **the awkward age** – adolescence. 'Don't mention Janine's untidy bedroom to her, Dad. She's at an awkward age.'

12. **at a ripe old age** – very old. 'He lived to a ripe old age.' cf. **'a green old age' 4/16**.

13. **to take/be an age** – to take a long time over something, to keep someone waiting. 'What an age you've been, Simon!'

14. **it's ages since . . .** – it's a very long time since . . . 'It's ages since we met.'

15. **to be/act one's age** – to behave like a grown-up person. 'For heaven's sake, be your age, Martin! You are 18, not eight!'

16. **to feel one's age** – admitting to less energy, various ailments and the decline of mental and physical capability that come with increasing age. 'Feeling exhausted after playing with his two little grandchildren all afternoon, Mr Higgins really felt his age.'

17. **to look/looking good for one's age** – to look younger than one's years. 'I would never have thought your mother was 70. She looks really good for her age.'

18. **to show one's age** – to betray one's age by trying to look younger than one really is. 'She showed her age when she dressed like a teenager.'

19. **the Age of Aquarius** – the New Age, a time of great spiritual freedom and thirst for knowledge. The Earth's axis traces a circle in outer space, divided by astronomers from ancient civilizations into the twelve signs of the Zodiac. This cycle is completed every 26,000 years. Aquarius is the 11th sign of the Zodiac, named after a group of stars known as the Water-bearer. Water symbolizes knowledge. See *Gods of the New Millennium* by Alan F. Alford.

20. **New Age** – a spiritual movement which has its roots in Paganism. Being in harmony with nature, loving and protecting the environment are important aspects of the New Age movement.

1. **the electronic age** – a time when we are dependent on devices run by electricity, such as computers, telecommunication systems, electronic shop checkouts, banking, and so on. 'The young are far happier about entering the electronic age than older people.'

Date

2. **to date something** – (1) to establish the date an object was made, implying that it is the product of an earlier age. (2) also used in reference to elderly people. 'His manners and speech date him.'

3. **to have a date** – to arrange a meeting with a member of the opposite sex. 'I've just made a date with Philip. We are going to the theatre tomorrow evening.'

4. **date rape** – rape of a woman by a man whom she has met socially. 'Be very careful who you go out with, Josie. Half of all rape victims are attacked in date rapes.'

Clock

5. **to work round the clock** – to work without ceasing at a task until it is finished. 'For that money I'm prepared to work round the clock.'
   round-the-clock presence – (1) uninterrupted presence, both day and night, usually of nurses working in intensive-care stations in a hospital, giving round-the-clock service. (2) round-the-clock surveillance by bodyguards or detectives.

6. **a clock-watcher** – someone who has lost interest in his work and does the absolute minimum required. 'Alan was an enthusiastic teacher when he started here, but now he is a clock-watcher – just like the rest of the staff.'

7. **a nine-to-five job** (short for nine o'clock in the morning till five o'clock in the afternoon) – usual working hours; the idiom is sometimes used to imply a humdrum and boring routine. 'Jonathan is getting bored with his nine-to-five job. He is thinking of going to sea as a ship's steward.'

8. **five o'clock shadow** – a man showing signs of needing a shave again by the afternoon or evening. 'Be sure to shave away your five o'clock shadow, Dennis, before we go out tonight.'

9. **to put the clock back** – to recapture an earlier period of time. 'You can't order young people about any more. Times have changed, and it is useless trying to put the clock back.' Frequent usage: **if only we could turn back the clock!**

10. **to go/run like clockwork** – to go exactly according to plan. 'We got the group to Edinburgh without the least difficulty. Everyone cooperated, and it all went like clockwork.'

By-gones

11. **let by-gones be by-gones** – let's forgive and forget.

Life

1. **a walk of life** – an occupation or profession. 'I have travelled all over the world and have met people from every walk of life.'

2. **the prime of life** – the best moments of one's life after one's youth; a time filled with achievement and satisfaction. 'Mr Forbes is in the prime of his life and is now seriously looking for an attractive woman to marry.'

3. **for the life of me** – even if my life depended on it. 'I can't for the life of me see why you should take your holiday in Yorkshire just because you were born there.' The phrase is used negatively, generally with 'can't' or 'couldn't'.

4. **as large as life** – in person. 'I had just posted a letter to James in Cologne – when suddenly there he was, as large as life, standing right in front of me!'
   larger than life – outstanding, extravagant, unrealistic. 'In a special memorial service the dead hero was described as a larger than life character.'

5. **a fact of life** – a truth which must be accepted, no matter how unfair or unreasonable it may seem. 'I'm sorry that you find the rule unreasonable, but there is nothing I can do about it; it is a fact of life.'

6. **not on your life!** – in no circumstances, certainly not. An emphatic way of refusing a request. ' "If you are going to the theatre this evening, would you mind very much taking my aunt along?" "Not on your life!" '

7. **you (can) bet your life** – you can be absolutely certain. This phrase is often used ironically of people who are expected to act in a particular way, judging by what one knows of their past behaviour. 'You can bet your life that, if Edward comes, Mary will come too. She won't let him out of her sight for a second.' Also: **to stake one's life on something**.

8. **for dear life** – as if one's life were in danger. 'When the two burglars saw Patrick come into the hall, they ran for dear life out of the house and down the garden.'

9. **to cling to life** – to do everything possible to stay alive. 'The seriously ill man was determined to cling to life for as long as possible and tried all kinds of herbal remedies.'

10. **to hang on to life** – just about surviving; there is hope, but one's life is still in danger. 'After that tragic accident, he is still hanging on to life.' cf. **'at death's door' 38/11; 'on the verge of death' 38/12**.

11. **within an inch of one's life** – very near to losing one's life. Often used as a hyperbole. 'If I catch you stealing again, I will thrash you to within an inch of your life.'

12. **to the life** – an exact likeness, a living likeness. 'The portrait has been very well done; it's you to the life.'

13. **to come to life** – (1) to regain consciousness after a faint. (2) to gain in vigour and excitement. 'The first act of the play was rather dull, but in the second act it really came to life.'

1. **a new lease of life** – an opportunity to enjoy a happier/longer life. 'Robin's change of job has given him a new lease of life. He is his own master now, and looks 10 years younger.'

2. **to get one's life back** – to stop doing a job, work, etc. which makes one deeply unhappy, unfulfilled and dissatisfied, and start doing something completely different, which brings joy and fulfilment. 'How I love breeding dogs! I've got my life back at last and I'm so happy!'

3. **to pick up one's life** – to try to get back to leading a normal life. 'Lesley ran away from home to be with a pop star, but he dropped her after a few weeks and now she is trying to pick up her life.'

4. **to bear/lead a charmed life** – to escape unscathed from many dangers as if one were protected by a magic power. 'Henry's companions were all injured but he returned without a scratch; he must lead a charmed life.'

5. **the life and soul of the party** – the person who brings the most sparkle and excitement to a party. 'Janice is so quiet and demure in the office that you'd never think she was the life and soul of the party last night.'

6. **a cushy life** – a soft and easy life. 'With parents as rich as that, what else can the boy expect but a cushy life.'

7. **the high life** – a luxurious, pleasure-loving way of life. 'Donald will find Bromley rather quiet after the high life he has been living in Bermuda.'

8. **the low life** – the life led by riff-raff, vagabonds, tramps and petty criminals.

9. **a high-profile life** – a very noticeable way of life, very much in the public eye. ' "Your high-profile life is getting me down, Thomas," his wife complained. "You never have time for me any more!" '

10. **to see life** – to broaden one's experience by mixing with men and women of all types, including the immoral and dissolute. 'Tom should see life before he marries and settles down.'

11. **to put one's life on hold** – to wait for everything to be just right. 'This job may not be perfect, Steven, but accept it. It's no use putting your life on hold.'

12. **to turn one's life upside down** – to change one's life beyond recognition. 'The big win on the lottery has turned our lives upside down.'

13. **to lead a double life** – to lead the life of two distinct and separate people. The classic example is R. L. Stevenson's *Dr Jekyll and Mr Hyde* in which the same man is depicted as a respectable scientist by day and a monster by night.

14. **one's life falls apart** – the most important aspects of one's life go badly wrong. 'David got into such severe financial difficulties and trouble with his wife that very soon his life began to fall apart.'

15. **there's life in the old dog yet** – I may not be as young as I was, but I am still full of energy. Often said by elderly people to counter suggestions that their powers are failing.

16. **I can't do it to save my life** – it wouldn't be possible, even if my life depended on it. 'I can't play tennis to save my life, but I enjoy watching it.'

Live, Living

17. **to live beyond one's means** – to live in a style one cannot afford. 'No wonder the Howards have gone bankrupt; they have been living beyond their means for years.'

18. **you live and learn** – a comment on a new and unexpected fact. 'Who would have thought that Mr Saunders of all people would be arrested for shop-lifting? You live and learn.'

19. **to live up to** – to match someone else's standards. 'I don't want to go to the same school as my brother; I could never live up to him.'

20. **to live up to one's reputation** – to behave in a manner that may be expected by one's friends and acquaintances. 'The headmaster is certainly living up to his reputation. He is a real disciplinarian.'

21. **to live on one's reputation/name** – to rely on one's past achievements to earn a living. 'It's easy enough to live on one's

reputation; the real problem is to win a reputation in the first place.'

1. **to live something down** – to repair damage to one's reputation by improving one's behaviour or skill in one's calling. 'The operation was a disaster; I shall never live it down.'

2. **to live a lie** – to be a hypocrite, to mislead people as to one's true nature. 'Mr Holmes had lived a lie for the past five years: by day, he worked as a parson in the parish of St Giles; by night, he frequented the night clubs in the West End.'

3. **how the other half lives** – how people in a different class from oneself live. 'You should get around and see how the other half lives.'

4. **to live rough** – to live in uncomfortable conditions. 'However long you live rough, you never really get used to the hardship.'

5. **to live with something** – to put up with something unpleasant that one cannot rid oneself of, especially ailments. 'The doctor tells me that it is only a minor inconvenience which I must learn to live with.'

6. **live and let live** – to be tolerant and not interfere in other people's lives. 'What does it matter to you who your brother spends his free time with? I believe you should live and let live.'

7. **to live in sin** (old-fashioned) – to have a sexual relationship with a person to whom one is not married. 'When are Steven and Pamela going to get married, or are they going to live in sin for ever?'

8. **to live it up** – to spend money recklessly on one's own pleasure. 'I should have thought the Wallaces had better things to spend their money on than living it up in Paris.'

9. **to live in the fast lane** – to live a hectic life full of parties, alcohol- and drug-taking. 'Veronica is in a clinic for drug addiction and general ill-health. She has been living in the fast lane far too long.' The 'fast lane' refers to the outer lane in the motorway which is used by drivers who enjoy driving very fast, sometimes even recklessly, just for the thrill of it.

10. **alive and kicking** – very much alive. 'You needn't worry about Robert. He was alive and kicking when I saw him this afternoon.' The phrase derives from the kicking of a baby in the womb.

11. **a live wire** – a person with enormous energy and initiative who is never inactive. 'If you want to raise money for the orphanage, you should put Bill in charge of the fund-raising; he is a real live wire.' Literally, a live wire is the wire that is charged with electricity.

12. **plain living and high thinking** – moral philosophy and tasteless food. 'After a week's plain living and high thinking at my cousin's, I'm in the mood for a good pub-crawl.'

13. **a living will** – a document which states that if one becomes terminally ill, artificial means should not be used to prolong one's life. Copies of this should be given to a lawyer and also to several close relatives or friends.

Existence

14. **an empty existence** – a meaningless, aimless life. 'Those two high-society girls live such an empty existence, just going to parties all night and sleeping all day.' cf. the opposite: **a packed existence** – being occupied and very busy all the time. cf. **'empty time' 28/14.**

Death

15. **sick to death** – exasperated beyond endurance. 'I am sick to death of his stories. He tells me the same ones every time I meet him.'

16. **to be tickled to death** – to be extremely amused. 'We were tickled to death when we heard Roger had come top in the exams after his terrible school report.'

17. **to frighten someone (half) to death** – to give someone a terrible shock or fright. 'Don't ever creep up on me like that again! You frightened me to death!'

1. **to bleed to death** (not of a person) – to collapse, in consequence of mounting costs, debts, etc. 'If we don't get fresh orders soon, we shall bleed to death. There is no money to pay the bills.'

2. **to hold/hang on like grim death** – to hold very tightly, as if one's life depended on it. 'The old man was hanging on to his briefcase like grim death. I wonder what he had in it.'

3. **to work oneself to death** – to exhaust oneself from overwork. 'We have worked ourselves to death and all for a pittance!' cf. **'to break one's back' 104/7**.

4. **to work something to death** – to over-work something so much that it can no longer produce useful results, such as when an idea loses its force through constant repetition. 'You've been saying the same thing in your publicity for 20 years. You have worked our idea to death; it's time you thought of something new.'

5. **to catch one's death (of cold)** – to catch a very bad cold. 'You'll catch your death if you go out into the cold night air after that hot bath.' Often used as a warning.

6. **as pale as death** – pallid and wan. Used only to describe someone's face. 'Steven's face was as pale as death when he was told his parked car had rolled over the cliff.' cf. **'as pale as pastry' 180/4**.

7. **to feel/look like death / like death warmed up** – to look gravely ill, to be seriously indisposed. 'Poor Nancy could not manage her physics exam and left the examination hall looking like death.' cf. **'to feel like a wet rag / like a washed-out rag' 201/16**.

8. **the kiss of death** – an act of betrayal that effectively destroys a project, relationship or life. 'On the pretext of showing concern for her husband's well-being, Mrs Andrews gave him the kiss of death by telephone. Having established his presence at home, she sent two hired assassins to murder him.' The allusion is to the betrayal of Christ by Judas Iscariot by means of a kiss.

9. **a death wish** – being tired of life, contemplating suicide. 'Mr Wilkins became depressed after losing his job and developed a death wish, driving recklessly everywhere in his car.'

10. **to be in at the death/kill** – to be present at the climax, at the final phase. 'Everyone is expecting the chairman to resign this afternoon. Do you want to be in at the death?' The phrase is taken from hunting when the fox is caught by the hounds and killed.

11. **at death's door** – to be dying. 'I'm afraid there is no hope left. Your father is at death's door.'

12. **on the verge of death** – very close to dying. 'The patient was on the verge of death after being bitten by the snake, but luckily the serum was administered just in time.'

13. **a brush with death** – to have been close to getting killed. 'When the plane crashed on take-off, the passengers had a brush with death which they will never forget.' cf. **'to escape by the skin of one's teeth' 110/21**.

14. **to cheat death** – to escape with one's life. 'Don't ever skate near that thin ice again, Henry. You can't cheat death twice!'

15. **to sound the death knell for something** – to announce that the end of something is near. 'Shocked by the bad standards in maths, the education minister sounded the death knell for classroom calculators.' The death knell is the sound of a bell that is rung to mark a death or burial.

16. **a near-death experience (NDE)** – people who have almost died tell of how they travelled through a dark tunnel towards a welcoming light. Here they met divinities, according to their religion, saw their loved ones who had previously died and then were told by an angel that it was not yet their time to die; they must return to life. cf. **'an out-of-body experience' 80/7**.

Die

17. **to die hard** – to resist change, especially changes in tradition, customs and ideas.

'The dogma dies hard that a student should master the grammar of a foreign language before starting to speak it.'

1. **to die in the last ditch** – to resist (something) to the very end, to fight to the death. 'If the government tries to demolish the Health Service, that is the last ditch in which many of us will die' (*Observer*, 8 January 1983).

Dead

2. **to cut someone dead** – to refuse to return someone's greeting, to ignore someone with intentional rudeness. 'Mrs Hammond must be very angry with you to have cut you dead; she is normally so polite.'

3. **to make a dead set at** – (1) to make a vigorous attack on a person (usually verbal). (2) to make a strong bid for a person's affection. 'From the moment I entered the ballroom, Susan made a dead set at me; she ruined my evening.'

4. **drop-dead beauty / drop-dead gorgeous** – to be stunningly beautiful, striking. 'The film star charmed the crowds in London with her spectacular clothes and drop-dead beauty.'

5. **a dead loss** – completely unproductive, useless. 'That course Pietro went on was a dead loss; after three months, he still couldn't speak a word of English.'

6. **a dead letter** – a law (or rule) which has not been repealed but is no longer enforced. 'The punishment for high treason under the Treason Act is death, but it has become a dead letter.'

7. **dead wood** – superfluous material. 'If you cut out all the dead wood, we might consider your book for publication.'

8. **dead-beat** – completely exhausted. 'After a day's shopping in London, I am always dead-beat.' cf. **'to be whacked' 271/2**.

9. **to be dead on one's feet** – to be absolutely exhausted. 'Do let Andrew sleep in tomorrow morning. He seems dead on his feet.'

10. **the dead spit / spit and image of** – exactly alike. 'The twins are the dead spit

of each other. How do you tell them apart?'

11. **in the dead hours of the night / in the dead of night** – in the middle of the night. 'We'll leave in the dead of night when everyone is asleep; no one will hear us.'

12. **to refuse to be seen dead in / I wouldn't be seen dead in** – to have a violent dislike of particular clothes. 'Just look at the price they are asking for that horrible dress in the window. I wouldn't be seen dead in that rag!'

13. **over my dead body** – against my strong opposition. 'If that man wants to marry Joanne, it will be over my dead body.'

14. **dead and buried** – an old quarrel or dispute that was disposed of and forgotten long ago. 'I thought that quarrel you had with Jack over the house was dead and buried.'

15. **to end in deadlock** – to end without agreement. 'Talks between the two warring leaders have ended in deadlock once again.'

Grave, Graveyard

16. **as silent/quiet as the grave** – deathly still, soundless, very quiet. 'Our town centre is as silent as the grave every evening; there's never anything to do.'

17. **to dig one's own grave** – to lose out through one's own fault. 'Tim dug his own grave when he told the taxi driver about his new invention. He marketed it as his own and Tim got nothing.'

18. **a graveyard spiral** – complete loss of control of a plane or helicopter, diving to earth. 'John Kennedy Junior was piloting his plane when it fell in a graveyard spiral, killing him.'

19. **a graveyard shift** – working overnight on the late shift that begins at midnight or 2 a.m. 'Poor Robert has the graveyard shift all this week, but he'll be able to go shopping with you on Saturday.'

Shroud, Pall

1. **to shroud someone/something in secrecy** – to keep someone/something out of the public eye, to mask or obscure something. 'For some years the planting of GM crops had been shrouded in secrecy, but then it became public knowledge after all.' Also: **shrouded in darkness/mist/mystery/confusion**. A shroud is a piece of cloth in which a dead body is wrapped prior to burial. cf. '**a veil of secrecy' 196/8**.

2. **to hang over something like a pall** – to be like an invisible cloak over something; a sad, depressing presence looming over one. 'After the big department store was destroyed by fire, quiet hung over it like a pall.' A pall is a large, heavy cloth that is draped over a coffin or tomb. Also: **a pall of dust / a pall of darkness / a pall of smoke hangs over something; to throw a pall of gloom over something**.

Ghost

3. **a ghost writer** – a person who is employed to write for someone else, but to keep this a secret if possible. 'It is believed that the journalist will be ghost-writing the film star's memoirs, as she herself has no talent for writing.'

4. **a ghost patient** – an imaginary patient thought up by corrupt doctors, dentists or opticians as a way of getting extra money from the British National Health Service. 'The doctor made £1 million by swindling the NHS with a long list of ghost patients.'

5. **a ghost driver** – someone who drives on the wrong side of the road, either by mistake or in an attempt to commit suicide.

6. **a ghost town** – a town that is no longer inhabited. 'Now that the last shop has closed down, the village looks like a ghost town.' It is said that Great Britain has more ghosts than any other country in the world.

7. **to be only a ghost of one's former self** – to have been very ill and lost a lot of weight, vitality and happiness. 'I got such a shock when I saw Margaret after her accident. She was only a ghost of her former self.' Also: **a ghost of a smile**.

Spirit

8. **to be with someone in spirit** – to be thinking of someone with sympathy, anxiety, etc., without being with him/her in person. 'I wish you every success, Tina; I shall be with you in spirit.'

9. **the moving spirit** – the originator of an idea or project. 'I would like to know who the moving spirit is behind this idea. How stupid of him to put us on shift-work when business is so slack!'

10. **to take something in the right spirit** – to accept advice or criticism without bitterness or resentment. 'We have completed our report on the efficiency of your office staff and are sorry that they have not taken our advice in the right spirit.'

11. **to dampen one's spirits** – to discourage a good mood or stifle good humour. 'Jane had so been looking forward to the dance; trust her jealous brother to dampen her spirits.'

    to lift/raise someone's spirits – to cheer someone up.

12. **to spirit away** – to remove quickly and secretly. 'I wonder what has happened to the vase Aunt Sheila gave us for Christmas. One of the children must have spirited it away!' The original meaning was to abduct or kidnap, when young Africans were 'spirited away' to the plantations in the West Indies.

Fortune

13. **a hostage to fortune** – a risky act or unwise remark which should have been made more carefully as it might be used against one sometime in the future. 'The young prince said he never wanted to become king, but one day he might regret having offered this hostage to fortune.' 'Hostages' used to mean those dearest to one, as in 'He that hath wife and children hath given hostages to fortune' (*Essays: Of Marriage and Single Life* by Francis Bacon).

Fate

1. **to tempt fate** – to provoke fate by taking a needless risk, or by taking the same risk again, especially after a lucky escape. 'To go climbing again today after your lucky escape yesterday would be to tempt fate.'

2. **to seal one's fate** – to have no means of escape, no alternative. 'If you swim about in those shark-infested waters, Michael, you will seal your own fate.'

3. **a quirk of fate** – a strange and unexpected occurrence. 'By a quirk of fate Brenda found herself on the same Mediterranean cruise as her English teacher.'

4. **a fate worse than death** – the most terrible thing that can happen to one (used humorously). 'Having to listen to their neighbour's piano-playing all evening was a fate worse than death.'

Miracle

5. **nothing short of a miracle** – quite astounding, utterly remarkable. 'After the earthquake, the old woman emerged from the ruined house unharmed. It was nothing short of a miracle.' Also: **a miraculous escape/recovery**.

Holy Grail

6. **the Holy Grail** – a highly prized aim or ambition. 'The quest for turning sea water into inexpensive salt-free drinking water has now become the Holy Grail of modern science.' In medieval legend, Jesus drank from the grail (a cup, chalice or platter) at the Last Supper. Later, when Jesus was dying on the cross, Joseph of Arimathaea caught some drops of his blood in this very same grail, and brought it to Glastonbury in England. This is where it disappeared and King Arthur's knights had many adventures in their never-ending quest to find it again. See *The Holy Grail* by Malcolm Godwin.

Halo

7. **the halo effect** – judging people only by appearances, such as by the clothes they wear, the cars they drive, their social circle; assuming, for instance, that people who wear glasses are very intelligent; that elderly professors with beards are absent-minded. Nowadays the halo effect is also used in educational circles. If a good child mixes with a bad child, by association, he will also be regarded as bad by the teacher, even if he is innocent of any wrong-doing. The idea that every living thing has an aura originated thousands of years ago in the Far East. The aura varies in colour – ranging from a gloomy grey aura for bad people, and going through various other colours until one reaches perfection in a bright yellow or white aura. This aura culminates in the halo around the head, such as has been depicted in famous paintings where saints have been shown to have a yellow, white, silver or golden halo around their heads, showing their saintliness. If a good child is near a bad one, it is suggested – figuratively – the grey colour of the bad child's halo will spill into the lighter colour of the good child's halo, thus corrupting him. cf. **'birds of a feather' 67/1**.

Mantra

8. **to repeat mantra-like / like a mantra** – repeat in succession. 'The words "too much stress" are repeated mantra-like by all the girls in our office.' A mantra is a sacred word or sound used during meditation in Hinduism and Buddhism.

Idol

9. **to treat someone like an idol** – to adore or worship someone without question.

10. **a fallen idol** – a disgraced person in the eyes of someone who had worshipped him or her, and now been disillusioned. 'Malcolm had always adored the film actress but she became a fallen idol after she smashed up her hotel room in a fit of rage.'

Icon

1. **to become an icon** – to become an object of veneration, to be greatly admired and held up as an example for people to follow. 'Princess Diana became an icon to many women after her death.'

Heaven, Nirvana

2. **heaven on earth** – perfect conditions in which to live or work. The phrase is often used to draw a comparison. 'Having laboured for three years on his first novel in a Glasgow slum, it seemed like heaven on earth to the young writer to work on his second in Nice.'

3. **in heaven's name!** – an interjection used to express impatience or annoyance. 'What have you done with the plane tickets? In heaven's name, you haven't lost them, have you?'

4. **manna from heaven** – something that arrives unexpectedly to help someone out of his or her difficulties. 'The spare can of petrol the farmer produced when he found Paul stranded on the moor with his motorbike, was like manna from heaven to him.' Manna was the name given by the Israelites to the miraculous food they found on their journey out of Egypt (Exodus XVI, 15). The word might come from the Egyptian *mennu* for tamarisk. A tamarisk is a tropical or Mediterranean shrub or tree which secretes a sticky honeydew, gathered by Middle Eastern desert nomads every June.

5. **to stink/smell to high heaven** – to be a public outrage, a scandal. 'The behaviour of these officials stinks to high heaven; there should be a public inquiry.'

6. **like nirvana** – in a state of absolute bliss, to be supremely happy. 'It would be like nirvana to own one's own home and have an enormous garden!' Nirvana is a Buddhist beatitude, i.e. a state in which individuality is extinguished and absorbed into the supreme spirit.

God

7. **a (little) tin god** – a self-important, dictatorial person. 'Now Sanders has been made manager, he's behaving like a little tin god.'

8. **to put the fear of God into** – to terrify. 'When Ralph takes me out in his racing car, he puts the fear of God into me.'

9. **there, but for the grace of God, go I** – I have been just as blameworthy but, thanks to good luck, have escaped the consequences. 'All my friends are in hospital with food poisoning except for me – I only ate some salad. There, but for the grace of God, go I.' Shakespeare expresses the same idea in *Hamlet* (II, ii, 561): 'Use every man after his desert, and who would 'scape whipping?'

10. **as true as God's in heaven** – to be completely sure of something. cf. '**to take as Gospel**' 274/11.

11. **to think that one is God's gift to** – to overestimate one's intelligence, skill or attractiveness. 'Just because Joe is moderately goodlooking, he thinks he is God's gift to women!' cf. '**to fancy oneself**' 125/8.

12. **an act of God** – (1) a legal term for a catastrophe of nature that no one could reasonably have foreseen. (2) in ordinary parlance, what seems like an act of divine mercy. 'It was an act of God that everyone escaped from the aeroplane unhurt.'

13. **to play God / to play at pretending to be God** – doctors who do not allow terminally ill patients to die a natural death, and who do all they can to prolong their lives and prevent them from dying, by means of sophisticated modern machinery, etc. This also applies to doctors and scientists who experiment with embryos, cloning and gene technology. 'Scientists are now doing genetic experiments on human embryos. We mustn't let them play God.'

14. **a godsend** – an unexpected gift or offer of help. 'When Pamela broke her leg, the arrival of her sister was a godsend to her.'

Angel

1. **enough to make the angels weep** – so foolish that even an angel would despair. 'The way you have treated Helen is enough to make the angels weep.' The allusion is to Shakespeare's *Measure for Measure* (II, ii, 117): 'But man, proud man, / Drest in a little brief authority . . . / His glassy essence, like an angry ape, / Plays such fantastic tricks before high heaven / As make the angels weep.'

2. **like an angel** – with the utmost innocence and purity. 'Thomas sings like an angel in the school choir, but you should see him on the football field!' Also: **to have a voice like an angel; to write/ dance like an angel**.

3. **to be on the side of the angels** – to be on the right side in the struggle between good and evil; to have the right principles or opinions, from the speaker's point of view. 'We shouldn't be critical of George; with all his faults, he is on the side of the angels.' The phrase has been taken from Disraeli's speech (made at Oxford, 1864): 'Is man an ape or an angel? I, my Lord, I am on the side of the angels.'

4. **a guardian angel** – one who protects another's interests from the purest and most unselfish of motives. 'Margaret has done so much for us without expecting anything in return; she has been a true guardian angel.'

5. **a library angel** – an invisible angel who appears to direct one's attention to books which may change one's future life by stirring up an interest in a completely new subject.

Soul

6. **a soulmate** – someone who has the same characteristics as another person and therefore gets on extremely well with him or her. 'Those two really are soulmates. They understand each other so well and are quite inseparable.' cf. **'kindred spirits'** 140/14.

7. **soul-searching** – consulting one's conscience on how to react to something. ' "Do I really love Irene enough to marry her?" It was a soul-searching experience for Norman.'

8. **like balm to one's soul** – healing and soothing. 'Luckily James had a kind and devoted nurse. She was like balm to his soul.'

Charm

9. **to work like a charm** – to turn out beautifully, to one's great satisfaction. 'Robin had trouble going to sleep at night. Then his mother decided to read him a bedtime story and it worked like a charm. He quickly fell asleep.' A charm is a spell or an enchantment, something which possesses magical power. A charm such as an amulet or trinket on a chain may be worn to avert evil or ensure good luck. cf. **'like magic / to work like magic'** 320/14.

Doom

10. **doom and gloom / gloom and doom** – an impression of depression and despair. 'This television programme is full of gloom and doom. Let's turn over to something more cheerful.'

11. **prophet(s) of doom** – a person or people who forecast bad events. 'Many prophets of doom proclaim the end of the world every few months.'

12. **harbinger of doom** – something which tells one of some impending catastrophe. 'Through the ages, comets have been frequently mentioned in myths as harbingers of doom.'

Damned

13. **damned if you do, damned if you don't** – it is impossible to satisfy everyone. 'Should we intervene in this nightmarish conflict? We're damned if we do and damned if we don't.' cf. **'a Catch-22 situation'** 261/15.

Disaster

14. **a recipe for disaster / a disaster waiting to happen** – to have all the ingredients for misfortune. 'Are you seriously

thinking of crossing the English Channel in that little sailing boat? That's a recipe for disaster!'

Dire Straits

1. **to be in dire/desperate straits** – to be suffering great hardship, difficulties. 'What happened to the old lady? She seems to be in dire straits by the look of her.'

Sin

2. **sin bin** – a special room in a school where unruly pupils are sent in order to show that they are in disgrace, and to keep them away from the better-behaved pupils. 'Setting up sin bins in schools might cut down the high number of expulsions of unruly pupils.'

Hell

3. Similes with 'hell': **like going to hell and back; like hell on earth; to hurt/ache like hell; as sure as hell; to be as angry/frustrated/lonely/ guilty as hell; as weird/peculiar as hell; as curious/shrewd/cunning as hell**.

4. **all hell broke loose** – there was a state of uproar and disorder. 'If you tell the men that they won't be getting the increase in wages you promised them, all hell will break loose.' Also: **merry hell broke out**. The derivation is from Milton's *Paradise Lost* (Book IV, 918): 'All hell broke loose.'

5. **come hell or high water** – whatever the obstacles. 'Come hell or high water, I am determined to succeed.'

6. **for the hell of it** – for no particular reason except to give oneself pleasure. 'Asked why he had beaten up a complete stranger, the young man replied that he had done it for the hell of it.'

7. **who/what/how (etc.) the hell** (slang) – an emphatic exclamation expressing anger. 'Who the hell do you think you are, talking to me like that!'

8. **hell for leather** – at a mad speed, reck-lessly fast. 'Jack was driving his motorbike hell for leather down the country lane.'

9. **to play (merry) hell with** – to aggravate or cause harm. 'This constant damp weather plays hell with my rheumatism.'

10. **to give someone hell** – (1) to make someone's life very unpleasant. 'I love my father dearly, but really, he does give me hell sometimes.' (2) to berate someone. 'The manager gave his team hell at half-time when they were losing 3–0.'

11. **to go through hell** – to have a dreadful experience. 'Marion went through hell when she was wrongfully accused of drug-dealing.'

12. **to hell with** – to be not in the least concerned with. 'To hell with all your complaints; I shall play the piano all day long if I want to.'

13. **go to hell!** (rude) – go away and leave me in peace. Often said in reply to offensive comments or threats.

14. **hellbent on** – absolutely determined, regardless of the consequences. 'I don't know what's the matter with Roger; he seems hellbent on killing himself with those stunts of his!'

15. **hellhole** – an unpleasant and disreputable place. 'The arcades under some railway stations are absolute hellholes, filled with tramps, beggars, alcoholics and drug addicts.'

16. **neighbours from hell** – aggressive and abusive neighbours. 'I can't bear to live next door to such neighbours from hell any longer. I'm moving house' cf. '**a sink estate**' 150/7.

Devil

17. **the devil's own job** – an immensely difficult task. 'Disentangling all this barbed wire is the devil's own job.'

18. **give the devil his due** – however bad someone may be, give that person credit for any good quality he or she may have. 'Sergeant-Major Andrews used to bully the young recruits without mercy, but, to give the devil his due, he always treated me fairly.'

1. **to have the luck of the devil** – to have a great deal more luck than one deserves. 'Brian always invests his money in rubbish, but instead of going down, his shares always go up; he has the luck of the devil.'

2. **to talk/speak of the devil** – to be talking about someone when he suddenly appears. 'It's bad manners of Dennis always to keep us waiting. Shall we go? Oh, talk of the devil, there he is!'

3. **the very devil** – an appalling nuisance. 'Little Martin is so sweet most of the time, but, when he gets cross, he can be the very devil.'

4. **daredevil** – someone who risks his/her life doing something dangerous just for fun. 'Gary's latest daredevil stunt was to jump over the river on his motorbike.'

Demon

5. **the demon in the bottle / the demon drink** – strong alcoholic drinks. 'Even young children should be warned about the demon in the bottle and its harmful effects.'

6 Trees and Plants

Flowers

1. **flower power** – a social movement of the 1960s, begun in the USA, which believed that love could overcome enmity and hate. Flower power rejects the laws and morality of contemporary society. 'Mr Tebbit, the Trade and Industry Secretary, blamed the end of National Service and the emergence of flower power . . . for the violence in our society' (*Daily Mail*, 25 July 1985).
   flower people – advocates of flower power.

2. **as welcome as flowers in May** – to be welcomed with much joy and happiness.

3. **say it with flowers!** – women often prefer the gift of flowers to protestations of love.

Rose

4. **the English rose** – the delicate beauty of a young English girl.

5. **roses in her cheeks** – the tender, delicate pink colour in her cheeks. ' "We'll get the roses back into her cheeks, Monica," the doctor told her.'

6. **rose-petal skin / petal-soft cheeks** – very soft, delicate skin/cheeks. 'The mother looked at her sleeping child lovingly and then kissed his petal-soft cheek.' Also: **rosebud mouth; rosebud lips**.

7. **it was roses, roses all the way** – a wonderful success in which everybody cooperated without any difficulty or unpleasantness.

8. **a path strewn with roses** – a career free from obstacles.

9. **a bed of roses** – a pleasant, enjoyable situation without any drawbacks or irritations. 'His job is a bed of roses compared with mine: short hours, a good salary and interesting work.'

10. **it isn't a bed of roses** – it isn't an easy life, the conditions are hard and disagreeable.
    it's not all roses – there are difficulties to be overcome, as well as pleasures to be enjoyed.

11. **the white rose** – a symbol of innocence and purity.

Other Flowers and Plants

12. **the primrose path** – the path of self-indulgence that ends in ruin. From two references from Shakespeare: 'the primrose path of dalliance' (*Hamlet*, I, ii, 47), and 'primrose way to the everlasting bonfire' (*Macbeth*, II, iii, 22).

13. **as pale as a lily** – to look deathly pale, to have white, pallid skin. 'The Marquis de Casalduero is as pale as a lily because the bats drained his blood while he slept' (*Of Love and Other Demons* by Gabriel García Márquez).

14. **lilies and roses** – a clear, fresh, beautiful complexion.

15. **a shrinking violet** (facetious) – a shy, self-effacing person. 'Adrian expressed his views very freely at the meeting last night; he is not such a shrinking violet as we imagined.'

16. **a wallflower** – a girl who has not been invited to dance, but sits with her back to the wall in the ballroom without a partner.

1. **to lay up in lavender** – to treat something as very precious, carefully preserved for a future occasion.

2. **as fresh as a daisy** – full of energy.

3. **to be in clover** – to be in a comfortable situation, enjoying the best things in life without having to make an effort. From cattle feeding in a field of clover.

4. **an open sesame** – a means of gaining immediate access to influence and patronage. The word comes from the Greek, sesame, a tropical and sub-tropical plant that is grown in the East Indies.

5. **to grasp/seize the nettle** – to take drastic action to overcome an unpleasant difficulty. 'It's time you grasped the nettle and told your friend that you can no longer support him.'

6. **'The ivy can grow no higher than its host'** – a remark made by the French philosopher Descartes about critics: No matter how brilliant and learned a critic may be, he can never surpass the writer on whom he is dependent.

The Garden

7. **to lead someone up the garden path** – to deceive, mislead someone. 'We never realized we were being led up the garden path until it was too late.'

8. **everything in the garden is lovely** – everything is splendid, and there is nothing to worry about. (Often used to express the contrast between appearance and reality.) 'The food was perfect and the management were so friendly; everything in the garden was lovely until the waiter handed us the bill.'

9. **in the bloom of youth / in her first bloom** – in the full beauty of youth.
   past her bloom – past her best, when the beauty of her youth is beginning to fade.

10. **to blossom out into** – to develop very well. 'When Lloyd George became prime minister in 1916, he blossomed out into a statesman.'

11. **the pick of the bunch** – the best, the outstanding one in a group.

12. **to nip in the bud** – to frustrate a plan, plot, etc., before it has time to gather strength; to destroy at an early stage. 'The police inspector proudly presented his ideas for nipping criminal behaviour in the bud.'

13. **a budding writer/politician/artist** – one who is just beginning to make a name for him- or herself.

Thorn

14. **a thorn in the flesh/side** – a constant irritant, a source of continuous annoyance. 'The boy was a thorn in his father's flesh for many years, always contradicting him and criticizing his way of life.'

15. **to sit on thorns** – to be in a painful or embarrassing situation; to be in constant fear of being found out. 'For many years he was sitting on thorns; he had never qualified as a doctor, although he cured many of his patients.'
   a bed of thorns – an extremely painful or embarrassing situation.

16. **a crown of thorns** – a legacy of trouble, a source of great tribulation. The phrase suggests that the troubles are pushed on to an innocent and unwilling victim. ' "I have inherited a crown of thorns," the young king said sadly.' Taken from Matthew XXVII, 29.

The Farm

17. **to reap a rich harvest** – to gain a splendid reward for one's efforts.

18. **a corny joke** – a hackneyed joke. cf. **'an old chestnut' 49/24**.

19. **to sow one's wild oats** – to experience youthful pleasures and excesses before settling down. 'What, 22 and still living at home! It's time he went abroad and sowed his wild oats.'

20. **a crop squat** – a group of people who settle on a field without legal right in order to prevent genetically modified crops being grown there. 'Protesters staged a two-week-long crop squat on the farmer's field, causing the trials of GM crops to be abandoned.'

Hay

1. **to hit the hay** – to go to bed. 'I think I'll hit the hay now. I have to be up early in the morning.' In former times, hay was used to fill mattresses.

2. **to make hay from** – to take advantage of an opponent's mistakes. 'The Republicans may be able to make almost as much hay from the misdeeds of a few Democrats as the Democrats did from the fall of President Nixon' (from *NOW!* magazine). The origin is from the proverb 'to make hay while the sun shines'.

3. **to make hay of something / to make hay with** – to throw into disorder, to confuse, to make a mess of.

4. **to go haywire** – to go crazy, to lose control of oneself. 'When his cat was run over, Michael went completely haywire and wrecked the motorist's car.'

5. **like looking for a needle in a haystack** – to look for something that is impossible to find. 'Robert's office is in such a mess; finding your letter will be like looking for a needle in a haystack.'

Straw

6. **a man of straw** – a worthless man, one without means or character.

7. **a straw poll / straw vote** – an impromptu, unofficial vote taken to test the direction in which public opinion is moving.

8. **a straw bid** – a worthless bid, one made without any financial backing.

9. **to draw straws** – to draw lots by picking straws of different sizes.

10. **to clutch at a straw** – to employ any means, however useless, to save oneself.
    a drowning man will clutch at a straw – a desperate person will resort to any expedient, no matter how impractical or hopeless.

11. **not worth a straw** – worthless. cf. '**not worth a fig**' 184/12.

12. **not to care/give a straw** – a straw stands for something worthless; the expression '**not to give a straw for**', or '**not to care two straws**', means to place no value upon a person or object. 'I don't give a straw for his opinion.'

13. **the last straw** – beyond the limit; the breaking point. From the proverb 'It's the last straw that breaks the camel's back.'

14. **a straw in the wind** – a slight indication of future developments. 'It may only be a straw in the wind, but she left half an hour after the dinner party last night. I don't think she is so keen on doing business with us as she was.'

Cud, Seed, Grain

15. **to chew the cud** – to ponder, consider a problem from every angle, think over carefully and deliberately.

16. **to run/go to seed** – to deteriorate in one's habits and appearance, to become shabby. 'When I called on him this morning, he was unshaven and wearing an old, stained dressing-gown. I am afraid he has run to seed.' The reference is to plants which, instead of developing new shoots, only produce seeds and lose their beauty.

17. **to sow the seeds of doubt, etc.** – to insinuate doubt, often with the idea of starting something without being noticed. 'He set to work sowing the seeds of doubt in their minds by hints and innuendoes.'

18. **seeded players / seeds** – players ranked by the organizers of a tournament in order of merit, and drawn so as not to meet one another until the closing rounds.
    an unseeded player – one not so ranked who may win, contrary to the opinion of the organizers; an 'outsider'.

19. **a grain/grains of truth** – some truth. 'I know it seems unbelievable, but there is a grain of truth in what he says.'

Grass, Reeds, Weeds

20. **to put someone out to grass** – to retire someone compulsorily on grounds of age. The phrase derives from putting horses that are too old to work out to pasture.

to go to grass – to retire on grounds of age.

1. **to hear the grass grow** – to have very acute hearing.

2. **keep off the grass!** – don't intrude on someone else's sphere of activity.

3. **grass roots** – the ordinary folk, those with their origins in the soil. In politics, the grass roots of a party are the ordinary membership, as opposed to the leadership. 'Ministers must take care to keep in touch with the grass roots of their party.'

4. **not to let the grass grow under one's feet** – to waste no time in getting a task done, to set to work quickly, without waiting for other people's agreement.

5. **the turf** – the world of horse-racing.

6. **to turf out** – to oust a person from a position, physically eject.

7. **a broken reed** – a weak, untrustworthy person; someone on whom it would be folly to rely. 'If you ever found yourself in serious trouble, Alex would abandon you without the least hesitation. He is a broken reed.'

8. **a reed shaken by the wind** – someone whose opinions are swayed by the latest fashion.

9. **to grow/spread like weeds** – to proliferate very fast. 'There is a crazy demand for his products. His business will grow like weeds.'

10. **to weed out** – to eliminate the undesirable.

Roots

11. **to take root** – to grow, become established. 'The ideas of Karl Marx have never taken root in the United States or Germany.'

    to have its roots in – to stem from, to be caused by. 'All crime has its roots in the loveless childhood of the criminal.'

12. **to grow/put down roots** – to develop interests and friendships. 'We have grown too many roots here to emigrate.'

13. **to uproot someone** – to part someone from a life and home he is used to.

'Moving to New Zealand meant uprooting his family but they hoped for a better life there.'

14. **to be/stand rooted to the ground/ spot** – to be transfixed or rendered immobile through fear, astonishment or shock.

15. **to get to the root of something** – to find the cause or source of something. 'This rumour has been circulating in the classroom for some time. I am going to get to the root of it.' cf. '**to get to the bottom of something**' 104/21.

16. **a deep-rooted habit** – a long-established or chronic habit. 'It won't be easy to rid him quickly of such a deep-rooted habit.'

17. **root and branch** – in its entirety, without any exceptions being made. 'The old customs in China have been destroyed root and branch by the new regime.'

Trees

18. **a family tree** – a genealogical record in the form of a diagram. 'My family tree goes back to the Normans.'

19. **the tree is known by its fruit** – you can judge someone best by his actions; deeds are more eloquent than words. The origin is from the Bible (Matthew XII, 33).

20. **up a tree/gum tree** – in great difficulty; unable to make any further progress.

21. **at the top of the tree** – at the top of one's profession.

22. **to bark up the wrong tree** – to accuse or blame the wrong person. 'Alison couldn't have stolen your watch. She was out all day. You are barking up the wrong tree.'

23. **a heart of oak** – someone loyal and brave on whom one can rely. 'You can always count on William in a crisis. He has a heart of oak and will stand by you, whatever the consequences.'

24. **an old chestnut** – an old hackneyed joke, one that has been over-used. 'His speech was full of old chestnuts. People in the audience groaned at each one.' cf. '**a corny joke**' 14/18.

1. **to give the palm to** – to acknowledge as champion.

2. **to bear/carry the palm** – to signal one's triumph.

3. **to carry off the palm** – to win the victor's crown.

4. **to yield the palm** – to admit defeat, to acknowledge the victory of one's opponent.

5. **palmy days** – the days of one's triumphs, past glories.

6. **to look to one's laurels** – to be aware of a new challenge to one's supremacy.

7. **to rest on one's laurels** – to be content with past achievements without making any further effort.

Bush, Hedge

8. **to beat about the bush** – to broach a subject indirectly, to delay coming to the point. 'Stop beating about the bush and tell me what you want.' A shooting idiom: the 'beaters' beat about the undergrowth in order to put the birds up.

9. **to take to the bush** – to withdraw oneself to the wild country, away from civilization. The 'bush' is an Australian term, meaning wild woodland which was originally inhabited by the Aborigines.

10. **bush-telegraph** – the rapid unofficial communication of news or gossip. 'Europe's bush-telegraph spread the news of the abdication crisis long before the British public got to hear of it.' Originally, the spreading of information by the beating of drums, etc.

11. **to hide one's light under a bushel** – to be modest about one's achievements or virtues. The reference is to Christ's parable: 'Neither do men light a candle and put it under a bushel, but in a candlestick' (Matthew V, 15).

12. **to hedge one's bets** – to reduce one's potential betting losses by betting on more than one result.

13. **dragged through a hedge backwards** – very untidy and bedraggled. 'What have you done to your hair,

Rachel? You look like you've been dragged through a hedge backwards.'

Wood

14. **not to see the wood for the trees** – not to be able to make out the essential because of all the detail. 'You have put in so much unnecessary detail that one loses track of the story; one can't see the wood for the trees.'

15. **to be out of the wood** – to be out of trouble or danger. Often used negatively. 'Business is looking up, but there's still a lot of money to repay; we aren't out of the wood yet.'

16. **to touch wood** – a superstitious belief that after congratulating oneself on one's good fortune, one should touch wood in order to avoid supernatural retribution.

17. **to crawl out of the woodwork** – someone unwelcome and who had previously kept in the background, who only now appears in order to take advantage of the situation. This originates in the idea of unwelcome insects, e.g. woodworm, cockroaches, which crawl out of their hiding places in the house to damage one's furniture or harm one's body.

18. **against the grain** – against one's instincts, against one's inclinations. 'It goes against the grain to rebuke a man old enough to be my grandfather.' Wood can be cut more easily if it is cut in the direction of the grain than across the grain.

Log, Branch

19. **to sleep like a log** – to sleep soundly, without stirring. From the idea of someone in a deep sleep lying absolutely still, 'like a log'.

20. **as easy as falling off a log** – something that needs no skill or effort to accomplish. cf. '**as easy as shelling peas**' **185/3**.

21. **to hold out the olive branch** – to make a peace offering. 'I thought it was time we held out the olive branch to Angela, so I invited her to dinner tomorrow. This quarrel has gone on long enough.'

Stick

1. **a dry old stick** – a dull, boring man, with very little to say for himself.

2. **the policy of the big stick** – the threat of force. From Theodore Roosevelt's speech on the need for the USA 'to speak softly and carry a big stick'.

3. **to get hold of the wrong end of the stick** – to misunderstand an explanation. The phrase is often used in reply to an unjust suspicion or accusation. 'You've got the wrong end of the stick; it was your friend, not I, who went through your things.'

4. **to be caught in a cleft stick** – to be forced to choose between two disastrous courses of action. 'Yvonne had promised to pay Susan's fine but then found she hadn't enough money. She would either have to let her friend down or sell her engagement ring; she was caught in a cleft stick.'

5. **to get the dirty/rough end of the stick** – to be treated unfairly, to bear all the blame. 'Whenever anything goes wrong in this house, I get the dirty end of the stick.'

6. **to be as cross as two sticks** – to be in a bad temper.

7. **a few sticks of furniture** – only a few pieces of furniture. 'Everything in the house had been taken except for a few sticks of furniture.'

8. **to up sticks** – to move house. 'I heard you are to up sticks, Mrs Stevens. Will it be to the seaside?'

Leaf

9. **to turn over a new leaf** – to repent one's way of life and make a fresh start; to reform. 'Each time he comes out of prison, Jack promises to turn over a new leaf – but he never does.'

10. **to take a leaf out of someone's book** – to follow someone's example. 'I am going to take a leaf out of your book and go into business.' Originally the phrase meant to plagiarize by taking a leaf, i.e. a page, out of someone else's book and making a copy of it.

11. **to leaf through a book** – to turn over the pages of a book without reading it thoroughly, in order to get a general idea of what it is about.

12. **to shake like a leaf** – to tremble with fear.

13. **to read the tea-leaves** – to foretell someone's future by examining the tea-leaves at the bottom of the cup. This refers to an old superstition that the tea-leaves have a hidden meaning for the drinker.

Rot

14. **to start the rot** – to begin the downward trend. 'Experimenting with soft drugs started the rot for the addict.' Also: **the rot sets in**; **to stop the rot**.

7 Animals

Animal

1. **to behave like an animal / worse than an animal** – a term of abuse for persons of great villainy and cruelty, since animals are not credited with a moral sense. 'They have behaved like animals; not even the youngest children were spared.' A common variation of this phrase is **'lower than the animals'**.

2. **a political animal** – someone with a special talent for politics. 'The ancient Greek was a political animal.'

3. **a party animal** – someone who adores going to parties and mixing socially with others. 'Sara is a real party animal but I wish she wouldn't drink so much.'

4. **animal spirits** – the exuberance and cheerfulness of youth that characterize a healthy body. 'He didn't mean any harm; it was only animal spirits.'

5. **animal passions** – what used to be called a person's 'lowest instincts'. Often used in reference to lust and lechery.

6. **a rare animal** – an unusual person who may combine two contradictory features or interests. 'He was that rare animal, a scientist turned artist.' cf. **'a rare bird' 66/5**.

Creature

7. **creature comforts** – those luxuries which make life pleasant and enjoyable, especially on a material level.

Beast

8. **it's the nature of the beast** – it's inherent in the character of the person, which will never change.

9. **to nail the beast** – to conquer an illness, overcome something/someone brutal and unpleasant. 'Mr Tilbrook fought hard against his cancer and eventually managed to nail the beast.'

10. **Beauty and the Beast** – a beautiful woman accompanied by a repulsively ugly man. A humorous phrase derived from the old fairy tale 'Beauty and the Beast'.

Pet

11. **pet name** – a special name expressing affection, such as 'Honey', 'Angel', 'Bunny', 'Kitten'.

Dog

12. **a dog in the manger** – one who denies to others the pleasures he can't enjoy himself. From Aesop's Fables, in which the dog prevented the cows from eating the hay in the manger by lying in it and snarling at them, while not wanting the hay himself.

13. **to lead a dog's life** – to lead a thoroughly miserable existence.

14. **to treat someone like a dog/a whipped dog/worse than a dog** – to treat viciously. cf. **'to feel like/treat someone like a leper . . .' 135/9**. 'He is a cruel, callous bully; he treats her worse than a dog.'

1. **a dog's dinner** (slang) – a horrible mess. **to dress up like a dog's dinner.** 'Wherever did you get those dreadful clothes? You look like a dog's dinner!'

2. **a hang-dog air/expression/demeanour** – a shame-faced, woebegone look. 'I wish something could be done to cheer up these office girls with their hang-dog expressions.'

3. **give a dog a bad name and hang him** – once someone has acquired a bad reputation, it is almost impossible for him to shake it off, and even his most innocent actions will be misunderstood. 'He had a reputation for stealing, so when he handed in a £10 note at the office, he was suspected of having come by the money dishonestly. Give a dog a bad name . . .'

4. **to help a lame dog over a stile** – to help a struggling person. 'He lent me £1,000 to start up my business. It was good of him to help a lame dog over a stile.'

5. **any stick will serve to beat a dog with** – it is easy to find fault with a person if you want to; any excuse will serve your purpose.

6. **not to have a dog's chance** – to have no chance at all. 'He is so much heavier than you; you haven't a dog's chance against him, however cleverly you box.'

7. **to work like a dog/like dogs** – to work very hard, to exert oneself to the point of exhaustion. 'The refugees found work on the black market but they had to work like dogs for very little pay.'

8. **love me, love my dog** – if you want to love me, you must put up with my faults, my friends and my relations.

9. **dog doesn't eat dog** – people of the same profession, school, etc., never make trouble for one another. 'It would be useless for you to appeal to the Law Society about your lawyer's behaviour. Dog doesn't eat dog!'

10. **to be top dog** – to dominate, to make oneself the master. By contrast, the '**under-dog**' – the loser in a fight, the inferior in strength. 'She always sympathizes with the under-dog, right or wrong.'

11. **a watchdog** – an authority looking after the interests of the consumer. 'Letters of complaint to the government watchdog over rip-off mortgages have risen alarmingly.'

12. **a dog-fight** – (1) a fight between two people. 'I don't want a dog-fight between the two of you, so behave!' (2) a battle between two aeroplanes.

13. **to be in the dog-house** – to be in disgrace, usually with one's spouse. 'His wife isn't speaking to him. He has been in the dog-house since he came home from a party at four in the morning.'

14. **a dog's-body** – one who does the routine or mechanical work. 'When I was at Bader's, I was only a dog's-body; none of the work I did required any skill.'

15. **dog-eared** – said of the pages of a book which have been turned down or have curled at the corners through excessive use.

16. **a dull dog** – someone who has nothing to say for himself, whose conversation is always uninspired and boring.

17. **a dirty dog** – an evil character; but the phrase is often used humorously for a sly fellow who gets what he wants by dubious methods.

18. **a sly dog** – one who keeps his pleasures to himself, a man who is discreet about his vices.

19. **a lucky dog** – one who enjoys undeserved luck. 'He isn't in the least good-looking or impressive, but all the girls fall for him – the lucky dog!'

20. **to take a hair of the dog that bit you** – to take more of the alcohol in which one has been over-indulging in order to cure a hangover. It was thought at one time that the hair of the dog that bit one was a cure for rabies.

21. **to be a lap-dog** – to be pampered and over-protected. 'She never lets her son play with other children. She has turned him into a lap-dog.'

22. **dog-Latin** – inferior or degenerate Latin

used by clerics, lawyers and doctors with an imperfect knowledge of the language. cf. **'cod Latin'** 216/8; **'pidgin English'** 215/8.

1. **dog-days** – the hottest weather. The phrase is a translation from the Latin *caniculares dies*, meaning the hottest days of the summer (in July and August). According to Roman theory, the hottest weeks of the year were determined by the rising of the dog-star Sirius which they believed contributed to the heat of the sun.

2. **to call off the dogs** – to abandon an investigation when inquiries are leading nowhere. Huntsmen call off their dogs when they follow a wrong scent.

3. **sick as a dog** – horribly sick.

4. **dog-tired** – exhausted after a hard day's work. 'I was dog-tired after working the whole day in the garden.'

5. **to let sleeping dogs lie** – to leave well alone and refrain from stirring up trouble. 'You must have known that mentioning his ex-wife would upset him. You should have let sleeping dogs lie!'

6. **his bark is worse than his bite** – (1) bullies generally prefer bluster to fighting. (2) a person is not as unkind or fierce as he pretends to be.

7. **the dogs of war** – a term of abuse for war-makers, mercenaries and war profiteers. Its original meaning was the horrors of war, e.g. famine, killing and atrocities (from *Julius Caesar*, III, i).

8. **to die like a dog** – to die without honour or dignity, to die in shameful circumstances.

9. **to go to the dogs** – to ruin oneself by licentious or degenerate living.

Poodle, Spaniel

10. **nobody's poodle** – someone with a mind of his own, one who is not easily led or persuaded to act against his better judgement. A poodle is commonly regarded as a foppish breed of dog, due perhaps to its mincing gait. Always used negatively.

11. **spaniel-like** – fawning behaviour. ' "Our party is displaying a spaniel-like devotion to the tobacco company," the health minister complained.'

Pup

12. **to sell someone a pup** – to swindle, to sell something under a false description. 'When we arrived at the hotel, we found we were paying twice as much as the other guests. The travel agent had sold us a pup.'

13. **a puppy/young puppy** – an arrogant or conceited young man. A cocksure young man who corrects his elders.

14. **puppy-fat** – plumpness that the boy or girl will shed on reaching maturity. 'She's a little on the tubby side, but it's only puppy-fat.'

15. **puppy love** – the love of a very young, immature person. cf. **'calf-love'** 58/9.

Tail

16. **to tail / put a tail on someone** – to keep watch on someone. This is usually done by the police or by a private detective. 'The baker was under suspicion of burglary, but to prove it the police had to tail him.'

17. **nose-to-tail traffic** – cars travelling bumper to bumper in one solid line. 'On public holidays the traffic on Britain's main roads is nose to tail.'

18. **a tailback** – a long queue on a motorway due to an obstruction such as a roadblock or crash. 'This summer Norman is going to avoid the tailbacks when he goes on holiday by going everywhere by train.'

19. **to chase one's tail** – to lead an extremely hectic life without achieving anything satisfactory. cf. **'to go round in circles'** 266/15; **'to run hard just to stand still'** 307/10.

20. **the tail wagging the dog** – the transfer of power from the leaders of a group to its least valued members. 'Instead of the doctors giving the porters orders, we were telling the doctors what to do! It was a case of the tail wagging the dog.'

Cat

1. **to lead a cat and dog life** – used to describe a husband and wife who quarrel furiously with each other most of the time.

2. **to play cat and mouse** – to alternate harshness and leniency in one's treatment of a helpless victim, in the manner of a cat playing with a mouse. When human beings indulge in this game, there is a strong element of sadism in the character of the dominant party.

3. **to put/set the cat among the pigeons** – to provoke quarrelling and dissension. 'You shouldn't have criticized the vicar in the local newspaper; now you've really put the cat among the pigeons!'

4. **to be catty** – to make spiteful remarks. 'I thought it was catty of her to ask at dinner whether Jim was doing better at school. She knows how sensitive we are about the trouble he has been in.'

5. **a cat-fight** – a fight between two women. 'It's really not nice having to share a holiday home with these girls. They have so many cat-fights over the boys next door.'

6. **a cat nap** – a short sleep, usually in an armchair instead of in bed. 'Roger, will you please see that no one disturbs me? I need a cat nap before going to the theatre tonight.' cf. **'a power nap' 233/3**.

7. **a cat-call** – a whistle indicating one's disapproval. 'There were so many cat-calls from the gallery that the management were obliged to ring down the curtain.'

8. **a cat burglar** – someone who burgles houses by climbing up the drainpipe and entering by the window.

9. **to let the cat out of the bag** – to blurt out a secret. 'You let the cat out of the bag when you said you were pregnant.'

10. **like a cat on hot bricks** – extremely awkward and uneasy. 'He dropped in by accident at an ante-natal clinic and was like a cat on hot bricks while the exercises were in progress.'

11. **to have the morals of an alley-cat** – to behave without propriety or decency. 'Have nothing to do with those girls, Nigel. They have the morals of alley-cats.'

12. **no room to swing a cat** – a very small, cramped space. The original phrase was probably 'not room to swing a cat-o'nine-tails', and dates from the time when sailors were flogged on board ship. The floggings took place on the deck because the cabins were too small to swing a cat in.

13. **not a cat in hell's chance** – no chance at all. 'You haven't a cat in hell's chance of getting that job. There are half a dozen other men after it who are better qualified than you.'

14. **curiosity killed the cat** – excessive curiosity can lead one into trouble. A common rebuke by mothers to their offspring.

15. **there's more than one way to kill/skin a cat** – there is more than one method for achieving an object. If the more conventional method fails, one should try other methods.

16. **to see which way the cat jumps** – to remain uncommitted before coming to a decision until it becomes clear which way public opinion is moving.

17. **to bell the cat** – to attack a common enemy at great personal risk to oneself for the sake of others. The phrase is taken from Piers Plowman's fable of the mice who wanted to hang a bell around the neck of a cat.

18. **has the cat got your tongue?** – have you lost your power of speech? A question often put jokingly to children who are shy.

19. **to be made a cat's paw of** – to serve as a tool for someone else. From Aesop's fable of the monkey which made use of the paw of his friend the cat for pulling hot chestnuts out of a fire.

20. **a cat may look at a king** – spoken by an inferior, meaning 'I have as much right to look at you as you have to look at me. We are both equal.' The remark can also be understood as a snub to the snobbish,

viz.: 'However grand you may think you are, you can't stop me looking at you.'

1. **like the cat that swallowed the cream** – looking elated, very pleased with oneself.

2. **the cat's whiskers / the cat's pyjamas** – a US colloquialism for 'the very best'. 'Now that he has beaten the champion, Paul thinks he is the cat's whiskers.'

3. **a fat cat** – any wealthy and powerful businessman or woman, especially a boss of a privatized utility who is receiving a high salary and bonuses out of all proportion to his or her ability. A whiff of corruption surrounds some fat cats. 'The public is demanding a curb on the pay bonuses of fat cats.' Frequent usage: **a fat-cat row**; **fat-cat pay**; **cut fat cats down to size**; **fat cats on gravy train**; **fat cats cream off millions**; **a fat-cat image**.

4. **a wild-cat strike** – an unofficial strike, called without the approval of the trade union, by a number of individuals acting on their own initiative.

5. **to be a copy-cat** – to imitate someone else's behaviour. The expression '**Copy-cat!**' is much used by schoolchildren.

Kitten

6. **as weak as a kitten** – feeble, very weak. 'After her operation, she felt as weak as a kitten.'

7. **to have kittens** – (1) to be very worried or tense. 'Poor Catherine's having kittens. She's taking her driving test today.' (2) to be very excited or angry. 'Mrs Meek will probably have kittens when she finds out that her daughter did a bungee jump.'

Pussy

8. **to pussy-foot** – to aim soft blows at your opponent which are not intended to hurt him or her. The blows may be verbal as well as physical. 'Say what you really think about Mark and stop pussy-footing!' The allusion is to the soft paws of the cat.

Horse

9. **a dark horse** – a person of unknown abilities or one who has kept his abilities to himself and may spring a surprise. This is a racing metaphor indicating an unknown horse which could win the race unexpectedly.

10. **a stalking horse** – a pretext to conceal one's real designs. 'Democracy has been used as a stalking horse for caucus rule.' Hunters would stalk game by hiding themselves behind their horses as they advanced on their prey.

11. **an old war horse** – a veteran of many battles who likes to reminisce over them.
    to sniff the air like an old war horse – to anticipate a battle, to sense a war atmosphere.

12. **to back the wrong horse** – to put your reliance on a person who then lets you down. 'If you think Walsh will ever repay you, you are mistaken; I'm afraid you've put your money on the wrong horse.'

13. **to eat like a horse** – to overeat, to eat without restraint. cf. '**to eat like a pig**' **59/9**.

14. **to work like a horse** – to do a huge quantity of work. 'It's time you had a rest; you've been working like a horse all the afternoon.' cf. '**to work like a dog**' **53/7**.

15. **a willing horse** – one who is eager to work and do other people's as well.

16. **a horse-laugh** – a loud guffaw usually expressing derision or incredulity. 'When I told him the government had promised to reduce taxes next year, he gave a horse-laugh and said he had heard that one before.'

17. **horseplay** (school slang) – rough but good-natured games.

18. **horse sense** – rough, earthy common sense.

19. **horse-trading** – hard, shrewd bargaining with no sentiment on either side. 'After a lot of horse-trading we have at last agreed a price for the house.'

1. **to flog a dead horse** – to repeat the same outdated argument over and over again. 'Whatever you think, capital punishment will never come back. Why do you flog a dead horse?'

2. **to ride a hobby horse (to death)** – to introduce one's favourite subject into a conversation at every opportunity.

3. **a horse of another colour** – a completely different matter. ' "I don't want the money for myself but for my brother." "For your brother! That's a horse of another colour." '

4. **to be/climb on one's high horse** – to assume an attitude of moral superiority. Note also the phrase '**don't get on your high horse with me**,' meaning 'don't set yourself up as my moral superior.'

5. **straight from the horse's mouth** – information received from someone with actual experience whose testimony cannot be questioned. 'I've had it straight from the horse's mouth; he was there when the man was killed.'

6. **to lock the stable door after the horse has bolted** – to take precautions after the event has occurred, instead of before.

7. **to put the cart before the horse** – to mistake the effect for the cause. 'To say that Alex can't take exercise because of his poor health is to put the cart before the horse. Alex is in poor health because he doesn't take any exercise.'

8. **to drive a coach and horses through a law, rule or regulation** – to find a very big loophole in it. cf. '**a loophole in the law**' 275/13.

9. **if wishes were horses, beggars would ride** – a wish that cannot possibly be fulfilled. Most wishes are impractical, otherwise the strangest results would arise.

10. **to swap horses in midstream / halfway across the stream** – to make a critical change of plan after a contest has begun. Often used negatively to indicate that a mistake was made. 'It's always a mistake to swap horses halfway across the stream.'

11. **wild horses would not drag it out of me** – I won't give away the secret in any circumstances.

12. **to frighten the horses** – to be indiscreet, to shock public opinion. 'It doesn't matter what you do in the bedroom so long as you don't frighten the horses.' Mrs Patrick Campbell (1865–1940), a famous actress, is said to have spoken these words.

13. **hold your horses!** – wait a moment, don't do anything rash. 'Hold your horses! I only broke the window; I didn't burn the hole in the carpet.'

14. **horses for courses** – different jobs require different skills. 'An employer will only offer you a job if you have the particular skill he is looking for. It's horses for courses as far as he is concerned.'

15. **a horse whisperer** – a person who has an exceptional understanding of horses and uses his or her skill to communicate with them. See *The Horse Whisperer* by Nicholas Evans.

Mare, Ass, Mule, Donkey

16. **to find a mare's nest** – to make a discovery that turns out to be worthless. The idiom is based on the idea that it is nonsense to suggest that a mare can have a nest like a bird.

17. **to make an ass of oneself** – to behave in a ridiculous manner. The ass has always been a symbol of stupidity.

18. **as stubborn as a mule** – one who is unwilling to yield or make any concessions in a dispute.
    as obstinate as a donkey – unwilling to listen to reason or change one's mind. A donkey is proverbial for both its obstinacy and stupidity.

19. **to talk the hind leg off a donkey** – to talk endlessly.

20. **donkey-work** – the hard, boring part of a job; that which requires little or no intelligence. 'It was Joan's idea. I only did the donkey-work.'

21. **like a carrot to a donkey** – a strong inducement or incentive. 'They offered

the men a carrot in the shape of a 10 per cent rise in wages, and double overtime.'

1. **not for donkey's years** – not for a very long time. 'Wherever have you been all this time? I haven't seen you for donkey's years!' The phrase may have come from a play on the words 'ears' and 'years', which are pronounced the same in some parts of the country.

Cow, Bull, Calf

2. **the sacred cow** – a derogatory term for any institution or custom generally regarded as sacrosanct which, in the opinion of its critics, is useless and should be abolished, such as parliamentary sovereignty and the National Health Service. The phrase originates in the Hindu belief that cows are sacred and should not be slaughtered, even in times of famine.

3. **a milch cow** – a universal provider, one from whom it is easy to obtain money. 'The boys are old enough to get a job. You are becoming the milch cow of the family.' 'Milch' means 'milk giving' and derives from Anglo-Saxon *milch* (milk). It is still used in the phrases 'milch cow' and 'milch ewe'.

4. **till the cows come home** – for ever. 'You can argue about that till the cows come home. You won't ever agree.' cf. '. . . until you are blue in the face' **3/11**.

5. **to take the bull by the horns** – to grapple fearlessly with a problem. 'The young man took the bull by the horns and asked his boss for a rise.'

6. **to score/hit a bull's eye** – to achieve one's exact aim, to make a spectacular success. 'John hit the bull's eye with his invention, and now he is a very rich man.'

7. **like a bull in a china shop** – very clumsy and destructive. This phrase is often used when tact and diplomacy are notably absent. 'In the short time Jack was with us, he upset every member of my family. He was like a bull in a china shop.'

8. **to kill the fatted calf** – to treat a person with special hospitality, usually after a long absence from home. 'We are all longing to see you, Peter. Father is going to kill the fatted calf for you.' The allusion is to 'The Prodigal Son' (Luke XV, 30).

9. **calf-love** – the first adolescent love-affair. cf. **'puppy-love' 54/15**.

Sheep, Lamb

10. **to look sheepish** – to look embarrassed, guilty. 'Henry looked sheepish when the doctor told him to take off his clothes.' **as silly as a sheep; a sheepish grin**.

11. **like a flock of sheep** – with mindless obedience. 'As soon as the trade-union leader set off towards the police cordon, the rest of the strikers followed like a flock of sheep.'

12. **to count sheep** – the monotony of counting sheep in one's imagination is a powerful inducement to falling asleep.

13. **to separate the sheep from the goats** – to separate the good from the bad, the virtuous from the wicked. The allusion is to the Day of Judgement (Matthew XXV, 32), when the good are rewarded with a place in heaven and the wicked are sent to hell. Nowadays, the distinction is more often drawn between efficient businesses and those that are inefficient or untrustworthy.

14. **like a lamb / as meek as a lamb** – meekly, without resistance. 'It must have been a terrible shock to Harry when I told him he would have to give up his room, but he took it like a lamb.' **to go like a lamb to the slaughter(-house)** – to await one's destruction with complete docility.

15. **like being savaged by a dead sheep** – a reprimand which one cannot take at all seriously, a completely ineffective rebuke. 'Daniel's mother really should be a lot stricter with him. When she scolds him he finds it's like being savaged by a dead sheep.' The expression derives from the occasion when Sir Geoffrey Howe's pedestrian style was memorably summed up by his opponent Denis Healey: 'Being attacked by him was like being savaged by

a dead sheep' (*The Penguin Book of Twentieth-Century Speeches*, edited by Brian MacArthur).

Goat

1. **to get one's goat** – to annoy, exasperate. 'It gets my goat the way he lays down the law on every subject under the sun.'

2. **to play the giddy goat** – to behave wildly, irresponsibly. Goats have always been associated with wildness and lack of control.

3. **to be a scapegoat** – to be punished for the sins or crimes of others. 'He was made the scapegoat because he had been in trouble before.' From the sacrificial goat that was allowed to escape from the Hebrew temple after the high priest had transferred his sins and those of his people to it. The word would appear to be a contradiction in terms because, in modern speech, the 'scapegoat' does not escape but is wrongly punished in the place of the guilty party.

4. **a goatee beard / a goat-like beard** – a small tuft of a beard on the point of the chin.

5. **to show the cloven hoof** – to betray one's evil intentions. The devil is depicted in art and legend as having the cloven hoof of the goat which he can never conceal, thus betraying his evil motives.

Pig, Guinea-pig

6. **to look/stare like a stuck pig** – to be petrified with amazement or fear, to stand with mouth and eyes wide open.

7. **pig-headed** – stubborn, unwilling to listen to advice or change one's mind. cf. '**to be stiff-necked**' 134/3.

8. **a male chauvinist pig** – a term of abuse coined by the Women's Lib movement for any man who is domineering or aggressive in his attitude to women. 'Chauvinist' derives from Nicolas Chauvin, a French soldier, well known for his exaggerated nationalistic views; 'pig' stands for male greed and insensitivity.

9. **to eat like a pig** – to eat a huge quantity of food noisily and greedily. Also: **as greedy as a pig**. cf. '**to eat like a horse**' 56/13.

10. **to pig it** – to live in squalor.

11. **pigs in clover** – people with more money than manners.

12. **a pig in a poke / to buy a pig in a poke** – something unsatisfactory, bought unseen by the buyer. 'What a pity you didn't get a surveyor to look over the house before you signed the contract. I am afraid you have bought a pig in a poke!' The word 'poke' originally meant 'bag'. Thus an animal in a bag that was taken to market and sold as a pig in a poke might, when the purchaser had time to inspect the bag, turn out to be a cat.

13. **a guinea-pig** – someone who allows himself to be used as a subject for experiments in hospitals and laboratories. (The animal of the same name is in great demand for experimental work on account of its docile nature.) 'My boyfriend is letting himself be used as a guinea-pig by a pharmaceutical company to test a new drug for acne.'

Sow, Swine, Hog

14. **you cannot make a silk purse out of a sow's ear** – it is not possible to make something fine out of inferior material. 'I am afraid you'll never get that lad into the university, however much time you spend on him. You can't make a silk purse out of a sow's ear.' James Howell (1594–1666) wrote of the impossibility of making a 'satin purse out of a sow's ear'.

15. **to cast pearls before swine** – to waste gifts on those who are too uncultured to appreciate them.

16. **a road-hog** – a motorist who monopolizes the road by driving very slowly in the middle, or who drives too fast without any consideration for other road-users.

17. **to hog (conversation, food, wine, attention, publicity, etc.)** – to monopolize, to take more than one's fair share.

18. **to go the whole hog** – to go through with something to the very end. 'I wanted to perfect my knowledge of French so I

went the whole hog and spent all my savings on a six months' stay with a family in Paris.' 'Hog' was originally slang for 'shilling'; so to go the whole hog meant to spend the whole shilling at once.

Mouse

1. **a little mouse** – a very shy, insignificant person. 'Who would have thought Maureen would marry such a wealthy man? She is such a little mouse!' Also: **as quiet/timid as a mouse**.

2. **mouse-like appearance** – to look inconspicuous, wearing plain, dull clothes. 'Beneath her mouse-like appearance and timid ways, Agnes held strong views' (*The School at Thrush Green* by Miss Read).

3. **mousetrap cheese** – the cheapest of cheeses. 'Alan's party last night was so disappointing – he just offered us some mousetrap cheese, salt sticks and the cheapest wine you can imagine.'

Rat, Lemming, Squirrel

4. **a rat** – someone who will betray a cause to further his own interests. A traitor may be motivated by principle, but a rat is interested only in his own advantage.

   to rat on somebody – to inform on someone behind his/her back. 'After having promised to confirm my alibi, my friend ratted on me and told the police the truth.'

5. **a love rat** – a highly promiscuous and unfaithful boyfriend or husband. 'I've had enough of that love rat husband of mine. I'm divorcing him!'

6. **a gym rat** – a keep-fit fanatic who spends hours working out in the gym. 'Are you sure you want Eddie as your boyfriend, Pauline? He's such a gym rat!'

7. **a political rat** – one who leaves his or her party and joins the opposition. cf. '**to cross the floor of the House**' 161/7.

8. **the rat race** – the frenzied scramble for success in one's job. 'I wish I could opt out of the rat race and just enjoy myself, but I can't afford to.'

9. **rat pack** – a gang of rowdies or thugs. 'The rat pack of reporters who pursued Princess Diana's car have been found innocent of causing her death.'

10. **the/a rat run** – short cuts used by drivers in the rush hour to avoid the traffic. 'This used to be such a quiet, peaceful road until all these horrible cars started using it as a rat run.'

11. **to smell a rat** – to suspect that something is not quite right, to have grounds for suspicion. 'I smelt a rat when he kept on postponing the wedding, even though his explanations seemed reasonable enough.'

12. **to look like a drowned rat / to be as wet as a drowned rat** – to be soaking wet and to look very dejected. 'The strong gale broke Mary's umbrella and she came home looking like a drowned rat.'

13. **like a lemming/lemming-like** – self-destructive, suicidal. ' "I have an uneasy feeling that investors will soon rush like lemmings to get out of the single currency," the professor warned the bankers.' Lemmings are small rats which migrate across Norway to the sea, where they drown in huge numbers.

14. **to squirrel away** – to hide away a hoard of money or valuables. 'Before he was arrested, the cunning criminal was able to squirrel away the millions of pounds he had stolen from the bank.'

Rabbit, Hare

15. **to produce/pull the rabbit out of the hat** – to produce what seems an impossible result with no effort, as if by magic. 'When I told him I had no fancy dress for the party, he produced the costume of a toreador for me just like a rabbit out of a hat.'

16. **to breed like rabbits** – to breed very fast, to multiply at great speed.

17. **as mad as a March Hare** – insane. The March Hare was one of the characters in Lewis Carroll's *Alice in Wonderland* who vied with the Mad Hatter in making crazy remarks. The month of March is the rutting season when hares go mad.

18. **hare and hounds** – a paper-chase, a trail

of paper scattered along the ground by the 'hares' for the 'hounds' to follow.

1. **to run with the hare and hunt with the hounds** – to support both sides in a dispute at the same time. Also: **to run like a hare**; **as swift/fast as a hare**.

Fox, Wolf

2. **a sly fox / an old fox** – someone who is very experienced and has acquired much guile. 'You won't take in an old fox like me with such a story.'

3. **as cunning as a fox** – very cunning indeed, as cunning as a fox is reputed to be.

4. **to be foxed** – to be outwitted, baffled or deceived. 'I was completely foxed by the crossword puzzle.'

5. **to shoot someone else's fox** – to demolish or destroy someone else's enemy. 'I was on the point of ordering Stanley's arrest when Scotland Yard did it for me; they shot my fox!'

6. **to hound someone into a corner like a trapped fox / to corner someone like a trapped fox** – to pursue someone relentlessly and without mercy. 'The drug-pushers hounded the spy into a corner like a trapped fox.'

7. **to wolf (food) down** – to swallow one's food without chewing, in the manner of a ravenously hungry wolf.

8. **a lone wolf** – someone who likes to be independent and live alone without having to co-operate with other people. 'Tony will never join your association, however much he sympathizes with your aims. He is too much of a lone wolf.'

9. **a wolf in sheep's clothing** – someone who looks respectable and harmless but whose behaviour is quite the opposite. 'Young children have to be aware of strangers who are kind and generous to them but could turn out to be wolves in sheep's clothing, such as paedophiles.' Also used with reference to trees, plants, food, etc. 'Golden Rain is a magnificent-looking tree but it is like a wolf in sheep's clothing – the seeds are extremely poisonous.'

10. **to keep the wolf from the door** – to have sufficient funds to pay one's bills and keep the bailiffs out. 'Here's £100. That should be enough to keep the wolf from the door!' The original meaning was to have enough money not to starve.

11. **to cry 'Wolf'** – to sound a false alarm so many times that, when at last you sound a genuine alarm, no one will come to your help. This phrase is taken from 'The Shepherd Boy who cried Wolf' in Aesop's Fables.

12. **to throw to the wolves** – to sacrifice a friend or dependant to appease one's enemies. 'He won't hesitate to throw you to the wolves to protect himself.'

13. **a wolf-whistle** – the whistle of a man at the sight of an attractive girl or woman in the street, made for the purpose of catching her attention.

Hyena

14. **to laugh like a hyena / a hyena-like laugh** – to have a loud, high-pitched laugh, only of a woman. 'Oh, what a bother! Cynthia has also been invited to the party. I can just hear her hyena-like laugh.' When a hyena approaches the dead body of an animal it utters a hysterical cackle which sounds like a human laugh.

Stag, Doe

15. **a stag party / night** – a social gathering for men only.

16. **doe-eyed / doe-eyed image** – a pretty, young woman, with large (usually brown) eyes, who is vulnerable, self-pitying, and in need of protection and sympathy. 'The film actress's doe-eyed image stared out from the pages of many tabloid newspapers after her husband was caught having an affair with another woman.'

Beaver, Badger, Ferret, Weasel

17. **to beaver away** – to work hard at a task. 'He has been beavering away at his job for the last three months.' The beaver is renowned for its energy and perseverance.

1. **to badger someone** – to make persistent demands on someone. 'Whenever he sees me, he badgers me to join his club; he won't give me any peace until I do.'

2. **to ferret out** – to find out something after a very diligent search.

3. **weasel words** – words which weaken the force of the words that immediately precede them. They suck the life out of the words, just as a weasel sucks the egg out of its shell. 'We must expand our exports and at the same time protect our home industries' – the first half of the sentence is contradicted by the weasel words in the second half; if we stop countries exporting to us, they will not have enough foreign exchange to import our goods.

Opossum

4. **to play possum** – to avoid trouble by lying low, feigning illness or pretending to be unaware of the facts. The allusion is to the habit of the opossum which feigns death when it is attacked.

Hedgehog, Mole

5. **as prickly as a hedgehog** – someone who takes offence very easily.

6. **a mole** – a traitor who undermines from the inside the organization in which he is employed. Sir Francis Bacon used 'mole' in his *History of the Reign of King Henry VII* in 1622. In his spy stories, John Le Carré acquainted his readers with the word 'mole', saying it was used by the KGB.

7. **to make a mountain out of a mole-hill** – to exaggerate a difficulty. 'Aren't you making a mountain out of a mole-hill? There's no need to cancel our holiday just because the airlines are grounded. We can go by boat-train instead.'

Bat

8. **as blind as a bat** – completely blind. 'You must have been as blind as a bat not to have seen me; I was sitting at the next table!'

9. **to run like a bat out of hell** – to run as fast as one possibly can. 'When the fire started in the Australian bush, people were running like bats out of hell to save their lives.' Western legend associates bats with nightmares, vampires, witches and the devil. Therefore the object of one's fear must be really terrifying if it frightens even a bat.

10. **bats in the belfry** – slightly mad.

Chameleon

11. **chameleon-like** – a person who easily adapts to different circumstances, is changeable and not always reliable. 'You cannot trust or take that politician seriously. He has a chameleon-like personality.' A chameleon can change the colour of its skin to fit in with its surroundings. It can even let another chameleon know that it is angry by turning black with rage.

Frog

12. **to frogmarch** – to carry an obstinate or unruly person face downwards by holding the arms and legs. 'When I asked Crouch for my money, his servants practically frogmarched me out of his house!'

13. **to have a frog in the throat** – to have an obstruction in the throat which causes hoarseness or loss of voice.

Snake

14. **a snake in the grass** – a hidden, treacherous enemy. 'Your friend has been telling your boss tales about you. She's a real snake in the grass!'

15. **to cherish a snake in one's bosom** – to have one's kindness repaid with spite or ingratitude.

16. **to scotch the snake** – to spoil a plan.

17. **snakes and ladders** – the ups and downs in life. From the name of a children's game of chance played on a board that contains rewards and penalties.

Turtle

18. **to turn turtle** – to turn round and run away in the face of danger. The allusion is

to the turtle which turns upside down in the water. When the phrase is applied to a boat, it means that the boat capsizes and sinks.

1. **to come out of one's shell** – to overcome one's natural reserve and speak freely. 'Mark was always so shy but, since he has made friends with Nancy, he has come right out of his shell.'

    to withdraw into one's shell – to be shy and unsociable. 'It is better to leave her alone when she has withdrawn into her shell.'

Whale

2. **to have a whale of a time** – to have a splendid time. The whale stands for something very big, and also something fine or splendid.

    a whale of a job – a wonderful job; **a whale of a task** – a huge task.

3. **to look like a beached whale / to be left to flap about like a beached whale** – when something important, famous or very big is rejected and left all alone, away from where it should belong. ' "Why does my brilliant project suddenly look like a beached whale?" the politician said crossly.'

Dragon, Lizard

4. **a dragon** – a formidable, aggressive woman who makes a lot of trouble. 'She's a real dragon. You had better keep away from her.'

5. **to chase the dragon** – to take heroin by burning it on aluminium kitchen foil and breathing in the smoke. 'Too many rich and successful models chase the dragon nowadays.' In myth and fable, dragons are sometimes represented as breathing out fire and smoke. The dragon is also a symbol of the Orient, where much heroin comes from.

6. **a lounge lizard** – a man who mingles with the rich at fashionable parties, hoping to meet someone advantageous to himself. He usually meets these people in the lounges of expensive hotels. In US English: **a parlor** [*sic*] **lizard**.

Crocodile

7. **a crocodile** – schoolchildren walking in a procession two by two, usually with a teacher at the back.

8. **to shed crocodile tears** – to shed false, insincere tears. 'Take no notice of her crocodile tears. She's not in the least concerned about your injury.' The crocodile was believed by many people to shed tears of remorse as it devoured its victim. In fact, the crocodile is getting rid of surplus salt from its nasal glands.

Rhinoceros, Elephant

9. **to have a skin like a rhinoceros** – to be insensitive to insults. cf. '**to be thick-skinned / have a thick skin**' 111/19.

10. Similes with 'elephant': **as heavy as an elephant**; **as clumsy as an elephant**.

11. **a rogue elephant** – someone who flouts authority in order to vent his spite on everyone and everything. 'Your son is making enemies of all our customers; he's a real rogue elephant!' A rogue elephant is a vicious elephant that deserts the herd and runs amok, causing great damage.

12. **an elephant's memory** – a long memory, especially for an ill-turn or an insult. Elephants are proverbial for their long memories.

13. **an elephant race** – on the motorway, when a lorry goes on to the fast lane and tries to overtake another lorry but finds this very difficult, sometimes even impossible. The two lorries run neck and neck for miles, much to the annoyance of car drivers behind the lorry in the fast lane.

Camel

14. **to swallow a camel and strain at a gnat** – to tolerate a great wrong while protesting at a minor lapse.

Kangaroo

15. **to kangaroo** – to convict and punish unjustly without giving the accused a fair hearing.

1. **a kangaroo court** – a court without any legal authority which tries and punishes people who have endangered the interests of some group or association. The term was originally employed for the illegal trials that were held in jails for offences against the prison community. Today the same term is used for trade unions when they try members for breaches of union rules and regulations.

Monkey, Ape

2. **to monkey with** – to interfere, usually with harmful results. 'Dennis has been monkeying with the grandfather clock. Now it won't chime.'

3. **monkey tricks** – spiteful, malicious behaviour.

4. **to make a monkey of someone** – to make someone look ridiculous. 'I don't like being made a monkey of in front of my friends; don't play your jokes on me again when we have guests.'

5. **to get one's monkey up** (slang) – to annoy or irritate someone very much. 'Whenever I turn on my radio, my neighbour knocks on the wall; he really gets my monkey up.'

6. **as clever as a cartload of monkeys** – very artful and sly.

7. **monkey business** – underhanded business, business that is not quite honest or straightforward. 'Paul has been getting up to some of his monkey business again. He needs watching.'

8. **to have a monkey on one's back** – to be a drug addict. 'I don't want you to be friends with Richie. He's got a monkey on his back.'

9. **to ape one's superiors** – to imitate people in a higher position than oneself.

Lynx, Leopard

10. **to be lynx-eyed** – to have very sharp eyesight.

11. **the leopard can never change its spots** – one can never change one's character; thus a man with an evil past never changes his ways.

Lion

12. **as brave as a lion** – very brave, the lion being a symbol of courage.
    to have a heart like a lion; lionheart / lion-hearted – to have great courage; **as fierce as a lion; to roar like a lion** – to shout very loudly; **to feel like a lion** – to be in the best of health.

13. **a lion-hunter** – hosts or hostesses who seek out celebrities with whom to impress their guests.

14. **to lionize someone** – to make a celebrity of someone by lavishing praise and hospitality on him or her.

15. **the British Lion** – the symbol of Great Britain.
    to twist the lion's tail – to humiliate or provoke Great Britain.

16. **the lion's share** – much more than one's fair share, almost everything. 'He took the lion's share, and by the time he had finished there was nothing left for the rest of us except for a few crumbs.' Taken from Aesop's Fables.

17. **the lion's den** – a place of great danger.

18. **to beard the lion in his den** – to challenge a formidable enemy on his own ground.

19. **to put one's head in the lion's mouth** – to put oneself needlessly at the mercy of an enemy. 'The English girl put her head in the lion's mouth when she sang pro-democratic songs in a country run by a dictator.'

Tiger

20. **he's a tiger** – an expert, a person of dynamic energy.
    to fight like a tiger – to fight with savage, relentless ferocity.

21. **paper tiger** – a sham, a cowardly adversary who is unable to offer any real resistance. The phrase was coined by the Chinese leader Mao-Tse-tung at the height of the Vietnamese civil war in reference to the capitalist countries who, the Chinese claimed, were too cowardly to

defend their interests, although they made a lot of threats against their enemies.

1. **to ride a tiger** – to find that the person you are trying to make use of is your master and is in control of you.

2. **to have a tiger by the tail** – to get involved in unexpected trouble or danger, to find that the person you are hunting is much more formidable than you had supposed. 'You can't shake a tiger by the tail and not expect to get bitten' (from *NOW!* magazine).

Bear

3. **like a bear with a sore head** – in a specially bad mood or temper. 'Father is like a bear with a sore head this morning. I wonder what has upset him.' Bears are notoriously bad-tempered; hence the phrase. Also: **as cross/savage as a bear with a sore head**.

4. **to give someone a bear hug/a friendly bear hug** – to embrace someone tightly, squeezing the chest and shoulders towards one. 'None of your bear hugs for me, Peter. Remember I have a broken arm!'

5. **bears and bulls on the Stock Exchange** – a bull expects a share to rise, and a bear expects it to fall in price. So you can be '**bullish of a share**' and expect its price to rise, or '**bearish of a share**' and expect it to fall.

6. **a bear garden** – a place that is full of noise and contention. The name originated in the bear gardens of Tudor times when bears were baited and attacked by dogs. These 'bear gardens' were well known for the rowdy behaviour of the spectators.

8 Birds

Bird

1. **bird** (Cockney) – girlfriend. D. H. Lawrence is known to have used the phrase.

2. **an old bird** – someone who is too experienced and shrewd to be taken in. 'You won't get an old bird like him to believe that tale!' From the proverb 'You can't catch an old bird with chaff'.

3. **an early bird** – someone who rises early. 'My husband was always an early bird.' From the proverb 'It's the early bird that catches the worm'.

4. **an odd bird** – an eccentric person.

5. **a rare bird** – an exceptional person who combines two contradictory interests. 'He was that rare bird – a poet and a chemist.' cf. 'a rare animal' 52/6.

6. **a bird of passage** – someone who never stays long in the same place but is always on the move, a wanderer, like a swallow which migrates according to season.

7. **like a bird in a cage/a caged bird** – imprisoned, trapped. 'Lucy had a beautiful house and garden in the middle of the countryside, but her husband was at work all day. She told me that she felt like a bird in a cage.'

8. **a jail-bird** – someone who spends his life in and out of prison.

9. **bird-strike** – a bird accidentally hitting a plane. 'We are lucky, that bird-strike could have ended in disaster!'

10. **to get the bird** – to suffer a severe rebuff, to be greeted with abuse. 'He offered to give a talk on his travels in India, but he got the bird!'
    to give someone the bird – to hiss or boo at a person in order to express one's disapproval.

11. **the bird has flown** – the person you want has disappeared. 'The birds have flown' was said by Charles I when he and his henchmen arrived at the House of Commons too late to arrest his political enemies. cf. 'to fly the nest' 67/11.

12. **free as a bird** – free to come and go as one pleases.

13. **to eat like a bird/a sparrow / to pick at one's food like a bird** – to eat very little, to have no appetite. 'I'm very worried about Maria. She eats like a sparrow and is getting so thin.'

14. **a little bird told me** – someone whose name the speaker prefers not to reveal. Often used when speaking to an inquisitive child, in reference to some gossipy information.

15. **a bird's-eye view** – a general view.

16. **a bird of ill-omen** – someone who brings bad luck, like Jonah (in the Bible), or a messenger who is always bringing bad news. From a bird whose presence signifies misfortune, like the albatross or crow.

17. **to kill two birds with one stone** – to achieve two results with the same means. 'We can kill two birds with one stone by combining our honeymoon with our business trip.'

18. **to be able to charm the birds off a tree** – to have so much charm that one can achieve almost anything with it. 'Richard could charm a bird off a tree if he put his mind to it.'

to be unable to charm birds off a tree – to be lacking in charm.

1. **birds of a feather** – you can judge the character of a person by the company he or she keeps. The phrase is derogatory and derives from the proverb 'Birds of a feather flock together'. cf. '**the halo effect' 41/7**.

Feather, Hackles, Wing

2. **in fine feather** – in splendid condition, lively and cheerful. 'Alan was in fine feather. He has quite recovered from his depression.'

3. **you could have knocked me down with a feather!** – I was so overcome with surprise that even an object as light as a feather would have been enough to knock me down.

4. **to smooth someone's ruffled feathers** – to soothe someone's injured pride. 'The vicar was very upset at the way you spoke to him this morning. You had better do something to smooth his ruffled feathers.'

5. **to make the feathers/fur fly** – to start an angry controversy which leads to quarrelling and fighting. 'Your scheme to convert the local church into a community centre has made the feathers fly.'

6. **to make someone's hackles rise** – to make someone very angry, to infuriate him. 'It's not so nice having all these hooligans hanging around at the end of our road. They make everyone's hackles rise.' The hackles are the long feathers on the neck of the domestic cock which rise when it is angry and preparing for a fight.

7. **to take someone under one's wing** – to give a person one's help and protection. 'Since Lady Montague has taken Tim under her wing, the teachers at his school haven't given him any more trouble.'

8. **to spread one's wings** – to try and find new experiences elsewhere. 'Let Rebecca go to Australia. She should spread her wings before settling down.'

9. **to clip someone's wings** – to tame someone, to curtail his or her powers. 'Every time I ring my doctor for an appointment, I am cross-examined by his receptionist. It's time her wings were clipped.'

Nest, Roost

10. **to feather one's nest** – to make wrongful use of one's position, in order to make or save money for oneself. 'He is not going to feather his nest at our expense!'

11. **to fly the nest** – one's children are mature enough to leave home and start their own lives without their parents. ' "Poor us!" the mother sighed. "Our children have flown the nest and now our house is so empty." ' Also: **an empty nest**. cf. '**the bird has flown' 66/11**.

12. **to foul one's nest** – to speak ill of one's own family to strangers. 'You shouldn't have fouled your nest like that at Susan's wedding. Your family will never forgive you.' The phrase comes from the proverb 'It's an ill bird that fouls its own nest'.

13. **a nest-egg** – a small amount of money that is kept in reserve, in case of need.
    to break into one's nest-egg – to spend money that has been saved up. 'Prices have gone up so fast in recent years that many people have been obliged to break into their nest-eggs.'

14. **a love nest** – a house, flat, etc., where lovers live together, sometimes in secret. 'Malcolm and Ina quarrelled, but Ina decided to stay in their love nest while Malcolm went sulking back to his parents.'

15. **to rule the roost** – to dominate or govern a group. 'In the early part of the century, it was the eldest son, not the widow, who ruled the roost.' The roost is the resting place of the hens where they perch at night.

16. **to come home to roost** – to recoil on the person responsible for a folly or wrong. 'There is always a price to pay for our follies; sooner or later they come home to roost.'

Robin, Lark

17. **a round robin** – a letter of protest with the signatures in circular form in

order to conceal the identity of the ring-leader.

1. **'Who killed Cock Robin?'** – the first line of a nursery rhyme which in modern parlance means 'Who is responsible for the fall of a prominent figure?', a question often posed by political commentators when a minister is replaced.

2. **to have a lark / lark about** – to play jokes or indulge in horseplay with other children. 'I told the children to stop lark-ing about – and go to sleep.'

3. **to be up with the lark** – to be up early in the morning.

4. **to be as happy as a lark** – to be very happy, carefree, jolly. 'Steven is as happy as a lark, playing with his new model railway.'

Jay, Magpie, Cuckoo

5. **a jay-walker** – a pedestrian who crosses the road without looking. Jay (from the bird) is US slang for a country bumpkin.

6. **to chatter like a magpie** – to chatter incessantly, without interruption; often used in reference to children.

7. **a cuckoo in the nest** – an unwelcome intruder. 'Hicks has been a cuckoo in the nest ever since he joined the association. Why join if he doesn't agree with our aims?'

Crow

8. **to crow/crow over** – to gloat, to rejoice at the defeat of an opponent. 'I don't like the way Rolf crows over his opponents when he wins. It is very unsporting of him.'

9. **as the crow flies** – as an imaginary bird would fly; the distance as measured by a straight line from one point to another.

10. **crow's feet** – the little lines or wrinkles which appear under a person's eyes in middle age.

11. **a scarecrow** – the name given to a woman who wears shabby, torn or dowdy clothes. 'I can't possibly wear this at the ball; I shall look a proper scarecrow in it.'

Literally, some old tattered clothes put on a stick in a field to frighten the crows away.

Pigeon, Dove

12. **to pigeon-hole** – to delay action on a request or complaint indefinitely. A pigeon-hole is one compartment among many reserved for the filing of documents.

   to put someone into a pigeon-hole – to consign someone to a certain cate-gory, often prematurely. ' "People keep on wanting to put me into a pigeon-hole," the well-known composer com-plained.'

13. **to be as gentle as a dove** – to behave in a peace-loving, tender manner.

14. **don't get lovey-dovey with me!** – don't get amorous with me, don't get the wrong ideas about me.

15. **to flutter the dovecotes** – to cause a lot of excitement in a peaceful community. 'If you return to the village after all the publicity you've had, you will flutter the dovecotes all right!'

Hen

16. **a hen party / night** – a party to which only women or girls are invited.

17. **a hen-pecked husband** – a man who is domineered over by his nagging wife.

18. **like a hen with one chicken** – over-protective of one's only child.

Cock

19. **to be all cock-a-hoop** – to be exultant, triumphant. 'Hudson was all cock-a-hoop at the news. He had never expected to get a first-class degree.' The origin is unknown.

20. **to be cock of the walk** – to be the champion or victor in one's own particu-lar field, to dominate all one's rivals.

21. **a cock and bull story** – a wildly improb-able story, often invented to glorify the speaker or to excuse some wrongful action. 'Harry told me a cock and bull

story about a man robbing him of the money he owed me while he was on his way to my house.'

1. **a cock sparrow** – a bold, aggressive little fellow, always spoiling for a fight.

2. **a cock-eyed scheme** – a wild, foolish scheme, one that is bound to fail.
   that's cock-eyed – that's all wrong.

3. **to take a cockshot at** – to throw something at an object without taking much care; to make a wild throw at it.

4. **at cock-crow** – at sunrise.

Chicken

5. **to be chicken/chicken-hearted** – to be cowardly, easily frightened, to be afraid of a fight. 'Don't count on him when you need a witness; he'll be chicken.'

6. **to chicken out** – to wriggle out of an obligation through cowardice.

7. **she's no (spring) chicken** – she's no longer young. 'No chicken' is often used in reference to a woman who is no longer as young as she would like to appear, and whose behaviour does not become a woman of her age.

8. **as tender as a chicken** – very soft, delicate.

9. **don't count your chickens** – don't rely on your gains until you have them in your possession. 'Don't count your chickens. Your uncle may not leave you any money at all.' From the proverb 'Don't count your chickens before they are hatched' from Aesop's Fables.

10. **that's like asking which came first, the chicken or the egg** – there are some questions to which there is no rational answer.

11. **to run around like a headless chicken** – to run around busily but without achieving very much. 'We're moving house tomorrow and our poor parents are running around like headless chickens.'
    to run something like a headless chicken – to be completely disorganized; **a headless-chicken look** – a confused look, a perplexed expression.

12. **to look like a plucked chicken/hen** – to have had too much hair cut away or tweaked out. 'Lucy came back from the hairdresser looking like a plucked chicken. Her beautiful long hair had all been cut off.'

13. **to look like a trussed chicken** – to wear clothes which are far too tight. 'Oh dear, Hannah! That dress is two sizes too small for you. You look like a trussed chicken!'

14. **chicken feed** (slang) – a poor, meagre reward for work done.
    to make something look like chicken feed – to make the cost of something look absolutely small and insignificant in comparison with something else. 'If the Balkan war had spread to Macedonia, it would have made the death toll of Bosnia look like chicken feed.'

15. **the pecking order** – the order of seniority in an organized group of people. 'I am pretty low down in the pecking order, so I don't enjoy my job much.' The phrase is taken from the social order of domestic chickens which ranks chickens according to their strength. Each bird is pecked by the one immediately above it in rank, but pecks the one immediately below it.

Duck

16. **a sitting duck** – someone who is vulnerable to attack from his or her enemies. 'These tourists in the shopping centre are sitting ducks for the town's professional pickpockets.' From the idea that it is easy to shoot a duck which is sitting still. cf. **'a sitting target' 241/1.**

17. **a lame duck** – a person who is incompetent and in need of financial assistance. Also a company or industry that is running at a loss and needs public money to survive. Second-term US presidents who have lost their power of patronage, and consequently their influence in the legislature, are known as **'lame ducks'**.

18. **a dead duck** – a cause or campaign that no longer has relevance to modern life.

19. **like a dying duck in a thunderstorm** – all forlorn, bedraggled and miserable.

'You do sound sorry for yourself – like a dying duck in a thunderstorm.'

1. **an ugly duckling** – a plain, unprepossessing child who grows into a beautiful woman. The phrase comes from Hans Andersen's fairy tale *The Ugly Duckling* in which an ugly duckling, after much ridicule, grows into a beautiful swan.

2. **(like) water off a duck's back** – without making the slightest impression. 'She scolded her son again and again for his dishonesty, but her words were water off a duck's back.'

3. **to take to something like a duck to water** – to adapt oneself to a new situation without any conscious effort or difficulty. 'Although he had never worked in an office before, he took to the routine like a duck to water.'

4. **to duck an inquiry/a challenge / to duck out of** – to avoid, get out of, shirk one's responsibilities. 'The politician ducked the challenge of going up against his rival in the leadership election.' 'Duck' derives from the Old English *ducan* – to dive. One associates this word with the duck that quickly dives under water to catch a fish.

5. **to play ducks and drakes with one's money** – to take unjustifiable risks with one's money, to throw it away. The game of ducks and drakes consists in throwing a flat stone along the surface of the water and counting the number of times it bounces on the water.

6. **to score a duck / be out for a duck** – in cricket, to be out without scoring any runs. 'The crowd groaned as the opening batsman was out for a duck yet again.'

Goose, Swan

7. **to be unable to say boo to a goose** – to be so timid that one cannot make even the mildest protest, however badly one is treated. 'If you were to move your family into his house, he wouldn't try to stop you. He can't say boo to a goose!'

8. **to cook someone's goose** – to destroy one's opponent's chances by some dramatic coup. 'That's cooked his goose once and for all. He'll never survive the scandal.'

9. **a wild goose chase** – to go on a profitless journey, to take part in a useless search. Most wild goose chases are unsuccessful because wild geese fly very high and fast and are therefore difficult to shoot.

10. **the goose-step** – a kind of military step with the legs pushed aggressively forward.

11. **goose flesh/skin/pimples** – a rough condition of the skin resembling the skin of a plucked goose, which comes about as the result of cold or fear.

12. **to kill the goose that lays the golden egg** – to destroy the source of one's wealth. 'I know you don't like the way your father paints, but if you discourage him too much, you will be killing the goose that lays the golden egg.' From Aesop's Fables.

13. **all your geese are swans** – you overestimate the value of your possessions or ideas, just because they are yours.

14. **all your swans are geese** – all your hopes have been disappointed.

15. **swan-song** – the last achievement of a writer, painter, musician, and so on. According to legend, the swan only sings when it is about to die.

Turkey

16. **to talk turkey** – to talk bluntly, usually about business.

17. **that's cold turkey** – (1) the plain truth. (2) withdrawal from drug-taking.

18. **like turkeys voting for Christmas** – someone planning his or her own downfall or destruction. 'The standards at this school are extremely poor, but no teachers are going to complain. It would be like turkeys voting for Christmas as the school would then be shut down.'

Stormy Petrel, Coot, Albatross

19. **a stormy petrel** – a turbulent, restless character who stirs up trouble wherever he or she goes. A stormy petrel is a small

sea-bird whose appearance on the surface of the sea foretells a storm. The word 'petrel' is derived from St Peter, the apostle who walked on the water.

1. **as bald as a coot** – completely bald; so called because the coot has a featherless pate on its forehead which resembles the head of a bald man.

2. **to have an albatross round one's neck** – to suffer from some crippling disadvantage. ' "This park is like an albatross round our necks," the councillor sighed. "It's turning into a wilderness but we simply haven't got the money to pay for its upkeep." ' The albatross has always been regarded as a bird of ill-omen. Also: **to hang round one's neck like an albatross; a secret weighs upon one like an albatross**. cf. '**to carry a millstone round one's neck**' 95/6.

Kingfisher

3. **halcyon days** – times of undisturbed happiness and peace. 'Those were the halcyon days of Athens [fifth century BC] when she produced her finest poetry and drama, architecture and sculpture.' Halcyon is Greek for 'kingfisher', being a compound of Greek 'sea' and 'conceiving'. Thus the halcyon days were the calm days, when the kingfishers were able to breed in peace, undisturbed by wind and storm. cf. '**a hey-day**' 31/9.

Parrot, Canary

4. **parrot-fashion / parrot-like / parrot-wise** – learnt by heart without regard to the meaning.

5. **as sick as a parrot** – a cliché often used by football managers, meaning 'very disappointed'.

6. **to sing like a canary** – when a criminal gives information or evidence about his/her comrades to the police. 'Secret documents proved that one of the criminals must have sung like a canary to police officers.'

Peacock, Phoenix, Dodo

7. **as proud as a peacock** – conceited and vain. The comparison is based on the outstandingly beautiful plumage of the peacock's tail, which opens out like a fan to attract the hen.

8. **to rise like a phoenix from the ashes / to rise from the ashes** – a force which has apparently been destroyed, but which emerges once again to triumph over its opponents. 'The Pagan religion is rising from the ashes of persecution as we enter a new age of spiritual tolerance.' According to legend, the phoenix was an Eastern bird which set fire to itself and then rose again from the ashes. The Egyptians associated the phoenix with immortality. Also: **to emerge like a phoenix; reappear like a phoenix; phoenix-like**.

9. **as dead as a dodo** – finished, dead, extinct. 'I thought that jazz was as dead as a dodo, but now it seems to have made a comeback.' The dodo was a large bird which died out at the end of the 17th century. A humorous but ungrammatical variation: **deader than the dodo**.

Owl

10. **as wise as an owl / a wise old owl** – owls have a solemn look, and solemnity is often associated with wisdom; hence the phrase.

11. **a solemn owl** (derogatory) – an excessively solemn person who is lacking in humour.

12. **a night owl** – someone who does not go to bed until the early hours of the morning. 'Since Philip has started work on his book he has become a regular night owl.'

Hawk, Eagle

13. **to watch/watch over someone like a hawk** – to keep a very close eye on someone. 'You must watch that young man like a hawk. Everyone knows that he is a thief.' Also: **to have eyes like a hawk**.

1. **hawks and doves** – in British politics, the 'hawks' are the hardliners of the Conservative right wing, and the 'doves' those on the left wing who favour conciliation and compromise with the other parties. There are also 'hawks' and 'doves' on both wings of the Republican and Democratic parties in the USA, where the meaning is much the same.

2. **an eagle eye** – a very sharp gaze which takes in the smallest detail; a look from which it is impossible to escape. 'The refugee was left in the interrogation room under the eagle eye of one of the guards.'

Vulture

3. **like a vulture** – a grabbing, mercenary person. The vulture is a scavenger that feeds on the corpses of rotting animals. Consequently, the word is often used to describe the relations who gather round the rich man's death-bed. cf. **'to circle around someone like a shark . . .'** **75/5**.

4. **a culture vulture** – a person who likes to show off his/her knowledgeable interest in the arts. 'My Auntie Lydia is coming and she expects me to show her all round London's museums and art galleries. She's such a culture vulture.'

Ostrich

5. **like an ostrich (with its head in the sand)** – someone who wilfully conceals the truth from him- or herself, who refuses to face reality. Ostriches are generally believed to hide their heads in the sand in the mistaken belief that, if they cannot see the danger, the danger no longer exists. (Ostriches do not really hide their heads in the sand but bend their long necks so that they are parallel with the ground. Thus they may in fact hear approaching danger better.) Hence all the phrases connected with ostrich, such as **'ostrich policy'**, **'ostrich belief'**, **'ostrich-like'**, which imply a refusal to face reality. cf. **'to bury one's head in the sand' 82/16**.

Fish

1. **a big fish** – a very important person.
   only a small fish – only an unimportant person.

2. **a big fish in a small pond** – someone whose authority and influence is limited to a small area. 'I'd rather run my own shop in the village, where I'm a big fish in a small pond, than work in a large store, where I'd only be one in two hundred.'

3. **a queer fish** – an odd character.

4. **a cold fish** – a cold, unfeeling person.

5. **to land a fish** – to score a big success, e.g. winning an important contract.

6. **to be like a fish out of water** – to find oneself in an unfamiliar situation, to be ill-adapted to new conditions. 'When he was transferred from the air force to the army, he felt like a fish out of water; the work was so different.'

7. **a pretty kettle of fish** – an awkward predicament with no easy solution. When Queen Mary learnt that her son, King Edward VIII, was faced with the choice of giving up Mrs Simpson or of abdicating, she exclaimed: 'This is a pretty kettle of fish!'

8. **to be/seem/smell fishy** – suspicious, dubious, questionable. 'Marion says she got that gold watch as a present from her boyfriend, but it smells fishy to me. Do you think she is telling the truth?'

9. **to drink like a fish** – to be a hard drinker, a habitual, excessive drinker. Many fish swim open-mouthed, and look as if they are continually drinking. Fish do, however, drink water now and again, sometimes accidentally when they eat.

10. **to cry stinking fish** – to disparage one's own wares. 'You shouldn't criticize your father's price rises in front of our customers. You'll lose us business, if you cry stinking fish.'

11. **neither fish, flesh, fowl nor good red herring** – to be neither one thing nor the other, with the result that it doesn't satisfy anyone. The idiom is usually shortened to '**neither fish, flesh nor fowl**'. 'This is neither a game of chance nor skill. It is neither fish, flesh nor fowl.' The expression relates to the strict dietary laws of the Catholic Church many centuries ago: monks were not allowed to eat fish; people in general were not allowed flesh (meat); and the poor were not allowed red herring.

12. **to have other fish to fry** – to have other more important things to engage one's attention. 'I tried to interest him in our venture, but he seemed preoccupied with something else. No doubt he has other fish to fry.'

13. **there are plenty more fish in the sea** – often said with the object of consoling a person crossed in love. 'There are many other people, besides your boyfriend, who would suit you just as well, so there is no need for you to despair. There are plenty more fish in the sea.' From the proverb 'There are as good fish in the sea as ever came out of it'.

14. **to feed the fishes** – (1) to be seasick. (2) to drown.

15. **to fish in troubled/muddy waters** – to meddle in matters which may cause

one a lot of trouble, to try to make capital out of somebody else's misfortune.

1. **to fish for compliments** – to invite compliments by making disparaging remarks about oneself in the hope that they will be contradicted. ' "I'm not nearly as pretty as Isabel." "What are you saying! You are a hundred times prettier! You really are fishing for compliments!" '

2. **to fish for information** – to seek information by asking leading questions. The phrase suggests that the interrogator is relying on the witness to supply the missing evidence. 'The reporters were here all morning fishing for information about your intention to divorce Helen.'
   to go on a fishing expedition – this is similar but more explicit. It means to visit someone and interrogate him in the hope that he will incriminate himself.

3. **life in a goldfish bowl/fish bowl / like being in a goldfish bowl** – a situation in which it is impossible to keep anything secret, to be in the spotlight and without any privacy. 'Many famous personalities feel on display all the time – like living in a goldfish bowl.'

4. **to need something like a fish needs a bicycle** – to have absolutely no need of something. 'We need GM food like a fish needs a bicycle.' Humorous feminist variations: **a woman needs a man like a fish needs a bicycle; a woman without a man is like a fish without a bicycle.**

Mackerel

5. **to throw a sprat to catch a mackerel** – to invest a small sum in the hope of making a big profit.

Herring

6. **to draw a red herring across the path** – to introduce an irrelevant issue into a discussion. The 'red herring' may either be introduced intentionally, in order to confuse one's opponent, or accidentally.

Eel

7. **as slippery as an eel** – difficult to pin down, difficult to catch. 'I couldn't get anything in writing out of him; he is as slippery as an eel.' Eels have snakelike bodies and a slimy skin. They can dig themselves into sand or mud, tail first, with astonishing speed.
   as nimble as an eel in a sandbag – moving in a slow and clumsy fashion.

Sardines

8. **to be packed like sardines** – to be squashed together among a lot of people; hence the phrase '**sardine class**', a humorous term for economy class. 'We were packed like sardines on the train. I could hardly move my arms.' The oil in which the sardines are packed is more expensive than the sardines. Therefore the profit is bigger if there are more sardines squashed into a tin, and less oil. cf. '**economy-class syndrome' 133/9**; '**jam-packed' 178/5**.

Fry

9. **small fry** – unimportant people. 'He was too snobbish to greet the small fry.'

Caviare

10. **caviare to the general** – something special that is wasted on the uncultivated. The reference is from Shakespeare's *Hamlet* (II, ii, 465): 'The play, I remember, pleased not the million; 'twas caviare to the general.' The word 'general' refers to the general public, not to the military rank. Caviare was introduced to England at the end of the 16th century and it took a while for people to get used to the taste.

Oyster

11. **as close as an oyster** – secretive, reluctant to give information. 'You can trust me with your secret. I'll be as close as an oyster.' Also: **as close as a Kentish oyster**.

12. **the world is my oyster** – to have abun-

dant opportunities, unlimited scope. 'Why, then the world is mine oyster, Which I with sword will open' (Shakespeare, *The Merry Wives of Windsor*, II, ii).

Whelk

1. **not to be able even to run a whelk-stall** – to be hopelessly incompetent. 'Don't give me advice on how to run my business; you couldn't even run a whelk-stall!' A whelk is a small shellfish which is sold as a cheap food, especially at the seaside.

Clam

2. **to shut up/close up like a clam / to be as tight-mouthed as a clam / to clam up** – to become silent and refuse to speak. ' "It's a complete waste of time questioning him," the detective said in exasperation. "He just clams up." ' In US slang, one says, **'Shut your clamtrap/clam-shell'** (mouth) or **'clam-shells'** (lips). In English, **'Shut your trap!'** is a rude way of saying, 'Be quiet!' ('trap' being short for 'clamtrap'). cf. **'a wall of silence'** 156/12.

Limpet

3. **to cling/stick like a limpet** – to cling tenaciously. 'I met Tom on the bus yesterday. He clung like a limpet to me the whole afternoon.' A limpet belongs to a group of sea snails which have shells shaped like tents. When disturbed, it clings very tightly to rock and is extremely difficult to dislodge. cf. **'to stick/cling like a leech'** 78/11.

Crab

4. **to catch a crab** – when rowing, to dip the oar too deep into the water or to miss the water altogether. In either case, the effect is to stop the boat.

Shark

5. **a shark** – a swindler, a money-grabber, one who charges an extortionate price for his services. The verb 'shark' is derived from the northern French *cherquier* (English – 'search'), but has the added meaning of 'searching greedily'. See *Hamlet*, I, i, 98 – 'shark up', meaning 'to snap up'. The name has been given to the fish in the same sense.

to circle around someone like a shark smelling blood / like a shark with its prey – to move around someone in order to trap that person and do him or her harm. cf. **'like a vulture'** 72/3; **'to swarm like locusts'** 78/15.

10 *Insects*

Worm

1. **a worm** (derogatory) – someone lacking in moral fibre, despicable. 'What a worm!'

2. **a bookworm** – someone who loves books and reading. 'Bookworms were delighted when the new bookshop gave away 100 books on its opening day.'

3. **the worm of conscience** – the nagging voice of conscience.

4. **a worm's eye view** – viewed from underneath.

5. **even a worm will turn** – there is a limit to the extent that even the weakest person can be bullied. The day will come when that person will stand up for him- or herself.

6. **to worm out information** – to extract information in a cunning underhand way.

7. **to open/open up a can of worms** – to create an unpredictable and complicated problem which may lead to embarrassment. 'The scientist will open up a whole can of worms if he can prove that amalgam fillings in teeth really do damage the health.' Frequent usage: **This is opening/going to open a real can of worms**. cf. **'a recipe for disaster'** 43/14; **'Pandora's box'** 225/6.

8. **to worm oneself into another's favour or confidence** – to ingratiate oneself by devious means with another person.

Spider

9. **to blow the cobwebs away** – to clear one's mind of out-of-date notions. 'Beethoven was a great innovator in his day who blew away the cobwebs in the world of music.'

Fly

10. **a fly in the ointment** – a small blemish that spoils one's pleasure. 'I would like to go to Spain next summer. The only fly in the ointment is we shall have to take our aunt with us.'

11. **he/she couldn't hurt/harm a fly** – a gentle person who would never hurt anyone. 'You can trust the new nanny, Amanda. She wouldn't hurt a fly.'

12. **a fly on the wall** – a secret observer. 'A fly-on-the-wall documentary on TV has followed the daily lives of a family for six months.'

13. **there are no flies on him** – he is too sharp to be deceived or swindled.

14. **to die/dying off/killed/drop/shoot down like flies** – dying easily and in large numbers. 'Millions of people died like flies during the flu epidemic after the First World War.' There are about 90,000 species of flies in the world. More than 5,000 species live in the British Isles.

15. **to descend/be like flies on or around someone** – to pounce eagerly upon someone. 'The reporters and cameramen descended like flies upon the film star when he left the hotel.'

16. **to swarm like flies around some-**

one/something – to gather in very large numbers around someone/something. 'Commuters swarm like flies around Victoria Station during the rush hour.'

1. **to trap/catch/capture something like a fly in amber** – to keep a special event in one's memory, never to forget it. 'Those summer days in Devon were the happiest in our lives. Our photos captured us like flies in amber and will always remind us of them.' All kinds of insects were trapped in the sticky resin which oozed out of trees and then hardened to form amber. They are perfectly preserved and some are tens of millions of years old.

Grasshopper, Butterfly, Moth

2. **a butterfly/grasshopper mind** – being unable to concentrate on one thing for any length of time, flitting from one interest to another. 'I was still thinking about what Hazel had said about rabbits but her grasshopper mind had leapt on to a completely different subject.'
   like a butterfly / butterfly-like – fickle, flighty. 'The handsome pop star flitted like a social butterfly from one beautiful woman to another.' **as elusive as a butterfly** – unattainable.

3. **to break a butterfly on a wheel** – to use superfluous strength in order to secure a result.

4. **to have butterflies in one's stomach/tummy** – to have an attack of nerves before an important event.

5. **like a moth (that flies) round a light** – like someone who is unable to resist temptation. 'The children gathered eagerly around the jar of jelly beans, like moths around a light.'

6. **moth-eaten ideas** – out-of-date ideas. 'He has such moth-eaten ideas that he would be more at home in the Victorian age.'

Bee, Drone, Wasp

7. **to be as busy as a bee** – to work non-stop.

8. **to be the bee's knees** – to be the best person or thing; exceptionally good. 'To play the part of Hamlet in the school play really is the bee's knees for Thomas.'
   to think one is the bee's knees – to think one is superior to everyone else. 'Janet thinks she's the bee's knees just because she is so good at computer programming.'

9. **to make a bee-line for** – to make one's way directly towards. 'Whenever I visit Mr Smith, his sister makes a bee-line for me.'

10. **to draw/attract someone like bees to a honey pot** – to attract someone strongly to something. 'Conflict attracts mercenaries like bees to a honey pot.' Also: **to take to something like a bee to honey.** cf. 'a honey-pot town' 177/14.

11. **to drone on** – to talk monotonously and at length on a subject.

12. **to bring a hornets' nest about one's ears / to put one's foot in a wasps' nest** – to bring down an avalanche of retribution on one's head by interference and criticism. 'When the government announced its intention of cutting out the waste in the National Health Service, it put its foot in a wasps' nest.'

13. **a wasp waist** – an exaggeratedly small waist. 'That tailor has given you a wasp waist. You'll have to have the jacket let out.'

14. **with a sting in its tail** – a speech or article that reserves its venom until the end.

15. **to take the sting out of something** – to make something seem less painful. 'The teacher had to tell Malcolm off for being so late but took the sting out of the reprimand by praising his essay.'

16. **to get stung** (slang) – to be cheated. 'I bought a beautiful vase on the market thinking it was an antique, but I got stung – it was just a very good modern fake.'

Bug

(see also *Bug* in Chapter 13)

1. **a big bug** – a very important person, often self-important.

2. **a fire-bug** – a compulsive fire-raiser.

3. **a litter bug** – someone who drops litter in the street and doesn't make use of a litter bin.

4. **as snug as a bug (in a rug)** – to feel very cosy and comfortable. 'The old lady looked as snug as a bug sitting there in her favourite armchair in front of the fire, sipping her hot cocoa.' This is probably the bed bug which lives in people's beds and feeds on particles of dead skin.

5. **to be bitten by the travel bug** – to be obsessively fond of travelling. ' "Has John come back from Australia yet?" Mary asked. "No, he has been bitten by the travel bug and is on his way to South America." '

6. **to have a room bugged** – to install an electronic device in a room for taping conversation.

Flea, Nit, Leech

7. **a (mere) flea bite** – a comparatively small sum of money. 'He was fined £500, but that was only a flea bite for a man of his wealth.'

8. **to send someone away with a flea in his ear** – to snub or rebuke a person. 'When he asked me for a loan, I sent him away with a flea in his ear. He must have felt very humiliated.'

9. **a flea-market** – an open-air market selling second-hand goods. 'Christine picked up a bargain at the flea-market today. Shall we go and have a look too?'

10. **nit-picking** (derogatory) – making small, pettifogging criticisms. 'The critics were all mean, nit-picking people, totally devoid of any artistic sense.' The nit is the egg of a louse, and therefore barely visible.

11. **to stick/cling like a leech** – to act like a parasite whom it is difficult to shake off. 'Whenever we invite Cousin Harry, we can never get rid of him. He sticks like a leech.' Also: **to leech on to someone**; **leech-like / like a blood-sucking leech**. Leeches are still being used by some doctors in Britain today. The action of blood sucking has beneficial effects on damaged skin. cf. '**to cling/stick like a limpet**' 75/3.

Stick Insect

12. **to look like a stick insect** – extremely thin, emaciated, lean and gaunt. 'Jordan and Samuel went hitch-hiking around India for several months and both came back looking like stick insects.' Also: **to have a stick-insect figure/silhouette**. cf. '**as thin/skinny as a rake**' 252/9; '**drainpipe-thin**' 158/6.

Snail

13. **at a snail's pace / at a snail-like pace / as slow as a snail / snail-like progress** – terribly slow, deliberate of movement, sluggish. 'I'm sorry I'm so late. My train went at a snail's pace all the way.' Often used to express annoyance at someone's excessive slowness.

   snail mail – post which takes a very long time to arrive; **snail rail** – trains which are delayed and slow to arrive.

Cricket

14. **as merry/chirpy/lively as a cricket** – cheerful, happy. So called because the chirp of a cricket has a merry sound.

Locust

15. **to swarm like locusts** – to appear in very great numbers. 'His poor relations swarmed like locusts around the rich man.' cf. '**like a vulture**' 72/3; '**to circle around someone like a shark . . .**' 75/5.

Pest

1. **a squeegee pest** – usually a teenage boy
who cleans car windscreens at red traffic
lights without the driver's permission and
then demands money for his work. He
uses a bucket of water and a 'squeegee' –
either a sponge or strip of leather. 'No
Squeegee' car stickers are available to
counter this problem.

Feelers

2. **to put out feelers** – to try to find out
the opinion of others before going ahead
with an action. 'Before we complain
about the teacher to the headmaster, let's
put out a few feelers to see who is telling
the truth.' cf. '**to test the water/
waters**' 12/15.

11 *Body*

Body

1. **to have body** – to have weight or substance. 'That wine has body, as well as bouquet and clarity.'
   to have no body – to be lacking in substance. 'Richard's novel was quite amusing but very light; it had no body.'

2. **to be a nobody** – to be a person of no significance, no importance. 'I won't take orders from a nobody like Smith.'

3. **a busybody** – someone who meddles or pries into other people's affairs. 'My neighbour has been asking me a lot of questions about my girlfriend. He is an appalling busybody.'

4. **to keep body and soul together** – to support life. 'When I left home, work was difficult to find, and I earned hardly enough to keep body and soul together.'

5. **to sell one's body** – to be a prostitute. cf. '**the oldest profession**' 273/4; '**to live by clipping**' 282/6.

6. **a body-blow to all one's hopes** – a very severe blow, a disastrous blow. 'Failing to qualify after so many years' study dealt a body-blow to all her hopes.'

7. **an out-of-body experience (OBE)** – some people believe that one's spirit is able to leave the physical body for a little while, to travel around and then return. An invisible 'thread' connects the spirit to the body and ensures its safe return. This 'thread' is severed only at death. Two similar kinds of spiritual voyages are the near-death experience and returning to another body after death in reincarnation. cf. '**a near-death experience**' 38/16.

Figure

8. **to cut a poor figure** – to look foolish. 'I must have cut a poor figure in front of the guests. I had quite forgotten how to dance.'

9. **a figure of fun** – an object of ridicule. 'When he was younger, the boys treated the master with respect, but now he's only a figure of fun.'

Head

10. **to head for** – (1) to go towards. (2) to ask for trouble, danger or disaster, etc. 'I warned you the company was heading for disaster.'

11. **a head start** – an advantage over one's competitors. 'You have a head start over your competitors; your business has been established longer than theirs.'

12. **to come to a head** (of ill-feeling, disagreements, etc.) – to reach a crisis.
    to bring to a head – to bring about a crisis. 'The minister brought matters to a head by resigning from the government.' The reference is to the 'head' which forms on a boil when it is about to burst.

13. **over one's head** – (1) intellectually too difficult to grasp. 'They talked advanced mathematics together. It was completely over my head.' (2) to appeal against the decision of one's immediate superior to someone higher up in the hierarchy. 'The sergeant-major went over the head of his company commander and complained direct to the commandant.'

14. **on one's head** – (1) to deserve blame if anything goes wrong. 'On your head be it if any of the patients suffer.' (2) to do

something without the slightest difficulty or effort. 'I could have answered all the history questions on my head' (literally, with my feet in the air, upside-down).

1. **to be off one's head** – to be mad. 'He must have been off his head to try to climb the mountain without a guide!'

   to go off one's head – to go mad, to act like a madman. 'When Philip's marriage ended, he went completely off his head.' The idiom may express only a temporary lapse. 'Have you gone off your head? You paid him all that money in advance! You'll never see him again!'

2. **to laugh one's head off** – to be seized by a fit of laughter. 'Harold was so keen to show off his dancing skill but he slipped and Susan laughed her head off.'

3. **to have a head for** – to have a gift or aptitude for. Often used in connection with figures, accounts and business. 'With your head for figures, you should go in for accountancy.'

   to have a head for heights – to feel comfortable at great heights. Often used in the negative form. 'I could never be a mountaineer; I have no head for heights.'

4. **to hold one's head high** – to be free from any taint of guilt. 'Now you have been acquitted on all the charges, you can hold your head high.'

5. **to turn someone's head** – to give someone a high opinion of himself, to give him a false idea of his own importance. 'Jack's election to the presidency of our union has turned his head. He has started talking about himself in the third person as if he were royalty!'

6. **to keep one's head / to keep a level head** – to remain calm and sensible.

   to lose one's head – to lose one's power of reasoning, to get into a panic. 'When the boat sprang a leak, Susan completely lost her head and began to scream hysterically.'

7. **to keep one's head down** – to avoid drawing attention to oneself. 'All this bad publicity is not doing you any good. You had better keep your head down for the next six months.'

8. **to fling oneself at someone's head/**

at someone – to pursue someone in a spirit of infatuation. 'The moment she saw the pop star, she flung herself at his head.'

9. **to snap off/bite off someone's head** – to speak sharply to someone, to snub or correct curtly. 'You needn't snap my head off. How was I to know?' Also: **to have a biting turn of phrase**.

10. **to let someone have his head / give someone his head** – to let someone use his own initiative, his own judgement. Compare '**to give the horse its head**' – to allow the horse freedom to decide the speed it will gallop at.

11. **to count heads / head-counting** – to accept the view of the majority. 'You are the only person on the committee who understands the subject, so what is the point of counting heads? You must decide.'

12. **to put their heads together** – to enlist someone else's advice in solving a problem, to discuss a problem with someone. From the proverb 'Two heads are better than one'.

13. **to knock their heads together** – to take drastic action to end a quarrel. 'I wish Ralph and Mike wouldn't quarrel in front of the reporters. Someone should knock their heads together.'

14. **to take it into one's head** – to have a sudden idea, often with the implication that the idea is a mistaken one.

15. **to get into one's head** – to learn, comprehend. 'I can't get this Latin grammar into my head.'

16. **to put ideas into someone's head** – to have a bad influence on someone, to indoctrinate. 'Mark has been putting ideas into Roger's head, and now he wants a bigger room and more food.'

17. **to put out of one's head** – to dismiss from one's mind some idea, hope or project.

18. **to make headway against** – to make progress, despite strong opposition; to prevail over. 'He made headway against the prejudices of the villagers.'

1. **to knock on the head** – to ruin a plan. 'Jane has broken her leg; that has knocked our skiing holiday on the head.'

2. **to scratch one's head** – to be puzzled, bewildered. 'I've been scratching my head over this game for the last half-hour, but I don't see how I can win; I give up!'

3. **a thick head / to be thick/thick-headed** – of limited intelligence, not very bright, stupid. 'You left the kitchen window open, you thick head! That's how the burglars got in!' Also: **as thick as a plank; as thick as two short planks**.

4. **soft in the head** – foolish, dense, mentally retarded; sometimes used as a reproach for some foolish action. 'Tim must be soft in the head to have believed that story.'

5. **to be bone-headed from the neck up** (slang) – to be completely stupid. From the idea of the bone replacing the brain.

6. **hot-headed** – easily aroused to anger. 'I don't know whether they will be happy together; she is mild and gentle, and her husband is quarrelsome and hot-headed, just the opposite of her.'

7. **to be at loggerheads** – to be in constant dispute with. 'He has been at loggerheads with his legal advisers throughout the proceedings.' Loggerheads were long poles with metal balls at the end which could be dipped into boiling tar. In medieval times these were hurled at enemy ships, or they could be used by embittered sailors who wished to fight each other.

8. **to go to one's head** – to be made vain or conceited by success. 'John was much applauded for his speech last night. I only hope his success will not go to his head.'

9. **to have a swelled head** – to be conceited, to have a high opinion of oneself. 'Winning first prize in the song contest has given Jane a swelled head. Now she shows off terribly.'

10. **to go bald-headed at** – to attack with great energy, in total disregard of the consequences. 'Michael went for his enemy bald-headed, although he was unarmed and outmatched by his opponent.'

11. **to rear/raise its ugly head** – to become a menace. 'The unemployment problem has raised its ugly head once more.'

12. **heads will roll** – those responsible for the blunder will be dismissed. In bygone times, guilty people in high places were sometimes executed. Today, they are removed from office, or transferred to positions of less importance, but the old phraseology has survived.

13. **to have something hanging over one's head** – to have an ordeal in front of one. 'This court case has been hanging over my head for the last six months. I shall be glad when it's over.'

14. **to need one's head examined** – to do something so stupid as to be almost insane. 'You drove at 90 miles an hour on that road! You should have your head examined!'

15. **to need/want something like a hole in the head** – to need or want something that is completely unnecessary because it will only cause problems. 'That trouble-maker, Mr Smith, wants to join our club. We need him like a hole in the head.'

16. **to bury one's head in the sand** – wilfully to close one's eyes to danger. 'I warned him the company would crash if we didn't economize, but he didn't want to listen to me. For the last three years he has buried his head in the sand.' cf. **'like an ostrich' 72/5**.

17. **to put one's head on the chopping-block** – to take some action which effectively ends one's career. 'For you to vote against the chairman after all he has done for you would be to put your head on the chopping-block.'

18. **to keep one's head above water** – to earn only just enough money to be able to live or to pay one's debts. 'I'm afraid Philip's business isn't doing at all well; he is barely keeping his head above water.'

19. **a head-on collision** – a violent disagreement with someone whose opinions are completely opposed to one's own.

20. **to be head over heels in love with** – to be madly in love with. Sometimes

abbreviated to '**to be head over heels**'.
   to fall head over heels in love – to fall in love very suddenly, very violently. Sometimes abbreviated to '**to fall head over heels**'.

1. **not to know whether one is on one's head or one's heels** – to be in a state of total confusion. 'After severely reprimanding me for my work, my boss offered me promotion at twice the salary. I didn't know whether I was on my head or my heels.'

2. **to stand logic on its head** – to argue illogically. 'To say that Brian isn't clever enough to benefit from a university education is to stand logic on its head. If Brian weren't clever enough, he wouldn't have passed the entrance examination.'

3. **to be head and shoulders better than** – to be altogether superior to.

4. **to have a head on one's shoulders** – to possess good judgement.
   to have an old head on young shoulders – possessing greater wisdom than might be expected of a young person. 'If you are a young man confronted with a difficult problem, you need an old head on young shoulders.'

5. **to put one's head in a noose** – to invite disaster.

6. **to win/beat/lose by a short head** – by a very small margin. 'Greatly encouraged by his cheering friends, Mark managed to beat the former darts champion by a short head.' The idiom derives from horse-racing and refers to the distance measured on reaching the end post first, the 'head' being the horse's head, and the 'short head' being less than the whole length of a horse's head.

7. **heads or tails?** – the call made when tossing a coin to decide the order of play, especially in a game. 'Heads' refers to the sovereign's head on one side of the coin, and 'tails' the reverse side.

8. **heads I win, tails you lose** – an unequal contest which only one person can possibly win. 'It's not fair. Whatever I decide to do, you will win the lot. It's heads you win, and tails I lose.'

9. **to make neither head nor tail of something** – to be completely baffled.

10. **to hit the headlines** – to achieve notoriety, to be the most important item of news on the front page of the national newspapers. 'What a scandal! If you publish that story, it will hit the headlines.'

Hair

11. **to have one's hair stand on end** – to be terrified. 'When he saw the ghost, his hair stood on end.'

12. **a hairy story** – an uncouth story.

13. **hair-raising** – startling and perturbing. 'When journalists dug a bit deeper into the MP's past, some hair-raising secrets came to light.'
   a hair-raising story – a horror story, one that shocks you.

14. **to raise the hairs on the back of one's neck** – very frightening indeed. 'The strange atmosphere of the dark passageways in the haunted castle was enough to raise the hairs on the back of my neck.'

15. **don't lose your hair over it / keep your hair on** – keep calm, don't get too excited over it. cf. '**to keep one's shirt on**' 192/9.

16. **without turning a hair** – without showing any emotion or surprise. 'When she was told her father was dying, she never turned a hair.'

17. **to tear one's hair (out)** – to be desperate, unbearably frustrated. 'He has been tearing his hair over the accounts.'

18. **to let one's hair down** – to speak one's mind, to give vent to one's feelings. 'When I'm with Peter, I can really let my hair down.'

19. **enough to make one's hair curl** – to shock very severely. 'If you could see our electricity bill, it would make your hair curl!'

20. **to have someone by the short hairs** (vulgar) – to have someone at a hopeless disadvantage, to have him in one's power. Also: **to have someone by the short and curlies; to short and curly** – to beat someone up.

1. **to split hairs / hair-splitting** – to make insignificant distinctions, to argue with exaggerated subtlety.

2. **see-through hair** – thinning hair, especially of a woman, usually due to hormone problems, lack of iron, zinc, vitamins and iodine, or to stress. See *The Hair Loss Cure* by Elizabeth Steel.

3. **flyaway hair** – unmanageable hair. cf. 'a bad hair day' 31/15.

4. **to escape by a hair's breadth / to be saved by a hair's breadth** – to escape very narrowly, by a tiny distance. 'She was only saved from falling under the train by a hair's breadth.'

5. **to a hair** – accurate or exact to the last detail.

6. **the bald truth** – the plain truth, to put it bluntly, the true state of things. 'The problem of drug addicts in this town has not been solved. That is the bald truth.' cf. 'full stop' 265/5; 'the bottom line' 265/13.

Face

7. **to be two-faced** – to support both parties in a dispute at the same time, to agree with a person to his face but disagree with him behind his back. 'Paul praised my painting while sitting for me, but I found out that he had made fun of it behind my back. He is very two-faced!'

8. **bare-faced** – open, shameless, daring; almost always used in connection with 'insolence', 'impudence', 'cheek' and words with similar meanings. 'He had the bare-faced impudence to ask me for a loan ten minutes after we had been introduced!' cf. 'as bold as brass' 123/8.

9. **to put the best face on something** – to accept a setback or defeat gracefully. 'Simon put the best face on his dismissal, saying that he had intended to take another job anyway.'

10. **to put a bold face on something** – to behave without any embarrassment or shame. 'When Peter was accused of the theft, he put a bold face on it, sat down, and lit a cigar before replying.'

11. **to put on a brave face** – to suppress one's feelings of fear or sadness. 'When the mother heard that her daughter had been injured in a train crash, she tried to put on a brave face for the sake of her other children.'

12. **to face a thing out** – to insist that one is in the right, often unreasonably.

13. **to look in the face** – to confront bravely. 'After the crash of his business, the future was extremely bleak; nevertheless, he looked it in the face.'

14. **to face off** – to confront. 'Animal rights activists faced off police in a clash at an animal laboratory.'

15. **to stare in the face** – to be certain, to be clearly unavoidable. 'Bankruptcy has been staring Tom in the face for a long time, but he won't admit it.'
    to stare death in the face. 'Brenda stared death in the face when the bank robber threatened her with his gun.'

16. **to make faces** – to grimace. 'The little boy made faces at his aunt when she wasn't looking.'

17. **to pull a face** – to make a grimace which may express disgust, anger, derision or dismay.
    to pull/make a long face – to look dismal. 'When I told him that he would have to pay for all the damage out of his own pocket, he made a long face.'

18. **to keep a straight face** – to look as if you really believe a story or are in agreement with the speaker, when in reality you would like to laugh. 'When he told me he was going to photograph the Loch Ness monster, it was all I could do to keep a straight face.'

19. **let's face it** – don't let us deceive ourselves. 'Let's face it, William will never get into college, not in a hundred years.'

20. **to face up to** – to confront a problem realistically without deluding oneself as to the nature of the difficulties. 'You must face up to the fact that we have no money.'

21. **on the face of it** – to all appearances, assuming that the facts have been correctly stated. 'On the face of it, your part-

ner is clearly in the wrong, but have you told me the whole story?'

1. **to have the face to** – to be insolent enough to. 'After I had caught Mark stealing my crystal bowl, he had the face to ask me if he could keep it as a souvenir.'

2. **to show one's face** – to appear, to make one's presence known. 'I wonder she dare show her face here, after the way she has behaved.'

3. **to shield one's face** – to hide one's face to avoid being recognized. 'The famous pop star shielded his face when he rushed from his taxi to the hotel.'

4. **to one's face** – in one's presence instead of behind someone's back. 'Let him make his accusations to my face!'

5. **to set one's face against** – to oppose strongly. 'He has set his face against any change in our plans.'

6. **at face value** – at its nominal or official value. 'The face value of an Elizabeth II sovereign is only £1, but its real value is at least £100.'

7. **to face both ways** – to support both contestants at the same time.

8. **to face about** – to change one's mind, to adopt a contrary opinion.

9. **a slap in the face** – a rebuff or snub. 'It was a slap in the face not inviting her old friend Sandra to her birthday party.' A statement, etc., can sting one like '**a slap in the face**' and the rain, etc., can hit one like '**a slap across the face**'.

10. **to lose face** – to be humiliated.

11. **to save face** – not to lose respect, to avoid humiliation.
    a face-saving formula – a form of words that seeks to avoid humiliation for the defeated party.

12. **to put a new face on something** – to show something in a different light. 'Higgs' presence at the house on the night of the crime has put a new face on the investigation.'

13. **a facelift** – to enhance the appearance of someone or something. 'The Royal Opera House in London has been given a facelift which has improved it immensely.' The term derives from the operation to 'lift' or tighten the skin of an ageing person's face to make it appear more youthful. cf. '**a nose job**' 89/12.

14. **to laugh in someone's face** – to mock. 'I told him he was to blame for the accident, but he laughed in my face and told me I must be joking.'

15. **to laugh on the other side of one's face** – to change from exultation to dismay. 'Andrew was looking forward to a few days' freedom, but he'll laugh on the other side of his face when he hears Joyce has gone away for good.'

16. **to wipe the smile off someone's face** – to destroy someone's complacency. 'Arnold has been boasting that he is the best heavyweight in our unit, but I'll soon wipe the smile off his face.'

17. **to be po-faced** – to be completely humourless, far too solemn. 'The po-faced landlady strongly disapproved of her student lodgers holding a party in her house.' The idiom may originally have been 'poor-faced' or 'pot-faced' (from the French word for 'chamber pot', *pot de chambre*, in which the 't' of *pot* is not pronounced).

18. **to fly in the face of** – to ignore the facts or logic of an argument, to deny or contradict unreasonably. 'You are flying in the face of all the authorities on this subject.'

19. **to throw in someone's face** – to reproach someone for a blunder or fault. 'Alice threw her husband's disgrace in his face.'

20. **to fall flat on one's face** – to make a dismal failure of something. 'A couple of years ago, Steven bought the book shop at the corner but, not having any experience of running a shop, he fell flat on his face.'

21. **his/her face fell** – he/she looked dismayed.

22. **her face is her fortune** – her beauty is her only asset.

23. **an alabaster face** – an extremely pale face. 'The alabaster face and large dark eyes of the model had made her rich and famous.' cf. '**alabaster skin**' 111/4.

1. **faceless men** – anonymous, unfeeling men. This phrase is used with special reference to civil servants who often use their traditional anonymity to escape responsibility for their actions.

   faceless wonders – the advisers of the British prime minister, part of his or her private staff. 'The minister complained that there were faceless wonders inside the government who were upsetting all his plans.'

Eye

2. **to see eye to eye** – to be in agreement with someone, usually over a wide range of subjects. 'We found it difficult to live together because we don't see eye to eye.'

3. **to be up to the eyes/ears** – to be overwhelmed with, to have an excessive amount. 'I am up to the eyes in work.'

4. **to have an eye on the main chance** (derogatory) – to be alert to any opportunity for betterment. 'She was a shrewd woman; she never did a kindness without a good reason, and she always had an eye on the main chance.'

5. **to meet one's eye** – to look straight in the face. 'He could not meet my eyes, but blushed and turned away from me.'

6. **there is more in something than meets the eye** – there is some hidden significance. 'Mrs Lewis rang up to say she and her husband couldn't come to dinner today. She said she had a cold, but I think she's offended with us. There is more in this than meets the eye.'

7. **to cast an eye over** – to read through very quickly, to check.

8. **to be all eyes** – to be very attentive. 'When she got up to sing, her admirer was all eyes.'

9. **through the eyes of . . .** – from the point of view of . . . 'When you play chess, you should look at the game through the eyes of your opponent.'

10. **to open the eyes to** – to make someone aware of a truth, usually some unpleasant fact. 'I opened his eyes to his wife's unfaithfulness.'

11. **to be an eye-opener** – to be a revelation. The phrase suggests a sudden surprise, which may be good or bad. 'Charles had always had romantic ideas about being a cowboy, so his first day at the ranch was a real eye-opener for him.'

12. **with one's eyes open** – fully aware of the risk one is running. 'He went into it with his eyes open, so he can't complain now if things go wrong.'

13. **with one's eyes shut** – with no difficulty or need for any assistance. 'I know my way to her house so well that I could take you there with my eyes shut.'

14. **to have an eye for** – to have good judgement of something. 'She has an eye for horses; she has bred them all her life.'

15. **to get one's eye in** – to get accustomed to the conditions so that one can display one's skill. 'Once he's got his eye in, he is very difficult to beat.' The reference is to ball games like cricket in which a player has to adjust his sight to the movement of the ball.

16. **to have/keep an eye on** – to watch carefully. 'You must keep an eye on that girl. She is very wild, and is not to be trusted on her own.'

17. **to have a roving eye** – to be always looking for a pretty face. 'It's a pity, Anne's husband has a roving eye and always seems to be with a pretty girl!'

18. **to shut one's eyes to** – to ignore or to pretend ignorance of someone's faults. 'She shut her eyes to all his shortcomings, although my brother was always pointing them out to her.'

19. **with an eye to** – with the aim of. 'I studied French with an eye to getting a job in one of the big fashion houses in Paris.'

20. **to see with one's own eyes** – to witness, to experience oneself without having to rely on anyone else's testimony. 'You can take my word for it; I saw it with my own eyes.'

21. **not to believe one's eyes** – to doubt the reality of what one has seen. 'When my sister returned from the beauty parlour, she was so changed that I couldn't believe

my eyes.' cf. **'to be unable to believe one's ears'** 90/16.

1. **the scales fall from one's eyes** – the sudden realization that one has been deceived. 'For Melanie, the scales fell from her eyes the moment she saw her boyfriend kissing her sister.'

2. **to cry one's eyes out** – to weep so much that one can't weep any more.

3. **there wasn't a dry eye in the house** – everyone in the audience was in tears. 'After screening the film *Message in a Bottle*, there wasn't a dry eye in the cinema.'

4. **to catch the eye / to be eye-catching** – to attract attention. 'With her splendid figure and her elegant gown, she soon caught the eye of the judges.'

5. **to catch the eyes of the world** – everyone is aware of something and highly interested in watching it. 'The spectacular eclipse of the sun caught the eyes of the world.'

6. **that's one in the eye for** – a snub or rebuff. 'She didn't invite him to her birthday party. That was one in the eye for him!'

7. **eye-wash** – humbug, hypocritical nonsense.

8. **in the twinkling/blink of an eye** – very quickly. 'The burglar dashed from the house and was gone in the blink of an eye.'

9. **to see out of the corner of one's eye** – to notice, usually for only a second, while one's attention is directed elsewhere. 'As I was entering the restaurant, I saw John out of the corner of my eye, jumping on a bus.'

10. **wide-eyed** – wide-open eyes that express surprise or innocence.

11. **a private eye** – a private detective. 'The police don't like private eyes as a rule, but they had to admit that Hugh was a first-class investigator.'

12. **to clap eyes on** – to see or meet. Nearly always negative. 'I've never clapped eyes on you before!'

13. **to cock the eye** – to look at knowingly. 'As soon as the vicar began to speak about the drinking in the village, she cocked an eye at me, and I felt myself going red in the face.'

14. **to keep one's eyes skinned** – to be extremely vigilant and alert.

15. **to take one's eyes off someone/something** – to turn one's attention away from someone/something. 'Can't you take your eyes off your book for one moment and look at me!'

16. **to make eyes at** – to gaze amorously at.

17. **to see with half an eye** – to realize at once. 'You could see with half an eye that Bob and Ruth weren't happy.'

18. **the naked eye** – without the aid of spectacles or a telescope. 'On a fine day, you can see the Bowden Rocks with the naked eye.'

19. **to view with a beady eye** – to look doubtfully or critically at someone. 'When I asked the boss for a day off so that I could nurse my sick mother, he viewed me with a beady eye.'

20. **to be starry-eyed** – to be full of fancies, to have a lot of impracticable ideas.

21. **the evil eye / to have an evil eye on someone** – a menacing, ominous look. In Voodoo, the evil eye casts its spell over the intended victim, even when they are separated by hundreds of miles.

22. **in the public eye** – very much in the news, much discussed.

23. **in one's mind's eye** – in one's imagination. 'In my mind's eye, I can still see him knocking out his pipe on the mantelpiece, although he's been dead these 20 years.'

24. **to have bigger eyes than one's stomach** – to over-eat, to be a glutton.

25. **to have/get square eyes** – to spend too much time watching television. 'To bed now, children. You'll get square eyes if you don't turn off the television this instant.'

26. **an eye for an eye, a tooth for a tooth** – a like punishment, a punishment that is as severe as the crime but not more so, in

accordance with both the Muslim and Judaic laws. It has come to be used in the sense of revenge. See the Bible, Exodus XXI.

1. **to throw dust in someone's eyes** – to mislead or deceive someone wilfully.

2. **the eye of the storm** – the centre of the storm where all is peaceful.

3. **eye-ball to eye-ball** – direct confrontation between two enemies.

Eyelid

4. **not to bat an eyelid** – to show no feeling or concern. 'No matter how outrageously the boy behaved, his father never batted an eyelid but just went on reading his newspaper.'

5. **to hang on by one's eyelids** – to hang by a thread, to maintain only a precarious hold.

Eyebrow

6. **a high-brow** – someone with an intellectual approach to literature and art. The high-brow is interested in style rather than content, and in ideas rather than action.
   a low-brow – a person who has no intellectual interests. He or she likes a story with plenty of action, looks for a pleasant tune in music, and prefers a painting that tells a story.

7. **to raise the eyebrows** – to express surprise, sometimes mild disapproval. 'When her boss ordered flowers for the manageress, the secretary raised her eyebrows.'

8. **to knit one's brows** – to concentrate. 'He knitted his eyebrows as he tried to work out a solution to the puzzle.'

9. **to be steeped to the eyebrows** – to be totally immersed in a subject. 'Since his childhood he had been steeped to the eyebrows in Greek mythology.'

10. **by the sweat of one's brow** – by very hard work, either physical or mental, without anyone's help. 'He reached his present position, not by influence, but by the sweat of his brow.'

Nose

11. **to nose about** – to pry, to make all sorts of inquiries. 'The inspector has been nosing about among my father's documents all the morning.'

12. **to nose out** – to discover a secret.

13. **to be nosy** – to be inquisitive, to ask too many questions.
    a nosy parker – someone who is forever asking questions about one's business and one's private life. A busybody.

14. **to poke one's nose into someone else's business** – to pry, to interfere in another person's private business. 'He has been poking his nose into my affairs again.'

15. **to keep one's nose out of something** – to leave well alone. 'Keep your nose out of his affairs. This matter has nothing to do with us.'

16. **a nose for trouble/scandal, etc.** – the ability to pick up bad or sensational news before other people do. 'That journalist has a fine nose for the latest scandal.'

17. **to get up someone's nose** (slang) – to exasperate, irritate. 'Harry gets up my nose with his never-ending complaints.'

18. **under one's nose** – something that happens very close to a person without his or her knowing. 'He stole my watch from right under my nose.'

19. **to follow one's nose** – to go straight ahead or by instinct. 'She couldn't be bothered to explain how to get there. She told me just to follow my nose.'

20. **to be led by the nose** – to be completely dominated by, totally influenced by. 'The employee led her boss by the nose until she had spent all his money.'

21. **to pay through the nose** – to pay an excessive price. 'I had to pay through the nose for that desk. I could have got it for a fraction of the price anywhere else.'

22. **to rub someone's nose in it** – to draw someone's attention repeatedly to a past blunder. 'It was bad enough for poor

Kenneth, losing all that money, without you rubbing his nose in it all the time.'

1. **to look down one's nose** – to regard with distaste or disdain. 'He looked down his nose at the youth for wearing his hair long.'

2. **to turn up one's nose at something** – to despise. 'She turns up her nose at Frinton and Bournemouth. Nothing but the Riviera is good enough for her.'

3. **with one's nose in the air** – in a snobbish manner. 'Judy never greets me; she always has her nose in the air.'

4. **to see beyond the end of one's nose** – to look beyond one's immediate surroundings, to use one's imagination and intelligence. 'He has no imagination. He can't see beyond the end of his nose.'

5. **to put someone's nose out of joint** – to upset or replace a favourite. 'Jenny is to replace Sally as the boss's confidential secretary. That will put Sally's nose out of joint!'

6. **to cut off one's nose to spite one's face** – to injure or deprive oneself while trying to hurt someone else. 'He was determined to punish his son, so he cancelled the cruise he had booked. But it was a case of cutting off his nose to spite his face, because his son went to Cornwall, leaving his father to be miserable at home.'

7. **to keep one's nose clean** (slang) – to keep out of trouble. 'Life in the army can be quite pleasant, provided you obey orders and keep your nose clean.'

8. **to keep/put one's nose to the grindstone** – to work hard and long at the same job without any rest. 'With so many debts to pay off, he'll just have to keep his nose to the grindstone for the next few years.'

9. **to make a long nose at someone / to thumb one's nose at someone** – to show contempt for a person or institution. 'When you are making £100,000 a year, you can thumb your nose at convention.'

10. **hard-nosed** – shrewd, tough, unsentimental.

11. **a nose-dive** – a vertical dive by an aeroplane. 'The aeroplane went into a nose-dive and crashed into the ground.'

12. **a nose job** – plastic surgery on the nose in order to improve one's appearance. 'Sandra's nose job has done wonders for her confidence.' cf. '**a facelift**' **85/13**.

13. **to get a bloody nose** – to suffer an unpleasant rebuff.

14. **as plain as the nose on someone's face** – extremely obvious. 'You failed your maths exam because you didn't do enough homework. It's as plain as the nose on your face.' cf. '**as plain as a pikestaff**' **248/12**.

15. **a Roman nose** – a rather large, bulbous nose.

16. **a Greek nose** – a straight nose that extends down from the forehead in a straight line.

17. **a political nose** – to have a flair for politics; a politician's instinct which tells him or her what the public wants. 'The minister's political nose tells him that people are worried about petrol prices and that he must do something about it.'

Ear

18. **long ears** – an inquisitive person who is always asking questions.

19. **to have sharp ears for any gossip** – alert to any gossip, not to miss any scandal.

20. **coming out at the ears** – having something in superabundance. 'Jack has found so much oil, it's coming out at his ears.'

21. **to gain the ear** – to arouse someone's interest on one's behalf. 'Now that I have gained the chairman's ear, we shouldn't have any more difficulty.'

22. **to lend an ear** – to pay attention, to listen. 'If you will lend me your ear for a minute, I will explain how the burglar alarm works.'

23. **to play it by ear** – to use one's intuition, to improvise. ' "I'm new to this school; so I'll have to play it by ear for the first few lessons," the teacher said.' The phrase

derives from playing a piece of music without looking at the musical score.

1. **in one ear and out the other** – heard without making any impression. 'Everything I say to that boy goes in one ear and out the other.'

2. **a word in the ear** – advice given in confidence.

3. **to be all ears** – to listen very attentively. 'What you say is very interesting. I'm all ears.'

4. **to have one's ear to the ground** – to be well-informed on what is going on, to be alert to future developments. 'Paul is always the first to know what's happening in the office. He keeps his ear to the ground.'

5. **to be still wet behind the ears** – to be naïve, inexperienced. 'He will be no match for them; he is still wet behind the ears.' The phrase has its origin in children's neglect to dry themselves behind the ears.

6. **are your ears burning?** – do you feel embarrassed to hear yourself talked about?

7. **to tickle the ears** – to flatter, to please. 'She said you were very handsome – yes, I thought that would tickle your ears.'

8. **to set people by the ears** – to stir up mischief. 'During his short stay, Philip set us all by the ears. We had no peace until he had gone.'

9. **to box the ears** – to strike the ears hard, usually as a punishment.

10. **to be out on one's ear** – to be ejected or sacked, often violently. 'The heckler was soon out on his ear, once he started interrupting the speaker.'

11. **to prick up one's ears** – to listen alertly, become suddenly interested in what is being said. 'He pricked up his ears when they mentioned the salary.' The idea comes from the pricking up of a dog's ears when it hears an unfamiliar sound.

12. **to grate on the ear** – to make a harsh, disagreeable sound. 'The lecturer's voice grated on the ears of his students.'

13. **an ear-splitting noise** – an unbearably loud noise.

14. **out of earshot** – out of hearing distance. 'Hi, Brenda! I'll tell you something interesting as soon as Linda is out of earshot.'

15. **to be up to the ears in work/debt** – to have a huge amount of work/debts.

16. **to be unable to believe one's ears** – to be astounded at what one has heard. 'When Anne told me she had been married to my brother two years ago, I couldn't believe my ears.' cf. **'not to believe one's eyes' 86/21**.

Mouth

17. **to look down in the mouth** – to look depressed, dejected, in low spirits. 'Henry was looking very down in the mouth today; his wife and children had just left for their holiday leaving him to look after the house.'

18. **to have a big mouth** – to speak a lot in a loud voice, to boast.

19. **to shoot off one's mouth** – to talk loudly and indiscreetly. 'Alex was shooting his mouth off in the pub last night about his domestic problems; he should keep all that to himself.'

20. **a mouthful** – a long and difficult name. 'Andrei Andreivitch – that's a mouthful, isn't it?'

21. **to be mealy-mouthed** – to describe something bad with undue mildness as if one were afraid to speak one's mind. 'If the man is a scoundrel, then say so; why be so mealy-mouthed about it?'

22. **to be foul-mouthed** – to use bad or obscene language. 'Don't let our children play with those boys down the road, Maggie. They are very foul-mouthed.'

23. **a loose mouth** – an indiscreet person.

24. **to stand convicted out of one's own mouth** – to condemn oneself with one's own words.

25. **to leave a nasty taste in the mouth** – to leave an unpleasant impression with someone. 'She apologized profusely for making such an accusation against me,

and we shook hands at once, but what she had said left a nasty taste in my mouth.'

1. **to put words into someone's mouth** – to accuse someone of saying things that he or she has not said. ' "I never said that," the witness protested angrily. "You are putting words into my mouth." '

2. **to take the words out of someone's mouth** – to say something before the other person has had time to say it himself. ' "This is an appalling play," I said. "You've taken the words out of my mouth. Let's go," Alan replied.'

3. **to open one's mouth too wide** (vulgar) – to ask for too much money. 'My plumber has started opening his mouth too wide. I shall have to find someone else.'

4. **to make one's mouth water** – to tantalize. 'He made my mouth water showing me all his beautiful carpets. I wish I had enough money to buy one!'

5. **to foam at the mouth** – to be overcome with fury, to be so angry as to lose all control over oneself. 'When the football squashed his prize dahlias, the gardener foamed at the mouth with rage.' The foam is the rush of saliva from the mouth.

6. **out of the mouths of babes and sucklings** – the truth is often spoken by children without their being aware of it.

7. **by word of mouth** – through the spoken word, as opposed to the written word. 'Many herbal remedies have been passed down by word of mouth from one generation of gypsies to the next.'

8. **the gift of the gab** – the gift of fluent speech. 'With your gift of the gab you should do well as a lawyer.' Gab derives from Gaelic *gob* meaning 'mouth', but is only used in this phrase. As legend has it, the 'gift of the gab' may be acquired by kissing the Blarney stone in Killarney, County Cork, Ireland. cf. '**to be full of Blarney / to talk Blarney**' 210/6.

Jaw

9. **to jaw away** (school slang) – to speak without interruption. 'Jaw, jaw is better than war, war' (Churchill) – to negotiate, even if it takes a long time, is better than making war.

10. **out of the jaws of death** – from the very brink of death. This phrase is often used with the verb 'snatch'. 'He was snatched from the jaws of death by his friend.'

Whisker

11. **within a whisker** – by a very narrow margin. 'We were within a whisker of being defeated. The result couldn't have been closer.'

Lip

12. **to have one's lips sealed** – to be obliged to keep silent, to keep a confidence or secret.

13. **to bite one's lip** – to regret having said something indiscreet. 'She bit her lip for having made such a clumsy mistake.'

14. **none of your lip!** – don't be cheeky/impudent.

15. **to put a finger to one's lips** – to make a sign to keep quiet.

16. **to curl the lip** – to show contempt.

17. **to keep a stiff upper lip** – to suffer in silence, to suppress all emotion. 'Lewis suffered dreadfully but he kept a stiff upper lip throughout his ordeal.' From the poem 'A stiff upper lip' by Phoebe Cary (1824–74).

18. **to pay lip service** – to respect a principle or custom in theory but to ignore it in practice. 'He pays lip service to his wife's wishes but, once she has gone away, he reverts to his old way of life.'

19. **to lick/smack one's lips** – to exult at the prospect of an appetizing meal or other future event to be enjoyed.

20. **to be tight-lipped** – unwilling to say more than is absolutely necessary. 'He

was very tight-lipped about his future plans.

1. **to hang on someone's lips** – to listen attentively to every word a person is saying, to give a person one's entire attention.

2. **read my lips** – take note of what I say (stressing the importance of one's words). ' "Read my lips," the politician said earnestly. "We pledge not to touch the pension funds." ' The phrase was coined by former US president George Bush during his election campaign when he promised, 'Read my lips: no new taxes.'

Tooth

3. **to cut a tooth** – (of a young tooth) to pierce the gum.

4. **to have a sweet tooth** – to have a liking for sweet food, sugar, honey, ice-cream, etc. 'Nicola has such a sweet tooth; it makes it very difficult for her to slim.'

5. **to go over with a fine-tooth comb** – to make a most thorough and painstaking examination

6. **to be long in the tooth** – old, too old, older than one cares to admit. 'He's a bit long in the tooth for her, isn't he? He must be at least 60!'

Teeth

7. **milk teeth** – the first teeth.

8. **to cut one's wisdom/eye-teeth** – to acquire sense or discretion.

9. **to give one's eye-teeth for** – to wish with all one's heart for, to be prepared to make any sacrifice for. 'I would give my eye-teeth for your job. You have a job in a million!'

10. **to show one's teeth** – to make threats or express hostility. 'Our landlord has always been such a kind, easy-going man, but when I accidentally smashed his window he really showed his teeth.'

11. **to give teeth to** – to give a person or organization special powers and sanctions. 'We must give the ombudsman teeth so that he can enforce his decisions.'

12. **to get one's teeth into** – to concentrate all one's energy on. 'Short stories are all very well, but I prefer a novel – something I can get my teeth into.'

13. **to get the bit between the teeth** – to throw off all restraint in achieving one's objective. 'Malcolm is determined to buy the house, whatever it costs. Once he gets the bit between his teeth, it is useless to argue with him.' A rider can control a horse by pulling on the bit in the horse's mouth. However, once the horse gets the bit between its teeth, the rider can no longer control it.

14. **in the teeth of** – against the strong resistance of. 'Henry married the girl in the teeth of her parents' disapproval.'

15. **to be fed up to the teeth/back teeth** – to be exasperated beyond endurance. 'I'm fed up to the back teeth with all his complaints.' cf. '**to be sick and tired**' **135/6**.

16. **to be kicked in the teeth** – to suffer a severe blow from someone from whom you least expect it. 'After I had given her son all those private lessons for nothing, she cut me dead at the party last night. It was a real kick in the teeth.'

17. **to set one's teeth on edge** – to grate or jar on the nerves. 'Her voice sets my teeth on edge, like scraping a plate with a knife.'

18. **to grind one's teeth** – to express one's fury. 'Herbert ground his teeth when he heard his daughter was going to marry his junior clerk.'

19. **to cast in the teeth** – to reproach a person to his face for some blunder or fault. 'She cast his drunkenness in his teeth.'

20. **to gnash one's teeth** – to regret bitterly, either one's own mistakes or the success of somebody of whom one is jealous. 'He gnashed his teeth at the idea of Michael marrying his old girlfriend.' A biblical phrase: '. . . there shall be weeping and gnashing of teeth' (Matthew VIII, 12).

21. **to grit one's teeth** – to suppress one's feelings when suffering a painful or fright-

ening experience. 'He gritted his teeth and dived into the cold water.'

1. **to lie through one's teeth** – to lie shamelessly. 'If Richard told you that he was a rich man, he was lying through his teeth. Why, only yesterday he asked me to lend him £50!'

2. **to draw someone's teeth** – to render a dangerous person harmless. 'The prime minister drew the teeth of the Opposition by announcing that there had been a drop of a quarter of a million in the number of unemployed.'

3. **like drawing/pulling teeth** – extremely difficult. 'Tell me more about your day at university, Tim. Getting information out of you is like pulling teeth!'

Tongue

4. **to have a sharp tongue** – to have a pointed, barbed way of speaking.

5. **to be loose-tongued** – to be garrulous, indiscreet.

6. **to keep a civil tongue in one's head** – to speak respectfully to one's superiors. 'The director ordered his manager to keep a civil tongue in his head.' A little old-fashioned.

7. **with the tongue in one's cheek** – words spoken insincerely. 'When he congratulated Martin on his 20 years' public service, he must have had his tongue in his cheek, because he is always talking about Martin's bad work in the office.'

8. **to wag one's tongue** – to talk behind someone's back, to gossip.
      to set tongues wagging – to give cause for gossip through one's indiscretions.

9. **to get one's tongue round** – to have difficulty in saying a word. 'Hypothesize? I can hardly get my tongue round it.'

10. **to have a tongue that runs away with one** – to talk too much, to be indiscreet. 'How your tongue ran away with you last night, Roy! You shouldn't have talked about your father like that to a stranger.'

11. **to hold one's tongue** – to say nothing, to be discreet. 'If I tell him something in confidence, do you think he can be trusted to hold his tongue?'

12. **a slip of the tongue** – a mistake in one's speech, through carelessness or, more often, a conflict of wishes. An example: a chairman in his welcoming speech to his co-directors declared the meeting closed instead of open because he didn't want to see them (*Psychopathology of Everyday Life* by Sigmund Freud).

13. **I could have bitten my tongue off** – I was angry with myself for having said something (usually something tactless or stupid). 'I thought my joke would amuse our guests but, instead, there was an embarrassed silence. I could have bitten my tongue off.'

14. **to give someone the rough edge of one's tongue** – to reprimand someone harshly. 'If he doesn't mend his ways, I shall give him the rough edge of my tongue, and he'll be sorry he was so impertinent.'

15. **to have a dirty tongue** – to use bad language.

16. **on the tip of one's tongue** – (1) to be on the point of saying something. 'It was on the tip of my tongue to tell Mervyn that I had already read the book he had given me, but I stopped myself just in time.' (2) very nearly remembered. 'Her name was on the tip of my tongue just now; it will come back to me.' This use is almost always confined to the names of people or places.

17. **tongue-tied** – unable to speak through shyness or fear. 'The student stood tongue-tied in front of the examiners.'

18. **have you lost your tongue?** – why can't you speak? Addressed to someone who is speechless, silent.

19. **to find one's tongue** – to regain one's speech. 'Oh, you've found your tongue again, have you?'

20. **a tongue-twister** – a sentence composed of similar sounds that are difficult to pronounce without stuttering, e.g. 'She sells seashells on the seashore.'

Throat

1. **to have a lump in one's throat** – to feel sad, to be on the verge of tears. 'When I waved goodbye to Angela, I had a lump in my throat. I had grown very fond of her.'

2. **to have the words stick in one's throat** – to find it impossible to say the words, owing to dislike, pride or prejudice. 'I wanted to congratulate him, but I disliked him so much that the words stuck in my throat.'

3. **to force/ram down one's throat** – to force a belief or idea upon someone. 'It's a mistake to force your own ideas down his throat. He is old enough to think for himself.'

4. **to jump down one's throat** – to criticize someone for some trifling mistake, to speak sharply to. 'However carefully the student spoke, the teacher jumped down his throat.'

5. **at each other's throats** – deadly enemies, constantly fighting each other. 'The two brothers will never make peace; they have been at each other's throats for the last 20 years.'

6. **to slit one's throat** – to damage one's own interests. 'You would be slitting your throat if you reduced your prices still further.' It can also be used to express a strong negative attitude. 'I would rather slit my throat than work together with that rogue Maynard.'

7. **cut-throat competition** – ruthless competition by any method, fair or foul. 'You will find it difficult to open a shop in the High Street. There is a lot of cut-throat competition in this town.' Also: **the cut-throat world of politics/business**.

Cheek

8. **to have a cheek** – to be extremely disrespectful towards someone. 'He has a cheek. The minute we were introduced, he asked me for a loan.'

9. **the cheek of the devil** – uninhibited insolence. 'She has the cheek of the devil,

asking her boss to post her letter for her.'

10. **none of your cheek** – don't be impertinent to me. 'Don't give me any of your cheek.'

11. **to turn the other cheek** – to submit to violence, not to resist the blows of one's oppressor. The charity of the Christian ethic, which distinguishes it from many other religions. 'Resist not evil. Whoever shall smite thee on thy right cheek, turn to him the other also' (Matthew V, 39).

12. **cheek by jowl with** – very close to one another.

Chin

13. **chin up!** – take courage, don't despair.

14. **to stick one's chin out** – to persist in one's own opinion, to defy other people's wishes. 'It was a stupid idea of the boss's, but I'm not going to stick my chin out.'

15. **to lead with one's chin** – to lay oneself open to a dangerous counter-attack when attacking an opponent. 'You were leading with your chin when you accused Williams of lying. You might have known he would say the same to you.' A boxer leads with the chin when he drops his guard as he moves forward.

16. **to take (it) on the chin** – to undergo a painful experience or punishment with courage. 'Rolf had a hard time when he was a recruit in the army but he took it all on the chin.'

17. **to have a chin-wag** – to have a talk or chat.

Neck

18. **neck and neck** – absolutely level. The phrase is taken from horse-racing.

19. **on the neck of** – immediately following.

20. **to get it in the neck** – to be severely punished.

21. **it's neck or nothing** – one must risk everything, one must gamble all on one throw.

22. **to stick one's neck out** – to make predictions which may be falsified by events.

1. **to break one's neck** – to be in a tremendous hurry. Used with such adverbs as 'almost', 'nearly', 'practically'. 'You might have told me you weren't coming. I nearly broke my neck getting to the station in time to meet your train.'
   at breakneck speed – recklessly, dangerously fast.

2. **to save someone's neck** – to help someone out of a very unpleasant situation. 'If I hadn't taken the blame, you would have got the sack. This isn't the first time I have saved your neck.'

3. **to rubber-neck** – to be very curious, e.g. to listen to somebody else's conversation or read his newspaper over his shoulder. This also refers to people in cars peering to catch a glimpse of a roadside accident.

4. **to breathe down someone's neck** (slang) – to supervise someone very closely. 'I would like the job much better if the boss wasn't breathing down my neck all the time.'

5. **to be up to one's neck in something** – to be deeply implicated in a crime or trouble. 'You knew very well what we were doing. You are in this up to your neck.'

6. **to carry a millstone round one's neck** – to be burdened with a responsibility from which it is impossible to free oneself. 'My brother-in-law, who depends on us financially, has been a millstone round my neck ever since we married.' A millstone is a heavy circular stone that rotates against another one in order to grind grain. See the Bible (Matthew, XVIII, 6): 'Whosoever shall offend one of these little ones which believe in me, it were better for him that a millstone were hanged about his neck, and that he were drowned in the depth of the sea.' cf. '**to have an albatross around one's neck**' 71/2.

Shoulder

7. **to carry/have on one's shoulders** – to bear responsibility for, to have to answer for. 'He had on his shoulders the whole burden of his father's debts.'

8. **to shoulder out** – to grab someone else's job.

9. **to shoulder the blame** – to accept full responsibility. cf. '**to shift the blame**' 122/9.

10. **straight from the shoulder** – frank, outspoken.
    to give it to someone straight from the shoulder – to tell someone the plain truth without sparing his feelings.

11. **to give someone the cold shoulder** – to treat someone with marked coldness, to ignore him in a noticeable manner. 'When I greeted Lucy this morning, she pretended not to see me. I wonder why she is giving me the cold shoulder.'
    to be cold-shouldered. 'I can't imagine what I have done to be cold-shouldered by him.'

12. **to rub shoulders with** – to meet frequently, or to come into frequent contact with, a person.

13. **to have broad shoulders** – to be able to bear the full weight of one's responsibilities.

14. **a chip on the shoulder** – a grievance on one's mind which colours one's attitude to life. 'Steven has had a chip on the shoulder ever since he was thrown out of the army.'

15. **to put one's shoulder to the wheel** – to throw all one's energy into a task.

16. **a shoulder to cry on** – someone you can rely upon to offer sympathy and comfort in a time of sorrow or depression, a good friend. 'If you ever want a shoulder to cry on, you know where to come.'

17. **to stand shoulder-to-shoulder with someone** – to work together with, or to support whole-heartedly. 'The teachers stood shoulder-to-shoulder with the headmaster in support of his stance on school uniforms.'

Arm

18. **to receive/welcome with open arms** – to accept/greet with great willingness, without any hesitation.

19. **at arm's length** – at a distance. 'Alan

wanted to get to know Helen better, but she kept him at arm's length.'

1. **to stand with arms akimbo** – to stand with each fist on the hip bones, with the elbows pushed forward, a posture which may express shock or anger. The word 'akimbo' is derived from the Icelandic *keng* ('into a crook') with the English doublet 'bow' unnecessarily added to it.

2. **a right arm** – the main supporter to whom one first turns for help when there is difficulty or trouble. 'Since Mother's death, Susan has been Father's right arm.'

3. **one would give one's right arm to . . .** – one would make a great sacrifice in order . . . 'I would give my right arm to see Janet again.'

4. **to chance one's arm** – to take a big risk.

5. **with one arm tied behind one's back** – without the slightest difficulty, in spite of a huge disadvantage. 'Why, my man could beat yours with one arm tied behind his back!' Originally used of boxers. Now used to indicate a decisive superiority in any competitive situation.

6. **arm twisting** – threatening, putting pressure on someone. 'After some arm-twisting by the management, the men withdrew their claim for a massive increase, for fear of the factory closing down.'

7. **an arm candy** – a good-looking person accompanying someone solely to enhance the other's appearance. 'The two famous pop stars entered the exclusive restaurant, each accompanied by an arm candy.'

Elbow

8. **at one's elbow** – within very easy reach. 'I have all the books I want at my elbow.'

9. **elbow-room** – space in which to move. 'I haven't got any elbow-room in this tiny office.'

10. **to elbow one's way through** – to push opposition to one side.
    to be elbowed aside – to be pushed out of the way. 'It can be very humiliating for a politician to be elbowed aside.'

11. **to give someone the elbow** – to get rid of someone. 'Hughes isn't worth his wages; it's time we gave him the elbow.'

12. **elbow-grease** – energy, industry and sweat.

13. **to be out at elbows** – shabby, poorly dressed; sometimes used with 'down at heel', to describe someone whose clothes are patched or torn.

14. **to lift the elbow** – to be a habitual drinker. 'Have you noticed? Peter lifts the elbow!'

Wrist

15. **a slap on the wrist** – a mild, ineffective punishment.
    wrist-slap diplomacy – a punishment inflicted by one government on another, which is too small and ineffective to serve any useful purpose. Diplomatic illnesses and cancellations of state visits both come into this category.

Hand

16. **to be a great hand at something** – skilful; generally used in an ironic sense. 'He is a great hand at giving advice, but when it comes to doing some work, he is not so good.'

17. **a dab hand** – to be clever at doing something, often something of a practical nature. 'Why don't you let me decorate your sitting-room for you; I'm a dab hand at decorating.'

18. **a free hand** – complete freedom, without any interference or restriction. 'My husband has given me a free hand as to how I bring the children up.'

19. **an old hand** – experienced, skilful. 'He'll finish the fence for you very quickly. He is an old hand at that kind of work.'

20. **to be even-handed** – to be fair, unbiased, equally critical of both parties to a dispute.

21. **to be high-handed** – to be tyrannical, unwilling to listen to reason.

22. **to be under-handed** – to be unfair, dishonourable. 'That was an underhanded

trick he played on you, telling you your friends were at the airport waiting for you, when they were not.'

1. **to come away empty-handed** – to return with nothing to show for one's efforts. 'He went on a business trip to Rome and came back empty-handed.'

2. **to be short-handed** – to be short of assistance. 'We are very short-handed just now. Three of our staff are ill.'

3. **a handful** – a person who is always up to some mischief, in need of strict supervision. 'Their small son was quite a handful while they were on holiday.'

4. **to have one's hands full** – to be fully occupied, to be unable to accept any fresh work. 'I have my hands full running the business, so I've had to resign from the village council.'

5. **to have only one pair of hands** – to be incapable of working any faster. 'I can't look after the children and cook the dinner at the same time; I've only got one pair of hands.'

6. **to be tied/bound hand and foot** – to have obligations which severely restrict one's freedom. 'I'd love to take a holiday with you but I'm tied hand and foot to my business.'

   to have one's hands tied – similar in meaning to the above, but a little less emphatic. 'I'm not allowed to advance you any money without your father's permission. I'm sorry that I can't oblige you, but my hands are tied.'

7. **hands off** – do not interfere.

8. **a cool hand** – someone with good nerves, calm, not easily flustered. 'When the staff walked out, the employer sat down and lit a cigar. He's a cool hand all right.'

9. **with an open hand** – generously. 'Whenever we asked Mr Jones for money for the charity, he responded with an open hand.'

10. **with a heavy hand** – severely, oppressively. 'We were brought up with a heavy hand. None of us dared contradict our parents.'

11. **to hold a good hand/a bad hand** – to hold good cards/bad cards. 'You dealt me a good hand, but Martin has had one bad hand after another.'

12. **one's right-hand man** – someone's principal support and adviser.

13. **a left-handed compliment** – an apparent compliment which is really just the opposite. ' "Your sister is very well preserved, isn't she? She doesn't look a day over 40." "My sister is 35!" '

14. **close at hand** – within easy reach. 'If you need help, we are always close at hand.'

15. **at first hand** – direct from the person concerned and not from someone else. 'I got the news at first hand, so I know it's true.'

16. **at second hand** – indirectly, from somebody not immediately concerned. 'I have only received the news second hand, so it may not be reliable.'

17. **second hand** – sold for the second time, no longer new, having been used already.

18. **to change hands** – to change ownership. 'The service is much better now the restaurant has changed hands.'

19. **to have clean hands** – to be above reproach. 'He who seeks equity must come to court with clean hands' (a legal maxim).

20. **when the left hand doesn't know what the right hand is doing** – when the activities of an organization are not properly co-ordinated and, as a result, there is confusion. 'My offer was accepted by the director but refused by the manager. The left hand of Vernon's doesn't know what the right hand is doing.'

21. **to soil/dirty one's hands** – to do something dishonest or shameful. 'I wouldn't soil my hands doing business with that firm; they are cheating the public.'

22. **to give a slow handclap to** – to show one's disapproval of a public speaker.

23. **a backhander** – (1) a sudden surprise blow given with the back of the hand; which can also be used metaphorically. (2) a bribe.

1. **to hand it to someone** – to give someone credit for something he or she has done. 'I'm sorry Philip has failed his examination again, but you've got to hand it to him for trying.'
   I've got to hand it to you – I must congratulate you.

2. **to work hand in hand** – (1) to work together in close agreement. (2) to be closely linked. 'Regular attendance at school and good school reports often work hand in hand.'

3. **to make a poor hand at** – to work unskilfully at something. 'I should make a poor hand at doing your job. Bookkeeping is not in my line.'

4. **with a strong hand** – firmly, vigorously, severely. 'The officer dealt with the man's insubordination with a strong hand.'

5. **to gain the upper hand** – to obtain a decisive advantage over someone, to master him. 'He was much stronger than his opponent and soon gained the upper hand.'

6. **to accept with both hands** – to accept most eagerly. 'If I'd been in your place, I'd have accepted his offer with both hands. You won't get a better one.'

7. **to join hands** – to unite with, work together with. 'We must join hands with our friends in Europe.'

8. **to go down on one's hands and knees** – to beg most humbly. 'I won't go down on my hands and knees to him, no matter how important he is.'

9. **a hand-out** – a free distribution of money, goods, etc., which may amount to bribery. 'When Lewis was leader of the local council, there were plenty of hand-outs to his friends.'

10. **to have in hand** – (1) to put money on one side, or in reserve, usually for a special purpose. 'I have £300 in hand, in case the job works out dearer than they estimated.' (2) to attend to a job. 'We have the matter in hand and will inform you as soon as the work has been completed.'

11. **to get something in hand** – to have under control. 'I am making the holiday arrangements now, so you needn't worry. I have got everything in hand.'

12. **to be out of hand** – (1) to be undisciplined, out of control, ill-behaved. 'When his son was in Paris, the boy got out of hand and ran up big gambling debts.' (2) without any discussion. 'He refused the offer out of hand, and broke off negotiations.'

13. **to take in hand** – to take control of someone, usually for some particular purpose. 'He is 10 kilos overweight. The dietician is taking him in hand.'

14. **to get one's hand in** – to regain one's skill. 'After a couple of games, you'll soon get your hand in.'

15. **off-hand** – (1) without referring to one's notes or records. 'I can't tell you off-hand, but, as soon as I get back to the office, I'll telephone you.' (2) casual, lacking in respect. 'She was off-hand with me, and went on with her housework while I was speaking.'

16. **to be in one's hands** – to be under one's control, to be one's own responsibility. 'It is in your hands now whether or not you succeed. I can't help you any more.'

17. **to have on one's hands** – to have a responsibility to attend to, often an irksome one. 'I shall have their boy on my hands all through his summer holidays.'

18. **to have something taken off one's hands** – to be relieved of an irksome responsibility. 'I am grateful to you for taking Judy off my hands. She was getting too much for me.'

19. **to raise/lift one's hand to** – to strike. 'I've never raised my hand to him, but one day I shall if he goes on like this!' cf. '**to lay hands on**' 99/10.

20. **hand-to-hand fighting** – fighting at close quarters with the enemy, with bayonets, knives or even fists.

21. **to keep one's hand in** – to retain one's skill by practising. 'Mike keeps his hand in during the winter on the indoor tennis courts.'

1. **to have a hand in something** – to play a part in something, bear some of the responsibility for. This is often used in reference to something illicit. 'I suspect he has had a hand in the robbery, although I can't prove it.'

2. **to show one's hand** – to make one's intentions clear. 'When I asked Digby if he was planning to take over our company, he pretended to be very surprised. He doesn't want to show his hand yet.' The idiom comes from card-playing, e.g. from bridge in which it is important for the players not to show their cards during the bidding.

3. **to try one's hand** – to see how well one can do in an activity, instead of just watching others. 'Why don't you try your hand at weaving? You might do just as well as us.'

4. **to shake hands on it** – to signify one's assent to an agreement.

5. **to wring one's hands** – to show dismay but offer no practical support. 'For some time the response from the UN and the rest of the world to the latest war was just to wring their hands.' Also: **hand-wringing**.

6. **to wash one's hands of something** – to absolve oneself from responsibility. 'That boy is quite impossible. From now on I wash my hands of him!' The allusion is to Pontius Pilate who washed his hands in a bowl of water in order to show that they were innocent of the blood of Jesus Christ (Matthew XXVII, 24).

7. **to have blood on one's hands** – to be responsible for the injury or death of a person. 'I don't think we should stop the surgeon operating; we don't want the patient's blood on our hands.'

8. **to sit on one's hands** – to wait passively, without doing anything.

9. **to win hands down** – to win very easily, by a large margin.

10. **to lay hands on** – to strike. 'If you lay hands on me, I will charge you with assault.' cf. '**to raise/lift one's hand to**' 98/19.
    to lay hands on – this also has two

negative meanings: (1) to seize, arrest. 'The police have not yet laid hands on the wanted man.' (2) to find an object that has been mislaid. 'I know it's somewhere in the office, but I can't lay my hands on it.'

11. **to give a hand with** – to help, usually for only a short time. 'Please give me a hand with the suitcase. It's rather heavy.'

12. **to hold one's hand** – to refrain from taking any action, on receiving certain assurances. 'If you undertake to pay us by Tuesday, we will hold our hand.'

13. **to throw in one's hand** – to yield, to stop trying. 'When he was told that his men had called a strike, Fison threw in his hand and closed the factory.' From card-playing, when a player who had been dealt a bad hand threw his cards on the table and stopped playing.

14. **to be on one's hands** (commercial) – to be lying in the shop unsold. 'The antique furniture is still on our hands; we just cannot get rid of it.'

15. **to play into someone's hands** – to use the tactics which most benefit one's opponent/enemy. 'You should never have confided your business troubles to your competitors. Now they can make matters worse for you. You have played into their hands.'

16. **to overplay one's hand** – to press one's advantage too far. The phrase is derived from games of cards where a player with good cards bids or calls higher than the hand justifies.

17. **to turn one's hand to** – to turn one's attention to, to apply oneself to, to attempt. 'Everything your father turns his hand to, he does well.'

18. **to force someone's hand** – to bring pressure to bear on someone. 'I didn't want to mention your name but, by going to the police, they forced my hand.'

19. **to lend someone a (helping) hand** – to be of assistance to someone. 'Can you lend me a hand in the kitchen. It's in such a mess.'

20. **to be caught with one's hand/ fingers in the till** – to be caught

stealing from one's employer. 'You would think I had been caught with my hand in the till from the way my boss talks to me.'

1. **hand on heart / cross my heart and let me die** – I promise you, I am telling you the truth. 'I didn't smoke one cigarette while you were out. Hand on heart!'

2. **hand over fist** – (1) very rapidly. 'My son is very bright. He is making progress hand over fist.' (2) to make money very fast. 'Since Andrew started his own business, he has been making money hand over fist.' The phrase has probably been taken from rope-climbing, when the free hand is passed over and above the fist that is holding the rope.

3. **to wait on someone hand and foot** – to serve somebody with complete dedication. 'I was waited on hand and foot; I only had to ring a bell and a servant came to my room in a few seconds.'

4. **to live from hand to mouth** – to make only enough money to supply one's immediate needs, not to know where one's future income is coming from. 'I'm sick of this hand-to-mouth existence; I think I'll look for a regular job.'

5. **to bite the hand that feeds you** – to injure the person on whom you depend for your living. 'You shouldn't have criticized your father in front of his guests. You were biting the hand that feeds you!' (*Thought and Details on Scarcity* by Edmund Burke).

6. **to eat out of someone's hand** – to submit willingly to someone's wishes, to do anything to please someone. 'After our talk, Mary was eating out of my hand.' A tame animal will eat from its keeper's hand.

7. **a show of hands** – the taking of a vote by asking all those present who are in favour of a proposal to raise their hands.

8. **sleight of hand** – skilful trickery (often used humorously). 'With a sleight of hand, the prime minister was able to persuade the workers that they had won a victory over the employers, and the employers that they had got the better of the workers.' Literally, the clever use of the hands in conjuring and juggling.

9. **to know a place like the back/palm of one's hand** – to know a place intimately. 'I know London like the back of my hand.'

10. **all hands to the pumps** – Please help, everyone. It's urgent!

11. **to be man-handled** – to be moved by physical force. 'When I called for the money at Pearson's home, I was man-handled by his servants and thrown out of the house.'

12. **to have time hanging on one's hands** – to be in a state of boredom, when time passes slowly. 'Time hung heavy on the hotelier's hands in the winter when the tourists went home and her children were at boarding school.'

13. **to take one's life in one's hands** – to risk losing one's life. 'If you let him drive you there, you will be taking your life in your hands. He is the worst driver I've ever met.'

14. **with an iron hand** – with great severity. 'The leader crushed the rebellion with an iron hand.' cf. **'an iron hand in a velvet glove' 194/12**.

15. **to be in good hands** – to be well looked after. 'If your mother goes to the Lavington Sanatorium, she will be in good hands; the doctors and nurses there are really good.'

Palm

16. **to palm someone off with / be palmed off with** – to be offered something inferior. Usually used in a negative sense. 'They made me a much better offer to start with, so I'm not going to be palmed off with such a rotten job now.'

17. **to have someone in the palm of one's hand** – to have someone completely in one's power. A somewhat melodramatic expression.

18. **to grease someone's palm** – to bribe. Often used in connection with the bribing of minor officials.
    palm oil – money used for bribery, on

the analogy of greasing the palms; **to have an itching palm** – to accept bribes eagerly. 'In that country the officials all have itching palms; they are only too anxious to take bribes.'

Fist

1. **to be close-fisted** – to be miserly, stingy, mean. The term expresses reluctance to open one's fist and let go of the money one is holding.

Thumb

2. **to have someone under one's thumb** – to dominate, or domineer over. 'She has her son completely under her thumb. He would never dare contradict or disobey her.'

3. **rule of thumb** – a rough, practical calculation made without the benefit of theoretical knowledge or scientific measuring instruments. 'Although his methods are more or less rule of thumb, he gets excellent results.'

4. **to give the thumbs down** – to veto a plan or course of action. 'After consulting together for an hour, the committee gave the thumbs down to the young architect's proposals.' The 'thumbs down' derives from a modern misinterpretation of the signal given by Roman spectators to indicate that they wanted a defeated gladiator slain.

5. **to give the thumbs up** – a sign indicating a positive answer, good news or approval of a person or scheme. 'When I asked the young man whether he had enjoyed his evening with Jenny, he smiled and gave me the thumbs-up sign.'

6. **to thumb a lift / thumb one's way** – to ask for a lift from a vehicle driver.

7. **to twiddle one's thumbs** – to be idle, to have nothing to do. 'We had to twiddle our thumbs for an hour while Helen was getting dressed.'

8. **to stick out like a sore thumb** – to be conspicuous on account of some odd or peculiar feature. 'Why did you have to paint your house that colour? It sticks out

from the others like a sore thumb.' cf. '**an eye-sore**' 136/13.

9. **to thumb through (the pages of a book)** – to turn the pages of a book, usually without reading properly, but out of curiosity.

10. **a thumb-nail sketch** – a very abbreviated or miniature sketch – so small that it can be done on a thumb nail. 'The novelist only gave a thumb-nail sketch of his characters, as he thought their actions were more revealing than mere description of their appearance.'

11. **to be all thumbs / all fingers and thumbs** – to be clumsy, as if each finger were a thumb, which would result in a loss of dexterity. 'I can't thread this needle; I am all thumbs today.'

Finger

12. **to be light-fingered** – to have a strong inclination to steal whenever the opportunity arises.

13. **to have money stick to one's fingers** – to wrongly keep money that belongs to someone else.

14. **to burn one's fingers** – to suffer the consequences of some error of judgement. 'I burned my fingers badly by investing money in your friend's company. I shan't make that mistake again.'

15. **to twist someone round one's little finger** – to know how to impose one's will over someone, or to have a strong influence on someone.

16. **to have at one's fingertips** – to be an expert in a subject, to know a subject to perfection. 'He has parliamentary procedure and the rules and traditions of the House of Commons at his fingertips.'

17. **to one's fingertips** – in every respect, completely. 'Evans never made a decision without consulting his book of rules first; he was a bureaucrat to his fingertips.'

18. **to keep one's fingers crossed** – to hope and pray for success. 'Good luck with your driving test; I'll keep my fingers crossed for you.' Making the sign of the cross – in this case with the fingers – was

believed to preserve one from bad luck. Today, the phrase is only used light-heartedly.

1. **I can't put my finger on it but . . .** – I have a feeling that something is wrong, without knowing exactly what it is.

2. **to work one's fingers to the bone** – to work until one is exhausted.

3. **to slip through one's fingers** – to miss a good opportunity. 'I took too long making up my mind, and let the house slip through my fingers.'

4. **to snap one's fingers at** – to show contempt for a person or institution.

5. **to point the finger at** – to blame a person/organization for a blunder or crime. 'The finger has been pointed at the government for the high level of unemployment.'

6. **to be able to count on the fingers / on the fingers of one hand** – to emphasize the smallness of a number by counting it on the fingers / fingers of one hand. 'You could count on the fingers of one hand the number of times old Westwood arrived late at the office during the 30 years he worked for the firm.'

7. **to lay a finger on** – to hurt or harm. 'If you lay a finger on the child, you will regret it.'

8. **a two-fingered gesture** – a rude gesture indicating contempt. The gesture is made with the palm of the hand facing inwards. Contrast the V-sign, which is made with two fingers but with the palm facing outwards.
    to put two fingers up to something. 'The controversial art exhibition, full of blood, excrement and dead animals, seemed to be putting two fingers up to the art establishment.'

9. **to put the finger on** – to determine or diagnose the cause. 'You've put your finger on it: too many late nights and parties. That's no way to prepare for an examination!'

10. **to have a finger on the pulse** – to be aware of all the latest news, gossip, current affairs. 'Don't you know what's happening in the Far East? Go and ask Edward – he's got his finger on the pulse.'

11. **not to lift a finger** – to refuse to do the least thing to help. 'All the time we were staying there, the girl didn't lift a finger to help her mother.'

12. **pull/take your finger out** – get on with the job. 'Prince Philip appealed to British industry to pull its finger out.' The complete phrase is 'pull/take your finger out and get stuck in' (a naval phrase).

13. **to have more (of something) in one's little finger than someone else has in his whole body** – to be greatly superior in one quality (such as intelligence, knowledge, skill, ability, talent) to another person. 'Mary has more talent in her little finger than you have in your whole body, which isn't saying much!' Often said in the heat of an argument.

Quick

14. **to cut to the quick** – to hurt someone's feelings very deeply. 'Robert was cut to the quick when his wife told him that she didn't want to go abroad with him.' The quick is the sensitive part of the flesh beneath the fingernail.

Knuckle

15. **too close to the knuckle** – too realistic for comfort, embarrassing. 'Genet's plays are too close to the knuckle to be entertaining.'

16. **to knuckle down** – to accept discipline.

17. **to knuckle under** – to submit to authority. The phrase suggests that the submission is unwilling.

18. **to give someone a rap on the knuckles** – to reprimand someone severely. 'He was given a rap on the knuckles for his bad work.' The person who gives the rap is always in a position or rank of superiority. This phrase is often abbreviated to '**take the rap**', with the same meaning: 'Why should I take the rap for you?'

Chest

1. **to play one's hand/cards close to one's chest** – to be secretive about one's plans. 'I know he is up to something, but he is playing his cards very close to his chest.' cf. **'to keep one's own counsel' 276/13.**

2. **to get something off one's chest** – to talk freely about something one has concealed. 'It's been on my conscience for a long time but, now I've got it off my chest, I feel a lot better.'

Breast

3. **to make a clean breast of the matter** – to make a full and complete confession. 'If you have stolen the money, you had better make a clean breast of it to your boss at once.'

Bosom

4. **bosom friends** – very close friends who confide all their secrets to each other (applicable to either sex). 'The two girls were bosom friends and kept nothing back from each other.'

5. **to be in the bosom of one's family** – to live with one's family, surrounded by one's parents and brothers and sisters.

Belly

6. **a pot-belly** – a large, protruding stomach. 'If you drink so much beer every day, you will get a pot-belly.' Also: **a beer belly**.

Navel

7. **navel-gazing** – looking back on one's mistakes instead of forward to new solutions. ' "I don't think much of navel-gazing," the chairman said sternly. "Let's look to the future and not repeat our past mistakes." ' The expression originates in a 19th-century religious sect whose members would gaze at their navels in order to fall into a trance.

Lap

8. **to drop into someone's lap** – to acquire something easily, without the least effort. 'All the best things in life must be worked for – love, friendship, success . . . they won't just drop into your lap.'

9. **to live in the lap of luxury** – to live in a state of great comfort and ease, having all one's material needs supplied without having to make any effort.

10. **in the lap of the gods** – completely unpredictable. 'I have no idea whether we shall win or not. It's in the lap of the gods.'

Back

11. **to turn one's back on** – to abandon someone/something. 'Hayley has turned her back on studying art and is going to study music instead.'

12. **a back-up service** (commercial) – visiting a customer to check that the equipment sold to him/her is working properly. 'This firm provided a back-up service free of charge.'

13. **to give one's (full) backing** – to give one's (full) support to a person or a plan of action.

14. **a backlash** – a strong reaction to excessive provocation. 'If the judges continue handing out these ridiculously light sentences, there could be a nasty backlash from the public and people will take the law into their own hands.'

15. **get off my back!** – leave me alone; stop making demands on me.

16. **behind one's back / when one's back is turned** – in a person's absence, without his or her knowledge. 'Christine has been saying some very nasty things about you behind your back, George.'

17. **to get one's own back on someone** – to revenge oneself on someone. 'I mean to get my own back for the injury he has done me, even if it takes me 10 years.'

18. **to get someone's back up** – to provoke

someone to anger. 'You really got his back up with your criticisms of his house.' From the idea of a cat being threatened by a dog, when the cat arches its back to show its anger.

1. **the backbone** – the main support. 'He has been the backbone of the team for the whole of the season.'

2. **to have no backbone** – to lack strength of purpose, to be morally submissive. 'That boy has no backbone. He gives in to the slightest opposition.'

3. **to the backbone** – completely, absolutely, without any question. 'She was a Tory to the backbone.'

4. **to be morally straight-backed** – to be absolutely honest and trustworthy. 'Our firm needs a director who is morally straight-backed.'

5. **broken-backed** – damaged, lacking the ability or means to survive. 'It's been a broken-backed business ever since it lost its major customer.'

6. **to break the back of a task** – to finish the hardest part of a task. 'By the time his brother arrived, they had broken the back of the work, and there was little left for him to do.'

7. **to break one's back** – to exhaust oneself with overwork. 'I have broken my back trying to keep this business going, but I couldn't go on any longer.' cf. '**to work oneself to death**' 38/3.

8. **to stab in the back** – a forceful phrase for betrayal, indicating the indignation of the victim. 'He has been my best friend for the last 20 years. I would never have dreamed he would stab me in the back like that.'

9. **with one's back to the wall** – in a desperately dangerous situation from which there is no escape. On 18 April 1918, Field Marshal Haig gave this famous order to the Allied forces: 'With our backs to the wall and believing in the justice of our cause, each one must fight on to the end.'

10. **to make a rod for one's own back** – to create difficulties for oneself. 'Why did the silly man argue with the magistrate? He made a rod for his own back.'

11. **to be glad to see the back of someone** – to be glad to see the last of someone.

12. **to have a good background / to have no background** – to be from a good/poor family. 'I don't want her to marry Steven. He has no background.'

13. **to have a broad back** – to be willing to accept responsibility for other people's mistakes. 'Put all the blame on me if it makes you feel better. I have a broad back.'

14. **backscratching / you scratch my back and I'll scratch yours** – you praise me and I'll praise you; you help me and I'll help you.

15. **to give someone a pat on the back** – to praise or applaud, to congratulate, often in a mild manner. 'Although his plan had not completely succeeded, she gave him a pat on the back for having tried so hard.'

16. **to put one's back into** – to put all one's energy into a task.

17. **to back the field** – a betting phrase for wagering one's money against one particular horse – usually the favourite.

18. **the back of beyond** – a remote, inaccessible place. 'I wish you didn't live in the back of beyond.'

19. **to look like the back end of a bus/ tram** – to look unattractive and very overweight. 'We really can't employ that girl as an air stewardess. She looks like the back end of a bus!' cf. '**to look like the side of a house**' 155/9.

Spine

20. **to send shivers down one's spine** – a feeling of apprehension or fear. 'I shouldn't really be reading this ghost story. It's sending shivers down my spine.'

Bottom

21. **to get to the bottom of something** – to find out the truth. 'Who spread this nasty rumour about me? I'm going to get

to the bottom of it!' cf. '**to get to the root of something**' 49/15.

1. **to knock the bottom out of an argument** – to prove the falsity of an argument, to refute an argument. 'Pauline knocked the bottom out of our argument in a short but effective speech.'

Leg

2. **not a leg to stand on** – without any reasonable justification in a dispute, without the semblance of a case. 'Mark accused the doctor of negligence, but when he admitted he hadn't taken the medicine prescribed, he hadn't a leg to stand on.'

3. **to be on one's/its last legs** – to be on the point of collapse, worn out. 'Mrs Jones hasn't enough money left to renew her stock; her business is on its last legs.'

4. **a leg-up** – a helping hand. 'He gave me a leg-up when I was starting work by introducing me to some new customers.'

5. **the final leg** – the last section of a journey or a race. 'The final leg of the race was the most beautiful – alongside the River Thames from Tower Bridge to Westminster Bridge.'

6. **to stretch one's legs** – to take exercise by walking about after a period of inactivity. 'We've been sitting here all the morning. It's time we stretched our legs.'

7. **to pull someone's leg** – to play a joke on someone, to tell someone a misleading story that momentarily shocks or frightens him or her but which amuses everybody else.
   a leg-pull – a joke or untrue story with the same meaning as above.

8. **to leg it** – (1) to run away. (2) to walk when other means of transport have failed.

9. **to shake a leg** – to take part in a dance.

10. **to be bow-legged** – to have one's legs bent outwards so that there is a big space between them. The opposite of 'knock-knees'.

11. **to be legless** (slang) – to be so drunk that

one cannot walk straight. cf. '**to keep one's feet**' 107/19.

Knee

12. **on one's knees** – in a position of submission.

13. **to bend the knee** – to submit to a stronger force, to obey submissively.
    on one's bended knees / on bended knee – in a position of abject submission. 'My husband treated me so badly during our marriage that I wouldn't have him back if he came to me on his bended knees.'

14. **to bring to his/its knees** – to defeat or force to submit. 'The recession has brought our company to its knees.'

15. **a knee-jerk reaction** – an unthinking, automatic response. 'We got the usual knee-jerk reaction to our request for a rise in our salaries.' When the knee is tapped below the joint, it kicks involuntarily; this is known as the knee-jerk reflex.

16. **weak-kneed** – someone who is unable to resist pressure. 'He was so weak-kneed that he allowed the man to ransack his flat, although he was twice as big as the burglar.'

17. **to go weak at the knees** – to fall in love.

Foot

18. **my foot!** – a comment expressing disbelief. 'Paul's too weak to carry his suitcase upstairs! Too weak, my foot! He's twice as strong as I was at his age.'

19. **to put one's foot in it** – to cause embarrassment with a tactless remark. 'You put your foot in it when you told her how much you admired her husband. They were divorced last year!'

20. **to shoot oneself in the foot** – to damage one's interests by one's own incompetence. 'Our country has shot itself in the foot by refusing to bargain with the leader of the rebels.' cf. '**an own goal**' 300/13.

21. **to put one's foot down** – to impose one's authority, to call a halt to some action of which one disapproves. 'When

his 18-year-old son wanted to start a business with his girlfriend, his father put his foot down and told him he wouldn't allow it.'

1. **to have a foot in both camps** – to have an interest in supporting both parties in a contest. 'Sooner or later, you'll have to choose between Labour and the Conservatives; you can't have a foot in both camps indefinitely.'

    to have/get a foot in the door – to have/gain access to a business, market, occupation, etc., in spite of opposition. 'Now we've got a foot in the door, we are hoping to open up a big market in China.' The commercial traveller puts his foot in the door to prevent the housewife from shutting it in his face, so that he can persuade her to buy his merchandise.

2. **to gain a foothold / to get a foothold in** – to establish a basis. 'The ambitious young woman gained a foothold in the firm and hoped she would soon be promoted.'

3. **to set on foot** – to initiate, to get things moving. 'The mothers of the district intend to set on foot plans for opening a kindergarten.'

4. **to start on the wrong foot** – to make a mistake at the very beginning (of a relationship). 'You started on the wrong foot, asking the boss for a week's leave only a few days after you had joined.' The reference is to starting to march with the right foot instead of the left.

5. **to put a foot wrong** – to make a mistake, to break the rules. 'Since Alan came out of prison, he hasn't put a foot wrong.'

6. **to wrong-foot someone** – to put someone at a disadvantage in a contest, to surprise him or her. 'Mr Jukes wrong-footed us by calling our manager as a witness. We hadn't expected him to do that.'

    to catch someone on the wrong foot – to take advantage of an opponent's mistake.

7. **to be on a friendly/good footing** – to enjoy a friendly relationship with someone.

    on a firm footing – on a solid foundation. 'We have put our business with Phillips on a firm footing.'

8. **to be light-footed** – to be nimble, light on one's toes. 'Although he is such a fat man, he is light-footed when he dances.'

9. **footloose and fancy free** – unattached, free of romantic ties.

10. **to put one's best foot forward** – to walk briskly, to walk faster, to hurry. Usually with the meaning of reaching a place by a particular time. 'If you want to catch your train, you'll have to put your best foot forward.'

11. **to be forced on to the back foot** – to have to withdraw a statement. 'After enormous protest from parents and pupils, the headmistress was forced on to the back foot about making girls wear skirts to school. Now they are allowed to wear trousers instead.'

12. **to follow in someone's footsteps** – to do the same as he. 'So, young man, you are going to follow in your father's footsteps and be a doctor!'

13. **to trample/tread underfoot** – to beat down all opposition, to crush the body and the spirit of one's enemy.

14. **with one foot in the grave** – so old or ill that one is on the point of dying. 'With one foot in the grave, I am afraid he is in no position to help you.' The idiom is often used humorously (as in the title of the famous sit-com of the same name).

Feet

15. **to be on one's feet** – to stand, to be standing. The phrase is often used to emphasize the length of time the subject has been standing. 'The medical students have been on their feet all day long in the operating theatre.'

16. **to set someone on his feet** – to give someone a fresh start, to help that person over his or her difficulties.

17. **to fall/land on one's feet** – to adjust oneself to new conditions (after a setback) with unexpected success. 'No sooner had she lost her job than she obtained

another at twice the salary. She always falls on her feet.'

1. **to find one's feet** – to get adjusted, to settle down. 'The boy soon found his feet at his new school.'

2. **to drag one's feet/heels** – to show reluctance. 'It's over a month since Hughes had the contract, but he hasn't signed it yet. I wonder why he is dragging his feet.'

3. **to walk someone off his feet/legs** – to walk a long way with a companion until he is exhausted. 'Whenever we go out together, Alan walks me off my feet.'

4. **to be rushed off one's feet** – to have so many claims on one's time that everything has to be done in a great hurry.

5. **to sweep off one's feet** – to make a swift conquest. 'She was so captivated with his good looks that he swept her off her feet within a few minutes of meeting her.'

6. **one's feet haven't touched the ground** – to be extremely happy. 'Since Lisa met her new boyfriend, her feet haven't touched the ground.'

7. **to get back on one's feet** – to make a full recovery, to become adjusted again. 'Once you've got back on your feet, you will feel quite differently about your work.' The idiom is often used in the sense of recovering from the effects of an illness.

8. **to cast oneself at someone's feet** – to throw oneself on the mercy of another, to submit to another person's will.

9. **to have/get cold feet** – to feel afraid to commit oneself to a decision or action which may prove risky or dangerous. 'Simon is getting cold feet about advancing you the money, now that your firm is in difficulties.'

10. **to have feet of clay** – to have an insecure base. The phrase is often used in reference to persons or governments of seemingly great power which conceals some fatal weakness. From the Bible (Daniel II, 31–45). cf. **'Achilles' heel' 225/13**; **'a chink in someone's armour' 249/3**.

11. **under someone's feet** – in the way, obstructing one's movements. 'I can't cook the lunch with you under my feet all the time.'

12. **to have one's feet under the table** – to have a friend in whose home one is made welcome. cf. **'to hang up one's hat in a house' 195/12**.

13. **to cut the ground from under one's feet** – to take an opponent by surprise by suddenly depriving him of his advantage. 'When Nancy's father complained about the teaching at the school, the headmaster cut the ground from under his feet by announcing that Nancy had won a scholarship at Marlborough College.' cf. **'to pull the rug from under one's feet' 167/13**; **'to take the wind out of someone's sails' 22/14**.

14. **to stand on one's own (two) feet** – to be independent, self-reliant, in an economic or emotional sense. 'My son must get a job and learn to stand on his own two feet.'

15. **to put one's feet up / take the weight off one's feet** – to sit down and rest. Often said to a guest who has arrived after a tiring journey.

16. **to sit at a person's feet** – to listen with respect to an intellectual authority. 'We all admired Professor Stanton for his original thinking and sat at his feet when we were at the university.'

17. **to vote with one's feet** – to show one's dissatisfaction with one's country, place of work, etc., by leaving it instead of voting for better conditions. 'If conditions in this company don't get any better, we'll all vote with our feet and find other jobs.' cf. **'to vote with one's wallet' 198/10**.

18. **to think on one's feet** – the ability to speak in public, and to respond quickly to unexpected questions.

19. **to keep one's feet** – to avoid falling. 'After three glasses of whisky, he found it difficult to keep his feet.' cf. **'to be legless' 105/11**.

20. **with both feet on the ground / to have one's feet planted firmly on the ground** – free from fanciful,

impractical ideas; sensible and practical. 'Margaret won't get carried away by a lot of silly notions; she has both feet on the ground.'

to keep one's feet on the ground – not to be carried away by fame and success. 'The famous gardener and writer is keeping her feet on the ground in spite of her tremendous success on television.'

1. **the patter of tiny feet** – the sign of a toddler in the family. The idiom is often used when referring to an expected birth. 'Colin, our dream has come true at last! Soon we'll hear the patter of tiny feet!' cf. **'a happy accident' 138/2**.

Heel

2. **to be down-at-heel** – (1) to be shabbily dressed. Sometimes the phrase is combined with **'out-at-elbows'**. 'I found my friend sadly changed for the worse; he was down-at-heel and out-at-elbows.' (2) slovenly, neglected. 'Our down-at-heel transport system really could do with a lot more money being spent on it.'

3. **well heeled** (derisive) – well off. 'Judging by the size of their house, they must be very well heeled.' The original meaning was 'well armed'. The phrase is taken from cock-fighting, when cocks were fitted with metal spurs or 'heels'.

4. **to dig one's heels in** – to resist a request by all the means at one's disposal. 'When the parents told the headmaster they had decided to send their daughter to another school and demanded a refund of the fees, he dug his heels in and refused point blank.'

5. **to kick up one's heels** – to enjoy one's newly gained freedom. 'When the teachers at our school went on strike and walked out of the classrooms, we kicked up our heels with joy.'

6. **to lay by the heel** – to arrest and subdue. The reference is to 'laying by the ankles' of petty criminals in the stocks in the Middle Ages.

7. **to come to heel** – to obey, to submit after being disciplined. 'Once I have talked to them, they will come to heel quickly enough. They will soon learn who is the master here!' From the command given to a dog to rejoin its master.

8. **to tread on the heels of / follow upon the heels of** – to follow close behind. 'The recession trod on the heels of the oil crisis.'

to be hard on someone's heels – to walk close behind someone.

9. **to show a clean pair of heels** – to remove oneself from the scene as quickly as possible. 'As soon as I asked them for money, they showed a clean pair of heels!'

to take to one's heels – to run away.

10. **to turn on one's heel** – to turn round abruptly.

11. **to kick/cool one's heels** – to be kept waiting a long time. 'I had to kick my heels outside his office for a whole hour.'

Toe

12. **a toe-hold** – a small and precarious entry, often used in a business sense. 'He gained a toe-hold in Japan, but it will take him some time to consolidate his position.'

13. **to toe the line** – to obey the rules and regulations. The phrase implies that the person 'toeing the line' is being pressured, against his or her will. 'Unless he toes the line, he will be expelled from the party.'

14. **to tread on someone's toes** – to offend someone with a tactless remark. 'You trod on his toes when you told him his novel was very promising. He has been five years writing it!'

15. **to keep someone on his toes** – to keep someone alert and attentive. 'The sergeant-major kept the recruits on their toes by continually firing orders at them.'

16. **to go/walk on tip-toe / to tip-toe** – to walk on the tips of the toes. 'When their mother was ill, the children tiptoed up and down the stairs so as not to wake her.'

Brain

17. **to have the brain of a pigeon** – to be quite brainless. Pigeons are supposed to have a very small brain.

1. **hare-brained** – wild, mad.
   a hare-brained scheme – a wild, mad scheme.

2. **to be scatterbrained** – to be careless and disorganized. 'I hope he won't forget the theatre tickets. He is so scatter-brained.'

3. **a brainwave** – a sudden insight into a problem, a flash of inspiration. 'She didn't know what to wear at the fancy dress ball. Then she had a brainwave; she put on her oldest clothes, smeared some soot on her face and went as Cinderella.'

4. **a brainstorm** – a violent reaction with loss of emotional control. 'When he was told that all his possessions had been destroyed in the fire, he had a brainstorm.
   a brainstorming session – a meeting at which all the members are encouraged to contribute suggestions and solutions, however far-fetched, to a problem.

5. **brain-washing** – to control a person's thinking and ideas by psychological and physical torture, disorientation and other forms of coercion.

6. **Brains Trust** – a panel of intelligent people who express their views on questions of current interest put to them by television or radio audiences.

7. **the brain drain** – the emigration from Britain to the USA of many college and university graduates who were tempted by the higher salaries and better facilities. 'Now America is also experiencing a brain drain – to Britain, the most popular destination for Americans.' The French phrase for brain drain is the 'Eurostar Effect'. Thousands of French job-seekers and business entrepreneurs are starting a new life in Britain – to them, a land full of opportunity and low taxes – coming in by train through the Channel Tunnel.

8. **to have something on the brain** – to have an obsession, to be preoccupied with an idea that won't give one any rest. 'Our plumber has fishing on the brain. He talks about it all day long.'

9. **to pick someone's brains** – to enlist the aid of someone more clever or expert in a given subject. 'This is much too diffi-cult for me. Do you mind if I pick your brains?'

10. **to rack/cudgel one's brains** – to make a great intellectual effort, e.g. by working for a long time on a problem, or trying to recollect some forgotten experience, name, etc.

11. **to turn someone's brain** – to madden or drive insane. 'The news that his daughter had married a criminal turned his brain.'

Nerve

12. **to have the nerve to . . .** – to have the impudence to . . . 'When I caught him helping himself to the things in my larder, he had the nerve to ask me where the mayonnaise was.' cf. '**to have the gall to**' 117/2.

13. **to nerve oneself to / nerve oneself for . . .** – to brace oneself mentally to . . . 'He nerved himself to ask his boss for a rise.'

14. **to get on someone's nerves** – to exasperate someone by the repetition of some irritating action. 'Her never-ending complaints got on my nerves.'

15. **to touch a nerve** – to affect someone emotionally. 'A recent case where a man was arrested for having killed a burglar has touched a nerve with a lot of people.'

16. **to touch a raw nerve** – to inflict pain on someone by mentioning a subject which the person would rather forget. 'You touched a raw nerve when you asked Mrs Wilde why her son failed all his exams.'

17. **a bag of nerves** – someone who is unable to control his/her anxiety or irritability. 'Since her divorce, Pamela has been a bag of nerves.' Also: **one's nerves are in shreds**.

18. **to be a strain on one's nerves** – to be a source of intense irritation or anxiety. 'Living with two other men in one cell was a great strain on all our nerves.'

19. **not to know what nerves are** – to be fearless, to be free from fear. 'He goes at tremendous speeds on the race-track

without any fear. He doesn't know what nerves are!'

1. **to have nerves of steel** – to have very strong nerves, to have nerves that are strong enough to withstand any fear.

2. **to have a fit of nerves** – to have an uncontrollable bout of anxiety.

3. **to live on one's nerves** – to be in such a nervous state that one's whole life is affected. 'Since the car accident when she was badly injured, she has been living on her nerves.'

4. **to strain every nerve** – to exert oneself to the utmost. 'He strained every nerve to remain cool and collected and not to let his fingers shake when he opened the telegram.'

5. **to lose one's nerve** – to be reduced by fear to a state of helplessness. 'After hitting an air shot on the first tee in front of a big crowd, Henry lost his nerve and bolted.'

6. **nerve-racking** – extremely distressing. 'It's such a nerve-racking experience trying to find a really good school for one's children.'

Vein

7. **in the same vein** – in the same style or mood. 'He wrote many stories in the same vein, humorous and light-hearted.'

Flesh

8. **in the flesh** – in bodily form. 'I knew him better than any of you. In fact, I saw him in the flesh just before he died.'

9. **flesh and blood** – human, with all the weaknesses of human nature.

10. **one's own flesh and blood** – one's parents, brothers and sisters and one's children. 'You can't cut yourself off from your son; after all, he is your own flesh and blood.'

11. **to flesh out** – to add weight to, to make more substantial. 'You can flesh your article out by adding a descriptive passage.'

12. **to put on flesh** – to put on weight.

'Harold has put on a lot of flesh since he was here last. He'll have to cut down on cakes and sugar.'

13. **to make one's flesh creep** – to frighten or horrify with some dreadful tale. The allusion is to 'the fat boy' in Charles Dickens' *Pickwick Papers*.

14. **to have one's pound of flesh** – to exact what is due, to the very last ounce. 'All right, if you are going to insist on your pound of flesh, I'll work for you all next weekend, although you've paid me little enough for the work.' From Shakespeare's *The Merchant of Venice*.

15. **to press the flesh** – to canvass support in an election campaign by mixing with the voters, shaking hands, kissing babies and so on. 'I've done my share of pressing the flesh for the last six months; now I want a rest.' A US phrase.

16. **the sins of the flesh** – love of physical pleasure like eating, drinking, fornication. 'The priest told his parishioners to resist temptation and fight against the sins of the flesh.'

17. **the spirit is willing but the flesh is weak** – because of our human frailties, we are not always able to resist the demands made on us by our bodies, even when we want to. Often used facetiously: 'I wanted to get up at six o'clock this morning and study, but I just couldn't. The spirit was willing but the flesh was weak!'

18. **to go the way of all flesh** – to die. 'However rich and important they are, they will go the way of all flesh like the rest of us.'

Skin

19. **to save one's skin** – to escape from a disagreeable predicament. 'She saved his skin by telling the police he had spent the evening with her.'

20. **to escape with a whole skin** – to escape without injury.

21. **to escape by the skin of one's teeth** – to have a very narrow escape. 'That was a near thing! I only escaped being conscripted into the army by the skin of my

teeth.' cf. '**a brush with death**' 38/13.

1. **to jump out of one's skin** – to receive a tremendous shock. 'She nearly jumped out of her skin when she unlocked her front door and found a burglar standing in her hall.'

2. **to be in someone else's skin** – often used negatively to indicate some kind of trouble. 'I wouldn't be in his skin if he paid me £1,000.' cf. '**to be in another's shoes**' 190/5.

3. **to get under one's skin** – to exasperate, to irritate. 'I can't stand the way he patronizes us. He gets under my skin.'

4. **alabaster skin** – white, translucent skin. cf. '**alabaster face**' 85/23.

5. **to fit someone like a second skin** – to fit perfectly, to follow the contours of the body exactly. 'The film star wore a long silver-sequined evening dress which fitted her like a second skin.' In the words of Austrian artist Friedensreich Hundertwasser: 'Man has three skins. He is born with his first skin. His clothing is his second. And the façade of his house is his third. If the second and third skins don't match the person inside, the organism falls ill.' cf. '**to fit like a glove**' 194/10.

6. **skin-tight** – tight-fitting. 'The lead singer of the group wore skin-tight jeans and a skimpy T-shirt.'

7. **to be all skin and bones** – to be undernourished, very thin. 'We must give that stray cat some food. It's all skin and bones.'

8. **skin-deep** – superficial, shallow. 'Her emotions were only skin-deep. She was incapable of any deep feeling.'

9. **to be thick-skinned / have a thick skin** – to be insensitive to criticism, insults, or the broadest of hints. 'Don't worry, you won't hurt his feelings. He is very thick-skinned.' cf. '**to have a skin like a rhinoceros**' 63/9.

10. **to be thin-skinned** – to be oversensitive to criticism, to take offence at the slightest provocation. 'I didn't mean him to take my remarks personally. He is very thin-skinned!'

11. **to be a skin-flint** – to be mean, miserly. 'You won't get a penny out of him. He's a real skin-flint.'

12. **to skin alive** – to punish very severely. 'If Paul finds out that you've been using his movie camera, he'll skin you alive.' cf. '**to come down on someone like a ton of bricks**' 157/10.

Bone

13. **a lazy bones / to be bone idle** – slothful, idle. 'His son is a lazy bones. He never gets up before lunch!'

14. **a bone of contention** – an unresolved quarrel or dispute. 'The ownership of the ancestral home has been a bone of contention between the two brothers for the last twenty years.' The phrase derives from two dogs fighting over a bone.

15. **the funny bone** – that part of the elbow whose nerve is unprotected; so called because a person will react with laughter instead of tears to a blow on the 'funny bone'. The 'humerus' is the bone found in the upper arm (from the Latin *umerus*), which sounds very much like 'humorous'.

16. **to feel it in one's bones** – to have a premonition that something (probably unpleasant) is about to happen, although one cannot give a reason for it. ' "I know I'm going to have trouble with this class," said the teacher to her friend. "I can feel it in my bones." '

17. **to have a bone to pick with someone** – to have cause for making a complaint to someone. 'I have a bone to pick with you. My sister saw you take a £5 note out of my handbag this morning.'

18. **to make no bones of/about** – to speak very frankly, without holding anything back. 'I'll make no bones about it: my father was from a working-class family.'

19. **the bare bones** – just the essentials but no more. 'Those are the bare bones of the system. I'll fill you in on the details later.'

20. **to cut to the bone** – to reduce to an absolute minimum, to eliminate all inessentials. 'We have cut our housekeeping

to the bone, but we still have a struggle to pay the bills.'

1. **to be bone dry / as dry as a bone** – to lack moisture. 'I can't grow anything in my garden. The soil is bone dry.' The same idiom can be used humorously for wanting a drink very badly. 'Let's stop at the pub; I'm as dry as a bone.' See the Bible (Ezekiel XXXVII) for 'the valley which was full of bones [that were] . . . very dry'.

Skeleton

2. **a skeleton in the cupboard** – a source of embarrassment and shame to a family, which is kept secret from strangers. 'I'm sure there is a skeleton in the Wellards' cupboard. Don't they have a relative who has been in prison?'

3. **a skeleton at the feast** – a reminder of sorrow or trouble on even the merriest occasions. The Greek biographer and moralist Plutarch describes in his *Opera Moralia* how the ancient Egyptians had the custom of displaying a skeleton in a prominent position at their banquets and celebrations so as to remind guests of their mortality. cf. '**the sword of Damocles . . .' 226/4.**

4. **a skeleton key** – a special key that will unlock many doors, a master key. 'Don't worry if you have lost your bedroom key. Reception has a skeleton key.'

5. **skeleton staff/ crew, etc.** – a much-reduced staff, crew, etc., which is capable of maintaining the minimum service required for the organization to function.

Breath

6. **save your breath** – the words used to scold someone who has given unwanted advice. 'I told you before, Angela, I will do what I like – so save your breath.' The expression derives from Rabelais: 'Save your breath to cool your porridge' (*Works*, Book V, Ch. 28).

7. **to waste one's breath** – there is no point in trying to persuade one to think otherwise. 'You're wasting your breath, Steven. I'm going to stay on at university

and pass my exams before I marry you.'

8. **to catch one's breath** – to stop breathing for a brief moment after receiving a surprise or a shock. 'Mrs Higgins caught her breath when she heard a strange noise, but it was only the cat.'

9. **to hold one's breath** – to wait expectantly for something. 'I only need one more correct number to win the lottery – my whole family is holding its breath!'

10. **don't hold your breath** – don't be too impatient as it may take some time. 'We won't know the result of the X-rays for some time, so don't hold your breath.'

11. **to take one's breath away** – some shocking action which leaves one speechless/amazed. 'Louisa's outrageous behaviour took my breath away and made me feel very embarrassed.'

12. **with bated breath** – nervously, excitedly. 'Mr Wilcox waited with bated breath to see if his wife would give birth to a girl or a boy.'

Marrow

13. **chilled to the marrow** – freezing cold, frozen through and through. 'We had better turn up the heating. Jack was chilled to the marrow, watching that football match.'

Sinew

14. **the sinews of war** – the means to wage a war: money, arms, etc. 'Without the sinews of war, we have no power to defend our rights.'

Limb

15. **to be out on a limb** – having taken the initiative, to find oneself without effective support. 'As soon as the organizers saw they were out on a limb, they cancelled their campaign.'

16. **to escape with life and limb** – to escape without any broken bones.

17. **a danger to life and limb** – anything which threatens the health and security

of other people. 'The way you drive your car is a danger to life and limb.'

Muscle

1. **not to move a muscle** – to be immobile, motionless. 'All the time we were watching the sentry, he didn't move a muscle.'

2. **to use one's muscle** – to use superior strength. 'The printers have used their muscle to obtain far higher wages than they deserve.'

   to carry a lot of muscle – to make one's influence felt. 'The money you earn today depends on the muscle your union carries, nothing else.'

3. **to muscle in** – to take away the business of a competitor by force, or by the use of unethical methods. 'It's a good idea, but Philpot's will muscle in on you if they can. They are quite ruthless.'

4. **to be muscle-bound** – to have stiff, unwieldy muscles, as a result of excessive exercise and training. 'The crew practised too hard at the beginning of the season, with the result that they were muscle-bound on the day of the race.'

Blood

5. **a man of blood** – a man of violence.

6. **to make bad blood between** – to cause two people to quarrel with one another. 'He made bad blood between the two brothers.'

7. **to be after/out for one's blood** – to seek revenge. The idiom can be used humorously: 'Now that you have beaten him in the finals, Tom is after your blood.'

8. **to get one's blood up** – to become enraged. 'He is furious with the way they behaved to the old woman. They have got his blood up.'

9. **it makes one's blood boil** – it exasperates one beyond endurance. 'It made my blood boil to see him stealing our roses and then presenting them to his girlfriend.'

10. **to shed blood** – to kill or wound.

   to shed one's blood – to be wounded or killed in a war. 'They shed their blood that we might live.'

11. **to the last drop of blood** – till death.

12. **to sweat blood** – to work until one is exhausted. 'I've sweated blood to make a success of your company and you haven't given me a word of thanks!'

13. **to spit blood** – to be outraged. 'The minister's money-saving ideas have members of the teaching profession spitting blood.' cf. **'to spit poison' 189/13**.

14. **to act in cold blood** – to act coldly and deliberately, with premeditation. 'The jury found that the man had murdered his wife in cold blood, not in the heat of the moment.'

15. **to make the blood run cold / to chill the blood** – to terrify someone. 'The sight of the masked man climbing through her bedroom window was enough to make Julie's blood run cold.'

16. **to act in hot blood** – to act in anger, to be motivated by passion, not reason.

17. **to be hot-blooded** – passionate, easily aroused to either anger or amorousness.

18. **a full-blooded attack / to make a full-blooded attack** – to attack with one's whole strength, keeping nothing in reserve. 'He has made a full-blooded attack upon your policy, your character and your motives.'

19. **to draw blood** – to make a damaging attack on a person's pride or reputation. 'The minister has been forced to write an angry letter to the *Daily Telegraph* in reply to our article. We have drawn blood!'

20. **to give someone/something a blood transfusion** – to give fresh life to, to reinvigorate. 'North Sea oil has given Britain a blood transfusion, and only just in time.'

21. **to bring in new/young blood** – to employ people with fresh ideas. 'Now that they have brought in new blood, the marketing should be more energetic.'

22. **a blood-sucker** – a person who obtains money by blackmail or extortion.

1. **you can't get blood out of a stone** – you won't get pity or sympathy from someone who is completely unfeeling. 'It's no good appealing to Uncle Joe. You can't get blood out of a stone.' Also: **like getting/drawing blood from a stone**.

2. **blood money** – the reward paid for information that secures the death or betrayal of a person.

3. **a blood-bath** – murder and bloodshed on a large scale. 'The revolutionaries are demanding a blood-bath.'

4. **blood and iron policies** – the attainment of political objectives by the use of brute force. 'Blood and iron was at the core of Bismarck's *Realpolitik*.'

5. **blood will tell** – one's innate qualities will come to the surface sooner or later. 'The adopted child was given the same opportunities as the other children, but he turned out completely different from them. Blood will tell.'

6. **it runs in the blood / it's in one's blood** – it is an inherited quality. 'The Mayers have been distinguished doctors for generations. It runs in the blood.'

7. **blood is thicker than water** – the ties between relations are closer than those between friends.

8. **to squeeze the lifeblood out of something** – to destroy an essential element of something. 'If your father withdraws his money, he will squeeze the lifeblood out of our business.'
    money is the lifeblood of commerce – money is the essential means for exchanging goods.

Heart

9. **be of good heart** – take courage, don't lose hope!

10. **in good heart** – in good spirits, cheerful.

11. **to do one's heart good** – to cheer up, make one happy. 'It does my heart good to watch the children opening their Christmas presents.'

12. **after one's own heart** – with one's full approval and admiration. 'Saving the baby seals from the fishermen was an action after my own heart.'
    a man/woman after my own heart – the kind of man/woman whom I most admire. 'Peter is a man after my own heart. He fights for what he believes in and never gives up.'

13. **to steel one's heart against** – to suppress one's natural pity. 'He steeled his heart against the cries for help of the sick children.'

14. **a heart of stone** – pitiless, unfeeling. 'To turn away your own son! You must have a heart of stone!'

15. **with a light heart** – cheerfully, happily, in a carefree manner. 'I came home with a light heart. I had paid off all my debts at last.'

16. **with a sinking heart** – with growing dismay. 'The schoolboy listened to his examination results with a sinking heart. He realized that he would never get into university.'

17. **to be sick at heart** – to feel very miserable about something. 'When we saw our champion being knocked about in the boxing ring, we all felt sick at heart.'

18. **to break one's heart / broken-hearted** – to suffer a personal loss from which it is impossible to recover, to be reduced to a state of complete despair. 'Emily was broken-hearted when her husband left her.'

19. **a heart-throb** – a charismatic personality, one who captivates members of the opposite sex. cf. **'a lady killer' 235/5; 'he's a real Casanova' 229/10**.

20. **a hearty** – a low-brow, someone lacking in intellectual tastes, loud-mouthed and vulgar.

21. **to be hearty** – to be noisy and boisterous.

22. **the heart of the matter/problem** – the essential problem. 'Too many children are playing truant. We must get to the heart of this problem.'

23. **heart and soul** – passionately in a totally committed way. 'Charles worked heart and soul for the cause.'

1. **to put one's heart (and soul) into something** – to work at something with energy and enthusiasm. 'Research is tiring and laborious work. If you can't put your heart into it, you should try something else.'

2. **to open one's heart** – to confide one's innermost feelings to someone. 'Newspapers often publish stories of famous people opening their hearts.'

3. **one's heart is not in it** – to be not interested in or to feel unenthusiastic about something. 'In the last few weeks your heart hasn't been in your work. Would you like to talk to me about it?'

4. **from the bottom of one's heart** – with the utmost sincerity, most deeply. 'I wish you every success from the bottom of my heart.'

5. **at heart** – fundamentally. 'He has many faults, but at heart he is a very decent young man.'
   to have at heart – to feel deeply about; to be extremely concerned about. 'I am sure your mother has your best interests at heart.' The phrase can be used with 'health', 'happiness', 'safety', etc.

6. **a heart-to-heart talk / a heart-to-heart** – a confidential and serious discussion between two people about some personal problem. 'I had a heart-to-heart talk with Lucy's father about our plans to marry, and my prospects.'

7. **to take heart** – to be encouraged. 'You can take heart from Robert's success. If he can pass the exam, so can you!'

8. **to take to heart** – (1) to take something badly, to be very much hurt by. 'When Martin forgot his date with Susan, she took it very much to heart.' (2) to take a warning very seriously. 'I hope you will take to heart what I have told you.'

9. **to take to one's heart** – to accept someone with love and joy. 'The people have taken Your Royal Highness to their hearts.'

10. **to give one heart** – to encourage, make one bold. 'You have given me heart. I'll try again.'

11. **to put (fresh) heart into** – to encourage, to give someone confidence. 'After so many failures, I was going to give up, but you have put fresh heart into me.'

12. **have a heart!** – the phrase is used as a plea in reply to some unreasonable demand. 'I've already typed 30 letters for you today, and now you want me to do another 13. Have a heart!'

13. **to have no heart** – to be unfeeling, inhumane. 'A man who shoots dumb animals can't have any heart at all.'

14. **to be half-hearted about something** – not very keen. 'Will you join the tennis club, Margaret? Kathy is very half-hearted about it.'

15. **to find it in one's heart to** – to be generous enough to . . . 'If you can find it in your heart to forgive Jenny, you will never regret it.'
    not to have the heart to – not to be able to . . . 'I didn't have the heart to tell Martin the bad news on his birthday and spoil his fun.'

16. **to lose heart** – to lose courage, to despair. 'When the skating champion tumbled on the ice, he lost his heart and did not complete his programme.'

17. **to lose one's heart to** – to fall in love with. 'She lost her heart to the new arts teacher.'

18. **in one's heart of hearts** – if one is absolutely honest with oneself. 'In his heart of hearts, he knew that he wasn't cut out to be a lawyer, despite his academic success.'

19. **with all my heart** – with the utmost sincerity, with all best wishes. 'I hope with all my heart that your marriage will be a happy one.'

20. **close to one's heart** – especially valued by someone. 'The work you are doing for the sick children has always been close to his heart.'

21. **to learn (off) by heart** – to know a piece so well that one can recite it from memory. 'Our teacher makes us learn everything off by heart.'

22. **to set one's heart upon** – to want above all else, to have an intense longing

to . . . 'His grandfather has set his heart on sending the boy to his old school.'

1. **to allow the heart to rule the head** – to be influenced by one's emotions and not by one's reason. 'In business, it is a mistake to allow the heart to rule the head.'

2. **to one's heart's content** – to one's complete satisfaction. 'There's a piano in your room, and you can play it to your heart's content. No one will disturb you.'

3. **a change of heart** – a change of mind or decision, prompted by a change in one's feelings. 'His father was against the marriage at first, but, after getting to know the girl better, he had a change of heart.'

4. **my heart goes out to** – I feel intense pity and sympathy for. 'My heart goes out to the victims of the bomb explosion.'

5. **one's heart bleeds for someone** – to feel extremely sorry for someone. Often used ironically: 'I'm sorry you won't be taking your usual holiday in the Bahamas this year. My heart bleeds for you.'

6. **to eat one's heart out** – to suffer intense grief, often resulting from failure or disappointment, especially over the loss of a person's love. 'Elizabeth has been eating her heart out ever since Dennis broke off their engagement.'

7. **with one's heart in one's mouth** – in a state of great fear. 'When the postman handed me the telegram, my heart was in my mouth.'

8. **to have one's heart in the right place** – to be kind and well-meaning. This idiom is almost always used when appearances are to the contrary. 'He may be a bit of a show-off sometimes, but his heart is in the right place.'

9. **to warm the cockles of one's heart** – to raise someone's spirits, to gratify. 'It warmed the cockles of her heart to have all the children and grandchildren seated at her dining-table at Christmas time.'

10. **to pour out one's heart** – to confide all one's sorrows, fears, anxieties, hopes and joys to another person. 'When we were

alone, she poured out her heart to me about her broken marriage.'

11. **to have heart failure** – to suffer a great shock, to be demoralized. 'It was the audacity of its contents which gave them heart failure and persuaded them to surrender . . .' (*New Statesman*).

12. **one heartbeat from the presidency** – on the death of the American president the immediate assumption of office by the vice-president without any action by the legislature or judiciary.

Stomach

13. **to have a strong stomach** – to be not easily shocked or disgusted. 'You'll need a strong stomach if you are going to be a surgeon.'

14. **to have no stomach for** – to have no courage for, no desire for. 'He hated quarrelling and had no stomach for a fight.'

15. **to turn the stomach** – to disgust, to nauseate. 'Your hypocrisy turns my stomach.'

16. **to stomach (an insult, etc.)** – to accept, to submit to. 'If you want to be his friend, you'll have to stomach his insults.'

17. **on an empty stomach** – a stomach that lacks food. 'You must take these pills on an empty stomach.'

18. **to have a sinking feeling in the pit of one's stomach** – to have a great fear, a premonition of disaster.

19. **one's stomach feels like water** – to feel nervous and queasy. 'Ruth's stomach felt like water at the thought of her dinner date with a complete stranger.'

20. **one's stomach is as tight as a knot** – to feel tense, apprehensive.

21. **a stomach-churner** – used to describe a ride, e.g. on a roller-coaster, which involves one being tossed about violently in all directions, just for the thrill of it. 'Theme parks are always building new stomach-churners to attract the crowds.' The term derives from 'churning' milk to make butter, by stirring and turning the milk forcefully until the fat is separated

from the liquid. cf. **'a white-knuckle ride'** 6/12.

Gall

1. **as bitter as gall** – extreme bitterness. 'Gall' is the old synonym of 'bile', the bitter liquid secreted into the stomach by the liver.

2. **to have the gall to . . .** – to have the impudence to . . . 'Sandra had the gall to ask for her job back two days after we had sacked her for dishonesty.' cf. **'to have the nerve to'** 109/12.

3. **to dip one's pen in gall** – to write with venom and bitter sarcasm.

4. **gall and wormwood** – that which arouses the most bitter resentment. Both words stand as symbols of extreme bitterness. 'It was gall and wormwood for him to have to make a public withdrawal of his accusations.'

Bile

5. **to be full of bile** – to be full of resentment and bitterness. 'His speeches were full of bile.'

Spleen

6. **to vent one's spleen on** – to express pent-up anger and vexation. 'In his autobiography, he vented his spleen on all his enemies.'

Gut

7. **to have the guts to . . .** – to have the courage to . . . 'He didn't have the guts to stand by his friend when he was in trouble.'

8. **to hate someone's guts** – to detest, loathe someone.

Liver

9. **yellow-livered** (a term of abuse) – cowardly. There was a superstition that a coward's liver contained no blood; hence the phrases **'yellow-livered'**, **'white-livered'**, **'lily-livered'**, etc. cf. **'to be yellow'** 5/8.

12 Mind

Mind

1. **mind over matter** – the triumph of willpower and courage over physical pain or infirmity. 'Whether a patient recovers from a dangerous illness often depends on his own willpower. It's a case of mind over matter as a rule.'

2. **to make up one's mind** – to come to a decision. 'I have made up my mind to sell my house and go abroad.'

3. **to have a good mind to do something** – to have a strong inclination. The phrase usually expresses irritation. 'He has behaved so badly, I've a good mind not to go to his party.' More often than not, the inclination is suppressed.

4. **to be in one's right mind** – to be sane. 'No one in his right mind would do a thing like that!'

5. **to be out of one's mind/senses** – to be extremely stupid or insane. 'You must have been out of your mind to talk like that to your boss.'
   to be driven out of one's mind – to be driven insane with worry, fear, suspicion, anxiety, etc. The phrase is often used with the adverbs 'nearly' and 'almost'.

6. **one's mind goes blank** – a sudden inability to think. 'Poor Louise! She got so nervous reading through her maths exam paper that her mind suddenly went blank.' cf. **'a mental block' 120/4**; **'writer's block' 287/14**.

7. **to have in mind** – to consider or propose. 'Yes, we have a number of four-bedroom houses on our books. What price did you have in mind?'

8. **an open mind** – an unprejudiced mind, one that is receptive to new ideas. 'I have an open mind whether to take him on. I will decide after I have seen him.'
   a closed mind – a mind that is prejudiced, one that is not receptive to new ideas. 'Rupert has a closed mind on the subject of politics, so you are wasting your time arguing with him about it.'

9. **the mastermind** – the person in charge of an operation, the originator of the plan on which the success of the operation depends. 'The police believe they know the mastermind behind the bank robbery.' Also: **to mastermind**.

10. **to call to mind** – to recall, remember. Usually used negatively. 'I can't call to mind her ever having mentioned it, but she may have done so.'

11. **to cast one's mind back** – to make a conscious effort to recall an incident. 'Can you cast your mind back to the day you first visited him?'

12. **to know one's (own) mind** – to have a clear and firm conviction, usually as to what should be done. 'She never had any doubts about being a doctor; she always knew her own mind.'
    not to know one's own mind – to be undecided, usually as to what should be done. 'It would be a mistake putting Jim in charge; he never knows his own mind.'

13. **to have a mind of one's own** – to be capable of making decisions without depending on other people's opinions. 'Why do you always ask your father what to do? Surely you are old enough to have a mind of your own.'

1. **to be in two minds (over a matter)** – to be undecided. 'I could see the advantages and disadvantages of living in New Zealand. I was in two minds about moving there.'

2. **to change one's mind** – to change one's decision or opinion.

3. **mind you** – even so, all the same. 'Paul did wrong. Mind you, many people would have done the same in his place.' (An interjection used to qualify a statement.)

4. **to set one's mind on** – to be absolutely determined on a course of action. 'I can see you have set your mind on taking the job, so I won't try to dissuade you.'

5. **to be of one mind** – to be unanimous, to be of the same opinion.

6. **to my mind** – in my opinion. The phrase is often used to indicate a difference of opinion. 'I know you won't agree with me but, to my mind, the whole idea was a mistake.'

7. **to put/give one's mind to** – to concentrate on. 'If he would only put his mind to his studies, he could be a brilliant scholar.'

8. **to bear/keep in mind** – to pay heed to, to take into consideration. 'You must bear in mind that Alan is very young.'

9. **to cross one's mind** – to occur to one, to have a momentary thought. 'It did cross my mind that the maid might have stolen the money.'

10. **to slip one's mind** – to forget, usually as a result of carelessness rather than a defective memory. 'It quite slipped my mind that Maureen was coming to tea today.'

11. **to prey/weigh on one's mind** – to worry, preoccupy or make one feel guilty. 'The interview preyed on Kate's mind and made her feel very nervous.' 'My unkindness to the old woman weighed on my mind for a long time.'

    to have something on one's mind – to be worried, preoccupied or feel guilty about something. 'I can see you have something on your mind; would you like to tell me about it?'

12. **a weight off one's mind** – relief from an anxiety or feeling of guilt. 'It was a weight off my mind to know that he was being well looked after.'

13. **to put someone's mind at rest/at ease** – to dispel someone's anxiety. 'I can put your mind at rest – your wife is out of danger.'

14. **to be easy in mind** – to be calm, to be free from anxiety.

15. **to put to the back of one's mind** – to dismiss (an idea) from one's mind for the time being.

16. **to get something out of one's mind** – to free oneself from an idea. 'I have made a terrible mistake and now I can't get it out of my mind.'

17. **to take one's mind off something** – to seek distraction from one's troubles. 'There is nothing like a good book to take one's mind off one's troubles.'

18. **to have something imprinted on one's mind** – something which is impossible to forget. 'The picture of women and children injured by bombs and half-starved would be imprinted on the reporter's mind for ever.'

19. **to speak one's mind** – to speak very frankly. 'She said exactly what she thought; she spoke her mind.'

20. **to give someone a piece of one's mind** – to scold someone severely, to tell someone what one thinks of him/her. 'When James didn't trouble to see the girl home after the party, I gave him a piece of my mind.'

21. **presence of mind** – a quick response in an emergency. 'When the child fell out of the moving train, she had the presence of mind to pull the emergency cord.'

22. **to make the mind boggle** – to astonish. The alternative phrase is '**the mind boggles**'. 'The mind boggles at the bills he ran up in such a short time.'

23. **to broaden the mind** – to develop new interests. 'Why don't you learn a foreign language and travel? That will broaden your mind.'

24. **to have a mind like a steel trap** – to possess an enormous amount of

knowledge. 'It's no wonder Emma was chosen to be editor of the new encyclopaedia. She has a mind like a steel trap.' A steel trap is for catching animals, allowing entrance but not exit. In this comparison, information would enter the mind but would not be allowed to escape from it or be forgotten.

1. **to have a mind as sharp as a razor / a razor-sharp mind** – to be astute, smart, keen-witted, quick. 'The game of chess went on for hours. Both players had minds as sharp as razors.'

2. **to have a mind like a cesspool/cesspit/sewer** – to have a mind that harbours 'unclean' thoughts, i.e. usually sexual or scatological in nature. 'You should be ashamed of yourself. Your mind is like a sewer!'

Mental

3. **mental** – mad or idiotic.

4. **a mental block** – a psychological obstruction to the free flow of ideas. 'Whenever the psychiatrist asks me questions about my childhood, I have a mental block.' cf. '**one's mind goes blank**' 118/6; '**writer's block**' 287/14.

5. **quick/slow in the uptake** – quick or slow to understand. 'I kept looking at my watch, but he made no move to leave; he must be a little slow in the uptake.'

Think

6. **to think the unthinkable** – to plan radical action in order to change a poor state of affairs. 'When it came to power, New Labour promised to think the unthinkable on welfare.'

7. **to have another think coming** – to have to change one's mind. 'If you think I'm going to drive you to school every day, you've got another think coming. You can easily walk, you lazy bones!'

8. **a think-tank** – a group of researchers using their expertise to find the solution to a problem. 'The government think-tank will have to find a solution to the problem of truancy.'

Wits

9. **to have quick wits / to be quick-witted** – to have a quick understanding, to be quick with an answer.
   to be slow-witted – to be slow in understanding.

10. **to have/keep one's wits about one** – to be alert and resourceful. 'If he hadn't had his wits about him, he might have been drowned.'

11. **to live by/on one's wits** – to resort to expedients from day to day for a living rather than take a regular job.

12. **a battle of wits** – a contest in which people's minds, rather than bodies, are pitted against each other. 'Playing chess with your father is a real battle of wits!'

13. **out of one's wits** – mentally disturbed, mentally disabled or senile.
    to frighten someone out of his/her wits – to terrify someone so much that he or she is unable to think properly. 'That Alsatian of the Masons frightens me out of my wits whenever I pass their house; they should keep it chained up.'

14. **at one's wits' end** – in despair of finding a solution to one's problems.
    to drive someone to his wits' end – to drive someone to despair. 'The boy was so slow that he drove his teacher to his wits' end.'

Sense, Senses

15. **out of one's senses** – mad.
    to take leave of one's senses – to go mad. 'Have you taken leave of your senses? The wedding is tomorrow; you can't possibly cancel it now!'

16. **to come to one's senses** – to start behaving sensibly again. 'You should warn John that you will stop his allowance unless he behaves himself; then he will come to his senses.'
    to bring someone to his senses – to persuade someone to stop behaving foolishly.

17. **a sense of loss** – a feeling of sadness that a person or thing is irretrievably lost.

'When Lucy saw her younger brother off to India, she felt a strong sense of loss and wondered whether she would ever see him again.'

1. **a sense of proportion** – the ability to see things in their proper perspective. 'So you have failed your examination, but there are worse things in life than failing exams; you mustn't lose your sense of proportion.'

2. **to make sense** – a sensible course of action to follow. 'Now that we know the destructive force of the sun causes skin cancer, it makes sense to use sun tan oil.'
   to make sense of something – 'I can't understand this scribbled note, Isa. Can you make sense of it?'

3. **to see sense** – to be reasonable. 'You can't go out in this freezing weather without your coat. Do see sense!'

Touch, Sight

4. **a soft touch** – an easy target. 'Eddie never asks me for a loan. You seem to be the soft touch, as he always asks you and you always oblige.'

5. **touchy-feely** – to seek out physical contact with other people, such as hugging them, shaking hands, rubbing their backs, or stroking their hair or their arms. 'Princess Diana will always be remembered as a touchy-feely princess who drew people to her in great numbers.' cf. **'kissy-kissy' 126/8**.

6. **the common touch** – to show understanding of the ordinary people. 'To be a good politician, you have to have the common touch.'

7. **to be/keep in touch** – to remain in communication with one another; to stay informed about something. 'When the two friends parted at the airport, they promised to keep in touch.' Note the opposite: **to lose touch with someone**.

8. **to be out of touch** – (1) to be no longer in contact with someone/something. (2) to have no information about/be unaware of current trends. 'There was no need for prices to go up again, and the head of the company was described as being out of touch with the current situation.'

9. **to lose one's touch** – to lose one's ability to do something really well. 'The opera singer's voice sounded a bit strained, I thought. She's getting older and, sadly, losing her touch.'

10. **to be touchy** – to be very sensitive about a certain subject. 'My aunt is very touchy about being childless. Whatever you do, don't mention the subject of children to her.'

11. **the magic touch** – to be successful in all one's enterprises. 'It would be a good idea to go into business with Gordon. He has the magic touch.' cf. the opposite: **'the kiss of death' 38/8**.

12. **touch-and-go** – a very critical situation. 'It was touch-and-go whether she would survive the operation.'

13. **a touchstone** – a test for determining the quality of something. 'For a long time the Social Services have been a touchstone of everything that has been neglected by the welfare state.'

14. **with the benefit of hindsight** – only knowing after something has happened what could have been avoided or improved. 'With the benefit of hindsight, that accident need never have happened. We all know that Paul can never resist stopping at a pub for several drinks.' cf. **'to be wise after the event' 123/5**; **'to second-guess' 258/10**.

Reason

15. **to listen to reason** – to adopt a sensible approach to a question without being influenced by one's emotions. 'I warned you that the idea would never work; what a pity you wouldn't listen to reason.'

16. **it stands to reason** – there is only one conclusion to be drawn. 'It stands to reason that if the railway is losing money, fares should be reduced to attract more passengers.'

17. **without rhyme or reason** – nonsensical, illogical. 'At first, I could see no rhyme or reason in Gertrude Stein's

writing, but later I changed my mind about her.'

Conscience

1. **in all conscience** – taking a fair and reasonable view. The phrase is often used to emphasize one's doubts about the reasonableness of a demand. 'I should have thought that his charges were high enough in all conscience without his asking for any extra money.'

2. **to make something a matter of conscience** – to be guided by one's sense of right and wrong. 'I agree with you that many laws are unjust, but if you make every law a matter of conscience you will end up in gaol!'

3. **conscience money** – money paid anonymously to ease one's conscience, e.g. when income tax has been evaded.

Moral, Err, Fault

4. **a moral certainty** – such a strong probability as to exclude almost any doubt. 'This time next year, it is a moral certainty that we shall be living in America.'

5. **moral support** – encouragement which stops short of physical or financial help. 'I am making my first speech at our local debating society. I hope you'll be there to give me moral support.'

6. **a moral victory** – a defeat that should by rights have been a victory. 'We played better football than Honiton and would have won easily if two of our men hadn't been injured. Honiton agreed with us that it was a moral victory for our side.'

7. **to err on the right side** – to make a mistake which benefits someone else. 'You are not late; in fact you are erring on the right side coming in at half past eight instead of nine.'
   a fault on the right side – a mistake which benefits someone else. 'Molly got the account wrong. We owe her £80, not £60. At least, it's a fault on the right side.'

8. **to see/realize, etc., the error of one's ways** – to admit that one has been behaving in the wrong way and agree to act more sensibly in future. 'It took the stern

words of my uncle to make my brother see the error of his ways.'

Blame, Lie

9. **to shift the blame** – to consider someone else responsible. 'When their dog escaped from the park, John shifted the blame on to his sister.' cf. '**to shoulder the blame**' 95/9.

10. **to peddle lies** – to spread untruths. 'The regime is still peddling lies about the atrocities that took place in the village.'

11. **a tissue of lies / a pack of lies** – a series of untruths. 'What the witness said in court was a tissue of lies. You really mustn't believe her!'

Character

12. **in character** – in accordance with a person's usual behaviour; in a way anyone knowing him or her would expect.
    out of character – not in accordance with a person's usual behaviour; in a way anyone knowing him or her would not expect. 'I was surprised Francis was so rude to you; it was completely out of character.'

13. **(quite) a character** – peculiar, eccentric. 'Mr Fraser goes out in long flowing yellow and scarlet robes. Yesterday he stopped the traffic in the Strand. He is quite a character.'

Purpose, Desire, Willing, Will

14. **to all intents and purposes** – in essence, effectively. 'To all intents and purposes, the property was a complete loss; only the kitchen remained, the rest of the house having been burned to the ground.'

15. **to be at cross-purposes** – to have a misunderstanding because of conflicting intentions. 'I am afraid we are at cross-purposes; I am offering you a job, not asking you for one.'

16. **to leave a lot to be desired** – to be unsatisfactory in many respects. 'Although the hotel charges were very high, the cuisine and service left a lot to be desired.'

1. **to show willing** – to show that one is ready to co-operate even if one has no desire to. 'You may not want to strike, but you should show willing to protect your rights.'

2. **with a will** – with strength and determination. 'When the old man was attacked by the mugger, he defended himself with a will.'

3. **willy-nilly** (literary) – whether one wishes it or not. 'Paul wanted to keep aloof from his companions but, willy-nilly, he was drawn into their revels.' 'Willy-nilly' is a corruption of 'will he, nill he', 'nill he' deriving from Anglo-Saxon *nillan*, short for *ne willan*, 'not to wish'.

Wise, Wiser

4. **to be wise to** – to be fully aware of, to be alert to. 'He is wise to all their tricks; he won't let them make use of him.'
   to put someone wise to – to make someone aware of the facts, to warn him or her as to the true position. 'I thought I had better put you wise as to what's going on here. Your conduct is being criticized in the officers' mess.'

5. **to be wise after the event** – to know what should have been done to prevent something happening when it has already taken place. 'Aren't you being wise after the event? How could we have known that the burglar would get in by the window on the second floor?' cf. '**to second-guess**' 258/10; '**with the benefit of hindsight**' 121/14.

6. **none the wiser** – knowing no more than one did before. 'I have spent six hours interrogating witnesses and I am none the wiser.'

Courage, Bold, Virtue

7. **to have the courage of one's convictions** – to declare one's principles openly, regardless of the danger to oneself or to one's reputation. 'I don't agree with you, but I admire you for having the courage of your convictions.' cf. '**to stand up and be counted**' 265/12.

8. **as bold as brass** – impertinent, shameless. 'Colin asked me what my income was the first time we met. The man is as bold as brass.' cf. '**bare-faced**' 84/8.

9. **to make a virtue of necessity** – to turn an unwanted obligation into a positive advantage. 'I am being sent to northern Europe. I didn't want to move but they are going to teach me skiing free of charge; so I'll be making a virtue of necessity.'

Kindness, Kindly, Generous

10. **to kill with kindness** – to spoil someone's character, especially a child's, by indulging all his wishes and not correcting his faults. 'They've sent their daughter to a modern school where she can do exactly as she likes, and where punishments are forbidden. The teachers are killing her with kindness.'

11. **not to take kindly to** – not to welcome or approve (only used in the negative). 'These men and women are experienced teachers; I am afraid they won't take kindly to being told how to do their job by your inspector.'

12. **generous to a fault** – excessively generous, so generous as to cause difficulties or embarrassment. 'Matthew is generous to a fault; people are always taking advantage of him.'

Proud, Pride

13. **to do someone proud** – to treat someone with great generosity. 'Meg's parents did us proud; they treated us to a box at Wyndham's Theatre followed by dinner at Claridge's.'

14. **to swallow one's pride** – to submit humbly, to accept a humiliation. 'You made a mistake resigning in a temper like that. You had better swallow your pride and ask the boss to take you back.'

15. **a blow to one's pride** – to be humiliated. 'It was a blow to Mr Berry's pride when his opponent was chosen for the job.'

Cruel, Mercies, Pity

1. **to be cruel to be kind** – to inflict pain on or punish a person in order to rid him or her of a distressing habit or fault. 'Mrs Fry warned her daughter that if she continued taking drugs, she would turn her out of the house. She explained she had to be cruel to be kind.'

2. **to leave a person to someone's tender mercies** – to abandon a person to rough, brutal treatment. 'I could see at once that Harry's new guardian was a bully, and I was sorry to leave the boy to his tender mercies.'

3. **more's the pity** – so much the worse, that only makes it worse; generally used as a rejoinder to an excuse or explanation. ' "I didn't send you a Christmas card this year. I haven't sent one to any of my friends." "More's the pity," replied Joan.'

Grace

4. **a saving grace** – one good quality which redeems many faults. 'Anne is lazy, untidy and disrespectful; her one saving grace is that she is good with the children.'

5. **with a good/bad grace** – in a good-humoured/ill-humoured manner. 'Rose paid me back the money, but with a bad grace, as if I had done her a wrong.'

6. **to fall from grace** – to lose favour. 'Since smashing up Lady Robinson's car, I have fallen from grace, and expect very soon to lose my job.'

Patience, Faith, Charity

7. **to try the patience of a saint** – to be so tiresome or stupid that even the most tolerant and easy-going of people would get annoyed. 'If I've explained it to you once, I've explained it a hundred times. You would try the patience of a saint!' cf. '**to try the patience of Job**' 224/8.

8. **in (all) good faith** – honestly and sincerely. 'I acted in good faith when I sold you that washing-machine. As far as I knew, it was in perfect condition.'
   in bad faith – dishonestly.

9. **an article of faith** – a crucial element in someone's philosophy. 'It is an article of faith among Conservatives that competition should be encouraged and state monopolies should be abolished.'

Happy, Humour, Laugh

10. **a happy event** – the birth of a child. 'Will your daughter be back in England for the happy event, or are you going to look after her in Germany?'

11. **a happy medium** – a middle way which avoids extremes. 'You should take plenty of exercise but avoid anything too strenuous like tennis or squash. Golf would be a happy medium for a man of your age.'

12. **a happy hunting-ground** – a place which offers good chances of success for hunters, collectors and other people with special interests. 'The International Club was always considered a happy hunting-ground for young men who were looking for a girlfriend.' 'The happy hunting-ground' was the name given by the Native Americans to their life after death.

13. **to be out of humour** – to be in an ill-humour, in a bad mood. 'William is out of humour this morning because he didn't get a letter from his daughter.'

14. **a laughing-stock** – to be the object of ridicule. 'You can't go out dressed like that, Lizzy! You'll be the laughing-stock of the whole street!'

15. **to be no laughing matter** – something to be taken seriously and no subject for jokes. 'It's no laughing matter that poor Mr Lenning slipped on the ice. He broke his leg.'

16. **a laugh a minute** – quite hilarious, usually meant ironically for 'not funny at all'. ' "That was a laugh-a-minute show!" sneered Angela. "I don't know why it got such good reviews." '

17. **to have the last laugh** – to be successful in the end, after quite a few setbacks. 'Time and again they said his invention

would never sell, but he had the last laugh because it turned out to be a great success.'

Bored, Sleep

1. **bored stiff/bored to tears** – very bored, uninterested. 'I am bored stiff by many of the television programmes.'

2. **a yawning chasm** – a deep division. 'Concerning attitudes to the euro, a yawning chasm is opening up between the government and ordinary people.'

3. **do not lose sleep over something/someone** – there is no need to be restless or worried about something/someone. 'I know I should have worked much harder at school but I found a good job, so I've never lost any sleep over it.' Frequent usage: **don't lose any sleep over it**.

4. **a sleeper** – someone who looks ordinary and innocent, but is really a spy, waiting (sometimes for many years) for orders before springing into action. 'Where has Mr Alders gone, and all our valuable documents? Do you mean to say he was really a sleeper? We had a spy in our midst?'

5. **a sleeping policeman** – a low ridge or flowerbed which juts partly into the road to stop drivers speeding. 'It's time we had a few sleeping policemen here to stop all these cars using our road as a short cut.'

Fancy, Dream, Nightmare

6. **to take a fancy to someone/something** – to take a sudden liking to someone/something. 'You do take a fancy to the most extraordinary things. Where are we going to put a palm tree in this tiny flat?'
    to take someone's fancy – to attract. 'I don't really know why I bought it; it just took my fancy.'

7. **to catch/tickle one's fancy** – to appeal to one's liking. 'How about joining the sailing club? Does that catch your fancy?'

8. **to fancy oneself** – to have a high opinion of one's looks or of one's abilities, to be conceited. 'Derek fancies himself as a ladies' man, but he spends too much

time admiring himself in the mirror for my liking.' cf. '**to think that one is God's gift to**' 42/11.

9. **a flight of fancy** – a free, unrestricted use of the imagination. 'Jack's play has nothing to say about our social or political problems. It is a flight of fancy, nothing else.'

10. **not dream of** – not think of, not consider. The phrase is used in order to make an emphatic denial. 'I wouldn't dream of charging you a fee for doing your portrait; please accept it as a gift.'

11. **a dream team** – the absolutely perfect set of people working in combination. 'In the 1990s two supermodels and an Olympic athlete formed a dream team to launch a new brand of sportswear.'

12. **to go like a dream** – to move with power and smoothness. The phrase is usually applied to cars, yachts or aeroplanes.

13. **to live in a dream world** – a world of make-believe or wishful thinking. 'You know you'll never be able to afford your own swimming pool. You're just living in a dream world.' cf. '**never-never land** 212/7; '**to live in Cloud-cuckoo-land**' 22/6.

14. **beyond one's wildest dreams** – far more exciting than one ever thought possible. 'Winning the lottery was beyond her wildest dreams.'

15. **the American Dream** – the idea that anyone and everyone has the opportunity to become rich and successful in America. 'The American Dream may turn sour for some unfortunate people, but it made my friend a millionaire.'

16. **a bad dream** – a situation so upsetting and terrible that it doesn't seem real. 'Surely I can't have failed my A levels – not after all that hard work. This is all a bad dream.'

17. **to live (in) a nightmare** – to live in a state of great fear and anxiety. 'With the threat of imminent invasion, the inhabitants of the war-torn city lived in a nightmare.'
    a nightmare – a really stressful or difficult situation/state of affairs. 'With

my secretary on holiday, it has been a nightmare getting these letters out on time.'

Love

1. **a labour of love** – a work done without payment, either for its own sake or for the sake of a loved one. 'Miss Watts had worked for three years on the tapestry; it was a labour of love done for the church.'

2. **love-birds** – two people who are very much in love with each other. 'Mr and Mrs Sanders always walk hand in hand, although they are over 60; they are still love-birds.'

3. **there's no love lost between them** – two people who dislike each other very much. The original meaning was the exact opposite. Goldsmith writes in *She Stoops to Conquer* (I, v): 'As for mumures, Mother, we grumble a little now and then, to be sure. But there's no love lost between us' (meaning that none of the love between them was wasted).

4. **not for love or money** – not at any price. 'The London hotels are booked out at this time of the year; you can't get a room for love or money.'

5. **to play for love** – to play a game without gambling on it. 'I never gamble, but I'll play you for love if you like.'

6. **to love someone to bits** – to love someone very much indeed.

7. **a love–hate relationship** – to have conflicting feelings of love and hate towards one's partner or friend. cf. **'a roller-coaster relationship'** 314/10.

Kiss

8. **kissy-kissy** – to try to ingratiate oneself to one's advantage. 'I need to see my true friends again, not all these show-business stars. I'm tired of all this kissy-kissy affectation.' cf. **'touchy-feely'** 121/5.

9. **kiss and tell** – famous or well-known personalities publicizing their sexual experiences, or having these publicized by a (former) partner, on television or in the newspapers. ' "These kiss-and-tell stories

are quite disgraceful," my grandmother said indignantly. "Fancy disclosing your private life like that." '

Hate, Fury, Rage

10. **a pet hate/aversion** – a special dislike. 'My pet hate is the shift-workers who march past our house singing at the top of their voices at three o'clock in the morning on their way to work.'

11. **hate mail** – threatening letters, usually sent anonymously. 'My boss down at the factory has been getting a lot of hate mail recently. He's very upset.' cf. **'a poison-pen letter'** 269/14; **'to blackmail someone'** 8/8.

12. **fast and furious** – excited, wild, noisy. 'Bill and Alison danced the waltz fast and furious round the room until they became too giddy to go on.'

13. **like fury** – with demonic energy and determination. 'After being a goal down, we played like fury and beat the champions 2–0.'

14. **all the rage** – in great demand, the height of fashion. 'Please, Dad, let's have a Dolby Surround for our hi-fi set. It's all the rage!'

15. **to vent one's rage/anger at/upon** – to release one's fury at someone/something. 'The teacher always vents his anger upon Tony, but he's never done anything wrong. It's most unfair.'

16. **road rage** – losing control of oneself in hectic traffic conditions, resulting in aggressive behaviour towards other road users. 'When I got the very last parking space, the man behind me jumped out of his car and screamed at me in a fit of road rage.' Also: **office rage**; **supermarket-trolley rage**; **bus-stop-queue rage**; **cigarette-smoke rage**.

17. **air rage** – when airline passengers become angry and uncontrollable, thus threatening the lives of everyone in the confined space of a plane. Some experts think this may be caused by lack of oxygen on the plane, as the same air is constantly recycled. 'Two victims of air rage

forced a jet to make an emergency landing at Dublin airport.'

1. **to seethe with rage** – to be absolutely furious. ' "How often have I told you not to touch my computer, and now you've spilt your drink all over it!" Colin's father was seething with rage.'

2. **with a vengeance** – in far greater measure than one expected or wanted. 'When the weather finally broke, it rained with a vengeance every day and all day for the next two weeks.'

Row, Annoyance

3. **to be locked in a row** – to be stuck in a series of bitter arguments. 'The ministers have been locked in a row over whether to build the new motorway or not.'

4. **a cross-patch** – an ill-tempered person. 'How can you be such a cross-patch on a beautiful day like this?'

5. **to be in a huff** – to feel annoyed and offended. 'I didn't ask her to come with me to the meeting. She's been in a huff ever since.'

Shouting

6. **to be all over bar the shouting** – to be in a situation (contest or game) where there is no doubt about the winner apart from being acknowledged officially. Also used humorously. 'Another boat race won by Oxford – it's all over bar the shouting.'

Shame, Crying, Doubt

7. **shame on you!** – you should be ashamed of yourself. 'Do you mean to say you let Doris carry all her luggage down the stairs without helping her? Shame on you!'

8. **a crying shame** – a great wrong that calls for action. 'It's a crying shame that the children should be separated from one another because of their parents' divorce.'

 a crying need – an urgent need that demands action. 'There is a crying need to place orphans with families who are anxious to adopt.'

9. **to put someone to shame** – to make someone feel inferior by showing up his or her faults. 'While you were sunning yourselves in Tenerife, Vivien worked over Christmas without once complaining. She has put you all to shame.'

10. **a nagging doubt** – a doubt that continually troubles the conscience. 'I had a nagging doubt whether we had been right to send William abroad with no one to accompany him when he was only 13.'

11. **no room for doubt** – to have a feeling of absolute certainty. 'He is the man who broke into my house. There is no room for doubt.' Also: **without a shadow of doubt**.

12. **to give someone the benefit of the doubt** – to accept the most charitable explanation of someone's actions. 'Very well, Mrs Brown, we will give you the benefit of the doubt this time, but in future please make sure you have paid for everything in your bag before you leave the shop.'

Fear, Afraid, Scare, Horror

13. **without fear or favour** – completely fair, without prejudice or fear of threats. 'It's expensive going to law, but one thing you can be certain of: your case will be heard without fear or favour.'

14. **there's not much fear of . . .** – it's not very likely that . . . (used in reference to future events). 'The only way to save our jobs would be for all of us to accept a 10 per cent cut in our wages, but there's not much fear of that happening, worse luck.'

15. **in fear and trembling** – in a state of great fear, shaking with fear. 'When the boss sent for me, I went to her office in fear and trembling, but she only wanted to praise my work.'

16. **to give someone the creeps** – to feel very uneasy about someone. 'That man follows me about each time he sees me. He really gives me the creeps.'

17. **to play on someone's fears** – to exploit to one's own advantage. 'The salesman played on the old widow's fears when he

recommended that she buy his burglar alarm system.'

1. **scared stiff** – terrified, overcome with fear. 'When the Alsatian leapt at me, I was scared stiff and couldn't move.'

2. **to scare the pants off someone** – to give someone a terrible fright. 'Spending the night in the haunted room of that castle would scare the pants off me.'

3. **a scaremonger** – a person who spreads alarmist and pessimistic rumours. 'I don't want to have anything to do with John. He's such a scaremonger and someone like him can really spoil my day.' Also: **scaremongering**.

4. **a horror scenario** – the absolute worst sequence of events imaginable. ' "Are we prepared for the horror scenario of a plane crashing into a nuclear power station?" the chief fireman asked.' See *Worst Case Scenario Survival Handbook* by Joshua Piven and David Borgenicht.

Nervousness, Breakdown

5. **to snap under the pressure** – to have a breakdown. 'If you make any more demands on the boy about his school-work, he will snap under the pressure.' cf. **'to be driven/tipped over the edge'** 16/14.

6. **to be close to breaking point** – to be on the verge of having a nervous break-down. 'Don't nag her any more, Mother. Rose is close to breaking point as it is.'
   to reach breaking point – unbear-able circumstances which one can with-stand no longer. 'After having looked after her severely disabled husband for five long years, she had reached breaking point and could no longer cope.' Also: **to have a nervous breakdown**.

7. **to fall/go to pieces** – to lose control of oneself completely. 'After his wife ran away, Jerry's life fell to pieces and he started drinking.'

8. **to pick up the pieces** – to make good or pay for someone's mistake or negligence. 'Many single mothers have not got adequate means of support, and the tax payer has to pick up the pieces.'

9. **to have the jitters** – to have a fit of nerves. 'How can Harry think of going on stage when he has the jitters just meeting a small group of people?'
   to give someone the jitters – to make someone extremely nervous.

10. **to be shaken to the core** – to be deeply shocked, to be profoundly affected. 'The major skiing accident in Switzerland has shaken holiday-makers to the core.' Also: **to be numbed to the core**.

11. **to be in turmoil** – to be deeply troubled and upset. 'Richard has been kidnapped in a foreign country and his father's mind is in turmoil.'

Sorrow, Grief, Misery, Tears

12. **more in sorrow than in anger** – with feelings of sadness and disappointment rather than anger (at someone's wrong-doing). 'When Kenneth told his wife that he had gambled away her money, she looked at him more in sorrow than in anger.'

13. **to drown one's sorrows** – to drink heavily to console oneself for a setback or misfortune. 'Margaret has just told me she won't be seeing me again, so I am drown-ing my sorrows.'

14. **to be in a state / in a sorry/right/ proper state** – in a pitiful condition. 'When I called on Oliver, I found him in a sorry state; he was lying in great pain on the floor.'

15. **to come to grief** – to fail disastrously. 'Owing to his lack of experience, all Gerald's ventures came to grief.'

16. **to swallow one's grief** – to stifle one's sadness. 'At the news of her grand-mother's death, Julia swallowed her grief so as not to upset her children.'

17. **to put someone out of his misery** – to put an end to someone's suspense by giv-ing him the information he was hoping for. 'The doctor has put me out of my mis-ery; there's nothing wrong with my lungs.' The original meaning was to kill a sick or injured animal that was suffering unnecessarily.

18. **to be prone to tears** – to cry easily. 'You

really must treat her gently, Melissa. She is very sensitive and prone to tears.'

Suffer, Woe, Throes

1. **to suffer fools gladly** – (almost always used in the negative) to tolerate stupidity in others. 'Alan is too impatient to suffer fools gladly.'

2. **woe betide you** – you will be sorry . . . 'Woe betide you if you miss your interview. You won't get another chance.' The phrase is sometimes used humorously. 'Betide' means 'happen to' and derives from Anglo-Saxon 'tide', 'time', 'hour'. It is only used in this phrase.

3. **to be in the throes of something** – struggle with the task of. 'Please don't come over just now; I'm in the throes of filling in my tax return.'

Ill-will, Ill at Ease

4. **to harbour ill-will** – to bear a grudge, produce bad feeling, hostility. The fast-growing Leylandii hedge provoked long-lasting resentment and ill-will between the two neighbours.' Also: **to provoke/ produce ill-will**.
   to bear no ill-will – to be well disposed towards someone/something.

5. **to be ill at ease with** – to feel awkward in the presence of someone. 'Bernard always felt ill at ease when he was with his father; he never understood why.'

Dumps, Damper

6. **in the dumps / down in the dumps** – depressed, miserable. 'Yvonne has been down in the dumps ever since her brother went to Canada.' 'Dump' is a cognate of Dutch *dompen* (to quench, extinguish) and English 'damp'. cf. **'a wet blanket' 165/1**.

7. **to put a damper on someone** – to discourage or depress someone. cf. **'in the dumps' 129/6; 'a wet blanket' 165/1**.
   to put a damper on an idea, enthusiasm, hope – to discourage someone's idea, enthusiasm or hope. 'I wish John weren't so negative; he puts a

damper on all my ideas.' cf. **'to pour cold water on' 12/18**.

8. **a party-poop / party-pooper** – someone who spoils the happy atmosphere of a party. 'You're a real party-pooper, Linda. I know you've quarrelled with your boyfriend, but can't you talk about something else?' cf. **'a wet blanket' 165/1**.

Joy, Hope

9. **to be someone's pride and joy** – to be the special object of someone's love and pride. 'The bird sanctuary which the old man had built himself was the pride and joy of his life.'

10. **to wish someone joy of a person/ thing** – to express pleasure at being rid of a person/thing one doesn't like. An ironic comment on the person/thing one has been parted from. 'So Mrs Anderson has deserted us for Henry Boyd; I wish him joy of her!'

11. **to get no joy from** – to get no help from. 'I've been looking everywhere for a room; I tried the information bureau, but got no joy from them.' cf. **'to get no change out of' 290/18**.

12. **to hope against hope** – to keep on hoping even though there are no longer any grounds for hope. 'We were hoping against hope that Grandfather would get better, although the doctor had given him up.'

13. **a fond hope** – a foolish hope. 'The old man nourished the fond hope that his grandson would qualify as a doctor, although the boy had no interest in medicine.' 'Fond' derives from East Friesian *fone, fon* meaning a girl, weakling, simpleton; hence 'foolish', the meaning it has retained to the present day, but only in this phrase.

14. **to pin one's hopes on** – to rely on a single thing or person for the fulfilment of one's hopes. 'We are pinning our hopes on a new German drug to cure our son.'

15. **to build up someone's hopes** – to encourage someone's wishes. 'Don't build up the child's hopes, Dennis. She hasn't

got a chance of getting into the
orchestra.'

Feel, Feelings

1. **to feel small** – to feel humiliated or
   ashamed. 'When Martin found he hadn't
   enough money to pay the bill, he felt very
   small.'

2. **to get the feel of** – to become accustomed to. 'After tapping away all day on
   the typewriter, it took me very little time
   to get the feel of the computer keyboard.'

3. **to feel out of it** – to feel as if one
   doesn't belong. 'All the guests at the party
   were teenagers. I was much too old and
   felt quite out of it.'

4. **to get the feeling that** – to suspect
   without understanding the reason. 'I get
   the feeling, Marion, that you don't want
   to come out with me.'

5. **to acquire a feeling for something** –
   to develop a sympathy for something. 'If
   you want to speak a foreign language
   well, you must acquire a feeling for it.'

6. **to feel the draught/pinch** – to suffer
   discomfort through lack of money. 'Now
   that people are short of money, the shops
   in the High Street are feeling the draught/
   pinch.'

7. **no hard feelings** – no ill-feelings or
   resentment. 'Since we don't agree,

wouldn't it be better for us to part, with
no hard feelings on either side?'

8. **to have mixed feelings about** – to be
   undecided, to feel regret as well as pleasure about a certain course of action.
   'When my parents decided to emigrate to
   Australia, I had mixed feelings about us
   going.'

9. **to vent one's feelings on** – to find an
   outlet for one's anger in; to divert one's
   anger on to. 'Just because you didn't get
   an increase in your salary, you needn't
   vent your feelings on me!'

10. **to hide one's feelings** – not to show
    one's emotions. 'How could she hide her
    feelings when she was so much in love
    with him?'

11. **feelings are running high** – exuberant
    feelings or feelings of anger, outrage.
    'After winning the World Cup, football
    fans were celebrating the victory and feel-
    ings were running high.'

12. **not to feel oneself** – to feel slightly
    unwell or depressed. 'I am sorry if I was a
    little short with you just now; I don't feel
    myself today.'

13. **the feel-good factor** – a sense of con-
    tentment from which political capital can
    be made. 'Now that the government is los-
    ing popularity, there is no longer the
    same feel-good factor throughout the
    country.'

Blind

1. **to be blinded by hatred** – to hate to such an extent that one's judgement of a person is distorted.

2. **to turn a blind eye to** – deliberately to overlook a fault in another person, which one does not wish to acknowledge, even to oneself. 'The old man adored his grandson and always turned a blind eye to his misbehaviour.'

3. **to have a blind spot for** – to have uncritical enthusiasm for. 'Most parents have a blind spot for their children, and ignore their faults.'

4. **to have a blind trust/faith in someone** – to trust someone absolutely and without question. The idiom **'a blind trust'** has also come to mean a trust which manages a politician's private capital, making sure that there is no link between policy and donation, and thus preventing a conflict of interest. Blind trusts might not be so blind after all and that is why they are to be abolished.

5. **a blind date** – an introduction to an unknown person arranged by an agency or a third party.

6. **to be blind drunk** – completely drunk. 'At weekends you'll always see those two boys in the alley, wandering around blind drunk.'

7. **a blind-alley occupation/job** – one that offers no chance of promotion. It is always unskilled and therefore badly paid in the long run. cf. **'a dead-end job'** 146/8.

8. **the blind leading the blind** – an ironic comment on leaders who are as ignorant and incompetent as the people they are leading. From the Bible (Matthew XV, 14): 'And if the blind lead the blind, both shall fall into the ditch.'

9. **to be blindingly obvious** – to be very clearly evident.

Deaf

10. **to turn a deaf ear to** – to refuse to listen, usually to some request for help.

11. **to fall on deaf ears** – to meet with no response, to be ignored. 'Maria so wanted to go on that school trip, but all her pleas fell on deaf ears.'

12. **a dialogue of the deaf** – a fruitless discussion, one in which all the participants have closed minds and are unreceptive to any rational argument.

13. **to be as deaf as a door-post** – completely deaf. Sometimes said of a person who is not conscious of his or her deafness. 'He's as deaf as a door-post but he gets very angry if you shout at him.'

14. **a deafening silence** – a silence which expresses more embarrassment than any words could do. 'When Jack asked the bride at the wedding reception whether she had been married before, there was a deafening silence.' Also: **the silence was deafening**.

15. **hard of hearing** – having difficulty in hearing.

Dumb

16. **to strike dumb** – to render someone speechless with surprise.

to be struck dumb/dumb-struck – to be made speechless with astonishment.

1. **to dumb down / dumbing down** – to make everything very much simpler, so that one does not have to learn much any more, or make the effort to learn, and everyone knows less and less. Current school textbooks and television programmes are said to play a major role in this dumbing-down process. 'If you ask me, cheap American cartoons and soap operas are responsible for the dumbing down of TV.' 'Dumbing down' comes from the German word *dumm* for 'stupid'. cf. '**to be spoon-fed' 170/14**.

2. **the dumb millions** – the masses who have no say in the way they are governed.

3. **our dumb friends** – our animal friends.

4. **dumb animals** – a phrase used in pity because animals are unable to complain of ill-treatment.

5. **a dumb blonde** (US) – a girl who is good-looking but lacking in intelligence. The Americans use the word 'dumb' in the sense of 'stupid' in the same way as the Germans use the cognate *dumm*.

6. **a dumb-waiter** – an arrangement of revolving shelves introduced in the 18th century for replacing servants in the drawing-room. The object of the device was to ensure greater privacy rather than save labour.

Lameness

7. **a lame excuse** – an excuse that is weak and unconvincing.

8. **crippling taxes** – a tax that is so high that it discourages businessmen from expanding their enterprises or taking risks.

9. **a fractured sentence** – a sentence in which the subject and the object have been separated by one or more subordinate clauses, e.g. 'I wanted, when I was staying with my friends in Massachusetts, in the spring of 1983, to pay a visit to the Niagara Falls' instead of: 'When I was staying with my friends in Massachusetts in the spring of 1983, I wanted to pay a visit to the Niagara Falls.'

Fever, Colds

10. **at fever heat/pitch** – with the utmost exertion and excitement. 'The children worked at fever heat to get their play ready in time for Christmas.'

11. **spy fever** – an enormous interest in spies.

12. **not to be sneezed at** – not to be despised, considerable. 'An income of £30,000 a year is not to be sneezed at, even today.'

13. **to cough up** (vulgar) – to pay up.

Infections

14. **an infectious laugh** – a laugh that is quickly echoed by the other people present. 'His laugh was so infectious that we all joined in, even though we didn't understand the joke.'

Plague, Virus, Disease

15. **to plague someone** – to pester someone with constant requests.

16. **to avoid like the plague** – to keep something you consider harmful or dangerous at as great a distance from you as possible. 'If you hate musicals, you should avoid the new show like the plague.' A plague is any epidemic disease. In the 14th century, fleas on the black rats carried the bubonic plague which killed 25 million people in Europe and was called the Black Death.

17. **to sweep across like a plague / to spread like the plague/a virus/a contagion/a disease/a dose of flu** – to spread very quickly, to be very infectious, contaminating, demoralizing. 'These road cones are spreading like a disease on our roads.' Also: **to spread like a rash; to spread like flu in winter; to spread like a fungus**.

18. **a plague on both your houses** – a phrase of disgust with both parties in a contest. It is often said by Liberals about the two major parties in British politics, the Conservative and Labour parties. The

reference is to Shakespeare's *Romeo and Juliet* (III, i, 96).

1. **an epidemic of something** – a widespread outbreak of a particular, often social, problem. 'An epidemic of pickpocketing has broken out in the cathedral town.'

2. **a doomsday virus** – a virus that is so dangerous and spreads so quickly that it spells potential doom for humankind, having the power to kill millions of people in a short time. One doomsday virus is ebola fever, which originated in Africa and is named after the River Ebola in Zaïre, where there was an outbreak in 1976. Other dangerous viruses are: yellow fever, malaria, influenza, smallpox, syphilis and Aids. See *The Fourth Horseman: A Short History of Epidemics, Plagues and Other Scourges* by Andrew Nikiforuk.

3. **germ warfare** – war waged with germs instead of bombs. cf. **'biological warfare/weapons'** 268/8.

4. **the kissing disease** – glandular fever, caused by a virus which can be passed on by kissing and affecting mostly teenagers and young adults.

Bug

(see also *Bug* in Chapter 10)

5. **to catch the bug** – to become addicted to a particular pastime such as gardening, cooking, theatre-going, etc. 'Now that my father has retired, he has caught the gardening bug and spends nearly all his time out of doors.'

6. **a computer bug** – a fault or defect in a computer system which adversely affects the software or hardware. 'Gerald needed two whole hours to track down the computer bug which had disrupted his program.'

7. **a computer virus** – this causes a whole series of defects to multiply, spread and cause destruction throughout various computer systems, especially if they are connected to each other via the Internet. ' "How could I have been so stupid?" Malcolm groaned in despair. "I opened 'a secret message' e-mail and now a computer virus has destroyed my software!" '

Syndrome

8. **sick-building syndrome** – a sickness caused by dust which is attracted to computer screens, photocopiers and other modern office equipment. It causes headaches, fatigue, runny noses and itchy eyes. 'If we fill the office with lots of plants and air the rooms every hour, hopefully we won't get this sick building syndrome.'

9. **economy-class syndrome** – a thrombosis caused by having to sit for a long period on a plane without being able to stretch one's legs. 'Make sure you move your feet and legs about during the flight, or you could end up getting economy-class syndrome!' cf. **'jam-packed' 178/5**; **'sardine class' 74/8**.

10. **foreign-accent syndrome** – waking up, usually after a stroke, and speaking one's mother tongue with a foreign accent.

11. **the Jerusalem syndrome** – on entering Jerusalem, to be so overwhelmed by the feeling that Jesus Christ was once also in exactly the same place, that one is suddenly convinced that one is a prophet too, and behaves accordingly.

12. **dying-baby syndrome** – the inability of reporters to remain objective when writing about the horrors they have seen, especially the suffering of women and children in war-torn countries.

13. **simulation syndrome** – are we coming, staying or going? This is a sensation most commonly experienced when you sit in a stationary train and look out of the window at another train travelling past. You often think you yourself are moving. Also, when looking at the clouds passing in front of the moon, one can think the moon itself is moving.

14. **handbag syndrome** – backache caused by always carrying a very heavy handbag on the same shoulder.

Other Afflictions

1. **intellectual myopia** – a phrase recently coined for 'stupidity'.

   a myopic view of a problem – a short-sighted or narrow-minded conception of a problem.

2. **to have teething problems/trouble** – to have initial difficulties that stem from inexperience or novelty of design. 'When we bought our new television set, the salesman warned us that we might have teething trouble with it, since the design of the model was a new and complicated one.' The reference is to the pain associated with the cutting of a tooth. cf. '**to have growing pains**' 136/2.

3. **to be stiff-necked** – to be very obstinate, impossible to argue with; unwilling to listen to reason. cf. '**pig-headed**' 59/7.

4. **to cramp someone's style** – to hinder or spoil what someone is trying to do. 'My husband loves to entertain our guests with his funny stories but, when Father comes to dinner, Alan always forgets what he wants to say. I don't know why, but Father seems to cramp his style.'

5. **to work in spasms** – to work irregularly, some days many hours on end and some days not at all.

6. **with a jaundiced eye** – with a sour, disapproving look. 'Having already lost a lot of his money on his wife's wild schemes, Philip viewed her new project with a jaundiced eye.'

7. **a measly reward** – a mean, miserly reward.

8. **like the measles** – something one must go through. 'Mrs Anderson expects her two teenage girls to fall in love with some pop star and worship him like mad, but then to get it over with – like the measles.' The expression comes from *Idle Thoughts of an Idle Fellow* by Jerome K. Jerome: 'Love is like the measles; we all have to go through it.'

9. **a rash of new ideas, etc.** – one (idea) very quickly following another.

10. **to be all over somebody like a rash/ a bad rash** – to be overly familiar with someone. 'Diana felt "fairly intimidated" by the atmosphere on board the royal yacht *Britannia* during Cowes Week. She found Charles' friends too friendly and too knowing. "They were all over me like a bad rash," she told her friends' (*Diana: Her True Story* by Andrew Morton, © Michael O'Mara Books).

11. **to have itching fingers** – to have a strong impulse to hit someone. 'My fingers were itching to smack Peter's face.'

12. **warts and all** – with all its faults and imperfections, a realistic portrayal. The modern artist tries to render a true likeness, 'warts and all', and avoid flattering his or her subject. The expression is used in writing as well as in painting. 'The former minister announced that she would get her revenge by writing a warts-and-all memoir about her fellow politicians.' The phrase comes from Oliver Cromwell's statement that he wanted his portrait to show him accurately, 'warts and all'.

13. **acne Majorca** – a bad outbreak of spots, probably caused by oily suntan lotions and too much sun, affecting holiday-makers who enjoy sunbathing in hot, sunny places like Majorca. 'Fancy that! Yvonne's acne Majorca has completely disappeared after four days of this wet, windy weather.'

14. **like a monstrous carbuncle** – something that looks hideous and out of place. Prince Charles invented this simile when he criticized the proposed design for the new wing of the National Gallery in London at the 150th anniversary dinner of the Royal Institute of British Architects on 30 May 1984: '. . . but what is proposed is like a monstrous carbuncle on the face of a much loved and elegant friend.'

15. **an anaemic character** – a weak, subdued character.

16. **to get dizzy with success** – success has often been compared with climbing to the top of a pole, when it would be natural to feel dizzy on looking down.

17. **verbal diarrhoea** – compulsive talka-

tiveness. 'Hewitt spoke to the conference for three hours, scarcely pausing to draw breath; a bad case of verbal diarrhoea.'

1. **only a hiccup / a mere hiccup** – only a small, temporary setback in one's progress, or in a relationship with someone. 'We look forward to doing a lot of business with you; your dispute with our director was only a hiccup.'

2. **a barren harvest** – a worthless reward.

3. **cancerous growth** – a pathological tendency to grow and spread. 'In the last few years there has been a cancerous growth in drug-taking which has affected all sections of society.' Note the simile: **to spread/grow/invade like cancer**.

4. **to be the cancer at the heart of it all** – to be the root of some evil. ' "The children in my class used to be so friendly and willing to learn," the teacher sighed. "Now they seem bored and are so rude. I think that new boy Fred is the cancer at the heart of it all." '

5. **sick humour / a sick joke** – humour that is morbid or sadistic, e.g. when an armless person is given a tennis racquet for his or her birthday. cf. '**a black joke**' 7/20.

6. **to be sick and tired** – to be completely fed up with something. 'I'm sick and tired of having to tell you to put your dirty clothes into the laundry basket and not leave them on the floor!' cf. '**to be fed up to the teeth/back teeth**' 92/15.

7. **serial sickies** – workers who often succumb to the temptation of taking a day off work, especially on Fridays or Mondays so that they can enjoy a long weekend holiday – and still get their wages paid.

8. **to add insult to injury** – to aggravate a wrong that one has done someone by adding another. 'Having failed to pay the doctor's bill, the patient then complained about his treatment to the medical association. He added insult to injury.'

9. **to feel like/to treat someone like a leper** – to feel like an outcast, to be shunned, to avoid someone at all costs. 'After peace was declared in 1945, the air force pilot was treated like a leper for his part in the bombing and devastation of Dresden.' Also: **to become a social leper**. cf. '**to treat someone like a dog**' 52/14.

10. **to come to a sticky end** – to end badly. 'If Bertie doesn't stop gambling and borrowing money all the time, he'll come to a sticky end.'

Aches

11. **to be a headache** – to be a great trial to other people, due to one's misbehaviour and bad temper.

12. **a real headache** – a big problem. 'All these regulations are a real headache for my little business.'
    the main headache – the biggest problem. 'With the awful traffic jams, Eddie's main headache was to get to the examination centre on time.'

13. **to belly-ache** (Australian) – to complain continually. The phrase is now fashionable in Great Britain.

Pains

14. **to be a fool for one's pains** – to work hard, or try to help someone else without proper reward or acknowledgement. 'Only £10 for all that work! You were a fool for your pains!'

15. **to be at pains / to take pains to** – to exert oneself to, to make a great effort to. 'They were all at pains to make me feel at home, and I soon forgot I was homesick.'

16. **to spare someone pain** – to avoid a subject that might upset a person. 'Don't let's talk about the plane crash in which her father died. We want to spare her the pain of remembering.'

17. **to give someone a pained look** – to look at someone in either an annoyed or offended way.

18. **no pain, no gain** – nothing can be achieved without making an effort or sacrifices. 'If you want to get slim, Joanna, you'll have to stop eating all those sweets and cakes and do some exercise every day, otherwise no pain, no gain.' cf. '**you**

can't make an omelette without breaking eggs' 175/14.

1. **a pain in the neck** (slang) – a pest, a real nuisance, a source of continuous annoyance. 'That man has been a pain in the neck ever since we took him on. He quarrels with all our customers and staff.' Also: **to be the biggest pain in the backside**.

2. **to have growing pains** – just as a child has 'growing pains' in its limbs, so an industry may have 'growing pains' when it has difficulties in getting itself established on a profitable basis. cf. **'teething trouble' 134/2**.

Agony

3. **to pile on the agony** – to aggravate the pain. 'There was no need to tell Dennis he would have to get a job now that he has failed his exams and can't go to university. That was piling on the agony.'

4. **an agony aunt/uncle** – a person who answers readers' problems in letters sent to her/him for advice. Nearly every magazine has an **'agony column'** which is devoted to these letters. 'The agony aunt of our local paper had a nervous breakdown after hearing about so many of her readers' problems.'

Wounds

5. **to lick one's wounds** – to console oneself after a severe blow. 'After having been dropped by her boyfriend, Lilly locked herself in her room to lick her wounds.'

6. **like a wound / to fester like an open/internal wound** – to be vulnerable to grief and anguish. 'Be kind to your neighbour, Darren. She's lonely and miserable since her husband died, and her grief is like an open wound.'

7. **to reopen old wounds / to open old wounds** – to lay bare old hurts or grievances. 'The public inquiry into the train crash reopened wounds for the relatives and friends of the dead and injured.'
   to be deeply wounded by someone's behaviour/remarks – one's feelings have been badly hurt.

8. **to heal one's wounds** – to restore one's hurt feelings. 'It's going to take a long time to heal her wounds after her boyfriend dropped her so suddenly.'

Sores

9. **to be sore about** – to feel aggrieved about. 'He is still sore about Vivien going out with Norman.'

10. **a sore spot** – a subject about which someone is particularly sensitive. 'You shouldn't have mentioned his father's bankruptcy. You touched a sore spot with him.'

11. **a sore point** – a hurtful subject. 'Mentioning his failed exam was a sore point for Philip.'

12. **a sight for sore eyes** – an object of outstanding beauty, capable of inspiring the most jaded observer.

13. **an eye-sore** – hideous, offensive to the eye. 'The new building was an eye-sore, quite out of place in its surroundings.' cf. **'to stick out like a sore thumb' 101/8**.

14. **to open old sores** – to revive old quarrels. 'Why did you talk to Martin about Father's will? What was the point of opening old sores?'

Madness

15. **midsummer madness** – madness has always been associated with the full moon, so that the midsummer heat, combined with the full moon, was the time when madness was at its fullest intensity.

16. **there is method in his madness** – although he seems to be acting illogically, he has, in fact, a purpose in everything he does. 'Our approach to our clients may surprise you at first, but you will soon see there is method in our madness.' (See Shakespeare's *Hamlet*, II, ii, 211.)

17. **to drive someone mad** – to annoy someone intolerably. 'The marriage ended in divorce because Andrea's constant nagging drove Roger mad.'

18. **hopping mad** – absolutely furious. 'When the bus went all the way at walk-

ing pace, the passengers were hopping mad with the driver.'

1. **to throw a fit** – to experience an attack of nerves, brought on by shock, anxiety, rage, etc. 'Your father would throw a fit if he knew what you were up to!'

2. **by fits and starts** – irregularly, spasmodically. 'Mary works by fits and starts. One day she will work for ten hours; the next two days she won't work at all.'

3. **a mania for (fresh air, fast driving, stamp-collecting, etc.)** – an overwhelming desire for or interest in some object or activity.

4. **a schizophrenic attitude to** – mixed or contradictory feelings and views about a particular topic. Schizophrenia is a mental illness characterized by a dissociation between the reason and the emotions.

5. **the lunatic fringe** – the fanatics in a political party who seek to impose their extremist policies on the country by force.

6. **to behave like a raving lunatic / drive/grin like a lunatic / grin like a loon** – like someone completely mad. 'It was a funny carnival party. When my boyfriend saw me, he grinned like a loon and offered me some plastic popcorn.' 'Lunatic' is derived from the Latin *luna* for 'moon'. Some mental conditions do seem to be influenced by the lunar cycle. Also: **as crazy as a loon; to sound like a loony idea** – a mad idea.

7. **like a man/someone possessed/obsessed** – like someone mad, his/her mind taken over by demons. 'Jeremy was determined to have finished repairing the car before nightfall and worked like a man possessed.'

Addiction

8. **a Net junkie** – someone who is addicted to surfing the Internet or to computer gambling on the Internet. 'You'd better see a shrink, Mike. I think you've turned into a Net junkie.' The opposite is an **'Internot'** – someone who is not in the least interested in the Internet.

9. **a quick fix** – a short-term solution to a problem. 'So far, no quick fix has been invented to stop the ageing process.'

10. **a pill popper** – a person who habitually takes pills or drugs. 'We really must try and help that pill-popping friend of yours, Fiona, or she'll end up in hospital.' cf. '**to kick the habit**' 300/2.

Illness

11. **a diplomatic illness** – a sham illness to provide an excuse for non-attendance at a party or function. Diplomatic illnesses are sometimes pleaded in order to extricate someone from an embarrassing situation; at other times, to express annoyance or resentment.

Medicine, Health

12. **to give someone a dose/taste of his own medicine** – to treat a wrongdoer in the same way as he has his victims. 'While Johnson was breaking into the vicarage, his own flat was burgled. He was given a taste of his own medicine!'

13. **the medicine could be worse than the illness** – sometimes it is better not to interfere, but to leave well alone. The phrase is used especially as a warning not to interfere in other countries' wars.

14. **to go through something like a dose of salts** – quickly and effectively. 'The mathematician went through his income tax documents like a dose of salts.' The phrase derives from Epsom Salts, which are used as a laxative.

15. **a bitter pill to swallow** – to be obliged to accept a great disappointment or humiliation. 'It was a bitter pill for him to swallow when he discovered that after 20 years of marriage his wife did not love him.'

16. **to use as a sticking plaster** – a temporary repair to something that needs a more permanent solution. 'The transport minister was being accused of using the £1 billion as a sticking plaster when much more money was needed over a longer period.'

17. **to give a clean bill of health** – after a medical check-up, to inform someone

that he or she is in good physical condition. 'Now that the doctor has given me a clean bill of health, I can start training for the European Championship.'

1. **a health farm** – a place where people go to improve their health, undergoing special programmes of diet and exercise. ' "Health farms are expensive but the results are worth the money," my friend enthused.'

Accident

2. **a happy accident** – an unplanned pregnancy. 'Melissa's husband was rather taken aback when she told him about their happy accident.' cf. **'the patter of tiny feet'** 108/1.

3. **to look like an accident waiting to happen** – an accident is bound to take place if steps are not taken to prevent it. ' "The nurses don't check the oxygen supplies often enough," the doctor said crossly. "It looks like an accident waiting to happen." ' cf. **'like a disaster waiting to happen'** 42/14.

Ambulance

4. **an ambulance chaser** – a lawyer who tries to persuade people who have been in accidents to take legal action. 'If you ever have an accident, Jimmy, beware of ambulance chasers. They just want to make money out of you!'

Clinic

5. **a drying-out clinic** – a clinic which specializes in treating alcoholics and trying to curb their addiction. 'The politician's wife had to spend six whole months in a drying-out clinic before she recovered.'

6. **a well-woman/well-man clinic** – a clinic for the treatment of women with gynaecological or sexual problems, and the male equivalent.

Patient

7. **a heartsink patient** – a patient suffering from illnesses which no doctor can pin down, and which may even be imaginary. ' "If I get one more heartsink patient today, I think I'd rather work in the casualty department," the young doctor groaned.'

Recovery

8. **on the road to recovery** – an improvement in one's health after an illness. 'After his liver transplant, he was at last on the road to recovery.'

9. **to be on the mend** – recovering, getting better. 'Vanessa is on the mend after falling off her horse and breaking her arm.'

Relations

1. **poor relations** – relatives who are despised for their lack of money. The phrase is often applied to people who beg from their richer relations; but it can also be used ironically. 'My sister-in-law is a terrible snob. She always makes me feel like a poor relation when I visit her.'

2. **race relations** – social relations between people of different races and cultures living in the same country. 'Race relations are improving within the police force, thanks to the great efforts of the home secretary.'

3. **relations are rather strained** – a change for the worse in the feelings of two persons or parties towards one another, e.g. between the USA and the former Soviet Union; a cooling-off of a friendship, usually brought about by some unresolved problem or dispute. 'Since I told my fiancée that I wanted to take a job in America, our relations have been rather strained.' Also: **relations are at freezing point** – extremely bad; **relations between them have hit rock bottom**.

4. **cracks in a relationship** – faults in a relationship between two lovers, etc., such as laziness, quarrels, jealousy and money problems. 'Lack of money sometimes causes cracks in a relationship.'

Romantic Attachments

5. **a (teenage) crush / a schoolgirl/boy crush** – to be infatuated with someone, usually a teacher, a pop star, a famous actor, etc., often for only a short time. 'The Wilmots were shocked when their daughter's crush on her Latin teacher turned into a serious love affair.'

6. **to be an item** – being a unit, being together as one. 'After having lived apart from her boyfriend for some time, the actress declared happily: "We are an item again!" '

7. **a love contract** – the legal term for this is 'a consensual relationship agreement'. If one falls in love at work with one's boss, one of the office staff, etc., one may have to sign a love contract, promising not to cause trouble if one is jilted.

8. **a matchmaker** – a person who likes to arrange marriages or romantic liaisons. 'I keep away from matchmakers at parties. Once they get hold of you, they never give up trying to find someone for you.'

9. **to have a fling / to embark on a fling** – to have a short-lived affair outside marriage. 'The wife of a racehorse owner caused a stir when she had a fling with one of his jockeys.'

Marriage

10. **marriage lines** – a marriage certificate.

11. **a shot-gun marriage** – one that the couple are forced into by circumstances beyond their control (e.g. the pregnancy of the bride). It has come to mean any partnership that is forced on the parties. 'There may well be a shot-gun marriage between the trade unions and small business if the economic depression continues.' This is a US idiom which owes its origin to the old days when a young man who had seduced a girl would be forced

by her angry parents to marry her at the point of a shot-gun.

1. **a see-saw marriage** – a marriage in which both partners have a job and take it in turns to stay at home looking after the children and the house.

2. **a broken marriage** – where the husband and wife have divorced or separated. 'Melinda had three young children from a broken marriage and did not think she would ever find another husband.' Also: **(their) marriage is in tatters**.

Family, Community

3. **nearest and dearest** – the immediate family. 'Time is too short to keep in touch with cousins and uncles. I prefer to stick to my nearest and dearest.'

4. **to be family** – someone who is entitled to special consideration because he or she is one of the family. 'We always keep a room free for Pamela; she is family.'

5. **in the family way** (vulgar) – pregnant.

6. **a person of family** – born into a good family.

7. **the head of the family** – usually the father or, in his absence, the eldest son.

8. **to run in the family** – (of a characteristic or talent) to pass from one generation to the next. 'Jack's three children are all musical, just like their father; it must run in the family.'

9. **a ready-made family** – a second or third marriage into which a partner brings children from a previous marriage. 'The second marriage failed because Henry could not cope with a ready-made family consisting of seven children.'

10. **a close-knit family** – members of a family who get on very well together, united by love and loyalty to one another. 'The Hardings don't mind what the neighbours say about their handicapped daughter. They are a very close-knit family.'

11. **a close-knit community** – a group of people united in daily life. 'The village I come from has always been a close-knit community.'

Class

12. **the chattering classes** – journalists, artists and other intellectuals who meet regularly to discuss topical affairs from home and abroad. 'The appointment of the new health minister was the talking point among the chattering classes.' This phrase was first used by the editor of the *Spectator*, Frank Johnson, in *NOW!* magazine in 1981.

13. **a touch of class** – in good taste. 'The way Sue dresses really has a touch of class.'

Kindred, Generation

14. **kindred spirits** – two people who share the same ideas and interests. 'Anne and I must be kindred spirits; we have the same views on everything.' cf. **'a soulmate' 43/6**; **'sisters under the skin' 143/15**.

15. **a lost generation** – a whole group of people, in this case children and young adults, who have wasted their lives by playing truant or dropping out of school altogether, ending up without an education and therefore unemployable. ' "These young lads are a lost generation," the social worker sighed. "They can hardly read or write, so it's no wonder they are unemployed." '

Father

16. **a father figure** – a man who takes the place of a father. He may play the part of a father to a young man, as Dr Johnson did to Boswell, or to a whole nation, as President Tito did to Yugoslavia.

17. **the father of (literature, history, modern psychology, etc.)** – the originator or the first example of. Chaucer is the father of English literature. Freud is the father of psycho-analysis.

18. **to be gathered to one's fathers** (biblical) – to die.

19. **the sins of the fathers are visited on the sons** (biblical) – later generations suffer the consequences of their ancestors' vices.

20. **like father, like son** – resemblance of

the son to the father from the intellectual or emotional point of view.

1. **the child is father of the man** – the child's behaviour indicates how the character of the man will develop. 'The childhood shows the man / As morning shows the day' (Milton, *Paradise Regained*, Book IV, l.220). 'The child is father of the man' (Wordsworth, 'My heart leaps up when I behold . . .').

2. **on the father's/mother's side** – a relative of the father, e.g. the father's parents, or his brother, sister or cousin, etc. The same applies to the mother.

3. **to stand godfather** – to pay the bills, godfathers being people from whom one expects generous gifts.

Daddy

4. **a sugar daddy** – a rich old man who keeps a girl young enough to be his daughter.

5. **Big Daddy** – a father who is very protective of his daughter.

Man

6. **a family man** – a man whose interests are in his home, rather than outside it, e.g. in his career, or in sport, socializing, etc.

7. **a fancy man** – a male lover of a mature woman, who may or may not be married. 'When Lisa's husband goes to work in the morning, her fancy man slips in through the back door.' cf. '**toy-boy**' **143/2**.

8. **a marked man** – a man who is sought for purposes of revenge or retribution because of his betrayal or actions against someone. 'Richard was a marked man after he was discovered spying for the enemy.'

9. **a self-made man** – someone who becomes rich and famous through his own efforts. 'You've got to hand it to him, Dad – with his millions, he's the best example of a self-made man.'

10. **to be one's own man/woman** – to do what one likes without being answerable

to anyone. 'His royal connections did not stop him from being his own man.'

11. **Mondeo man** – the emblematic 'middle England' figure. 'Mondeo man will in the end decide which one is the political party of the future.'

Wife

12. **a fish-wife** – a woman who is vulgar and uses bad language.

13. **an old wives' tale** – an old story or belief that has no foundation in fact, a myth. Here are a few examples of old wives' tales: that a drowning man rises to the surface twice before sinking for the last time; that children suffer from 'growing pains'; that you will catch a cold if you sit about in wet socks; and that musical people learn a foreign language quicker than unmusical people.

Mother

14. **like motherhood, we are all for it** – to declare one's support for a policy which has the support of everybody; like saying: 'I'm in favour of a fair and just society.'

15. **mother tongue** – the first language one learns to speak.

16. **a mother-complex** – an unhealthy or abnormal emotional tie between the son and his mother, resulting in the son's emotional dependence on the mother and coolness towards other women.

17. **a mother's boy/darling** – a boy who is indulged or spoilt by his mother.

18. **the wicked step-mother** – stepmothers are often regarded as wicked by the step-children who look upon them as intruders.

19. **a fairy godmother** – a person who provides one with every possible blessing. 'You've been a real fairy godmother to me.' A figure of speech taken from fairy stories in which a woman with supernatural powers protects the interests of the young heroine.

20. **the mother and father of** – the biggest and the worst. 'I'm sorry I can't go out

with you tonight. I've got the mother and father of a toothache.'

Child

1. **like a child / child-like / like children** – having the innocent and frank qualities of a child. 'The professor's boundless enthusiasm had a child-like quality about it.' Frequent usage: **child-like charm**; **child-like innocence**; **a child-like excitement**; **to act/behave like a child/like a spoilt child**.

2. **child's play** – a simple task for anyone who has the gift or experience to accomplish it. 'It was child's play to teach the boy English; he was so quick and intelligent.'

3. **spare the rod and spoil the child** – without strict discipline, a child's character will be ruined by his parents' indulgence. A Victorian adage which has been rejected by later generations of parents.

4. **child of nature** – someone who is innately good, even if unpolished.

5. **love child** – a child whose parents are not married to each other.

6. **wild child** – a young, unrestrained girl or boy who experiments with drugs and drink, and mixes with the wrong people at lots of parties. 'The parents were respectable enough, but fame and money had turned their daughter into a promiscuous wild child.'
   a child of the 1980s/1990s, etc. – someone who displays all the characteristics of his or her generation.

7. **a child wife** – a wife who is too young to carry out her duties, e.g. David Copperfield's first wife (in *David Copperfield* by Charles Dickens).

8. **a brain-child** – one's original idea. It can be used in a derogatory way when the speaker disclaims responsibility for an idea that has failed in practice. 'The new shift system at the office was the manager's brain-child, not mine. He is to blame for its failure.'

9. **second childhood** – the simple-mindedness of old age which resembles in some ways the mind of a child.

10. **to achieve something like a virgin comes to a child** – to achieve something without knowing how it happened. 'The business tycoon came to his wealth like a virgin comes to a child.'

Kid

11. **whizzkid** – a person who achieves success early through his or her ability, competence and expertise. ' "My Dorothy's going to marry a wealthy City whizzkid!" Mrs Hyde boasted.'

Baby

12. Similes with 'baby': **to be/behave like a baby**; **to be baby-like**; **to sleep like a babe/baby**; **as innocent as a baby**; **as smooth/soft as a baby's bottom**.

13. **a cry-baby** – someone who cries or complains at the smallest provocation. 'That boy cries out whenever he is touched. He's a real cry-baby.'

14. **baby-face** – round cheeks, innocent air and adolescent appearance, though advanced in years.

15. **to baby-sit** – to look after a baby or small children while the parents are out. This is done by a **'baby-sitter'**. cf. **'to house-sit / house-sitter' 155/5**.

16. **to throw out the baby with the bath water** – to destroy the good while trying to eliminate the bad. 'When the new director dismissed a large number of his staff to make the company more profitable, he also got rid of some of his best engineers. He had thrown out the baby with the bath water.'

17. **to be left holding the baby** – to be forced to take over someone else's responsibility. 'When the firm started to lose money, Harry resigned, and I was left holding the baby.'

18. **the babes in the wood** – innocent, naïve people lacking in experience and over-trustful. 'We've been doing this work for many years; we aren't exactly babes in the wood.'

19. **a babe-in-arms** – someone who is completely naïve and inexperienced in the

ways of the world. 'How can John think of starting a business at his age! He is only a babe-in-arms.'

1. **a babe magnet** – a very good-looking young man who is able to attract lots of women to him.

Boy

(see also *Boy* in Chapter 29)

2. **a toy-boy** – a handsome young man who is chosen as a lover by a much older but wealthy woman. 'I need a good-looking young man who likes listening to me and is prepared to flatter and pamper me. Do you know where I can get a toy-boy, Lydia?' cf. **'a fancy man' 141/7**.

Girl

3. **It Girls** – upper-class girls famous during the 1990s for their aristocratic connections and wealth, and who enjoyed partying and being photographed. 'The picture of the It Girl, arm in arm with the famous pop star, was front-page news.'

Son

4. **he is his father's son** – he resembles his father in character.

5. **the prodigal son** – someone who returns home after a long absence, and is received with great joy by his family despite his past behaviour. Today the phrase is used in a humorous sense. 'Are you going to kill the fatted calf for the prodigal son, Tom?' The allusion is to the parable of the prodigal son in Luke XV, 30.

6. **son of the soil** – a person who has been brought up on the land, e.g. a farm labourer.

7. **a son of a bitch** (vulgar) – an Americanism meaning a mean, nasty man who will take unfair advantage of you to further his own ends.

8. **a natural son/daughter** – an illegitimate son/daughter.

Daughter

9. **a daughter language** – a language which derives from an older one, e.g. the Romance languages, French, Italian, Spanish, etc., from Latin.

Brother

10. **the brotherhood of man** – human society considered as one big family.

11. **Big Brother** – in George Orwell's novel *1984*, Big Brother is the dictator of an imaginary country who dominates the lives of all its citizens. Big Brother is able to observe each citizen through an electronic eye, so that there is no escaping him, however cautiously his opponents conspire against him. Big Brother has become a symbol of power and tyranny against whom it is useless to struggle.

12. **Am I my brother's keeper?** – often used as a disclaimer of responsibility for the actions of one's close associates. From Genesis IV, 9: 'And the Lord said unto Cain, Where is Abel thy brother; and he said I know not. Am I my brother's keeper?'

13. **brothers in arms** – originally fellow soldiers, but used metaphorically in the sense of participants in the same struggle.

14. **blood brothers** – two men who have sworn to behave like brothers towards each other.

Sister

15. **sisters under the skin** – two women with the same tastes, or abilities, friends, regardless of race. ' "I didn't know you were both interested in joining Amnesty International. You seem so unalike." "Oh yes, we are sisters under the skin." ' cf. **'kindred spirits' 140/14**.

Twin

16. **a twin-set** – matching jumper and cardigan.

Cousin

1. **country cousins** – people from the country rather than the town, who are presumed to be ignorant and unsophisticated.

Grandmother

2. **don't teach your grandmother to suck eggs** – don't try to instruct someone who is more experienced than you.

3. **grandmother's funeral syndrome** – in the workplace, the absence of workers who are pretending to be ill. Originally, lying about a grandmother's death was used as an excuse to be absent from work.

Nanny

4. **a nanny state** – the state or institutions interfering with one's private life under the guise of wanting to be protective. 'We have to guard against being turned into a nanny state.'

Aunt

5. **an Aunt Sally** – an object of ridicule whose policies have failed or become unpopular. 'The prime minister has no intention of allowing the home secretary to be made an Aunt Sally for the increase in crime this year.' An Aunt Sally was originally a female effigy stuck on the end of a pole at which sticks and stones were thrown with the object of knocking the pipe out of its mouth; hence an object of derision.

Uncle

6. **Uncle Sam** – a nickname for the typical American. cf. '**John Bull**' 221/18.

7. **Uncle Tom** – a derisive term used by black nationalists for black people who collaborate with the white authorities. Uncle Tom was the black hero of *Uncle Tom's Cabin*, a story by Harriet Beecher Stowe.

8. **Uncle Tom Cobbleigh and all** – all and sundry, including the most ordinary people you can think of.

Bachelor

9. **a bachelor girl** – an unmarried girl.

10. **a bachelor's wife** – the perfect wife in the mind of the unmarried man.

Widow

11. **a grass widow** – a woman whose husband is away temporarily; originally, an unmarried woman who has lived with one or more men. The phrase suggests illicit relations out of doors rather than in the marriage bed.
    a green widow – a wife who has to spend all day by herself in her home in the country while her husband goes to work in the town.
    a golf widow – a woman whose husband spends much of his time on the golf course, so that she is alone for most of the day.

12. **not for widows and orphans** – not for investors of limited means who cannot afford to take risks with their money.

13. **a merry widow** – merry because she is now free to make new friends and have a merry time. The reference is to Franz Lehár's operetta *The Merry Widow*.

14. **widow's weeds** – a widow's mourning dress. 'Her widow's weeds become her.'

Neighbour

15. **beggar my/your neighbour** – to gain an advantage through someone else's loss. 'The French are using beggar-my-neighbour policies by refusing to accept that British beef is safe, so that they can sell their own.' Originally a card game in which the winner has all the cards and the other players have none at all.

Town, City

1. **to go to town** – to spend one's money recklessly. 'The Howards have really gone to town on a house for their daughter. They have bought her an absolute beauty.' 'Go to town' is a US colloquialism referring to the people who come into town from the countryside to spend their money. It was originally used about cowboys and ranch hands.

2. **a man about town** – a sociable man who attends many fashionable parties and has a wide circle of wealthy friends. 'My brother has become quite a man about town; when he was young, he hated going to parties.'

3. **a lady of the town** – a woman of loose morals.

4. **the talk of the town** – someone whose behaviour and wild way of life give rise to gossip and scandal-mongering. 'You had better behave yourself, Pauline. You are becoming the talk of the town.'
   it's the talk of the town – it's the most talked-about or fashionable place or thing.

5. **city slickers** – people living in cities thinking of themselves as worldly-wise and sophisticated.

Street

6. **to take to the streets** – to demonstrate against authority, to make a show of force. 'The students took to the streets in support of the health workers' claim for higher wages.'

7. **to go on the streets** – to work as a prostitute.

8. **streets ahead of** – far superior to, very much in advance of. 'You are streets ahead of us in technology.'

9. **mean streets** – very poor areas, full of crime and violence. 'Talented children can escape the mean streets if they do well at school and get into university.'

10. **not in the same street** – far inferior to, in no way comparable. 'All right, I'll have a game with you, but you know very well I'm not in the same street as you.'

11. **the man in the street** – the ordinary, typical man or woman. 'We are doing market research work, and we want the reaction of the man in the street to our suggestions.'

12. **to go back to Civvy Street** – to return to civilian life after serving in the armed forces. 'What are you going to do when you go back to Civvy Street?'

13. **grub street** – an inferior writer, inferior writing. '. . . any mean production is called grubstreet' (Dr Johnson, *Dictionary*). Grub Street near Moorfields in the East End of London (now Milton Street) was inhabited in the 17th century by a group of inferior writers and literary hacks.

14. **right up my street** – that's a subject I'm very familiar with. 'I'll be glad to advise Brian about his advertising. Advertising and publicity are right up my street.'

15. **street cred** – being accepted into the urban culture of one's friends. 'Those clothes you're wearing won't do if you want to become one of us. Look at mine. They have more street cred.' 'Cred' stands

for 'credibility', from the Latin *credere*, 'to believe'. cf. **'street-speak' 216/10**.

1. **streetwise / streetsmart** – being acquainted with the problems of city life and being able to survive in the big city without much money or support from anyone. 'Young girls working as prostitutes in big cities are not always streetwise and can end up in the gutter.'

Highway

2. **the information highway** – the Internet, which transfers digital information to computers from worldwide sources.

Road

3. **one for the road** – a final drink before one leaves a social gathering.

4. **to take to the road** – to become a tramp. 'I would rather take to the road than work in an office from nine till five each day. I want to be free.'

5. **at the end of the road** – (1) towards the end of one's life. 'I have come to the end of the road, my dear; the doctor has given me only another six months.' (2) to reach a stage where continuation is hopeless. 'With no further evidence available, the investigation into the death of the student on a Far East expedition has reached the end of the road.'

6. **at the cross-roads** – at a point in one's life when important decisions have to be made. 'Peter and Sue are at the cross-roads; they will have to decide very soon whether to make their home in England or emigrate.'

   to reek of dirty work at the cross-roads – suspicions of foul play and dishonourable practices.

7. **to make inroads into/on something** – (1) to make good progress with something. 'It is hoped that the new Asylum Bill will make inroads into the asylum and immigration backlog.' (2) to have a harmful effect on something. 'This old house we have bought is making inroads into our savings.'

Dead End

8. **a dead end** – (1) a road which is closed at the end, a cul-de-sac. 'We should never have gone down this narrow road. It's a dead end and now we must reverse all the way back!' (2) leading nowhere. 'We must make up our minds now and stand firm. All this friendly talk is just leading us down a dead end.'

   a dead-end job – a job with no prospects or advancement. 'Brenda was stuck in a dead-end job when she saw an advertisement looking for a nanny in America.' cf. **'a blind-alley occupation/job' 131/7**.

Turning-point

9. **the turning-point** – a change in attitude. 'The turning-point in Jill's relationship with her husband came when he changed from a full-time to a part-time job.'

Landmark

10. **a landmark** – an occurrence of great consequence. 'Landmark legal action is being taken by parents whose children were allegedly harmed by the measles, mumps and rubella vaccine.' Also: **a landmark case**.

11. **to reach a landmark** – to achieve an important stage or point in something. 'He reached a landmark when he rode his motorbike again after months in hospital.'

Way

12. **to pave the way for** – to create the necessary conditions for . . . , usually followed by some event. 'The Second World War paved the way for the independence of India.'

13. **to go all the way with** – (1) to be in complete agreement with. 'I'm not sure whether I would go all the way with you, but I certainly sympathize with your aims.' (2) to have full sexual intercourse with.

14. **way out** – (1) quite wrong, totally mis-

taken. 'You are way out in your calculations. The holiday will cost £300, not
£200.' (2) out of the ordinary, bizarre.
'Some of the costumes at the party were
way out, especially the exotic pyjamas
which would have been more suitable for
the bedroom.'

1. **to rub someone up the wrong way** –
to be tactless, to say the very thing that is
certain to annoy someone. 'You certainly
rubbed Mrs Parker up the wrong way, telling her you don't like Sussex. She has lived
there all her life and adores the county.'

2. **to go about something the wrong
way** – to use the wrong method of
approach to achieve an object. 'If you
wanted Howard to back your project, you
went about it the wrong way contradicting him at dinner.'

3. **at the parting of the ways** – a time
when it is best to separate. 'I am so sorry,
Tim, but I'm afraid we've come to a parting of the ways. We are only making each
other unhappy.' From the Bible (Ezekiel
XXI, 21): 'For the king of Babylon stood
at the parting of the way, at the head of
the two ways . . .'

4. **to go one's own way** – to follow one's
inclinations, to rely on one's own judgement and ignore other people's. 'All right,
Tom, go your own way, if that's how you
feel about it, but I wish you would listen
to us just once.'

5. **to have a way with one** – to have a
natural charm, which is very persuasive.
'Jenny certainly has a way with her. I
found myself agreeing with everything
she said.'

6. **to have come a long way** – to have
accomplished a great deal. 'You've come a
long way since we last met. You were a
clerk then, and now you own your own
factory.'

7. **in a big way** – on a large scale. 'Ian is
very ambitious, he does everything in a
big way.'
   in a small way – on a small scale,
only to a small extent. 'If you could help
me, even in a small way, I should be most
grateful.'

8. **to find out the hard way** – to learn the

truth from one's own painful experience.
'We warned you that you wouldn't like
boarding school but you wouldn't listen.
Now you've found out the hard way.'

9. **to make way for** – to surrender one's
position to someone else. 'You've done a
wonderful job for the company, but we
think, Sir, that at the age of 70 it is only
fair you should make way for a younger
person.'

10. **to have it one's own way** – to insist on
doing what one wants despite arguments
to the contrary. 'Have it your own way,
Hugh, but if things go wrong, don't blame
us.'

11. **to have it both ways** – to support two
incompatible arguments or courses of
action at the same time. 'If you want an
absolutely safe investment, then you can't
expect a high rate of interest. You can't
have it both ways.'

12. **to cut both ways** – to have advantages
and disadvantages at the same time. 'This
new drug will relieve your arthritis, but
you must put up with the side-effects; it
cuts both ways.'

13. **set in one's ways** – having fixed ideas
and habits. 'Turner is too set in his ways
to adopt your ideas; you had better look .
for a younger man.'

14. **to look the other way** – to pretend not
to see, to overlook a breach of the rules or
some irregularity. 'Even a disciplinarian
like the sergeant-major has to look the
other way sometimes.'

15. **on its way out** – becoming unfashion-
able. 'The mini-skirt was already on its
way out by 1969.'

16. **to pay one's way** – to support oneself
without having to borrow money. 'Many
American students pay their way through
college by taking a part-time job.'

17. **to mend one's ways** – to change one's
behaviour or habits, for the better. 'If you
want your uncle to help you, you'll have
to mend your ways. That will mean cutting out night clubs and starting to study
seriously.'

18. **a way of life** – a set of principles according to which one lives one's life. 'Alan

soon got used to the Muslim way of life, but his sister found it more difficult.'

1. **to see one's way to** – to feel justified in. 'After Peter's ingratitude to her, his cousin didn't see her way to giving him any more help.'

2. **well on the way to** – progressing towards something. 'Rita will be well on the way to becoming an alcoholic unless she stops drinking all day.'

3. **to go out of one's way to** – to put oneself to some trouble to . . . , to make a special effort to . . . 'When we visited London, our hosts went out of their way to make our stay enjoyable.'

4. **no way** (colloquial US English) – out of the question, impossible. ' "Could you please lend me £50?" "No way, I haven't got that much myself." '

5. **by the way** – incidentally, which reminds me. 'I'm sorry your cousin is ill. By the way, have you got his new address? I have some letters for him.'

6. **there are no two ways about it** – there is no other possibility or explanation. 'When you are in the army, you have to obey orders, no matter how unreasonable or stupid they may be. There are no two ways about it.'

7. **to stand in someone's way** – to obstruct or hinder someone in his or her aims. 'If you want to take a job abroad, don't let me stand in your way.'

8. **in a bad way** – physically or mentally in a serious condition. 'Your brother has had an accident. Will you go to the hospital at once; he's in a bad way.'

9. **not to know which way to turn** – to be in desperate difficulties. 'I was stranded in New York one winter without money or friends; I didn't know which way to turn until the British Consulate helped me out.'

10. **to put business someone's way** – to be the means of placing custom or orders with someone. 'If you are interested, I can put some business your way.'

11. **to fall by the wayside** – to fail to achieve one's aim, because of laziness, lack of strength or distractions. This phrase is generally used humorously. 'My father put me into accountancy, but I am sorry to say I was one of those who fell by the wayside.' The allusion is to Luke VIII, 5: 'A Sower went out to sow his seed, and as he sowed, some fell by the wayside; and it was trodden down and the fowls of the air devoured it.'

Lane

12. **to go down memory lane** – to revive old memories. 'Let's be sentimental, Joan, and go down memory lane this afternoon.'

Avenue

13. **to explore every avenue** – to make the most thorough inquiry. 'We are exploring every avenue to obtain the information you are asking for.'

Track, Trail

14. **to be on the right/wrong track** – to make/not to make progress in one's search for . . . 'The police believe that they are at last on the right track in their hunt for the murderers.' 'If you think I had anything to do with it, you're on the wrong track.'

15. **life on the wrong side of the tracks** – the 'bad' side of life (night clubs, prostitution, etc.). 'Joanna was bored with her library job and was tempted by life on the wrong side of the tracks.'

16. **back on track** – following the right course again. 'At last the peace process in Northern Ireland was back on track after many weeks of confrontation and rows.'
    to backtrack – to change one's mind and withdraw from an earlier opinion.

17. **to keep track of** – to keep oneself informed of someone's movements, activities, etc. 'I try to keep track of all my old school friends, but it isn't easy.'
    to lose track of – not to be informed of the movements, etc., of someone. 'Joyce has been married so many times that I've quite lost track.' **to lose (all)**

track of time – not to be aware of the passage of time.

1. **to be on a fast track** – to be in a position to achieve success quickly. 'After the launch of his new TV game show, he was on a fast track to fame and riches.'

    to put on the fast track – to deal with quickly.

2. **to make tracks for** – to leave quickly for. 'It's getting late. We had better make tracks for home.'

3. **a track record** – a record of one's successes/failures. 'I think we should consider Holmes for the headship. His track record for getting his pupils into the universities is very good.'

4. **in one's tracks** – in the very place where one is standing at a particular moment. 'Hugh was on the point of hitting his son when his wife entered the room; that stopped him in his tracks!'

5. **to cover one's tracks** – to conceal traces of one's movements. 'The bank robbers have covered their tracks very cleverly.'

6. **a trail-blazer** – someone who is the first to make progress successfully into new territory; an innovator. 'Former German Chancellor Helmut Kohl was the trail-blazer who united East and West Germany.'

Path

7. **to keep to the straight and narrow (path)** – to resist temptation and lead a virtuous life. 'As a clergyman, I am naturally expected to keep to the straight and narrow path, but it hasn't always been easy.' The phrase comes from the Bible (Matthew VII, 14): 'Because strait is the gate, and narrow is the way which leadeth into life, and few there be that find it!'

8. **to beat a path to a place** – to visit in large numbers. 'Now that Vivien has become famous, all sorts of people will be beating a path to her door.' The path to a place is beaten flat by the feet of so many people.

9. **to cross someone's path** – (1) to meet someone accidentally. 'Since I left school, I haven't crossed Smith's path, and I can't say I have any wish to.' (2) to thwart someone. 'If Jones crosses your path again, let me know and I'll put a stop to his interference.'

10. **to smooth the path** – to ease problems and thereby make better progress. 'Having listened carefully to the children's problems, the teacher was able to smooth the path to a sensible solution.'

Short Cut

11. **to take short cuts** – actions that save time or money. 'If the builders of those apartment blocks had not taken short cuts by using inferior materials, many lives would have been spared when the earthquake struck.'

River

12. **to sell down the river** – to betray, to act deceitfully towards. 'When we went back to the bookie's office to collect our winnings, he had already run off with the stakes; he had sold us down the river.' The phrase was first used by the black slaves who were sold by their owners to plantation owners further down the Mississippi, where conditions were usually much harsher.

Bridge

13. **to cross one's bridges before one comes to them** – to worry unnecessarily about something that may never happen. 'I don't know why you are worrying about Father catching one of those tropical diseases in Africa. His company hasn't decided yet whether to send him to Africa. Don't cross your bridges before you come to them.'

14. **to burn one's bridges / burning bridges** – to leave the old ways of life behind and to start anew. 'What good is it burning my bridges when the old problems follow me everywhere?'

15. **to build bridges / bridge-building** – to try to come to an agreement, to establish a link or communication between two disagreeing parties or opponents.

'Building bridges between two warring nations is always a difficult task.'

1. **to be a bridge between two things** – to link two sides. 'The Labour transport minister is a bridge between the Old and the New Labour Party.'

2. **to bridge a gap** – to make up a difference. 'It is difficult to bridge the gap between the older and the younger generation.'

3. **that's (all) water under the bridge** – that is all past now, and there is nothing that can be done about it. 'Yes, it's a pity you didn't accept Fred's offer, but it's useless to reproach yourself now. It's all water under the bridge.'

4. **to pull up the drawbridge** – to keep visitors out in order to ensure privacy for oneself and one's family. 'We enjoy entertaining, but at Christmas we like to pull up the drawbridge and be on our own.'

Joint

5. **to case the joint / casing the joint** – to watch a house, telephoning the owners or ringing the door-bell to find out whether anyone is at home and if it is safe to burgle it. 'Don't answer the phone, Mark. It is the sixth time it rang, so it's probably someone casing the joint.'

Back Yard

6. **not in one's back yard** – as long as it is far away from one's own property, it doesn't matter what happens there. 'Did you know that the duke is going to sell off some of his land to build a housing estate there? It won't be in his back yard so he couldn't care less.' Note: **NIMBY** – 'Not In My Back Yard'; **NIMBYism**.

Estate

7. **a sink estate** – a large area of developed land that has been filled with council houses, inhabited mostly by 'problem' families, people without jobs, drug-pushers and addicts, burglars and all kinds of criminals. Poor and old people also live here but, unable to move away, they suffer accordingly. cf. '**neighbours from hell**' 44/15; '**a sink school**' 263/6.

Church, Tower

8. **a church-like stillness** – very quiet and peaceful. 'It was nearly closing time and the museum had a church-like stillness about it.'

9. **to head down the aisle** – to get married in a church. 'I've got some great news, Tania. James and Stella will soon be heading down the aisle!'

10. **an ivory tower** – a haven from the harsh realities of life. 'Living in your ivory tower at Oxford, you can't imagine, can you, what it's like to go hungry?' The term *tour d'ivoire* (ivory tower) was first used by Sainte-Beuve in 1837 to describe the retreat of the French poet Vigny. Also: **an ivory-tower existence**.

11. **a tower of strength** – a person one can always turn to for sympathy and support in times of trouble. 'When my parents' marriage broke up, my eldest sister was a tower of strength to the children. We couldn't have managed without her.'

Ruins

12. **to be/lie in ruins** – completely destroyed, finished. 'After the teacher was caught shop-lifting, her reputation lay in ruins.' Frequent usage: **one's life is in ruins**. cf. '**to lie in tatters**' 202/3.

Prison

13. **like a prison / like being in a prison** – a place where one feels confined, restricted. 'I didn't like the look of the university hall of residence. With its dark walls and small windows, it felt like a prison.'

Museum

14. **a museum piece** – something antiquated or worn-out. 'We can't go to Scotland in that museum piece. Surely the car-hire company can do better than that!' The literal meaning is a specimen of an earlier civilization exhibited in a museum.

Exhibition

1. **to make an exhibition of oneself** – to invite public ridicule or contempt by one's behaviour. 'I wish Henry wouldn't make an exhibition of himself shouting at the waiter like that. It is so embarrassing.'

Public House

2. **to have someone over a barrel** – to have a person in one's power, so that he can be forced to do whatever is asked of him. 'The boss has got you over a barrel. If you don't withdraw your accusations, she will take you to court, and if you do withdraw, you will lose the respect of the staff.'

3. **to scrape the barrel/the bottom of the barrel** – to content oneself with poor quality when all other possibilities have been exhausted. 'Dorothy must have scraped the bottom of the barrel to have married a man like that!'

Market

4. **a captive market** – a monopoly of an essential product or service which the consumer is obliged to accept without exercising his or her normal freedom of choice. 'We can ask any price we like for our water supply; we have a captive market.'

5. **downmarket** – of poor quality, cheap; of low standing, appealing to the lower social classes. 'I know downmarket papers cost less, but I would rather pay a bit more and get one of the broadsheets.'
   a downmarket area – an area where housing is relatively cheap and therefore lived in by people who are less well off.

6. **upmarket** – catering for the more discerning public, with more prestige and higher prices. 'This restaurant in Mayfair is very upmarket and will appeal to our overseas business colleagues.'
   an upmarket area – an area at the higher end of the housing market. 'This area is going to be demolished and rebuilt with houses for the well heeled, so this whole neighbourhood will move upmarket.'

7. **to be a drug on the market** – to find no customers, something for which there is no demand. 'Gramophone records have become a drug on the market since cassettes were introduced.'

8. **to be in the market for** – to be interested in obtaining or buying something. 'We are not in the market for diamonds at present.'

9. **to play the market** – to speculate in the buying and selling of stocks and shares or commodities. 'Herbert calls it playing the market; I call it gambling.'

10. **to put something on the market** – to offer something for sale. 'We have decided to leave London, so we are putting our house on the market.'
    to come on the market – to be offered for sale.
    to come off the market – to be no longer offered for sale.

11. **to corner the market** – to obtain a monopoly of the supply of particular goods or services. 'Once a government has cornered the market, as for instance in gas or electricity, there is always a huge rise in prices.'

12. **a rising/falling market** – a rising/falling demand for goods or services which will be reflected in their prices.

13. **to price oneself out of the market** – to ask so much more money for one's services or products that customers go elsewhere. 'The school fees you are charging are so high that you are in danger of pricing yourself out of the market.'

14. **to spoil the market for** – to reduce the demand for services or products by lowering their quality or putting too many on offer. 'The dishonest advertising agencies will spoil the market for the good ones.'

15. **to flood the market** – to offer services or goods far in excess of the demand for them.

16. **to drive a hard bargain** – to come to an agreement on one's own terms without making any worthwhile concessions. 'You drive a hard bargain, but I suppose I'll have to accept your offer.'

1. **under the counter** – of goods illegally sold in shops, secretly, without the knowledge of the authorities. 'Johnson always sold the stolen jewellery under the counter to clients who could be trusted not to go to the police.'

Hill

2. **up hill and down dale** – everywhere. Idiomatically, this phrase is only used with verbs like 'look for', 'search for', 'hunt for'. 'Wherever have you been all this time? We have been looking for you up hill and down dale.'

3. **as old as the hills** – very old indeed. 'That car of yours is as old as the hills. Don't you think you ought to buy a new one?'

4. **to be over the hill** – (1) to be past one's best, one's most successful times are over. 'Mr Simpson will have to retire soon. He's getting forgetful and I think he's over the hill.' (2) to have conquered some obstacle. 'Don't worry about Bill's operation any more. He is recovering and is over the hill.'

5. **to go downhill** – to suffer a decline in one's health or fortunes. 'Poor Bill, he has gone steadily downhill since he lost his job.'
   to go down – to suffer a decline in its reputation, quality or appearance. This is only used of things, not people, especially of neighbourhoods and districts. 'This was one of the most fashionable districts in London, but it has gone right down in the last ten years.'

6. **an uphill struggle/task** – something that costs a great deal of effort but shows very little result. 'It's an uphill struggle teaching Henry Greek; he has absolutely no aptitude for languages.'

Slope

7. **a slippery slope** – a decision or action that will eventually have dire consequences. 'Allowing euthanasia is seen by some people as a slippery slope to killing off old patients.'

Peak

8. **to be at the peak of** – to be at the top of something. 'Christine shouldn't retire just yet. She is at the peak of her career.'

Pitch

9. **to carve out a pitch** – a prostitute touting for business in a certain part of a road or district. 'Nearly every large city has regions where prostitutes have carved out their pitches.'

Area, Zone

10. **a no-go area** – dangerous territory, an area to be avoided. 'New spy cameras have been installed around the town's no-go areas to reduce crime.'
    a no-go – something that cannot be considered. 'Tobacco advertising on television is a no-go.'

11. **a no-go zone** – forbidden territory. 'A three-mile Mediterranean beach has been declared a no-go zone while a high-standing government official is on holiday there.'

Directions, Bounds

12. **left, right and centre** – all around, everywhere. 'When the victim of an accident was taken to a pub and then found to be unhurt, drinks were bought for him left, right and centre.'

13. **to know no bounds** – to disregard limits and restrictions. 'The child's cheekiness towards his teacher knows no bounds and he ought to be reprimanded.'

Wilderness

14. **in the wilderness** – to have been ousted from high political office and to find that one has been forgotten by the public. 'Having served his country as a minister for some years, a personal mistake lost him his position and he found himself in the wilderness.' Also: **to be plunged into the political wilderness**.

Transport, Traffic

1. **the jet set** – a section of society which is rich and fashionable, able to travel anywhere and enjoy all the luxuries that go with such a lifestyle. 'The film actress claimed that her waiter boyfriend was only after her money, so that he could also enjoy her jet-set life of expensive hotels, luxurious yachts and lavish parties.'

2. **to railroad someone into doing something** – to force someone to do something against their will. 'When Annabel became pregnant, her parents railroaded her into marrying the baby's father.'

3. **to be/go off the rails** – not behaving properly. 'The students had much too much to drink and started to go completely off the rails.'
   to go careering off the rails – to get out of control very quickly.

4. **to be a slow coach** – to be very slow in one's actions, to keep one's companions waiting impatiently. 'What a slow coach you are! Do hurry up; everyone is waiting for you!'

5. **to jump the queue** – to try to seize an advantage without waiting one's turn. 'Everyone queues up in England. You'd make yourself very unpopular if you jumped the queue.'

6. **to miss the bus** – to lose an opportunity. 'I am 50 years old but I still haven't been promoted. Now it's too late; I've missed the bus.' cf. **'to miss the boat' 204/2**.

7. **to tell someone where to get off** – to give someone a stern rebuke. 'When Joe started lecturing me on how to paint, I soon told him where to get off. He seemed to forget that I've had years of experience at it and he is only a beginner.' The phrase refers to the bus-conductor's right to order any passenger off a bus if he or she makes trouble.

8. **to fall off the back of a lorry** – a euphemism for 'to be stolen'. 'I wonder where Philip got that crate of very expensive wine. Did it fall off the back of a lorry?'

9. **a free ride** – something for nothing. 'Whenever Jill got an invitation to a party, her younger brother came along for a free ride.'

10. **to pick up speed** – to accelerate. 'You'll have to pick up speed if you want to finish that job before the television programme starts.'

11. **a backseat driver** – someone who offers unwanted advice to the person in charge, while having no responsibility him- or herself for the way a task is performed. 'We'd manage much better without the help of backseat drivers like Williams.' The phrase refers to the passenger in the back of a car, who is always telling the driver what to do.

12. **to be the driving force** – to be the strength behind some scheme. 'Zöe's mother was the driving force to get her into university.' cf. **'the power behind the throne' 235/13**.

13. **a driven man/woman** – a highly motivated person, possessing the power to fulfil his or her aims. 'Heather Mills is the perfect example of a driven woman – someone who has suffered many setbacks in life but who is still determined to ease the suffering of amputees.'

14. **to be on a collision course with someone** – to be heading for a disagreement, confrontation with someone. 'When Mr Tibbs was promoted to head of the science department, he was soon on a collision course with the chemistry teacher who had also wanted the job.'

15. **to put a spoke in someone's wheel** – to stop someone's plans on purpose. 'Mr Jones put a spoke in his daughter's wheel by not allowing her to join her friends on the very expensive trip to New York.'

16. **the wheel of fortune** – comparing one's fate to a wheel spinning round and stopping at various points, bringing one good or bad luck. 'The wheel of fortune let Melanie become a millionaire while her sister had to live in poorer circumstances.' cf. **'a lottery / life's lottery' 311/9**.

16 The House

House

1. **to keep open house** – to be at home to visitors at all times; to offer them hospitality regardless of who they are.

2. **a rough house** – a fight, a violent disturbance. 'The soldiers are getting very aggressive. We had better leave before there is a rough house.'
   rough-house treatment – disorder and affray. 'Riders going out fox-hunting got the rough-house treatment from protesters.'

3. **a full house** – a theatre that is fully attended.
   an empty house – an empty theatre. 'The ageing actress refused to retire, even though she was playing to empty houses.'

4. **the House of God** – a church or chapel.

5. **to be houseproud** – to take pride in keeping one's house clean and tidy. 'Anne is so houseproud, her drawing-room is like a shop window.'

6. **to be housebound** – to be an invalid, unable to leave the house. 'Mrs Collins' grandmother needs a daily help very urgently because she is housebound.'

7. **a house-hunter / house-hunting** – to look for a house to live in. 'I've spent all day house-hunting in London and now I'm exhausted.'

8. **a housing boom** – a sudden rise in house prices. 'Let's take advantage of the housing boom and sell up now. We could go on a world cruise!'

9. **a household word** – something that is familiar to every household in the country.

10. **a drink on the house** – a drink that is paid for by the landlord of the public house. 'Have another; it's on the house.'

11. **in the best houses** – in the best society. The phrase suggests a country house with a retinue of servants to which the most distinguished people are invited.

12. **a house of cards** – an idea that has no foundation in fact, a wildly impracticable idea. 'His schemes for the future are no more than a house of cards that may topple over any moment.'

13. **a house of ill-fame** – a brothel.

14. **a clearing house** – premises that can be used for illegal purposes such as disposing of stolen property or exchanging drugs and money. 'That innocent-looking Mr Squires was in fact using his home as a clearing house for the gang of robbers.'

15. **a madhouse** – one in which there is great commotion and disorder. 'I'll never visit my friend again. There was so much noise all through the night that it was impossible to sleep. It was a madhouse!'

16. **house arrest** – confinement to one's own home by order of the authorities.

17. **to bring the house down** – to receive resounding applause. 'The prime minister made a powerful speech which brought the house down.' The reference is to the applause of a theatre audience.

18. **to shout the house down / don't shout the house down** – to make a terrible commotion. 'I can't study while our brother is shouting the house down.'

19. **to cry/shout something from the**

housetops – to tell everyone. 'If I'd known you were going to shout it from the housetops, I wouldn't have said anything.' The phrase derives from the East where the roofs are usually flat and are used as meeting places for the family.

1. **a house-warming party** – a party given in celebration of the new owners taking possession of their house. 'Let's have a house-warming party as soon as possible and invite all the neighbours.'

2. **to get on like a house on fire** – to be in whole-hearted agreement with someone. The idiom suggests that the relationship of the two people grows in warmth. 'We have a great deal in common and work very well together. We are getting on like a house on fire.'

3. **to be as safe as houses** – to be absolutely safe. 'Your money will be quite safe in that company. It's well managed and it has huge assets. It's as safe as houses.'

4. **a safe house** – (1) secret accommodation for someone in need of protection, arranged by the police or Social Services. 'The witness whose evidence had led to the arrest of the leader of the drugs ring was taken to a safe house by the police for his own protection.' (2) a hiding place used by a criminal trying to avoid arrest.

5. **to house-sit / house-sitter** – someone who takes the owners' place in the house while they are away, and looks after it. 'I am so glad we found a house-sitter. Now we needn't worry about burglars while we're away on holiday.' cf. '**to baby-sit** **142/15**.

6. **to have the run of the house** – to have free access to every room in the house. 'You can have the run of the house while we are on holiday.'

7. **to hang around the house** – time spent at home waiting or not doing much. 'You went to the cinema while I was hanging around the house. You might have told me!'

8. **to eat someone out of house and home** – to eat an excessive amount of one's host's food. 'My son William has a terrible appetite. At the rate he is going, he will eat us all out of house and home.'

9. **to look like the side of a house** – very fat, corpulent. 'Did you eat all my chocolates? You'll end up looking like the side of a house!' Also: **as big as a house / as tall as a house**. cf. '**to look like the back end of a bus/tram**' **104/19**.

10. **to set/put one's house in order** – to correct one's own mismanagement, often used with reference to business. 'Before we criticize others, we ought to put our own house in order.'

Home

11. **to be/feel at home with** – to be on familiar ground, to be well informed on a given subject.

12. **to feel like home** – to feel perfectly comfortable and at ease in a place which is not one's home but which feels very similar to it. 'We loved our new tent. After we had unpacked all our camping equipment into it, it felt like home.'

13. **to be 'at home' to people** – to be willing and prepared to receive friends in one's home.
    an 'at home' – a meeting of selected guests in one's own house.

14. **not at home** – a euphemism for not wishing to receive an unwelcome guest. 'The maid was instructed to tell John Lane that her mistress was not at home.'

15. **a home from home** – a place or situation where one feels completely happy and at ease, where one is treated like one of the family.

16. **home-shopping** – shopping from home, usually by mail-order catalogues or the Internet. 'This home-shopping is a great idea, Daniel. Now we have more time for other things!'

17. **to be homesick** – to have a painful longing for one's own home and family.

18. **the last home** – the last resting-place, i.e. the grave.

19. **a broken home** – family life that has been unsettled by the break-up of the parents. 'Eileen told the social worker that she turned to crime because she came from a broken home.'

1. **to be home and dry** – to succeeded in one's aim. ' "If the accused can prove he was at his mother's between 2 p.m. and 4 p.m., then he is home and dry," said the judge to defending counsel.'

2. **to do one's homework** – to be properly prepared, to master the facts before presenting one's case. 'Counsel paused for a few minutes to look at his papers before resuming his speech. It was obvious he hadn't done his homework.'

3. **to bring something home to a person** – to make someone aware of the truth, often painfully. 'His wife's nervous breakdown brought it home to Donald how cruel he had been to her.' This idiom is often connected with the idea of punishment.

4. **a home truth** – a statement that hurts someone because it points to a fault or weakness of which he or she is ashamed.
   close to home – very near the truth. 'Father's guess about our truancy yesterday hit very close to home.'

5. **nothing to write home about** – nothing special or out of the ordinary. 'Mary plays the piano quite competently but she's nothing to write home about. We were expecting much more.' The phrase suggests that a person's expectations have been disappointed.

6. **to romp home** – to leave all the others in the race far behind.

7. **to home in on** – (of a missile) to seek out and destroy a moving target after it has been launched.

Wall

8. **to go to the wall** – to fail, go bankrupt or collapse.
   the weakest go to the wall – the weakest are forced out of business by their more powerful competitors.

9. **to drive someone up the wall** – to irritate someone unbearably. 'When Alec talks about all the illnesses he has had, he drives me up the wall.'

10. **walls have ears** – you must be very careful what you say because someone may be eavesdropping. There is always a danger of being overheard, however private the conversation may be.

11. **within these four walls** – in confidence.

12. **a wall of silence** – solid unresponsiveness. 'When the politician explained the new proposals, he was met with a wall of silence.'
    to meet with/come up against a wall of silence – to receive no cooperation or assistance. 'Everyone in this village knows who the terrorist is, but all police questioning is met with a wall of silence.' cf. **'a cloak of secrecy' 193/19**; **'to be kept in the dark' 26/1**; **'to shut up/close up like a clam' 75/2**.

13. **the writing on the wall** – a warning of impending doom. 'Sanders & Duke are dismissing their staff. I am afraid the writing is on the wall for them.' From the Bible (Daniel V, 31), where King Belshazzar sees a hand writing on the wall of his palace prophesying the end of his kingdom.

14. **a hole-in-the-wall** – a cash machine which has been built into the wall of a bank. These are used to obtain money, even outside banking hours. ' "I wouldn't dream of using a hole-in-the-wall," the elderly woman muttered crossly.'

Stone

15. **to stonewall** – to defend oneself with great caution in order to avoid mistakes and thus deny one's opponent any advantage. Originally, cricketing slang for playing purely defensively, by blocking every ball and making no attempt to score.

16. **to leave no stone unturned** – to spare no effort to attain one's ends. 'The policeman promised the antique-shop owner that he would make painstaking inquiries into the theft and leave no stone unturned.'

17. **only a stone's throw from here** – within easy calling distance, a very short walk.

18. **to break stones** – to do useless, unrewarding work.

1. **a stony stare** – to stare without any recognition or feeling.

2. **to be stony-broke** (slang) – to have no money.

3. **to be stone deaf** – to be completely deaf.

4. **the water was stone cold** – the water was devoid of any warmth.

5. **to lay the corner-stone** – to complete the most essential part of a work. The corner-stone is the most important part of the building.

6. **to cast the first stone** – to make the first accusation. From the New Testament (John VIII, 7): 'Let those among you who are without sin cast the first stone.'

7. **a stepping-stone** – something that furthers one's progress. 'Jenny took the low-paid job in the bank as a stepping-stone to a higher career.'

Brick, Block

8. **a brick / a regular brick** (slang) – a kind-hearted, unselfish person. 'Jean looked after the children all the time I was in hospital. She is a regular brick.'

9. **to drop a brick** – to make a tactless remark unintentionally. 'Have you ever seen such a horrible colour for a car? It's your car! Oh dear, I have dropped a brick, haven't I?'

10. **to come down on someone like a ton of bricks** – to punish someone with great severity. 'If Brian catches you reading his diary, he'll come down on you like a ton of bricks.' cf. **'to skin alive'** 111/12.
    as heavy as a brick – extremely heavy.

11. **like talking to a brick wall** – to waste one's breath trying to persuade someone who is too obstinate to listen to reason. 'He is so dogmatic; it's like talking to a brick wall arguing with him.'

12. **to knock one's head against a brick wall** – to waste time and energy attempting the impossible. 'I told you that you would never get Alan to change his mind. You have been knocking your head against a brick wall!'

13. **to see through a brick wall** – to understand a truth which is beyond the grasp of ordinary people.

14. **to make bricks without straw** – to try to achieve some result with inadequate means. 'We were unable to give you an opinion because you didn't give us the information we needed. We can't make bricks without straw.' The reference is to the captivity of the Israelites in biblical times when they were commanded by the Egyptians to make bricks without straw: 'There is no straw given unto thy servants and they say to us make brick . . .' (Exodus V, 16).

15. **redbrick** – a modern or recently built university, as distinct from the traditional universities like Oxford, Cambridge and St Andrews, whose colleges were built of stone. The term is sometimes used in a derogatory sense.

16. **a building block** – basis of or means towards further development. 'The headmistress of a school in London suggested abolishing GCSEs as in her opinion they were not the best building blocks for A levels.'

17. **a stumbling block** – an obstacle, a hindrance. 'Research is going on into dyslexia, a condition which is an educational stumbling block for many highly intelligent children.'

Roof

18. **not to have a roof over one's head** – to be homeless. 'These poor tramps haven't got a roof over their heads. Let's do something for them.'

19. **to raise the roof** – to arouse tremendous applause.

20. **to hit the roof / to go through the roof** – (1) to be furiously angry, to explode with rage. 'When I told my father I had crashed his car, he went through the roof.' (2) **prices have gone through the roof** – prices have shot up, become very high. 'House prices in central London have gone through the roof.' cf. **'to fall through the floor'** 161/10.

Tiles

1. **to be (out) on the tiles** – to be out all hours of the night, drinking and having a good time. 'I'll give George a piece of my mind when he gets home. He's been on the tiles again.'

Chimney, Gutter, Drain, Pipe

2. **to smoke like a chimney** – to smoke incessantly.

3. **out of the gutter** – from the lowest and poorest family; without any education or breeding; with nothing to commend one socially.
   to be determined to pull oneself out of the gutter – to make an effort to achieve something again.

4. **a guttersnipe** – a hooligan, someone of very bad character. The snipe is a bird that lives on the refuse in the gutters.

5. **to go down the drain** – to be irretrievably lost, usually as a result of waste or extravagance. 'He gambled away all his inheritance; every penny went down the drain.'

6. **drainpipe-thin** – to be very thin indeed, lean, lanky, gaunt. 'The model was drainpipe-thin and very pale.' cf. **'as thin/ skinny as a rake'** 252/9; **'to look like a stick insect'** 78/12.

7. **in the pipe-line** – in preparation, not yet complete. 'John has two more novels in the pipe-line.'

Pillar, Pedestal

8. **to be driven from pillar to post** – to be driven all over the place; to find it impossible to settle down.

9. **a pillar of society** – a prominent, important member of the community who can be relied upon to give it his or her support.

10. **a pillar of strength** – a strong support in a particular cause. 'Our vicar proved to be a pillar of strength after my father's death.'

11. **to put on a pedestal** – to credit someone with qualities that he or she does not possess, to consider someone to be above criticism. 'It is a pity that Helen puts all her friends on a pedestal. Sooner or later she is disillusioned, and all her friendships end in disappointment and bitterness.'

Corner

12. **to drive someone into a corner** – to deprive an opponent of any possibility of retreat. The phrase is often used in boxing.

13. **in a tight corner** – in a dangerous position from which it is difficult to escape.

14. **to fight one's corner** – to fight hard for one's own interests. 'A minister will always resist cuts in public money for his own department. I don't blame a minister for fighting his corner' (former premier James Callaghan on TV, 1981).

15. **a hole-and-corner affair** – a love affair between two people that is kept secret to avoid shocking public opinion.

16. **to turn the corner** – to make a recovery, often said with reference to health or finance. 'The doctor says that Mary has turned the corner and is out of danger.'

17. **to cut (off) a corner** – to achieve one's objective by breaking or stretching a rule to one's own advantage.

18. **to knock the corners off someone** – to make someone conform in his or her behaviour to the accepted pattern. 'I wouldn't worry about Peter being a problem child; once he gets to boarding school, they will soon knock the corners off him.'

19. **to stand someone in a corner** – to rebuke a subordinate publicly. 'The prime minister stood the young under-secretary in the corner for attacking government policies in a newspaper article.' It used to be the custom in primary schools to stand children in the corner for misbehaving in class.

20. **all the corners of the earth** – every part of the earth.

Door

1. **to shut the door in someone's face** – to terminate any further negotiations.
    to slam the door in someone's face – this is the same as above, but more violent.

2. **to show someone the door** – to request someone to leave.

3. **to let someone/something in through the back door** – to introduce a measure in a way which one's opponents will not notice. 'The private motorcar has not been abolished yet, but there has been a great deal of back-door legislation making its use more expensive and less enjoyable – by increasing road tax, restricting parking facilities, making driving tests more difficult and so on.'

4. **to lay at someone's door** – to blame a person for something that has gone badly wrong. 'The delay in bringing relief to the victims of the earthquake was laid at the door of the government.'

5. **to leave a door open** – to offer an opportunity for further discussion.

6. **to open the door/doors** – to create new possibilities. 'The appearance of a fresh witness opened the doors to new inquiries into the fraud case.'

7. **to open the door to** – to create an opportunity for some abuse. 'When a government acts as an agent for private business, it opens the door to bribery.'

8. **behind closed/locked doors** – in complete privacy. Often used in the sense of denying a hearing to an interested party. 'The decision was reached behind closed doors and so was contrary to natural justice.'

9. **to darken someone's door** – when someone unwelcome tries to enter one's house. 'I gave the salesman a good telling-off and I don't think he will ever darken our door again.' Frequent usage: **never darken my door again!** It is often used humorously. cf. 'a cold-calling salesman' 283/7.

10. **to be next door to something** – so close as to be almost identical. 'To suppress the truth about dry-rot in the house was next door to fraud.'

11. **on one's doorstep** – very close by. 'When a man was shot down in their street, the inhabitants just couldn't believe that such a crime could happen on their doorstep.'

12. **to be a doormat** – to endure unfair treatment by others without complaining. 'I've been a doormat to you and your mother long enough, Edward. Now I'm going to leave!'

13. **the revolving-door problem** – the problem of mentally ill patients having to leave hospital, completely unprepared for life outside, and then becoming even more ill, and in some cases dangerous to the public. After this, they are forced to go back into hospital once again, and the problem repeats itself. cf. '**a Catch-22 situation**' 261/15; '**a vicious circle**' 266/18.

14. **a hand-on-the-doorknob consultation** – a patient visiting a doctor with a minor ailment who, on leaving, raises another health problem he or she was too embarrassed to mention earlier.

Hinge

15. **to hinge on** – to depend on. 'Her future career will hinge on her success in the June examinations.'

Key

16. **to have the key of the door** – to have free access to the house. A privilege granted to the children when their parents think that they are old enough to be trusted.

17. **a latch-key child** – a child who has been given a key to let himself into his home after school while his parents are still out at work. 'Most of the pupils who get into trouble at our school are latch-key children.'

18. **under lock and key** – (1) in prison. (2) well secured. 'The documents which would reveal the secret financial

transactions of the minister are being kept under lock and key.'

they can throw away the key – the prisoner's crimes are so terrible that he or she can stay locked up for ever.

1. **keyed up** – in a state of nervous expectation, as one would feel before making an important speech. 'He was all keyed up, knowing that his big moment had arrived.'

2. **to keep something low-key** – to attract little attention, to keep things subdued. 'The young couple wanted to keep their wedding low-key and so only invited their parents and closest friends.'

3. **the key to the problem** – the essential means of solving a problem.

4. **the key position** – a position of vital strategic importance.

5. **to play a key part** – to be of crucial importance. 'In the 1930s and 1940s, British scientists were the first to develop radar, which in turn played a key part in developing the atom bomb.'

6. **the key word** – the word that is needed for breaking a code.

7. **a key speech** – the most important speech. 'The prime minister was about to give his key speech on education.'

8. **a key industry** – an essential industry without which other industries cannot function properly.

9. **a key player** – (1) the most important player. 'We really can't start the game without him. He is the key player!' (2) an important businessman or politician who is determined to gain what he wants, through his intelligence or by use of cunning. The idiom can also refer to a company. 'The new travel company was seen as a key player in the fast-growing world of e-commerce.' cf. **'like *Hamlet* without the prince'** 227/7.

10. **keyhole surgery** – surgery requiring only a very small incision thanks to modern miniature instruments and the use of laser beams. Operations are monitored on a screen via fibre optics.

11. **a keyhole dress** – a dress with a hole

which enables one to catch a glimpse of cleavage. 'The film actress looked particularly seductive in her keyhole dress as she went to receive her award.'

Bell

12. **as clear as a bell / a voice like a bell** – very clear, easily heard or understood. 'Now that my tinnitus has been cured, I can hear you as clear as a bell again.' cf. **'crystal clear'** 169/16.

13. **to be as sound as a bell** – to be in the best of health. In this context, 'sound' is a cognate of the German *gesund*, meaning 'healthy' or 'in perfect order'. It alludes to the pure tone of a finely tuned bell, whereas a cracked bell is useless. cf. **'as fit as a fiddle'** 315/9; **'as right as rain'** 19/10.

14. **that rings a bell** – that sounds familiar, I've heard that before.

15. **to sound alarm/warning bells** – to warn of possible difficulties ahead. 'The transport system is in a terrible mess although warning bells have been sounding for decades.'

16. **to set alarm bells ringing** – to alert someone to danger. 'The low price for such a beautiful house set alarm bells ringing.'

17. **like the clappers** – very quickly. 'The rain suddenly came down and Melanie ran like the clappers to reach home.' A 'clapper' is the tongue or striker of a bell. It moves very quickly when it is rung. cf. **'as quick/fast as lightning'** 24/6; **'run like a bat out of hell'** 62/9.

18. **a ding-dong** – a fierce quarrel. 'My brother and I had a right old ding-dong over who should have the car at weekends.'

Window, Shutter

19. **window shopping** – looking at articles in a shop-window without buying anything.

20. **window dressing** – to display things of little or no value so that their deficiencies are concealed. 'The chief executive

manipulated the figures very cleverly to conceal the company's heavy losses. It was all window-dressing.' One dresses a window by arranging the merchandise to the best advantage so that it will attract the attention of the passers-by.

1. **to put all one's goods in the window** – to show off all one's good qualities without holding anything in reserve. To be immodest.

2. **the window of the soul** – a poetic term for the eyes.

3. **to go/fly out of the window** – not to be interested any more. 'Since she met that awful man, all her good intentions about studying economics have gone out of the window.'

4. **to throw caution out of the window** – to be unconcerned about taking risks. 'In spite of the warning, Jim threw caution out of the window and dived into the water from the tall bridge.' cf. '**to throw caution to the winds**' 23/4.

5. **a window of opportunity** – a chance to start a new project that could well be rewarding. 'With the election of a Mayor of London, a window of opportunity has arisen for improving the transport system in London.'

6. **to put up the shutters** – to close a house or business; to go into liquidation. 'The famous TV party-host will soon be putting up the shutters after 30 years in show business.'
   this is where the shutters come down – no more information is forthcoming.

Floor

7. **to cross the floor of the House** – to change political parties, to take one's seat on the opposite side of the House. The reference is to the House of Commons. 'Winston Churchill crossed the floor of the House twice during his parliamentary career.' cf. '**a political rat**' 60/7.

8. **to wipe the floor with** – to defeat decisively, to humiliate one's opponent.

9. **to have/take the floor** – (1) to be the centre of attention, when everyone is listening to you. (2) to start dancing.

10. **to fall through the floor** – to collapse, fall steeply in value; to be greatly reduced in price. 'The dollar has fallen through the floor.' 'With constant strides in new technology, the price of second-hand computers has fallen through the floor.' cf. '**to hit the roof / to go through the roof**' 157/20.

11. **to sink through the floor** – to feel extremely embarrassed. 'When she asked me in front of all the guests why I had been expelled from school, I was so embarrassed I could have sunk through the floor.' By sinking through the floor, the subject would no longer be visible and would thus avoid any further embarrassment.

12. **to get in on the ground floor** – to join forces with an enterprise that is still in an early stage of development with a view to profiting later.

13. **floor show** – a cabaret which is performed on the floor of a club or restaurant as opposed to the stage of a theatre.

Ceiling

14. **a glass ceiling** – an invisible limit to rising in one's profession. Women are generally hardest hit by this. 'Some high-powered female stockbrokers are complaining about a glass ceiling to their careers.'

Corridor, Stairs

15. **the corridors of power** – that part of Whitehall where the Civil Service Establishment wields power. From a novel of the same name by C. P. Snow.

16. **backstairs** – something underhanded, e.g. backstairs intrigue/gossip/influence, etc. 'As a result of a backstairs intrigue, she got a well-paid job in one of the ministries.' Originally, in a large house, one staircase was for the family and their guests, and a second staircase was for their servants.

Ladder

1. **the first rung of the ladder** – the first step of one's career. ' "Once you have climbed the first rung of the ladder," Jane's mother said confidently, "the rest will follow in no time!" '

2. **to take a step up the ladder/to go up the ladder** – to be promoted. 'Just one more step up the ladder and Alan will have achieved what he always wanted – to be director of the company.'

3. **the top of the ladder** – the summit of one's career or profession. 'If you want to get to the top of the ladder, you must work like a demon, and be completely ruthless.' Benjamin Disraeli likened the premiership to 'the top of the greasy pole'.

Gate, Fence

4. **a gate-crasher** – an uninvited guest.
   to gate-crash – to gain admittance to a party without having been invited.

5. **between you, me and the gate-post** – what I am telling you must not go any further, it is a secret.

6. **to be a fence** – a criminal who deals in stolen goods. 'The fence boasted to the burglar that he could easily sell all kinds of stolen goods.'

7. **to sit on the fence** – to be unwilling to make a decision or to commit oneself to either party in a dispute. 'The government is still sitting on the fence about who should fund the new and very expensive art gallery.' Frequent usage: **to be open to fresh charges of fence-sitting on . . .**

8. **to come off the fence** – to make one's intentions clear. 'The government is under increasing pressure to come off the fence over the payment of long-term care for the elderly.'

9. **to come down on the right/wrong side of the fence** – to ally oneself with the successful/unsuccessful party in a dispute.

10. **to rush one's fences** – to take premature action, to take action without proper preparation. 'Aren't you rushing your fences proposing to Christine? You've only known her a week.' The phrase is taken from show jumping.

11. **to mend one's fences** – to improve relations with someone by removing the cause of the annoyance or dispute. 'If we want to trade with that country, we had better mend our fences with it without delay.' When fences are broken, disputes between neighbours often arise over their rights to the land.

12. **garden-fence disputes** – neighbours quarrelling over various things connected with their houses and gardens, such as noisy dogs or children, broken fences, hedges or trees that grow too high and block the sunshine. 'I'm getting really tired of all these garden-fence disputes with my neighbour. If it's not his leaves blowing into my garden, it's my weeds and creepers that annoy him.'

Room

13. **to prefer someone's room to his company** – to like someone for his money rather than for his own sake.

14. **in a smoke-filled room** – senior politicians having discussions and making decisions undemocratically behind closed doors. 'It appears that the government has agreed in a smoke-filled room that some genetically modified food can be released for consumption several years before the GM safety trials end.' cf. **'a smokescreen' 15/14**; **'behind closed/locked doors' 159/8**; **'shroud someone/something in secrecy' 40/1**; **'smoke and mirrors' 168/5**.

Hall

15. **to have the hallmarks of** – to show a person's characteristics. 'The article wasn't signed but it had all the hallmarks of S. Jones.' Literally, to bear the stamp of the Goldsmiths' Company, which certifies the standard of the gold or silver article tested.

16. **Liberty Hall** – a state of chaos, a place where people may do just as they please.

'I would never send my son to that school – no discipline there at all – pure Liberty Hall!' (Goldsmith, *She Stoops to Conquer*, Act II).

1. **in the hall of fame** – the imaginary hall in which all the famous characters in history are placed.

Kitchen

2. **kitchen talk** – uneducated talk, consisting for the most part of gossip and idle chatter. 'That is only kitchen talk.'

3. **if you can't stand the heat, get out of the kitchen** – if you find the responsibilities of office too nerve-racking, you should relinquish your post. It is a saying associated with US President Harry S. Truman (1884–1972).

4. **kitchen cabinet** – a group of advisers at the disposal of the prime minister, whose salaries are financed privately. These advisers are not civil servants but have access in some cases to Cabinet minutes and other confidential documents. The term was first used in 1829 when Andrew Jackson, the US president, dismissed large numbers of civil servants and installed his own friends at the White House as his personal advisers.

Cellar

5. **to have a good cellar** – to possess a cellar that is stocked with plenty of good wine.

17 Furniture and Household Articles

Furniture

1. **part of the furniture** – a person whose presence is ignored because he or she no longer plays any part in the life of a family or enjoys their respect. 'I've been a servant here for 50 years, but no one thought of telling me that we are moving. But then, I'm only a part of the furniture.'

Bed, Cradle

2. **a good bedside manner** – a manner that inspires a patient with confidence in the doctor; a willingness to listen to the patient's complaints and to reassure him or her whenever possible.

3. **to get out of bed on the wrong side** – to get up in a bad temper. 'What's the matter with you this morning, Paul? You got out of bed on the wrong side, didn't you?'

4. **to have made one's bed and have to lie on it** – to be forced to accept the results of one's own bad decision-making. 'I warned you not to invest in those shares and now their value has gone down. You have made your bed and now you must lie on it.' From the proverb 'As a man makes his bed, so he must lie on it.'

5. **to make good/bad bedfellows** – being a good/bad partnership. 'Steven and Joshua are so different in their views. They make bad bedfellows.'

6. **to featherbed** – to cushion an industry from the effects of rising costs or competition from abroad by means of government grants and subsidies.

7. **a bed of nails** – a duty or situation which brings much annoyance or pain to a person. 'With my boss changing his instructions from one day to the next, my job has become a bed of nails.'

8. **a hotbed (of vice, sedition, reaction)** – a place where the tendency in question is nourished and developed. 'In biblical times, Sodom and Gomorrah were hotbeds of vice.'

9. **cradle-snatcher** (derogatory) – a woman who has a boyfriend much younger than herself.

Pillow, Bolster

10. **pillow talk** – confidences exchanged between husbands and wives or between lovers when they are in bed.
    to fish for pillow-talk information – said of a spy who befriends and seduces the wives of important figures solely to find out top secrets from them.

11. **to bolster up** – to give one's support to a weak or unconvincing theory, argument, etc. 'Although Reed bolstered up his theory with many new arguments, he got no support from the experts.' The bolster is used as an under-pillow for supporting the sleeper's head.

Blanket

12. **to blanket** – to cover something completely. 'Fog and rain blanket the Highland mountains in the late autumn.'
    like a blanket – (1) to feel protected by something. 'People were very kind to us. I felt their kindness like a blanket, wrapping us round' (*Mrs de Winter* by Susan Hill). (2) to feel smothered, stifled by something. 'It seemed a very long five miles, and the heat stifled us like a heavy

blanket' (*The Flame Trees of Thika* by Elspeth Huxley). cf. '**to hang over something like a pall**' 40/2.

1. **a wet blanket** – one who spoils other people's fun by ill-humour or excessive seriousness; a depressing influence. The idiom has its origin in the 17th century when farmers used wet blankets for extinguishing fires in their cornfields. Later, by association of ideas, spoilsports and killjoys were dubbed 'wet blankets'. cf. '**in the dumps / down in the dumps**' 129/6; '**to put a damper on someone**' 129/7.

2. **to be born the wrong side of the blanket** – to be illegitimate.

3. **a blanket regulation** – one that is applied to all alike, regardless of differences in size, quality and so on. 'If the minister applies this blanket regulation to every school, she will destroy many of the best.'

4. **a blanket ban** – to forbid/outlaw something completely, often in the form of an official announcement. 'A blanket ban was imposed on the sale of Belgian lamb after EU officials discovered that the sheep had been fed on fodder mixed with sewage.'

5. **blanket coverage** – a general analysis or reportage not directed at any particular group. 'The subject of race relations needs blanket coverage for the public at large.'

6. **blanket bombing** – an indiscriminate bombing campaign which completely destroys a large area. 'The war-torn country suffered greatly from the blanket bombing and begged the other countries for help.' cf. '**a scorched-earth policy**' 16/9.

Table

7. **table talk** – light conversation, talk that avoids any serious or gloomy topic.

8. **to keep the table laughing** – to keep one's guests at table entertained.
   to set the table in a roar – to set the guests at table laughing uproariously at a joke or story.

9. **to keep a good table** – to provide good cuisine and excellent wine.

10. **table manners** – polite, considerate behaviour at meals. George Mikas remarked that the French have a good table, and that the English have good table manners.

11. **to turn the tables** – to reverse the position, to seize the advantage from one's opponent. 'The Rangers were three goals down at half-time, but in the second half they turned the tables on Wandsworth and won by 5–3.' The idiom originates in the one-time custom of turning the table round in the middle of a game of chess or draughts, so that the player who had the inferior position could then take advantage of the stronger position of his opponent.

12. **to put a proposal on the table** – to make a definite offer in the course of negotiations.

13. **to table a motion** – to put forward a proposal for debate.

14. **a round-table conference** – a conference at which the participants can confer on equal terms, the shape of the table ensuring that none of the seats takes precedence.

15. **High Table** – the table in a college that is reserved for the president, the fellows and the most distinguished guests.

16. **to drink someone under the table** – to defeat one's companion in a drinking contest.

Chair, Armchair

17. **to take the chair** – to act as chairperson at a meeting, to take charge of the meeting.

18. **to address the Chair** – to direct one's remarks to the chairperson.

19. **to appeal to the Chair** – to ask for the protection of the chairperson.

20. **playing musical chairs** – a children's game. Idiomatically, it means the shuffling of portfolios among the same ministers in a government to avoid the unpleasantness of making dismissals.

1. **an armchair strategist** – one who plans a military operation from the security of his or her own home without having to fight.

2. **an armchair critic** – one who is in a position to criticize the way a job is done, without actually being involved in the work. His or her criticism therefore tends to be vague and unrealistic.

3. **an armchair traveller** – someone who looks at travel films on television or reads books on travelling from the comfort of an armchair instead of visiting the countries themselves. 'It's much safer to be an armchair traveller – and cheaper, too.'

Seat

4. **a hot seat** – a position of responsibility carrying great risks. 'The president of the United States is in the hot seat of world power.'

5. **to keep a seat warm for someone** – to keep a job until another person is ready to take it. 'Martin should have resigned his office this year, but he is staying on an extra year to keep the seat warm for you.'

6. **to take a back seat** – to retire from the active conduct of a concern and let someone else take control. 'I've been managing this company for the last 20 years; it's time I took a back seat.'

7. **to lose one's seat** – to lose a position of influence. The phrase often refers to a seat on a committee, local council or in Parliament.

8. **a seat of learning** – a retreat for scholars where learning is an end in itself, like the universities.

9. **the seat of the trouble** – the source of the difficulty or pain.

Stool

10. **to fall between two stools** – to fail through hesitation between two different courses of action, or through trying to combine both. 'Holmes fell between the stools of philosophy and mathematics. Having divided his time equally between

both subjects, he left university without a degree in either.'

11. **a stool-pigeon** – someone employed to inform on his or her companions.

12. **the stool of repentance** – a low seat in Scottish churches on which sinners were set in full view on the congregation. The phrase may be used to indicate that someone has fallen into disfavour with the authorities.

Bench

13. **to be on the bench** – to be a judge or magistrate.
    to be raised to the bench – to be appointed to a judgeship either in the High Court or the County Court.

Desk

14. **a desk general** – a general whose experience has been limited to administration, and who has had no battle experience. In the Second World War, General Eisenhower was dismissed by his critics as a 'desk general' before the invasion of Europe in June 1944.

Cupboard, Closet

15. **cupboard love** – a display of affection motivated by selfish interest. 'Jane's dog always gives me a wonderful welcome, but I'm afraid it's only cupboard love.'

16. **to come out of the closet / to come out** – homosexual men and women who declare their sexual preference, having previously kept it a secret. 'What a relief it must be to some people to be able to come out of the closet, and not hide their feelings any more.'

Shelf

17. **to be on the shelf** – to have reached an age when a woman is unlikely to receive a proposal of marriage.

18. **a shelf-life** – something that is good for only a limited period. 'Your friendship with Anne has a limited shelf-life, but our friendship will last for ever.' cf. **'to pass one's sell-by date' 283/6.**

1. **to shelve (a plan or proposal)** – to postpone indefinitely, often with the idea of putting it out of one's mind for good.

Drawer

2. **not out of the top drawer** (almost always used negatively) – not a lady or a gentleman.

Curtain

3. **it's curtains for . . .** (slang) – it's the end of, or the finish of . . . 'It will be curtains for Norman if he doesn't find the money by next Wednesday.'

4. **to draw a curtain over** – to pass discreetly over an incident, to suppress it. This is done when the scene is too painful or embarrassing to relate. cf. **'to draw a veil over' 196/8**.

5. **the Iron Curtain** – the military and political barrier which separated the Western democracies from the Warsaw Pact countries. The phrase first appeared in Dr Goebbels' diaries but was made famous by Winston Churchill in numerous speeches made after the Second World War.

Purdah

6. **to be/live/keep something in purdah** – to keep from public view. 'The minister was advised to enter a period of pre-Budget purdah to escape the wrath of the public.' The idiom derives from the veil or curtain that kept Muslim women from view by separating their living quarters from the rest of the household.

Carpet

7. **to sweep something under the carpet** – to banish from one's mind a subject that is unpleasant or embarrassing, to discourage its discussion. 'Sooner or later, you'll have to discuss Jane's marriage; it's no good sweeping the whole thing under the carpet.'

8. **to be carpeted** – to be rebuked by one's employer. In the old days when there was a carpet only in the boss's office, an employee stood on the carpet to hear complaints about his work, or to be dismissed.

9. **to roll out the red carpet** – to treat a new arrival as a very important person. 'He had a wonderful tour of the United States. Everywhere he went, they rolled out the red carpet for him.'

10. **to bite the carpet** – to be very angry. 'He was so angry at the news that he almost bit the carpet.'

11. **a carpet-bagger** – a candidate for election who has no roots or interest in the constituency he wishes to represent. The original meaning was a Unionist financier or adventurer who exploited the cheap labour in the American South after the Civil War. These adventurers carried bags made of carpet material.

12. **like a magic carpet** – as if one could be transported by magic to any place one wanted to visit. The phrase is often used in a sarcastic sense. 'I'm sorry we can't deliver the furniture before next week. We haven't got a magic carpet.'

Rug

13. **to pull the rug from under one's feet/under one** – to take one's opponent by surprise by suddenly depriving him of his advantage. 'Thomas got 50 customers to sign a complaint against the manager, but when he presented the petition to the company, they pulled the rug from under his feet by announcing the manager had already retired.' cf. **'to cut the ground from under one's feet' 107/13**; **'to take the wind out of someone's sails' 22/14**.

Picture, Frame

14. **to see/look at the whole picture** – to visualize the whole situation. 'The government must look at the whole picture when it closes rural post offices. Closure may save money on staff, but it will deprive the villagers of amenities.'

15. **to put someone in the picture** – to bring someone up to date with the latest

developments. 'As you are new to this particular project, I had better put you in the picture before we go any further.'

do you get the picture? – do you understand what I'm trying to tell you?

1. **big-picture issues** – highly topical and interesting themes shown on television news or current affairs programmes.

2. **a perfect picture** – (1) a full and accurate description. 'The author has given us a perfect picture of Tasmania.' (2) lovely to look at. 'The bride was a perfect picture.'

   picture-perfect – absolutely perfect, faultless, immaculate. 'Now, we all want this play to be picture-perfect, so let's work really hard at it.' Also: **as pretty as a picture / picture-pretty**.

3. **to be the picture of health** – to exhibit all the qualities of a healthy person: rosy cheeks, glistening skin, shining eyes, etc.

4. **a frame-up/to frame** – the fabrication of evidence with the object of incriminating an innocent party. 'Can you help me? I've been framed.'

Mirror

5. **smoke and mirrors** – to conceal a truth, show deceit in a situation. 'The taxpayer must once again pay more taxes thanks to the latest smoke-and-mirrors settlement.' The truth is obscured by, figuratively speaking, smoke, which can hide one's real intentions, and mirrors, which can give one false information – as with the distorting mirrors at a funfair which can make one look extremely fat or thin. cf. **'a smokescreen' 15/14**; **'in a smoke-filled room' 162/14**.

6. **mirrors of the universe** – various objects which have a striking similarity to natural phenomena.

   natural mirrors of the universe – examples: a sunflower closely resembles the corona of the sun during a total eclipse; a human embryo looks like Pangea (the earth long ago); a plankton cell dividing looks just like a supernova. See *Spiegelbilder des Universums* by Albrecht Ploum.

   man-made mirrors of the universe

(deliberately designed to mirror nature) – examples: a parachute has copied a dandelion clock; a plane has been modelled on an eagle; a high-jump pole has been designed to be as flexible as a wheat stalk.

Lights
(see also *Light* in Chapter 3)

7. **the lights were on but nobody was (at) home** – to be mentally deficient.

Laser Beam

8. **to focus like a laser beam on something** – to concentrate completely on one thing. 'Desperate to get more votes, the politician promised to focus like a laser beam on the economy.' 'Laser' is the abbreviation for 'light amplification by the stimulated emission of radiation'.

Torch

9. **to carry a torch for someone** – to be in love with someone who does not return one's love, or perhaps does not even know about it. 'The maths teacher carries a torch for the history teacher but he can only see her during school hours and then she is surrounded by children.' The torch meant here is a long stick set alight at the top. In former times, if a boy held a torch for a girl, it meant he was in love with her.

Candle

10. **not fit to hold a candle to / cannot hold a candle to** – not fit to compare with someone, to be in every way inferior. 'He paints quite well but he isn't fit to hold a candle to his brother.' The literal meaning was not fit to hold a light for the person doing the work to see by.

11. **to burn the candle at both ends** – to exhaust one's energy recklessly, to allow oneself insufficient rest or sleep. Often said of students who prepare hastily for an examination by working late into the night and getting up early in the morning to resume their studies. The night is thus shortened at both ends like the candle.

1. **candle-end economies** – small paltry economies that serve no purpose. 'The government should stop making candle-end economies which only annoy the public.'

Junk

2. **a pile of junk** – a lot of rubbish. 'An elderly man looked at the "Angel of the North" statue and shook his head disapprovingly: "This is just a pile of junk." ' cf. '**junk food' 174/2**; '**junk mail' 286/ 18**.

Can

3. **to carry the can** – to take the blame. 'Don't blame me if everything goes wrong. It was your decision – you must carry the can.'

Cup, Mug, Chalice

4. **my cup was full** – my happiness/bitterness was complete.

5. **to mug up** (slang) – to learn as fast as one possibly can, almost always in preparation for an examination.

6. **a poisoned chalice** – something which appears to offer something good but which could be deadly. 'The high-profile job is seen by many as a poisoned chalice and only two candidates have applied for it.'

Bottle, Crystal, Glass

7. **to hit the bottle** – to drink too much (alcohol). 'Whenever my husband has a bad day at the office, he hits the bottle.'

8. **to beat the bottle** – to conquer alcoholism. 'You said once an alcoholic, always an alcoholic, but that's not true. My uncle managed to beat the bottle.'

9. **to be on the bottle** – to be a habitual drinker. 'She's been on the bottle ever since her husband died.'

10. **to have/show a lot of bottle** – to show courage and lack of fear. 'The garage attendant showed a lot of bottle when a car thief threatened him. He threw him on the ground and held him there till the police came.'

11. **to bottle out of something** – to withdraw out of cowardice or fear. 'Alex was going to be a member of our team sailing across the Atlantic, but he bottled out at the last moment.'

12. **to bottle up (one's feelings, anger, etc.)** – to suppress one's feelings, to prevent them coming to the surface.

13. **to let the genie out of the bottle** – to bring about an unforeseeable chain of events which is difficult to stop. 'A biogenetic mistake cannot be rectified. Once a modified gene mutates in a dangerous way, it is like letting the genie out of the bottle.' Frequent usage: **it is proving immensely difficult to get the genie back in the bottle**. A genie is a spirit sealed in a bottle or other receptacle which will appear when the bottle is rubbed and fulfil the owner's wishes three times. (From the story of Aladdin in *The Thousand and One Nights*.) cf. '**opening Pandora's box' 225/6**; '**to open/open up a can of worms' 76/7**.

14. **a bottle-neck** – (1) an accumulation of unfinished goods in a factory whose production is interrupted owing to shortages of labour or materials. (2) the narrow part of a street in which the passage of traffic is constricted and delays consequently occur.

15. **a bottle blond/blonde** – someone who has dyed his or her hair blond. 'Do you think Sheila is a natural or a bottle blonde?'

16. **crystal clear** – transparently clear, so that there is no room for misunderstanding. 'I thought I had made it crystal clear that I was very much opposed to your idea.' cf. '**as clear as a bell . . .' 160/12**.
crystal air – beautiful, fresh air.

17. **a cut-glass accent** – a refined way of speaking, as spoken by the upper classes. 'My lawyer made a good impression on me. She is very well educated, very confident and speaks with a cut-glass accent.' cf. '**Queen's English' 215/5**.

Plate, Dish, Saucer

1. **to have enough on one's plate** – to have enough work or responsibility. 'I should have thought she had enough on her plate without playing nursemaid to her niece.'

2. **to be handed something on a plate** – to obtain an important advantage without having had to work for it in the usual way. 'Peter was handed the directorship on a plate, his uncle is the chairman of the company!'

3. **a signature dish** – a special dish or delicacy ordered from a well-known chef. 'Here's a special treat for your Silver Wedding anniversary: dinner in a top London restaurant with a signature dish by the most famous chef in town!'

4. **to dish out** (slang) – to supply in plentiful measure. 'They enjoy dishing out advice.'

5. **a flying saucer** – possibly an unidentified object from another planet, but its existence has never been proved.

6. **eyes as big as saucers** – eyes that become very large and round, usually with delight. 'Oliver's eyes were as big as saucers when he saw his birthday present – a new flat-screen computer.' Also: **eyes as big as plates**. cf. **'eyes look/are like golf balls' 301/15**.

Knife, Fork

7. **an accent you could cut with a knife** – a very strong accent, one that is immediately noticeable. 'As soon as he opened his mouth, I knew he was a Yorkshireman. You could have cut his accent with a knife.'

8. **words go through one like a knife** – words which are painful to hear, which cause one anguish. ' "I'm very sorry, but I don't love you any more, Philip." Her words went through me like a knife.' Also: the wind cuts into/through someone **'like a knife / like a thousand knives'**; a tree goes through a house **'like a knife through butter'**; words, actions, etc., slice through officialdom

'like a hot knife through butter'. cf. **'words/actions feel like a sword through one's heart' 245/1**.

9. **to be/walk on a knife-edge** – to be in the uncomfortable position of having to please both parties in a dispute. 'My two best friends are having a fierce quarrel. I have to walk on a knife-edge between them.'

   a knife-edge vote – a very closely drawn vote. 'The ministers were in great suspense over the next day's crucial, knife-edge vote on Europe.' cf. **'within a whisker' 91/11**.

10. **under the knife** – on the operating table.

    to have a horror of the knife – to be in great fear of an operation.

11. **from pen to knife** – from the first visit to a doctor to the eventual referral to a surgeon for the operation. ' "At last my operation is behind me," Glenda sighed happily. "It has taken one whole year from pen to knife." ' cf. **'the golden hour' 10/4**.

12. **a fork in the road** – the junction of two divergent roads.

13. **to fork out** – to pay out money on behalf of another person who has accumulated a big bill.

Spoon

14. **to be spoon-fed** – to be given so much assistance that the subject has no need to make any effort on his own behalf. 'The nationalized industries had been spoon-fed for so long that they no longer cared whether they gave value for money, or made a profit or loss.' cf. **'to dumb down / dumbing down' 132/1**.

15. **to be awarded the wooden spoon** (ironical) – to get a bad mark for doing something wrong, in contrast with winning the gold or silver spoon. 'Richard got the wooden spoon for failing to stand up for his members.' The 'wooden spoon' is similar to the 'booby prize', wood being material of very small value. Formerly a custom at Cambridge University when a wooden spoon was awarded to the

student who did worst in the examinations.

1. **to need a long spoon** – to need extreme caution in one's dealings with an evil person. 'If you do business with Roberts, you will need a long spoon; he is a terrible liar.' The phrase is derived from the proverb 'He needs a long spoon who sups with the devil'.

2. **to count one's spoons** – to make sure one's guest hasn't stolen any valuables, the suggestion being that the guest is a bad character. 'The more he talked of his honour, the faster we counted the spoons' (*The Conduct of Life* by R. W. Emerson).

3. **like digging a ditch with a spoon/ teaspoon** – to go about something in a completely ineffective way; to undertake a laborious task with inadequate equipment. 'Why do you want to write the whole manuscript with a typewriter when you have a brand new computer? It'll be like digging a ditch with a spoon.'

Sieve

4. **to have a memory like a sieve** – to have a very bad memory. 'When it comes to people's names, I have a memory like a sieve.' The sieve, being full of holes, is unable to retain liquid poured into it. Similarly a bad memory is incapable of retaining information, impressions, etc.

Pot

5. **to go to pot** – to ruin oneself or one's prospects. 'Harry has let his business go to pot.'

6. **to take pot luck** – to eat whatever has been cooked just for the family. This is often said to an unexpected guest.

7. **to keep the pot boiling** – (1) to keep things moving at a lively pace, to maintain the momentum. 'If you want to keep the pot boiling, you'd better think of a new game or the children will get bored.' (2) to maintain one's living standards. 'While Father is looking for a new job, Mother is working part-time to keep the pot boiling.'

8. **a pot-boiler** – work that is well below the level of the writer's ability, done for the sake of making money quickly. Potboilers are often produced quickly by well-known writers to capitalize on their reputation.

9. **in the melting pot** – in a fluid condition when the outcome is still uncertain. 'In mid-term, with more than three million unemployed, the fortunes of the government were in the melting pot.' From the title of a novel by Israel Zangwill.

10. **a case of the pot calling the kettle black** – to blame someone for a fault that one has oneself in equal or greater degree.

11. **a pot of money** – a large sum of money obtained all at once from speculation or gambling.
    to have pots of money (slang) – to be in possession of a fortune. 'He spends every winter at St Moritz. His father has got pots of money.'

12. **a pot shot** – a shot taken at a sitting target, considered unsporting.

13. **a tin-pot** (army slang) / **tin-pot official** – (1) a self-important official who inspects an active unit in the army and expects a lot of ceremony and fuss. (2) a small, uninteresting place which considers itself important – '**a tin-pot fair**', '**a tin-pot village**', etc. Used as an adjective, it means 'cheap', 'paltry', 'inferior'. 'Be very careful when you go to that country, Simon. It's being run by a tin-pot dictator.' Tin pots are known to shine very conspicuously but the metal they are made out of is very thin compared with that of other traditional cooking pots, e.g. ones of copper or iron. cf. '**banana republic**' 183/13; '**little tin god**' 42/7.

14. **pot** (slang) – soft drugs, like marijuana.

Pan

15. **a flash in the pan** – a chance success which is unlikely to be repeated. 'Robin's book was a great success, but he hasn't written one since; I'm afraid it was only a flash in the pan.'

16. **out of the frying-pan into the fire /**

to jump out of the frying-pan into the fire – to exchange a bad situation for one that is even worse. 'Rolf changed his job because he wanted more freedom, but in his new job he couldn't leave the office without the manager's permission. It was a case of out of the frying-pan into the fire.'

Pressure Cooker

1. **like a pressure cooker** – to be full of tension; one's nerves are near breaking point. 'The children at this school are having to work far too hard. The pressure-cooker atmosphere is causing many of them to have nervous breakdowns.'

Grill, Griddle

2. **to grill someone** – to interrogate someone very intensively, with the object of breaking a person's resistance and extracting a full confession.

3. **as hot as a griddle/furnace/oven** – boiling hot, burning, scalding. 'Jennifer quickly put her sandals on when she noticed the pavement under her feet was as hot as a griddle.'

Aga, Backburner

4. **an Aga saga** – a novel showing middle-class English country life, describing the ups and downs of the local community. 'The English novelist Joanna Trollope became famous for her Aga sagas and has sold more than five million books.' The Aga is a British-manufactured stove, and there are about 250,000 of them scattered around the world.

5. **to go/put something on the backburner** – to postpone, attend to something later. 'We can't do all the work at once; some of it will have to be put on the backburner.'

Bucket

6. **to kick the bucket** (slang) – to die. One explanation of the phrase is that the suicide kicks away the bucket on which he is standing after he has tied the rope round his neck.

7. **to sweat buckets** – to be very anxious and apprehensive. 'Although Gerald was innocent, he sweated buckets waiting for the verdict of the Court.' cf. '**to be in a cold sweat**' 20/13.

Brush

8. **to have a brush with** – to come into conflict with someone else. 'He had a brush with the law yesterday.'

9. **a brush-off** – the dropping or rejection of a friend. 'After I had waited an hour for her, she rang up to say she didn't want to see me again. It was a real brush-off.'

10. **to brush to one side/aside** – to ignore or make little of.
    to brush over – to disregard. 'When I told him I hadn't enough money to repay him, he brushed over the incident with a wave of his hand.'

11. **to be tarred with the same brush** – to be suspected of having the same faults as one's relations or associates. 'Just because Dennis has been in prison, no one will have anything to do with his brothers and sister. They have all been tarred with the same brush.'

12. **as daft as a brush** – very silly, stupid. 'Why on earth did you plant the oak tree right in front of your kitchen window? You're as daft as a brush, Linda.' The idiom might once have been 'as soft as a brush' (in northern England, 'soft' means 'a bit slow', 'stupid'), or 'as daft as a brush without bristles'.

13. **to brush up (one's French, Spanish, etc.)** – to renew one's knowledge of a subject; often used in connection with a foreign language that has been neglected. 'I'll be staying in Hamburg for the next four weeks to brush up my German.'

14. **a toothbrush moustache** – a short, bristly moustache. Also: **a pencil moustache**. cf. '**a goatee beard / a goat-like beard**' 59/4.

Sink, Tap

15. **a sink/den of iniquity** – a place of vice and corruption. 'The vicar denounced the village as a sink of iniquity.'

1. **on tap** – always available, like water from a tap.

Sponge, Soap

2. **to soak something up like a sponge** – to be able to take in an enormous amount of information without any effort. 'Melvin can soak up general knowledge like a sponge. I'm sure he'll do well in the TV quiz show.' A natural sponge consists of a colony of thousands of tiny creatures and it can absorb a large amount of water.

3. **to throw up the sponge** – to admit defeat, to be guilty of cowardice. The phrase is taken from boxing, when the second throws the sponge into the ring to indicate that his man is unable to go on with the fight.

4. **to sponge on someone/a sponger** – to squeeze money out of another person without giving anything in return; someone who does this.

5. **to soft soap** (slang) – to conciliate a person one has wronged with false reassurances and compliments. cf. **'soothing syrup' 178/1**.

6. **soap opera** – an inferior play in serial form on radio or television.
   a docu-soap – a documentary in the form of a soap opera. 'The docu-soap featured the progress of four overweight women who worked in a food factory and who were determined to lose weight.'

7. **soap-box oratory** – speaking in public on a make-shift platform or soap-box. 'If you want to enjoy soap-box oratory, you should go next Sunday to Speaker's Corner in Hyde Park.'

Razor

8. **as sharp as a razor/razor-sharp** – very sharp indeed. 'Careful with those scissors, Sam. They're razor-sharp.'

9. **razor-sharp brain/wit** – to be highly astute, keen-witted. 'The actors were all very nervous when they saw Roy Hawthorn in the front row – a critic famous for his razor-sharp brain and merciless pen.' Also: **a razor-sharp observation**; **razor-tongued**.

10. **razor-thin** – extremely thin.
    a razor-thin margin – an extremely narrow margin.

Peg

11. **square pegs in round holes** – people who are not suitable for their work or surroundings. 'That man should never have become a lawyer. He's a square peg in a round hole.'

12. **to take down a peg** – to reduce someone's self-importance, deflate his or her pride. The idiom suggests corrective action which falls short of total humiliation. 'The office-boy has been taking too much on himself lately. He was beginning to forget his position. I had to take him down a peg this morning.'

13. **a peg to hang something on** – an opportunity or excuse for discussion. 'The inspector said that he only used grammar in his English language classes as a peg for conversation, and that grammar had no value in itself.'

Handle

14. **to fly off the handle** – to lose one's temper, speak violently, to lose one's self-control. 'When I told Harry that I would have to charge him for the work I had done for him, he flew off the handle and started to shout at me.' cf. **'to go up in the air' 12/4**.

15. **to have a handle to one's name** – to have a title of rank or honour, such as Viscount, Lord, Professor. 'Please remember I have a handle to my name. I am Professor Chapman to you.'

16. **to give a handle to** – to provide evidence for rumour-mongers and gossips.

17. **to be good at handling people** – to know how to deal with people. The phrase has a commercial sense, and often suggests the idea of making use of people to suit one's own interests.

18 *Food*

Food

1. **food for thought** – something that is worth considering seriously. 'The idea of accepting the euro gives a lot of people food for thought.'

2. **junk food** – an unhealthy diet of ready-made food which has little nutritional value, such as chips, hamburgers, crisps, sweets. 'Joey would lose a lot of weight if only he would cut out all that junk food and take some exercise.'

3. **fast food** – convenience food, usually frozen or processed food, such as pizzas, chips and hamburgers, which can be cooked and served very quickly. 'Jane is so busy at work – for lunch she either buys a sandwich or eats at a fast-food restaurant near the office.'

4. **slow food** – mostly fresh and locally grown food which is prepared in restaurants with loving care, and eaten at one's leisure. Slow food is the complete opposite of fast food – it takes much longer to prepare and to eat.

5. **mood food** – food that releases the chemical endorphin, which has the power to make one feel really happy. Examples are: fresh strawberries (especially with sugar and cream), chocolate and ice cream. Other life-enhancing foods are: **magic food** – honey, yogurt, potatoes, apples, pasta; **brain food** – fish; **beauty food** – milk, fruit, vegetables; **super foods / wonder foods** – seaweed, kiwi fruit, cabbage, prunes, bilberries, black-bread, sardines, ginger, garlic, soya milk.

Milk

6. **to milk** – to swindle or cheat. 'The tourists were milked by the souvenir sellers.'

7. **the milk of human kindness** – compassion, sympathy. 'Pamela is clever and hard-working but she lacks the milk of human kindness.'

8. **it's no use crying over spilt milk** – it is useless to regret one's past mistakes. We cannot undo the past.

9. **milk and water** – insipid, feeble. 'These milk and water policies won't help the country. We need something more drastic.'

10. **a land of milk and honey** – a land overflowing with the good things of life, a land abounding in riches.

11. **mother's milk** – that which supplies an essential need. 'The professor's revolutionary ideas were mother's milk to his students.'
    to imbibe with one's mother's milk – to adopt instinctively. 'He imbibed a hatred of the old order with his mother's milk.'

Cream

12. **to cream off / to skim the cream** – to take the best. 'Oxford and Cambridge are still creaming off the most brilliant scholars, despite all the social changes that have taken place since the end of the war.'

13. **the cream (of society, etc.)** – the aristocracy, the most highly favoured class. The phrase is often used ironically. From the French '*la crème de la crème*'.

Cheese

1. **to be as different as chalk and cheese** – to be completely different, to have nothing in common. 'You'd never think that Paul and Sue were brother and sister. They are as different as chalk and cheese.'

2. **not to know chalk from cheese** – not to know one thing from another. 'Don't offer Susan our most expensive wine. Let her have a cheaper one – she doesn't know chalk from cheese anyway.'

3. **cheese-parings** – objects of no more value than cheese-parings, junk or trash. 'When the old man died, they found only cheese-parings in his house.'

    to be cheese-paring – to be extremely mean, to give grudgingly. 'The father was so cheese-paring with his son's pocket money that the boy hadn't enough money to buy a table-tennis bat.' Frequent usage: **official cheese-paring**.

4. **a big cheese** – a very important person with much power and influence. 'The big cheese at the town hall is going to introduce new parking meters in the town centre.' cf. **'a big fish in a small pond' 73/2**; **'a big-wig' 196/9**.

5. **to be cheesed off** (slang) – to be fed-up, bored, disgruntled.

6. **hard cheese!** – bad luck! 'That was hard cheese spraining your ankle just at the start of your holiday.' The phrase usually indicates a lack of sympathy for the victim.

Eggs

7. **to have egg on one's face** – to be humiliated. 'Paul couldn't understand Marie-Louise when she asked him a simple question in French, although he has always boasted that he can speak French fluently. When he left, he had egg all over his face.'

8. **a bad egg** – a bad character, a rascal. 'We are so worried; our daughter has made friends with a very bad egg.'

9. **an egg-head** (US English) – an intellec-

tual, probably from the belief that a long head with a high forehead, i.e. an egg-shaped head, is a sign of superior intelligence.

10. **to tread upon eggs** – to broach a subject with the utmost delicacy, as if treading on eggs, trying not to break them.

11. **like walking/treading on egg-shells** – to proceed with the utmost delicacy and caution. 'There's an important business deal coming up and my boss is very tense and short-tempered. It's like walking on egg-shells working for her today.' Also: **something is egg-shell thin**.

12. **as sure as eggs is eggs** – absolutely certain, as certain as night follows day. 'Eggs is eggs' might be a humorous or misunderstood version of the mathematical 'x is x'; 'eggs' and 'x' do sound quite similar.

13. **don't put all your eggs in one basket** – don't invest all your money in one thing, but spread your risks.

14. **you can't make an omelette without breaking eggs** – you can't achieve anything in this life without causing somebody pain. cf. **'no pain, no gain' 135/18**.

15. **to over-egg the cake/pudding** – to exaggerate very badly. 'When Jones told the chairman that it was a privilege to work for him, and then called for a vote of thanks for him from his workmates, we all felt that he was over-egging the cake.'

16. **to unscramble** – to undo, to change back. 'Now that so much money has been spent on the plans, it will be difficult to unscramble them.' The reference is to scrambling eggs; once they have been scrambled, they cannot be cooked in any other way.

Butter

17. **as soft as butter** – (1) very soft, mushy. 'The little boy stepped on to the newly cemented driveway, but to his surprise the cement was still as soft as butter.' (2) effeminate; submissive, weak. 'You needn't be afraid of my father, Patricia. He looks very stern but I promise you he's as soft as butter really.'

18. **to butter up** – to flatter, to pay insincere

compliments to someone. 'The boys buttered up the new master in the hope of getting less homework.'

1. **to spread the butter too thick** – to flatter, to exaggerate one's praise.

2. **butter-fingers** – someone who lets something slip between his or her fingers as if they were made of butter. 'That's the third time you've dropped the ball. What a butter-fingers you are!'

3. **to look as if butter wouldn't melt in one's mouth** – to look very innocent, although one is not innocent at all. 'He looked as if butter wouldn't melt in his mouth, but he didn't take me in. I knew he had done it.'

4. **a butter mountain** – the name given to the huge reserve of butter maintained by the EU in order to ensure that the butter brought to market is not sold too cheaply. Note the similarity to the term '**wine lake**' which serves to maintain the prices of wine in the EU.

Fat

5. **the fat will be in the fire** – there will be an explosion of anger. This happens when news of someone's misbehaviour gets out. 'If Father hears you've been gambling on the Stock Exchange with his money, the fat will be in the fire.' The derivation is from the spitting and spluttering of a fire when fat is thrown into it.

6. **to live on/off the fat of the land** – to live in the most luxurious conditions.

7. **a fat lot** (ironical) – nothing at all, none at all. 'A fat lot of good that will do you.'

Bread

8. **the bread-winner** – the wage-earner who supports the family. 'With Father ill, our eldest brother has become the bread-winner of the family.' Note that '**bread**' and '**dough**' are slang words for 'money'.

9. **on the bread-line** – in a state of great poverty, when one is obliged to queue up for one's ration of food. It has come to mean poverty in general.

10. **to take the bread out of someone's mouth** – to deprive someone of his or her living. 'If you open your shop next door to Harry's, you will be taking the bread out of his mouth.'

11. **as easy as slicing bread** – extremely easy, not at all difficult. 'Now that Mr Higgins had a new electric saw, getting the logs ready for the fire was as easy as slicing bread.' Note also the phrase '**the best thing since sliced bread**'. cf. 'as easy as falling off a log' 50/20; 'as easy as shelling peas' 185/3.

12. **one's bread and butter** – one's living. 'I can't afford to give it up. It's my bread and butter.'

13. **bread-and-butter issues** – political questions concerning health, education and employment. 'I think the most important task for a government is to concentrate on bread-and-butter issues.'

14. **the bread and butter of a business** – the main source of a business's income. 'The business they are doing with Japan is coming along nicely, but the bread and butter is with Europe.'

15. **to quarrel with one's bread and butter** – to find fault with one's livelihood. 'I wouldn't quarrel with your husband's bread and butter if I were you. If he gives up his job, you will have nothing to live on!'

16. **to know which side one's bread is buttered** – to know where one's interest lies. 'However much he sympathizes with you, he won't say anything to offend his boss. He knows which side his bread is buttered.'

17. **to have one's bread buttered on both sides** – to have a very easy life, to obtain an easy comfortable living.

18. **a bread-and-butter letter** – a thank-you letter for hospitality from a departed guest.

Loaf, Crust

19. **use your loaf!** (vulgar) – use your brain; think.

20. **to earn a crust** – to earn some money.

1. **to be crusty** – to be cantankerous, peevish, irritable.

Sandwich

2. **to sandwich between/in between** – to squash between, insert between, like the filling in a sandwich. 'On the flight, I was sandwiched in between two very fat passengers so that I scarcely had room to raise my fork to my mouth.' 'Sandwich' derives from the Earl of Sandwich (1718–92), a passionate gambler who did not like to leave the gaming-table to dine but instead would ask his servant to bring him two slices of bread with meat in between which he ate while still playing.

3. **a sandwich generation / the meat or filling in the sandwich** – people who find themselves trapped between two completely different situations, such as looking after their children and caring for their elderly parents. 'Poor Brenda – she really is a member of the sandwich generation. She's stuck in the house nearly all day, having to look after her ageing parents and her small children.'

4. **a sandwich course** – a course which provides practical instruction as well as lectures on theory, the practical being 'sandwiched' between the theoretical.

5. **a sandwich child** – the middle child of three siblings.

6. **a sandwich man** – a man who carries advertising boards both in front and behind; so called because the man is sandwiched between the two boards.

7. **a jam sandwich** – a white police car with a red stripe along its side.
   a lettuce sandwich – a white Royal Parks Constabulary police car with a green stripe along its side.

Toast

8. **to be as warm as toast** – to be comfortably warm, very warm.

9. **to have someone on toast** – to have someone in one's power, to enjoy a decisive advantage over someone, usually in consequence of some mistake he or she

has made. 'Now, I've got you on toast. You must do as I say.'

Crumb

10. **a crumb of comfort** – a small consolation, a small mercy. 'One crumb of comfort is that, although he will be bedridden, he can continue with his writing.'

Wafer

11. **one's patience is stretched/wearing wafer-thin** – one's patience is wearing out. 'Robert was a most unwilling pupil and his maths teacher's patience was stretched wafer-thin.'

Honey, Syrup, Treacle

12. **to be as sweet as honey** – to be unnaturally sweet, perhaps from some ulterior motive. 'The girls were as sweet as honey as long as I did what they wanted.' cf. '**to be as sweet as pie**' 180/3.

13. **a honey trap** – to lure someone into a desirable situation, often sexual, which can later be exploited. 'The famous footballer fell into a honey trap when he became deeply attracted to a pretty blonde journalist and told her that he took drugs.' Common usage: **to be compromised in a classic honey trap**. cf. '**to blackmail someone**' 8/8.

14. **a honey-pot town** – a town which has a very good infrastructure, the very best hospital and schools, well-kept buildings and parks, a good shopping centre and well-organized leisure activities. This kind of a town attracts people in great numbers – like bees to honey. 'I've always wanted to live in a honey-pot town. Let's consult an estate agent and try to buy a house in one.'

15. **honey-pot areas** – beautiful parts of the countryside. 'The government is planning to put a tax on tourists visiting the honeypot areas of England, such as the Cotswolds or the Peak District.'

16. **the honeymoon is over** – criticism which was muted for the first few weeks (of a new government's term of office, a

new appointment, and so on) now becomes unrestrained. The allusion is to the change in attitude of the newly married couple which often occurs when the honeymoon is over.

1. **soothing syrup** – words designed to comfort rather than tell the truth. cf. **'soft soap'** 173/5.

2. **a voice as smooth as syrup** – smooth-spoken, soft, suave, flattering. 'The door-to-door salesman was tall and handsome, and his voice was as smooth as syrup.'

3. **like thinking through treacle** – to be unable to think clearly. 'After drinking too much at the party and coming home too late, Philip had trouble with his physics exam the following morning. "It was like thinking through treacle," he later told his friends.' Also: **like walk-ing/wading through treacle**.

Jam

4. **to be in a jam** – to be in great difficulties, to be in a mess, like a fly caught in a jar of jam from which it is unable to extricate itself.

5. **jam-packed** – squeezed together very tightly. 'The underground trains are always jam-packed during the rush-hour.' cf. **'economy-class syndrome'** 133/9; **'sardine class'** 74/8.

6. **money for jam** – money that is made with no effort. 'All I had to do was to walk up and down the room and smile at the customers. It was money for jam.'

7. **do you want jam on it?** – don't be so greedy; be content with what you've got.

8. **it's jam tomorrow, jam yesterday, but never jam today!** – you are always boasting about what you have given us in the past and what you are going to give us in the future. Unfortunately, nothing ever comes of your promises, and we are still as badly off as ever. From Lewis Carroll's *Through the Looking-Glass*: 'The rule is, jam to-morrow and jam yesterday – but never jam to-day.'

Sugar, Sweets, Chocolate

9. **to sugar the pill** – to make something which is unpleasant seem less so. 'I shall sugar the pill by sending Owen on a week's paid holiday before I make him redundant.'

10. **a toffee-nosed person** (mildly derogatory) – an upper-class person. A 'toffee-nose' is one that points upwards in a snobbish, disdainful manner.

11. **I can't jump for toffee** – I jump very badly; the idea behind the phrase being 'I couldn't jump well, even if you offered me a toffee to do it'.

12. **to dole something out like toffees** – to hand out liberally, in generous amounts. 'Unfortunately, it is still common medical practice to dole out antibiotics like toffees.'

13. **a lollipop man/lady** – nickname for a traffic warden who escorts children across the road.

14. **chocolate box** – a face which possesses pretty features but is lacking in individuality or distinction, the kind of 'pretty' face one sees on the lid of a chocolate box. 'She was a nice chocolate box – nothing more.' Also: **chocolate-box image/portrait**. 'The chocolate-box image of that part of the coast isn't true to life. The weather there is usually terrible.'

15. **as useless as a chocolate kettle** – of no use at all, ineffectual. 'The wind's blowing all my papers away and you're just standing there, staring. You're as useless as a chocolate kettle!' Also: **as useless as a chocolate fireguard**.

Jelly, Blancmange

16. **to shake/tremble/quiver like a jelly** – to shake, tremble with fear, anxiety or nervousness. 'Our neighbours' dog frightened Josh; the poor little boy was shaking like a jelly.' Also: **to turn someone to jelly with a glance**; **to laugh like a jelly**.

17. **to run one's legs to jelly** – to exhaust oneself running around. 'Mrs Wilby ran

her legs to jelly trying to buy all the odds and ends for her daughter's birthday party before the shops closed.' Also: **legs like jelly/blancmange; jellied legs**.

1. **like gripping blancmange** – to attempt the impossible, a hopeless task. ' "Getting that burglar to admit to all his crimes will be as difficult as gripping blancmange," the detective sighed.' cf. **'as easy as juggling with soot' 15/15; 'like swimming through porridge' 180/7**.

Cake, Pancake, Bun, Biscuit

2. **you can't have your cake and eat it** – you have a choice, meaning either/or, not both. 'You must make up your mind whether you want to buy a house with Uncle Tom's legacy, or invest the money. You can't have your cake and eat it.'

3. **a piece of cake** – something very easy to do, requiring little or no effort. 'The general knowledge examination was terribly easy. It was a piece of cake.' The full phrase was originally 'It's as easy as eating a piece of cake'.

4. **a cake walk** – something thought to be very easy, completely unproblematic. ' "I've studied hard these last three years, so the exams should be a cake walk," Martin assured his parents.'

5. **icing on the cake** – an extra incentive which is not necessary, but gives a great deal of pleasure. 'If they send me to Saudi Arabia, I shall get a salary increase of 25 per cent with my promotion, but the icing on the cake will be a two months' paid holiday every two years.'

6. **a slice of the cake** – a share of the profits. 'After such a wonderful year, your workers will want a slice of the cake.'

7. **to go like hot cakes** – to sell very quickly, to be snapped up. 'The new line in sports cars is going like hot cakes; there is a crazy demand for them.' Hot cakes, fresh out of the oven, taste very delicious and are eaten very quickly. The idiom is of US origin and has been in use since the end of the 19th century when one began to buy hot cakes, freshly baked from market stands and carts, and ate them on the spot. cf. **'to go like a bomb' 247/5**.

8. **as nutty as a fruitcake** – mad, eccentric. 'When Bill dressed up as a clown and joined the carnival parade, his friends thought he was as nutty as a fruitcake.' In the 19th century, 'nutty' meant 'spicy'. 'Nutty' is also one of many English expressions for 'insane' or 'mad'. cf. **'a nut-case' 186/6; 'to be off one's nut / to be nuts' 186/5**.

9. **to fall as flat as a pancake** – to have no effect at all. Sometimes abbreviated to **'fall flat'**. 'The joke fell flat; nobody laughed.'

10. **one's chest is as flat as a pancake** – to have a small bosom. 'You can't wear that low-cut dress. Your chest is as flat as a pancake!' Also: **one's hair is as flat as a pancake**.

11. **the fishcake syndrome** – a deep yearning in an adult for the food cooked by one's mother when one was a child.

12. **hair done in a bun** – with the hair piled up in the shape of a bun.

13. **the doughnutting of a town** – this is what planners term the neglect of inner-city areas (hence the empty inner ring of the doughnut), leading to slums and impoverishment. It also refers to the building of enormous supermarkets, leisure centres, etc., on the outskirts of towns. cf. **'a brownfield site' 8/15; 'a greenfield site' 5/4; 'greenbelt' 5/5**.

14. **that takes the biscuit!** – used ironically for something scarcely credible because it is so absurd. 'That takes the biscuit. The teacher has proposed to his granddaughter's schoolfriend.' Note US form: **that takes the cake!**

15. **that's the way the cookie crumbles** (US English) – that's life; words used to comfort someone when things have gone wrong.

Pie, Pastry

16. **pie in the sky** – hopes and dreams that will never be realized. 'Universal brotherhood and peace is a wonderful ideal but, I am afraid, it is all pie in the sky.' cf.

'castles in Spain' 211/3; 'castles in the air' 12/1.

1. **to eat humble pie** – to submit or apologize humbly. 'After boasting that he would win the boxing tournament, he had to eat humble pie when he was knocked out in the first round.' 'Humble pie' was made from the offal of deer and offered to the footmen at a banquet.

2. **to have a finger in every pie** – to take a meddlesome interest in many affairs. 'When Mark heard there was to be a jumble sale, he was soon busy organizing the stalls. He has a finger in every pie.'

3. **to be as sweet as pie** – very charming, often used sarcastically. 'She could be as sweet as pie if she wanted to get something out of me'. cf. '**to be as sweet as honey**' 177/12.

4. **as pale as pastry** – very pale, to look ill. 'Jane was in bed with flu and looked as pale as pastry.' cf. '**as pale as death**' 38/6.

Pudding

5. **the proof of the pudding is in the eating** – the test is whether it works or not. 'The yacht has elegant lines all right, but how will she sail? The proof of the pudding will be in the eating.'

6. **a roly-poly** – someone who is short and rather plump. 'Is that our new biology teacher? She's quite a roly-poly, isn't she!' Roly-poly is a pudding, in which jam or fruit is spread on dough and rolled up, then baked.

Porridge

7. **like swimming through porridge** – to find something extremely difficult, heavy-going. 'Trying to understand the complicated treaty was like swimming through porridge for the politicians.' cf. '**as easy as juggling with soot**' 15/15; '**like gripping blancmange**' 179/1.

Spaghetti

8. **spaghetti junction** – the centre of a whole network of roads near Birmingham; so called because the pattern of the roads resembles spaghetti.

Meat

9. **there's a lot of meat in it** – something which gives one plenty to think about. 'I like a novel with plenty of meat in it, for instance Tolstoy's *War and Peace*.'

10. **it must have been meat and drink to you** – it must have given you enormous satisfaction. Often used when a person's critics acknowledge they have been in the wrong. 'The apologies of her old rival were meat and drink to her.' cf. '**music to one's ears**' 315/1.

11. **one man's meat is another man's poison** – what favours one person, injures another. 'The epidemic kept the young doctor busy all day. One man's meat is another man's poison.'

12. **to make mincemeat of someone** – to win a devastating victory over an opponent. 'She made mincemeat of his arguments. Under her cross-examination, his case collapsed.' The idea comes from chopping meat up into tiny pieces and serving it as mince.

13. **to beef about** (Australian colloquialism) – to complain about.

14. **as dead as mutton** – completely dead. cf. '**as dead as a door-nail**' 250/11; '**as dead as Queen Anne**' 229/11.

15. **mutton dressed as lamb** – an older woman who dresses up to look like a young one. The phrase can be extended to ideas. 'Their ideas are exactly the same as 20 years ago; only the jargon has changed. Mutton dressed as lamb.'

16. **to talk tripe** – to talk utter nonsense. As well as being slang, the phrase can be very rude. 'I don't agree with a word you are saying. You are talking tripe.' Tripe is the lining of a cow's stomach, and is considered a delicacy in the north of England.

17. **salami tactics** – achieving one's object-

ive in small steps, like cutting salami up into slices.

1. **to be in a stew** – to be in a mess, to be in an awkward situation. 'Can you help me out, Andrew? I'm in such a stew; I have to pay my rent tomorrow and have run out of cash.'

2. **to stew in one's own juice** – to take the consequences of one's own actions. 'How many times have I told you not to borrow money? This time I am not going to help you out. You can stew in your own juice.' This originates from the time when people were burnt at the stake and had to 'fry in their own grease'.

3. **to bring home the bacon** – to succeed, achieve one's aim, to supply the needs of one's family. 'With all his faults, her husband certainly brings home the bacon. She can't complain on that score.'

4. **to save someone's bacon** – to get someone out of a difficulty. 'If you hadn't hidden me in your cupboard, I should have been terribly embarrassed. You really saved my bacon.'

5. **to go together like bacon and eggs** – to go together perfectly. 'In an ideal world, rail travel and safety should go together like bacon and eggs.'

6. **ham-fisted/ham-handed** – clumsy with one's hands. 'That girl is too ham-fisted to wait at table. She drops everything.'

Soup, Sauce, Gravy

7. **to be in the soup** – to be in trouble. 'If you lose our passports, we shall be in the soup!'

8. **to soup up** (slang) – to make an engine more powerful by tuning it up. A souped-up version of an engine is one that has been developed into a racing model.

9. **a soup run** – the Salvation Army and other charities supply the homeless who live on the streets with soup several times a day.

10. **a mess of potage** – something of little or no value. 'They have sold their comrades for a mess of potage' (Arthur Scargill, president of the National Union of Miners, referring to the working miners in the coal strike, December 1984). The allusion is to Esau's birthright which he sold to his brother Jacob for a mess of potage (Genesis XXV, 33).

11. **don't give me any of your sauce!** – don't give me any impertinence, insolence, cheek.

12. **to join/get on the gravy train** – to take one's share of the rewards. 'When a new party comes to power, there is always a scramble to join the gravy train.' Unaccounted-for expenses, bribery, corruption and easily earned money are also associated with the gravy train.

Salt, Pepper

13. **to be above/below the salt** (humorous) – to be in favour/out of favour with one's host or hostess. 'Since his rudeness to his sister-in-law, Donald no longer sits above the salt when he visits his brother at Maybrick Hall.' In the old days when the family and the servants ate at the same table, the salt was placed halfway up the table to mark the dividing line between them. The master of the house sat with his family and guests 'above the salt', and their servants, including the governess and tutor, sat 'below the salt'.

14. **to eat salt with** – to enjoy a person's hospitality. There is a tradition among the Arabic people that you may not accept someone's hospitality and abuse him afterwards. 'If you eat salt with your Arab host, he will provide you with his benevolent protection.'

15. **to salt away** – to hide away, used in reference to money secretly hoarded. 'He must have salted away the best part of a fortune in the last 10 years of his life.'

16. **to take with a pinch of salt** – to believe only a part of what you have been told, to allow for considerable exaggeration. This phrase is a translation from the Latin *cum grano salis*, which has the same meaning.

17. **to rub salt in a wound** – to add deliberately to someone's misery, to make an

injury even worse. 'As you have just given your tenant a week's notice, I wouldn't ask him to clean up the flat before he leaves. You will only be rubbing salt in the wound.' Also: **like salt on a raw wound**.

1. **worth one's salt** – worth one's pay, worth having. 'Any boy worth his salt wants to get into the school football team.'

   not worth one's salt – not worth one's pay. The phrase is taken from the Latin word *salarium*, which meant the salt money that was paid to Roman soldiers instead of their salt. A man not worth his salt was considered worthless.

2. **the salt of the earth** – God's elect, God's own people. The phrase comes from Matthew V, 13, in reference to Christ's disciples: 'You are the salt of the earth.' The distinction has been claimed by many people since the time those words were spoken.

3. **an old salt** – an old sailor, one whose skin has absorbed a lot of salt from the sea.

4. **salt-and-pepper hair / pepper-and-salt hair** – brown hair that becomes streaked with white as one grows older. 'I'm glad they've invented a shampoo which brings back the natural colour of the hair. No more salt-and-pepper hair for me!' Also: **a beard/hair peppered with grey**.

5. **to pepper someone with questions** – to put many questions quickly to someone. The questioning is similar to sprinkling pepper on one's food; the holes in the pepperpot determine the way the pepper comes out.

Mustard

6. **as keen as mustard** – very keen, full of enthusiasm. This might derive from the advertisements for Keen's mustard at the beginning of the 20th century which bore the caption: 'Nothing is as keen as Keen's Mustard'.

7. **to cut the mustard / not cut the mustard** – able/not able to achieve a set aim or to fulfil certain requirements. 'We must replace the head teacher. Her job also involves skills of organization, and she just hasn't cut the mustard.' This phrase is used mostly in the negative.

Pickle

8. **to be in a pickle** – to be in chaotic disorder, to be in a mess. 'Your bedroom is in such a pickle, I wonder you can find anything in it.'

   to be in a nice/fine pickle – to be in trouble; used ironically for an awkward situation. 'We'd have been in a fine pickle if we had missed the last bus home.' cf. '**to be in a jam**' 178/4; '**to be in the soup**' 181/7.

Ginger

9. **to ginger up** – to put life into, to stir up. 'The new manager was determined to ginger up his staff if they didn't work harder.'

Fruit

10. **to bear fruit** – to produce results.

11. **stolen fruit / forbidden fruit** – a sin which is regarded as a pleasure. 'Forbidden fruit is always the most desirable.' The phrase is connected with the forbidden fruit in the Garden of Eden, taken by Adam in disobedience of God's commandment.

12. **Dead Sea fruit** – a thing of great promise which turns out to be worthless. 'Poor Andrew, he never got his invention to work; after five years of ceaseless effort, he had only produced Dead Sea fruit.' The reference is to the legendary apples of Sodom, which grew on the shores of the Dead Sea. The apples were very beautiful but would dissolve into ashes as soon as they were touched or tasted.

Orange, Lemon, Lime

13. **to squeeze the orange until the pips squeak** – to extract information by questioning someone until he or she is exhausted.

   to squeeze until the pips squeak – to put extreme pressure on someone; to get every last penny from someone/something. 'The politician stated firmly that she would squeeze the health budget until the pips squeaked. Only then would things improve.'

1. **a sucked orange** – someone who has served his or her purpose and is no longer wanted. 'After working 20 years for the company, Alex was discarded like a sucked orange.'

2. **the answer's a lemon** – a joking retort to a long, complicated problem which is not worth the time and effort needed to solve it.

3. **as sour as limes** – to be peevish, querulous, irritable. 'Malcolm left the party long after midnight and was as sour as limes the next morning.' cf. '**to be crusty**' 177/1.

Apple, Pear

4. **as sure as God made little apples** – with absolute certainty, as sure as night follows day.

5. **the Big Apple** – New York.

6. **the rotten apple** – the one bad person among a number of good ones. 'His youngest son was the rotten apple.'

7. **like a ripe apple** – one only has to be patient and then one will get what one wants. 'Independence will fall to us one day like a ripe apple' (Mahatma Gandhi talking about India gaining its independence from Great Britain).

8. **to upset the apple cart** – to spoil a carefully laid plan. 'That has upset the apple cart! We can't go away while the men are on strike.'

9. **to be the apple of one's eye** – to be the one for whom a person has the tenderest affection. 'He loved his sons, but his daughter was the apple of his eye.'

10. **to be in apple-pie order** – to be clean, tidy, well organized. 'The room is in apple-pie order for our guest.' From the French '*nappe pliée en ordre*' for neatly folded linen.

11. **to go pear-shaped** – to go badly wrong. ' "Everything's gone pear-shaped," the

managing director sighed. "There's been another robbery at the factory." '

Banana

12. **a banana skin** – a pitfall for the unwary which makes the victim look ridiculous. 'The government has slipped on too many banana skins for its own good.'

13. **a banana republic** – a republic in one of the hotter parts of the world (i.e. where bananas grow) whose governments are repeatedly overthrown and replaced by new ones, equally unstable. cf. '**a tin-pot / tin-pot official**' 171/13.

14. **to go bananas** – to get into a rage, to lose all control over oneself.

15. **fingers like bananas / banana fingers** – large, fat fingers. 'Olivia has fingers like bananas. No wonder she can't play the piano.' 'Banana' comes from the Arabic word *banan* meaning 'finger'.

Gooseberry

16. **to play gooseberry** – to accompany a pair of lovers, to be a chaperon to them. 'I am not playing gooseberry to you two. You will be perfectly all right without me.'

Raspberry

17. **to give a raspberry** – to give someone a rebuke (slightly dated).

18. **to blow a raspberry** – to make a rude noise with one's tongue.

Grape

19. **sour grapes** – to disparage something because it is unattainable. 'It is sour grapes to say you wouldn't accept the car, even if it were given you. Of course you would!' From Aesop's fable of the Fox and the Grapes.

20. **I heard it through the grapevine** – the grapevine is a source of information, rumours, gossip, which is forever churning out new items. 'I heard it through the grapevine that the boss and his secretary

are getting married at the end of the month.'

1. **to wither on the vine** – to die through neglect (with special reference to ideas or proposals). 'Our new manager had lots of ideas about reorganizing the business. Instead of arguing with him, we allowed his proposals to wither on the vine.'

Plum, Cherry, Peach

2. **a plum role/job/post, etc.** – the most desired, the very best.

3. **to land / be offered a plum job** – to obtain, by good luck or good management, the most sought-after job. 'Leonard was offered a plum job in the Foreign Office.'

4. **a plummy voice** – an upper-class voice which is either affected by the speaker, or which sounds affected to the listener.

5. **to take two bites at a cherry / a second bite at the cherry** – to make a second attempt, having failed the first time. 'You really wanted that job and now you've lost it due to sheer laziness. Why should you get a second bite at the cherry?'

6. **a peach / she's a peach/a peach of a girl** (slang) – an outstandingly beautiful girl, stunningly attractive.

7. **a peaches-and-cream complexion** – to have soft, silky skin and peach-coloured complexion. 'Victorian ladies looked down on sunburnt skin and always wore large sun-hats to protect their peaches-and-cream complexions.' Also: **to have skin like a peach/as soft as a peach/peach-soft skin**.

Juice

8. **juicy bits of gossip** – spicy and often malicious pieces of gossip. 'It's such fun when our cousin visits us. She always has such juicy bits of gossip about the rest of the family.'

Prune

9. **facts, dates, etc., go through one like prunes** – to have a very poor

memory for facts, dates, etc. 'You needn't bother to tell me all the dates connected with this castle. I'm sorry to say that dates go through me like prunes.' Prunes, soaked in water, are a very effective laxative as they contain diphenylisatin (a laxative). cf. '**to have a memory like a sieve**' **171/4**.

10. **to prune a book, thesis or story** – to eliminate all unnecessary words and passages.

11. **prunes and prisms** – a mincing way of speaking (from *Little Dorrit* by Charles Dickens).

Fig

12. **not worth a fig** – worth nothing at all. cf. '**not worth a straw**' **48/11**.

13. **not to care a fig / not to give a fig for** – to care nothing for. 'I don't care a fig (I don't give a fig) for his opinions.'

Vegetables

14. **to be a vegetable** – to be alive but without the proper use of one's faculties. 'If he had survived the head injuries he got in the crash, he would have been a vegetable for the rest of his life.'

Bean

15. **to be full of beans** – to be bursting with energy and health, to be in high spirits.

16. **to spill the beans** – to talk indiscreetly, to let information slip out. 'She has spilt the beans about your engagement. It will be all over the town by now.' cf. '**to let the cat out of the bag**' **55/9**.

17. **not to have a bean** – to have no money, to be penniless.

18. **not worth a bean/row of beans** – worthless.

19. **to know how many beans make five** – to be alert, shrewd. From the custom of teaching small children to count with beans.

Pea

1. **a pea-souper** – a thick yellow fog. 'I can't see my hand in front of me. It's a real pea-souper!'

2. **to be as like as two peas** – to be indistinguishable from one another. 'The twin boys are as like as two peas.'

3. **as easy as shelling peas** – something so easy that it requires no skill or effort. cf. **'as easy as falling off a log'** 50/20; **'a cake walk'** 179/4; **'as easy/simple as ABC'** 265/3; **'a piece of cake'** 179/3.

Potato

4. **to drop something like a hot potato** – to withdraw quickly from a commitment as soon as one discovers how embarrassing it could become. 'When he heard that his brother-in-law was an alcoholic, he dropped his temperance campaign like a hot potato.' Also: **to be handed a hot potato; a political hot potato.**

    to be thrown like a hot potato – no one has the desire to be involved with one. 'No one wanted to help the young man. He was thrown like a hot potato from one department to another.' cf. **'to avoid like the plague'** 132/16; **'to feel like/treat someone like a leper'** 135/9; **'to play pass the parcel'** 313/12.

5. **a couch potato** – someone who lazes about at home, snacking and watching a great deal of television, and taking no exercise. 'Why don't you come jogging with me round the park? It's not healthy for you always lounging around like a couch potato.' cf. **'the Patsy problem'** 232/1.

    couch-potato children – children who hardly take any exercise but watch television all day. 'You two really must join a youth club! I don't want you to become couch-potato children!' Also: **a couch-potato culture; a couch-potato lifestyle; couch-potato syndrome.**

6. **a mouse potato** – someone who spends a lot of time amusing him- or herself by playing computer games, programming,

etc. ' "How about doing some maths on your computer for a change, you little mouse potato!" Jill's father laughed.' A 'mouse' is a small device connected to the computer, which one moves by hand in order to control the cursor on the screen.

Other Vegetables

7. **the stick and carrot policy** – rewarding success and punishing failure, just as one rewards a donkey for obedience and punishes it for disobedience. 'In every school, no matter how progressive, the stick and carrot policy is employed. The good children are rewarded and the bad children are punished.' Also: **more carrot and less stick; it's a case of stick and carrot.** cf. **'like a carrot to a donkey'** 57/21.

8. **to know one's onions** – to know one's job, to be extremely capable. 'If you want any information, ask Mrs Jones to give you a demonstration. She knows her onions.'

9. **to mushroom** – to multiply very fast. Almost always used in a bad sense. 'The number of travel agencies has mushroomed in the last 10 years.' The mushroom is a vegetable that is well known for its phenomenal rate of growth.

10. **as red as a beetroot** – red with embarrassment, or from excessive heat.

11. **a cauliflower ear** – an ear that has been permanently swollen and disfigured as a result of having been repeatedly struck. Often a feature of veteran boxers.

12. **fine words butter no parsnips** – actions are more important than words; speeches are no substitute for hard work. 'When I was dismissed, the boss gave me a marvellous reference, but what's the good of that, now I can't get a job! Fine words butter no parsnips.'

13. **as cool as a cucumber** – serene, calm, undisturbed when under stress. 'While the rest of us were getting tremendously excited, she remained as cool as a cucumber and went on with her sewing as if nothing special had happened.'

14. **salad days** – inexperienced youth.

'My salad days / When I was green in judgement' (Shakespeare, *Antony and Cleopatra*, I, v).

1. **as limp as last week's lettuce** – slack, dull and inactive. 'Her men friends were as soft as butter and as limp as last week's lettuce' (*The Ladies of Missalonghi* by Colleen McCullough, © Arrow).

2. **the pumpkin has not turned into a coach** – the early promise has not been fulfilled, and disenchantment has followed. In the fairy story of Cinderella, the fairy godmother turns Cinderella's pumpkin into a golden coach to convey her to the palace ball.

Nuts

3. **to be nuts about someone** – to be madly enthusiastic, infatuated with. 'You know, don't you, that he is nuts about you?'

4. **to drive someone nuts** – to drive someone mad (used humorously). 'Stop talking for a moment, Kathy! You are driving me nuts with all your questions!'

5. **to be off one's nut / to be nuts** – to be mad, insane. 'You mean to tell me you left all our money on the bus. You must be off your nut!' Nut is slang for 'head', so the phrase has the same meaning as 'off one's head'.

6. **a nut-case** – a mad person. 'Don't waste your time explaining it to her. She's a nut-case.'

7. **a hard nut to crack** – a tough, intractable problem or person to overcome. 'He is a difficult man to convince. You will find him a hard nut to crack.'

8. **to put in a nutshell** – to explain in a few words, to give a bare summary. 'That's right – we are broke. You've put it in a nutshell.'

9. **as crinkled/wrinkled as a walnut** – very much creased and puckered. 'The old farmer's face was as crinkled as a walnut from being out in the sun all day.'

   as brown as a walnut – suntanned; **a pickled walnut**. 'An alcoholic's liver is like a pickled walnut.'

10. **eyes like almonds / almond-like eyes** – big, beautiful, oval-shaped eyes. 'Mambi was a very attractive girl with eyes like almonds and long, shining black hair.' Also: **almond-shaped eyes**.

11. **hazel eyes / hazel-eyed / hazel gaze** – light-brown eyes the colour of hazelnuts.

12. **to pay peanuts** – to pay a ridiculously small sum of money. 'They pay him a salary of £6,000 a year; that's peanuts for a man of his experience and qualifications!'

Tea, Coffee

13. **not one's cup of tea** – not to one's taste. 'I was offered quite a well-paid job in the City, but the work wouldn't have been my cup of tea.'

14. **that's another cup of tea** – that's another matter, that puts a different complexion on it.

15. **I wouldn't do it for all the tea in China** – I wouldn't do it whatever you offered me. 'I wouldn't live with them for all the tea in China.'

16. **wake up and smell the coffee!** – to realize that one lives in the present with all its disadvantages. ' "Come on, Linda!" Sheila cried impatiently. "Someone's been snooping round our flat! Wake up and smell the coffee!" '

Wine, Champagne

17. **to wine and dine** – to entertain on a lavish scale.

18. **good wine needs no bush** – if your products are good, they will speak for themselves without needing to be advertised. The bush was the bunch of ivy hung outside which advertised the vintner's business.

19. **to put new wine in old bottles** – to put new ideas into an old framework which cannot accommodate them. 'Some physicists tried to put Einstein's theory of relativity into a Newtonian framework – like putting new wine into old bottles.'

20. **a champagne lifestyle** – a way of living which is only possible for the seriously

rich, such as travelling only first class, visiting the most exclusive resorts, buying *haute couture* and eating and drinking only the absolute best – including champagne. The idiom comes from the expensive white sparkling wine produced in Champagne in France.

1. **a champagne socialist** – someone who is not a true socialist, having a high-class lifestyle. 'They may support New Labour but they are really champagne socialists. Look how they send their children to that expensive public school.' Note the Russian equivalent: **'Bollinger Bolsheviks'** (Bollinger being the name of a champagne). cf. **'to pay lip service' 91/18**.

Cork

2. **to float as light as a cork** – to keep afloat very easily. 'The children watched the empty beer barrel floating down the river as light as a cork.' Cork comes from the outer layer of bark of the cork tree, an oak called *Quercus suber*, which is cultivated in Spain, Portugal and France.

3. **corkscrew curls** – hair twisted into a spiral shape.

Beer, Lager

4. **small beer** – people or things of trifling importance. 'He didn't trouble to acknowledge our greeting. Now that he has become famous, we are only small beer!'

5. **'Life isn't all beer and skittles'** – life is not just a game; it has a serious side to it as well. From *Tom Brown's Schooldays* by Thomas Hughes.

6. **lager louts** – groups of youths who get drunk and adopt aggressive manners, often found at football matches. 'Some lager louts were kicking against the lamp post, trying to put out the light.' cf. **'a Lycra lout' 200/5**.

Meal, Picnic

7. **a square meal** – a substantial meal. 'Kenneth is terribly thin, isn't he? He looks as if he could do with a square meal.'

8. **to make a meal of it** – to make an unnecessary fuss about someone's mistake. 'All right, we should have warned you earlier, but there's no need for you to make a meal of it.'

9. **meals on wheels** – Social Services delivering meals by car to the homes of the elderly or disabled who are unable to cook for themselves. 'Meals on wheels are an enormous help to all those elderly people who are homebound and can't do their own shopping and cooking.'

10. **a meal-ticket** – a means by which one can live without working. 'I don't think that Eve loves Paul. She is just using him as a meal-ticket.'

11. **it's a picnic** – something very pleasant which costs no effort. 'Last year's play was a picnic to produce compared with this year's.'

    no picnic – something that is both difficult and disagreeable. ' "You must put up with a lot of hardship and discomfort. War is no picnic," the major told his soldiers.'

Breakfast

12. **to eat someone for breakfast** – a strong character who can easily dominate a weaker one. 'Beware of the new boss, James. He will eat you for breakfast!'

13. **breakfast television** – television programmes which begin early in the morning. 'Breakfast television is a good way of catching up with the latest news and gossip.'

Lunch

14. **there is no such thing as a free lunch** – accepting a free gift or favour but realizing that in one way or another it has to be paid for in the end. The phrase comes from the US: if one bought an alcoholic drink in an old-time saloon, one was entitled to a free lunch.

15. **ladies who lunch** – wealthy women who don't have to work and have much time on their hands for socializing, gossiping and dining in exclusive restaurants. 'The ladies who lunch have decided to support a charity for stray dogs this year.'

to '**do lunch**' – to meet one's friends for lunch.

Dinner

1. **to have done something more times than one has had hot dinners** – very many times indeed. 'We really must do something about getting Amanda to school on time. She's been late more times than I've had hot dinners.' cf. '**to change/spin like a weather-cock**' 19/8.

Drink

2. **to drive someone to drink** – to behave so badly towards someone that he or she is driven to taking desperate measures, like an alcoholic turning to the bottle for solace.

3. **a stiff drink** – a strong alcoholic drink.

4. **binge-drinkers** – people who drink a lot of alcohol in a short time and then become aggressive. 'Binge-drinking can lead to child abuse and domestic violence.'

Bite, Eat

5. **to bite off more than one can chew** – to undertake more than one can fulfil. 'I shall have to cancel some of my orders; I've bitten off more than I can chew.'

6. **a soundbite** – a brief and clearly expressed statement that has been taken or summarized from a longer speech of some personality, reporter or politician, etc., for news on television or radio. Sometimes this is quoted out of context. ' "Rip-off Britain" was a damaging soundbite which angered many shopkeepers and traders.'

7. **to eat one's words** – to suffer a humiliation by having to withdraw a statement that has been proved wrong. 'Our critics said that we would never make a success of our magazine; now that we have proved them wrong, they will have to eat their words.'

8. **what's eating you?** – what's bothering

you? 'You've been sulking for days, Marion. What's eating you?'

9. **to be eaten up with jealousy** – to be consumed with jealousy, obsessed with jealousy. 'Maureen told me that if I bought a large car, she would drop me. The poor woman is eaten up with jealousy.'

10. **to eat someone alive** – to defeat someone completely. 'I could eat you alive, Bernard. You've taken my girlfriend away from me!'

11. **to eat up one's time** – something that takes up a lot of one's time. 'I should never have offered to help make things for the Christmas bazaar. It's eating up all my spare time.'

12. **a comfort eater** – a distressed person who finds consolation in food. Comfort food is usually fattening and sweet, e.g. ice cream, chocolates, sweets, cakes and biscuits. Also: **comfort eating**.

13. **serial eating** – members of a family who don't take their meals together but one after the other. ' "I don't think much of our serial eating habits," Irene complained. "It's much more fun when we all eat together, like at weekends." '

Appetite

14. **to whet someone's appetite or interest** – to sharpen or stimulate. 'Your story about sailing has really whetted my appetite for the sport.'

15. **not to lose one's appetite for . . .** – not to lose interest in, or be discouraged. 'In spite of all the setbacks, the students have not lost their appetite for reform and will continue to demonstrate.'

Taste

16. **in good taste** – in a pleasing, agreeable manner.
    in bad taste – in a vulgar, offensive manner. 'All his jokes were in bad taste.'

Sour, Sweet

17. **to turn sour** – to become unpleasant, disagreeable. 'Steven and Brenda's marriage

turned sour after only a few weeks.' cf. **'as sour as limes'** 183/3.

1. **all sweetness and light** – amiable and reasonable behaviour. 'It is amazing to watch Roy's mood swings – one moment he is all sweetness and light; the next, sullen and difficult.'

2. **in one's own sweet time/way** – just when it suits one. 'Don't bully Kenneth about mowing the lawn. He'll do it in his own sweet time.'

3. **to keep someone sweet** – to please and charm someone with an ulterior motive in mind. 'It's quite a strain keeping Grandad sweet, but I do need the extra cash for my holiday abroad.'

4. **sweet nothings** – words of endearment that lovers say to each other. 'Alex was enraptured by his girlfriend and whispered sweet nothings in her ear.'

Pounds, Weight, Dieting

5. **to pile on the pounds** – to put on a lot of weight. 'By eating such an unhealthy diet, Nick really piled on the pounds and could no longer take part in sporting competitions.' Note the opposite: **to shed pounds**.

6. **to throw one's weight about** – to show off, to behave arrogantly or superciliously. 'I know you are the chief receptionist of this surgery, but there is no need to throw your weight about.' cf. **'not to pull one's weight'** 302/13.

7. **to throw one's weight behind** – to support someone/something fully. 'Yvette would never have got the job if her father hadn't thrown his weight behind her.'

8. **a dead weight** – a heavy burden. 'He is too young to join the expedition. He would just be a dead weight.'

9. **middle-age spread** – putting on weight around the stomach between the ages of 40 and 60.

10. **to be on a crash diet** – to severely restrict one's intake of food in order to lose weight very quickly. 'My mother says a crash diet should only be done under a doctor's supervision.' cf. **'to diet like a yo-yo / yo-yo dieting'** 312/12.

    a diet buddy – someone who encourages you to slim.

11. **to waste away** – to become weak and thin, to be without energy. 'Alice has anorexia and is wasting away. We must get some professional help really quickly.'

Poison

12. **to look like poison at someone** – to look at someone with utter hatred. 'Mrs Tomlin looked like poison at her husband's mistress and said she would get a divorce as quickly as possible.' cf. **'to look daggers at'** 245/4.

13. **to spit poison** – to pour out damaging remarks or accusations. 'Sometimes rival film stars spit poison at each other, and this quickly finds its way into the newspapers.' cf. **'to spit blood'** 113/13.

14. **name your poison** – tell me which alcoholic drink you would like (jokingly asked in a pub).

19 Clothes

Shoe

1. **where the shoe pinches** – the source of the discomfort. 'Helen is bringing up four children on £80 a week with no help from her husband, so she knows where the shoe pinches.'

2. **to work on a shoe-string** – to run a business with practically no capital. 'We had to work on a shoe-string, with hardly any staff.'

3. **to step into another person's shoes** – to replace a person, taking over his or her responsibilities (often someone who is occupying an important position). 'I hope that, by the time you retire, your son will be old enough to step into your shoes.'

4. **to step into a dead man's shoes** – to benefit from the death of a person by inheritance or by taking over his job.

5. **to be in another's shoes** – to be in someone else's situation. 'Betty told me you smashed up the car last night. I shouldn't like to be in your shoes when Father hears about it.' cf. **'to be in someone else's skin'** 111/2.

6. **to shake in one's shoes** – to tremble with fear. 'He shook in his shoes when he heard he was wanted by the police.'

7. **a goody-two-shoes / to have a goody-two-shoes image** – to be extremely well behaved and not do anything shocking. 'The film star wanted to shake off her goody-two-shoes image and act the part of a villainess.' Similar to: **a goody-goody**. The idiom comes from a children's book, *The History of Goody Two-Shoes*, probably written by Oliver Goldsmith in 1765.

Boot

8. **the boot is on the other foot** – the circumstances are the other way round. 'The boot is on the other foot. It was your son who stole the money from the beggar, and not the beggar who stole from your son.'

9. **to boot out of a job / to be given the boot** – to dismiss someone / to be dismissed on the spot, without ceremony. 'Mr Potts was caught stealing from the till and was immediately given the boot.' cf. **'to sack / to get the sack'** 285/3.

10. **to pull oneself up by one's own boot-straps** – to make one's way by one's own exertions without help from anyone.

11. **to lick someone's boots** – to flatter someone in a servile manner to obtain an advantage, to fawn on someone. 'It's nauseating the way he licks his boss's boots all the time.'
    a bootlicker – a person who does this.

12. **too big for one's boots** (slang) – conceited, pleased with oneself. 'Ever since that boy won the tennis tournament, he has been too big for his boots. He needs putting in his place.'

13. **a bossy boots** – an overbearing, tyrannical person. 'It's no fun working in an office alongside such a bossy boots.'

14. **smarty-boots** – a know-all, someone who knows all the answers. cf. **'smarty-pants'** 192/7.

15. **to have one's heart in one's boots / to have one's heart sink into one's boots** – to be dismayed, to be in despair. 'When I saw the nurse's face, my heart sank into my boots.'

1. **as tough as old boots** – to be extremely tough, strong and unaffected by severe conditions. 'I wouldn't worry about Stephen if I were you. He's as tough as old boots and can look after himself.' Food can also be as '**tough/hard as old boots**' – completely hard, unpalatable.

2. **to be booted and spurred** (humorous) – to be ready for action.

3. **to hang up one's boots** – to retire. 'I'll be hanging up my boots next year. I think I deserve a rest after running the business for 30 years.' The allusion is to the football player who hangs up his boots after the match.

4. **to die with one's boots on** – to die while still at work. Originally a military phrase, meaning to die in battle.

5. **to put the boot in** – to make a brutal attack on someone when he is at a serious disadvantage. 'After ransacking the widow's house, the burglars put the boot in by smashing up the place.'

Sock

6. **to pull up one's socks** – to work harder, to reform. 'You've had another bad school report. If you don't pull up your socks, you will have to work in the holidays.'

7. **to sock a person / to sock on the jaw** (slang) – to hit someone hard.

8. **to put a sock in it** (slang) – to keep quiet, to hold one's tongue.

Stocking

9. **a Christmas stocking** – it is the custom in England for children to hang their stockings at the end of their beds on Christmas Eve for Father Christmas to fill with Christmas presents. The custom is based on the belief that Father Christmas comes down the chimney of the child's bedroom.

Dress

10. **to dress up** – (1) to dress with the greatest possible care, usually for a special occasion. (2) to wear fancy-dress costume.

11. **a fancy-dress ball/dinner** – a ball or dance at which the guests are dressed in the costumes of historic or fictional characters or anything else that takes their fancy.

12. **to dress down / to give someone a dressing-down** – to reprimand severely. 'The colonel dressed the regiment down for their untidy appearance.'

13. **dressed to kill** – to be sumptuously dressed with the object of arousing interest or making a seduction. cf. '**dressed up to the nines**' 260/14.

14. **the dress circle** – the seats on the first floor of the theatre overlooking the stalls – so called because it was the custom for the audience in the dress circle to wear evening dress.

15. **to dress the soil/ground** – to make the soil ready for sowing and planting. 'The gardener has been dressing the soil – hoeing and raking in compost in time for the spring sowing.'

16. **to dress a fowl, etc.** – to pluck a fowl, clean and prepare it for cooking.
    to dress a lobster – to prepare a lobster for the dining-table.

Skirt

17. **to hide behind a woman's skirts** – to try to avoid the consequences of one's actions by putting the blame on a woman. 'Mary was acting on your instructions, and now that things have gone wrong you are hiding behind her skirts.'

18. **a skirt / a piece of skirt** (slang) – any young woman.

19. **to like a bit of skirt** – to enjoy the companionship of women. The phrase always has a sexual significance.
    to run after anyone in skirts – to chase women, to womanize. Neither of these phrases is in good taste.

20. **to skirt round** – to talk round a subject, to avoid the main issue.

21. **to skirt the coast** – to sail close to the coast to avoid squalls.

22. **to live on the outskirts** – to live on or near the boundary of a town.

Frock, Gymslip

1. **to unfrock a priest** – to expel a priest from the church for misconduct, neglect of duties, immorality and so on.

2. **gymslip pregnancy** – said of a school-girl when she becomes pregnant, some-times as young as 12. 'Sociologists are wondering why Great Britain is suffering from such large-scale gymslip pregnancy.' A gymslip was a pinafore dress which was, and in some schools still is, the uniform for schoolgirls. It has no sleeves and no collar. Also: **a gymslip mum**.

Petticoat

3. **to be under petticoat government** – to be ruled by a woman domestically, socially, economically or politically. 'We haven't had a petticoat government since Mrs Thatcher.'

Frills

4. **without frills** – the essence, without adornment. 'I would like a simple, straightforward account of what hap-pened, without the frills, please.'

Apron

5. **to be tied to a woman's apron-strings** – to be emotionally dependent on a woman, often used in reference to boys and young men. 'It's time that young man left home; he is tied too much to his mother's apron-strings.'

Pants

6. **to bore the pants off someone** – to bore someone very much. 'For goodness sake, don't invite Major Williams; he will bore the pants off our guests.'

7. **smarty-pants** – a know-all. cf. **'smarty-boots' 190/14**.

Trousers

8. **to wear the trousers** – to be the dom-inant party in the marriage, to command or rule. The idiom is more often used when the wife dominates her husband. 'From her wedding day until her death, she wore the trousers.'

Shirt

9. **to keep one's shirt on** – keep calm, don't get excited or angry. It used to be the custom for men to take off their shirts to give them more freedom to fight, and to keep their shirts clean. cf. **'to keep your hair on' 83/15**.

10. **to put one's shirt on something** – to wager or bet on. 'I am putting my shirt on that horse. It is certain to win.' The idea behind the idiom is that it is such a strong runner that you can put your last remain-ing possession on it in complete safety.

11. **without a shirt to one's back** – in dire poverty, with practically no possessions.

12. **to put on a hair-shirt** – to punish one-self for some sin. Politically, to sacrifice one's present comforts in order to strengthen the economy of the country. 'There is no need for you to put on a hair-shirt – the accident wasn't your fault.' Some monks put on hair-shirts to do penance.

13. **a stuffed shirt** – someone who is always on his dignity, a pompous bore.
    stuffed-shirt ideas – unnatural and affected ideas.

14. **to be shirty** – to be in a bad temper. A word which usually implies that the person in question is being unreasonable. 'Don't get shirty with me; I didn't take your book.'

Suit

15. **a suit** – derogatory term for a corporate executive. 'The company audit started today – the place was simply crawling with suits.'

16. **to be in one's birthday suit** – to be naked, just as one was born. cf. **'skinny-dipping' 306/4**; **'without a stitch' 200/15**.

Jacket

1. **an Eton jacket** – a short jacket reaching only as far as the waist, similar to the jacket worn by junior boys at Eton College.

2. **to put someone in a strait-jacket** – to restrict someone's freedom. 'I feel as though I were in a strait-jacket; I can't do anything at that school without asking permission first.' A strait-jacket is a tight-fitting garment that is put on violent patients to restrict their movements.

3. **strait-laced** – strict, puritanical, keeping one's feelings under strict control. 'You had better be careful what you say to Julian. He is strait-laced and easily shocked.' Literally, having the laces in the corset pulled very tight, so that the wearer has a stiff rigid posture.

Tie

4. **the old school tie** – the badge of former public school pupils. In the eyes of many people, the old school tie has become a symbol of class privilege which provides an elite with important social and business advantages. This charge is hotly denied by advocates of the public school system.

Collar

5. **a dog-collar** – the name given to the collar worn by the clergy; so called because of its resemblance to a dog's collar.

6. **to be hot under the collar** – to be angry, excited. 'There's no reason for you to get hot under the collar. No one has stolen your room key; there it is on the hook.'

7. **to collar someone** – to tackle, grab someone by his collar.
   to collar something (school slang) – to help yourself to something without the permission of the owner.

Cuff

8. **off the cuff** – without prior thought. 'In a case like this, off-the-cuff advice is use-less. You must make a careful study of the problem before deciding what to do.'

9. **to cuff/give someone a cuff** – to slap or strike a light blow.

Brace

10. **brace up!** – a command often used in the army, meaning: 'Stand up straight, and pay attention!'

11. **brace yourself for a shock** – prepare yourself for a shock so that, when it comes, you won't be overwhelmed.

Belt

12. **to hit below the belt** – to make a mean or unfair attack. 'When he made fun of his opponent's deafness, he was roundly condemned for hitting him below the belt.' The idiom originates from boxing, hitting below the belt being expressly forbidden by the Queensberry Rules.

13. **to have under one's belt** – to have an achievement already to one's credit. 'Gerald already has two novels under his belt.'

14. **to tighten the belt / to pull in one's belt** – to make economies, eat less when food or money is scarce. Applicable to nations as well as individuals. 'The Chancellor warned the nation it would have to pull in its belt if the balance of trade figures showed no improvement.'

15. **to belt away / to belt along** – to drive very fast.

16. **to belt up** (slang) – to keep quiet or stop talking (rude).

17. **to belt someone** (slang) – to hit someone hard.

Cloak

18. **under the cloak of** – under the guise or pretence of. 'Under the cloak of assisting the vicar, he did a lot of business with the parishioners.'

19. **a cloak of secrecy** – an attempt to conceal something of importance. 'Some people feel that sperm donation should not be shrouded in a cloak of secrecy.'

cf. '**to draw a veil over**' 196/8; '**to shroud someone/something in secrecy**' 40/1.

1. **a cloak and dagger play** – a Victorian melodrama of mystery and intrigue.

2. **a cloak and dagger operation** – an operation in espionage, involving secrecy, danger and often undercover violence and assassination.

Gown

3. **Town and Gown** – the age-old feud between the undergraduates at Oxford and Cambridge, and the townspeople.

Coat

4. **to cut one's coat according to one's cloth** – to live within the limits of one's income. Often said of someone who has suffered a big drop in his or her earnings and who will be obliged to accept a lower standard of living. 'Now her husband has lost his job, she will be obliged to cut her coat according to her cloth.'

5. **to ride on/hang on someone's coat-tails** – to advance one's own career by associating with someone who is currently achieving quick promotion. 'If you want promotion, all you have to do is to ride on Crane's coat-tails; he's the favourite of the boss.'

6. **to be dragged by one's coat-tails** – to be forced against one's will into taking a particular action. 'Britain is being dragged by its coat-tails into abandoning the pound and accepting the euro.'

7. **to trail one's coat** – to provoke a fight. Trailing one's coat-tails, in the hope that someone would tread on them and thus give one the excuse to start a fight, used to be popular, especially in Ireland.

8. **to be a turncoat / to turn one's coat** – to change sides in a dispute, to betray one's principles.

Glove

9. **to be hand in glove with** – to be in very close cooperation with someone else, almost always in a bad sense. 'The two of them were working hand in glove, and were arrested by the police together.'

10. **to fit like a glove** – (1) to fit perfectly, to follow the contours of the body exactly. 'She looks very elegant in her ski-suit. It fits her like a glove.' (2) to describe exactly. 'The description in the *Police Gazette* fitted the suspect like a glove.' cf. '**to fit someone like a second skin**' 111/5.

11. **to treat someone with kid gloves** – to treat someone with the utmost gentleness and tact, so as not to cause offence. The significance of the phrase lies in the fact that leather made from kid skin is of the softest texture.

12. **an iron hand in a velvet glove** – forceful action concealed in mild, restrained words. cf. '**with an iron hand**' 100/14.

13. **to fight with the gloves off** – (1) to fight ruthlessly, without showing mercy. Boxing is normally conducted with the gloves on. (2) to fight over some principle. 'Gloves came off in the battle for the new leader of the Party.'

Gauntlet

14. **to throw down the gauntlet** – to challenge someone to a contest. 'Gauntlet' is derived from the French word *gant*, meaning a 'glove'. In medieval times, one knight would challenge another by throwing down his gauntlet (glove). cf. '**to throw one's hat into the ring**' 195/6.
    to take up the gauntlet – to accept the challenge by picking up the gauntlet (glove).

15. **to run the gauntlet** – to submit to a punishing ordeal. 'The minister ran the gauntlet of protesters who were fighting to keep the greenbelt free of housing developments.' The phrase has been taken from the custom in the army and public schools of making an offender run between two lines of soldiers or schoolboys who would beat him with straps, sticks, etc., in order to demonstrate their disapproval of his misconduct.

Hat

1. **a bad hat** – a bad character.

2. **to pass round the hat** – to ask for money.

3. **to talk through one's hat** – to talk nonsense.

4. **I'll eat my hat if I'm wrong!** – a promise to do something impossible if one is wrong; in other words, a declaration of absolute confidence in the correctness of one's judgement. 'I'll eat my hat if he hasn't passed his exam this time.'

5. **to take off one's hat to someone** – to show one's admiration for someone by (figuratively) taking off one's hat. 'I take off my hat to him for having the courage of his convictions, even if I don't always agree with him.' Removing one's hat has always been the traditional way of showing respect.

6. **to throw one's hat into the ring** – to challenge one's rivals to a contest for office. It is similar in meaning to the medieval custom of '**throwing down the gauntlet**', see **194/14**.

7. **that's old hat** – that is old-fashioned, out of date. 'Everything he told me was old hat. I've heard it all a hundred times before.'

8. **at the drop of a hat** – without warning, without any special reason. 'She is quite capable of deserting you whenever she feels like it – at the drop of a hat.'

9. **to keep something under one's hat** – to keep something secret, confidential. 'I was told this in confidence, so I'd be grateful if you would keep it under your hat.' The allusion is to the art of the magician who conceals a number of articles under his hat in the performance of his act.

10. **to wear different hats** (e.g. judge's hat, director's hat, politician's hat, etc.) – the role played by a person at any particular time. 'When he speaks from the pulpit, he is wearing his clergyman's hat. When he writes a newspaper article, he is wearing his journalist's hat.'

11. **to get one's bowler-hat / to be bowler-hatted** – to be dismissed from the armed services. The phrase is much used in the army, despite the virtual disappearance of the bowler-hat.

12. **to hang up one's hat in a house** – to be accepted as one of the family. cf. '**to have one's feet under the table**' **107/12**.

13. **a hat trick** – to score three victories in succession. 'By scoring a hat trick in the most important football match of the year, he won thunderous applause from his fans.' From taking three wickets in successive balls in cricket.

14. **as mad as a hatter** – completely insane. Hatters used to go mad as a result of mercury poisoning, mercury being used in the making of certain hats.

Cap

15. **that caps it all! / to cap it all** – (1) to give something the finishing touch, to crown a person's achievements. 'He capped a wonderful year by winning a scholarship at Balliol.' (2) that is the limit! 'You were expelled from school, you lost your job, and now you are in trouble with the police. That caps it all!'

16. **to put on one's thinking cap** – to give something the most careful thought. 'I don't know what the answer is to your problem. I shall have to put on my thinking cap.'

17. **to wear a dunce's cap** – to be scoffed at for one's stupidity. It used to be the custom in schools to put a big conical hat on the head of the most stupid pupil or 'dunce' and hold him or her up to the mockery of the class.

18. **a mad-cap** – a crazy, reckless person. 'He took that corner at over 100 miles an hour. He is a real mad-cap!'

19. **a night-cap** – a soothing drink, such as cocoa or hot milk, taken last thing at night before going to bed.

20. **a feather in one's cap** – something one can be proud of, that does one credit. 'That's a feather in his cap, being asked to perform for them twice in one year!'

1. **if the cap fits, wear it** – no one is making any accusations against you, but if you are to blame, then by all means say so! Often used in reply to someone who claims he or she is being falsely accused, and is becoming aggressive.

2. **to throw up one's cap / to throw one's cap in the air** – to rejoice, to exult.

3. **to go cap in hand** – to beg humbly for favours or money. 'Why should I go cap in hand to him? I have a right to the money.'

4. **to set one's cap at** – to flirt with a man with the object of friendship or marriage. 'That girl sets her cap at all the young men she works with. She is mad keen to marry, and not particular whom she does.'

5. **to cap a story** – (1) to finish off someone else's story. (2) to go one better with a story of one's own. 'Whenever I try to tell a story, he interrupts and caps it before I have finished.'

Bonnet

6. **to have a bee in one's bonnet** – to be obsessed with a strange idea. 'Joan has a bee in her bonnet about illnesses; she thinks they only exist in the mind, so that it's a waste of time calling in the doctor.'

Veil

7. **to take the veil** – to become a nun.

8. **to draw a veil over** – to hide the facts, maintain a complete silence over. 'I will draw a veil over the events that followed, in order to spare the lady's feelings.' Also: **a veil of secrecy**. 'The government will soon throw a veil of secrecy over genetically modified crop trials'; **a thinly veiled attack**; **to unveil plans**. cf. '**to draw a curtain over**' 167/4; '**a cloak of secrecy**' 193/19; '**to be kept in the dark . . .**' 26/1; '**to shroud someone/something in secrecy**' 40/1.

Wig

9. **a big-wig** – a very important, influential person. 'She must have invited a big-wig or she wouldn't have spent so much on the dinner.' In the 17th and 18th centuries, it was the custom for judges, bishops and aristocrats to wear large, impressive wigs to stress their importance. Judges in Britain still wear wigs today in court, although some opposition to wigs is growing. cf. '**a big cheese**' 175/4.

Sleeve

10. **to laugh up one's sleeve** – to conceal one's amusement at the discomfiture of someone. 'Martin pretended to be so sympathetic when you lost the game, but I am sure he was laughing up his sleeve at you.' When wide, loose sleeves were worn, one could 'laugh up one's sleeve' without being detected.

11. **nothing up my sleeve** – in an open, frank manner with nothing hidden or secret. 'You can trust me. I have told you the whole truth and I promise you I have nothing up my sleeve.' Conjurors conceal cards, birds, small animals, etc., up their sleeves when performing their tricks.

12. **to wear one's heart on one's sleeve** – to show one's feelings too obviously, to lack self-control in concealing them. 'I always know when Anne has quarrelled with her boyfriend. She wears her heart on her sleeve.' From Shakespeare's *Othello* (I, i): 'But I will wear my heart upon my sleeve / For daws to peck at'.

13. **to roll up one's sleeves** – to get ready for some hard work; to prepare to fight someone. 'You had better roll up your sleeves, Eddie, and give Dad the help you promised.'

Button

14. **on the button** – exactly right. 'I totally agree with his political opinions – he's right on the button.'

15. **as bright as a button** – intelligent, lively; often used in reference to small children. In former times, nearly all but-

tons were made of brass or silver and needed polishing, after which they looked very bright.

as cute as a button – a US colloquialism with the same meaning.

1. **to button-hole someone** – to detain someone in order to talk to him or her. The phrase comes from the habit of grasping a man by his button-hole so as to gain his attention.

2. **to press the button** – (1) to press the fatal button which would unleash a nuclear war. (2) to set in motion various kinds of machinery (administrative or otherwise). 'When you press buttons in Whitehall, things really do start to move' (said by Harold Wilson in November 1964, soon after being elected to power).

3. **to have something buttoned up** – an idiom much used in the army, meaning that all the necessary preparations have been made. 'Our unit is being sent overseas at the end of the week. Everything has been buttoned up.'

Label, Tag

4. **to put a label/tag on something** – to give a name to some person or organization, such as 'vegans' for people who don't eat or use any animal products, or 'four eyes' for those who wear glasses.

Pocket

5. **to be in pocket** – to show a gain after deduction of all expenses.

   to be out of pocket – to show a loss after deduction of all expenses. 'The money he paid me for looking after his children wasn't enough. At the end of the school holidays I was £100 out of pocket.'
   out-of-pocket expenses – expenses incurred in doing a job, which may or may not have been foreseen.

6. **to hit the pocket** – to make someone pay. 'One should hit the pockets of rail operators each time there is a serious complaint. That should make them try harder.'

7. **to line one's pocket** – to make an unlawful profit. 'The government officials

lined their pockets with bribes and commissions.'

8. **to pick someone's pocket** – to steal money from someone's pocket without being noticed.

9. **a pickpocket government** – a government which levies oppressive taxes on its subjects. ' "We have a pickpocket government," my penfriend complained. "We work round the clock, but after tax we are left with barely enough to feed our family." '

10. **to dig into one's pocket** – to contribute money to some good cause, to spend money on something. 'I have to sell 20 raffle tickets, Daddy. How about digging into your pocket and buying a few!'
    to dig deep into one's pocket – to spend a great deal of money on something, somewhat reluctantly.

11. **to put one's hand in one's pocket** – to pay out of one's own resources. 'The soldiers were given a splendid welcome by the people in the pub and didn't have to put their hands in their pockets once during the whole evening.'

12. **to make a hole in one's pocket** – to have to spend a large amount of one's money. 'Going motor-racing every weekend is making a hole in Malcolm's pocket.'
    something is set to blow a big hole in one's purse/wallet – something will cost an enormous amount of money.

13. **money burns a hole in one's pocket** – to have money, usually newly acquired, which one is impatient to spend. 'My lottery win is burning a hole in my pocket. Come on, Robin – help me to spend it!'

14. **to pocket something** – to take possession of something one is usually not entitled to. 'The beggar saw a £5 note in the road and, after looking round, he pocketed the money.'

15. **to pocket an insult** – to accept an insult without protest. 'I am not going to pocket his insults any longer.'

16. **to pocket one's pride** – to submit to a humiliation. 'The agent walked about my house giving orders to my staff as if he

owned the place; but although I felt very offended, I pocketed my pride in order not to lose the contract.'

1. **in one another's pocket/pockets** – two people who are dependent on each other. 'You can't invite Paul without inviting Harold as well. They are in one another's pocket.'

2. **to have someone in one's pocket** – to have someone under one's control. The phrase derives from the days of the 'pocket borough' when some constituencies contained only a handful of voters, under the control of one man who was able to decide the outcome of the election and send his own Member to Parliament. The owner of the borough was said to 'have it in his pocket'. Pocket boroughs were abolished by the Reform Act of 1832.

Purse, Wallet

3. **purse-proud** – proud of one's wealth.

4. **to hold the purse-strings** – to keep the finances under one's control. 'She let her husband do the talking, but she held the purse-strings.'

5. **to loosen one's purse-strings** – to give one's money, make money available. The idiom often suggests that the donor is mean and has been persuaded against his or her inclination to spend money.

6. **to dig (deep) into one's purse** – to pay out more money when one hasn't very much left. 'A ski-ing holiday in Switzerland! I don't like to ask Father to dig into his purse again just after he's paid all those bills.'

7. **to put up a purse** – to collect a sum of money for the giving of a prize.

8. **out of the public purse** – out of the taxpayers' money. 'Money from the public purse is soon spent, with nothing to show for it.'

9. **to be hit hard in the wallet** – to be forced to pay out large sums of money. 'A father who had denied paternity was proven responsible for the baby and was hit hard in the wallet.'

10. **to vote with one's wallet** – to show

one's disgust at exorbitant prices and do one's shopping elsewhere. 'Petrol prices are far too expensive in this town. Drivers should vote with their wallets to force the prices down.' cf. **'to vote with one's feet'** 107/17.

Bandbox

11. **bandbox fresh / bandbox neat** – very neatly dressed, spruce, trim, smart. 'Our teacher is always bandbox neat, and expects us to be as well.' A bandbox is a paper-covered cardboard box for storing millinery. It was formerly used by parsons for keeping their bands in, i.e. their clerical vestments, collars and ruffs.

Bag

12. **bag and baggage** – completely, without anything left behind. 'The angry landlady threw her student-lodger out of her house, bag and baggage.' First used in this sense by Gladstone when he called for the expulsion of the Turkish army from Bulgarian soil, 'bag and baggage'.

13. **to be a bag of bones** – to be reduced to almost a skeleton through illness or undernourishment. 'When I saw the dog last, he was a bag of bones. I hope he'll put some flesh on in his new home.'

14. **it's in the bag** – we have as good as accomplished our objective. 'After three hours with the director, I was offered a position in the firm. It's in the bag!'

15. **to pack one's bags** – to leave as the result of a quarrel, usually with one's employer. 'When I told Martina that she would have to pay for all the broken china, she packed her bags and left.'

16. **a mixed bag** – a collection of people/ objects of very uneven quality. 'The passengers on the cruise were a mixed bag. We were disappointed.'

17. **growbag** – a plastic bag filled with compost and earth for growing plants in. ' "My tomato plants grew out of a growbag," Mrs Almond said proudly. "Aren't they enormous!" ' Also: **Gro-bag; growing bag.**

18. **body-bag** – a bag especially designed to

transport a dead body, usually during war or after plane crashes, etc. The **'body-bag factor'** plays a political role where large numbers of body-bags might be needed. 'The body-bag factor played an important role for the Americans in the last Balkan war, discouraging them from entering the fray.'

1. **bum-bag** – a small bag tied round the hips and used, especially by tourists, for carrying money, tickets, passports, etc., safely.

2. **to look like an old bag** – to look untidy and unkempt, slovenly. 'At home I do my best to look smart and well-groomed. My sons don't want me to look like an old bag.'

   an old bag – a derogatory reference to an older woman for whom one (usually) has little respect or liking.

3. **to look like a bag-lady** – to look dirty and untidy, unkempt, frumpy. ' "I know you're the mother of six children, but you really must spend more time looking after yourself," Emily scolded her friend. "You look like a bag-lady." ' A bag-lady is a homeless woman who lives on the streets.

4. **bag-people** – people living on the streets, carrying their possessions around with them in plastic bags. 'There seem to be more bag-people hanging round the town centre this year.'

5. **a verbal handbagging** – a good telling-off; scolding someone severely. 'The astonished prime minister received a verbal handbagging about the National Health Service from an old lady.' Former prime minister Margaret Thatcher always had a handbag with her. Cartoonists loved drawing pictures of her hitting with her handbag the ministers she was displeased with.

Suitcase

6. **a suitcase economy** – an economy that suffers from raging inflation. The phrase comes from the inflation in Germany after the First World War, when prices were so high that people were obliged to carry huge quantities of banknotes in their suitcases to do their shopping.

Cloth

7. **to respect the cloth** – to show the respect that is due to a clergyman, 'the cloth' being the traditional name for the clergy.

8. **in sackcloth and ashes** (facetious) – showing extreme remorse and penitence for one's wrongdoing. 'I must have been in a bad mood when I reviewed Sarah's book. I shall have to go to her in sack-cloth and ashes and beg her forgiveness.' In biblical times, it was the custom for sinners to wear sackcloth and sprinkle ashes over their hair to make a public show of their penitence. Sackcloth is made from flax or hemp – the coarsest of material.

9. **to steal someone's clothes** – to adopt someone else's ideas and pass them off as your own. A favourite phrase in politics when one party is said to steal the clothes of the other.

Silk, Satin, Velvet

10. **to take silk** – to become a Queen's Counsel at the British Bar and wear a silk robe in court in place of a junior counsel's stuff gown.

11. **as soft/smooth as silk** – very soft, like silk. 'A baby's skin is as soft as silk.' Also: **a silky voice**.

12. **like satin** – with the smooth, glossy appearance of satin. 'In the evening light, the calm surface of the sea looked like satin.'

13. **as smooth as velvet / velvet smooth / like velvet** – with the soft, smooth texture of velvet. 'The lawns, gently sloping to the bend in the drive, were mown like velvet' (*Jericho* by Dirk Bogarde, © Penguin). Frequent usage: **a deer's velvety nose**; **a velvet sky at night**; **velvety-brown eyes**.

Linen

14. **to wash one's dirty linen in public** – to advertise in public the moral lapses and difficulties of one's private life. 'Of course, your brother has behaved very badly to

you, but you will only make matters worse by washing your dirty linen in public.'

Cotton, Wool

1. **to cotton on to** – to grasp, understand. 'When I explained for the second time how to perform the task on the computer, he finally cottoned on and was able to continue working without referring to me again.'

2. **to wrap someone up in cotton wool** – to pamper, to be over-protective, generally used in reference to a child. 'It's time you stopped wrapping Ronald up in cotton wool and let him play with other children.'

3. **to pull the wool over someone's eyes** – to deceive, mislead, cheat. 'You certainly pulled the wool over our eyes with that sob-story of yours!'

4. **to be woolly-headed** – to be unclear or muddled in one's thinking.

Lycra

5. **a Lycra lout** – a cyclist who behaves in an aggressive or irresponsible manner towards pedestrians. 'Nearly a hundred pedestrians were injured by Lycra louts last year.' Lycra is a light, stretchy, brightly coloured fabric made from synthetic fibre. It has become the uniform of the serious cyclist. cf. **'lager louts' 187/ 6.**

Elastic

6. **an elastic term** – (1) (school, university term) flexible, possible to lengthen. 'Marie had started studying French and German, but, it being an elastic term, halfway through she was allowed to take Spanish.' (2) (an expression) not fixed; may be stretched to mean many things. ' "Being secretary at our primary school is a highly elastic term," the head teacher said. "We would like you to take charge of the correspondence and telephone, but also to apply some basic first aid, and comfort the children when they cry." '

7. **to be/feel like an elastic band about**

to snap – to be under enormous stress, to be close to breaking point. 'I felt like an elastic band that had snapped. I had never felt so lonely; suicide seemed to be the only way out. Thank you for saving my life.'

Patch, Sew

8. **to patch up a quarrel** – to put an end to a quarrel without going into the rights and wrongs of the dispute. 'It's time we patched up our quarrel with Johnson, otherwise we shall lose a lot of business.'

9. **not a patch on . . .** – nothing like as good as . . . 'I play tennis reasonably well but I'm not a patch on my brother.' A patch is a piece of cloth sewn on to a garment to cover a hole. The patch is of minor importance compared with the garment itself.

10. **to sew up** – to come to an agreement on all the details of a plan. 'Now that the agreement has been sewn up, we can begin to work.'

Pins, Needles

11. **as neat/clean as a new pin** – very neat and tidy. 'After two hours' hard work, the kitchen was as neat as a new pin.' cf. **'spick and span' 203/8.**.

12. **pins and needles** – a tingling feeling in fingers or toes due to the interruption of the blood circulation. 'My fingers are absolutely white and frozen, and now I have pins and needles in them. I don't know which is worse.'

Stitch

13. **to be in stitches** – to laugh so much that one's sides hurt. 'The comedian's jokes had the audience in stitches.' A 'stitch' in this case is a pain felt in the side after exerting oneself.

14. **to stitch someone up** – to betray or wrongly accuse someone. 'I wasn't in town at the time of the burglary. Someone has stitched me up!'

15. **without a stitch** – naked, without clothing. 'Zöe got a surprise when she went to

the wrong beach. Everyone was sun-bathing without a stitch on.' cf. '**skinny-dipping**' 306/4; '**to be in one's birthday suit**' 192/16.

Thread, Yarn

1. **to lose the thread** – to be unable to follow an argument, either because it is too hard to understand or because the listener's concentration has failed.

2. **to pick up the threads** – to resume one's work after a period of inactivity. 'It will be difficult for Alex to pick up the threads after neglecting his book for so long.'

3. **to hang by a thread** – to be in a precarious position. 'After the collision with the lorry, Oliver's life hung by a thread.'

4. **to wear someone's patience threadbare/thin** – to exhaust someone's patience. 'I'm sorry I can't continue with the lessons. After three months, Toby has worn my patience threadbare.' When an article of clothing is worn out, the threads of the material show.

5. **to spin a yarn** – to excuse oneself to someone for being late, etc. by telling a rambling, improbable story. 'I don't believe a word of it! How often have you spun me that yarn!'

Knot

6. **to tie the knot** – to get married. 'Andrea and William were in a rowing boat in the middle of Loch Ness when they decided to tie the knot.' cf. '**to head down the aisle**' 150/9.

7. **to get tied up in knots** – to be disorientated, confused. 'Stop shouting at me for a moment – I can't think properly. You're getting me all tied up in knots!'

Wear

8. **the worse for wear** – damage done through drinking too much alcohol or through fatigue. 'Did you see Paul's uncle yesterday? He seemed very much the worse for wear after the party.'

9. **wear and tear** – damage done through continuous use. 'Will Stonehenge survive the wear and tear of millions of tourists?'

    wear-and-tear arthritis – osteoarthritis, a joint problem affecting the hips and knees.

Rags, Tatters, Holes

10. **the local rag** – the local newspaper. Local newspapers, especially in London, are rightly or wrongly looked down on. Hence the phrase.

11. **the rag-tag and bob-tail** – the poorest of the poor. People dressed in rags and tatters. Also: **a rag-tag army**.

12. **a ragbag** – a haphazard collection of things. 'The Green Party leader became famous due to his ragbag of highly original ideas concerning environmental issues.'

13. **a rat-bag** – someone who is or who has done something extremely unpleasant.

14. **a toe-rag** – a scoundrel, good-for-nothing. 'Have nothing to do with those toe-rags, Nigel. They are in trouble all the time.' A '**toe-ragger**' is a tramp.

15. **to treat someone like a toe-rag** – to look down on someone with distaste, treat someone contemptuously. 'My boss is treating me like a toe-rag just because I'm a woman. I'll look for another job somewhere else.' A toe-rag was a cloth or strip of rag wrapped around the feet of people who could not afford shoes. The insult 'toe-rag' was much used by writers of Cockney crime stories. Another possible origin is that toe-rag is really 'tow-rag', the 'tow' being the coarse broken part of hemp after spinning which was used in former times to wipe away grease and dirt from steam engines. Hence, a tow-rag was a dirty, despicable person. cf. '**to feel like/treat someone like a leper**' 135/9; '**to treat someone like a dog**' 52/14.

16. **to feel like a wet rag/like a washed-out rag** – to feel completely exhausted, worn out, overtired, drained. 'Thank goodness the school holidays are over tomorrow. I feel like a washed-out rag.' cf. '**a nervous wreck**' 206/2; '**to feel/look like death . . .**' 38/7.

1. **glad rags** – a woman's best clothes, usually worn for a special occasion. 'You'd better put your glad rags on, Mary. I've invited the admiral and his wife to dinner.'

2. **from rags to riches** – from extreme poverty to great affluence. 'It was like a fairy story. After a few months in America, he had gone from rags to riches.' The opposite of this, '**from riches to rags**', is sometimes used humorously.

3. **to be in tatters / one's life is in tatters** – one's hopes/dreams/plans are shattered; one's life/career/reputation is destroyed. 'When Pamela's husband went bankrupt, her dream of a world cruise lay in tatters.'

4. **to pick holes in** – to find fault with. 'It was most discouraging. He picked holes in every single scheme she suggested.'

Ship

1. **all shipshape** – everything in good order, all neat and clean. 'The rooms are all shipshape for our guests.' The phrase was originally 'all shipshape and Bristol fashion', meaning that the ship was properly prepared for sea. The port of Bristol was well known for its efficiency in preparing ships for sea.

2. **when my ship comes home** – when I get rich, when I make my fortune. 'When my ship comes home, we'll buy that house by the sea.'

3. **ships in the night / ships that pass in the night** – casual acquaintances and friendships that last only a very short time. 'A pity you've been posted overseas just when we've met. Ships in the night!'

4. **like rats leaving the sinking ship** – like traitors who desert the losing side in a contest. Rats are said to have a premonition when a ship is about to sink, and to leave it.

5. **to go down with the ship** – to stay at one's post until the bitter end. There was a tradition that the captain should go down with his ship. When the *Titanic* sank (1912), both the captain and designer went down with the ship, although they were offered places in the life-boats. In modern times, the rule has been relaxed, and the captain is expected to be the last to leave the ship.

6. **to run a tight ship** – to apply a strict regime, to be in firm control of an organization or business and run it efficiently. 'Two prison officers were suspended and accused of running too tight a ship following allegations of brutality.'

7. **the ship of the desert** – the camel. The journey of the camel across the desert has been compared with the voyage of a ship. Both are dependent on their own resources during the journey.

8. **spick and span** – clean, neat, tidy. 'Everything is spick and span now for our visitor. It has taken me all the morning to get his room ready.' A nautical phrase meaning that, on a new ship, every spick (nail) and span (chip) is new. cf. **'as neat/clean as a new pin'** 200/11.

9. **in the wake of** – immediately after, in consequence of. 'In the wake of their electoral defeat, the divisions in the Party came out into the open.' The wake is the track of smooth water left by a moving ship.

Boat

10. **in the same boat** – to suffer the same predicament as somebody else. 'We are affected by rising prices just as much as you; we are all in the same boat.'

11. **to push the boat out** – to go to great efforts to prepare a special meal or celebration for friends, etc. 'Mike and Julie are coming to lunch. We haven't seen them for ages so let's really push the boat out for them.' It used to be the custom to have a celebration before starting on a voyage.

12. **to rock the boat** – to hinder the success of a concern in which one is involved. 'For goodness sake, don't criticize the management in front of our

customers; you won't help us by rocking the boat.'

1. **to burn one's boats** – to commit oneself to a course of action that cannot possibly be changed. 'Now you have resigned your position in the company, you can't ask them for it back; you have burned your boats.'

2. **to miss the boat** – to miss an important opportunity. 'I'm afraid my husband is too old at 60 to be promoted; he has missed the boat.' Frequent usage: **don't miss the boat!** cf. **'to miss the bus'** **153/6.**

Sail

3. **to sail through** – to succeed without any difficulty. 'Philip simply sailed through his exams – no trouble at all.'

4. **plain sailing** – an easy, uncomplicated plan of action. 'Nobody is opposing your application; it should be plain sailing for you from now on.' The term was originally 'plane sailing', meaning that the sailing was as simple as if you were sailing on a flat instead of a spherical plane.

5. **to sail into someone** – to scold or attack someone. 'Without more ado, Geoffrey sailed into the man with his fists.'

6. **to trim one's sails** – to change one's views, to withdraw them in the face of opposition. The full phrase was 'to trim the sails before the wind', meaning to adjust one's sails when the direction of the wind changed. In politics, a **'trimmer'** is someone who will change his or her principles under pressure of circumstances.

7. **to sail against the wind** – to oppose the prevailing view. 'Andrew never minded how much opposition he provoked; he liked sailing against the wind.'

8. **to strike one's sails** – to submit to a more powerful opponent, to accept humiliation. From the custom in the days of sail of a smaller ship lowering its sails as a sign of defeat by another ship.

Beam

9. **broad in the beam** – broad-hipped.

10. **on one's beam ends** – in extreme financial difficulties, very short of money. 'Can you lend me some money? I'm on my beam ends.' A ship is on its beam ends just before it goes under.

Board

11. **to go overboard** – to be extravagant. 'A Chippendale dining-suite and a Chinese carpet; you have gone overboard with your dining-room, haven't you?'

12. **to go by the board** – to manage without, often used in the sense of sacrificing everything to one purpose. 'Everything went by the board – holidays, new clothes, entertaining, lunches out – in order to get Vivien into college.' The original meaning was to throw unwanted articles overboard, i.e. over the side of the ship.

13. **to take on board** – to tolerate or acknowledge the truth of an idea. 'Today, people are taking on board the view that unemployment is a worldwide phenomenon and not the fault of any particular government.'

Other Parts of the Ship

14. **to be on an even keel** – calm and undisturbed. 'After the children had left home, life for the elderly couple continued on an even keel.'

15. **to be at the helm** – to be in charge. 'It must be very stressful for you, Mr Williams, to be at the helm of such a big chain store.'

16. **a shot across the bows** – a warning signal. 'We've had a shot across the bows from the solicitor, warning us not to repeat our accusations.' A shot across the bows was a cannon-ball warning a ship either to surrender or to turn about.

17. **to clear the decks** – to get ready for action, clearing all unfinished business well out of the way. 'We are clearing

the decks for the launching of our new campaign.' The derivation is from naval warfare when the decks are cleared of any unnecessary objects which could obstruct the free movement of personnel and weapons during the action.

1. **to batten down the hatches** – to take every possible precaution to preserve one's money. A phrase that is much used by financial correspondents, meaning that when there has been a bad fall on the Stock Exchange, the only thing to do is to wait for the market to recover. When there is a storm at sea, the hatches, i.e. the openings in the ship's deck, are closed and secured to prevent the water getting in and sinking the ship.

2. **full/packed/stuffed to the gunnels/ gunwales** – to be absolutely full. 'I've heard that the government in that country is stuffed to the gunnels with a lot of useless bureaucrats.' Guns point from the 'wale', which is situated on the upper edge of the side of a ship.

3. **Davy Jones' locker** – the sea bed which receives the bodies of drowned sailors. 'Jones' is thought to be a corruption of 'Jonah', who was swallowed by a whale.

4. **the sheet anchor** – the basis of someone's livelihood, what he or she relies upon when everything else fails. 'I earn some money from my compositions, but the music lessons are my sheet anchor.'

5. **to throw a life-line** – to help somebody who is in trouble. The life-line is thrown from a ship to a person in danger of drowning.

6. **to show someone/know the ropes** – to be familiar with the way a business is organized. 'You'll find everything strange at first, but Jeremy will show you the ropes.' From the ropes used for sailing a ship.

Berth, Tack, Leeway

7. **to give someone a wide berth** – to avoid someone's company, to keep a good distance away from someone. 'If you quarrel with Jakes, he can get very nasty; I would give him a wide berth if I were you.' In this instance, the berth is the space in which a ship rides at anchor.

8. **to be on the right/wrong tack** – to take the line that leads to the right/ wrong conclusion. If one took the wrong line in sailing, one went in the wrong direction.

9. **to make up leeway** – to compensate for time that has been wasted. 'You have a lot of leeway to make up, if you want to pass your examinations in June.' The leeway is the distance that the ship has deviated from its proper course.

Coast, Sea

10. **the coast is clear** – there is no danger of interference from the authorities. Much in use at schools when the pupils are on the look-out for a teacher. This was a smuggling term which meant that the coast was free from coastguards.

11. **a sea change** – a fundamental change, a transformation. 'The prime minister is convinced that there will soon be a sea change in the relations between East and West.'

12. **at sea / all at sea** – bewildered, confused. 'After listening a few minutes to their conversation, I was all at sea. Botany is not my subject.'

13. **to find one's sea-legs** – to adjust oneself to the roll and pitch of the ship. 'Once you've been on board a day or two, you'll soon find your sea-legs.' cf. '**to be a good sailor**' 278/13.

Canoe, Barge, Ark

14. **to paddle one's own canoe** – to use one's own ability and efforts to make one's way without anyone's help. 'In future I will paddle my own canoe without asking for my parents' support.'

15. **not to touch with a barge-pole** – to dislike somebody or something intensely, to avoid. 'That man is a thoroughly disreputable character. I wouldn't touch him with a barge-pole.' cf. '**not to**

touch someone with a pair of tongs' 252/6.

1. **out of the ark** – excessively old, ancient. 'Wherever did you get that wardrobe from? It looks as if it has come out of the ark!' The reference is to Noah's ark which Noah and his family built to escape from the Great Flood (described in Genesis).

Wreck

2. **a nervous wreck** – mentally and physically exhausted. 'I feel a nervous wreck after looking after Jenny's children.' cf. **'nerve-racking'** 110/6; **'to feel like a wet rag . . .'** 201/16.

World

1. **it's a small world** – to be surprised at meeting a person one knows in an unexpected place. 'Fancy meeting you here, in the middle of a highland moor! It's a small world!'

2. **to make/get the best of both worlds** – to enjoy the advantages of two different situations or ways of life. 'As a day-pupil at a nearby boarding-school, Peter has the benefit of a good education, while enjoying the advantages of living at home with his parents. He gets the best of both worlds.'

3. **to carry the world before one** – to enjoy a resounding success. 'Stephen carried the world before him with his new invention.'

4. **to set the world on fire** – to achieve fame. 'I see you've set the world on fire with your latest symphony, Jack!' cf. '**not to set the Thames on fire**' 209/13.
   to make a noise in the world – to be talked about, to become famous.

5. **the world at large** – worldwide; to the public. 'Some models are prepared to expose much of themselves to the world at large.'

6. **to come up in the world** – to improve one's professional and social standing. 'You've come up in the world since we last met.'
   to come down in the world – to lose one's professional and social standing.

7. **to make one's way in the world / to make one's way** – to advance in one's job. 'My three sons are all making their way in the world without any help from me.'

8. **a man of the world** – a man with a good understanding of men and women, and experienced in the ways of the world. 'If you are in trouble, Valerie, would you like to talk to my father; he is a man of the world and very understanding.'

9. **to take the world as one finds it** – to adapt oneself to the ways of the world without trying to change it, to respect social convention. 'It's best to take the world as you find it, then you won't be disappointed.'

10. **for all the world like somebody/ something** – exactly like . . . 'Angela stood there in her mother's long white dress, for all the world like her mother when she was Angela's age.'
    for all the world as if – just like. 'When I visited my old university, I felt for all the world as if I were back in my student days.'

11. **not for all the world** – in no circumstances. 'I wouldn't leave London for all the world.'

12. **to be worlds apart** – to be completely different; there is a huge division. 'They should never have married. They are worlds apart.' 'The lives of teenagers of today and those of 20 years ago are worlds apart.'

13. **it's not the end of the world** – things could be worse. 'It's disappointing not getting into university but it's not the end of the world for you. You have a good job waiting for you.'

14. **it's a funny old world** – a world full of

coincidences, strange occurrences and odd happenings. 'Fancy meeting you here in the swimming pool after all these years! It's a funny old world, isn't it!' Also: **it's a crazy world; a mixed-up world.** cf. '**a topsy-turvy land . . .**' **213/1.**

1. **the world falls apart for someone / one's world is torn apart** – to be devastated. 'Many children nowadays see their world torn apart when their parents get divorced.'
   one's world is turned upside down – one's life has changed completely.

2. **to do someone a world of good** – to make a huge improvement to someone. 'You don't look well, Susan. Three weeks at the seaside will do you the world of good.'

3. **on top of the world** – elated by one's own success. 'No one thought Simon would win the by-election; he is on top of the world.'

4. **out of this world** (slang) – fantastically beautiful, marvellous. 'Just wait until you have seen the house. We must buy it; it is out of this world.'

5. **with the best will in the world** – no matter how much one tries. 'With the best will in the world, we can't help you if you won't cooperate with us.'

6. **the old world** – Europe, Asia and Africa, as distinct from North and South America.

7. **a parallel world** – the idea that everyone has a double is taken one step further in the theory put forward by some physicists that there is a parallel world to ours somewhere in outer space. This parallel world is a mirror image of our world.

8. **in the something world** – associated/connected with a particular sphere of life. Frequent usage: **in the animal-rights world; in the (ruthless/cut-throat/smoke-and-mirrors) world of politics; in the show-business world**.

9. **a phoney world** – a world full of sham and insincerity. 'I've had enough of this phoney world of show business. I think I would rather be a teacher than a film star.'

10. **a twilight world** – to have a lifestyle that avoids the rules and regulations normal people abide by. 'Some youngsters live in a twilight world where alcohol and drugs and sleeping rough are usual.' Frequent usage: **the twilight world of prostitution**.

11. **in a world of one's own** – in a make-believe world of one's own, in a world of fantasy. 'I don't think my sister recognizes me any more. She is living in a world of her own.'

12. **dead to the world** – in a deep sleep, very difficult to awaken. 'Alec must have drunk an awful lot. He is lying on his bed, dead to the world.'

13. **the world to come** – the life after death.

The Globe

14. **a global village** – the world being looked at as one unit due to easy communications by satellite, website, etc. 'Our ancestors would never have thought a global village possible.'

15. **globe-trotters** – people who delight in travelling the world. ' "Globe-trotters like you need these really big rucksacks, not those tiny suitcases," the shop assistant laughed.'

Place

16. **in place** – suitable, appropriate.
    out of place – unsuitable, inappropriate. 'The elegantly dressed woman felt out of place at the party where all the other women were wearing jeans.'

17. **all over the place** – in disorder, untidy. ' "Keep to your positions," the football manager shouted angrily at the players. "You are all over the place!" '

18. **to keep someone in his place** – to keep in order, to keep under control. 'The teacher only had to look at the children to keep them in their place.'

19. **to put someone in his place** – to discourage familiarity. 'When the young lad took the girl by the hand, she promptly took her hand away from his, intending to put him in his place.'

1. **there's a time and place for everything** – a good thing can be spoilt by bad timing or an unsuitable setting. 'I love the *Moonlight Sonata*, but I should hate to hear it at breakfast! There's a time and place for everything.'

2. **not to be one's place to** (always used in the negative) – not to be right or proper to . . . ' "It's not my place to give you advice," the clerk said to the manager.'

3. **to know one's place** – to accept the limits of one's position in society. In England up to the beginning of the Second World War, there was a deferential society in which everyone had a certain place or station in life, and respected their social superiors. This has now been largely replaced by an egalitarian society, with people claiming the same rights and privileges as the upper classes.

4. **a place in the sun** – a share of the good things in life. 'No one can dispute with us the place in the sun which is rightly ours' (said by Kaiser Wilhelm II, the German emperor, in 1911 during the Agadir crisis).

5. **pride of place** – the best position, often the most central or conspicuous, for the honoured guest, the most valuable *objet d'art*, and so on. 'He had a number of interesting ornaments on his mantelpiece, but pride of place was given to a silver snuffbox he had inherited from his father.'

6. **to fall into place** – to make sense, to follow a logical order. 'The work was difficult at first but, after a few weeks, everything fell into place.'

7. **in high places** – having power and influence. 'You had better be careful how you talk to me; I have friends in high places.'

8. **to go places** – to achieve great things, be very successful in one's career. 'You can be very proud of your daughter. That young woman will go places.'

9. **to come to the right place** – (1) to approach the best person for advice or help. (2) (vulgar) to sound a warning. 'If you are looking for trouble, you have come to the right place!' meaning: 'If you don't behave yourself, you'll be sorry.'

In London

10. **to put someone in Chancery** – (1) to hold a person's head under one arm, leaving you free to punch him. (2) to put someone into an awkward position from which it is difficult to extricate him- or herself. The reference is to the Court of Chancery which at one time had a reputation for delaying lawsuits and ruining the parties in dispute.

11. **the old lady of Threadneedle Street** – a nickname for the Bank of England.

12. **to talk Billingsgate** – to talk like fishmongers at Billingsgate. Billingsgate was formerly the principal fish market in London, and notorious for its bad language.

13. **not to set the Thames on fire** – not to distinguish oneself in any way, to be quite ordinary. 'Martin gets a lot of pleasure from his painting but I'm afraid he'll never set the Thames on fire.' cf. '**to set the world on fire**' 207/4.

14. **to be/end up in Carey Street** – to go bankrupt. 'We shall end up in Carey Street at the rate we are spending money.' The Courts in Bankruptcy are situated in Carey Street, off the Strand.

15. **bedlam/absolute bedlam** – a mad commotion. 'The chairman was quite unable to keep order. Everyone was on his feet shouting and swearing. Absolute bedlam!' Bedlam, a corruption of 'Bethlehem', was the name of a madhouse in the Middle Ages. (Today it would be called a hospital for the mentally ill.)

16. **you are not at the Ritz!** – the Ritz is a hotel in Piccadilly (London) which has made a name for the excellence of its cooking and accommodation. When servicemen complained about the bad cooking in the army during the Second World War, they were often told that there was a war on and that they were not 'at the Ritz'.

In England

17. **to send to Coventry** – to punish someone for disloyalty to his companions or

workmates by refusing to speak to him. 'Sending to Coventry' is a common practice in schools and trade unions. The idiom has its origin in the Civil War between King Charles I and Parliament (1642–6). In his *History of the Great Rebellion*, Volume 2, VI, 83, Clarendon says that Royalist prisoners captured at Birmingham were sent to Coventry, a Parliamentarian stronghold, where some of them were beheaded; whence the association of 'sending to Coventry' with the punishment of disloyalty, which later took the form of not speaking to the offender.

1. **to carry coals to Newcastle** – to bring a thing to a place which is famous for its production, like trying to sell wine to the French, or kimonos to the Japanese, and so on.

2. **a Norfolk dumpling** – a person who is dull and stupid. The inhabitants of East Anglia have this reputation, for reasons which are not apparent.

In Scotland

3. **off to Gretna Green** – couples who were under age (in English law) would run away together to get married at Gretna Green, a small town on the English–Scottish border. The conditions for marrying under Scottish law being less strict than under English, this was a favourite device for couples who had not obtained the consent of their parents.

4. **like painting the Forth Bridge** – a never-ending task. ' "Keeping this school clean with all the children running in and out is like painting the Forth Bridge," the cleaner complained.'

5. **the West Lothian Question** – why should Scottish MPs interfere in English matters when English MPs are not allowed to interfere in Scottish matters? The West Lothian Question was first raised by the Labour MP for Linlithgow, Tam Dalyell, in the 1970s. West Lothian is in southern Scotland.

In Ireland

6. **to be full of Blarney / to talk Blarney** – to make wild promises, to flatter and deceive. The Irish have a reputation for making wild promises. From kissing the Blarney Stone in Blarney, County Cork, Ireland.

7. **beyond the Pale** – socially unacceptable; any form of serious misbehaviour. 'I won't invite those boys; I saw them throwing stones at Jane yesterday. They are beyond the Pale.' The word 'Pale' is derived from the Latin *palus*, a stake, stakes having been used, in the 14th century, to mark out the boundary between the land settled by the British colonists in Ireland and the rest of the country. The people living beyond the Pale were regarded by the colonists as uncivilized. The same phrase was adopted by the English in their own country to indicate people of 'inferior class', who were not received in polite society. There was also a Pale of Settlement for the Jews in Czarist Russia from 1792.

In Belgium

8. **to meet your Waterloo** – to suffer a final, decisive defeat. The phrase has been taken from Napoleon's defeat by Wellington and Blücher at the Battle of Waterloo. It is usually applied to an unexpected defeat after a string of successes.

In Italy

9. **Rome was not built in a day** – nothing of value has ever been achieved without great effort.

10. **to fiddle while Rome burns** – to occupy oneself with trifles during a crisis. Legend has it that Emperor Nero fiddled while Rome burned.

11. **all roads lead to Rome** – Rome has always possessed a special importance – as capital of the ancient world, then as capital of Christendom. As the seat of the papacy, Rome commands the allegiance of millions of Catholics.

12. **see Naples and die** – Naples is the most

beautiful city in the world and, when you have seen Naples, you may die happy. There is a small town near Naples called Mori, the Italian for 'die', where thousands once died of typhoid and cholera, so this is a joke phrase.

1. **the Venice of the North** – there are three cities in the north of Europe which boast that they are comparable with Venice: Bruges, Amsterdam and Stockholm.

2. **to cross the Rubicon** – to do something irrevocable. In ancient Rome, generals were guilty of treason if they failed to disband their armies before crossing the Rubicon. Caesar took the decision to cross the Rubicon with his army to seize power.

Other Countries in Europe

3. **castles in Spain** – unreal wealth and splendour which only exists in the mind of the dreamer. cf. **'castles in the air' 12/1**; **'pie in the sky' 179/16**.

4. **the gnomes of Zurich** – Swiss bankers, so called because they were the guardians of huge treasures under the earth, i.e. in the vaults of their banks. The name was intended humorously.

5. **the Stockholm syndrome** – this occurs when hostages, kidnap victims or abused children gradually acquire a deep attachment to their captors or abusers. The idiom derives from an incident where robbers besieged a bank in Stockholm in 1973 and took hostages, who developed sympathetic feelings for the criminals.

6. **an Olympian detachment** – an impersonal, unemotional view of human conflict. From Olympus, the home of the Greek gods where Zeus reigned. The gods of ancient Greece were endowed with all the human passions and weaknesses – love, jealousy, vindictiveness and anger; so the modern meaning of the idiom has changed.

7. **a marathon** – a long-drawn-out contest, an event which calls for great endurance. 'The conference began at eight this morning and went on all day until 11 o'clock at night. It was a real marathon!' The name has been taken from the Battle of

Marathon between the Greeks and the Persians, fought in 490 BC. The messenger, who announced the result of the battle, fell dead on his arrival in Athens after running nearly 23 miles.

In America

8. **la-la land** – Los Angeles in California, USA. But la-la land can also mean a fantasy land where one has lost touch with reality. ' "Why ever should we build two enormous cinemas in this little town," the councillor muttered crossly. "That's la-la land stuff." ' There are many drug addicts and drunks in Los Angeles, a town notorious for its crime. Therefore **'to be in la-la land'** means to be high on drugs or completely drunk, i.e. completely unaware of what is happening around one.

9. **Tinseltown** – Hollywood in Los Angeles, California, centre of the US film industry; a place that is full of glitter and make-believe. 'Tinseltown's latest celebrity couple flew to London to be present at the première of their latest film.' Tinseltown got its name from all its glittering electric night lights. 'Tinsel' is the name for shiny metallic threads, usually in gold, silver or pink, which one uses to decorate a Christmas tree, birthday cake, or for other celebrations.

In the East

10. **Sodom and Gomorrah** – synonym for a centre of vice (Genesis XVII, 19).

11. **the Gadarene swine** – to stampede with the herd (or crowd) to destruction. From the Bible, when Jesus told the people how the evil spirit that had been cast out entered the Gadarene swine, causing them to hurl themselves in a fit of madness over the edge of the cliff to their destruction (Matthew VIII, 28–34).

12. **a perfect Babel / a Babel of sounds** – an uproar in many different languages. In the Bible (Genesis XI, 9), we may read about the confusion of tongues at Babel.

13. **to part like the Red Sea / like the Red Sea parting** – to make way for someone; divide, separate in a very

noticeable way so as to allow someone to go through a crowd. 'When the prime minister walks into a crowded room, it's like the Red Sea parting.' In the Old Testament, we are told how Moses led the Israelites away from their Egyptian enemies to freedom: he stretched out his hand over the Red Sea and a great wind blew all night and divided the waters. The children of Israel went into the midst of the sea upon the dry ground; and the waters were like a wall on either side of them.

1. **to fall like the walls of Jericho** – any sudden unexpected collapse. 'Don't worry about the court case. His arguments will fall like the walls of Jericho.' The allusion is to the collapse of the walls of Jericho when the Israelites blew their horns outside the city.

2. **the walls of Jericho didn't fall down in a day** – if you want to defeat your enemy, you will have to fight very hard.

3. **his/her road to Damascus / a road-to-Damascus(-style) conversion** – a dramatic change of mind on some burning issue. 'Mrs Gibbs was always against her son playing football because it was such a rough game, but she has since gone through a road-to-Damascus conversion after seeing how many friends he has made at the club.' When Saul of Tarsus, who had for a long time been a vigorous persecutor of the Christians, was on the road to Damascus, he heard the voice of God and immediately became an ardent disciple of Christ, adopting the name of Paul.

4. **Mecca** – a place which has a strong appeal for the enthusiast. 'Between the wars, Paris was the Mecca of painters and artists.' Mecca is the birthplace of the prophet Mohammed, and a holy place for Muslims.

5. **Delhi belly** – food poisoning sometimes suffered by tourists visiting Delhi or other places in India. ' "It's so unfair," Hazel groaned. "I had all my inoculations and anti-malarial pills and then I picked up Delhi belly and had to spend one whole week in my hotel bed." ' cf. '**Montezuma's revenge**' 231/4.

6. **to go doolally** – to go crazy; to be mentally unbalanced. 'Oh Mike! Your father will go doolally when he hears you've crashed his car!' From the name of a town near Bombay in India called Deolali. British troops were sent here to the sanatorium for mentally ill patients to wait for the next ship back home. Unfortunately they sometimes had to wait an exceedingly long time in Deolali, the heat, boredom and frustration driving them mad.

Imaginary Places

7. **never-never land** – a non-existent but very attractive place or state of affairs. 'You must live in never-never land if you think a millionaire is waiting for you round the corner.' From the imaginary country in *Peter Pan* by J. M. Barrie. cf. '**to live in a dream world**' 125/13; '**to live in Cloud-cuckoo-land**' 22/6.

8. **an El Dorado** – an imaginary country where the traveller can make a fortune without any effort.

9. **to live in Eden** – a place of sheer bliss and delight. The place where Adam and Eve were created.

10. **to consign to limbo** – to put out of one's mind once and for all. Limbo was a place adjoining hell which accommodated unbaptized infants.
    to be in limbo – to be in a state of uncertainty or doubt. 'Philip doesn't know whether he will get the job and has been in limbo since the interview.'

11. **in the land of Nod** – asleep. Note the related phrase '**to nod off**', meaning to fall asleep.

12. **Shangri-la / like Shangri-la** – a state of mind lacking in drive or interest, dull placidity. Shangri-la is the paradise described in James Hilton's *Lost Horizon* (1933) up in the mountains of a Buddhist country. In Hilton's city, the people lived in perfect peace and serenity, with no quarrelling or strife, but also with an absence of emotion or ambition.

13. **a fool's paradise** – a comfortable illusion which could have deceived only a fool. 'I knew all along that the business

would never recover. You have been living in a fool's paradise all these years!'

1. **a topsy-turvy land/world/way/tax,
etc.** – a chaotic, mixed-up world, etc.
'What a topsy-turvy tax! Due to an
anomaly, owners of large, expensive
London homes will have to pay less tax
than owners of much cheaper homes.'

Also: **topsy-turvy weather** (e.g. snow,
rain, storms and blazing sunshine all in
one day); **topsy-turvy teaching
methods** (where children are in charge
and teaching by old-fashioned methods is
frowned upon). cf. **'it's a funny old
world'** 207/14.

22 *Languages and Nationalities*

Language

1. **to pick up a language** – to learn a language by listening to native speakers talking together, without taking lessons or studying the grammar.

2. **a second language** – the first foreign language that one learns. Hundreds of millions of people have learned English as a second language. Usually the English learn French as their second language.

3. **bad/strong language** – language that is full of swear-words and obscene expressions.

4. **to talk the same language** – to share a common background with the person one is speaking to, to share the same problems and difficulties. 'We have both been running English language schools for the last 20 years. We talk the same language.'

5. **like talking to people who speak another language** – to be unable to communicate with others because their social background, outlook on life and ideas are so completely different from one's own. 'Unemployed teenagers generally stick with other unemployed teenagers and not with those who have a really good job. They don't mix. It's like talking to people who speak another language.' Worldwide, there are about 5,000 languages and dialects being spoken today. The most widely spoken language is Mandarin, the second most widely spoken language in the world is English. German is the most widely spoken language in Europe.

6. **to use the language of violence** – to resort to intimidation and force instead of common sense or the courts. 'I know you have been treated disgracefully, but to write threatening letters is to use the language of violence.'

7. **body language** – communicating with someone by conscious as well as unconscious movements of the body. These include: a slight movement of the eyebrows if one recognizes someone; shrugging the shoulders if one doesn't know something; clutching one's hands together with anxiety; rubbing one's hands gleefully; twiddling one's thumbs in boredom or nervousness; clenching one's fists in anger; tapping the feet with impatience, etc. Body language often reveals something one didn't intend.

8. **the language of clothes** – the clothes you wear tell others what kind of a person you are.

9. **to watch one's language** – to be careful not to use offensive words to anyone. 'You had better watch your language when you talk to your teacher or you'll be thrown out of the school.' cf. '**a dirty word' 324/13**; '**to mind one's p's and q's' 286/16**.

10. **to murder a language** – to make every conceivable mistake in the course of learning a foreign language. One school of thought holds that in order to learn a language one must 'murder' it first, because practice is more important than theory.

11. **a dead language** – a language that is no longer spoken today, except by scholars, theologians and experts. The classical languages of ancient Greek, Latin and Sanskrit are dead languages. Cornish is a dead language; the last person known to have

spoken it was Dolly Pentreath (1685–1778).

1. **a global language** – a language which is understood all around the world. English is a global language, spoken by about one and a half billion people, a quarter of the world's population. cf. **'a global village' 208/14; 'globe-trotters' 208/15**.

2. **the lingua franca** – the one language chosen by various groups of nationalities, who speak several languages, to be used as a means of communication. 'You never know, Carmen, but in a hundred years Spanish might be the lingua franca instead of English!'

British

3. **the best of British** – good luck! Originally: the best of British luck to you!

English

4. **broken English (French, Spanish, etc.)** – badly spoken English/French/Spanish, etc., containing many mistakes in grammar and pronunciation.

5. **Queen's English** – correct, grammatical English. It may be spoken in any accent, provided it is clear and intelligible. cf. **'a cut-glass accent' 169/17**.

6. **Standard English** – the dialect, one of many in the British Isles, that has won recognition as the standard form of spoken and written English. Standard English emerged as the national or official language during the 14th and 15th centuries. Its major components were the East Midland dialect and the London dialect spoken by the king and the court. It is now a universal form that has no necessary connection with England, nor is it tied to any special country or region. At the present time, words from more than 150 other languages have found their way into Standard English.

7. **received English** – a phrase coined by Professor Daniel Jones for the socially most acceptable accent. It is the only accent that is not tied to any particular region but is local to the whole country.

Jones called it 'received' because at one time this pronunciation was an essential condition for being received in the best society.

8. **pidgin English** – a corrupt, simplified form of English used by many people in Papua New Guinea and the Far East for trading. cf. **'dog-Latin' 53/22**.

9. **Estuary English** – a regional accent spoken in Essex and Kent but spreading northwards from the Thames Estuary. School-children and young adults in particular are greatly influenced by soap operas on television, disc jockeys, the world of rock and pop music, in which Estuary English is spoken. The accent, which is a bastardized form of the London Cockney dialect, is marked by its avoidance of the 'th' sound which turns into an 'f' or a 'v', e.g. mouth – mouf; truth – truf; think – fink; thing – fing; another – anuvver. Glottal stops are also apparent, in which the middle 't' or the end 't' of a word are left out: button – bu-on; skirt – skir.

10. **plain English** – (1) blunt, outspoken English. 'I told him in plain English what I thought of his idea', meaning I expressed my disapproval frankly and forcefully. (2) good, clear, easily understood English as opposed to the jargon that is sometimes employed by civil servants. We give below an example of bureaucratic English which we have rendered into plain English.

    Bureaucratic English: a distinction should be made at an age appropriate to the background and nationality of the student, below which the concept of the course should be for juveniles and above it for young adults (British Tourist Authority, 1979 BLE/1980).

    Plain English: The courses should take into account the ages, background and nationality of the students.
    cf. **'gobbledygook' 216/11; 'long-winded' 23/10**.

Celtic

11. **the Celtic Fringe** – the population of Wales, Northern Ireland and the Highlands and Islands of Scotland, which has

strong Celtic roots and therefore differs from the rest of Britain in its culture, Celtic language and customs. This term is sometimes used condescendingly by the English.

Dutch

1. **to go Dutch** – each person pays his or her own bill in a restaurant. A practice favoured by students or young people who are working.

2. **a Dutch party** – a party to which each guest contributes some food or drink.

3. **double Dutch** – nonsense, meaningless words. 'I didn't understand a single word. It was all double Dutch to me.'
   triple Dutch – even more incomprehensible. cf. **'all Chinese to someone' 219/6.**

4. **to talk to someone like a Dutch uncle** – to lecture with excessive seriousness.

5. **Dutch courage** – false courage acquired by drinking. 'I ordered myself a double whisky to give myself some Dutch courage.'

6. **I'm a Dutchman if . . .** – a way of denying a supposition. 'If you're right, I'm a Dutchman', means I am quite sure you are wrong.

7. **a Dutch auction** – an auction at which the starting price is pitched high and then slowly reduced until a bid is made.

Latin

8. **cod Latin** – fishy Latin ('cod' is a jest or hoax); there is something strange about this Latin! *Caesar ad erat forti* – Caesar had a rat for tea; *Brutus ad sum iam* – Brutus had some jam; *Caesar sic in omnibus* – Caesar sick in omnibus; *Brutus sic intram* – Brutus sick in tram; *Itis Apis Spotanda Fineo Ne* – It is a piss pot and a fine one.

Other 'Languages'

9. **rhyming slang** – a secretive language common to a group of people, e.g. the London Cockneys, whereby words are replaced by rhyming words to conceal their meaning to outsiders. The following are examples of Cockney rhyming slang. 'he had to do bird for two years' – he was sent to prison for two years ('bird' comes from 'birdlime' = time). A thief's fingers are 'sticky' from stealing, just as a bird is caught on the sticky birdlime of twigs (cf. **'a jail-bird' 66/8**). 'Use your loaf ' – use your head (loaf = loaf of bread = head, cf. **176/19**). 'I'm feeling housy-housy' (to rhyme with 'lousy' = ill). Also: high noon = spoon; wild west = vest; Roman candle = sandal; ding dong bell = hell. (From *The Penguin Dictionary of Rhyming Slang*.)

10. **street-speak** – slang spoken by teenagers. An example: 'Nick was out of dollars and looking wack so he knew he wouldn't pull anyway. Then he had a wicked idea. He'd invite his homies over and have a kicking time. The music would be wax.' Actual meaning: 'Nick was without funds and looking far from his best, so he had no chance of attracting the opposite sex. Then he had a promising thought. He'd invite his male friends round and have an enjoyable evening in their company. The music would be excellent' (Denna Allen, *Woman's Own*, 13 September 1999). cf. **'street cred' 145/15.**

11. **gobbledygook** – high-sounding, complicated language often used by bureaucrats in documents, or by people wishing to be politically correct. 'It's time to cut through all this gobbledygook and use only words which can be understood by everyone.' Some gobbledygook phrases: a localized capacity deficiency – a traffic jam; a revenue enhancer – a tax collector; an unpremised business person – a hawker or street trader; a non-discretionary fragrance – body odour; festive embellishments of an illuminary nature – Christmas lights; domestic service engineer – housewife; chronologically gifted – old; vertically challenged – short; follicly challenged – bald; a grain-consuming animal unit – a cow. Maury Maverick, a US congressman, invented this word in 1944 after hearing the pretentious nonsense spouted by colleagues on his war committee and compared it to the

gobbling sounds of turkeys. Also: **ecobabble** – green gobbledygook; **Eurobabble** – EU gobbledygook; **psychobabble** – psychology gobbledygook; **technobabble** – technical gobbledygook.

1. **mumbo jumbo** – nonsensical talk; also used by ignorant onlookers of religious or tribal worship. 'Activities connected with positive thinking and yoga were at first dismissed as mumbo jumbo, but they have helped seriously ill patients to become well again.' The idiom derives from onlookers watching the Khassonkee tribe of Senegal worshipping their protective spirit, Mama Dyumbo, which they understood to be 'mumbo jumbo'.

2. **claptrap** – rubbish, pretentious nonsense. 'His talk about actually having seen the Loch Ness monster is a load of claptrap.' Frequent usage: **I have never heard such claptrap in my life**; **to spout the same old claptrap**; **emotional claptrap and absolute codswallop**.

3. **a stock phrase** – a phrase which is used all the time, often without meaning. 'When I get my newspaper in the mornings, the newsagent's stock phrase is: "How are we?" not caring whether I am well or not.'

Talk, Gossip

4. **to give someone a pep talk** – to inspire and encourage someone to do a certain action. 'Our teacher gave us all a pep talk before our Latin exam.' From 'pepper', which adds 'spice' to one's actions.

5. **small talk** – conversation about trivial matters practised at parties or by people meeting for the first time. 'I won't go to Irene's party. All that small talk is so boring and such a waste of time.' cf. **'table talk' 165/7**.

6. **yackety-yack** – aimless chattering.

7. **loose talk** – careless talk which can get people into trouble. 'Investigating the burglary, the police relied on loose talk in the local pub and soon caught the criminals.'

8. **to talk a load of codswallop** – nonsense, rubbish. 'Wallop' is Australian

slang for 'beer'. In 1875, Hiram Codd invented a bottle with a special top to keep mineral water fizzy. Beer drinkers looked down on fizzy mineral water which they regarded as rubbish and called it 'Codd's wallop'.

9. **to talk bosh** – colloquial for 'to talk rubbish'. *Bosh* is Turkish for 'valueless', 'worthless', 'empty'. Also: **tosh / a load of tosh; to talk bullshit**. cf. **'to talk tripe' 180/16**.

10. **to scotch talk** – to stop/put an end to people talking about a certain subject. 'The film star was keen to scotch talk that he had broken up with his girlfriend.'

11. **a gossip-monger / a rumour-monger** – someone who spreads gossip/rumours. Also: **the latest hot gossip**.

12. **tittle-tattle** – light talk or gossip not to be taken seriously. 'Buckingham Palace sources described the latest book about the Royal Family as complete nonsense and tittle-tattle.' Frequent usage: **tittle-tattle and complete fantasy; downmarket/newspaper tittle-tattle; rumours and tittle-tattle; dinnerparty tittle-tattle; to tell real sleaze and scandal from tittle-tattle**. Note that in Australia one calls a gossip a **'tittle-tat'**.

13. **blah, blah, blah** – never-ending, uninteresting prattle (rather rude and disrespectful). 'Here comes Mrs Thomas, complaining about the children as usual – blah, blah, blah.' A variation is: **di-da, di-da, di-da**. In New York they say: **'yada, yada, yada'**.

Other Nationalities

14. **Prussian efficiency** – a general term for all the qualities associated with the history of Prussia: energy, thoroughness, industry, patience and discipline.

15. **Teutonic thoroughness** – especially characteristic of Prussia. The Germans have always had a reputation for studiousness, theoretical analysis and research in depth, in contrast with Anglo-Saxon empiricism.

16. **to take French leave** – to leave without

first obtaining permission. The French have a similar saying to the English: *'filer à l'anglaise'*.

1. **excuse/pardon my French** – excuse my bad language (used humorously).

2. **the French enigma** – the inexplicable ability of the French to eat a great deal of fatty foods and yet not have any cholesterol problems leading to heart disease. Some experts think it is because of counterbalancing factors in their diet, such as lots of fresh fruit and vegetables, olive oil, garlic and red wine.

3. **French letter** – a contraceptive.

4. **Gallic humour** – humour that is logical and intellectual, wit rather than humour.

5. **to make a Roman holiday** – to organize a gruesome spectacle for the public. The words are from a quotation from Byron's *Childe Harolde's Pilgrimage* (IV, cxli): '. . . butchered to make a Roman holiday'. Public executions and whippings would both come into this category.

6. **when in Rome, do as the Romans do** – you should adopt the manners and customs of the people you are living with. First said in a slightly different form by St Ambrose (Epistle 36, II Kings VI, 18): 'When I am in Milan, I do as they do in Milan. But when I go to Rome, I do as Rome does!'

7. **when Greek meets Greek** – when two men of formidable strength engage in combat, the contest will be hard fought and severe.

8. **a Greek gift** – a gift which brings only trouble and sorrow. The reference is to Vergil's *Aeneid* II: 'I fear the Greeks, even when they bring gifts'.

9. **it's all Greek to me** – I can't understand a word of it, it's like listening to a foreign language. From Shakespeare's *Julius Caesar* (I, ii): 'But for my own part, it was Greek to me.'

10. **Young Turks** – young agitators, young militants who are in a hurry to make changes in the established order.

11. **a Bohemian life** – in some countries, the name 'Bohemian' was a synonym for 'gypsy' in the mistaken belief that gypsies came from Bohemia. It means an irregular, unconventional way of life, and is often applied to writers and artists.

12. **Bohemian tastes/dress** – bright, colourful, unconventional tastes or dress.

13. **the Russian soul** – a vague, unfulfilled yearning for a better, spiritual life which would bring consolation and relief to the suffering masses. Copiously described and dramatized in the works of Dostoyevsky and other Russian novelists of the 19th century.

14. **a Tartar** (term of abuse) – a grim, uncivilized, bad-tempered person who makes a lot of trouble. The Tartars are Asiatics of Turkish origin, and are said to be notorious for their savagery in war.

15. **to catch a Tartar** – to take prisoner a man who makes so much trouble that one regrets ever having captured him.

16. **the Amazons** – active, assertive women in different walks of life. The Amazons were a legendary tribe of women who fought on horseback against the ancient Greeks. They were renowned for their bravery in battle.

17. **Spartan simplicity** – absolute simplicity in one's way of life, the simplest diet and the avoidance of luxury or comfort in any form. The phrase has been taken from the Spartans, who were the most disciplined and austere people in ancient Greece.

18. **Spartan endurance** – great fortitude and discipline – a characteristic of the Spartan way of life.

19. **like the laws of the Medes and the Persians** – unchangeable – a rule or law that is always followed. 'You must surely have realized by now that you can't hope to change the school rules. They are like the laws of the Medes and the Persians.' From the Bible (Daniel VI, 8): 'Now, O King, establish the decree and sign the writing, that it be not changed, according to the law of Medes and the Persians which altereth not.'

20. **a Trojan horse** – an enemy concealed within. 'I think it would be dangerous to

elect that man to the board; he could be a Trojan horse.'

to work like a Trojan/like Trojans – to work extremely hard, to be very industrious. See *The Aeneid* by Virgil.

1. **a Parthian shot** – a cutting remark made by someone on leaving, which gives the victim no opportunity of retaliating. It often means one final insult in addition to many others, with the idea of getting in the last word. The Parthian horsemen used to shoot at their enemy while retreating at full speed from them.

2. **a Philistine / to have Philistine tastes** – someone without cultural interests. The phrase was coined by Matthew Arnold but is really a misnomer because the Philistines who lived around 1200 BC were highly cultured, combining discipline and efficiency with a taste for luxury.

3. **a good Samaritan** – someone who goes out of his way to help a stranger in distress, although the stranger has no claim on him. The phrase has been taken from Christ's parable of the Good Samaritan (Luke X, 29).

4. **there are too many chiefs and not enough Indians** – there are too many highly paid directors and managers, and not enough staff to carry out the orders.

5. **a Mexican wave** – various groups of spectators in a stadium taking it in turns to stand up and sit down so that this action resembles a wave. It first took place in Mexico during the 1986 World Cup. 'When the famous footballer scored another goal, a Mexican wave went across half the stadium.'

6. **all Chinese to someone** – to be incomprehensible. 'Don't try to explain this computer program. It's all Chinese to me.' cf. **'double Dutch'** 216/3.

7. **like Chinese water torture / the drip-drip-drip Chinese torture of something** – something which gets terribly on one's nerves. 'Hearing the mobile phones ringing throughout the train journey home was like Chinese water torture for the tired businessman.' One form of Chinese torture was to force the victim to listen to the drip, drip, dripping of a tap, day and night.

8. **the Mandarin mentality** – Mandarin was the name given to the officials in the Chinese Civil Service who ruled China for centuries before the Communist Revolution. The Mandarin mentality means the mentality of the ruling class, self-satisfied, domineering and very conscious of its superiority to the rest of the country.

23 Names

Name

1. **one's good name** – one's reputation. 'He had a good name for honest dealing.'

2. **a bad name** – a bad reputation. 'That hotel has a bad name for its accommodation and food.'

    to give someone a bad name – to do harm to someone's reputation. 'You'll give us a bad name if you talk to our customers like that!'

3. **to have a name for** – to be well known for. 'He has a name for his wit.'

4. **with nothing to one's name** – without any possessions. 'The refugee lost his home and livelihood and came to Britain with nothing to his name.'

5. **to make a name for oneself** – to distinguish oneself, usually used in a good sense. 'Arthur has made a name for himself in physics.'

6. **to know by name** – to know a person's name, but not to know him or her to speak to.

7. **to call someone names** – to address someone insultingly.

8. **to clear one's name** – to be acquitted of a serious accusation. 'The inquiry cleared Peter's name of all blame for the death of his patient.'

9. **to win a name for** – to be well known for. 'He has won a name for his rowdiness and bad manners.'

10. **to pass by the name of** – to assume the name of. 'He used to pass by the name of Thorn. His real name is Jones.'

11. **to lend one's name to** – to allow the use of one's name in support of a campaign or crusade.

12. **in the name of** – at the command of. 'In the name of the law, let me pass!'

13. **what's in a name?** – a name by itself has no significance. It is the associations which give it meaning. Shakespeare makes the same point: 'What's in a name? That which we call a rose / By any other name would smell as sweet' (*Romeo and Juliet*, II, ii).

14. **to name names** – to make accusations against certain people. 'I don't want to name names, but I will if the stealing doesn't stop.'

15. **to name and shame** – to publish the names of wrongdoers so that they might try to improve their performance or behaviour. 'Government inspectors named and shamed our local school, and if it doesn't make improvements, it might even have to close down.'

16. **maiden name** – a wife's family name prior to her marriage.

17. **nickname** – an extra name often coined by friends or school fellows to describe some physical characteristic, such as 'Tubby', 'Fatty', 'Ginger', 'Sandy', 'Tiny'. The word is derived from Middle English *ekename*; *eke* meaning 'other' or 'additional'.

18. **a household name** – a name familiar to every household in the country.

19. **to drag someone's name through the mud** – to damage someone's reputation by denigrating him or her in public. cf. **'to dig the dirt on someone'** 17/18.

one's name is mud – one is in disgrace. cf. '**to fling/sling mud at someone**' 18/3.

1. **to drop names / name-dropping** – mentioning the names (especially the Christian names) of important people in one's conversation to give the impression that one is friendly with them.

   a name-dropper – someone who 'drops names'. 'I really don't enjoy talking to Mrs Eliot. She is always name-dropping like crazy.'

2. **to trade on one's name** – to use one's famous family name for business. 'Some members of the Royal Family were accused of trading on their name.'

3. **no names, no packdrill** – it's better not to mention the people involved because one doesn't wish to make trouble for them. 'Just as I was locking up the office, I overheard someone telephoning a friend in Tokyo. No names, no packdrill.' Pack-drill was a punishment used in the British Army which obliged offenders to march up and down with heavy packs on their backs.

Boys' Names: Jack

4. **I'm all right, Jack!** – the slogan of the self-seeking opportunist who will forget his friends for the sake of his own interests.

5. **a jack in office** – a self-assertive official who misuses his authority.

6. **to be a cheap jack** – to sell shoddy goods; to indulge in mean, dishonest tricks to sell one's goods.

7. **every man jack of them** – every single one. 'All the men on the building site went on strike, including the foreman, every man jack of them.'

8. **to climb like a steeplejack** – to be agile in climbing and sure-footed.

9. **Jack is as good as his master** – there is no difference between the boss and the worker. We are all equal and we should all have equal rights.

10. **a Jack of all trades** – a man who knows a little of many jobs but none properly. The phrase derives from 'A Jack of all trades is a master of none'.

11. **Jack Sprat** – a small, undersized boy or man. The sprat is a very small fish. From the nursery rhyme: 'Jack Sprat could eat no fat and his wife could eat no lean, but 'twixt them both they licked the platter clean.'

12. **every Jack has his Jill** – every man can find the right woman if he looks for her. From the nursery rhyme 'Jack and Jill went up the hill . . .'.

13. **before one could say Jack Robinson** – in a moment, before one could turn round. The phrase was used, probably for the first time, by Fanny Burney, in her novel *Evelina* (Letter 82), 'I'd do it as soon as say Jack Robinson.'

14. **Jack/Jack Tar** (nickname) – an ordinary sailor.

15. **a jack-in-the-box** – a toy man who springs out of a box as soon as the lid is lifted. Sometimes used as an idiomatic comparison. 'They were jumping to their feet like jacks-in-the-box on points of order.'

16. **to hit the jackpot** – to get a huge return on one's money all at once; to make a lucky gamble. The phrase is taken from the card game poker, when one scoops the pool.

17. **to jack up** – to increase suddenly. 'By installing new machinery, they were able to jack up production by more than half.' One jacks up a car by raising one end of it to change a wheel.

John, Roger, Peter, Paul and Other Boys' Names

18. **John Bull** – he is supposed to personify the typical Englishman, having been described by Arbuthnot in his *History of John Bull* in 1727: 'The Englishman is honest, straightforward, irascible, bold and quarrelsome, plain-dealing and independent.' cf. '**Uncle Sam**' 144/6.

1. **long johns** – long-legged underwear which keeps you warm in the winter.

2. **to go to the john** – US slang for 'to go to the lavatory'.

3. **to hoist the Jolly Roger** – to challenge the authority of the state. The Jolly Roger is the black flag of piracy.

4. **to rob Peter to pay Paul** – to give to one person what rightfully belongs to another. 'To reduce income tax by doubling VAT is to rob Peter to pay Paul.'

5. **to be a Peter Pan** – to be a male adult who mentally remains fixated on his childhood. Peter Pan was the boy in Barrie's play of the same name who never wanted to grow up.

6. **to be a Paul Pry** – someone who is always interfering in other people's affairs, an objectionable busybody.

7. **a doubting Thomas** – a sceptic, someone who will believe only the evidence of his own eyes. Thomas, a disciple of Christ, was unwilling to believe in His resurrection until he had seen the marks left by the nails on the hands of Christ.

8. **Tommy / Tommy Atkins** – a generic name given to the English infantry soldiers in the First World War.

9. **a peeping Tom** – a voyeur, a man who takes pleasure in looking secretly at nude women. The 'peeping Tom' of Coventry was a tailor from the 11th century who peeped at Lady Godiva, riding naked through the town. Her husband, Leofric, Earl of Mercia and Lord of Coventry, had promised her that if she were to do this, his tenants would no longer have to pay such high taxes. Everyone was ordered to stay indoors so that they would not see Lady Godiva naked, but Tom could not resist taking a look.

10. **tommy-rot** (slang) – the most utter nonsense. 'He's talking tommy-rot as usual.'

11. **a tomboy** – a young girl, below the age of adolescence, who behaves like a boy, preferring the company of boys and their games.

12. **Tom, Dick or Harry** – any nonentity. 'I'm not going out with any Tom, Dick or Harry. If Ronald doesn't invite me, I won't go out at all.'

13. **a simple Simon** – someone who is easily taken in. From the nursery rhyme 'Simple Simon met a pieman going to the fair . . .'.

14. **a proper Charlie** – a fool. The name refers to the pensioners who were employed by King Charles I. These men had a reputation for stupidity.
    to make a Charlie of someone – to make a fool of someone.

15. **to take the micky out of** – to make fun of someone.

16. **a smart Alec** – a disagreeable know-all.

17. **Hooray Henry** – rich, snobbish young man who moves in fashionable circles, gets drunk easily and enjoys showing off. 'Most ordinary people disapprove of their prince mixing with Hooray Henrys.'

18. **Joe Public/Joe Bloggs** – the ordinary person in the street. 'I can't tell the princess from Joe Public. Perhaps she should wear a little crown on her head?'

19. **and Bob's your uncle!** – now you have what you want. When the young Balfour was given a ministerial post by his uncle, Lord Robert Salisbury, the prime minister, members of the opposition said 'Bob's your uncle', meaning that with such an uncle he could have whatever he wanted.

20. **a silly Billy** – a foolish fellow. The nickname for William IV who was considered none too bright. This phrase is often used in the plural form. 'The silly Billies in the Ministry!'

21. **like billy-o / billy-oh / billio** – very quickly, vigorously.
    to fight like billy-o – to fight very fiercely.

22. **jerry-built** – a badly built house without a foundation.

23. **to gerrymander** – to manipulate the boundaries of a parliamentary constituency so as to gain an unfair advantage, e.g. by transferring a large number of one's opponents to another constituency. Gerry was a governor of Massachusetts.

24. **Pipsqueak** – a small unimportant man who irritates people with his bossy

manner. 'I'm not going to be pushed around by that Pipsqueak!' From the name Pip.

1. **to give a Roland for an Oliver** – to give as good as one gets, to retaliate effectively.

2. **a Valentine** – a letter or card sent anonymously by someone on St Valentine's day, expressing love and admiration to the recipient.

3. **to go the full Monty** – to be absolutely determined to do everything necessary. ' "This slum must be cleared away," the minister declared. "We shall go the full Monty here and build a beautiful new housing estate in its place." ' The origin of the word Monty is uncertain: it could derive from *monte* (Spanish for 'mountain'), 'monty' (Australian slang for 'a sure thing'), Monte Carlo (winning lots of money) or even General Montgomery eating a 'full' English breakfast. The most probable derivation is Montague Burton, a British gentlemen's outfitters from which one could hire the whole outfit for a wedding.

Girls' Names

4. **plain Jane** – a plain girl.

5. **a dear Jane letter / a dear John letter** – a letter which informs the person addressed of the end of their relationship, meaning, to put it bluntly, that the person has been dropped in favour of someone else.

6. **a Black Maria** – the black van used by police for bringing suspected criminals to the police station. (Pronounced: Mar-eye-a.)

7. **a Bloody Mary** – an alcoholic drink consisting of tomato juice, vodka and Worcestershire sauce.

8. **not on your Nelly** – a derisive refusal. 'Not on your Nelly; you won't catch me doing that.'

9. **a nancy boy** – an effeminate young man; a homosexual.

10. **Lady Bountiful** – a country lady who gave half her money to charity. ' "I am not going to play Lady Bountiful with taxpayers' money," was said by Mrs Thatcher soon after becoming prime minister.'

Biblical Names

11. **the old Adam** – the primitive, sinful nature of a man which is concealed under the veneer of good breeding and education.

   as old as Adam – very old, ancient. The Bible tells us that Adam was the first man on Earth (Genesis I–IV). According to orientalists and Bible scholars, the book of Genesis is based on ancient Sumerian texts in which the first earthling was called Adamu. See *Genesis Revisited* by Zecharia Sitchin. cf. **'as old as Methuselah'** 225/7; **'as old as the hills'** 152/3.

12. **not to know someone from Adam** – to have no knowledge or recollection of someone. 'I can't think why the man by the window keeps waving at me; I don't know him from Adam!'

13. **the mark of Cain** – the stain of a crime or misdeed on one's reputation. 'You will bear the mark of Cain for the rest of your life for your cruelty to her children.' The allusion is to the murder of Abel by his brother, Cain. 'And the Lord set a mark upon Cain lest any finding him should kill him' (Genesis IV, 9).

14. **to raise Cain** – to create a terrible row, to explode with anger. 'He will raise Cain when he hears his son has been expelled from school.' So called because the name of Cain is associated with the most violent temper.

15. **Jacob's ladder** – a very steep ladder, flight of steps or staircase; also a rope ladder with wooden rungs used by sailors to climb up and down the side of a ship. 'We had to climb up a Jacob's ladder to get into the lighthouse. It was terrifying but well worth the effort.' From the Bible (Genesis XXVIII, 12): 'the ladder seen by Jacob leading up to heaven'.

16. **to be a Daniel come to judgement** – to show judgement and wisdom beyond one's years. 'A Daniel come to judgement, yea, a Daniel! O wise young judge, how I

do honour thee!' (Shakespeare, *The Merchant of Venice*, IV, i).

1. **to walk like Agag / to walk with the delicacy of Agag** – to take the greatest possible care so as not to provoke or irritate another person's feelings. 'Your new boss is a very touchy, difficult man; you will have to walk like Agag when you talk to him.' From the Bible (I Samuel XV, 32, 33): 'Then said Samuel, bring ye hither to me Agag the King of the Amalekites. And Agag came unto him delicately. And Agag said, surely the bitterness of death is past . . . And Samuel hewed Agag in pieces.' cf. **'like walking/treading on eggshells' 175/11; 'like walking through a minefield' 247/16**.

2. **they are like David and Jonathan** – inseparable friends. A perfect friendship (II Samuel I, 26).

3. **a David and Goliath situation** – a situation in which one adversary is hopelessly outmatched by the other. 'How can you possibly compete with the shop across the road? They have a hundred times more capital than you. It's a David and Goliath situation.' See Matthew XX, 1–16.

4. **to drive like Jehu** – to drive recklessly. 'That young lad should have his driving licence taken away. He drives like Jehu.' In the Bible, Jehu was a chariot-driver who drove dangerously fast (II Kings IX, 20): 'The watchman told, saying . . . the driving is like the driving of Jehu, the son of Nimshi; for he driveth furiously.'

5. **as wise as Solomon** – very wise, sagacious, rational; to have a capacity for sound judgement. 'Let's ask old Mr Reeves how to invest our money. He's as wise as Solomon.' Solomon was the king of Israel (he died in about 930 BC) and was well known for his wisdom.

6. **a Jeremiah** – one who always sees everything in the gloomiest light. 'What a Jeremiah you are. You are always prophesying disaster!' Jeremiah was a prophet of gloom of the Old Testament.

7. **the worship of Mammon** – an excessive love of wealth which is pursued at the cost of one's duty to family and friends. Mammon is a synonym of avarice and the worship of money. 'You cannot serve God and Mammon' (Luke XVI, 13).

8. **to try the patience of Job** – to provoke even the most patient person. 'I've explained it to you a hundred times and you still don't understand! You would try the patience of Job!' Job was afflicted with every possible calamity but learned from God to bear his misfortunes with courage and patience. From the Old Testament. cf. **'to try the patience of a saint' 124/7**.

9. **a Job's comforter** – someone who calls to offer sympathy but makes matters worse by blaming the bereaved person for what has happened. 'I was so sorry to learn of your little boy's death. What a pity he was never inoculated.' In the Book of Job (Old Testament), Job is reproached by his friends for bringing calamity on himself by his disobedience to God.

10. **to out-herod Herod** – to exceed Herod in cruelty and wickedness. It was King Herod who had the babes of Bethlehem put to death (Matthew II, 16). The phrase comes from Shakespeare: 'I would have such a fellow shipped for o'erdoing Termagant; it out-herods Herod' (*Hamlet*, III, 2, 1).

11. **as poor as Lazarus** – very poor. From the Bible (Luke XVI, 19–31).

12. **to play Judas** – to be a traitor. Judas Iscariot betrayed Jesus for 30 pieces of silver.

13. **the kiss of Judas** – any display of affection whose purpose is to conceal an act of treachery. It was the kiss of Judas that betrayed Jesus to the Roman soldiers (Matthew XXVI, 49).

14. **a piece of Jesuitry** – a very subtle argument, full of sophistry and logic carried to extremes.

Classical and Mythical Names

15. **an Adonis** – any young man of striking beauty. The phrase is sometimes used as a light-hearted compliment. 'With an Adonis like Mark at your side, you had better watch out. Half the girls in Tonbridge will be after him!'

an Adonis complex – the quest of young men to look good and feel good by having the strong, lean look, and sporting big powerful muscles on their arms and chest. 'Thomas has an Adonis complex and spends all his spare time at the gym.' In Greek mythology, the goddess Aphrodite was in love with the handsome young man, Adonis.

1. **beyond the dreams of Croesus** – unimaginable riches. Croesus, king of Lydia 560–546 BC, was reputed to be the richest man of all time. He was overthrown by Cyrus of Persia. King Croesus struck the first 2,500 coins made of pure gold. Also: **as rich as Croesus**; **richer than Croesus**.

2. **a clash of Titans** – a confrontation between two powerful adversaries. 'This court action should be really exciting: a clash of Titans.' In Greek mythology, the Titans were enormously giants who fought against the Olympian gods but lost.

   high-street Titans – big supermarkets.

3. **a Janus / Janus-like** – to be two-faced, hypocritical. 'Descartes (the French philosopher, 1596–1660) was a Janus with one face smiling at the conventional wisdom, and the other sceptical of it' (from Frederic Raphael's review of *Descartes: The Project of Pure Inquiry* by Bernard Williams). Janus was a Roman god of communication and guardian of the gate of heaven. He guarded doors and gates and had two faces, front and back, so that he could see everywhere, but each face had a contradictory expression and this is how he became associated with hypocrisy. cf. '**to be two-faced**' **84/7**.

4. **to stand like a Colossus** – someone outstanding on account of his great power or genius. 'For nearly 16 years Helmut Kohl stood like a Colossus among German politicians.' In ancient Greece, the Colossus was a gigantic statue of Apollo at Rhodes which stood in front of the harbour.

5. **to play Cupid** – to play the matchmaker. Cupid (Greek: Eros), son of Venus (Aphrodite), was the god of love. He is represented in fable as a boy of great beauty, with wings, carrying a bow and arrows.

6. **opening Pandora's box** – accepting a dangerous present which will bring every conceivable ill upon one's head. 'It looks as if some scientists are opening Pandora's box. They don't seem to care about the dangers of GM food.' From the Greek myth which relates how Pandora, the first woman ever made, was given a box by the gods whose contents when released would afflict the human race ever after. Only hope remained in the box. cf. '**to open/open up a can of worms**' **76/7**.

7. **to be as old as Methuselah** – the name is a symbol of longevity and the phrase is often used humorously, e.g. 'That joke is as old as Methuselah.' Methuselah is a mythical figure who was reputed to have lived for 969 years.

8. **Homer sometimes nods** – even the greatest of mortals errs from time to time. Horace excuses Homer's occasional drowsiness in view of the great length of his poem.

9. **platonic love** – pure love between men and women in which there is no sexuality. The phrase occurs at the end of the *Symposium* when Plato refers to the non-sexual love that Socrates felt for young men.

10. **socratic method** – the rigorous logical analysis that the Greek philosopher, Socrates, applied to every problem.

11. **a Caesarean operation / a Caesarean** – the cutting of the abdomen to effect delivery of the child, as with Julius Caesar. Caesarean is derived from the Latin *caesus*, the past participle of *caedere*, meaning 'to cut'.

12. **like Caesar's wife** – above suspicion (of any crime or immoral behaviour). Only used of important public figures. 'Ministers of the Crown must be like Caesar's wife. If their private lives give rise to scandal, they are expected to resign.' When asked why he divorced his wife, Caesar replied: 'I wished my wife to be not so much as suspected' (Caesar, *Roman Apothegms*).

13. **Achilles' heel** – the one and only weakness, but a fatal one. 'Brian could have

been a rich man today had it not been for his gambling, his Achilles' heel.' From the legend of Achilles whose body, when a baby, was immersed by his nurse in the river Styx to make him invulnerable (the *Iliad* of Homer). cf. **'a chink in someone's armour' 249/3**; **'to have feet of clay' 107/10**.

1. **Herculean efforts** – immense, almost superhuman efforts. Hercules earned immortality for himself by accomplishing 12 enormously difficult tasks set him by the Argive king. 'It will need Herculean efforts to master French in six months.'

2. **a Sisyphean task** – a laborious, futile and never-ending task. 'Sweeping the sand off the desert railway track is a Sisyphean task. One hour later, the sand has covered the track again.' Sisyphus, the king of Corinth, was forced to roll an enormous stone up a steep hill in Tartarus (part of the Underworld). Sadly, he could never reach the top with it because it kept on rolling down the hill again. He had to repeat this again and again.

3. **draconian punishments** – very heavy punishments. 'Soon shops not selling in metric weights and measures will face draconian punishments.' Draco was one of the nine chief magistrates in Athens in 621 BC who issued extremely severe laws and punishments that were so bad that Demades, an orator, said that they were written in blood.

   draconian measures / draconian laws – very harsh measures, laws; **draconian powers** – hard-hitting authority. 'The taxman is going to be given new draconian powers – so watch out!'

4. **the sword of Damocles / like the sword of Damocles hanging over one** – the danger that looms ahead and threatens our well-being. 'The danger of war hangs over humanity like the sword of Damocles. 'From the legend of King Dionysius, who made his courtier Damocles sit under a sword that hung from the ceiling by a single hair, in order to demonstrate to him the precariousness of a king's life which he so much envied. cf. **'a skeleton at the feast' 112/3**.

5. **the Midas touch** – a person is said to have 'the Midas touch' when all his business ventures prosper spectacularly. The phrase comes from the legend of Midas, king of Phrygia, whose prayer that anything he touched might turn to gold was granted by the gods as a reward for his hospitality to Dionysius' tutor.

6. **to cut the Gordian knot** – to take decisive action in order to gain one's ends. There was an ancient legend that the first person to untie the Gordian knot would gain the empire of Asia. Many travellers had failed to unravel the knot, but Alexander the Great solved the problem by cutting the knot with his sword, and then went on to win all Asia in accordance with the legend.

7. **a Pyrrhic victory** – an apparent victory which in fact is no victory at all. The phrase comes from the victory won by King Pyrrhus at Asculum in 279 BC which cost him many of his best men. After the battle, Pyrrhus remarked: 'One more such victory and we are finished.'

8. **a Procrustean bed** – a harsh, inhumane system into which the individual is fitted by force, regardless of his own needs or wishes. The phrase is taken from the name of the Greek robber who forced his victims to lie on a couch. If they were too long, he chopped off their feet, and if they were too short, he stretched their bodies to the required length. The phrase is often used in political debate.

9. **like a sphinx / sphinx-like** – mysterious, inscrutable. 'When the journalists asked the minister about her policies, she gave them a sphinx-like smile.' In Greek mythology, the Sphinx was a winged monster of Thebes with a woman's head and a lion's body. She proposed a riddle to the Thebans and devoured all those who could not guess it. Oedipus was able to solve it and so the Thebans were free from her terror at last. There is also a Sphinx in Egypt, a colossal statue near the pyramids at Giza. It was made in the shape of a man-headed lion, 19.8 metres high and more than 72 metres long, and carved out of natural rock.

10. **remember Ozymandias** – be humble, don't boast, for even the great will one

day fade from memory. 'Ozymandias' is the title of a sonnet written by Shelley in 1817 about the Egyptian ruler Ramses the Great, who died in 1237 BC.

1. **the Oedipus complex** – the association of patricidal fantasies and feelings of guilt in the mind of the young boy; a concept of the Freudian school of psychoanalysis based on the ancient Greek myth of Oedipus, who unwittingly slew his father and married his mother. cf. '**Othello's syndrome' 227/10**.

2. **the Hippocratic Oath** – the code of medical ethics contained in the writings of the Greek physician Hippocrates, the 'father' of medicine. The principal requirements of the oath are that the physician should act with absolute integrity towards his or her patient, and respect the confidentiality of a consultation.

Names from Literature

3. **an Aladdin's cave** – a place full of riches and good things. 'The little refugee girl spent the whole morning in the famous toy shop up in town. It was like an Aladdin's cave to her.' From the story of Aladdin in *The Thousand and One Nights*, a collection of Indian, Persian and Arabic stories first published in England in the early 18th century. Aladdin obtains a magic lamp from a cave full of treasures.

4. **like a Rip van Winkle** – a man who lives in the past, and is out of touch with modern life. 'You might have got the house for that price 30 years ago, but not today. Where have you been living all this time? You are a real Rip van Winkle!' In Washington Irving's fable, Rip van Winkle falls asleep for 20 years, and when he awakes, he finds his house deserted; he is bewildered and lost.

5. **a Darby and Joan** – an elderly married couple who have been happy together for many years. The names may derive from the characters in an 18th-century song.

6. **Lilliputian** – fussy, small-minded people. Taken from Jonathan Swift's *Gulliver's Travels*, whose purpose was to show how small-minded we all are by portraying mankind as a race of pygmies preoccupied with the pettiest pursuits.

7. **like *Hamlet* without the prince** – said when the most important person at an event is absent. 'To have the last day of the party conference without the leader would be like *Hamlet* without the prince.' In other words, the play would lose all its meaning if the part of Hamlet were omitted, because he is the main character. The idiom derives from an occasion long ago when the man who should have acted Hamlet was indisposed, and so the performance had to take place without the main actor.

8. **like Hamlet / Hamlet-like indecision** – to be as hesitant and indecisive as Prince Hamlet in Shakespeare's play of the same name. 'Now that everyone knows the politician has two mistresses, he doesn't know what to do. Like Hamlet, he cannot make up his mind – should he resign or not?' Note the famous line from Hamlet's speech in Act III, Scene i: 'To be, or not to be, that is the question.'

9. **to be a Shylock** – to be a ruthless, pitiless money-lender who will extract the last penny from his debtor. Taken from Shakespeare's *Merchant of Venice*.

10. **Othello's syndrome** – a psychiatric condition in which a husband is furiously jealous of anyone paying attention to his wife. It affects middle-aged men and can lead to the use of violence against their wives. In Shakespeare's play *Othello, the Moor of Venice*, Othello marries Desdemona but, thanks to the cunning Iago, believes that his wife is in love with Cassio. Othello smothers Desdemona in bed in a fit of frenzied jealousy. cf. '**the Oedipus complex' 227/1**.

11. **a Don Juan** – a man who is always falling in and out of love, one who has an insatiable love for women. 'He's a real Don Juan.' A notorious rake of the 14th century, Don Juan is the legendary hero of many stories, plays and poems. He is the central figure in Mozart's *Don Giovanni* and Byron's *Don Juan*.

12. **a Jekyll and Hyde personality** – someone who alternates great kindness and nobility of character with extreme

brutality and barbarism. The phrase is taken from Robert Louis Stevenson's novel which depicts the good Dr Jekyll changing into the evil Mr Hyde. The character created by Stevenson was intended as a symbol of the struggle between good and evil in each one of us.

1. **to be a Scrooge / Scrooge-like** – to be a miser. Scrooge is the main character in Dickens' *A Christmas Carol*, well known for being extremely mean.

2. **like a Micawber/Micawberish** – someone who makes no provision for the future and hopes something will turn up. Taken from a character in Dickens' *David Copperfield*.

3. **Robin Hood policies** – the policy of taking money from the rich and giving it to the poor. Robin Hood was the name of the legendary outlaw who lived with his men in Sherwood Forest in the 13th century and was reputed to rob the king's officers in order to help the peasants.

4. **to go Humpty Dumpty / like Humpty Dumpty** – to fall to pieces, to go badly wrong. 'When all the minister's plans went Humpty Dumpty, he tried to put the blame on his advisers.' Humpty Dumpty is the egg sitting on the wall who 'had a great fall' in the children's nursery rhyme. A person who is short and round and dumpy may also be called a Humpty Dumpty. cf. '**to go pear-shaped**' **183/ 11.**

5. **the Goldilocks way** – one's attempt to get things just right. 'The general was determined to stick to his "Goldilocks" war plans – he would fight the enemy in a way that was not too hard and not too soft.' From the children's story 'Goldilocks and the Three Bears', in which Goldilocks tries out the food, chairs and beds of the three bears, and finds them too hot, too cold, too hard, too soft, etc., until eventually she discovers the ones that are 'just right' for her.

6. **the Cinderella of** – the least admired. 'The problem of tramps and schizophrenics sleeping on the streets is still the Cinderella of spending priorities.' The phrase is taken from the fairy tale in which Cinderella was forced to drudge all

day at home while her step-mother and two step-sisters enjoyed themselves at palatial balls.

   a Cinderella disease – diseases such as Alzheimer's, prostate cancer and ME (chronic fatigue syndrome) which receive less attention and therefore less funding.

7. **like Alice in Wonderland / Alice-like** – illogical, incomprehensible, impractical. Ideas and projects which can exist only in the realm of fantasy and wild imagination. 'First I am blamed for taking the girl out, then the next day I am blamed for not taking her out. It's like something out of Alice in Wonderland.' From *Alice's Adventures in Wonderland* by Lewis Carroll, an imaginary world where the inhabitants are all insane, and the laws of logic and reason have been suspended.

8. **to grin/smile like a Cheshire Cat/ like the Cheshire Cat / like the Cheshire Cat's smile** – to grin widely from ear to ear. Lewis Carroll wrote about the Cheshire Cat in *Alice's Adventures in Wonderland*. One possible origin of the expression could be Cheshire cheese (from the English county of Cheshire), which might at one time have had the head of a grinning cat stamped on top.

9. **to be as pleased as Punch** – absolutely delighted, usually with oneself over some achievement. 'My daughter is as pleased as Punch. She has just had an article published in the *Daily Mail*.' Punch is always portrayed as laughing or singing with pleasure at his own escapades. Indeed, he can never change his expression as he has been carved out of wood.

10. **to play Punch and Judy over something** – in which two people have an enormous argument and fling accusations at each other. 'The architect and the builder are playing Punch and Judy over this new house. The architect is blaming the builder for shoddy workmanship and the builder is blaming the architect for his difficult plans.' Mr Punch is the hero of quite a violent puppet play, based on an Italian play, written about 1600. Punch kills his baby out of jealousy; his wife, Judy, then hits him with a bludgeon; Punch hits back and kills her.

1. **a Frankenstein monster** – the product of an inventor's imagination which destroys his creator. The phrase is taken from the famous horror story by Mary Shelley about a young student, Frankenstein, who makes a monster which becomes so powerful that it eventually destroys him. Parallels have been drawn with modern scientific discoveries, particularly in the biogenetic field.

    Frankenstein foods – genetically modified (GM) food. 'Frankenstein foods are secretly creeping into our diets.' In the words of Prince Charles: 'What right do we have to experiment Frankenstein-like with the very stuff of life?'

2. **Kafka-like / Kafka-esque** – relating to the bewildering and relentless officialdom/bureaucracy that is encountered in Kafka's work. 'We were passed from one official to another, nobody giving us an answer, but always referring us to another department. It was unbelievably frustrating, a really Kafka-like situation.' Franz Kafka (1883–1924) was a German-speaking Jewish novelist, born in Prague. In his novels, guilt is a major theme, and the individual is seen as totally alone, threatened and confused.

3. **an Orwellian future** – a nightmarish world of dehumanized beings, dominated by authoritarian organizations. 'In a recent speech, Prince Charles warned us about redesigning the natural world for the sake of convenience and embarking on an Orwellian future.' The novel *1984*, written by George Orwell in 1949, describes an authoritarian society rendered inhuman by the activities of the Thought Police, agents of 'Big Brother', who have stamped out all freedom of expression. Also: **Orwellian political correctness**.

4. **a Heath Robinson affair** – any machine that has been made amateurishly. 'Who ever installed your water-heater? It's a Heath Robinson affair!' W. Heath Robinson (1872–1944) illustrated the most complicated contraptions in the humorous magazine *Punch* and elsewhere.

5. **Noddy college courses** – near-valueless courses offered in colleges of higher education, courses that are unlikely to further one's future career. Noddy is a character invented by Enid Blyton, a famous writer of children's books.

6. **waiting for Godot** – waiting for ever because Godot never comes. From the play *Waiting for Godot* by Samuel Beckett.

Political and Historical Names

7. **like King Canute / Canute-like** – someone who tries to prevent the inevitable. 'The minister tried, Canute-like, to halt the stream of asylum seekers pouring into the country.' Canute was a Danish prince who became king of England (1016–35), Norway and Denmark. Supposedly he sat on the beach on his throne, surrounded by his flatterers, in order to demonstrate his power by forbidding the tide to come in and make him wet. In reality, however, he did this to show that he was not superhuman but in awe of nature and full of humility.

8. **Rabelaisian wit** – the earthy humour characteristic of the great French writer François Rabelais (1494–1553).

9. **Machiavellian cunning** – the most subtle, unprincipled cunning. In his treatise on state-craft, *The Prince*, Machiavelli (1469–1527) tried to establish the principles of political power which he maintained were based on realism rather than conventional morality. Machiavelli's book foreshadowed Bismarck's 'Realpolitik' in the 19th century.

10. **he's a real Casanova!** – he is irresistible to women. Also: **my Casanova of a son** – my amorous son. Casanova (1725–98) was an Italian adventurer who had a reputation for being one of the world's greatest lovers. cf. **'a heart-throb' 114/19**; **'a lady killer' 235/5**.

11. **as dead as Queen Anne / Queen Anne is dead** – said in reply to news that is no longer new. 'Did you say your brother is engaged to Judy? Yes and Queen Anne is dead. I knew about their engagement weeks ago.' cf. **'as dead as a dodo' 71/9**; **'as dead as a door-nail' 250/11**; **'as**

dead as mutton' 180/14; 'that's old hat' 195/7.

1. **like the Luddites** – a term of abuse for anybody who opposes the introduction of labour-saving machinery which may threaten his or her livelihood. The phrase comes from the 'Luddite' mechanics who attempted to destroy the new machinery in the Midlands and North of England which had been installed to replace their handicrafts, 1811–16.

2. **on a Napoleonic scale** – on a huge, ambitious scale.

3. **a maverick** – someone who is wild, reckless, out of control. Originally, an unbranded calf, named after a Texan ranger of that name who did not brand his cattle. Later, the name was given to politicians who refused to give allegiance to the party leadership.

4. **Houdini-like ability/skill** – someone who is able to wriggle out of difficult situations. The corrupt politicians in that country have a Houdini-like ability to escape conviction. Frequent usage: **a Houdini-like ability to save one's skin**. The escapologist Harry Houdini, born Erich Weiss (1874–1926), was the most spectacular showman of his time. He died at the age of 52 of internal injuries after being punched in the stomach. Note: a '**Houdini**' is US slang for someone who avoids (i.e. escapes from) work.

5. **to boycott** – to coerce a person by forbidding any social or commercial relations with him. In 1880, the Irish Land League resolved that anyone buying the farm of an evicted tenant should be treated like a leper. The first victim of this policy was Captain Boycott who had defied the League and was consequently '**boycotted**'. The term 'boycott' was later extended to similar action taken against organizations or countries, and has been used in this way ever since.

6. **Custer's last stand** – any man who goes down to defeat in a spectacular manner. Custer was an American general whose troops were wiped out in an Indian ambush.

7. **the Maginot Line** – something which is blindly, and foolishly, relied on, sometimes with dire consequences. 'The employment minister called the retirement age at 55 the Maginot Line of social progress.' André Maginot (1877–1932) was a French war minister, responsible for the French fortifications along the German border known as the Maginot Line. This line of defence was blindly relied on but proved a failure as the German forces entered France via Belgium, in 1940. cf. '**a glass ceiling' 161/14**.
   Maginot-minded – dull and boring, having no new ideas.

8. **Colonel Bogey** – a fictitious figure who established the par score for every golf course in the land. He was presumed to play every stroke correctly without ever making a mistake. Only the most brilliant golfers were able to beat Colonel Bogey's score.

9. **a Blimpish point of view** – any reactionary or unprogressive point of view that harks back to the pre-war period in Britain. Colonel Blimp, a red-faced elderly colonel, invented by David Low, the celebrated cartoonist, was a familiar figure of fun in the 1930s.

10. **to do a Thatcher** – to stay in power as prime minister for three consecutive terms. From the former Conservative prime minister Margaret Thatcher.

11. **a spoonerism** – the funny-sounding result of mixing up the initial sounds of two or more words by mistake. Some well-known spoonerisms are: a well-boiled icicle – a well-oiled bicycle; our queer old dean – our dear old queen; a half-warmed fish – a half-formed wish; 'Work is the curse of the drinking classes' (Oscar Wilde) – drink is the curse of the working classes. The Reverend William Spooner was Dean and Warden of New College, Oxford (1844–1930). A very nervous speaker, he often made funny mistakes like these, which his students referred to as 'spoonerisms'.

12. **malapropism** – the putting of words in the wrong place. From Mrs Malaprop in Sheridan's *The Rivals*. An 'allegory on the banks of the Nile' is an example of her speech.

1. **to have Hobson's choice** – to have no choice at all. 'You advertise a wide choice of holidays but you are only offering me one! It is Hobson's choice!' Tobias Hobson, a 17th-century Cambridge carrier, who hired out horses to the undergraduates of the university, never allowed his customers to choose a horse but insisted on their taking the horse nearest the stable door, so that they had no choice at all.

2. **Occam's razor** – the ruthless analysis of a problem which eliminates all superfluous factors. Occam of Ockham, Surrey (died 1349), held that entities must not be needlessly multiplied and that we were only entitled to generalize from experience.

3. **Parkinson's Law** – the title of a book by C. Northcote Parkinson in which he makes fun of the civil service. Parkinson's Law states: (1) the work done is in inverse proportion to the number of civil servants employed, and (2) public expenditure rises to accommodate the growth in bureaucracy. In other words, the more civil servants the state employs, the more work they will make in order to justify their existence and their salaries.

4. **Montezuma's revenge** – food poisoning with bad stomach pains and diarrhoea, caught by tourists in Mexico from eating Mexican food. Montezuma was the last Aztec emperor (1466–1520), who was seized, taken hostage and killed by the Spanish invaders led by Hernando Cortés, thus fulfilling the prophecy that strangers would come to rule in Tenochtitlán. From the day of his murder, all strangers coming to Mexico were supposed to suffer Montezuma's revenge. cf. **'Delhi belly' 212/5**.

5. **a grin like St Elmo's fire** – a flicker of a grin. ' "Now for my best spell!" So saying, the magician held up a sword to his audience, a grin flickering across his lips like St Elmo's fire.' St Elmo's fire is the ball of fire which is sometimes seen playing around the masts of ships in a storm. The name Elmo comes from the patron saint of seamen, St Erasmus, a bishop from Syria who lived in the fourth century.

Brand Names

6. **a Rolls-Royce mind** – a superior mind, to be outstandingly intelligent. 'We need to employ someone with a Rolls-Royce mind to steer the company out of this crisis.' Rolls-Royce is famous for the superior quality of its cars. The company was set up by Sir Henry Royce (1863–1933) and Charles Rolls (1877–1910).

    to move/run like a Rolls – to move/run perfectly and with the utmost smoothness (like a Rolls-Royce car).

7. **the real McCoy** – the genuine thing, not an imitation. 'My dad brought me back some jeans from America. They are the real McCoy!' McCoy (the name possibly deriving from a Scottish whisky which was imported to the US) was advertised as being 'the genuine liquor' in an American newspaper in 1930.

8. **the Barbour brigade** – members of the rich upper class, especially those who like hunting and shooting and walking about in the countryside in all kinds of weather. Barbour is the name of a very high-quality waterproof jacket or coat which has been made of waxed cotton, usually dark green, dark blue or black.

9. **to look like something from Woolworths** – to look rather cheap. 'Marion was wearing a beautiful evening dress but spoilt the effect by wearing a necklace which looked like something from Woolworths.' Woolworths is a large shop selling a wide variety of articles at a reasonable price. Snobbish people look down on Woolworths.

Show Business Names

10. **the Oprah effect** – Oprah Winfrey's powerful influence on the ordinary person, inspiring him or her to enjoy reading. Many books that have been recommended by her on her television bookclub programme have become bestsellers. The US talk-show queen, Oprah has become the most successful promoter of books of all time.

1. **the Patsy problem** – high-powered career women who might suffer a heart attack because they sit around in their offices too much, endure great stress and indulge in too much social drinking. From the television show *Absolutely Fabulous*, in which Joanna Lumley plays such a character, called Patsy. cf. **'a couch potato'** 185/5.

Surnames

2. **keeping up with the Joneses** – trying to maintain the same standards of material comfort as one's neighbours, who are represented by the very ordinary name of Jones. 'Just because our neighbours have bought a Daimler, that's no reason why we should buy one. I have no intention of keeping up with the Joneses.'

Power, Control

1. **pester power** – firms who wish to sell their products to children make them especially eye-catching and tempting to the youngsters by means of cartoon characters and bright colours, etc. The children will then pester their exhausted parents to buy these more expensive products instead of similar, cheaper products which do not use these hard-sell tactics. 'I'll do my shopping while the children are at school today. That means: no stress, no sulks, no pester power.'

2. **a power partnership / a power couple** – a young couple in which the man and the woman are both executives and have the same status in business. 'Philip and Lynette have a power partnership in this highly successful business.'

3. **a power nap** – a short sleep to replenish one's energies, especially in the case of businessmen and women. ' "Mrs Porton cannot see you at the moment," the secretary said. "She is taking a power nap." ' See: *Power Sleep* by Dr James Mass; *The Art of Napping at Work* by Bill Anthony. cf. 'a cat nap' 55/6.
   power breakfast, lunch, etc. – a meal during which one talks business with one's associates.

4. **to be power-mad/power-hungry / to thirst for power** – to long to be in power.
   to trade on the trappings of power – to make unfair use of objects connected with power, such as free rides on Concorde, etc.

5. **a second-class power** – no longer one of the first most powerful countries in the world. ' "We must fight this war and win it," the prime minister declared. "We don't want to become a second-class power." '

6. **girl power** – the influence that young women feel they can wield over social and economic issues. The Spice Girls took on the slogan of Girl Power, a term which has been current since the 1980s.
   power dressing – wearing smart suits.

7. **to do one the power of good** – something which makes you healthy and happy. 'Going cycling for one hour every day does my husband the power of good.'

8. **a power house** – an influential person who generates powerful ideas and is full of energy and strength to carry them out. 'Joseph John is this firm's power house, and with him in charge we shall soon be the most successful computer firm in Britain.'

9. **a control freak** – someone with an abnormal desire to control, command or dominate. 'Don't apply for a job with that firm. The director is a control freak.'

Emperor

10. **the emperor's new clothes** – there is really nothing interesting or spectacular there at all. This expression is used when, for example, famous critics, agents, art dealers, etc., praise a work of art which is quite without merit. But, because they praise it, people who wish to be regarded as clever and fashionable praise it too, and are willing to spend enormous sums of money on it. This idiom could also be used in the field of cosmetics, fashion, diet pills, fake medicine and some kinds

of bottled water. It derives from the fairy story 'The Emperor's New Clothes' by Hans Christian Andersen, in which the emperor is swindled by two crooks into believing they have made him a beautiful costume out of gold thread. In reality he is naked, as they have stolen the gold thread for themselves. None of his subjects dares to admit that they can't see the new clothes, until the illusion is finally broken when a little boy points at the naked emperor and laughs.

King

1. Similes with 'king': **as rich as a king** – wealthy, affluent; **to feel like a king** – to feel majestic and proud; **to be treated like a king** – to act or behave towards someone with the utmost respect, to see to his every need.

2. **fit for a king** – suitable for a king's use. 'That was a wonderful dinner you gave me – fit for a king.'

3. **a king-pin** – the most important person in any organization. 'You'd better not quarrel with Johnson; he's the king pin on the local council.' In the game of skittles, the king-pin is the most important piece.

4. **the king of the castle** – the most important person in the locality. From the children's game of the same name; one child stands on top of a sandcastle while the other children try to knock him off.

5. **a king's ransom** – a huge, excessively large sum of money. 'You'd have to pay a king's ransom 'for a house that size looking on to the sea.' Originally, the money that had to be paid for the release of a captured king.

Kingdom

6. **to send/blow to kingdom come** – to send/blow to the next world, to kill. The kingdom is the Kingdom of God. 'If the bomb explodes, we shall all be sent to kingdom come.'

Queen

7. **to feel like a queen** – to feel majestic and splendid.

8. **to queen/lord it** – to domineer over, to take advantage of one's rank to humiliate someone. 'I don't like the way your friend Doris queens it over the other girls in the office. Who does she think she is!'

9. **a media queen** – a beautiful woman who is the favourite subject of journalists and television reporters.

10. **a drag queen** – a man dressing up as a woman, often appearing on stage for entertainment. In the US, drag queens often appear on television chat shows.

Prince

11. **the prince of liars** – the biggest liar of all, the worst of liars. 'Peter is an awful liar but he is nothing compared with your brother, who must be the prince of liars.' The reference is to the Devil.

12. **put not your trust in princes** – men of power and influence can be just as fickle and unreliable as the rest of us. 'I am not in the least surprised that the boss has forgotten about your promotion. Put not your trust in princes.' The reference is to Psalms CXLVI, 3.

13. **a princely gift/sum** – a very generous gift, a magnificent, splendid sum of money. 'Mr Wallis was offered the princely sum of £30,000 for his old car.'

Princess

14. **to feel like a princess** – to feel elevated, magnificent and proud.

15. **the People's Princess** – Diana, the Princess of Wales (1961–97), ex-wife of Prince Charles and daughter-in-law of Queen Elizabeth II. Diana devoted herself to charitable and humanitarian causes. She secretly modelled herself on her ancestor Elisabeth Stuart (born 1595), who was stunningly beautiful and much beloved by her people – the very first Queen of Hearts. There was huge sadness from

people all over the world following her tragic death and that of her boyfriend, Dodi Fayed, in a car crash in Paris.

Duchess

1. **the Duchess of Death** – Agatha Christie (1890–1976), the most successful writer of detective stories of all time. She wrote 80 books, which were published in 103 countries, selling more than 2 billion copies. She was also called the Queen of Crime.

Lord

2. **to live like a lord** – to live in great luxury with the best food and wine, and be waited upon by many servants. 'I don't know where he gets the money from, but he seems to be living like a lord.'

3. **as drunk as a lord** – very drunk indeed. 'When I arrived at the party last night, your boyfriend was already as drunk as a lord.' Lords had a reputation for drunkenness, because they had so much money and nothing to spend it on except their own pleasure. In the 18th and 19th centuries, many rich men drank enormous amounts of wine. Their drunkenness got even worse after the Methuen Treaty of 1703 which allowed Portuguese wines, including port, to be imported very cheaply.

Lady

4. **like a lady / lady-like / in a lady-like way/manner/fashion** – to behave perfectly, faultlessly, to have excellent manners, to be exquisite. ' "Make sure you get out of the car in a lady-like way," the duchess warned her teenage daughter. "The photographers will be waiting for you!" ' Also: **a lady-like accent**.

5. **a lady killer** – a handsome man who believes that women cannot resist him and want him desperately. He will break many women's hearts. 'You're right, Rosemary, he is very handsome, but beware – he has a reputation for being a lady killer.' cf. **'a heart-throb' 114/19**; **'he's a real Casanova' 229/10**; **'to break one's heart' 114/18**.

6. **a ladies' man / a lady's man** – a man who enjoys being in the company of women.

Knight

7. **a knight in shining armour** – a man of great nobility and gallantry who will defend our rights without asking anything in return. 'If you want my advice, I'm afraid you'll have to pay for it; I'm a solicitor, not a knight in shining armour.'

Royal

8. **a battle royal** – a tremendous battle worthy of a contest between two kings. 'There was a battle royal going on between the two grandmothers who each wanted to look after the baby during the mother's absence.'

9. **the royal road to** – the easiest and quickest way to. 'There is no royal road to freedom; you have to fight for it.'

10. **a royal welcome** – a splendid welcome, one that is fit for a king. 'When we arrived at a small village in Lapland, we were surprised at the royal welcome the villagers gave us.'

11. **to feel like royalty** – to feel like a member of the Royal Family, to feel majestic. 'My uncle was a chauffeur and he sometimes gave me a lift in the firm's Jaguar. I felt like royalty sitting in the back.'

12. **right royal** – splendid, marvellous. 'Right royal' can also be used ironically in the sense of terrible or appalling. 'You made a right royal mess of the business while I was away; it will take months to put it right.'

Throne

13. **the power behind the throne** – someone with real, as opposed to nominal or symbolic, power. 'If you want a job in that company, you'd better apply to the secretary, not to the chairman. The secretary is the power behind the throne.' cf. **'the driving force' 153/12**.

Crown

1. **to take the crown** – to win the first prize. 'I wonder which baby will take the crown. They are all so beautiful.'

2. **to crown it all** – on top of everything else. 'Harry left his briefcase in the train, was told off by his boss for arriving late at the office, and, to crown it all, when he got home found that his house had been burgled.'

3. **one's crowning glory** – one's hair, or a wig. ' "I'm not going to let anyone cut off my crowning glory," the model told her agent defiantly.'

Court

4. **a friend at court** – someone in an influential position, who is able to help you. 'I'm not worried about the consequences; I have a friend at court.'

Ceremony

5. **to stand on ceremony** – to do something in the manner prescribed by custom or etiquette. 'Don't wait to be asked but help yourselves to the cakes. There's no need to stand on ceremony.'

The Upper Class

6. **'U' and 'Non-U'** – upper class and non upper class, based on Nancy Mitford's system of distinguishing social classes according to the words they use. For example: it is 'U' to say lavatory, and 'Non-U' to say toilet; 'U' to say napkin, 'Non-U' serviette; 'U' to have a bath, 'Non-U' to take a bath.

7. **the upper crust** (humorous) – the aristocracy. 'Joan is from the upper crust; you can tell by the way she walks and talks.'

Parliament

8. **the Mother of Parliaments** – the oldest Parliament in the world, a distinction that is claimed by the Parliaments in Westminster, the Isle of Man and the Swiss cantons; but, in England, the phrase is a synonym for Westminster.

9. **a hung Parliament** – one in which no single party commands a clear majority, and government can only be carried on by a coalition.

10. **a maiden speech** – the first speech a member makes in Parliament.

11. **a squeaky-clean candidate** – a person above reproach, with nothing to hide. 'In London the search was on for a squeaky-clean candidate to fill the office of mayor.'

12. **to lobby an MP** – to canvass an MP for support of one's case by going to Parliament and requesting to speak to him or her.

13. **to make a U-turn** – to pursue a policy in government that is directly opposed to one's party's election promises. **'There will be no U-turn'** means that there will be no change in policy. At the Conservative Party Conference in October 1981 Margaret Thatcher declared: 'The lady's not for turning', meaning that there would be no relaxation in the government's fight against inflation. (This was also a pun on the title of Christopher Fry's play *The Lady's Not For Burning*, about Joan of Arc.)

14. **to paper over the cracks** – to pretend that agreement on all important issues has been reached. 'Now that the election is approaching, the Party managers are papering over the cracks to impress the voters.' Papering over the cracks is a common device for concealing the structural weaknesses of a house from a buyer.

15. **to go/appeal to the country** – to call a general election.

16. **a floating voter** – a voter at a general election who has not decided which party to vote for. Having no strong opinions, he or she will be pushed in this direction or that like someone floating on the water. 'Preparing for the coming general election, the prime minister headed for a question-and-answer session with floating voters.'

17. **a focus group** – a small group of people who are asked about their opinions of pol-

itical parties and leaders. 'Quite often focus groups agree with opinion polls but now and again the difference is quite big.'

1. **to win by a landslide** (US colloquialism) – to win an election by an overwhelming majority of seats. A landslide denotes a fundamental shift in the political and social attitudes of the electorate. In 1945 in Britain, Labour won by a landslide; in 1980, Ronald Reagan won the presidential election in one of the biggest landslides in the history of America.

2. **to rig the poll** – to conduct a poll fraudulently, as by managing the poll in one's own interests instead of putting it under the control of an independent authority.

3. **to climb/jump on the bandwagon** – to join a popular trend for the sake of material advantage. 'When Krugerrands rose quickly in value, many investors jumped on the bandwagon and bought as many as they could in the hope of making an easy profit.' The reference is to the custom in the USA of putting a band on a wagon to advertise a politician's campaign at election time. When it becomes clear who is going to win, many of the local leaders will 'jump on the bandwagon' to show their support in the hope of obtaining a well-paid job in the newly elected administration.

4. **to kick someone upstairs** – to promote someone who has proved unsatisfactory to a position of nominal importance without responsibility where he or she can do no harm. This is done when it would be embarrassing to dismiss or demote that person. Senior Cabinet ministers are sometimes '**kicked upstairs**' to the House of Lords to save them from humiliation.

5. **a hue and cry** – an outcry, public protest and opposition to an unpopular measure of the government.

   to raise a hue and cry – to organize opposition to an unpopular measure. 'The opposition raised a hue and cry against the government's decision to increase the salaries of the top civil servants.' Originally (*c.* 1584), the hue and cry was a system for the pursuit and arrest of criminals in which all citizens were obliged to take part (from French *huer*, meaning 'to shout').

6. **a witch-hunt** – a campaign against a group of dissidents within a party for advocating views that are contrary to official policy. There have been similar witch-hunts against homosexuals who occupy positions of trust in the security services. The term takes its name from the witch-hunts in the Middle Ages when thousands of young women in Europe were denounced for practising witchcraft, and burned at the stake.

7. **to be beaten at the hustings** – to lose an election to Parliament. The hustings are the open-air meetings at which the rival candidates argue their case. Husting is an Icelandic word formed by *hus*, meaning 'house', and *thing*, meaning 'assembly'.

25 War and Peace

War

1. **all's fair in love and war** – conventional morality does not apply to the most important activities in life.

2. **a tug of war** – a disagreement between two opposing parties. 'A tug of war has been going on between the two teachers for the post of headmaster.'
   a tug of love – the struggle between the mother and father over the custody of a child. 'It is always the child who suffers most over a tug of love.'

3. **to be/have been in the wars** (humorous) – to suffer/have suffered from a number of minor mishaps to one's health, all at the same time. 'A cut lip, a stiff neck and now a sore throat! You *have* been in the wars, Tim!'

4. **on the war-path** – in an aggressive mood, in search of one's enemy in order to start a fight with him.

5. **a war chest** – money which is specifically to pay for a war or a political campaign, such as advertising one's party for the next general election. 'It is rumoured that the Chancellor is planning to take £20 billion from his war chest to fight the next election.' Originally a war chest contained personal things which a soldier might find useful during a war, such as writing utensils, a mug, a hairbrush, a little lamp for signalling, a periscope, etc.

6. **a war of nerves** – constant attacks on the nerves of one's opponent, as by making propaganda against him and writing abusive letters to him. 'John and his neighbour are fighting a war of nerves against each other.'

7. **a trade war** – commercial parties fighting to gain the upper hand. Also: **a tit-for-tat trade war; a price war; a bidding war** (to see who can bid the most for something); **a beef war; water wars**.

8. **a cold war** – a diplomatic and economic struggle reflecting a high state of tension between the two power blocs which stops short of armed conflict. 'There were signs that the cold war between the West and Soviet Russia would soon be resumed.'

9. **a far-flung war** – a war which takes place far away from one's native country, and which has no political significance to it. 'Mark was bored stiff selling cinema tickets, so he has become a mercenary and gone to fight in some far-flung war.'

10. **a shooting war** – an outbreak of fighting. A shooting war is often contrasted with a cold war, when the hostility of the adversaries is limited to economic and diplomatic measures.

11. **friendship wars** – the struggle to make friends and keep them. ' "These friendship wars going on in my class are such a strain," the teacher sighed. "So many sulks and so many tears." ' See *Best Friends* by Terri Apter and Ruthellen Josselson.

12. **to be at war with weight** – to be absolutely determined to get slim. 'Judging by all these advertisements for slimming products, I think we must be a nation at war with weight.' cf. '**the battle of the bulge**' 239/4; '**to diet like a yo-yo / yo-yo dieting**' 312/12.

Battle, Fight

1. **to win a battle** – to be successful in a struggle. 'After several operations and painful treatments, Mrs Tilbrook won her battle over cancer.'

2. **a pitched battle** – a battle in which large forces on both sides are committed. This phrase is used in contrast with 'skirmishes' or 'guerrilla warfare'.

3. **half the battle** – the first steps in accomplishing a difficult task which often decide the outcome. 'We have got the best equipment for the job; that is half the battle.'

4. **the battle of the bulge** – the struggle to lose weight. 'Poor Sam! Look at him stuffing himself with chocolate. I think he's lost the battle of the bulge.' cf. '**to be at war with weight**' 238/12.

5. **to fight a losing battle** – to engage in a struggle which one cannot hope to win. 'We all fight a losing battle with age; it's better to grow old gracefully.'

6. **to be locked in battle** – to be engaged in a legal fight. 'There is still no end in sight for the two neighbours locked in battle over a piece of land.'

7. **one's home/place of work/school becomes a battleground** – a place where there are perpetual arguments, or where one must struggle to assert oneself.

8. **to mark out the battle lines** – a politician or businessman states his intentions very clearly and names his supporters and his opponents. 'Now that the election is drawing near, the battle lines are being marked out. Those who are in favour of bloodsports will vote for one politician, and those who are against them will vote for the other one.'

9. **a running battle/fight** – a long-protracted dispute. 'William has had a running battle/fight with his local council about the rates ever since he bought his house.' The phrase comes from naval warfare. A running battle is one that takes place between two hostile fleets while they are on the move, one advancing and the other retreating.

10. **to fight shy of** – to avoid, to keep away from. 'Paul fought shy of the law courts because the costs were so ruinously high.'

11. **to put up a good fight** – to fight hard, to be a worthy opponent. 'Although we lost the match, we put up a good fight, losing by three goals to one.'

12. **a good, clean fight** – a fair fight in which all the rules are obeyed.

13. **to spoil for a fight** – to seize on any pretext for a fight. 'When you pay our landlord the rent, be careful how you speak to him. He is spoiling for a fight with you.'

14. **to take the fight out of someone** – to defeat one's enemy so severely that he has no wish to continue the fight.
    to have plenty of fight left in one – despite a bad defeat, to be willing and able to continue the fight.

15. **a fighting chance** – a fair chance, a reasonable chance. 'Harry is very ill, but he still has a fighting chance of pulling through.'

16. **to fight it out** – to settle a dispute by fighting. 'Those boys have been quarrelling the whole term and no amount of argument is going to settle the matter. The best thing is for them to fight it out.'

17. **to fight to control oneself** – to struggle to get a hold of oneself. 'Mr Smith had to fight to control himself when the drunken man started yelling abuse at him and his wife.'

18. **fighting fit** – in excellent physical condition. 'Andrew is fighting fit and ready to start work again.' This phrase derives from cock-fighting.

19. **to show fight** – to accept a challenge, to indicate one's willingness to fight. 'We've had a letter from the defendant. He disputes your claim and he is showing plenty of fight.'

20. **a bare-knuckle fighter** – someone violently aggressive. 'Don't disagree with him at the meeting. He is a bare-knuckle fighter.'
    a dirty fighter – someone who uses underhanded tricks to win a fight; also used in politics.

1. **to fight tooth and nail** – to fight with the utmost ferocity. 'Our son has been accused of stealing from another boy. We are going to fight tooth and nail to defend him.'

2. **to go on the offensive** – to change one's tactics from defence to attack in a contest or argument. 'Now we have refuted Anderson's accusations, it's time we went on to the offensive and attacked him.'

3. **to be on the defensive** – to be extremely sensitive to criticism, to imagine an insult when none is intended. 'I haven't accused you of anything, Henry. Why are you so much on the defensive?'

4. **to throw someone on the defensive** – to seize the initiative from one's opponent and turn from defence to attack. 'The manager was complaining about my work, but I threw him on the defensive by reminding him that he had absented himself for two weeks without permission.'

5. **barbed-wire defences** – blocking a hostile take-over bid of some company. 'An English telephone company that is trying to take over a German one, is facing barbed-wire defences.'

6. **to blunt the attack** – to weaken the attack of one's opponent, to reduce its effect. 'At the meeting, Johnson was very critical of Hazel Smith's record, but she was able to blunt his attack by showing that he had a private grievance against her.'

7. **to go for the jugular** – to attack one's opponent in the most vulnerable place. 'Harold Wilson, ex-premier, once said that during his political career he always went for the jugular.'

8. **to open (up) a new front** – to shift one's attack to a new target, to approach a problem from a new angle. 'The replacement of a human heart by an artificial one opens up a new front in the treatment of heart diseases.'

9. **to put up a brave front** – not to show one's true feelings but to try to act cheerfully. 'Maggie didn't really like her new surroundings in the southernmost part of the town, but she put up a brave front for her husband's sake.'

10. **to take the line of least resistance** – (1) when on the attack, to avoid obstacles so as to keep moving forward; a very effective strategy in the Second World War. (2) to avoid opposition of any kind and to submit to other people's demands. 'Henry always took the line of least resistance with his wife and did whatever she wanted.'

11. **to beat a retreat** – to withdraw, to abandon a position one has taken up. 'When Roger heard that there was going to be a collection, he beat a hasty retreat.'

12. **to make a tactical retreat** – to retreat with the object of advancing later in more favourable circumstances. 'Simmonds is not pressing his claim to our land, but I think he is only making a tactical retreat. He is trying to obtain more evidence, then he will go back to the court.'

13. **to steal a march on** – to obtain an advantage over an opponent by making a sudden surprise move. 'Davis & Hay have stolen a march on us by starting their spring sales on the same day as we open our new shop.'

14. **to give someone his/her marching orders** – to dismiss, to terminate someone's employment abruptly. 'Claude didn't get in until three o'clock this morning. If she does that again, I shall give her her marching orders.'

15. **to go over the top** – to act rashly, wildly. 'At the auction, Mary had £50 to spend, but when she saw a painting by her favourite artist, she went over the top and bid £100 for it.' The reference is to the First World War when soldiers had to go over the top of their trenches in order to move forward and attack their enemy.

16. **to leave oneself wide open** – to offer an easy target to one's opponent/enemy. 'If you complain about the noise your neighbour makes, you will leave yourself wide open when you give a party for your son's 21st birthday.'

17. **a pincer movement** – an attack from two opposite directions. Often used humorously. 'Let's make a pincer move-

ment on Father about our summer holidays. You tell him you are fed up with the south coast, and I'll show him some photographs of Crete.'

1. **a sitting target** – a target that is vulnerable to attack. 'The teaching profession is a sitting target for criticism and always has been.' cf. **'a sitting duck'** 69/16.

2. **bang/plumb on target** – right in the centre of the target, a perfect aim.

3. **to use brute force** – to use physical strength rather than one's intelligence. 'Jones was the better boxer of the two but was overwhelmed by brute force.'

4. **to hold the fort** – to accept responsibilities in the absence of the person in charge. 'I have to meet my friend this afternoon. Could you hold the fort for me until I get back?' A military phrase meaning to hold one's position and not retreat.

Military Operation

5. **like a military operation** – to carry something out precisely and effectively. 'The school outing was extremely well organized, like a military operation.'

Vendetta

6. **to run/wage a vendetta against someone** – prolonged enmity and bitterness between two or more people, or a family. 'The science teacher accused his colleagues of running a vendetta against him because he was so popular with the pupils.' cf. **'to make bad blood between'** 113/6.

Warrior, Trooper, Cavalry

7. **an eco-warrior** – a militant environmental campaigner. 'Eco-warriors are determined to protect the countryside and promote green issues.'

8. **a gender warrior** – an extreme feminist. 'Gender warriors are not interested in preserving traditional family life.'

9. **to swear like a trooper** – to use lurid language when swearing, such as an ordinary soldier is supposed to do. 'When Mr Spencer's car key slipped out of his hand

and fell down the drain, he began to swear like a trooper.' Also: **to lie like a trooper**.

10. **to charge in like the 7th Cavalry** – to rush into something, act impulsively. 'If we want to catch these criminals, we must plan things carefully and not go charging in like the 7th Cavalry.

Blows

11. **a bitter blow** – a great shock and disappointment. 'The freeing of the alleged killer of her daughter came as a bitter blow to her father.'

12. **to strike a blow at** – to cause damage to. 'A series of food-poisoning incidents struck a blow at the restaurant's reputation.'

13. **to cause mayhem** – to cause confusion, violent disorder and rioting. 'Recently, animal welfare protesters caused mayhem at a farm breeding cats for scientific research.' Mayhem derives from 'maim' – a bruise, injury, crippling hurt.

14. **to bear the brunt of** – to receive most of the blame. 'When his little sister broke the valuable vase, Philip, being the elder brother, bore the brunt of his mother's anger.'

15. **in the grip of** – in the power of. 'Last winter Europe was in the grip of a flu epidemic.' An even stronger phrase: **in the iron grip of**.
    to get a grip on oneself / don't lose your grip – pull yourself together / don't lose control over yourself.

16. **to take a swipe at** – to make a damaging comment or remark. 'While the MP was touring his constituency, he took a swipe at his opponent by mentioning a controversial topic which the other man endorsed.'

17. **a severe jolt** – a great shock. 'Jack is working very hard now. Failing his last exam gave him a severe jolt.'

18. **a knock-on effect** – one action sets off another. 'Looting started in one shop and soon the knock-on effect was inevitable – all the shops in the road suffered.' cf. **'domino theory'** 309/8.

Peace

1. **to hold one's peace** – to keep silent. 'I shall hold my peace until I have had the opportunity to study the facts of the case.'

2. **to make one's peace** – to put an end to a quarrel. 'It's time you made your peace with Betty. You and she have always been such good friends.'

3. **a peace offering** – a gift made with the object of ending a quarrel and restoring a friendship.

4. **peace at any price** – the avoidance of war or violence, whatever the cost. The phrase applies not only to nations but also to private relationships. 'It's no good asking Father to support you in your row with the headmaster. Father is for peace at any price.'

5. **peace of mind** – inward serenity. 'Please telephone us as soon as you arrive. We shall have no peace of mind until we hear from you.'

Weapon

1. **a weapon** – a powerful help towards achieving one's aim. 'A hawthorn hedge with its sharp thorns is a good weapon for keeping intruders out of your garden.' Different types of 'weapon': **a new weapon against crime/fraud/drug-pushers etc.; a smart weapon against illnesses** – a very effective pill; **a secret weapon** – (1) the intelligent and attractive wife of a politician. 'Raisa was Mikhail Gorbachev's secret weapon who helped him shoot to power.' (2) any clever strategy one has up one's sleeve.

2. **a double-edged weapon** – a weapon which cuts both ways so that it may harm as well as benefit the user, particularly in an argument. 'If you reduce your children's pocket money, you will save money but they will hate you. It's a double-edged weapon!'

Gun, Pistol

3. **to carry too many guns** – to possess strong superiority over one's opponent. 'In the debate, the proposers of the motion carried too many guns for us: they had a better grasp of the facts, and they were more experienced in public speaking.'

4. **to go down with all guns firing** – to suffer defeat fighting manfully to the very end. 'Robin was knocked out in the fifth round, but he went down with all guns firing.'

5. **to stick to one's guns** – to defend one's position against strong opposition. 'Alan has been asked by his boss to withdraw his complaints, but he is sticking to his guns.'

6. **to go great guns** – to act with energy and efficiency. 'Grandfather is going great guns and his business is booming.'

7. **to spike someone's guns** – to spoil someone's plans, to prevent him realizing them. 'When we heard the Simpsons were planning to buy the house next door to us to extend their shop, we spiked their guns by buying the house ourselves.' The spike (obsolete term for 'nail') was pushed into the barrel of the gun to stop it firing properly.

8. **to bring up the heavy guns/artillery** – the important people, the leaders. 'At the by-election, all the heavy guns were brought up to support the rival candidates.'

9. **to gun for someone** – to plot revenge on someone. 'Davey is gunning for us for taking his customers away from him.'

10. **a gun-runner** – someone who unlawfully smuggles guns into a country. Also the verb: **gun-running**. 'There was a rumour going around that the minister's assistant had once been a gun-runner for the IRA.'

11. **speech like machine-gun fire/like bullets from a machine-gun** – words spoken very rapidly, and in a staccato fashion. 'On the Continent, Civil Servants assume a certain military air. They consider themselves little generals; they use delaying tactics; they cannot withdraw armies, so they withdraw permissions; they thunder like cannons and their speech is like machine-gun fire; they cannot lose battles, they lose documents instead' (*How to be an Alien* by George Mikes).

1. **to hold a pistol to someone's head / to put a gun to someone's head** – to use a dangerous threat to achieve one's ends. 'I shall have to accept the workers' demands or close the factory. They are holding a pistol to my head.'

2. **to tell someone point-blank** – to make something absolutely clear in an abrupt and brusque way. ' "You simply cannot have another day off," the office manager told his assistant point-blank.' Also: **a point-blank refusal**. From a gunshot fired at very close range.

3. **to set one's sights on something** – to be ambitious and determined to achieve a particular goal. 'I don't know how she is going to afford it, but she has set her sights on studying law.' One looks through the 'sights' of a gun to focus clearly on the target.

4. **to go off at half-cock** – to execute a plan before the necessary preparations have been completed. 'Our attack went off at half-cock. We should have waited until we had won the support of our colleagues.' The phrase is taken from the inadvertent firing of a gun when the hammer is set at half-cock.

5. **calibre** – the relative worth of someone's mind or character. 'Sally is a nice girl with plenty of common sense but I shouldn't have thought she was university calibre.' Literally, the internal diameter of a gun.

6. **quick on the draw** – quick to attack, or defend oneself from, an enemy. The reference is to the drawing of their pistols by American cowboys when their lives would depend on the speed of their reaction to the approach of an enemy.

Cannon, Torpedo

7. **a loose cannon** – someone who is unrestrained in speech and action, therefore capable of doing damage unintentionally; a member of a group whose unpredictable behaviour makes him or her a danger or liability. ' "This minister has become very accident-prone," the spin doctor said disapprovingly. "He's turning into a loose cannon, firing off in all directions." '

8. **cannon-fodder** – soldiers who are regarded by the high command as unimportant enough to sacrifice in war. 'I would keep out of the infantry if I were you; they are only cannon-fodder.' Fodder is the food fed to the animals on a farm.

9. **to torpedo something** – to ruin/completely destroy a policy, a plan, peace talks, etc. 'The minister threatened to torpedo the whole Bill unless more concessions were made.'

Powder, Lock, Stock, Barrel

10. **to keep one's powder dry** – to hold oneself ready for action as soon as the need arises. 'Colonel Williams is sure to attack you in the local newspaper. In the meantime, all you can do is to wait and keep your powder dry.' Powder meant gunpowder, which it was necessary to keep dry for effective use (somewhat dated).

11. **to light the touch paper** – to set in motion events which might lead to a disaster/a scandalous revelation/a shocking conclusion, etc. 'Tony Blair lit the touch paper when he encouraged devolution in Scotland and Wales.' Touch paper is paper which has been placed in saltpetre, i.e. potassium nitrate, for the purpose of firing gunpowder.
cf. **'like pulling the pin from a grenade'** 247/15.

12. **lock, stock and barrel** – everything, with nothing excluded. 'Mr Hobson was obliged to sell the house and contents, lock, stock and barrel.' The lock, stock and barrel are the three parts of a gun.

Sword, Lance

13. **to cross swords with** – to fight or quarrel with. 'Jackson is a hot-tempered man; I wouldn't cross swords with him, if I were you.'

14. **to measure swords with someone** – to test one's strength against someone else. In duels, the swords were measured by the seconds in order to check that they were of the same length.

15. **to beat one's sword into a ploughshare** – to turn from war to peaceful pur-

suits. From the Old Testament: 'They shall beat their swords into ploughshares, . . . nation shall not lift up sword against nation . . .' (Isaiah II, 4).

1. **words/actions feel like a sword through one's heart** – to be deeply hurt by someone's words or actions. ' "This is the last night of freedom in your life, so make the most of it," the new bodyguard, Chief Inspector Paul Officer, told Lady Diana Spencer. "Those words," she would say, "felt like a sword through my heart." ' (*Behind Palace Doors* by Nigel Dempster and Peter Evans, © Weidenfeld & Nicolson). cf. **'words go through one like a knife' 170/8**.

2. **to break a lance with** – to have an argument with. 'It's a pleasure to break a lance with Tom; he is a very good-humoured man.'

Dagger, Knife, Stiletto

3. **at daggers drawn** – in open enmity, ready to attack one's enemy. 'The two brothers have been at daggers drawn for many years.' When the dagger has been drawn from its scabbard, it can be used at once without any further preparation.

4. **to look daggers at** – to look with hatred or fury at someone. 'Mrs Jessop looked daggers at her little son when he repeated to her guest what she had been saying about him behind his back.'

5. **to have one's knife in someone** – to bear malice towards someone, to bear a strong grudge against him or her. 'The manager has got her knife in me; she is making my life a misery.'

6. **to put the knife in** – to deal one's enemy a fatal blow. 'When you published Kenneth's letter, you put the knife in; his career is finished.'

7. **the knives are out for . . .** – a number of people are waiting for the opportunity to strike at their enemy. A phrase that is often used in politics, e.g. about an ex-prime minister who is blamed for the defeat of his or her party at the polls.

8. **stiletto heels** – high pointed metal heels on women's shoes. 'Marie-Louise, will you please take off your shoes. Your stiletto heels are cutting our carpet into ribbons.'

Sabre, Steel, Hilt

9. **to rattle the sabre / sabre rattling** – to make threatening noises, to attempt to frighten one's opponent/enemy into doing what one wants. 'Don't let Mr Ash frighten you. It's only sabre rattling.'

10. **to use cold steel** – to use bayonets or knives. 'Wars are no longer won by cold steel but by superior fire-power.'

11. **up to the hilt** – completely, to the very limit. 'Under the guarantee, your rights are protected up to the hilt.' The allusion is to the penetration of the full length of the sword into a body right up to the handle (hilt).

Arms

12. **up in arms** – in open revolt, as by demonstrating, shouting insults, etc. 'The students were up in arms when they heard that their privileges had been withdrawn.'

13. **armed to the teeth** – fully armed, armed with a variety of weapons so that one is prepared for any attack.

Shot, Shoot, Trigger

14. **like a shot** – at once, without the slightest hesitation. 'I would change jobs like a shot if I were 20 years younger.'

15. **a long shot** – an attempt to find an answer with very little information to assist one. 'It may be a long shot but I think Harry will marry again soon.'

16. **a shot in the dark** – a wild, random guess, one that has as little chance of being right as hitting a target in the dark.

17. **no more shots in the locker** – at the end of one's resources. The derivation of the phrase is from the lockers on board a warship in which the ammunition was stored.

18. **to call the shots** – to make the decisions. 'If you want anything done, you'd better ask Mary's housekeeper. She calls the shots in this house.'

1. **a shot in the arm** – a strong encouragement, a stimulus. 'North Sea Oil has been a shot in the arm for the economy of Great Britain.' A shot in the arm means an injection which stimulates the patient and gives him or her fresh energy.

2. **to have a shot** – to have a try to see how well you do. 'Table tennis is such an easy game. Why don't you have a shot at it?'

3. **to be shot of someone** – to be rid of someone. 'I'm glad my former boyfriend is emigrating to Canada. Then I'll be shot of him for good.'

4. **a fashion shoot** – posing for a magazine in designer clothes or highly fashionable outfits. 'Rich and famous young people are in great demand for fashion shoots by well-known magazines.'

5. **a shooting gallery** – a room, sometimes set up by a government, which provides heroin addicts with clean needles and a safe environment in which to inject themselves. There are also secret shooting galleries in squalid surroundings where addicts share needles and can become ill.

6. **a trouble-shooter** – an expert in industrial/diplomatic relations who is called in to mediate between the parties to a dispute. 'We shall need a trouble-shooter to settle our dispute with the boss.'

7. **to shoot down** – to demolish, to refute an argument. 'If you put forward that argument, the judge will shoot it down at once.'

8. **to shoot a line** (slang) – to tell a wildly exaggerated story in order to create an impression or mislead. 'Jerry was shooting a line that his parents are friends of the American president, but no one believed him.'

9. **to shoot from the hip** – to be quick with an answer. 'I'm not going to get into an argument with Sue again; she is very sharp, and she shoots straight from the hip.' This comes from the American Wild West, when firing the first shot was essential for survival.

10. **to shoot the (traffic) lights** – to drive a vehicle past the lights when they are showing red or amber.

11. **to shoot off** – to commence proceedings. 'Tom shot off by welcoming the delegates to the conference.'

12. **trigger-happy** – willing to use force on the slightest pretext. 'The workers have gone on strike without warning us. They are in a trigger-happy mood.'

13. **to trigger off** – to precipitate, to be the immediate, as opposed to the fundamental, cause. 'It was feared that a big increase in wages for the miners might have triggered off similar wage claims throughout the country.'

Bullet, Bomb, Grenade

14. **as hard as a bullet** – extremely hard, firm, solid, impenetrable. 'I can't eat these nuts, Mavis. They're as hard as bullets!'

15. **a head like a bullet** – a round-shaped head, with very short hair. 'Miss Violet said the chap was exceptionally tall and had cropped hair. Head like a bullet, she said' (*The School at Thrush Green* by Miss Read).
    a bullet-head – US slang for an obstinate person.

16. **to bite the bullet** – to accept with courage the prospect of a fight or unpleasant experience. 'Now that Father is dead, we must bite the bullet and learn to put up with hardship.'

17. **bullet train** – a passenger train travelling at high speed. 'What a thrill it is to travel in a bullet train!'

18. **like a bombshell / to land/hit like a bombshell / hit like a shell** – to make a big impact, to cause great astonishment. 'The revelations about the politician's past life have hit the United States like a bombshell.'

19. **to come as a bombshell** – to astonish, to dumbfound. 'The news that their father had left home came as a bombshell to his children.'

20. **a bombshell secret** – an important secret which, if revealed, would cause a great stir. 'The politician decided to keep

his policy bombshell secret until the first day of the Party Conference.'

1. **to drop a bombshell** – to inform someone of something terrible.

2. **to be shell-shocked** – to be gripped by a sudden violent emotion. 'He was shell-shocked by the sudden news that he had been adopted at the age of one.'

3. **to cost a bomb** – to cost a huge amount of money. 'A Persian carpet for our sitting-room would cost a bomb. It's out of the question.'

4. **to make a bomb** – to earn a lot of money. 'Let's work in the oil industry in one of the Arab countries – we'll make a bomb!'

5. **to go like a bomb** – (1) to sell in huge numbers. 'Our fur-lined boots are going like a bomb now the cold weather is coming on.' (2) (of transport) to travel very fast. 'The new train went like a bomb.'

6. **to go down like a bomb** – to be a nasty surprise or shock. 'The news that their cousin was a thief went down like a bomb in the family.' cf. '**to go down like a lead balloon**' 313/8.

7. **a time bomb / a silent time bomb / a ticking time bomb** – a life-threatening health defect of which one is unaware. 'The young sportsman had no idea that a time bomb in the shape of a congenital heart defect was ticking away inside him. It was this that caused his sudden death.' Frequent usage: **a financial time bomb for the future**.
   like a time bomb waiting to explode / like sitting on a time bomb – something damaging is going to happen in the near future. 'The blackmailer put the video cassette on the director's desk, and there it lay, like a time bomb waiting to explode.'

8. **a walking time bomb** – (1) someone in a dangerous state of mind. (2) a suicide bomber. 'With the explosives strapped to his body, the 22-year-old man was a walking time bomb.'

9. **to love-bomb someone** – to shower someone you love with all kinds of presents. 'The pop star's first two wives had left him and he was terrified his third wife might also leave him. That's why he love-bombed her, much to her amazement and delight.'

10. **a vitamin bomb** – food which is full of vitamins, such as a fruit salad.

11. **a calorie bomb** – delicious but very fattening food, such as a Christmas pudding.

12. **a sex bomb** – someone very sexy, usually a female film star (like Marilyn Monroe).

13. **to look like bomb-sites** – ground which is full of holes and badly devastated, as if it had been hit by bombs. 'The tornado left large areas of Florida looking like bomb-sites.'

14. **to look like a bomb-site / like a bomb's hit something** – to look a mess. 'Your bedroom looks like a bomb's just hit it!'

15. **like pulling the pin from a grenade** – like setting off an event which will have disastrous consequences. 'If the peace-keeping troops were to leave Kosovo, it would be like pulling the pin from a grenade.' cf. '**to light the touch paper**' 244/11.

Minefield

16. **a minefield** – an area fraught with problems/danger. 'There is so much conflicting advice about what food is safe to eat – the whole subject is like a minefield.' Other minefields: the home is a minefield (as most accidents happen there); secondary school is a '**minefield of emotion**' for teenagers entering puberty; rape laws are a '**legal minefield**'. A minefield is an area of land or sea sown with mines which are not always visible. It is therefore a highly dangerous place and one wrong move can result in disaster.
   like walking through a minefield – extremely difficult, highly risky. 'The police have to be especially careful when they pursue drug-dealers. It's like walking through a minefield for them.' cf. '**like walking/treading on egg-shells**' 175/11.

Arrow, Bolt, Bow

1. **to write arrow straight** – to write honest and genuine articles, etc. 'The young journalist wrote a harrowing and straight-arrow account about the war-torn country.'
    a straight arrow – an honest and trustworthy person; **as straight as an arrow** – in a direct line.

2. **to shoot one's last arrow** – to be left without resources in a contest. 'There are no further steps you can take against Mr Brown; you have shot your last arrow.'
    to shoot one's bolt – to spend one's resources prematurely in a contest. 'Jack attacked his opponent with all his strength but, by the fifth round, he had shot his bolt, and retired soon afterwards.'

3. **bolt upright** – absolutely straight. It is used to describe a sitting position. 'Bolt' was the old English word for a short arrow, for a cross-bow; hence 'bolt upright' means as straight as an arrow, and often expresses surprise.

4. **to draw the long bow** – to exaggerate.

Trap

5. **a booby trap** – (1) a practical joke played on someone unexpectedly. 'Don't place a booby trap for grandfather! It might give him a heart attack.' (2) a hidden bomb. 'The car was found to be booby-trapped; the driver had a lucky escape.'

6. **a poverty trap** – when a person finds it impossible to escape from a state of being very poor. 'If he does manage to earn a little money, he must pay tax on it and therefore lose the low-income benefits from the government.' Frequent usage: **he/she became locked in a poverty trap**. cf. **'a Catch-22 situation' 261/15**; **'damned if you do, damned if you don't' 43/13**.

7. **a death-trap** – (1) a highly dangerous situation. 'I wouldn't call pot-holing a sport but a death-trap.' (2) a very dangerous building, or part of one. 'This block of flats has no fire escape. If a fire were to break out, it would be a death-trap.'

Other Weapons

8. **hoist with his own petard** (literary) – injured or harmed by one's own weapon; ensnared in a trap intended for someone else. 'The strikers threatened to bankrupt their boss unless their wages were doubled. Their demand was granted, but the firm went bankrupt and they all lost their jobs. They had been hoist with their own petard.' (Shakespeare, *Hamlet*, III, iv: 'For 'tis sport, to have the engineer / Hoist with his own petard'.) The petard was a small bomb which was exploded to make a breach in a wall. Sometimes the military engineer firing the petard was blown up with it.

9. **to bury the hatchet** – to end a feud with one's enemy. The reference is to the old custom of the Native Americans who buried all their weapons so that they might not be reminded of past quarrels when they smoked the pipe of peace with their old enemies.

10. **a hatchet man** – a person who is expert at destroying the reputation of an opponent. 'Harvey is a marvellous hatchet man but he never says anything constructive.'
    a hatchet job / the hatchet work – the task of destroying the reputation of an opponent.

11. **a battle-axe** – a domineering, aggressive woman, one who likes to take charge of any activity. A battle-axe with its long handle was used as a weapon in the Middle Ages. It is not clear why the term should be applied only to women.

12. **as plain as a pikestaff** – quite clear and unmistakable; apparent, evident. 'The evidence is as plain as a pikestaff that this company is guilty of fraud.' The earlier form of the phrase (mid 16th century) was 'plain as a packstaff', i.e. the staff on which a pedlar carried his pack, which was worn plain and smooth from regular use (from *Brewer's Dictionary of Phrase and Fable*, © Cassel & Co.). cf. **'as plain as the nose on someone's face' 89/14**.

13. **a ramrod spine / a ramrod-straight back** – stiff and straight-backed, unyielding and proud. 'Nothing about Matsuy-

ama-San had visibly changed. He still sat there, stiff as a ramrod, a non-committal expression on his face, but there was no movement whatsoever' (*The Old Man and Mr Smith* by Peter Ustinov, © Michael O'Mara Books). A ramrod is a rod for cleaning the barrels of rifles and other small arms. cf. **'as stiff as a poker' 252/13**.

1. **an action/campaign/attack spear-headed by** – a drive initiated by. 'The campaign for more traffic lights and zebra crossings in the town was spearheaded by the head teacher of the secondary school and won the support of all the parents.'

2. **to take up the cudgels on behalf of a person or cause** – to defend a person or cause with great energy and determination. 'Now that the editor of the local newspaper has taken up the cudgels for your campaign, you have a good chance of success.' The cudgel is a thick stick or club.

3. **a chink in someone's armour** – a defect or weakness in someone which makes him vulnerable to attack. 'Robin was very sure of himself, but he had a chink in his armour: mention the name Yates and he would start shouting and swearing.' cf. **'Achilles' heel' 225/13**; **'to have feet of clay' 107/10**.

4. **like a suit of armour** – to have a protective shield around one. 'Our faith has been like an extra piece of armour in our battle against Roy's cancer' (*Give Us This Day* by Fiona Castle, widow of the entertainer Roy Castle, © Kingsway Publications).

27 Tools

Tools

1. **it's a poor workman who blames/ quarrels with his tools** – the inefficient and idle often put the blame for their failure on their tools, or the conditions in which they work. 'Jack blamed the school textbooks for failing his examinations although his classmates were successful. It's a poor workman who quarrels with his tools.'

2. **to down tools** – to refuse to work, to go on strike.

3. **a valuable tool** – a very useful means of helping. 'The Home Secretary announced that DNA screening of the entire population could act as a valuable tool to halt soaring crime levels.'
   a crucial tool – a most important means towards achieving something. Also: English is an important '**communications tool**'.

Screw

4. **to put a screw/the screws on someone** – to put pressure on someone, usually with the object of extracting money. In former times, the thumb-screw was a common instrument of torture. By turning the screw, one could increase the pressure on the victim until the pain became unbearable. Hence: **to tighten the screw; to give the screw another turn; to screw something out of a person**.

5. **to have a screw loose** (slang) – to be slightly mad, not quite sane. Often used humorously to express incredulity at someone's actions.

6. **to screw up one's courage** – to make up one's mind to do something courageous or daring, to overcome one's reluctance to act. 'Colin screwed up his courage and asked his boss for a rise in his wages.'

7. **to have one's head screwed on the right way** – to be sensible and intelligent. The very opposite of '**to have a screw loose**' 250/5.

Nail

8. **as hard as nails** – unrelenting, without feeling or sentiment.

9. **to pay on the nail** – to pay on the exact date that money becomes due.

10. **to drive a nail into one's coffin** – to make a blunder which will destroy one's reputation or happiness. 'If you resign from the Party, you will only be driving a nail into your coffin.'
    to drive a nail/another nail/a final nail into someone's coffin – to do someone an injury which will destroy his or her reputation or happiness. 'I've had a disastrous year anyway, but Joan's memoirs have driven the final nail into my coffin.'

11. **as dead as a door-nail / as dead as the nail in a coffin** – dead beyond any doubt. 'Old Marley was as dead as a door-nail. Mind! I don't mean to say that I know, of my own knowledge, what there is particularly dead about a door-nail. I might have been inclined, myself, to regard a coffin-nail as the deadest piece of ironmongery in the trade. But the wisdom of our ancestors is in the simile; and my unhallowed hands shall not disturb it, or the Country's done for' (*A Christmas Carol*

by Charles Dickens). It can apply to causes and campaigns, as well as people. 'The campaign for spelling reform is as dead as a door-nail.' Martin Manser suggests that the origin may be that the door-nail was the metal plate against which a door knocker banged. As this was hit so many times over the years, it could understandably have had all its life struck from it, and so be dead (*Dictionary of Word and Phrase Origins*, © Little, Brown). cf. '**as dead as a dodo**' 71/9; '**as dead as Queen Anne . . .**' 229/11.

1. **to nail a lie** – to produce certain, unquestionable proof of a lie. 'That's one lie we have nailed. I wonder how many more lies the witness has told.'

2. **to hit the nail on the head** – to find exactly the right answer to a problem in one or two words.

Tacks, Nuts, Bolts

3. **to get down to brass tacks** – to concentrate on the essentials. 'Let's get down to brass tacks, shall we? How much is each of you prepared to put into the project?'

4. **the nuts and bolts** – the practical considerations. 'We have talked enough about theory. It's time we considered the nuts and bolts.' The nuts and bolts are what hold the machinery together. They play a humble but essential part in any enterprise.

Chain

5. **a chain letter** – someone sends a letter to six friends requesting that each of them should in turn send a copy to six friends. If they comply the chain can remain unbroken for 10, 20 or even 30 years, but if they do not comply, the chain will be broken. Some chain letters contain the threat that very bad luck will befall those who break the chain.

6. **a chain** – a line of property buyers each of whom must sell his or her property before the next person can sell his or hers. 'Each time we saw a house we really would have liked to buy, we found that we were in a long chain.'

7. **a chain gang** – a group of prisoners who work outdoors but who cannot run away because their legs are chained to each other.

8. **to be a ball and chain on someone** – to be a hindrance to someone's progress. 'Mrs Parker felt sorry for the tramp and let him have a room in her house. But now he is a ball and chain on her and won't leave.' In former times, and in certain countries today, prisoners have a very heavy iron ball attached by a chain to one leg, so that they cannot run away. cf. '**to have an albatross around one's neck**' 71/2.

9. **to break links** – to sever connections. 'The Australians might break links with the British monarchy one day.'

Vice, Clamp

10. **a vice-like grip / a grip like a vice** – to have a really firm and secure hold on something. 'The dog held the burglar's arm in a vice-like grip.' A vice is an instrument with two jaws between which an object may be gripped securely. Also: **to hold someone in an iron vice**. cf. '**to have an iron grip on something**' 18/7.

11. **a clampdown** – to put a stop to something. 'Workers who absent themselves continually are going to face a clampdown and will be penalized.' Frequent usage: **a clampdown on absenteeism**; **a clampdown on football hooligans**.

Hammer, Tongs

12. **to come under the hammer** – to be sold by an auctioneer, to be put up for auction. The auctioneer indicates his acceptance of a bid by striking the table with his hammer.

13. **to hammer a point home** – to emphasize a point one has made in an argument by repeating it with great force. 'The father hammered home the dangers to his daughter about being out alone late at night.'

14. **to hammer out a scheme** – to decide on a scheme after the most thorough and

intensive examination of the difficulties, often in the course of discussion and argument.

1. **a hammer-blow** – a very bad shock which puts an end to one's ambitions or plans. 'The allegations of corruption came as a hammer-blow to his high-profile career.'

2. **to go for someone hammer and tongs** – to quarrel furiously with someone. 'At the meeting the hecklers were going for the speaker hammer and tongs until the chairman threatened to have them turned out.'
      to go hammer and tongs at a job – to work at a job with all one's might.

3. **to take a sledgehammer to crack a nut** – to use unnecessary force to achieve one's object. 'Surely, to disconnect a customer's electricity because he owes the electricity company £3 was taking a sledgehammer to crack a nut.'

4. **one's heart is thumping like a sledgehammer** – one's heart is beating very fast, one is in a state of great excitement or fear. 'When the lift suddenly got stuck, Sarah's heart began to thump like a sledgehammer.'

5. **pain/a smell/bad news hits someone like a sledgehammer** – to make a big and unpleasant impact on someone. 'The news that James would need one whole year to learn to talk again after his heart attack hit him like a sledgehammer.' Also: **a sledgehammer headache**; **a sledgehammer approach to something**.

6. **not to touch someone/something with a pair of tongs** – to avoid someone/something at all costs; said of someone with an evil reputation. cf. '**not to touch with a barge-pole**' 205/15.

Spade, Rake

7. **to call a spade a spade** – to speak plainly and bluntly, to tell the plain truth without bothering with polite phrases. 'In Yorkshire we don't use flowery language; we call a spade a spade.'

8. **the spadework** – the hard, detailed work. 'Peter's research workers took two years on the spadework before he was able to start on his book.'

9. **as thin/skinny as a rake** – very thin, gaunt, emaciated. 'The criminal was released from the foreign prison after six months, looking as thin as a rake.' Chaucer wrote in his Prologue to *The Canterbury Tales*: 'As lean was his horse as is a rake.' The thin prongs of a rake resemble thin ribs which can be seen through thin flesh.

10. **to rake up (the past, the ashes, old quarrels, etc.)** – to remind someone of disagreeable events in the past, to revive unpleasant memories. 'Why rake up the past? I thought it was all over and forgotten.'

11. **to rake in the money** – to make money very fast, to make huge profits. 'George's shop is raking the money in with their new product.'

12. **a rake-off** – an introduction fee, a commission. A rake-off implies that there is something dishonest about the transaction, e.g. when an information bureau, which states that it gives the public free and independent advice, takes commissions from the businesses it recommends.

Poker

13. **as stiff as a poker** – unyielding, unresponsive. 'De Gaulle has all the rigidity of a poker without its occasional warmth' (Harold Macmillan, prime minister of Great Britain, 1957–63). A poker is a metal rod used for moving coal or wood about in a fire.
      a poker-straight back – a very stiff and straight back/posture. cf. '**a ramrod spine / a ramrod-straight back**' 248/13.

Other Tools

14. **to throw a spanner in the works** – deliberately to obstruct or ruin the results of someone's efforts. 'You threw a spanner in the works, didn't you, telling the

manager your father wasn't paying him enough.'

1. **to have an axe to grind** – to allow one's private interest to affect the advice one gives. 'The patient joined the protest by the nurses against the doctor as she had an axe to grind for alleged neglect of her symptoms.'

2. **to axe a job** – to abolish a job in order to save money. The job may be in the private or the public sector.

     to be axed – to lose one's job, to be made redundant for the sake of economy. 'Paul is afraid he'll be axed from the navy; he'll be 50 next April.' **to face the axe** – to be due to be abolished. 'The monopoly the Post Office has on letters will soon face the axe.'

3. **the linchpin/lynchpin** – the most important person or feature to the success of a plan or relationship. 'An efficient ambulance service can be the linchpin in a hospital's efforts to save more lives.' The idiom derives from the pin that passes through the axle-end to keep on a wheel. 'Linch' comes from the Old English *lynis*.

4. **by hook or by crook** – by any means whatsoever, lawful or unlawful. 'Hugh will make money by hook or by crook; he won't let anybody stop him.'

5. **to be on tenterhooks** – to be in a state of acute suspense, waiting for news/results. 'We've been on tenterhooks the whole morning waiting for the results of the X-ray.' The term 'tenterhooks' means tenting or canvas that has been stretched by hooks, thus producing a state of tension.

6. **to lay something on with a trowel** – to flatter grossly, to exaggerate one's praise. 'You were laying it on with a trowel, weren't you, when you told Angela she had a divinely beautiful voice!' The phrase comes from Shakespeare: 'Well said; that was laid on with a trowel' (*As You Like It*, I, ii, 113).

7. **the thin end of the wedge** – a small concession which is used to obtain a very big and costly one. 'If we give our workers an increase of 5 per cent in a bad year

when we've made a loss, how much will they want in a good year? It's the thin end of the wedge.'

8. **to drive a wedge between** – to cause mischief, to cause people to quarrel with each other. 'Malcolm complained that his girlfriend's obsession with the famous pop star drove a wedge between them.'

Putty

9. **to be putty in someone's hands** – to be easily influenced. 'Some ministers are putty in the prime minister's hands.'

10. **as soft as putty / like putty / clay in someone's hands** – willing to do what you want, compliant, submissive. 'If you give her a box of chocolates, she'll be like putty in your hands.'

11. **to plug a gap** – to make up for a shortfall. 'As it seems clear that the singer won't turn up, let's plug the gap with some music.'

Concrete

12. **as hard as concrete** – very hard, impenetrable. ' "I wish it would rain," the gardener sighed. "The ground is as hard as concrete." '

Sandpaper

13. **skin/voice like sandpaper** – rough, stubbly skin; a harsh, scratchy voice. 'He was getting a sore throat, and his voice was like sandpaper.'

Bellows

14. **like a bellows / like a pair of bellows** – to breathe audibly. ' "We've just lost £20,000 because of you, Henry," his boss snarled at him, breathing like a bellows, his fists tightly clenched.' A bellows is a device for supplying a strong blast of air to something, e.g. to fan the flames of a fire. Note the verb '**to bellow**', to shout or utter in a very loud voice.

Electrical Items

1. **to have a short fuse** – to have a temper that flares up quickly. 'Try not to criticize his work, Mr Tomlin. Harry has a short fuse.'

2. **to hot-wire a car** – to start a car without the use of an ignition key but by connecting two wires and thus making a 'hot' electric spark. 'Today's young car thieves are clever enough to steal a car by hot-wiring it.'

3. **to pull the plug on someone** – to let a terminally ill person die by pulling out the plug from the hospital machine which keeps him or her alive. 'A clinical ethicist is to be employed by hospitals to advise doctors whether to pull the plug on terminally ill patients or to let them live.'

   to pull the plug (slang) – to commit suicide.

4. **to pull the plug on something** – to put a stop to something, to terminate abruptly. 'The youth leader pulled the plug on the gardening project because no one wanted to do the weeding.' The expression derives from pulling a plug out of its socket, so that there is no more electricity. cf. '**to pull the rug from under one's feet . . .**' 167/13.

5. **to recharge one's batteries** – to renew one's energy. 'I can't disturb my husband's rest as he needs it to recharge his batteries.' cf. '**a cat nap**' 55/6; '**a power nap**' 233/3.

Number

1. **an opposite number** – someone who holds a corresponding post in another firm, company, etc.

2. **a number cruncher** – someone who can easily carry out complicated arithmetic in his or her head; also a term for a computer. 'I'm not surprised that your sister found a job with a computer firm immediately. A number cruncher like her would find a top job anywhere.'

3. **a back number** – (1) someone who is no longer active in his or her work, retired or semi-retired. 'I'd have been glad to advise you, but I haven't practised for the last 10 years. I'm afraid I am a bit of a back number!' (2) any issue of a magazine or newspaper which has appeared prior to the current one.

4. **one's number is up** – all hope for a person has been abandoned, one is doomed.

5. **to take care of number one** – to put one's own interest before that of other people, an egoistic outlook.

6. **time out of number** – again and again, so frequently as to be uncountable.

7. **one's days are numbered** – one is approaching the end of one's life, or time in office, etc.

8. **in round numbers** – an approximate number, a number which is measured in tens, hundreds, thousands, and which does not include the numbers in between.

9. **safety in numbers** – protection provided by numerical superiority. 'I don't mind my daughter going out with a group, but I don't want her to be alone with one man. There is safety in numbers.'

Zero

10. **to zero in on** – to concentrate hard on something in particular. 'Police are zeroing in on a new wave of terrorism that takes the form of parcel bombs.'

11. **to have zero tolerance / a zero-tolerance policy** – to have no more patience with wrongdoers and to make no more allowances for them. 'Because the village policeman showed zero tolerance towards lager louts, thugs and petty thieves, the village was nearly free of crime.' Frequent usage: **zero tolerance for speeding motorists; to show zero tolerance to troublemakers; to have a zero tolerance of any harassment**.

12. **status-zero teenagers** – mostly boys who leave school at 16 with very little education, no hope of employment, no income and who sometimes get involved in crime and drugs. They are also called **'zero-status dropouts'**. 'The local youth leader managed to get ten status-zero teenagers interested in gardening.' cf. **'a lost generation' 140/15**.

Single

13. **to do something single-handed** – to accomplish a task without anyone else's help. Literally, to do something with only one hand.

Quarter

1. **to have a bad quarter of an hour** – to have a very unpleasant experience for a short period.

2. **no quarter was given** – no mercy was shown, no man's life was spared. One interpretation is that 'quarter' refers to the quarters, i.e. the lodging, given to prisoners of war by the victorious army. Hence 'no quarter given' meant 'no prisoners taken'.

Half

3. **to go halves** – to take an equal share with somebody else.

4. **to do something by halves** – to do something without finishing it, superficially, unenthusiastically. Also used in the negative: **'She doesn't do a thing by halves'** – she is extremely thorough in everything she does.

5. **not half** (Cockney) – very much indeed, with great pleasure. ' "Would you like a glass of beer?" "Not half!" ' '

6. **to meet halfway** – to make concessions to another person's position in a disagreement, to make a fair compromise. 'I do think you might meet us halfway, Lilian. We have agreed to go with you to the theatre, but why must it be the evening performance? What's wrong with the matinee?'

7. **one's better half** – a humorous reference to one's husband or wife.

8. **to have half a chance** – a very slight chance. 'If I had half a chance, I would go to America.'

9. **to have half a mind** – to feel somewhat inclined to do something, but without any real conviction.

10. **a half-baked idea** – an idea that has not been properly thought out; a stupid idea.
    a half-baked boy/girl (slang) – a foolish, stupid boy or girl.

11. **the flag at half-mast** – the flag that flies half-way down as a sign of respect for an important person who has died.

12. **halfway house** – a compromise between two conflicting systems. 'The college was a halfway house between a school and a university. There were no regular lessons but we were not allowed out without permission.'

One

13. **A.1.** – (1) the best possible. (2) in a military sense, enjoying perfect health.

14. **to be at one** – to be in full agreement (in the case of several people, to be unanimous).

15. **to be one too many for someone** – to outmatch somebody, to outwit him or her. 'When it comes to business, your sister is one too many for me.'

16. **to be the last one to** – to be the least likely to. 'You're the last one I would have expected to behave like that.'

17. **to have a one-track mind** – to be totally absorbed in a single topic. 'Harry has a one-track mind; he only thinks about sex.'

18. **one-sided** – to the advantage of one person and not the other, e.g. a **'one-sided agreement'** – an agreement which favours one party and not the other.
    to be one-sided – to be unfair or prejudiced.

19. **to go one better** – to outdo someone else. 'When Jack heard I had invited Mervyn to tea, he invited him to dinner. Jack always goes one better than me!'

20. **in one fell swoop** – in one fast and conclusive action. 'The police arrested the drug-dealers and the drug addicts in one fell swoop.'

21. **one-off** – once only. 'His novel has been selling very well but I doubt whether he can repeat his success. It was a one-off effort.'

22. **to take one with another** – to balance the advantages and disadvantages.

1. **it's all one to him** – it's all the same to him, he doesn't care.

2. **from day one** – from the very beginning. 'From day one, the business tycoon and the film actress were deeply attracted to each other.'

3. **back to square one** – back to the very beginning of some task or enterprise as a result of a setback. 'A miscalculation had occurred in the planning of the new bridge which meant going back to square one.' The allusion is to the game of ludo when a player is sent back to square one if he or she lands on the wrong square.

4. **a one-armed bandit** – a gambling machine in which coins are inserted, usually 'fixed' so that the gambler loses his or her money. Hence the name 'bandit'.

5. **to be a one-man band** – to do all the work oneself without employing staff.

First

6. **first come, first served** – whoever arrives first has a right to be served first. ' "Why do you always serve Mr Wood before me?" "Because Mr Wood always arrives before you. First come, first served." '

7. **first and last** – more important than any other consideration.

8. **there's always a first time for everything** – just because something has not happened in the past is no reason for thinking it will never happen in the future.

9. **at first sight** – the first impression, superficially. 'He fell in love with her at first sight.'

10. **in the first flush of** – fresh and blooming. 'The film star still looked very attractive, although he was no longer in the first flush of youth.' Also: **the first flush of love**; **the first flush of courtship**.

11. **first thing** – before doing anything else. 'I'll let you have the results first thing Monday morning.'
    not to know the first thing about something – to know nothing whatever about something. 'My father doesn't know the first thing about cooking.'

12. **to give the first refusal** – to give a person the first opportunity of accepting an offer, before others are considered. 'He's given us the first refusal of his house.'

13. **to get a first** – to obtain a first-class honours degree on graduation at a university.

14. **first fruit** – first benefits from one's work. From the first fruit that is ripe for picking.

Once

15. **once and for all** – for the last time. 'Once and for all, the answer is no! I'm not going to pay you any more money.'

16. **to give someone/something the once-over** – to give someone or something a quick or superficial examination.

17. **once/twice removed** – refers to family relationships between cousins. My cousin once removed is my first cousin's child. My cousin twice removed is my second cousin's child.

Two

18. **to put two and two together** – to draw an obvious conclusion.
    two and two make four – an obvious conclusion from the facts.

19. **two's company, three's none** – when there are three people there is always a tendency for two of them to make friends at the expense of the third. cf. **'three's a crowd' 259/7**.

20. **it takes two to tango** – when two parties are in disagreement, there is usually a fault on either side. 'I don't think this quarrel is entirely Tom's fault, Lynette. You know it takes two to tango!' A humorous variation: **it takes two to tangle**.

21. **two-timing** – to date two lovers or girl-/boyfriends at the same time. 'I'll never forgive Simon! He's been two-timing me with the girl down the road.'

22. **a two-edged compliment** – a comment

which can be understood in two contradictory ways, one of which is to the disadvantage of the person praised. An example might be: 'He has a phenomenal memory. He can remember every word of his old speeches.'

1. **to have two strings to one's bow / to have a second string to one's bow** – to have two means of achieving an objective. If the first fails, you can try the second. The allusion is to the second string that bowmen kept in reserve.

2. **not to care two hoots** – to be totally indifferent.

3. **not to give two pins for someone** – not to have any care or regard for that person.
   for two pins – without further thought or hesitation, although it might be unwise. 'For two pins I would join you on your world cruise, Maggie!'

4. **two-up, two-down** – a small terraced house with two rooms upstairs and two rooms downstairs, built before the First World War and found mostly in the coalmining districts of Britain in long rows.

Second

5. **to come off second best** – to lose a fight or a contest.

6. **to be second-rate** – to be in an inferior class. Frequent usage: **a second-rate mind**; **a second-rate painter**; **a second-rate teacher**.

7. **to be a good/bad second** – to run close behind the leader / a long way behind the leader.

8. **one's second self** – another person whose character, tastes and outlook are identical to one's own.

9. **second nature** – what can be done instinctively, without thought.
   to become second nature – to become habitual, almost instinctive. 'Bobby lies for the sake of lying. It has become second nature to him.'

10. **to second-guess** (US) – to give oneself credit for predicting an event correctly after it has already happened. 'It's no good trying to second-guess the result now – it will be on the news in a couple of minutes.' cf. '**to be wise after the event**' 123/5; '**with the benefit of hindsight**' 121/14.

11. **not to give it a second thought / not to think twice about something** – to be sure of one's intentions. ' "Are you sure you want to babysit for me on Sunday?" "Of course," Sara answered. "So don't give it a second thought." '

12. **to play second fiddle** – to play a subordinate part, to be second in command. 'I am tired of playing second fiddle to Jo. I am every bit as good as she is.'

13. **to have second thoughts** – to change one's mind. 'He was going to buy the house but, when he saw the neighbourhood, he had second thoughts.'

14. **second sight** – the possession of extrasensory perception.

Twice

15. **to think twice** – to make sure the action is the right one to take. 'I would think twice about going camping next to the lake, if I were you. There are millions of midges there.'

Double

16. **to see double** – to hallucinate under the influence of drink, drugs or disease.

17. **to be someone's double** – to resemble someone so closely that one can be mistaken for the other.

18. **double-talk** – talk that is calculated to mislead. Promises made dishonestly.

19. **to double-think** – this is a variation on 'double-talk' and means the ability to hold two contradictory opinions simultaneously. From George Orwell's *1984*.

20. **to double date** – two couples fixing the same date for their outing. 'I thought it might be fun to go on a double date with Peter, Simon and his girlfriend.'

21. **double-quick** – at great speed. The phrase is derived from the command 'double', meaning 'run'. 'Robin was in a

hurry to go on holiday and finished his office work in double-quick time.'

1. **double time** – twice the normal rate of pay, e.g. double the normal wage when the work is done outside the usual working hours.

2. **to double back** – to turn round and retrace one's footsteps.

3. **a double-barrelled name** – two surnames joined by a hyphen.

4. **in double harness** – two people working together.

5. **a double whammy** – two setbacks occurring at the same time. 'Charging drivers when they go to work and take their cars into town centres, as well as charging them for parking near their workplace really is a double whammy.' Also: **a triple whammy** – when there are three setbacks; **to be doubly hobbled** – to be up against two perplexing difficulties. A 'whammy' is a crippling curse or malevolent spell cast by someone putting the evil eye on someone or something. A double whammy is even more unsettling as it is cast by putting the evil eye twice on someone or something. In the American comic strip *Li'l Abner*, the character called Evil-Eye Fleegle is able to cast a double evil eye – a double whammy – and paralyse his enemies just by staring at them.

Three

6. **a three-cornered fight** – a contest (e.g. for Parliament) in which three candidates participate.

7. **three's a crowd** – when two people want to be together, a third person will be in the way. cf. **'two's company, three's none' 257/19**.

8. **the three R's** – Reading, Writing and Arithmetic; the three subjects which are taught in all elementary schools and are considered an essential part of anyone's education. A 'green' version of the three R's: Reduce, Reuse, Recycle (from *The Green Home* by Karen Christensen, © Piatkus Books).

9. **the three W's** – in order to protect themselves from strangers, children must tell their parents the three W's: (1) Who they are going out with, (2) Where they are going, (3) When they are going to be home (booklet from the National Society for the Prevention of Cruelty to Children).

10. **the three wise monkeys** – these are a symbol of discretion because they see no evil, hear no evil and speak no evil.

Third

11. **third degree** – the pressure put on suspects by the police by means of exhausting interrogation and intimidation in order to obtain information and confessions.

12. **the Third Way** – a third possibility, used mostly in politics, avoiding the extreme left and the extreme right and aiming at the centre. Tony Blair, New Labour prime minister, supported the Third Way and passed on his ideas to the German government. The SPD leader Gerhardt Schroeder admired it and called it *'Die neue Mitte'* (the New Centre), promising new social democratic politics in Europe.

13. **the third age** – the mature generation which is well-off, does not feel old and is still very active. cf. **'grey power' 9/6**; **'silver surfers' 10/15**.

Four, Fourth

14. **a foursome** – two partners who play against two other partners, especially at golf.

15. **to make up a four** – to join three others in a game, as in bridge or tennis.

16. **to stand four-square behind** – to be fully supportive of someone/something. 'Quite a number of people are standing four-square behind animal activists.'

17. **a four-letter word** – an indecent and offensive word, e.g. 'arse' (which dates back to before AD 1000 in English).

18. **the fourth dimension** – an imaginary dimension in addition to length, breadth and height.

19. **the fourth estate** – the press, the other

three estates being the monarchy, Parliament and the church.

Five, Fifth

1. **two and two make five in your case** – you have drawn the wrong conclusion.

2. **to give someone five** – to slap hands in greeting with a friend. 'Five' refers to the five fingers of one hand.

   to give someone high five – to slap hands in greeting high above the head. 'When Mervyn met his friend at the disco, he gave him high-five.' **a bunch of fives** – a fist, to make a fist.

3. **the fifth column** – a wartime phrase meaning those people in an occupied country who collaborated with the invaders.

Six, Sixth

4. **six of one and half a dozen of the other** – there is no difference at all between one course of action and another.

5. **at sixes and sevens** – bewildered or hopelessly confused, chaotic. The phrase comes from the figures on the dice which were once used in gaming.

6. **to hit/knock for six** – (1) to deal an enemy a crushing blow. 'We hit the newspaper for six! For libelling us, the court awarded us damages of £40,000 plus all our costs.' (2) to be astonished, completely taken aback. 'Richard was knocked for six when his girlfriend left him at the party and went home with another boy.' This is a cricketing metaphor: a batsman scores six runs when he hits the ball over the boundary line without it touching the ground first. cf. **'to be bowled out/ bowled over'** 301/12.

7. **six of the best** – six strokes with the cane, a school punishment. The phrase is sometimes used as the headline of a newspaper report: 'Six of the best – Mrs Todd gave birth yesterday to sextuplets. All are doing well.'

8. **sixth form** – the top form in any school.

9. **sixth sense** – a supernatural sense, a

special intuition in addition to the five senses (sight, hearing, touch, smell, taste).

Seven, Seventh

10. **the seven deadly sins** – in the Christian religion these are: pride, envy, anger, lust, sloth, avarice and gluttony.

11. **seven-league boots** – this phrase, which is derived from fairy tales, means boots which will carry the wearer seven leagues (21 miles) at a step.

12. **in (the) seventh heaven** – a state of exaltation, bliss or ecstasy. The seventh heaven in the Muslim religion is the dwelling of Allah; in Judaism it is the home of God and the highest angels. cf. **'on Cloud Nine'** 22/4.

Eight

13. **to have one over the eight** – to get drunk, so called because eight drinks are usually enough to intoxicate anyone.

Nine

14. **to be dressed up to the nines** – to be dressed for a special occasion, to be dressed to perfection. 'Up to the nines' is a corruption of medieval English 'to the eyne' ('to the eyes'), meaning from head to foot. cf. **'dressed to kill'** 191/13.

15. **a stitch in time saves nine** – a prompt correction saves a lot of labour and time later.

16. **a nine-days wonder** – something very sensational or scandalous which will be forgotten after a short time.

17. **to bowl over like ninepins** – to overcome with little or no resistance. 'The unexpected results of the election bowled them over like ninepins. They all sat silent and dejected.' Ninepins is a game, similar to skittles, which is played with nine 'pins' which are set up at the end of an alley and which must be knocked down with a ball. Once they are hit, the ninepins fall down very easily.

   to fall for someone like ninepins – to succumb very willingly to someone's charms. 'Kate is so beautiful and charming – men fall for her like ninepins.'

1. **possession is nine points of the law** – a legal maxim meaning that it is easier to defend one's possession of an object than to dispossess someone else.

Ten, Tenth

2. **ten out of ten** – full marks, 10 being the maximum marks given in English schools. 'I gave Andrew ten out of ten for his last novel. It was faultlessly written.'

3. **ten to one** – nine chances in 10 that something will happen.

4. **the submerged tenth** – the lowest and most under-privileged social class.

Eleven, Eleventh

5. **elevenses** – tea or coffee or other refreshments taken at 11 o'clock in the morning.

6. **at the eleventh hour** – at the last possible moment, only just in time to save the situation. 'The unpopular chairman agreed to resign and so, at the eleventh hour, a crisis was averted.' See the Bible, Matthew XX, 1–16.

Dozen, Teens

7. **a baker's dozen** – thirteen. Formerly, bakers were fined for giving short weight. In order to avoid the trouble of weighing their loaves, they threw in one extra to make sure their loaves were up to the required weight.

8. **to talk nineteen to the dozen** – to talk very fast without stopping in order to prevent others from interrupting, to be excited.

9. **in one's teens** – a boy or girl aged from 13 to 19 years of age.

Thirteen

10. **thirteen at table** – this is considered unlucky by many people who believe that the first person to rise from a table of thirteen will die. The superstition is based on 'The Last Supper' when Jesus and the 12 Apostles were seated at the table, and Judas Iscariot, the 13th man, went out and hanged himself after betraying Christ.

Seventeen

11. **sweet seventeen** – the age of sweetness and charm in a girl.

Nineteen

12. **the nineteenth hole** – the bar in a golf club, a humorous phrase because there are only 18 holes on a golf course.

Twenties, Twenty-first, Twenty-two, Twenty-four

13. **the Roaring Twenties** – the period immediately following the First World War when young men and women were enjoying a new freedom. Girls wore short skirts, smoked and danced the Charleston.

14. **a 21st-birthday party** – a party for the traditional coming of age when the boy/girl is acknowledged by the parents to have reached adulthood. Young people now 'come of age' at 18, but a 21st-birthday is still regarded as special.

15. **a Catch-22 situation** – a dilemma from which it is impossible to escape. 'The public are calling for less crowding in our prisons; at the same time they are demanding longer prison sentences for crimes of violence. It is a Catch-22 situation.' From *Catch 22* by Joseph Heller.

16. **24–7 / 24/7** – a shop or restaurant which is open non-stop for 24 hours seven days a week. 'Why can't there be more 24–7s? They're such a good idea.'

Thirties, Forty

17. **the hungry Thirties** – the 1930s were a period of depression and unemployment when many workers went hungry.

18. **forty winks** – a nap taken after lunch.

19. **fair, fat and forty** – refers to the middle-age spread in women (from Sir Walter Scott, *St Ronan's Well*, Ch. 7).

Fifty, Sixties

1. **fifty-fifty** – in equal proportions, half and half, often used in reference to chance. 'The chances of his recovering from the operation are only fifty-fifty.'

2. **the wrong/right side of fifty** – over 50 years of age / under 50 years of age.

3. **the Swinging Sixties** – the 1960s which ushered in the 'permissive Society', 'the pill' and the 'mini-skirt'. It was a new era when young people threw off traditional restraints on sexual behaviour and expression. The word 'swinging' is connected with the swinging hips of the young women.

Nineties

4. **the Naughty Nineties** – the period from 1890 to the end of the century which was dominated by the aesthetic philosophy of 'Art for Art's Sake' of Wilde, Beardsley and others. The exponents of this philosophy were notorious for their dandyism and decadence.

Hundred

5. **a hundred-and-one reasons** – many, many reasons which the speaker does not wish to enumerate.

6. **I've told you a hundred times** – I've told you over and over again. 'If I've told you once, I've told you a hundred times.'

7. **not in a hundred years** – never.

8. **not a hundred miles away** – very near here, closer than one might think. The phrase is used when the speaker does not wish to give an exact location.

Thousand

9. **one in a thousand** – very remarkable. '**She's one in a thousand**' – she has a very splendid character.
   a wife in a thousand – an outstandingly good wife.

10. **a thousand and one** – a huge number. 'He has a thousand-and-one ideas.'

Million

11. **a chance in a million** – either no chance at all or a very slim chance, a tremendous fluke.
    not one chance in a million – completely impossible.

12. **not/never in a million years** – absolutely never. 'Never in a million years would I have believed my son would want to become an airline pilot.'

Billion

13. **dot.com.billionbillionaires** – the wealthiest people in the world, usually young men and women, who have made their money only recently by working with new computer technology, especially the Internet. The term comes from one's Internet address, which is a mixture of letters and full stops or 'dots'.

School

1. **to tell tales out of school** – to talk maliciously about a person's private affairs behind his or her back. 'I don't want to hear any more. Don't tell tales out of school.' In this context, 'out of school' means after class, when the tale-bearer has the opportunity to speak to the teacher alone.

2. **to skip school/classes** – to play truant, to absent oneself. ' "If you skip school one more time, Ben," his mother threatened, "I'll accompany you all the way to your classroom and stay with you till your teacher comes." '

3. **a hard school** – a strict training. 'He was brought up in a hard school which stood him in good stead later when he explored the Antarctic.'

4. **a man of the old school** – someone whose education and point of view are based on traditional principles and loyalties. 'He is a strict disciplinarian and expects his staff to work hard, but he never asks them to do more than he does himself. He is a man of the old school.'

5. **a different school of thought** – a different body of opinion. When a problem has not been resolved with any certainty – in philosophy, science or art – then rival groups or schools may form which advocate a variety of theories, e.g. the empirical, idealistic and Marxist schools in philosophy.

6. **a sink school** – a school which is notorious for its failing standards. Sink schools are responsible for a lost generation of teenagers who leave school without any qualifications. cf. **'a sink estate'** 150/7; **'sin bin'** 44/2.

Class

7. **top/bottom of the class** – to excel/to do badly in a particular field or subject. 'I would recommend Rachel for the post; she is good at management and top of the class in administration.'

8. **in a class of one's own** – to be incomparably better than one's companions in a particular subject or skill. 'If you want a specialist in tax law, I would suggest we brief Mr Williams QC; he is in a class of his own.'

Lesson

9. **an object lesson** – a model of how something should/should not be done. 'The way the little boy acted when the burglar attacked his mother is an object lesson to us all.'

10. **to teach someone a lesson** – to punish or make someone feel sorry. 'The losses you made on the Stock Exchange last year should have taught you a lesson.'
    let that be a lesson to you – let's hope you will take warning from this unpleasant experience.

11. **to learn a lesson / draw a lesson from** – to heed a warning, to learn from a mistake. 'Mothers should draw a lesson from the fact that a baby died from eating adult food because it contained too much salt.' Also: there are signs that someone has **'learnt the right lesson'**; a lesson we should take to heart for the future.

Test

1. **to put to the test** – to examine or verify something. 'Tom always said he would be loyal to her under any circumstances. Let's put his promise to the test.'

2. **to stand the test of time** – to withstand the trials of age or time. 'Some oak trees have stood the test of time and are still going strong after several hundred years.'

3. **IQ test** – a test for measuring someone's 'intelligence quotient'. Hence: **to have a high/low IQ** – to be of high/low intelligence.

Questions, Answers

4. **ask me no questions and I'll tell you no lies** – don't be so inquisitive! ' "Where did that delicious cake come from, Barry? I know you're no good at baking, and you didn't buy it." "Ask me no questions and I'll tell you no lies," Barry laughed.'

5. **with no questions asked** – being able to do something dishonest with no one finding out or interfering. ' "I can easily get you a new passport with no questions asked," the agent said to the asylum seeker.'

6. **the big question** – a very important question. 'We've won the Lottery! Now comes the big question – what shall we spend the money on?'

7. **hard/searching questions** – farreaching inquiries. 'Hard questions need to be asked concerning the enormous amount of money spent on the new town hall.'

8. **to call into question** – to doubt/challenge an explanation or a statement. 'I'm afraid I have to call into question the excuse for your absence at school yesterday, Bill. I saw your "ill" mother cycling back from work in the evening.'

9. **to place/have a question mark over something** – to cast doubt over something, e.g. someone's position, post, job, etc. 'His bad behaviour places a question mark over his position as chairman of our committee.' Also: **a big question mark is hanging over something**. 'There are questions without answers and we, as human beings, must accept that in order to find peace' (Quentin Crisp).

10. **out of the question** – absolutely not; not worth considering. 'You are too young to take a trip abroad on your own, Kim. It is out of the question.'

11. **to be open to question / an open question** – a matter open for discussion or as yet undecided. 'The wisdom of opening a discothèque in this sleepy little village is open to question.'

12. **to pop the question** – to ask for someone's hand in marriage. 'You look radiant, Suzanna. Malcolm must have popped the question!'

13. **a straight answer to a straight question** – a direct, it is hoped truthful, answer to a direct question. 'It really infuriates me. Why on earth can't that politician give the journalist a straight answer to a straight question?' cf. '**to beat about the bush**' 50/8; '**to call a spade a spade**' 252/7.

14. **to know all the answers** – (1) to be an expert. (2) to take a smug satisfaction in one's knowledge and cleverness. 'George doesn't trouble to follow the lessons; he thinks he knows all the answers.'

15. **to answer back** – to answer insolently when corrected or rebuked. 'If you answer the teachers back, you will soon be in trouble.'

Reading, Writing

16. **to read between the lines** – to draw conclusions about the writer's feelings from the manner and tone of the work and not from his actual words. 'Reading between the lines of Miss Prout's reference, I have the impression that her employer was not satisfied with her work, although he doesn't actually say so.'

17. **to read something into (a document, letter, etc.)** – to put words into a work to suggest a meaning that was not intended by the author. 'We said the brochures should be ready by the end of

March, but we didn't promise anything; you are reading more into our letter than we intended.'

1. **to drop someone a line** – to write a note to someone. 'I must drop a line to Alex that I can't meet him next Monday.'

2. **to write something off** – to acknowledge that something no longer has any value. 'Malcolm's house was burned to the ground and he has written it off completely.' This is a book-keeping phrase for cancelling the value of an item shown in the accounts as an asset.

   to write someone off – (1) to acknowledge that someone is no longer capable of useful work in his/her occupation. 'It is too early to write Edwards off; he has had a disappointing season but he is still capable of championship tennis, once his health improves.' (2) to dismiss someone's chances of survival. 'After three days of intensive search, there is no trace of the missing mountaineers and their chances of survival have been written off.'

Spelling, A–Z

3. **to spell big trouble** – be warned: trouble is on its way. ' "Oh dear!" the head teacher sighed. "The school inspector is coming today to find out why the exam results are so bad. This spells big trouble." '

4. **as easy/simple as ABC** – very easy, not at all difficult; plain and understandable. 'It's a beautiful washing-machine and very modern. You'll find it's as easy as ABC to use.' cf. **'as easy as falling off a log' 50/20**; **'as easy as shelling peas' 185/3**.

5. **alpha and omega** – the beginning and the end; one's reason for being. 'Money is Mr Stansted's only joy in life, his alpha and omega, and he is not going to waste it on these fake works of art.' Alpha is the first letter of the Greek alphabet and omega is the last.

Punctuation

6. **full stop** – to emphasize a statement; that is the end of it! 'It is now time for the

Party to say if it is for or against cruel sports, full stop.' US English: **period!** cf. **'end of story' 286/12**; **'the bottom line' 265/13**.

7. **on the dot** – precisely at that time. 'I expect you home at 10 o'clock, on the dot!'

8. **to make one's point** – to stress one's opinion, make it known. 'You can take or leave my offer, but consider it thoroughly. I've made my point.' Frequent usage: **if you get my point**; **if you see my point** – if you understand what I'm trying to say.

Sums

9. **to do one's sums** – to make one's calculations or estimate. 'In the course of the minister's speech, it soon became clear that he had not done his sums.'

   to get one's sums right – to make a correct calculation or estimate. 'The borough treasurer was criticized by the chairman for not getting her sums right.'

10. **to reckon without one's host** – to make one's plans or calculations without taking other people's views into account, to ignore possible opposition. Originally, to calculate the bill at an inn without asking the landlord for the bill.

11. **to take someone's measure** – to judge someone's character and abilities, his or her strengths and weaknesses. 'If I have taken Lever's measure, he is just the man we want for the job.'

12. **to stand up and be counted** – to declare one's principles openly, whatever the cost to one's career or reputation. 'If you wish to help our cause, it is time for you to stand up and be counted.' cf. **'to have the courage of one's convictions' 123/7**.

13. **count me out** – I do not agree with you and do not wish to be counted among your supporters.

Geometry

14. **the bottom line** – the last thing that needs to be said and which sums it all up. 'Ten o'clock is much too late for you to go

to bed during term time. It's bed at 8.30 for you – and that's the bottom line!' Frequent usage: **lack of money is the bottom line**. cf. '**full stop' 265/5**.

1. **a fine line between two things** – there is no clear and easy-to-define distinction between two things. 'There is only a fine line between telling a white lie and being economical with the truth.'

2. **to drag someone/something into line** – to force someone or something to conform. ' "To drag the pound into line with the euro could trigger off inflation," the minister said gravely.'

3. **to take a clear line** – to keep firmly to a distinct and unmistakable policy. 'When John Major was prime minister, he was unable to take a clear line over Europe.'

4. **to take a tough/firm/hard line** – to adopt a strict approach towards someone/ something. 'If you don't take a tough line in the classroom, your pupils won't respect you.'

5. **somewhere along the line** – at some time or other. 'Somewhere along the line there was a loss of respect, and the relationship faltered.'

6. **to be on the line** – to be in danger of losing one's job, reputation. 'After having made such a bad mistake, his political future is on the line.'

7. **to keep something in line with** – to keep equal to or on the same level with. 'The finance minister told his audience that he would try to keep mortgage rates in line with the Bank of England's base rate.'

8. **to draw the line** – to set a limit to one's tolerance. 'I don't mind Carol bringing her friends home but I draw the line at strangers she's picked up in the bus.'

9. **to draw a parallel** – to point to similarities between two (historic) events or phenomena. 'It is difficult to draw a parallel between the ancient and the modern world.'

10. **to go off at a tangent** – to introduce an irrelevant subject in the course of a discussion. 'It's impossible to discuss anything with Molly; she will keep going off at a tangent.'

11. **to fit/suit to a T** – something that is absolutely right. 'This new exercise programme in the gym suits me to a T.' The 'T' in this idiom is the technical device called a T-square.

Circle

12. **a social circle** – a group of people meeting socially, usually in clubs. 'My neighbour boasted that her social circle included a famous opera singer, but I didn't know whether to believe her.' Other 'circles' of people include: **the royal circle; our circle of friends; in political circles; in diplomatic circles; in Hollywood circles; in theatre circles; in Catholic circles**.

13. **in smart circles** – groups of fashionable people. 'In smart circles, they've turned their backs on continental cuisine – traditional English cookery is now all the rage.'

14. **the inner circle** – the powerful but discreet group of people in charge of something important. 'The public doesn't really know the complete inner circle of the government.'

15. **to go round in circles** – to think for a long time about a problem without getting any nearer to a solution. 'We've been arguing for the last half-hour about what we are going to do and we are just going round in circles.' cf. '**to chase one's tail' 54/19**.

16. **to run round in circles** – to dash about in an agitated way without achieving one's purpose. cf. '**to run around like a headless chicken' 69/11**.

17. **to come full circle** – to return to one's starting point. 'After making and losing a fortune in America, Tom returned to his old job at Barclays. He had come full circle.'

18. **a vicious circle** – a chain of events in which the cause of the difficulty/disorder produces an effect which intensifies the cause. 'I didn't have enough lodgers to pay the rates (tax) on my house. To pay

the rates I had to sell some of the furniture. Without the furniture I lost some of my lodgers. As a result, I have less money than before to pay the rates; so I have to sell more of my furniture again. It's a vicious circle.'

1. **to square the circle** – to try to do the impossible. 'Trying to protect Snowdonia National Park from pollution and keeping it open to tourists is like squaring the circle.' cf. **'you can't have your cake and eat it' 179/2**.

Square, Triangle

2. **fair and square** – with the utmost frankness. 'I told Marion fair and square what I thought of her behaviour.'

3. **a square deal** – fair treatment. 'Tom always gave his workers a square deal.'

4. **to square accounts** – to revenge oneself on someone. 'Wallis has treated me with contempt in front of my friends; I intend to square accounts with him.'

5. **to square an account** – to pay a bill.

6. **all square** – a golfing phrase, meaning that the score is even. 'Dick won the 11th hole to make them all square.'

7. **on the square** – (1) honest, straightforward, dependable. 'Miles has always been on the square with me; you can trust him to act fairly.' (2) to be a Freemason. Freemasonry is a secret religious society which goes back to medieval times when a group of stonemasons are believed to have founded it.

8. **the eternal triangle / a love triangle** – a sexual relationship between two men and a woman, or two women and one man. 'The eternal triangle is the breeding ground for jealousy, conflict and tension.' See *Triangulation* by Phil Whitaker (a novel about a love triangle).

Units of Measure

9. **to go to great lengths / at great length** – to go to a great deal of trouble to achieve one's aim. 'Mrs Johnson went to great lengths to prepare a perfect birthday party for her daughter.' 'Often riots are not spontaneous but have been planned at great length.'

10. **to go to any length** – to do anything to suit one's purpose. 'If you are competing with Mary for the job, be careful. She will go to any length to get it.'

11. **to stand/stick out a mile** – to be absolutely obvious. 'However could you believe his promises? It sticks out a mile that he's a con-man.' cf. **'to stick out like a sore thumb' 101/8**.

12. **to win by a mile** – to win very easily. 'Yvette is an extremely good chess-player. She's going to win the competition by a mile.'

13. **to spot something a mile off** – to be blatantly obvious. 'One can spot a mile off that Cindy's taking drugs – her behaviour is so irrational.'

14. **to run a mile** – to get away from a distasteful situation as quickly as possible. 'The exam was so difficult. I would run a mile if I had to sit for it again.'

15. **a milestone** – a significant event. 'The move from England to New Zealand was a milestone in the life of the Brown family.' cf. **'a landmark' 146/10**.

16. **a yardstick** – a criterion by which to measure performance. 'Margaret Thatcher remains the yardstick against which all modern prime ministers are measured.'

17. **every inch of the way** – all the way through. ' "I'll stand by my pregnant daughter every inch of the way," said the mother of the 13-year-old girl.'

History

18. **to make history** – to do something important, for which one will be remembered. 'Professor Beloff has made history by establishing the first private university in Britain.'

19. **like holding a piece of history** – to have a deep and sensual experience of something which happened a long time ago. 'It was an amazing feeling, taking Queen Victoria's little onyx elephant in my hand. It was like holding a piece of history.' Also: **like making contact with**

a piece of history. 'The student was thrilled to be able to shake Prince Charles' hand. "It's like making contact with a piece of history," she sighed.'

1. **to consign something to the bin/ dustbin of history** – to relegate something to the past so that it is quickly forgotten. 'The idea of replacing the famous London double-decker bus with an ordinary bus manufactured according to EU regulations has been consigned to the dustbin of history.'

2. **to go down in history** – an action or deed that will never be forgotten. 'The conquest of Mount Everest by Sir Edmund Hillary and Sherpa Tenzing has gone down in history.'

3. **to airbrush someone out of history** – to paint over/blot out someone's deeds so that they are forgotten. 'After the latest scandal, there was a feeling that certain politicians should be airbrushed out of history.'

4. **ancient/past history** – an occurrence that is no longer of any importance. 'He was married twice, but that is ancient history. His third marriage has been a complete success.'

5. **history repeats itself / a case of history repeating itself** – past events recurring in a similar form in the present. 'His father spent years in prison and now his son is to be convicted. It's a case of history repeating itself.' Also: **history teaches us . . . ; we never/don't learn from history**.

Geography

6. **to put a place on the map** – to bring a place to the attention of the public, to make a place well-known. 'When the American film star returned to her birthplace, she put the small village on the map.'

Biology

7. **one's biological clock/body clock** – a system inside the human body which controls its functions, and which is triggered by the hypothalamus gland responding to light. 'Now I've reached 35, I can hear my biological clock ticking away. I think it's high time Simon and I tried to have a baby before it's too late.'

8. **biological warfare/weapons** – use of germs (which cause diseases) in armed conflict. There is a general understanding among countries not to use biological warfare in any armed conflict. cf. **'germ warfare' 133/3**.

9. **to be put under the microscope** – every aspect of someone's life is being scrutinized. 'I wouldn't really want to apply for a high-profile job because everything I did would be put under the microscope.'

Chemistry

10. **a special/strange chemistry** – a mysterious reaction to something; a special chemistry which can draw two people instinctively towards each other. 'Right from the beginning, there was a special chemistry between the two students and they fell in love immediately.'

11. **the litmus test** – an action that confirms an experiment or investigation. 'The candidates for the director's post will be chosen according to their views on certain litmus-test issues – the equality of women at all levels, friendly relations with Europe and their attitude to the environment.' Litmus paper is used in a chemical test for acidity (where it turns red), or alkalinity (where it turns blue).

12. **an acid test** – a crucial examination to prove something is genuine. 'The acid test of the new medicine is whether it will help your asthma in an emergency.' From the test with nitric acid to find out whether a specific material contains gold.

Art

13. **state-of-the-art** – the achievement of the latest technology in a particular field. 'We are very proud of our new, state-of-the-art television.'

14. **to go back to the drawing-board** – to try something again, right from the beginning. 'After all the time he had spent on

his plans, it was not a success and he had to go back to the drawing-board.'
cf. **'back to square one' 257/3**.

1. **to erase an image** – to do away with an impression. 'The teacher wanted to erase the image of being a strict disciplinarian and so did not tell his pupils off for being noisy.'

2. **to keep a low profile** – to avoid attracting attention, to be inconspicuous. 'I had no idea my proposal would arouse so much hostility. I had better keep a low profile for the next few months.'

3. **to raise one's profile** – to create a more favourable public image of oneself. 'The Prince of Wales went on a two-day visit to Scotland to raise the Royal Family's profile there.'

4. **to paint oneself into a corner** – to get oneself into an awkward situation from which it is difficult to escape. 'By promising the archaeologists to preserve the Roman remains, and the town to allow a new supermarket on the site, the minister has painted himself into a corner.'

5. **to paint a gloomy/sad/bleak/worrying picture** – to admit to a pessimistic outlook. 'Scientists paint a gloomy picture of the future, thanks to global warming.' Frequent usage: **no one can be flattered by the picture it (the report/article/book, etc.) paints**.

6. **as interesting as/like watching paint dry** – a dreary and dull activity or experience. 'I don't like billiards. It's like watching paint dry.'

7. **no oil painting** – not at all good-looking. 'Fred has plenty of girlfriends, although he is no oil painting.'

Copybook

8. **to blot one's copybook** – to make a serious mistake, which damages one's record. 'If you hadn't blotted your copybook borrowing the boss's car, you would have been promoted by now.'

Slate

9. **to wipe the slate clean** – to give someone another chance and overlook past offences. 'The judge told the prisoner that if he accepted the job offered him, he would wipe the slate clean.' The idiom has its origin in the former custom in schools of chalking up on a slate the names of pupils who had misbehaved. When the pupils had been punished, the slate was wiped clean.

Blackboard, Chalk

10. **the blackboard jungle** – lawlessness and violence in the classroom, with the pupils threatening and defying the teacher. The term has been imported from the USA.
    the concrete jungle – a big city where there are no trees or green spaces.

11. **not by a long chalk** – not ever, not at all. 'I'm sorry to say you're not good enough to join the Olympic skaters; not by a long chalk.'

12. **as white as chalk / chalk-white** – to have a very pale face, a face drained of blood and white with fear, shock, illness, etc. 'Mrs Sullivan's face went as white as chalk when she saw the huge spider crossing the carpet near her feet.'

Pen, Paper

13. **a pen-pusher** – an office worker who has to do a lot of paperwork. 'I'm only a pen pusher in this office. It's time I looked for a more exciting job!'

14. **a poison-pen letter** – a malicious or threatening letter, sent anonymously. 'Witnesses who have helped convict a criminal have received several poison-pen letters.' cf. **'hate mail' 126/11**; **'to blackmail someone' 8/8**.

15. **as white as paper / paper-white** – completely white; pale. 'The young man's back had never been exposed to the sun and it was as white as paper.'

16. **paper-thin** – very thin indeed, very narrow, flimsy. 'Why on earth have these

flats got such paper-thin walls? I can hear my neighbour practising on his piano and it is driving me mad.'

1. **not worth the paper something is written on** – absolutely useless. 'Before the election, the Party promised not to increase taxes. That pledge was not worth the paper it was written on. After the election, taxes went up instead of down.'

Seal, Glue

2. **to set one's seal to something** – to consent to or license something. 'If you want to borrow such a large amount of money, I'm afraid your father will have to set his seal to it.'

3. **to stick to someone/something like glue** – to keep/hold fast to someone at all costs.

4. **to be glued to the phone/to the television** – 'My daughter is always glued to the phone, gossiping about her new boyfriend to all her girlfriends.' cf. '**to cling/stick like a limpet**' 75/3.

Marks

5. **to give someone full marks for** – to give someone credit for a faultless achievement. 'Christine Bowles deserves full marks for the excellence of her latest biography.'

　　to give someone no marks – to give someone no credit for his or her work. One can award marks on a 10-point scale in the same way as marks are awarded in English schools. 'I give the local council only five out of 10 for its plan to clean up the town centre.'

6. **blind marking** – marking of papers by examiners of unidentified schools. 'Pupils and parents find blind marking of GCSE papers a much fairer system.'

7. **to make one's mark / to leave one's mark** – to leave a lasting impression. 'Princess Diana and Mother Theresa both left their mark on the world because of their kindness to others.'

Sneak, Egg On

8. **a sneaking sympathy** – a sympathy for someone or something that one is reluctant to admit. 'I have a sneaking sympathy for middle-aged housewives who are brought before me for shoplifting although, as a magistrate, I shouldn't talk like that.' The word 'sneak' means to complain about a fellow pupil behind his back to the teacher, and make trouble for him.

9. **to egg someone on** – to encourage someone to do wrong, e.g. by breaking rules. 'You shouldn't have egged Stephen on to play that joke on Mr Gibbs. Now he'll be in trouble.' The derivation is from Icelandic *egg* meaning 'edge', so that the literal meaning is to put someone on the edge.

Rules, Punishments

10. **a hard-and-fast rule** – a rule that is strictly enforced and cannot be changed or varied in any circumstances. 'We have a hard-and-fast rule about wearing uniform at our school and we cannot make an exception for your son.'

11. **to flout the rules** – to ignore procedure deliberately, not to obey orders, to show disrespect to an authority. 'When the boy entered the school, he was watched carefully by the staff as he was known to frequently flout the rules.' Also: something '**defies every (marketing) rule in the book**' and sells unexpectedly well.

12. **to bend the rules** – to adapt the rules to one's own advantage. 'I know that you are five years too old for this particular course, but I'll bend the rules and let you join in.'

13. **to play by the rules** – to strictly adhere to the rules. 'The prime minister insisted that Britain would play by the EU rules.'

14. **to rule with a rod of iron** – to use the utmost severity in maintaining order. 'Jack told us how his step-father ruled the family with a rod of iron; the teachers at school were quite gentle by comparison.'

15. **to kiss the rod** – to accept punishment meekly and submissively. 'If the boss

expects me to kiss the rod the way the others do, she is making a mistake.'

1. **to haul over the coals** – to rebuke severely. 'I was hauled over the coals for taking the day off yesterday. I won't do that again!' The phrase meant originally to torture a person by holding him or her over burning coal.

2. **to be whacked** (slang) – to be exhausted. 'I feel completely whacked after spending the day with Jill shopping in the West End.' To 'whack' is slang for to 'beat' or 'cane'. cf. **'dead-beat' 39/8**.

3. **a fair whack** (slang) – a fair share. 'If the company can afford an increase of 15 per cent for the directors, I don't see why we shouldn't get a fair whack of the profits too!'

4. **a whacking/thumping/whopping lie** – a huge, obvious lie. 'That's a whacking lie of the manager to say I am idle; I'm the first to arrive at the office and the last to leave.' The explanation for these phrases may be that whacking/thumping/whopping were regarded as a fit punishment for telling lies. The verbs 'whack', 'thump' and 'whop' mean to 'beat'.

Knack, Progress

5. **to have a knack for / to have the knack** – to be able to handle a situation skilfully, to have an ability. ' "However did Jim manage to repair the clock so beautifully?" "Oh, he has a knack for that kind of thing." '

6. **to lose one's knack/the knack** – not being able to do something efficiently any more. 'Grandfather used to be so skilful building ships in bottles. He's lost the knack now – it must be his age.'

7. **to get the hang of something** – to begin to understand something. 'Jennifer had spent hours trying to teach her brother fractions, when he suddenly got the hang of it.'

8. **to be a late developer** – a person who doesn't show much promise when young but makes up for it when growing older. 'Who would have thought that Andrew would do so well at the age of 20? He really is a late developer.'

Boy

(see also *Boy* in Chapter 14)

9. **a new boy** – someone who is new to a position of employment or a place of work. 'I'd be grateful if you could please explain the office routine to me; I'm a new boy here.' Boys in their first term at school (in particular, boarding school) are referred to as new boys.

10. **a whipping-boy** – someone who is made responsible for the mistakes and faults of another. 'The Cranes got badly sun-burned on their Pacific cruise and tried to make the travel agency the whipping-boy for their mishap for not warning them how hot the climate would be in those parts.' The whipping-boy was a boy who was educated with a prince and whipped whenever the prince deserved punishment, because tutors were not permitted to hit a child of the royal blood.

11. **bully-boy tactics** – shouting someone down and adopting violent and aggressive behaviour. 'The crowd used bully-boy tactics to prevent the speaker from being heard.'

12. **the old-boy network** – an association of ex-public school boys, i.e. old boys, who obtain jobs for one another on the basis of their common background, rather than merit.

Peer

13. **peer pressure/peer-group pressure** – a group of people of the same age and equal in every respect who feel a compulsion to behave in the same way as each other. Peer pressure is the main reason why so many school-children take drugs.

30 Work and Occupations

Work

1. **to have one's work cut out** – to accomplish a task only with the greatest difficulty. 'We shall have our work cut out to get the house ready in time for the wedding reception.' Literally, to work to a plan prepared by someone else.

2. **to make light work of** – to accomplish a task very easily, with little effort or trouble. 'Vivien made light work of her GCSE papers; they were much easier than she had expected.'

3. **to work to rule** – to obey the rulebook (i.e. one's working instructions), with exaggerated care, so as to bring about a slow-down in the service; a tactic of the trade unions for putting pressure on the employer.

4. **to work wonders** – to have an astonishing effect. 'That medicine the doctor prescribed for me has worked wonders for my rheumatism; I have no pain now.'

5. **to make short work of someone/something** – to dispose of someone or something very quickly and easily. 'The children made short work of the Christmas pudding, which disappeared very quickly.'

6. **to work off steam / to let off steam** – to find an outlet for one's energy or feelings. 'In the afternoons, the boys work off steam on the football field.'

7. **to do someone's dirty work** – unpleasant or contemptible tasks foisted on a person by someone else. 'I refuse to go round and apologize on your behalf. Why should I always do your dirty work for you?'

8. **a nasty piece of work** – someone of bad character, false and cruel. 'I am sorry you are going out with Beaney. He is a nasty piece of work.'

9. **a glutton for work/punishment** – someone who welcomes the opportunity of working hard for long hours. 'Don't tell me you've brought your work home after nine hours at the office; you are a glutton for punishment!'

10. **a workaholic** – someone who is unable to stop his or her addiction to work. 'Mr Parker's marriage failed because he was a workaholic and didn't have time for his wife.'

Job

11. **to have a job** – to have difficulty in doing something. 'I had a job making Pierre understand me. My French is very weak and he doesn't know any English.'

12. **an inside job** – a burglary committed with the assistance of an employee or relation of the person robbed. 'It must have been an inside job, otherwise how could the thieves have known where the jewellery was hidden?'

13. **a put-up job** – something arranged beforehand with a deceitful or criminal purpose. 'We were burgled two days after the new window-cleaner started work. The police think it was a put-up job.'

14. **just the job** – exactly what is wanted. 'Your car is just the job for London – cheap to run, and small enough to park anywhere.'

15. **it's a good job** – it's a good thing; it's lucky that. 'It's a good job you weren't at

home when Jim called; he was in such a bad temper.'

1. **to make the best of a bad job** – to try to gain as much advantage as possible from an unsatisfactory situation. 'At least the post will give you the opportunity to learn Spanish. Why don't you make the best of a bad job instead of grumbling all the time.'

2. **to give something up as a bad job** – to abandon an attempt to do something because it is too difficult or impossible. 'Having failed the driving test three times, Ralph gave it up as a bad job.'

3. **jobs for the boys** – the giving of the best positions by those in authority to their relations, friends and supporters. Selection for the jobs is based on favour not merit.

Profession

4. **the oldest profession** – prostitution. cf. '**to live by clipping**' 282/6; '**to sell one's body**' 80/5.

Occupations:

The Church

5. **to go into the church** – to be ordained as a priest in the church.

6. **a broad church** – an organization which tolerates a wide range of ideas and policies among its supporters. 'The traditional Labour Party has always been a broad church with room for social democrats and Marxists.'

7. **as poor as a church-mouse** – very poor, because there is little or no food in most churches for mice to feed on. As the Germans have the same phrase in their language – '*So arm wie eine Kirchenmaus*' – it is possible that the Saxons introduced it to Britain in the fifth- or sixth-century invasions.

8. **high priest** – the leading exponent of a theory or doctrine. 'Sigmund Freud was the high priest of psychoanalysis.'

9. **take a pew** – make yourself comfortable, sit down. Often said casually by the host to a visitor who can only stay a short time. The pew is the bench that is fixed to the floor of the church for seating the congregation. It has no place in a private house, so its use is a little facetious.

10. **the Vicar of Bray** – a 16th-century vicar who changed his views in accordance with the views of each new government. The phrase is occasionally used to describe anyone who changes his views for profit.

11. **like the curate's egg** – a euphemism for something that is bad or unsatisfactory. It derives from a joke in *Punch*: a young curate on being asked whether his egg was good replied: 'It is good in parts.' He was too polite to tell his host that his egg was bad.

12. **benefit of clergy** – a privilege enjoyed by members of the church in the Middle Ages which exempted them from criminal prosecution in the King's Courts, the Ecclesiastical Courts being much more lenient. The privilege was much abused and almost anybody who could read was able to claim 'benefit of clergy'.

13. **the parish pump / parish-pump politics** – (1) a preoccupation with trivialities. (2) a derogatory term for local government and council meetings. 'I am tired of parish-pump politics. We should be talking about our wages, not petty problems like canteen meals.'

14. **to give someone short shrift** – to treat someone curtly, impatiently. 'The colonel gave his men's complaints short shrift.' 'Short shrift' was originally the short time allowed a prisoner for making his confession before execution. 'Shrift' meant 'confession' and derives from Anglo-Saxon *schrift*, with the same meaning.

15. **to bear one's cross** – to bear suffering, affliction or annoyance. The suffering is usually the fault of someone else. 'To be underestimated by men is the biggest cross I have had to bear' (*Woman of Substance* by Barbara Taylor Bradford).

16. **an odour of sanctity** – an overpowering atmosphere of piety and virtuous living. 'Although I was made welcome at the vicarage, there was an odour of sanctity

about the place which made me uncomfortable.' The allusion is to a legend in the Middle Ages that when the saints were buried, their bodies gave off a sweet-smelling odour, which came to be known as the odour of sanctity.

1. **to make a martyr of oneself** (derogatory) – to make unnecessary sacrifices in order to win sympathy and pity from one's friends. 'Why shouldn't you take a holiday like the rest of the staff ? Are you trying to make a martyr of yourself ?'

2. **a holier-than-thou attitude/ expression** – to behave as though one were more virtuous than one's companions. 'Yes, I didn't get home until half-past two this morning, but you have come in later than that, so you needn't look at me with that holier-than-thou expression.'

3. **the holy of holies** – the most private room in a house. 'This is my husband's holy of holies where he can work without fear of being disturbed.' The Holy of Holies was the name given to the innermost apartment of the Jewish Temple where the Ark of the Covenant was kept. Only the high priest could enter this room on the Day of Atonement (Yom Kippur).

4. **a holy terror** – someone who causes a public disturbance by his rowdy misbehaviour. The term is often applied to a child who gets out of control and runs wild. 'That boy has become a holy terror to the whole neighbourhood, running his bicycle up and down the pavement all day long.'

5. **to take holy orders** – to be ordained as a priest in the Anglican Church. 'My son has just taken holy orders. He always wanted to be a priest.'

6. **to preach to the converted** – to waste one's persuasive powers on someone who is already of one's own opinion. 'I should like blood sports to be made illegal just as much as you do. You are preaching to the converted.'

7. **to count one's blessings** – to remember all the advantages that one enjoys, especially when complaining about the annoyances of present-day conditions. 'Yes, it

must have been disappointing not getting the job, but you should count your blessings: good health, a happy home, and a nice circle of friends.'

8. **a mixed blessing** – something that should bring joy but suffers from serious drawbacks. 'We were delighted when Mervyn gave us the puppy, but it has proved a mixed blessing; it has done so much damage to the furniture and curtains.'

9. **to give one's blessing to** – to give one's approval of. 'Although Julie is only 16, her parents have given us their blessing, and we are to be married in May.'

10. **a blessing in disguise** – what at first appears to be a misfortune turns out later to be a boon. 'Perhaps your son's failure to get into a university may be a blessing in disguise. He'll have no difficulty getting a job, and by the time he's 21 he'll have three years of practical experience behind him.'

11. **to take as Gospel** – to believe something to be true with absolute certainty. 'You must believe me; I'm telling you the Gospel truth.' The Gospel consists of the first four books of the New Testament (by Matthew, Mark, Luke and John) which describe the life and teaching of Christ. cf. **'as true as God's in heaven'** 42/10.

12. **to give/quote chapter and verse** – to produce evidence in support of one's statements. 'I can't quote chapter and verse for what I am saying; you'll just have to believe me.' The whole of the Bible is divided into chapters and verses; so that when a priest gives 'chapter and verse' as the authority for his statements, they can be immediately verified.

13. **a baptism of fire** – someone's first test, often painful. 'I have to visit a patient, so Dr Wake will have to take surgery; that will be his baptism of fire.' A baptism of fire is the first experience a soldier has of gun-fire.

14. **for one's sins** (humorous) – as a punishment for one's wrong-doing. 'I'm a teacher, for my sins.' Although the phrase is used humorously, it often implies dissatisfaction with one's occupation.

15. **to cover a multitude of sins** – to

include a great number of undesirable possibilities. 'She calls herself a consultant on personal problems, but that could cover a multitude of sins.'

1. **to be thankful for small mercies** – to be thankful for the small advantages and consolations that can be set against a misfortune or setback. 'Almost all the furniture was destroyed but we were able to save the jewellery. I suppose we should be thankful for small mercies.'

2. **that's your funeral!** (impolite) – that is your misfortune. 'You can't expect me to reduce your bill because your house has been burgled; that's your funeral!'

The Law

3. **to take the law into one's own hands** – to seek justice by using force or the threat of force without resorting to the law courts.

4. **to be a law unto oneself** – to live in accordance with one's own principles and ignore the law. In practice, this amounts to putting oneself above the law. 'You can't apply ordinary standards to that man. He is a law unto himself.' From Romans II, 14 (New Testament): 'These, having not the law, are a law unto themselves.'

5. **the rule of law** – the application of the law to all alike (institutions, local government, etc.), irrespective of differences in power or wealth.

6. **to keep on the right side of the law** – to obey the law but without troubling whether one's actions are honest or moral.
    to be on the wrong side of the law – to disobey the law. It is possible to get on the wrong side of the law unintentionally or through ignorance.

7. **the long arm of the law** – criminals are never safe from the law which has all the sources of the state behind it.

8. **in the eyes of the law** – the legal position, as distinct from the commonsense point of view. 'If a stranger enters your room and sits on your bed, he has done

you no wrong in the eyes of the law unless he uses force.'

9. **to lay down the law** – to be dogmatic and prejudiced on matters of opinion. 'It's no fun arguing with you; you lay down the law every time, and that's the end of the discussion.'

10. **to keep within the letter of the law** – to obey the law in every particular while defeating its spirit. 'There's nothing I can do about the noise my neighbour makes; he switches his radio off every night at the stroke of 10. In that way he can keep within the letter of the law and, at the same time, prevent me getting any peace.'

11. **to fall foul of the law** – to do something illegal. 'Hiring a van and smuggling all those bottles of alcohol in from France would be falling foul of the law – so don't do it, Tom!'

12. **the law of the jungle** – no law at all because, in the jungle, the strongest animals prevail over the weaker. Some economists have compared the free-market economy with the law of the jungle.

13. **a loophole in the law** – a way of avoiding the effect of the law without breaking it, when the language of the law is inaccurate or ambiguous.
    to close/plug a loophole – to correct a defect in the law. 'The government intends to close a loophole in the law so that illegal immigrants will no longer be able to stay in Britain by claiming political asylum.'

14. **to call in the law** – to request the assistance of the police to protect one's rights against criminal action.

15. **the unwritten law** – a law which is generally recognized, although it has not been committed to writing. Custom has the force of law in many parts of the world, even when it is not part of the written law. There is also an unwritten law of criminals, such as the trial and execution of men and women who betray their accomplices to the police.

16. **to have the law on someone** – to prosecute, to take legal proceedings against. 'I'll have the law on you for the damage you have done to my property.'

1. **to go beyond the law** – to go beyond the reach of the law, outside the jurisdiction. 'We can't sue him now. He is in Brazil and beyond the law.'

2. **to go to law** – to take proceedings in a court of law in defence of one's rights. 'I don't *want* to go to law, but I shall have to if he doesn't offer me fair compensation.'

3. **necessity knows no law** – someone who is desperate cannot be expected to keep the law.

4. **the law is an ass** – the laws of the land are often unfair and stupid. From *Oliver Twist* by Charles Dickens, when the beadle protests at being dismissed from his post.

5. **the law does not concern itself with trifles** – the courts will not listen to petty grievances, such as claims for a few pence or complaints that the neighbours' children make rude gestures over the garden fence. The derivation is from the Roman maxim '*de minimis non curat lex*'.

6. **to be laughed out of court** – to make such an absurd claim that it arouses derision instead of sympathy. 'The demands of the union leaders were so ridiculous that they were laughed out of court by the workers themselves.'

7. **to put oneself out of court** – to take any action which disqualifies one from receiving a benefit or advantage. 'By talking like that to the secretary about the boss, you have put yourself out of court for any promotion.' In a lawsuit, a party may '**put himself out of court**' if he behaves improperly, e.g. if he tries to bribe the judge or jury or threatens the other party with physical violence.

8. **special pleading** – an unfair way of arguing which consists in giving the words (e.g. of a contract) an unreal meaning to suit one's own case.

9. **an open-and-shut case** – a case whose outcome can be predicted with absolute certainty. 'There is no such thing as an open-and-shut case. Going to law is always a gamble.'

10. **to be as sober as a judge** – to be absolutely sober. Judges have a reputation for sobriety and seriousness.

11. **a Philadelphia lawyer** – one who is celebrated for his acuteness and quickness.

12. **a barrack-room lawyer** (derogatory) – a soldier without legal training who uses the Queen's Regulations to promote his own interests and make life uncomfortable for his military superiors. Such people are always disliked by their commanding officers.

13. **to keep one's own counsel** – to keep one's thoughts to oneself. 'There are times when it is wiser to keep one's own counsel. Even the best of friends may talk.' cf. '**to play one's cards close to one's chest**' 103/1.

14. **the devil's advocate** – an official appointed by the Catholic Church to refute the claims put forward for admitting a person to the calendar of saints. Counsel at conference with their clients sometimes play the part of devil's advocate to test them and, if possible, to anticipate the arguments of the other side.

15. **an honest broker** – an intermediary who brings two parties in dispute together in a fair and impartial manner without showing favour to either side. 'At the Congress of Berlin in 1876, Bismarck played honest broker to Russia and Turkey.'

16. **no respecter of persons** – to treat everyone equally, notwithstanding differences in rank or importance. 'Your senior position won't help you; the judges are no respecters of persons.' A biblical reference (Acts X, 34): 'Then Peter opened his mouth and said, Of a truth I perceive that God is no respecter of persons.'

17. **a gentleman's agreement** – an agreement that has no legal force but is based solely on the honour of the parties involved. 'We have a gentleman's agreement. When you are dealing with Malcolm, that is as good as a signed contract.'

18. **a sore trial** – a painful, disagreeable experience. 'The children were a sore trial to their mother and gave her no peace, only annoyance and hard work.'

1. **trial and error** – the use of experiment to find the correct solution to a problem by eliminating all the incorrect ones.

2. **a trial of strength with** – a contest to determine which of the two participants is the stronger. 'In 1972 and 1973, the government and the miners had a trial of strength; the miners won both times.'

3. **to put someone in the dock** – to make accusations against someone.

    not to be in the dock – not to have to defend oneself against an accusation. 'You are forgetting that *we* are not in the dock; *you* were responsible for what happened, not us.'

4. **to make a snap judgement** – to make a quick judgement without taking all the facts into account. 'It wouldn't be fair to you to give you a snap judgement on the telephone. If you would like to make an appointment, that will give me time to study your case.'

5. **against one's better judgement** – contrary to what one thinks is right or what should be done. 'I let her study art against my better judgement, and now she says she has not enough talent to go on with it.'

6. **to sit in judgement on** (derogatory) – to criticize and pass judgement on the behaviour of other people. 'You have no right to sit in judgement on Mary for coming home late; you aren't her father, and it's no concern of yours when she gets in.'

7. **to cloud one's judgement** – to obscure one's ability to diagnose something/someone correctly. 'Your dislike for the boy is clouding your judgement of his character.'

8. **to do oneself justice** – to realize one's true potential, to do work which reflects one's true abilities. 'When Roy takes an examination, he is always in such a state of nerves that he never does himself justice.'

    to do someone/something justice – to be fair in one's treatment and judgement of someone or something. 'Your portrait of Sue is a reasonable likeness but, in my opinion, doesn't do justice to her charm and vivacity.'

9. **poetic justice** – a misfortune which punishes a wrong-doer just as if it had been intended by divine providence. 'It was poetic justice that, after refusing his best friend a loan of £50, Mason was mugged on his way home and was robbed of twice that amount.'

10. **to hold no brief for** – to have nothing to say in defence of. 'I hold no brief for Stewart, but he has a right to a fair trial.' The brief is the bundle of papers relating to a client's case which is passed over to counsel by the solicitor.

11. **to read the riot act** – to threaten someone (usually a child) with severe punishment unless he stops his misconduct immediately. 'We were having a wonderful party, when the landlord suddenly appeared and read us the riot act. He threatened to give us notice if we didn't stop the commotion.' Under the Riot Act (1715), if 12 or more people make a riot, a magistrate may read the Riot Act to them, calling on them to disperse. If the riot continues for more than one hour, they are then guilty of a felony.

12. **the small print** – conditions which may not be noticed by one party to a contract because they appear in the small print. 'The computer had a 24-month guarantee. However, when I read the small print, I discovered the guarantee was null and void unless I had it serviced by the suppliers every year at a cost of £70 a time!'

13. **in my book** – it is a matter of principle, in my opinion. 'In my book, you don't complain about the staff to the boss until you have discussed it with them first.' The book is an imaginary book of rules that everyone follows.

14. **to bring someone to book** – to make someone answer for his or her misdeeds. 'We must bring these criminals to book; they deserve severe punishment.'

15. **to throw the book at someone** – to charge someone with as many offences as one possibly can. For example, a housebreaker who attacks the landlord can be charged with unlawful entry, trespass,

malicious damage to property, assault and battery. The book consists of the various sections of the Statutory Law under which the accused is charged.

1. **to go by the book** – to act in strict accordance with the rules and regulations, without taking personal factors into account. 'Edward would have been happier in the Civil Service than in business. Whatever the circumstances, he always goes by the book.'

2. **without prejudice** – without making any admission. If a letter in a legal dispute is marked 'without prejudice' the contents are treated as confidential, and the letter may not be shown to the judge. The writer of the letter can then make an offer, without fear that his letter will be used against him in court if his offer is refused by the other party.

3. **to sign one's own death-warrant** – to bring about one's own destruction or collapse. 'You have depended on your brother for your livelihood for the last 20 years. By quarrelling with him, you have signed your own death-warrant.' Before execution of a convicted murderer, it was necessary for the responsible authority to sign the death-warrant.

4. **to send someone down** – to send someone to prison after he or she has been convicted and sentenced.

Medicine

5. **to doctor something** – to add to, to dilute or otherwise interfere, as by poisoning, with the quality of wine, spirits or other drinks. The term usually has a sinister meaning.

6. **to doctor the accounts** – to falsify the accounts in order to make them appear better (or worse) than they really are.

7. **just what the doctor ordered** – exactly what is needed. 'A glass of iced lemonade? After two hours of tennis in the hot sun, that's just what the doctor ordered!'

8. **a spin doctor** – the adviser of a political party or a minister, especially concerning the press. 'A very important part in a min-

ister's political life these days is taken up by his spin doctor.' See *Spin-off* by Michael Shea (a thriller about a spin doctor).

9. **a cyber quack** – someone without any medical qualifications who pretends to be a doctor and who works on a medical website on the Internet and receives money for offering an ill person a consultation and diagnosis. 'That cyber quack gave me a completely wrong diagnosis for my headache. I haven't got a brain tumour after all – I just need new glasses!'

10. **to hold a surgery** – of a Member of Parliament: to listen to the complaints of his constituents and, if necessary, take up their case with the appropriate minister. The phrase has its origin in the doctor's surgery where the patients go for treatment.

11. **to nurse one's energy** – to keep one's energy in reserve, to save it for an important occasion.

12. **to nurse a grievance** – to feel resentment against someone or something. 'Having been dismissed from the Foreign Office, Peter nursed a grievance against it all his life.'

The Navy and Air Force

13. **to be a good sailor** – to adjust quickly to the movement of a ship at sea, without being sea-sick. cf. '**to find one's sea-legs**' 205/13.
    to be a bad sailor – to be frequently sea-sick. 'Nelson was a bad sailor all his life.'

14. **a sailor has a wife in every port** – sailors have always had a reputation for promiscuity, owing to their long absences from home.

15. **tell that to the marines!** – don't expect me to believe that! The phrase was originally: 'Tell that to the horse marines!' There is no such thing as a horse marine, so it is a joke phrase.

16. **a sky pilot** – a clergyman.

17. **to drop the pilot** – to dismiss an expert adviser. The classic example was the dis-

missal of the German Chancellor, Bismarck, by Kaiser Wilhelm II in 1891.

1. **a pilot scheme** – an experiment to test the demand for a product without incurring heavy expenditure on its production or sale. 'Before you spend a lot of money on your invention, you should try a pilot scheme to see whether there is any interest in the idea.' A pilot is a guide who steers ships into and out of harbour.

The Army

2. **to come the old soldier** – to offer advice on how to do a job instead of doing it oneself, to claim superior knowledge because of one's long experience of the work. 'You needn't come the old soldier with me. I've been in the job as long as you.'

3. **to soldier on** – to persevere, despite setbacks and defeats. Soldiers are expected to fight on, even when they suffer defeats. 'The government is expected to soldier on until the end of its term, although it has lost its majority in the House, and popular support in the country.'

4. **soldiers of fortune** – men who offer their services to any state; mercenaries.

5. **to get a rocket** (slang) – to receive a severe reprimand. 'Mary got a rocket from her boss for coming back from her holiday two days late.' 'Rocket' is a military term for a self-propelled missile.

6. **to fall into line** – to conform to routine or custom. 'Naturally, you'll be expected to fall into line in your uncle's office, just like the rest of the staff.'
    to fall out of line – not to conform to routine or custom. Both phrases are military, deriving from the falling into/out of line of soldiers on parade.

7. **when the balloon goes up** – when events become critical. 'Have you any idea what you'll do if the balloon goes up and the company goes bust?'

8. **spit and polish** – emphasis on appearances rather than on more serious matters. 'We do 90 per cent of our business on the telephone, so we don't have to waste time on spit and polish, or trying to

impress our customers with expensive wallpaper.'

9. **to pass muster** – to reach an acceptable standard, to pass inspection. 'I'm afraid I'm not a brilliant cook but the dinner should pass muster.' The 'muster' was the assembling of men for inspection, and introduction into the army or navy.

10. **to muster up one's courage/ strength** – to summon up or marshal one's courage or strength. 'I could barely muster up courage to ask for a rise, although I had a right to one.' Soldiers were mustered up or collected for the defence of the country.

11. **the top brass** – the most important people in an organization. 'The top brass are coming up from London to inspect the factory, so we had better clean the place up.' In the army, the generals and staff officers at the War Office are often referred to as the top brass.

12. **to pull rank** – to remind people in an organization of one's senior position. 'I didn't like the way the managing director's wife pulled rank at the office party. I didn't see why I should give up my seat to her.' In the army, officers pull rank when they act with stiff formality off duty.

13. **to close ranks** – to unite in defence of a common interest. 'Commuters are at last closing ranks against the policies of rail companies because of the high fares.' A military phrase for uniting in the face of attack by the enemy.

14. **to break ranks** – to fail to maintain unity with one's comrades. 'If we break ranks now, that will be the end of our fight for a fair wage.' Soldiers break ranks when they retreat against orders.

The Police

15. **off someone's beat** – outside one's subject. 'I'm sorry, chemistry is off my beat; I'm a physicist.' The phrase comes from the police constable's beat – the area he has to patrol when he is on duty.

16. **not to have a clue** – to be unable to account for a fact, problem, etc. 'I haven't a clue why I have been picked for this

job.' A clue is a fact which may point to the solution of an investigation, in particular the investigation of a crime.

Other Occupations

1. **to shepherd someone** – to guide, take care of. 'The verger shepherded us to our pews immediately behind the bridegroom.'

2. **to shepherd his flock** – (of a priest) to attend to the spiritual needs of his parishioners.

3. **the poacher turned gamekeeper** – said of anyone with a dubious record who has been appointed to a post of trust and responsibility. 'The Irish were among the most lawless of the earlier immigrants to the US. But today the majority of American policemen are of Irish stock. The poacher turned gamekeeper!'

4. **to be as hungry as a hunter** – to be very hungry. Hunters are presumed to be hungry because of all the exercise they are obliged to take in order to catch their quarry.

5. **to be an old maid** – to be a spinster long past marriageable age.
   to be old-maidish – to be like an old spinster in character: fussy, prudish, gossipy.

6. **what's cooking?** (slang) – I wonder what is going to happen? What are they scheming? 'When I went into the dining-room, I could tell from the expression on the men's faces that something was cooking.'

7. **a butcher** – someone who uses brute force instead of intelligence. 'The operation was a disaster. The man behaved like a butcher, not a surgeon.'

8. **stick to your last** – concentrate on your own speciality, and don't tell me how to do mine. 'Administrators should stick to their lasts' (Winston Churchill during the Second World War). The phrase comes from the old adage 'Cobbler, stick to your last'. The last is a wooden model of a foot used by shoemakers for shaping boots and shoes. cf. **'every man to his trade' 283/9.**

9. **tailor-made** – specially designed to suit a person's particular needs. 'These language courses have been tailor-made for business executives.'

10. **like a tailor's dummy** – an effeminate or immaculately dressed man, a dandy; used in a disparaging sense.

11. **not to care a tinker's cuss** – not to attach any value to . . . 'I don't care a tinker's cuss for her principles.'

12. **to tinker with** – to deal superficially with. 'It is only tinkering with the problem to give her sedatives. She should be examined by a specialist to find out the root cause of her illness.'

13. **a busman's holiday** – to spend one's time on holiday doing the same work as one does for a living. 'The teacher spent his summer holiday teaching at his friends' school in Italy. It was a real busman's holiday for him.'

14. **an empire-builder** – a civil servant who seeks to increase the size of his or her department at the expense of the taxpayer. It was originally used to describe the soldiers, explorers and administrators who extended the frontiers of the British Empire.

15. **shuttle diplomacy** – to negotiate an agreement by travelling between countries or parties. 'The US Secretary of State used shuttle diplomacy to achieve an agreement between the two warring countries.'

16. **to be taken to the cleaners / to be cleaned out** – to lose all one's money in business or gambling. 'We have been properly taken to the cleaners this time; we haven't a penny left.'

17. **to make a clean sweep** – to rid oneself completely of a thing or person that no longer serves a useful purpose. 'I have made a clean sweep of all my old papers that have been taking up too much space.'

18. **to come out in the wash** – of mistakes, difficulties and so on, to be soon forgotten, although they were embarrassing at the time. The reference is to the stains which disappear in the wash.

1. **that won't wash!** – nobody is going to believe that! The phrase is used with reference to explanations or excuses that are weak and unconvincing. 'The excuse Philip made for not keeping his appointment won't wash. If his train had really been stuck two hours in the tunnel, the story would have been in the papers.'

2. **everything is grist to his mill** – he can turn to good advantage everything you offer him. 'Your husband is a celebrity now, Mrs Holmes, so anything you tell us about him will interest our readers – everything is grist to our mill.'

3. **to put someone through the mill** – to subject someone to harsh training or unpleasant experiences. 'The army recruits were really put through the mill for the first three months of their training.'

   to go through the mill – to undergo harsh training or unpleasant experiences. cf. '**to go/put through the hoop**' 321/ 13.

4. **to be on a treadmill** – to be employed on exhausting never-ending work. 'The meals run into one another. No sooner have I cooked one meal than I have to start on the next. I am on a treadmill.' In the old days, treadmills were used in prisons as a punishment.

5. **yeoman service** – steady, effective service, a help in time of need. 'My manager has given me yeoman service for many years. I shall be sorry to lose him.' The phrase comes from Shakespeare – 'It did me yeoman's service' (*Hamlet*, V, ii, 36) – and refers to the military service of the yeomen in England's armies. The yeomen in Shakespeare's days were small middle-class farmers.

6. **to jockey for position** – to manoeuvre for advantage. Newly elected councillors jockey for positions in the most important committees, just as jockeys jostle one another for the best positions on the racecourses.

7. **a cowboy** – an unscrupulous businessman or a disreputable workman who exploits and swindles his customers. 'We had to call in another builder to make good the damage the cowboys had caused.' Hence: **cowboy airlines**; **cowboy contractors**; **cowboy language schools** (i.e. the bad ones).

Beggar, Thief and Others

8. **to beggar description** – to be so remarkable or appalling that no words can describe it. 'The conditions in which the family are living are absolutely horrible; they beggar description.' The phrase 'It beggared all description' appears in Shakespeare's *Antony and Cleopatra* (II, ii, 199) with reference to Cleopatra, but is always used today in a bad sense.

9. **to beggar belief** – something incredible, unbelievable. 'For my grandfather to have successfully tackled two thieves beggars belief – but he did!'

10. **to go begging** – to be unwanted. 'Quite a few houses on the south coastline are going begging as people fear land erosion.'

11. **to beg the question** – to assume what one is trying to prove. 'The statement that travelling is good because it broadens the mind begs the question whether travelling does broaden the mind.'

12. **as thick as thieves** – on very close, friendly terms with one another. There is a similar phrase in German, '*dicke Freunde*', meaning 'thick (i.e. close) friends'.

13. **a den of thieves** – a meeting place for criminals of all sorts. The phrase can be used as a term of abuse for a place.

14. **no honour among thieves** – criminals will not hesitate to give one another away to the police if they believe it is to their advantage.

15. **a ram-raider** – a criminal who steals a heavy vehicle and crashes it through a shop window so as to steal the goods inside. 'Did you know that ram-raiders crashed into the newsagent's shop last night? They made off with all the cigarettes.'

16. **to go joyriding** – to go for fast rides in a stolen car. ' "If only we had a proper youth club," the parish councillor said. "Then our children wouldn't be tempted

to go joyriding any more." ' Also: **a joy-rider**; **speed freaks/crash kids** – children who steal cars and then drive very fast in them.

1. **a ticket tout** – a person who buys large quantities of tickets for some event and then resells them at a higher price. 'Whenever there is an important football match, you can see many ticket touts about.'

2. **slave labour** – underpaid work. ' "I'm not going to work in this hotel kitchen any more," Paul exclaimed. "I work all hours for very little pay – it's just slave labour!" '

3. **a down-and-out** – someone without home or money, usually living on the streets. 'It's a great shame, but all cities in Europe have a high number of down-and-outs.'

4. **a dropout** – a student who leaves college or university without finishing his or her course. 'Philip is a drop-out. He studied the wrong subject, found it boring and just left.'

5. **a layabout** – someone who shuns work and prefers to be lazy. ' "Why on earth should the taxpayer support these layabouts?" Mrs Collins complained. "They ought to be made to work." '

6. **to live by clipping** – to pretend to be a prostitute but run off with the money before sex takes place. 'It's very sad, but I've heard of some girls who are only 12 or 13 years old who run away from home and live by clipping.' cf. **'the oldest profession'** 273/4; **'to sell one's body'** 80/5.

7. **an InterCity prostitute** – a woman who travels by InterCity train to London to earn her money in the more expensive areas of the city, such as Mayfair, South Kensington and Chelsea.

8. **a loose woman** – a woman who does not value her morals highly. ' "Keep away from our neighbour, young man," Fred's father warned. "She's a loose woman." '

Customer

9. **an ugly customer / rough customer** – a bad character who may become violent unless he gets what he wants.

10. **a slippery customer** – a deceitful person who will cheat and swindle to achieve his or her object.

Shop

11. **to shop** (slang) – to get somebody into trouble by reporting him or her to the authorities. 'I don't want to shop you, but I will do so if I catch you stealing the men's food again.'

12. **to talk shop** – to restrict one's conversation to one's own specialized subject. 'When two doctors get together, they always talk shop.'

13. **to mind the shop** – to look after and attend to someone's business, job, position (and also shop) in someone's absence. 'With the leader of the Conservative Party away on holiday, his deputy is minding the shop.'

14. **the other shop** – the rival establishment.

15. **to come to the wrong shop** – to apply to the wrong person.

16. **to shut up shop** – (1) to stop work, to cease business for the day. 'It has turned half-past five. It's time we shut up shop.' (2) to go out of business.

17. **to be all over the shop** – to lie untidily all over the place.

18. **a bucket shop** – a travel agency where one can buy cheap plane tickets. 'Jeff always gets his plane tickets from a local bucket shop and saves lots of money.'

19. **a tuck shop** – a small shop serving school-children with chocolates, sweets, snacks and drinks. ' "Where have all the tuck shops gone?" my mother asked. "There used to be one in every school when I was young." '

20. **shoplifting** – stealing articles from a shop. 'Shoplifters always say they did it on the spur of the moment!'

1. **shop floor** – the workers on the factory floor, as opposed to the office workers and management.

   shop-floor politics – action by the trade-union officials in a factory to obtain higher wages for the shop floor or factory workers, e.g. by ordering a go-slow, or calling a strike.

2. **to shop around** – to go from shop to shop in search of the best bargain. 'You are paying too much for your meat. You should shop around like me.'

Buying, Selling

3. **to buy someone's silence** – to pay someone not to tell a secret. 'The car driver gave the old woman £20 to buy her silence after she had seen him crash into a parked car and break its headlamp.'

4. **to sell oneself short** – to underrate one's own talent. 'Susan is always selling herself short. She has missed two good job offers as a result.'

5. **to sell something to the public** – to gain the approval and support of the public. ' "Our plans to enlarge the government office block will be difficult to sell to the public," the politician sighed. "We all know we would rather have a new school building." ' Also: **to sell ideas/plans to the voters; to convince the voters of the value of something**.

6. **to pass one's sell-by date** – (1) an age when one is considered not to be able to give one's best at work any more. 'Mrs Hilton has made so many typing errors these last few months. I think she's past her sell-by date and should retire.' (2) when things are past their best. 'More and more people are beginning to think that the National Health Service is past its sell-by date.' Also: **prejudice has no sell-by date** (saying). cf. '**to be on the shelf**' 166/17.

7. **a cold-calling salesman** – a commercial salesman soliciting prospective customers with his products by telephone or by canvassing on the doorstep. This is marketing jargon. Also called '**cold canvassing**'.

   a cold call – an unscheduled visit or telephone call from a salesman. 'I had three cold calls this week and am getting really tired of them.'

8. **dumping** – selling goods below cost price to squeeze out competition. 'Fiercer competition, especially dumping, will be of great benefit to the customer.'

Trade

9. **every man to his trade** – keep to your own job and don't meddle in other people's. cf. '**stick to your last**' 280/8.

10. **to be in trade** – to engage in an unlearned, commercial occupation, as distinct from a profession.

11. **to do a roaring trade** – to find that something sells extremely well. 'The street salesman did a roaring trade selling mini-fans during the heat-wave.' cf. '**to go like hot cakes**' 179/7.

12. **to ply one's trade** – said of prostitutes selling themselves. 'Lots of prostitutes ply their trade in the red-light districts of large cities.' cf. '**red-light district**' 3/1; '**to sell one's body**' 80/5.

13. **the tricks of the trade** – methods, dodges, short cuts and so on which are only learned with experience. 'That's a trick of the trade you can't learn out of a book or at college.'

14. **to trade on** – to take unfair advantage of someone's weakness to further one's own ends. 'He trades on his lameness to win sympathy.'

15. **to trade in** – to use an old article in part exchange for a new one, paying the difference in value in cash. 'I traded in my old car for a new one and got a 25 per cent discount.'

16. **to trade up** – to improve the quality of one's merchandise, thereby justifying an increase in prices. 'As they were unable to extend their premises, the chief executive proposed a policy of trading up.'

17. **in the trade** – among people employed in the trade.

18. **known in the trade as . . .** – to use a word that is peculiar to the trade in question. For example: in the theatre, actors

and actresses who are out of work are said to be '**resting**' (**320/6**); in business, salesmen who praise their merchandise 'talk up' its value; and advertisers who exaggerate the value of their products and services are said to 'puff' them.

1. **a bootleg trader** – someone who sells smuggled alcohol and tobacco cheaply. 'Customs and Excise are trying to stop bootleg traders selling their goods illegally.'
   a bootleg copy – an illegal copy of a CD, video or computer game.

2. **insider trading/dealing** – illegal dealing in shares by people who have advance knowledge through their connections with people who work on the Stock Exchange or in other high positions, and which is not known to the public. 'The crafty businessman got away with making an enormous profit because the Board of Trade failed to produce sufficient evidence of insider trading.'

Marketing

3. **marketing gimmicks** – special offers on certain goods as an incentive to customers to buy. 'Shoppers prefer permanently low prices to occasional marketing gimmicks.'

4. **a marketing tool** – a method to further business potential. 'The English language is more effective than any other as a marketing tool.'

Business

5. **to make something one's business** – to make it one's own responsibility. 'I will make it my business to see that he gets the job finished in good time.'

6. **to mean business** – to show that one's intentions are serious. 'She must mean business. She has paid £500 on account.'

7. **to have no business in a place / no business to do something** – to have no right to be in a place, no right to do a particular thing.

8. **mind your own business!** – attend to your own affairs and don't concern yourself with mine.

9. **to send someone about his business** – to dismiss curtly, to end an interview abruptly.

10. **unfinished business** – scores still to settle with one's enemies.

11. **not to be in the business of** – to have no intention of . . . 'Our school is not in the business of interfering with the upbringing of your children, Mrs Dale. We just want to help.'

12. **a bad business** – said when something has gone badly wrong. 'On his arrival he was robbed of all his money; a bad business!'

Service, Tipping

13. **to give tip-top service** – to give first-class service. 'I can always recommend this hotel. It gives tip-top service.'

14. **to be tipped for the top** – to be recommended for the highest position. 'Mr Green won't be a barrister for much longer. He's been tipped for the top.'

15. **a tip-off** – an anonymous or secret warning or hint. 'The police were only able to catch the criminal because of a tip-off from the public.'

At Work

16. **a sleeping partner** – a partner who has invested capital in a firm but plays no part in its management. 'It's no good going to Mr Parsons for advice; he is only a sleeping partner.'

17. **to be sent on a fool's errand** – to be sent on a pointless errand, one that has no purpose.

18. **to get the message** (slang) – to understand a warning or threat. 'I was polite but I made it clear we couldn't wait any longer for our money. He got the message all right.'

19. **to be in a rut** – to lead a boring, monotonous way of life which is difficult to change because it is so well established. 'I'm doing exactly the same work now as I was doing 14 years ago. It's too late now for me to get out of the rut.' The reference

is to the groove made by cartwheels in a soft road.

1. **to rob someone of his/her livelihood** – to prevent someone from earning a living. 'Discrimination robs people of their livelihoods.'

2. **to eke out a living** – to have a hard time making enough money to live on. 'Since the BSE crisis, some beef farmers have to eke out a living by taking another job on the side.'

3. **to sack / to get the sack** – to dismiss / to be dismissed. 'Harry got the sack for taking time off without permission.' In earlier times, workmen brought their tools in a sack to their place of work and on dismissal they were given back their sacks; hence, to get the sack. cf. **'to boot out of a job / to be given the boot'** 190/9.

4. **a rich man's hobby** – an occupation that enjoys a certain prestige but brings no money in. Before the Second World War, farming was described as a rich man's hobby because it was so uneconomic. The Bar was also so described shortly after the war because briefs were so scarce.

People at Work

5. **a wheeler-dealer** – someone who schemes in order to further his or her political or commercial interests. 'No political leader can do without the advice of his or her wheeler-dealer.' Also: **to wheel and deal**; **wheeling and dealing**.

6. **a big wheel** – someone very important, energetic, dynamic and powerful who gets things moving.

7. **movers and shakers** – powerful people in a position of influence. 'The finance minister has been entertaining the country's most influential movers and shakers.'

8. **a head-hunter** – someone who is paid to find the best executives or experts to fill a post by offering a higher salary or a more prestigious position. 'Our profits have shot up over this last year. I'm so glad that head-hunter found us such a good managing director.' Note the verb: **to be head-hunted**. The Dyaks of Borneo used to preserve as trophies the heads of those they killed in battle.

9. **a trendsetter** – someone who starts something new and is soon followed by others. 'Mavis has always been a trendsetter. Do you remember how she was the first one in our class to wear two rings in each ear?'

10. **a high-flyer** – a person aiming to be at the top of his or her profession. 'The bank director's birthday party was attended by more than a hundred guests, many of whom were City high-flyers.'

11. **dinky** – dual-income-no-kids. A husband and wife who have no children and each has a separate income. ' "I've got a dinky working for me," the boss chuckled. "He's very ambitious and doesn't mind working long hours." '

12. **a downshifter** – someone who decides to give up his or her high-powered career and choose another far less important job with a lifestyle that is not so hectic.

13. **career burn-out** – being drained of physical and mental energy through work pressure and stress. 'Sara's condition is due to career burn-out, and it's high time she had a long rest.' Also: **burn-out syndrome**; **burnt-out teachers/policemen, etc.**; **to be in danger of burning out**.

14. **a sorcerer's apprentice** – someone who has acquired a certain skill from his or her superior and applies it in that person's absence. This, however, causes a lot of harm and he or she is unable to stop it. 'This minister has proved a sorcerer's apprentice, allowing GM food to enter the human food chain.' From Goethe's poem *'Der Zauberlehrling'* (1797) about a sorcerer's apprentice. cf. **'to open/open up a can of worms'** 76/7; **'opening Pandora's box'** 225/6.

15. **backroom boys** – people such as scientists, engineers, researchers, etc., who do important work out of the public eye. 'Without the work and research of the backroom boys, no exploration of space would have been possible.' cf. **'faceless wonders'** 86/1; **'grey men'** 9/4.

The Press

1. **to have a good/bad press** – to be reported on favourably/unfavourably in the newspapers. 'The government have been getting a bad press recently for their handling of the unemployment problem.'

2. **the gutter press** – newspapers that depend on scandal, sex and violence to promote their sales.

3. **a press campaign** – an organized attempt by newspapers to promote a cause rather than report – and comment on – the news.

4. **on the record** – officially authorized for publication. When information has been given on the record, it is 'attributable', i.e. the name of the informant may be given, and he will accept responsibility for the story.
   off the record – not authorized for publication, given in confidence and 'non-attributable', meaning that the name of the informant may not be used by the newspaper.

5. **to set the record straight** – to clear up a mistake or wrong impression. 'A girl who was wrongly accused of shoplifting set the record straight after the story appeared in her local newspaper.'

6. **to sit on a story** – to delay publication of a story. A newspaper may sit on a story in order to obtain confirmation from an independent source, or to await a more favourable opportunity for publication.

7. **to cut a long story short** – to leave out many details when telling of an action or experience. 'To cut a long story short, the police came and arrested him.'

8. **a human-interest story** – to publish experiences of a sad or happy nature which people can identify with. 'Journalists sometimes risk their lives to present the public with a human-interest story.' Other types of story: **a hard-luck story**; **a front-page story**; **a cock and bull story** (68/21); **a hair-raising story** (83/13); **a hairy story** (83/12); **a tall story** (286/10).

9. **a likely story** – to show doubt about the truth of a matter. 'That's a likely story! I've heard that excuse a hundred times before.'

10. **a tall story** – a story that is so improbable that it will not be believed by the readers of the newspaper. 'That's a tall story! Show me your evidence.'

11. **to kill a story** – to suppress publication of a story. This may happen if the government objects to publication on security grounds, or if the editor believes that publication could damage the interests of the country.

12. **end of story** – that settles it! No more arguments. 'I've told you my answer is no: end of story.' cf. '**full stop**' 265/5.

13. **to break the story** – to be the very first one to give the public an exciting news item. 'The royal press officer broke the story to the journalists that the prince was going to divorce his wife.'

14. **to meet a deadline** – to have a story ready for publication by a specified date. The 'deadline' refers to the Andersonville prisoner-of-war camp in the American Civil War, which had a 'deadline' marked out round its perimeter; any prisoner of war caught crossing the deadline would be shot on sight. Also: **to beat a deadline**.

15. **to dot the i's and cross the t's** – to pay meticulous attention to detail so as to make oneself absolutely clear. From the confusion which arises when the letters 'i' and 't' are not properly written.

16. **to mind one's p's and q's** – to be on one's best behaviour, to take great care not to cause offence. 'If you are having tea with Aunt Jane, you had better mind your p's and q's; she takes offence very quickly.' The p's and q's refer to the type that the compositor sets up for printing.

17. **a free lance** – an independent, self-employed person, who works on his own initiative, and is his own master. A '**free-lance**' journalist or reporter contributes articles to a number of national provincial newspapers without being tied to any particular one.

18. **junk mail** – unwanted advertisements

and offers sent to householders. 'Nearly all the junk mail I get goes straight into the waste-paper bin.'

junk e-mail – (known as 'spam') advertisements sent through the Internet.

1. **in the know** – having access to information that is not available to the ordinary citizen. Being in the know depends primarily on having reliable sources of information.

The Book Trade

2. **to read someone like a book** – to know exactly what someone is thinking, even before he or she has spoken. 'When Sally comes to my office, it is always to ask for money. No matter how carefully she leads up to the subject, I can read her like a book.'

3. **to close the book on something** – (1) to agree to forget about something. 'Let's close the book on our previous difficulties and start afresh.' cf. '**to let bygones be by-gones**' 34/11. (2) to solve a mystery. 'Thanks to the efforts of the brilliant detective, the police were able to close the book on the bank-robbery mystery.'

4. **a closed book** – a subject about which one knows nothing, a mystery. 'Astronomy is a closed book to me.'

5. **like an open book / as open as a book / open as books** – easily understood, hiding no secrets. 'One of the prospective candidates for the ministerial post assured the public that his past was an open book.'

6. **the final chapter** – the end result of a series of happenings. 'Sentencing the accused to ten years in prison was the final chapter in a long struggle for justice.'

7. **a chapter of accidents** – a series of misfortunes and bad luck. 'My brother has a chapter of accidents behind him. I just hope that he'll be more fortunate in future.'

8. **to speak volumes / to speak volumes for** – (1) to be full of meaning. 'When the landlady showed Ralph his room, he was too polite to make any comment, but the expression on his face spoke volumes.' (2) to do a person or thing credit. 'Jack failed his examination three times before he finally passed; that speaks volumes for his determination.'

9. **to talk/to be like a walking dictionary/encyclopaedia** – to be very knowledgeable, sharp and intelligent. 'I have no idea who invented the television, Jennifer. Why not ask our neighbour – he's like a walking dictionary.'

10. **pulp fiction** – trashy, sentimental literature; publications printed on cheap paper and not worth reading. 'You can find a lot of pulp fiction on market stalls or car boot sales.' Also: **a pulp magazine**; **a pulp novel**.

11. **a tell-tale sign** – an indicator of something. 'When my small son began to develop the odd red spot on his body, I suspected they might be a tell-tale sign of chickenpox. There's a lot of it about at the moment.'

12. **to lose the plot** – to find oneself unable to follow a certain train of thought. 'I tried to follow the argument of the two bureaucrats but it got so complicated that I lost the plot.' See *Losing the Plot* by Paul Wheeler. cf. '**to lose the thread**' 201/1.

13. **the plot thickens** – the circumstances change to a more complicated situation. 'The corrupt politician won't say where he got the money from. He has many enemies who are willing to talk. The plot thickens . . .'

14. **writer's block** – an author's temporary inability to write. 'Malcolm has locked himself into his office and doesn't want to see anyone. He is suffering from writer's block.' cf. '**a mental block**' 120/4; '**one's mind goes blank**' 118/6.

Book-keeping

15. **to cook the books** – to falsify the accounts for a dishonest purpose. 'I don't believe the company made anything like that profit. Peter has been cooking the books so that he can get a good price for the business.' A clever cook can conceal the basic ingredients of a dish by adding all kinds of spices.

1. **to fudge the books** – to misrepresent or cover up something that may give the wrong impression. 'When it comes to opinion polls, it is not difficult to fudge the books by asking the wrong people.'

Bookmaking

2. **to suit/not to suit one's book** – to serve one's own interest / not to serve one's own interest. 'It may not suit his book to take the carpet back. He may not find another customer for it so quickly.'

3. **a turn-up for the book/books** – to be pleasantly surprised as a result of some action. 'It was the first time she had ever bought a lottery ticket, and she won handsomely. What a turn-up for the book!' The 'book' is a book of bets.

Computing

4. **a computer hacker** – someone who is very knowledgeable about computers and is able to programme them for good or bad purposes. 'The businessman was extremely upset because computer hackers had somehow penetrated his bank account and withdrawn a vast sum of his money.'

5. **a computer nerd** (derogatory) – someone who finds computers completely engrossing. 'Philip is a computer nerd and has no time for anything else.'

6. **a screenager** – a teenager who is an expert on computers.

Money

1. **money down the drain** – money wasted. 'Why do you spend all your money on a hobby like model trains; it's all money down the drain.'

2. **to be in the money / to be rolling in money** – to be extremely rich. Also: **to be made of money; to be awash in money.** 'My neighbour is always boasting that he is awash in money.' cf. '**to have pots of money**' 171/11.

3. **to have money burn a hole in one's pocket** – to be in possession of more money than one is used to and to be unable to stop oneself spending it. 'James can't wait to spend all that money you gave him; it is burning a hole in his pocket.'

4. **money is tight / finances are tight** – being short of money. 'I'm a single mum with three kids and money is tight, so it's a real struggle to buy the children all the things they need.'

5. **a money spinner** – a means of making money quickly with very little effort. It usually refers to ideas or projects.

6. **a licence to print money** – a business that is so profitable that it is like having permission to print money. These words were spoken by Lord Thomson when he took over the Independent Broadcasting Authority at its inception in 1967. cf. '**to coin money**' 291/1.

7. **funny money** – dubious currency, money gained fraudulently. 'I wouldn't trust him in business. He has the reputation of dealing in funny money.'

8. **black money** – secret money used illegally, in **slush funds (292/11)**, **money laundering (290/4)**, etc.; money accepted illegally for party funds without being declared. 'A black money scandal erupted recently around the former prime minister of Germany.'

9. **hush-money** – money paid to someone in return for keeping silent about a crime.

10. **ready money** – money that is immediately available.

11. **easy money** – money obtained without effort. 'It's easy money babysitting for our neighbours. Their little baby always stays fast asleep.'

12. **smart money** – money invested wisely. 'Smart money is now pouring into the City of London.'

13. **serious money** – very large amounts of money. 'I can't afford to become a partner in the law firm. It needs serious money to do that.'

14. **electronic money** – various kinds of plastic cards for obtaining money or credit. 'Electronic money is much easier to hide from pickpockets than notes and coins in a purse.'
    hard money – coins; **paper money** – notes.

15. **to knock some money off** – to offer a reduction in price.

16. **to spend money like water** – to spend large sums of money recklessly without considering the cost.

17. **to be after the big money** – to be determined to earn an enormous amount of money. 'You won't catch me working as an office girl, Chloe. I'm after the big

money, so I'll try and get a modelling job.'

1. **to throw good money after bad** – to try to recover money one has invested in an unsuccessful business by paying in still more, even though there is no chance of getting the money back. 'I wouldn't lend Henry any more money now he's lost so many of his customers. It would be throwing good money after bad.'

2. **to blow one's money on something** – to spend one's money in one go, to waste it. 'Adrian had inherited a large sum of money but he blew it all on fast cars.' cf. '**to blue one's money**' 3/6.

3. **to throw money at something** – to finance (usually at the taxpayers' expense) a business or enterprise which is losing money. 'You won't make the company efficient by throwing money at it. The only solution is to replace the management.'

4. **to launder money / money laundering** – to pay in at a bank money that is obtained illegally, usually by dealing in drugs. In this way, the source remains undetected. 'The businessman was accused of drug-running and money laundering, but he protested that he was innocent.'

5. **money is no object** – the amount of money spent is of no importance in comparison with the object desired.

6. **money for old rope** – money that is easily obtained. 'I have to do virtually nothing in this job. It's money for old rope.' cf. '**money for jam**' 178/6.

7. **to put one's money where one's mouth is** – to give practical assistance to a cause one has been openly supporting, e.g. contributing money to it. 'You have made so many speeches denouncing cruelty to animals. Isn't it time you put your money where your mouth is?'

8. **to put one's money on something/ someone** – to place a bet on. 'Are you going to do any betting at the Grand Prix? I put all my money on Mika Hakkinen. He had better win!'

9. **to give someone a run for his money**

– to put someone to a great deal of trouble before he gets what he wants. 'The visiting team beat us in the end but we gave them a run for their money.'

10. **to have a (good) run for one's money** – to get plenty of enjoyment for one's efforts, even if one doesn't achieve everything one hoped for. 'The air-balloon ride gave me a good run for my money – even though the weather turned bad towards the end.'

11. **to fork out money** – to pay with reluctance. 'We've just spent a lot of money at the school bazaar. Must we really fork out more for schoolbooks?'

12. **for my money** – if I had to make the choice. 'For my money, this bottle of champagne is better value than the others, even though it is a good deal more expensive.'

13. **like taking money from blind beggars** – to exploit defenceless people by taking advantage of them. 'How dare they do that to those poor investors! It's like taking money from blind beggars.' In *Nicholas Nickleby*, Charles Dickens refers to 'robber of pence out of the trays of blind men's dogs'.

Cash

14. **to cash in on** – to take advantage of. 'The young woman cashed in on her good looks to advance her career in modelling.'

15. **cash-in-hand** – money that is not declared to the Inland Revenue. 'There are a number of builders who will only work for you cash-in-hand.'

16. **hard cash** – money that consists of banknotes and coins as opposed to cheques. 'The advertising agency won't accept cheques any more, only hard cash.'

17. **to be cashstrapped / strapped for cash** – to be short of money. 'Schools are having to sell off their playing fields because they are so strapped for cash.'

Change

18. **to get no change out of** – to get no help or satisfaction from. 'We complained

to our neighbour about the behaviour of his children but we got no change out of him.' cf. **'to get no joy from'** 129/11.

Coin

1. **to coin money** – to make so much money from one's business that it is almost the same as minting it oneself. cf. **'a licence to print money'** 289/6.

2. **to pay back in the same coin** – to retaliate by using the same method. 'Jukes has attacked us in his advertising overseas; we will pay him back in the same coin.'

3. **the other side of the coin** – the opposite standpoint, showing the disadvantages as against the advantages.'Flying has enormous advantages over other means of transport; it is not only much faster but much less tiring. The other side of the coin is that it is boring and takes all the novelty out of travelling.'

4. **two sides of the same coin** – two contrasting characteristics of something. 'German unity and European integration are two sides of the same coin' (Konrad Adenauer).

5. **to be like twin faces of a coin** – to be irredeemably linked. 'Money and happiness are like twin faces of a coin.'

6. **to coin a phrase** – to invent a phrase in order to express a new idea. Hundreds of new phrases are coined every year, such as: software, meaning the contents of a computer program; hardware, the computer itself; video TV, for the storing and reproduction of TV programmes; to hijack, to seize an aeroplane for political or economic ends. All these phrases have been made out of existing words which are used in a new form.

Mint

7. **in mint condition** – as good as new, perfect. 'These books are as good as the day they were printed; they are in mint condition.' The reference is to coins newly produced at the Royal Mint.

Cheque

8. **a blank cheque** – permission to do whatever one considers desirable or necessary. 'I've been given a blank cheque to modernize the company's equipment.'

Penny

9. **to make an honest penny** – to make an honest living through hard work.

10. **to turn up like a bad penny** – a bad character who returns just when one was hoping to be rid of him. 'Oh no! There's my former boyfriend again. He's always turning up like a bad penny!'

11. **the penny drops** – the point of a remark is at last understood after a great deal of difficulty. 'I don't know how many times I told my husband that I was bored with fishing, but when he found me asleep over the rod one day, the penny dropped at last. He never took me fishing again.'

12. **to go/be two a penny** – to be in such plentiful supply that the pay offered is very small. 'You had better think of another way to make a living; artists are two a penny.'

13. **a penny for your thoughts** – what are you thinking about? May I know, or is it private? The person addressed is usually lost in thought. The phrase goes back to the 16th century.

14. **not to have/to be unable to rub two pennies together** – to be penniless, without any money; often said of someone who started without any money and got rich quickly. 'When I first met Tom three years ago, he couldn't rub two pennies together; look at him now!'

15. **not to care two pence for** – to be totally indifferent to. 'I don't care two pence what Martin thinks.' Two pence is almost valueless today.

16. **to cost a pretty penny** – to cost a considerable sum of money. 'It will cost you a pretty penny to take Lambert to court if you lose.'

17. **to spend a penny** – to pay a penny for the use of a public toilet. The price has

risen in the last few years, but the phrase remains the same.

1. **a penny pincher** – someone who is very mean with his or her money. Also: **penny-pinching**. ' "I wish I could buy an evening dress like yours," Elsie sighed, "but my penny-pinching parents would never allow it." '

2. **penny wise pound foolish** – by trying to save a little one can lose a large sum. 'Herbert insisted on taking the bus to London Airport instead of a taxi. As a result, he missed his flight and had to pay £150 extra for a later one. Penny wise pound foolish!'

3. **a penny-farthing organization** – an organization that is managed inefficiently for lack of money or resources. 'We would have won the election if we had had a computer and a properly staffed office instead of the penny-farthing organization we had to make do with.' The farthing was worth one quarter of the old penny, and was abolished when the decimal currency was introduced in 1971.

4. **as right as ninepence** – in good health, vigorous and strong. 'Spend a few days in bed and you'll soon feel as right as ninepence again.' This simile used to be 'as neat as ninepence', which meant 'very neat', an alliterative saying similar to 'as fine as fivepence'. (There used to be a ninepenny coin in Ireland in the early 17th century.) Another origin might be that the simile used to be 'as right as ninepins', referring to nine pins that were placed neatly and in the correct ('right') positions before the start of a game.

Shilling

5. **to cut off with a shilling** – to disinherit a child. In the old days it was the custom for a father, who had been displeased with his son, to pay him a shilling and tell him to leave.

Dollar, Buck

6. **as sound as a dollar** – very reliable, trustworthy, dependable, unfailing. ' "This vacuum cleaner has been on the market for many years and you may rest assured that it is as sound as a dollar," the shop assistant told his customer.'

7. **to bet one's bottom dollar** – to be absolutely certain that something is going to happen or not going to happen. 'If my stockbroker recommends a share, you can bet your bottom dollar that it will go down.' The bottom dollar is the dollar at the bottom of a stack of banknotes, so if one bets one's bottom dollar, that means all the money in one's possession. cf. **'you (can) bet your life' 35/7**.

8. **the million/64 million dollar question** – the question that everybody would dearly like to know the answer to.

9. **to feel/look (like) a million dollars** – to feel/look very attractive. 'Suzanna came back from the health farm 5 kg slimmer and looking like a million dollars.'

10. **to make a quick/fast buck/a quick pound** – the opportunity to make money fast. ' "You can make a fast buck by investing in these shares," the cunning agent said temptingly.' Note that 'buck' is a US dollar, not to be confused with buck meaning 'buckhorn', as in the phrases **'pass the buck' (311/1)** and **the buck stops here' (310/16)**.

Fund

11. **slush funds** – tainted money that is used by political parties to further their objectives. 'British political parties are permitted to accept cash from slush funds in Brussels.'

The Bank

12. **to break the bank** – to win the maximum amount at gambling. 'Did you really break the bank at Baden-Baden, or are you joking?'
    without breaking the bank – without spending too much money. 'If you want to buy a computer without breaking the bank, Alex, just look at your e-mail list of computer bargains.'

13. **to bankroll a party** – to help provide for a political party. 'All political parties

are bankrolled to a certain extent by rich members and the unions.'

Packet

1. **to make a packet / to cost a packet** – to make a great deal of money / to cost an enormous sum of money. 'Some people make a packet out of selling football souvenirs.'

Price

2. **to pay the price/a heavy price** – to be severely punished for some misdeed. 'Six whole months in prison! Our neighbour has to pay the price for drink-driving.'

3. **to slash prices** – to cut prices dramatically. 'After take-over bids from American giants, local supermarkets have already slashed prices.' cf. **'to blitz'** **24/9**.

Tab, Bill

4. **to keep tabs on someone** – to keep someone under observation. 'The police let the suspect go but made sure they kept tabs on him.'

5. **to pick up the tab** – to accept financial responsibility for something. ' "When the figures don't tally in our accounts department," Mr Tilbert complained, "I am always the one who has to pick up the tab." '

6. **to pick up the bill** – to pay the bill for everyone; to pay someone else's bill (which is usually large). 'Jill made a huge number of phone calls and her mother had to pick up the bill.' Frequent usage: **the taxpayer always picks up the bill**.

7. **to foot the bill** – to pay someone else's bill. 'Mr Brown had to foot the bill for his son's drunken escapades.' So called because the person called upon to pay was required to sign his or her name at the foot of the bill.

Toll

8. **to take its toll** – to exact a price. 'Too many parties and late nights have taken

their toll. Nadine looks exhausted and has dark shadows under her eyes.'
   to take a heavy toll – to demand a very high price (e.g. in suffering, devastation, etc.). 'The floods in southern France took a heavy toll in human misery and death.'

Rip-off

9. **a rip-off** – something that costs much more than it should. Also the verb: **to rip off**. ' "Why are the same goods so much cheaper on the Continent?" Peter asked. "I think we are being ripped off here in Britain." '

Pay

10. **to pay over the odds** – to pay artificially inflated prices. 'Parents of young football fans have been exploited for a long time by having to pay over the odds for replica football kits.'

11. **to pay with one's life** – to die on account of something. 'Mrs Biggins ignored the doctor's advice about giving up smoking and paid for it with her life.'

Finance, Economics

12. **financial clout** – financial weight and domination. 'Try and work for that firm, Angela. With their financial clout, you never need fear that you'll lose your job.'

13. **financial meltdown** – a crucial calamity or failure in financial affairs. 'The NHS will be facing a financial meltdown unless more money is forthcoming.' A 'meltdown' occurs when dangerous levels of radiation are released after a nuclear accident.
   a stock-market meltdown – when the stock market crashes.

14. **to be economical with the truth** – not to disclose all the relevant facts. 'When Mrs Wallace applied for the new job as teacher, she was economical with the truth about her qualifications. But she was found out and did not get the job.'

Dole

1. **to be on the dole** – to be without a job and receiving unemployment benefit. 'The greatest fear of professionals and workers alike is to be made redundant and put on the dole.'

Wealth

2. **liquid wealth** – assets such as shares, property, etc., which may be changed into cash with ease. 'It must be great fun being a shrewd businessman, watching one's liquid wealth increasing every day.'

Gold

3. **a gold-digger** – an adventuress who obtains money from men by making use of her physical attraction.

4. **as good as gold** – very well behaved. Often said of a child who has been looked after by a relative or friend in the absence of the parents.

5. **a gold-mine** – a lucrative source of income. 'This business could be a gold-mine if it were properly developed.'

6. **worth one's weight in gold** – someone whose services are considered invaluable. Often said of a trusted servant, or employee who cannot be easily replaced.

7. **to treat something like gold** – to look after something with the utmost care. 'When you are abroad, don't lose your passport or you'll be in trouble. Treat it like gold!'

8. **to have a heart of gold** – to be a kind, generous, forgiving person whose qualities are much appreciated.

9. **to strike gold** – to be extremely lucky; to perform some action that results in making a lot of money. 'Philip struck gold with his choice of university. It's the best one in the whole country for studying physics.'

10. **to go for gold** – to try to achieve the highest distinction at the Olympic Games: a gold medal. 'Mervyn is practising his long jump every day. He is going for gold at the next Olympic Games.'

11. **a crock of gold** – a large reserve of money which will support one in old age.
    the crock of gold at the end of the rainbow – a treasure that is unattainable, a mere dream.

12. **fool's gold** – a worthless product or venture which is mistaken by foolish or ignorant people for something of great value. 'Lured by promises of making a fortune quickly in a new venture, he found out it was fool's gold when the firm collapsed.' Literally, iron pyrites which, being yellow in colour, are sometimes mistaken for gold.

13. **to shine like pure gold / hair like liquid gold** – this is used to describe long blond hair which has been freshly washed and brushed. 'Once upon a time there was a little girl who lived on the edge of a big wood. She had very beautiful hair, which hung in long curls down her back. In the rays of the sun it shone like pure gold, and so she was called Goldilocks' (*Goldilocks and the Three Bears*, © Ladybird Books).

14. **like gold dust** – very rare, uncommon, infrequent. 'The Job Centre manager told Howard that new jobs in this part of the country are like gold dust. Now he is thinking of moving back to London.'

15. **a/the pot of gold at the end of the rainbow** – an unrealizable dream, something one can never find or fulfil. 'I want a baby more than anything in the world, but I'm getting too old. To me it's like the pot of gold at the end of the rainbow.' cf. **'castles in Spain' 211/3**; **'castles in the air' 12/1**; **'pie in the sky' 179/16**.

Golden
(see also *Golden* in Chapter 1)

16. **a golden hello** – securing the services of a highly desirable employee by giving him or her a large sum of money. 'I know we should pay a golden hello to attract the very best to our firm, but why should we pay a golden goodbye to our terrible boss?'

1. **a golden handshake** – a lump sum of money paid to a retiring director or manager, or to a redundant worker. Also called a '**golden good-bye/farewell**'.

2. **a golden parachute** – a large payment of cash or shares to a director as compensation for losing his job. 'Mr Peacock was offered a golden parachute for having to leave his job after 20 years of loyal service.'

3. **golden handcuffs** – a promise of special benefits, shares, pension, etc., to encourage one to stay in one's job. 'The talented businessman signed a five-year, £5 million, golden-handcuffs deal for himself and his company.'

4. **to worship the golden calf** – to worship money, to subordinate everything else to mercenary considerations. The reference is to the wrath of God at the worship of false idols by the children of Israel (Exodus XXXII).

Silver

(see also *Silver* in Chapter 1)

5. **to cross someone's palm with silver** – to bribe someone.

6. **born with a silver spoon in one's mouth** – born into a wealthy family, with all the advantages that that can give a child. 'I have to work for my living; I wasn't born, like you, with a silver spoon in my mouth.' The reference is to the custom of the godparents giving the child a silver spoon at the christening. Also: **to have a silver-spoon background**.

7. **thirty pieces of silver** – the money paid to Judas Iscariot for betraying Jesus Christ. This phrase is used as a symbol of betrayal.

Jewel, Gem, Precious Stones

8. **the jewel in the crown** – the most precious of all possessions. 'St Paul's Cathedral is the jewel in the crown of the City of London.'

9. **to shine/twinkle like a jewel** – to shine brilliantly. 'The lake shone like a jewel in the early morning sunshine.'

10. **like a jewel / like jewels** – something very precious and valuable. 'Bits of rubble that you could find on any construction site were passed on to eager customers like jewels, and at night, collectors combed the ground with flashlights and tweezers for the tiniest crumbs of painted cement' (*The German Comedy: Scenes of Life after the Wall* by Peter Schneider, © I. B. Tauris, London). Also: **a jewel of a book, etc.**

11. **like a rare gem** – something extremely precious, highly esteemed. 'Caroline's essay on horses is like a rare gem. I'm sure she'll be a writer when she grows up.'

12. **as bright as a diamond / diamond-bright** – brilliant, sparkling; vivacious and quick-witted. 'Your idea for the advertisement is brilliant, Alex. It's short and snappy and diamond-bright – just how I wanted it.'

13. **eyes sparkle/glisten like diamonds** – eyes that shine brightly. 'Louisa told me about her engagement to the handsome film star, and her eyes sparkled like diamonds.'

14. **a rough diamond** – someone whose kindness is concealed by a rough, unpolished manner. 'Jane's boyfriend is a bit of a rough diamond, but he's very nice when you get to know him.' A rough diamond is a diamond before it has been cut and polished.

15. **diamond cut diamond** – a contest between two equally sharp or cunning people. 'The two experts argued fiercely with each other the whole afternoon. It was diamond cut diamond.' The diamond is the hardest substance in the world, so it can only be cut by another diamond.

16. **ruby / ruby-red** – a deep, bright red. 'Vivien took a sip of port, thoughtfully savouring the ruby liquid before moving her bishop across the chessboard.'

17. **emerald-green** – bright green. 'We really must have a photo of this black cat on our magazine cover. Just look at its big emerald-green eyes!'

18. **sapphire-blue** – bright blue. 'Mary's blue dress brought out the sapphire-blue colour of her eyes to perfection.'

1. **a cameo role/part** – a star role, the outstanding part in a film or play. 'The young actress was thrilled when she was told that she had been cast in a cameo role in the new film.' A cameo is a precious stone which has two layers of colour: the upper layer is carved in relief and the lower layer serves as the background to it. Cameos were usually made into brooches and were very popular in Victorian times.

Pearl

2. **pearls of wisdom** – words of exceptional intelligence, knowledge and experience (often used humorously). 'Listen to him attentively. You may catch some pearls of wisdom.'

3. **the Pearly Gates** – the gateway to Heaven. (Christian believers hope to enter Heaven through the pearly gates.) From the Bible (Revelation XXI).

4. **pearl-white** – very white; sparkling white. 'On the toothpaste advertisement, the model laughed merrily and showed us her pearl-white teeth.'

Amber

5. **amber light** – a yellow traffic light (between green and red); a yellowish light. 'The light from the candle bathed the room in a romantic, amber light.'

Treasure

6. **a treasure trove** – a hoard of beautiful things which give one great pleasure. 'On our walking tour through isolated villages, we found a treasure trove of antique furniture in old farmhouses.'

   to open something up like a treasure chest – to discover objects of breathtaking beauty inside something.

Game, Match

1. **the name of the game is . . . .** – the outstanding feature or characteristic is . . . ; often said of a business, institution or school. 'The name of the game at our school is science.'

2. **two can play at that game / that's a game that two can play at** – in a contest, the opponent can use the same weapon or tactics. 'If you complain to the landlord about the noise, I will complain about the people you bring in at all hours; that's a game that two can play at.'

3. **like a game** – like a contest, full of schemes and stratagems. 'Politics is like a game, where the winners gain power and the losers are forced to retreat.'

4. **a dirty game** – unfair, unethical behaviour. 'That's a dirty game of yours, threatening your staff with dismissal unless they work overtime.'

5. **to raise one's game** – to better one's performance. 'If a political party wants to stay in power, it must continually raise its game.'

6. **to have the game in one's hands** – to enjoy a decisive advantage over one's opponent. Said of card games when one has a winning hand.

7. **to know what someone's game is** – to understand what someone is scheming. 'You don't deceive me; I know what your game is!'

8. **to give the game away** – accidentally to betray one's purposes. 'Philip told the girl there was a spider just behind her, but his smile gave the game away.'

9. **to be game to the end** – to show courage to the end. 'Hammersmith were easily beaten by the Rangers, but they were game right up to the end of the match.'

10. **to play the game** – to be fair and honest in one's dealings with other people.

11. **to play a waiting game** – to act with caution, waiting for one's opponent to make a mistake.

12. **to be on one's game/off one's game** – to be in good form / to be below one's usual form, when playing a game.

13. **the game is up** – the deception has been exposed. 'When the robbers saw the police had surrounded the bank, they knew the game was up and surrendered at once.'

14. **to put someone off his game** – to spoil someone's game, to cause him to play badly. 'I wish you wouldn't photograph me all the time; you are putting me off my game.'

15. **a winning game** – a venture with a strong probability of success. 'Judging by his past successes, Paul is playing a winning game.'
    a losing game – a venture with little chance of success. 'You are playing a losing game competing with such a large and well-established company.'

16. **a deep game** – a secret plan or scheme. 'Stephen is playing a deep game; he won't talk about it to anyone.'

17. **a mug's game** – an activity which would only appeal to a fool. 'Crime is a mug's game; criminals always get caught in the end.'

1. **the endgame** – the last phase. 'The endgame of the battle over the disputed inheritance had begun, and relations would never be the same again.'

2. **a completely/whole new ballgame** – a totally different situation in which to continue the contest or struggle. 'I have just heard the police will be charging your son with pushing drugs in addition to being in possession of them. We are now in a completely new ballgame.'

3. **a game of chance** – a gamble whose outcome depends on chance, not on skill. 'If you play a game of chance, you can always blame your bad luck when you lose.'

4. **to beat someone at his own game** – to compete successfully with someone in his own specialized field. 'Heinrich Schliemann, the discoverer of the ancient city of Troy, had had no training in archaeology, but he beat the experts at their own game.'

5. **so that's the game!** – so that's what you are trying to do!

6. **to play games with someone** – to conceal, in a teasing or cruel manner. 'Stop playing games with me and tell me what you want!'

7. **on the game** – engaged in prostitution.

8. **game, set and match** – the decisive point which wins an argument or debate. 'So you do agree with me! Game, set and match to me.' This is the final point in tennis that wins the player a match in a tournament or championship.

9. **a slanging match** – a fierce argument conducted in abusive language.

Sport

10. **to be a good sport** – to act honourably and fairly, not to complain when one is beaten.
    to be a bad sport – to act dishonourably and unfairly, to complain and make excuses when one is beaten. Also: **a spoilsport**.

11. **a sporting chance** – a fair or reasonable chance. 'The examiner didn't give me a sporting chance to answer her questions. She went on to the next question before I could get the words out.'

12. **to sport a beard/moustache** – to show off one's newly grown beard/moustache. 'The children stared at their teacher in amazement when he entered the classroom after the summer break, proudly sporting a beard.'

Exercise

13. **to exercise one's skills** – to apply or discharge one's talents and accomplishments. 'Students who are leaving university should be given the opportunity to exercise their skills in jobs of their choice.'

Gymnastics

14. **to bend over backwards** – to make an enormous effort to help or oblige someone. 'We have bent over backwards to get you this job. Now you must show us how hard you can work!' cf. **'to go out of one's way to'** 148/3.

To Play

15. **to play oneself in** – to get accustomed to the conditions before attempting anything bold or daring. 'The new minister only expressed his opinion after he had played himself in and learned the routine of the department.'

16. **to play someone up** – (1) to tease or annoy. 'That little girl is playing her mother up; she is only pretending to be ill so that her mother will give her some extra attention.' (2) (in the medical sense) when a part of the body causes pain from time to time. 'In the damp weather my left leg plays me up.'

17. **to play down** – to make little of, to discount. 'When I complained to the doctor about the pain in my elbow, I could tell he was trying to play it down.'

18. **to play hard to get** – to feign reluctance or unwillingness. 'Yvonne has refused your invitation to dinner again! Don't be discouraged; she is only playing hard to get.'

1. **to play safe** – to be extremely cautious, to avoid any risk. 'If you want to be sure of catching your aeroplane, you had better play safe and allow yourself two hours to get to the airport.'

2. **to play up to** – to flatter, with the object of gaining some advantage. 'I wonder why Julian has been playing up to Samantha all the evening; he never does anything without a reason.'

3. **to play along with** – to pretend to co-operate with someone for a limited period. 'If you have any proof that your boss is breaking the law, let us know. In the meantime, play along with him.'

4. **played out** – out of date, no longer in fashion. 'There are signs that TV is played out as the main source of entertainment in the home now that video has come in.'

5. **to play fast and loose with someone** – to alternate warmth with coldness in a person's affection. 'John has been playing fast and loose with Susan for months; she should find herself another boyfriend.'

6. **to play the fool** – to amuse oneself and one's companions joking and clowning.

7. **to play it cool / to keep one's cool** – to act calmly, in a restrained manner. 'Whatever you do, don't lose your temper with Paul; just play it cool.'

8. **to play havoc with / to wreak havoc** – to damage, ruin or destroy. 'Tony's chickenpox has played havoc with his complexion. I hope he will lose the scars one day.' Havoc is derived from the military command 'Havock' of medieval times, meaning 'Kill all without quarter'.

9. **to play upon words** – to pun, to make a joke by using a word in a double sense. e.g. Question: 'When is a door not a door?' Answer: 'When it is ajar.' (ajar = only a little open; a jar = a container, e.g. a jar of jam.)

10. **to play one person off against another** – to make mischief between two people, often in order to divert their annoyance from oneself. 'Don't take any notice of what Stanley says; he is trying to play us off against each other.'

11. **to play upon someone's feelings, sympathy, etc.** – to arouse someone's feelings in order to make use of him or her. 'Don't let him play on your sympathy, Monica. He is only trying to get some money out of you.'

12. **foul play** – an act of violence (or treachery) which may result in murder. 'The girl has been missing seven days from her home; the police suspect foul play.'

13. **a level playing field** – a situation where fair play is the rule. 'These egg farmers are not operating on a level playing field. They advertise their eggs as free range but they really come from a battery farm.'

Football and Other Ball Games

14. **to kick off** – to start. 'The quizmaster kicked off by asking the first contestant where he came from.' The phrase comes from football, when the centre forward gives the ball the first kick to start the game.

15. **a kick-back / a kick-back commission** – the commission paid to someone for introducing a client to an agency. The commission is usually split in equal shares between the agency and the person making the introduction. The 'kick-back' is not disclosed to the client, such payments being probably illegal. The phrase comes from football when a player kicks the ball back to one of his own side to prevent the other side getting possession of it.

16. **to do something for kicks / to get a kick out of something** – to do something just for the thrill and excitement of it. 'Most hooligans get a kick out of bullying someone weaker.'

17. **to kick against the pricks** – to rebel against control or domination. 'The new army recruit kicked against the pricks until he realized that the army training was necessary and that it was the same for all the soldiers.' Animals used to be herded into pens by using a stick with a sharp point which made them kick out. It is described in the Bible (Acts IX, 5).

18. **to kick up a fuss** – to complain loudly. 'Julia kicked up a terrible fuss when the

waiter took half an hour just to bring her the menu.'

to kick up hell / to kick up a stink – to make a huge fuss.

1. **to kick oneself** – to be very annoyed with oneself. 'I could have kicked myself for having forgotten our anniversary.'

2. **to kick an addiction / to kick the habit** – to conquer, put an end to a dependency on drugs, alcohol or cigarettes. 'Jeff used to smoke 30 cigarettes a day, but now he's trying to kick the habit.'

3. **to trust someone as far as one can kick/throw him/her** – to have absolutely no trust in a person at all. 'After you stole all that money from his wallet, Jim doesn't trust you as far as he can kick you.'

4. **a political football** – a cause which is good in itself but which has become a political issue so that it is no longer judged on its own merits. 'What a pity vivisection has become a political football.'

5. **to keep one's eye on the ball** – to concentrate on the situation one finds oneself in. 'When you're learning to drive, you must keep your eye on the ball or you'll have an accident.'

6. **the ball is in your court** – it is your turn to take the next step (in a negotiation, dispute, etc.). 'They have offered us £500 compensation. Are you going to accept or refuse their offer? The ball is in your court.' The reference is to tennis when the ball falls in a player's court and it is his turn to hit the ball back.

7. **to be in the ball-park** – a general estimate, figure, number, amount, etc., which may be considered possible. 'It was leaked to the press that the sum of £20 million was in the ball-park for funding a new hospital.' In the US, a ball-park is a baseball stadium. A **'ball-park figure'** is a rough estimate of something. This phrase originates in calculating approximately how many fans are sitting in a ball-park stadium watching a sporting event.

8. **to play ball** (US colloquialism) – to co-operate with. 'If he won't play ball, we

can always find someone who will.' Frequent usage: **they agreed to play ball**; **they refused to play ball**.

9. **to play hardball** – to act aggressively and forcefully in a given situation; often used with reference to politics or in business matters. 'The telecommunications firm Vodafone played hardball over several months before eventually succeeding in taking over its rival, Mannesmann.' Hardball is informal US English for 'baseball', a game similar to rounders. Very hard balls are used in this game.

10. **to have the ball at one's feet** – to have the initiative, to have the opportunity one has been waiting for. 'Now that the boss has put him in charge, Andrew has the ball at his feet.'

11. **on the ball** – (1) alert, quick, and very keen. 'I am very pleased with my new assistant. You don't have to say anything to him twice; he is on the ball all the time.' (2) to be perceptive and on the lookout for new ideas. 'The prime minister's new spin doctor is doing his job very well – he's always on the ball.'

12. **to keep the ball rolling** – to keep the interest alive. 'At the meeting, the chairman kept the ball rolling by inviting each person to ask questions.'

13. **an own goal** – an action carried out without realizing the harm done to one's own interests. 'The shopkeepers voted to close the High Street to traffic, but this was an own goal as no one could drive to the shops any more to do their shopping.' A goal scored by mistake by a player against his own side. cf. '**to shoot oneself in the foot**' 105/20.

14. **to reach one's goal** – to achieve one's aim. 'Alan reached his goal and won the cycle race, although everyone said he would never manage it.'

one's goal in life – one's aim, one's dearest wish. 'The politician's goal in life was to become leader of the Party.'

15. **to move/shift the goalposts** – to change conditions unilaterally after an agreement has been reached. ' "That's most unfair," Mr Skinner complained. "You've shifted the goalposts and I'm

going to lose a lot of money." ' Frequent usage: **we are afraid that the goal-posts have been moved yet again; we fear they are moving the goalposts**.

1. **to blow the whistle on** – to denounce publicly an illegal or dishonest activity. 'The blackmailer was finally exposed after his accomplice blew the whistle on him.' The reference is to football when the referee blows his whistle to stop foul play. Also: **a whistle-blower**.

2. **a cheerleader** – someone who tries to stir up enthusiasm for a project. 'Mr Pringle has been chosen as the firm's cheerleader to encourage expansion into the European market.' A cheerleader is usually a teenage girl in a brightly coloured costume who encourages the crowd to cheer on their team at a sporting event.

Cricket

3. **that's not cricket!** – that's not fair, not honourable. 'When I caught Sam listening in to their conversation on the extension, I told him in no uncertain terms that that was not cricket!'

4. **to catch out** – to find someone in the act of doing wrong. 'Tim was caught out by his teacher playing truant yesterday.' In cricket, a batsman is dismissed if the ball he has hit is caught by a fielder; he is then said to be caught out.

5. **to play a straight bat** – to act in an honest, straightforward manner. 'You can trust Mike; he always plays a straight bat.'

6. **off one's own bat** – without asking for anyone's assistance or permission. 'You shouldn't have invited Mr and Mrs Robinson to dinner off your own bat like that. You should have spoken to your parents first.' From cricket, meaning the score made by one player in a game.

7. **to bat on a sticky wicket** – to take action in unfavourable conditions. 'We have been batting on a sticky wicket all the morning; it was obvious that the judge was against us.' From cricket, when the ground is damp from the rain, and the bowler has the batsman at a disadvantage.

8. **to bat on that side of the wicket** – to be a homosexual. cf. **'a pink-pounder'** 9/20.

9. **a long stop** – a last resort, a person one can rely upon when everyone else has failed. 'Would you mind guaranteeing my loan from the bank? You can be the long stop.' In cricket, the long stop is the player who stands behind the wicket keeper to stop the ball if he misses it.

10. **to be 100 not out** – to be 100 years old and still alive. The reference is to a player's innings when a batsman has made 100 runs and is still in the game.

11. **to have had a good innings** – to have had a long life, marriage or career. 'I suppose I can't complain; I'm 80 years old and sound in health and mind. I've had a good innings.' The innings is the time the batsman spends at the wicket scoring runs.

12. **to be bowled out/bowled over** – to be taken completely by surprise, to be unable to explain one's actions. 'Poor Angela, she was bowled out by the first question on the TV show, and it was such an easy one, too.' The phrase comes from cricket, the batsman being dismissed when the ball hits his stumps.

13. **to bowl someone a googly** – an unexpected and unpleasant action which it would have been better to have avoided. 'I bowled my fiancée a googly when I asked her about the young man she was talking to in the park.' From the unexpected way a bouncing ball changes direction after being bowled (in a game of cricket).

14. **to be stumped** – to be baffled, to be unable to solve a problem or answer a question. 'When my pupils asked me for the meaning of "mundungus", I was stumped for an answer. I only remembered later that it meant bad tobacco.'

Golf

15. **eyes look/are like golf balls** – eyes opened wide in astonishment/amazement. 'We told the children about the forthcoming trip to Disneyland, and their

eyes were like golf balls!' cf. **'eyes as big as saucers' 170/6**.

1. **to be par for the course** – an action which does not cause surprise; something expected. 'In this safari park it is par for the course that the monkeys sit on your car and play with the windscreen wipers.' In golf, 'par' is the number of strokes needed by a good player to complete a course.

2. **to stymie / to be stymied** – to obstruct or hinder / to be obstructed or hindered. 'I was planning to sell the house, but my sister has stymied me by letting some rooms.' A 'stymie' is a golfing term meaning that a player can stymie his opponent's ball by interposing his own between it and the hole.

Boxing, Wrestling

3. **to keep up/to drop one's guard** – to keep one's defences in a state of readiness / to neglect one's defences. 'History shows that countries that drop their guard are often overrun by stronger and more aggressive ones.'

4. **to pull one's punches** – to struggle half-heartedly. 'If we are to compete successfully with Phillips, we can't afford to pull our punches; we must be ruthless.' A boxing term meaning to strike with less than one's full weight, to strike with a light blow.

5. **to pack a punch** – to be able to deliver a powerful blow. 'We must rewrite this article on the homeless so that it really packs a punch.'

6. **to beat someone to the punch** – to obtain an advantage over someone before he has time to do the same to you. 'Our book came out a week before Turner's. I'm glad we beat him to the punch.'

7. **to win a round** – to inflict a temporary but not a decisive defeat on the enemy. 'We have won a round, but we still have a hard struggle ahead of us.' A boxing match between amateurs is divided into 3 rounds, and between professionals 6–15 rounds.

8. **to win on points** – to win a useful

advantage without crushing one's opponent. 'At the college debate, we won narrowly on points.' In a boxing match the contestants are given points at the end of each round, and the one who has scored more points at the end of the fight is the winner, unless the match has been terminated by a knock-out.

9. **a heavyweight** – an important person with much influence. 'Some Tory heavyweights are beginning to question the policies of their leader.' In boxing, the boxer who belongs to the heaviest class must weigh above 79 kg.

10. **to wrestle with a problem** – to apply a lot of effort. 'Mr Parker would soon retire, and so he set up a high-powered group to wrestle with the problem of who would be the best person to take over as the new company director.'

Skating

11. **to put/get one's skates on** – to hurry up.

12. **to skate over** – to deal superficially with. 'When I discussed our project with my partner, he expressed his approval while skating over the difficulties.'

Rowing

13. **not to pull one's weight** – to leave one's share of the work to others. 'If Baxter doesn't pull his weight, we would be better off without him. He is putting too much strain on the rest of us.' A rowing phrase for moving the oar through the water without putting one's weight behind the stroke.

14. **to put one off one's stroke** – to distract someone from what he is doing. 'I wish you wouldn't criticize my driving; you are putting me off my stroke.'

Archery

15. **wide of the mark** – inaccurate, wrong. 'The auctioneer's estimate was wide of the mark. He overvalued the necklace by nearly 50 per cent.'

16. **to hit/miss the mark** – to get some-

thing right/wrong. 'How extraordinary! When Madame Vernet told Julie's fortune, she hit the mark every time.' The mark is the target in archery.

1. **to overshoot the mark** – to exceed the limit. 'You overshot the mark, didn't you? You spent £300 more than your grant.'

2. **nearer/closer to the mark** – almost correct. 'When you said that unemployment would go above four million, you were nearer the mark than you realized.'

Shooting

3. **fair game** – a legitimate target for attack or ridicule. 'Recruits in the army are fair game for the non-commissioned officers.' The phrase comes from the shooting of birds in the open season when they have a chance of escaping and are therefore fair game.

Hunting

4. **to give someone a fair crack of the whip** – to give someone a fair opportunity, a fair share, e.g. of time or attention. 'You can say a lot in five minutes. I thought the chairman gave you a fair crack of the whip.'

5. **to be at bay** – to be beset by a danger from which there is no escape. 'The robbers are at bay and the police are calling on them to give themselves up.'
    to keep at bay – to prevent a danger from materializing when one is already under threat, but usually for only a short time. 'The medicine won't cure the arthritis in your thumb but it will keep it at bay.' The 'bay' means the baying of the hounds in pursuit of their quarry.

6. **in full cry** – in eager pursuit. 'A pity you said that about Sandra in your book. Her relations and friends are in full cry.' The reference is to the barking of the hounds as they approach their quarry.

7. **to throw someone off the scent** – to mislead someone on purpose. 'The film actress used a look-alike to leave the studio, successfully throwing the press off her scent.'

8. **to come a cropper** – to fail disastrously.

'Even the most experienced businessman can come a cropper.' A hunting phrase meaning to fall heavily from a horse. The 'crop' is the head.

Angling

9. **to rise to the bait** – to respond to a hint, temptation or provocation in the way hoped for. 'Whenever I want to infuriate Dennis, I make a violent attack on modern art. He rises to the bait every time.' The reference is to fish which rise to the surface of the water for food.

10. **to swallow hook, line and sinker/anchor** – to believe every detail of a story. 'Ted is the most credulous person I have ever met. He swallowed my explanation hook, line and sinker.' From the fish that swallows the angler's hook, line and sinker, 'swallow' being a colloquialism for 'believe'.

11. **to be hooked on** – to be caught, to become addicted to a person or object. One can be hooked on a drug, tobacco, a hobby, a sport, or anything else that gives pleasure. A woman may hook a man and marry him.

12. **to let someone off the hook** – to release someone from an obligation, promise or admission of guilt. 'Now you have accepted Mike's apology, you have let him off the hook.'

13. **to slip through the net** – to avoid detection. 'A small number of children in the care of social workers slip through the net and come to harm.' Note the opposite: **to be caught in the net**.

14. **to tighten the net** – to take tougher measures. 'The transport minister wants to bring in more spy cameras to tighten the net on speeding motorists.'

Cycling

15. **to ride in tandem with** – to work in perfect harmony with. 'British scientists are working in tandem with American doctors in an attempt to find the cure for Parkinson's disease.'

16. **to back-pedal** – to withdraw quickly from an offer or statement one has made.

'Peter promised he would look after our dog if we wanted to take a holiday, but now he is back-pedalling on his offer.'

Motoring

1. **to kick-start** – to start something forcefully and effectively so that it will keep going. 'Giving each child a computer will kick-start the school's training programme.' To start a motor-bike you must push down a lever with your foot – hence 'kick-start'.

2. **a jump-start** – a great encouragement and incentive to achieve something difficult. 'By giving his grandson a hundred foreign stamps and an album, he gave him a jump-start in stamp collecting.' From trying to get a car's engine to start by using the power from jump leads attached to the battery in another car.

Flying

3. **to take a dive / to suffer a nose-dive** – to go down very abruptly. 'After the interest rates were put up by the Bank of England, shares on the Stock Exchange took a dive.' 'The government suffered a nose-dive in opinion poll ratings.' cf. '**a nose-dive' 89/11**.

Throwing, Catching, Gripping

4. **to throw in the towel** – to abandon a plan or idea, to give up. 'After having competed three times in the race and failed each time, Paul threw in the towel.' In the boxing ring, the loser used to admit defeat by throwing in the towel. cf. '**to throw in one's hand' 99/13**.

5. **to throw/have a tantrum** – to exhibit a sudden display of temper. 'You should not give it to him, Joanna, otherwise he will throw a tantrum each time you refuse him something.'

6. **to throw a wobbly** – to flare up with rage/anger. 'Children who scream and throw a wobbly if they don't get what they want ought to be punished and not humoured.'

7. **to be thrown on the scrap heap** – to be looked upon as useless, to be discarded and unwanted. 'Now that my uncle has reached the age of 65, he feels that he has been thrown on the scrap heap.'

8. **throwaway society** – a society which carelessly throws away things without thinking of the consequences for the environment; one which takes too many things for granted and without appreciating them; a society that is superficial and without substance. 'Today's throwaway society has become estranged from the beauty of nature and is surrounded by too many machines and gadgets.'

9. **a throwback** – someone who has inherited characteristics that go back to an earlier generation. 'Tim is a throwback – his grandfather was just as fond of gambling as he is.'

10. **to have a catch in it** – to suspect that there is a hidden drawback in something. 'The house is really beautiful and I'd love to buy it, but at that ridiculously low price there must be a catch somewhere.'

11. **to get a grip on oneself** – to pull oneself together, to control oneself. 'Don't moan and groan about something you can't change. Get a grip on yourself!'

12. **to tighten one's grip** – to take a firmer stand on something. 'As his daughter's schoolwork did not show much improvement, the father decided to tighten his grip on the situation and ensure she did her homework properly.'

Riding

13. **to take for a ride** – to make a fool of, to cheat. 'I wish I hadn't paid Hughes all that money in advance; he has taken me for a ride.'

14. **to ride roughshod over someone** – to show a complete lack of consideration for a person's wishes or feelings, to treat him with harshness. 'The landlord has ridden roughshod over us; we asked him for a month's notice, and he has given us 24 hours to get out.' The shoes of a horse that is roughshod have the heads of the nails projecting to prevent slipping.

15. **to give someone a rough ride** – to create a lot of difficulties for someone.

'The parents gave the head teacher a rough ride because they felt she wasn't doing enough to combat bullying at the school.'

1. **an easy ride** – a time passed without any difficulties or problems. 'With all the studying you've done, you'll have an easy ride when it comes to the exams.'

2. **riding high** – being successful and sought after. 'The popular politician was riding high and hoping for a top job in the Cabinet, but it wasn't to be.' cf. '**to be on the crest of a wave**' 13/13.

3. **to ride for a fall** – to bring disaster on oneself by behaving in an arrogant or provocative manner. 'Since Brian became the boss, he has made a lot of enemies among the staff; I'm afraid he is riding for a fall.'

4. **to keep someone on the trot** – to keep someone busy, always on the move. 'The sightseers kept me on the trot all day long. I am exhausted.'

5. **to trot out** – to exhibit for approval. 'When I asked the official for information about language schools in London, she trotted out a number of brochures, commenting on each with great enthusiasm.' The phrase comes from trotting a horse to show off its paces in front of a customer.

6. **to win in a canter/an easy canter** – to win easily, without having to make any real effort. 'Hazel Smith won the election in an easy canter.' A 'canter' is short for a 'Canterbury gallop', the slow easy pace that the pilgrims are supposed to have ridden on their way to Canterbury.

7. **to saddle with / to be saddled with** – to burden someone with responsibility for / to be burdened with responsibility for. 'On the death of my father, I was saddled with the debts of his estate.'

8. **to remain in the saddle** – to remain in a position of authority. 'Despite the attempts by the clergy in the diocese to remove him, the bishop remained in the saddle until his death.'

9. **to keep someone on a tight rein** – to keep someone under strict control. 'Andy's father keeps him on a tight rein;

he has to account to his father for every penny he spends.'

10. **to take up the reins** – to take over control of something. 'After his father's death, the eldest son took up the reins of the family firm.'

11. **to be back in harness** – to be restored to one's employment or office. Often said of someone returning to work after recovering from an illness. 'I am so glad to be back in harness. I'm miserable when I'm away from my work.'

12. **to die in harness** – to continue to work until the day of one's death. 'I hope I die in harness; I shouldn't know what to do with myself if I retired.'

13. **to kick over the traces** – to throw off all restraint. 'George is £2,000 in debt. He has been kicking over the traces again.' The traces are the harness a horse tries to get rid of so that it can kick more freely.

14. **to win one's spurs** – to win recognition for outstanding ability. Originally, to gain a knighthood in recognition of one's courage in battle. The knight was then presented with a pair of gilt spurs. cf. '**to win one's colours**' 1/8.

Swimming, Diving

15. **to swim with/against the stream** – to think or act in accordance with / contrary to the views of the majority. 'Original thinkers seldom swim with the stream.'

16. **it's sink or swim** – in a desperate situation, one must resort to desperate remedies. 'I had to dismiss half our staff this morning; we are simply not earning enough to pay the wages; it's sink or swim for us.'

17. **to be in the swim** – to be active in, or aware of, what's going on. 'You didn't know that Lloyd has resigned from the government? You can't be in the swim any more.'

18. **to take the plunge** – to take action after some hesitation, to make a final choice. 'My family has finally taken the plunge and is going to leave the city and find a house in the country.'

1. **to be out of one's depth** – to be unable to understand something. ' "I am out of my depth where computers are concerned. It must be my age," Nicole's grandfather admitted ruefully.'

2. **to dive in at the deep end** – to be put to the test without any preparation. 'I'm a great believer in diving in at the deep end. The sooner young barristers get into court the better.'

3. **to throw somebody in at the deep end** – to make someone do a task which he or she is completely unprepared for. 'Poor Kathleen got thrown in at the deep end today because of the flu epidemic. She had to teach French to advanced students, although she is only used to teaching beginners.'

4. **skinny-dipping** – bathing naked. 'Our neighbour told us she loves skinny-dipping in the early hours of the morning.'

Surfing

5. **to surf the net** – to browse through the Internet, stopping now and again at points of interest before moving on again. 'Let's surf the net and look for an exciting place to spend our next summer holiday!'

Jumping, Springing

6. **to be for/to be due for the high jump** (slang) – to incur a severe punishment. 'If Mrs Brown finds out that Yvette has been wearing her clothes, she will be for the high jump.' This expression might be military slang for having to face a difficulty. Army officers were fond of steeplechasing, during which their horses had to jump over high hedges and wide ditches.

7. **to jump at an opportunity / to jump at the chance** – to accept an opportunity eagerly. 'I am sure that Diane would jump at the opportunity of learning French in such pleasant surroundings.'

8. **to jump before being pushed** – to hand in one's resignation before one is dismissed from a job or post. 'After it had been proved that the politician had lied,

his colleagues hoped that he would agree to jump before being pushed.'

9. **to jump the gun** – to take premature action, with the object of gaining an unfair advantage. 'You jumped the gun, didn't you, calling here at this hour of the morning? Mrs Graham will be making a statement to the press at three o'clock this afternoon.' The reference is to a sportsman who starts the race before the gun has been fired.

10. **to jump ship** – to leave a post or a job, to quit, with the unspoken implication that the firm, factory, etc., is about to fail. 'Our company is in danger of going bust with Mr Grey as director. Some of our best employees might want to jump ship.' The idiom derives from a professional sailor secretly leaving his ship at a port without working for the full period for which he was employed.

11. **to jump to conclusions** – to draw an inference from insufficient evidence. 'Aren't you jumping to conclusions? Just because I have taken Jenny out a couple of times this week, it doesn't mean that I want to marry her.'

12. **to be one jump ahead** – to be in a position to anticipate the words or actions of someone else. 'I know exactly what he is going to say before he is halfway through his sentence. I am always one jump ahead of him.'

13. **with a spring in one's step** – feeling happy and light-hearted. 'Judith left the university with a spring in her step – she had passed all her exams.'

Skipping, Hopping

14. **to skip** – to do without, to dispense with. 'Shall we skip the introduction and start the game?' Also: **to skip a page**. 'I always skip the first few pages if a book is too boring.' The literal meaning is to jump lightly over something.

15. **to catch someone on the hop** – to take someone by surprise, to catch someone at an inconvenient moment. 'Sorry, Lisa, I can't stop. You caught me on the hop.'

16. **to be hopping mad** – to be absolutely

furious. 'You are terribly late coming home, Angela. Daddy is hopping mad!' cf. **'to drive someone mad'** 136/17.

Walking, Running

1. **to take a drastic step** – to take forceful action. 'Immediately Jane noticed that she had head lice, she took the drastic step of having her long hair cut very short.'

2. **step by step** – gradually. 'Let's do this maths problem step by step, Robin, and then you'll find it easier to understand.' cf. **'a stepping-stone'** 157/7.

3. **to be out of step** – not in sympathy or agreement with others. 'When Prince Charles was seen fox-hunting with his son, a number of people criticized him for being out of step with public sentiment.'

4. **to watch one's step** – (1) to walk carefully. 'Watch your step, Lily. I don't want you to slip on the ice!' (2) to act carefully and not offend anyone. 'Watch your step at the meeting, Alan, and let the others do the talking!'

5. **to take in one's stride** – to accomplish something difficult with ease. 'I don't know how he managed in the time, but the electrician didn't mind repairing the television, in addition to the hi-fi and the light-switch. He took it all in his stride.'

6. **walk-on-by society** – people who ignore crime and give no help to victims. 'Sadly, except for rare cases, we have become a walk-on-by society, afraid of getting involved.'

7. **a walkabout** – an unofficial stroll by some famous personality through a crowd of ordinary people. 'The Queen Mother went for a short walkabout on her birthday and was immediately surrounded by well-wishers.' Originally a solitary walk in the Australian outback by an Aboriginal.

8. **a walkover** – an easy achievement. 'Why don't you take French at A level, Olivia? Having spent so much time in France, you'll find it a walkover.'

9. **to run rings round someone** – to outmatch someone decisively. 'Amanda is a competent tennis player but her brother Ted can run rings round her.' From athletics, when one competitor runs so much faster than his rival that he can make a circle round him and still reach the winning post first.

10. **to run hard just to stand still** – to be under enormous stress and hardly able to cope any more. 'I'm so sorry I can't go out with you, Dennis. I've got a hundred things to do in the office before my holiday – I feel as if I'm running hard just to stand still.' cf. **'to chase one's tail'** 54/19; **'to run around like a headless chicken'** 69/11.

11. **to run amok** – to storm about in a frenzied manner. 'A maniac who ran amok in a church injured several people before being overpowered.'

12. **in the long run** – ultimately, looking a long time ahead. 'In the long run it is surely better to have your own house, even if it means having to pay a big mortgage for it.'
    in the short run – in the near future, looking only a short time ahead. 'In the short run, it is better to enjoy oneself while one can.'

13. **hit-and-run** – to knock someone down and drive away without stopping. 'They should increase the penalties for hit-and-run offences.'

14. **a running commentary** – a continuous account of an event while it is taking place. 'While the two boys were fighting together outside the girls' bedroom, Margaret gave her sister a running commentary.'

15. **to make the running** – to take the lead, to be the most prominent in any activity. 'All the Robsons were talented writers, but it was the mother who made the running with her magnificent biographies.'

16. **to be in/out of the running for** – to have a chance/no chance. 'Martin's headmaster has just told us that Martin is in the running for a scholarship, but he won't say more at the moment.'

17. **to be run down** – to be lacking in vitality and energy, easily tired. 'You look run down to me; you could do with a good holiday.'

1. **to run someone down** – to speak ill of / to find fault with someone. 'Joe is always running me down; I wonder what he's got against me?'

2. **the runner-up** – a competitor who comes second to the winner. 'Although she was the favourite to win, Jenny did not come first in the local half-marathon, but had to content herself with being runner-up.'

3. **to run out of steam** – to lose vigour/ momentum. 'Our new magazine did very well at first – we had lots of new ideas we wanted to experiment with – but after the first six numbers, we ran out of steam.'

4. **to be on the run** – to be in flight from. 'The jail-breakers are on the run, but it is only a question of time before they are caught.'

5. **to run someone/something close** – to rival, to compete strongly with. 'You are always saying how stupid our director is, but I must say his deputy runs him very close!'

6. **to run for president** – campaigning to become president. ' "Why do men always run for president in the US?" asked Josie. "Isn't it time we had a woman president?" '

7. **to run away with an idea** – to make a hasty assumption which is not supported by the facts. 'You shouldn't run away with the idea that because you haven't been elected leader, we don't appreciate your services to the orchestra.'

8. **to be an also-ran** – to be a failure. 'Hugh was an also-ran in everything he tried to do and deeply resented his failure.' The phrase refers to horse-racing: an also-ran is a horse that comes past the winning post after the first three.

9. **the first hurdle** – the first obstacle to one's plans. 'The first hurdle will be to obtain planning permission from the local council before we start building the new extension.' Also: **yet another hurdle**.

Leaping

10. **by leaps and bounds** – with great rapidity. 'Since Tom has been taking private lessons in maths, he has progressed by leaps and bounds.'

11. **a giant leap** – an enormous step. 'Landing on the moon was a giant leap for mankind.'

12. **a leap in the dark** – a hazardous undertaking whose results cannot be predicted. 'When Baden-Powell started the Boy Scout movement in 1908, he could have had no idea that it would be such a success; it was a leap in the dark.'

13. **to leap to mind** – to suggest itself immediately to one, usually through an association of ideas. 'When Stephen told us that his school-days had been the happiest time of his life, the memory of his being tossed in a blanket in the school dormitory leapt to mind.'

14. **to leapfrog someone/something** – to overtake or outdo someone/something so as to gain an advantage. 'The young financial genius made many enemies at his bank after he leapfrogged colleagues into the best-paid job.'

Climbing

15. **to climb down** – to withdraw an assertion or accusation one has energetically upheld, to accept a defeat. 'You had better climb down while there is still time, or you may find yourself in court.'

16. **a social climber** – a person who is trying to mix with people of higher social rank to gain in status him- or herself. 'Mrs Henderson doesn't really like you, Lord Travers. She's just a social climber, using you to get to the top.'

Scoring, Winning

17. **to settle a score** – to repay someone for a past offence, to avenge a grievance. 'Now that I have settled the score, can we be friends again?'

18. **a win-win situation** – circumstances where it is impossible to lose. 'The idea of

a crèche in the workplace is a very good one – good for the mother, good for the child, and good for the employer. It's a win-win situation for everyone.' Note the opposite: **a lose-lose situation**; **a no-win situation**. cf. **'a Catch-22 situation'** 261/15.

Games:

Chess

1. **an opening gambit** – the first step in a dispute or contest. 'Harvey's opening gambit was to call an emergency meeting.' In chess, the phrase means the offer of a sacrifice in the opening of a game in order to obtain a positional or tactical advantage. The idiom and the chess term do not therefore correspond in meaning. The 'opening gambit' (*gambito*) was first recorded in 1561 by the Spanish chess player Ruy Lopez.

2. **to checkmate** – to make a move which puts an end at once to one's opponent's plans. 'Our main competitors have checkmated us by taking us over.' Checkmate is a chess term meaning a decisive attack on the opponent's king which brings the game to a finish.

3. **only a pawn (in the game)** – only a person of very minor importance who is manipulated by stronger forces. 'We none of us have any say in our future; we are just pawns, nothing more.' In chess, the pawns are the weakest pieces which are often sacrificed in attacks on the opponent. Also: **a political pawn**.

4. **a stalemate** – a position in which neither party to a dispute can take effective steps against the other. In chess, stalemate occurs when one of the players is unable to move any of his pieces.

Dominoes

5. **to spread like a game of dominoes** – to spread in every direction. 'The lawyer's office was in a real mess, with his papers spread like a game of dominoes over every available desk and table.'

6. **to fall like dominoes / to collapse like a row of dominoes** – to fall down,

one after the other; one event inevitably leads to another. 'Government resistance to EU social measures is collapsing like a row of dominoes.' cf. **'a house of cards'** 154/12.

7. **a domino-type operation** – a double transplant operation, involving two patients, one immediately after the other.

8. **domino theory** – the idea or suggestion, using the image of dominoes knocking against each other and falling over, that if one thing is damaged, then all other things associated with it will also be damaged. The domino theory is frequently used in reference to neighbouring countries during a war. 'Under the domino theory, the latest war in Chechnya might spread to Uzbekistan, Kyrgyzstan, Turkmenistan, Kazakhstan and Tajikistan.' cf. **'a knock-on effect'** 241/18.

Mikado

9. **the Mikado syndrome** – used mostly in politics and business: to be afraid to make the wrong move or say the wrong thing for fear of losing one's post, job or voters. 'I think that politician is suffering from the Mikado syndrome. He is completely ineffective.' From the Japanese game where one holds thin sticks in one's hand and then lets them go. The object of the game is to pick up as many of the sticks as possible without causing the others to move. The moment just one stick moves, the game is over and one has lost.

Billiards

10. **as bald as a billiard-ball / a billiard ball head** – completely bald, without any hair on one's head. 'The pop star shaved off all his hair. Now he is as bald as a billiard-ball.'

Card Games

11. **to be a card/quite a card** – to be a notable character, to be eccentric. 'Old Mr Williams is quite a card, isn't he? He walks his dog up and down the road at all hours of the day and night.'

12. **one's leading/trump card** – one's

strongest point, one's main strength. 'Jane's leading card was her charm. She played it time and again to good effect.'

1. **to play one's best card** – to employ the best means at one's disposal to get the desired result. 'In the court action, Ian played his best card by calling a surprise witness.'

2. **to play one's cards well** – to act with skill and good judgement, to make the most of one's chances. 'At the interview, Jack played his cards well by trying to show how he could be useful to the company.'

3. **to hold all the cards in one's hands** – to be in a position to dictate the conditions. 'You will have to do as he says; he is holding all the cards in his hands.'

4. **to show one's cards** – to show one's intentions. 'I wouldn't show your cards if I were you. In business it is often best to keep one's intentions to oneself.'

5. **on the cards** – likely to happen, possible. 'It's on the cards that Julian will be getting married soon.' The phrase comes from fortune-telling, when the future is read in the cards.

6. **to have a card up one's sleeve** – to have some surprise or secret in reserve, unknown to one's adversary. The idiom is taken from cheating at cards, when a player conceals an ace up his sleeve.

7. **to stack the cards against someone** – to place obstacles in the way of someone's success. 'If you start a business, I'm afraid you will find the cards stacked against you. You have very little capital, and hardly any experience.'

8. **to put one's cards on the table** – to make one's intentions clear. 'Richard told me he was going to put his cards on the table but I had the impression that he was hiding something from me.'

9. **to have a raw deal** – to suffer an injustice. 'Only £100 compensation for all your injuries! You've had a raw deal.' The phrase comes from the dealing out of cards (at card games).

10. **one's long suit/strong suit** – one's principal strength, something one is

especially good at. 'I'll be glad to help your daughter with her GCSE in history. History was always my long suit.' ' "Don't trust him," the spin doctor warned the politician. "Loyalty to the leadership has never been his strong suit." '

11. **to follow suit** – to do exactly the same as the person immediately preceding you. 'When their host began to attack the government, Brian got up and left the room; soon afterwards, the other guests followed suit.' In many card games, a player is obliged to play a card of the same suit as the last card that has been played.

12. **to trump someone's ace** – to counter a strong argument/action of one's opponent with an argument/action that is even stronger. 'When the application of William Morris, the motor-car manufacturer, to join a golf club was refused by its members, he trumped their ace by buying the club.'

13. **to trump up a charge** – to concoct a charge against someone by producing false evidence. 'All these charges against me have been trumped up. There isn't a word of truth in any of them.' The word derives from the French *tromper* meaning 'to deceive'.

14. **to come/turn up trumps** – to prove surprisingly helpful. 'Our neighbour has never had anything to do with us, but when Nancy had a bad fall, he turned up trumps, rang the hospital and gave her first aid.'

15. **to play one's last trump** – to use one's last asset. 'When Mark was made redundant as a chemist, there was nothing for it but to play his last trump and return to his old school as a teacher.'

16. **the buck stops here** – the person who says this is the one who takes full responsibility for what has happened. No one else can take the blame. 'You are the owner of the building firm and it's your fault that our house is in such a mess. The buck stops with you.' Frequent usage: **he/she was unwilling to admit that the buck stops here**. And not so frequent: **the buck has stopped where it should**. The 'buck' is the buckhorn knife used in some card games, rather than

'buck' meaning 'dollar'. The player in charge of the buckhorn knife is responsible for the game.

1. **to pass the buck** – to blame someone else for one's own failure. 'Benny complained that he didn't pass his exams because his mum didn't buy him all the books he needed. That's just passing the buck, if you ask me.'

2. **a poker face** – a face that shows no expression so that one's feelings remain concealed. 'I never know whether Henry is pleased or annoyed; he has a real poker face.' The phrase comes from the card game poker, in which it is of vital importance to winning the game never to allow your facial expression to indicate the contents of your hand.

3. **to leave in the lurch** – to desert someone in need of one's help. 'James was only asking for a small loan. How could you have left such an old friend in the lurch!' In cribbage, the loser was said to be 'in the lurch' when the winner scored 61 before he or she had scored 31.

Board

4. **to be above-board** – to be honest, respectable. The 'board' is the table on which the card games were played. When the players had their hands 'above board', they couldn't change the cards or cheat. It follows that, if someone is 'above board', you can rely on him or her not to cheat you.

5. **to sweep the board** – to vanquish all one's opponents and win all the prizes.

6. **across the board** – as a rule, generally. 'When a business is taken over, salaries usually increase across the board.'

Gambling, Betting

7. **to take a gamble on** – to take a chance with. 'A TV channel took a gamble on an inexperienced hostess, and lost. The audience did not like her.'

8. **to look a good bet** – to have a good chance. 'Investing in mobile phones looks a good bet to me.'

Lottery, Scratchcard

9. **a lottery / life's lottery** – pure chance, uncertainty, a gamble on success. 'When you move into a students' home, it's a bit of a lottery who you must share a room with.' 'Life's lottery may have dealt you a blow, Emily, but you can fight back by working hard and being optimistic.' cf. '**the wheel of fortune**' 153/16.

10. **the postcode lottery** – towards the end of the last millennium, a postcode lottery existed in the National Health Service whereby it depended on the area you lived in whether you were given expensive life-saving drugs or not. 'My Auntie Barbara has been badly hit by the postcode lottery and is wondering if she'll ever get well again.'

11. **to draw a blank** – to be unsuccessful. 'Finding the kind of job she wants is difficult. She has drawn a blank for the third time.' From drawing a 'blank' lottery ticket, indicating that one has won nothing.

12. **a scratchcard solution** – a solution which can only come by good luck. 'Whatever shall we do about this enormously expensive empty tower block? We need a scratchcard solution, don't we, Mr Adams?' Frequent usage: **there are no scratchcard solutions to this problem**.

Dicing

13. **no dice** (slang) – no luck, no success. 'Sorry, no dice. I can't lend you any money this time.'

14. **to dice with death** – to risk one's life. 'The pilot of the small plane was dicing with death when he flew across the English Channel during a thunderstorm.'

15. **as straight as a die** – absolutely honest and fair. A 'die' was originally the single form of 'dice', but is obsolete except in the phrases 'straight as a die' and 'the die is cast'.

16. **the die is cast** – the gamble has been

taken and is irrevocable. The words used by Julius Caesar in 49 BC when he crossed the Rubicon.

Roulette

1. **Russian roulette** – gamblers used to risk their lives by putting a bullet in one of the six chambers of a revolver, spinning the chamber then holding it to their head and pressing the trigger. 'For those with a severe allergy to nuts, eating out is like playing Russian roulette.'

2. **ecological roulette** – there is bound to be some kind of ecological catastrophe/disaster, but there is no knowing when it will happen. 'Allowing oil tankers to travel close to the sandbanks of the Baltic Sea is playing a dangerous game of ecological roulette. One of them could get stranded any time and cause massive pollution.'

Children's Toys and Games:

Toy

3. **to treat something like a toy** – to play with something that is not a toy and should be taken more seriously. 'Put the kitten down, Emily. She's not a toy, you know.'

4. **to toy with an idea** – to consider a possibility but only half seriously. 'I toyed once with the idea of emigrating to Canada, but rejected it almost at once because of the climate.'

Doll

5. **like a doll / doll-like / like a little doll / as pretty as a doll** – to be very cute and pretty (usually describing a beautiful baby or little girl). ' "Your baby is as pretty as a doll," the nurse told the proud young mother.' Long ago, wooden figures of gods were given to children after religious ceremonies, and these were the very first dolls.

6. **as limp as a rag doll / like a rag doll** – to be lacking in energy and vitality; often used to describe a child/young girl lying unconscious, even dead. 'After

being rescued from drowning, little Sara lay limp as a rag doll in her rescuer's arms.'

7. **as pale as a wax doll** – very pallid, wan and sickly. 'The young couple adopted the little baby from an orphanage in Romania. He looked very sweet when they first saw him, but as pale as a wax doll.' About two hundred years ago, dolls' faces were modelled in wax and given round, chubby features.

8. **a china-doll complexion** – a pale, unblemished complexion. 'We need a pretty model with a china-doll complexion to model our new face cream.'

Puzzle

9. **like a puzzle / like a jigsaw puzzle / like piecing together a puzzle** – like a mystery; like trying to solve a mystery or resolve a difficult situation. 'Solving this crime will be like piecing together a puzzle, but I'm sure we'll manage it in the end.'

Kaleidoscope

10. **kaleidoscopic impressions / like a kaleidoscope** – constantly changing impressions and sensations. 'I leant back on the pillow of my gondola and let the colours and impressions of Venice unfold like a kaleidoscope before my eyes.' A kaleidoscope is a tube which contains pieces of coloured glass and reflecting surfaces and which can be rotated to reveal an endless variety of symmetrical forms.

Yo-yo

11. **to go/pop in and out like yo-yos/a yo-yo / to bounce up and down like a yo-yo** – to go in and out many times. 'My mischievous cousin Stephen popped in and out of my childhood like a yo-yo.' Long ago, the yo-yo was used as a jungle weapon by tribesmen in the Philippines. In their language, it means 'come back', as it was used like a boomerang.

12. **to diet like a yo-yo / yo-yo dieting** – to eat less in order to get slim quickly and then to eat more again, a constant cycle

of crash dieting followed by weight gain, followed by dieting. 'The Cabbage Soup Diet might offer the lifelong solution to yo-yo dieting.' cf. **'the battle of the bulge' 239/4**; **'to be at war with weight' 238/12**; **'to be on a crash diet' 189/10**.

1. **yo-yo wrist** – repetitive-strain injury in the wrist and arm caused by flicking a yo-yo up and down.

Top

2. **to sleep like a top** – to sleep very soundly. 'After her day out at the seaside, the little girl slept like a top.' A top remains motionless when it is spinning very quickly. This stillness, and the quiet and steady humming of the top, resembles someone fast asleep. cf. **'to sleep like a log' 50/19**.

3. **one's head is spinning like a top** – one feels very giddy, usually with having to absorb lots of information. 'I started my new job today. There's so much to learn that my head is spinning like a top.'

Marbles

4. **to lose one's marbles** – to behave foolishly, to go mad. 'You can't skate on that thin ice! Have you lost your marbles?' 'Marbles' derives from the French *meubles* (furniture). In the 18th and 19th centuries, one used the phrase 'the faculty and furniture of one's mind', meaning one's intellectual faculties.

Boomerang

5. **like a boomerang** – in a manner that indicates a suitable or inevitable response to one's previous actions. 'Some people believe that their actions in a previous life will come back at them like a boomerang, influencing their everyday lives.'

Kite

6. **to fly a kite** – to put forward an idea (usually in a ministerial speech) to test public reaction. If the reaction is favourable, the idea may be adopted; if it is not, the idea can be disowned. A kite is a frame-work of paper and cardboard that is flown at the end of a string, in the wind. The kite gives an indication of the direction and strength of the wind. The toy is so called because it hovers like the bird of the same name.

7. **to feel as high as a kite** – (1) to be blissfully happy. (2) to be drunk – in rhyming slang, 'kite' rhymes with 'tight', which means 'drunk'. (3) to be high on drugs (this meaning is the most frequently used). 'Marianne drifted past the two boys, a dreamy expression on her face, and as high as a kite.'

Balloon, Bubble

8. **to go down like a lead balloon** – something that does not have the desired effect; an idea, plan or speech that is unsuccessful and bound to fail; to leave one dismayed and completely shocked. 'Alan's decision to leave school shortly before taking his final exams and to become a pop singer went down like a lead balloon with his parents.'

9. **to balloon** – to become very fat. 'After eating too much junk food while on holiday, Harry's weight had ballooned to more than 100 kg.'

10. **to swell like a balloon** – one's stomach becomes full and round. ' "If you eat too many peas and onions," the doctor said to his patient, "your stomach will swell like a balloon." '

11. **to burst the bubble of something** – to shatter plans for an unrealistic venture. ' "Stop buying shares in his business," Jack warned his friend. "It's worthless. The bubble will soon burst!" '

Party Games

12. **to pass the parcel** – not to accept responsibility for someone/something and to pass this burden on to someone else, who acts in a similar fashion. 'No one wants this war criminal. Various countries have been playing pass the parcel with him.' Originally a children's party game in which a parcel is handed around a circle of players to music. cf. **'to be thrown like a hot potato' 185/4**.

Fireworks

1. **a damp squib / to sputter like a damp squib** – something which fails to generate enthusiasm; an anti-climax. 'The councillor's idea to spend the Lottery money on building a mountain of empty beer crates sputtered like a damp squib when everyone protested.' A squib is a small firework that burns with a hiss and finishes with a small explosion. If it becomes damp, it will no longer burn.

2. **to take off like a rocket** – to shoot up, be extremely successful in a very short space of time. 'Pamela's career as an actress took off like a rocket after she married the film director.'

3. **a rocket-like grower** – a plant, hedge or tree which grows extremely fast. 'This poplar tree really is a rocket-like grower. Surely it wasn't so long ago since we brought it back from the garden centre in the boot of our car?'

4. **prices/shares shoot up like a rocket** – to rise very rapidly in price, to become more expensive/valuable very quickly. 'If only we had bought some more of those stamp sets. Now they have shot up in value like a rocket.' cf. **'sky-high' 24/10**.

The Fairground

5. **in full swing** – of social events, going off well, a success. 'When we arrived, the party was already in full swing.'

6. **what you lose on the swings you gain on the roundabouts** – there is nothing to be said for or against a particular course of action because the advantages and disadvantages are evenly balanced. 'You eat better at the Victoria Hotel, but then it's much further from the beach than the Cavendish; what you lose on the swings you gain on the roundabouts.'

7. **to have/not to have a crystal ball** – to have/not to have the means to predict the future. This phrase is often used ironically, e.g. 'If I knew, Inspector Francis, how much money my company will be making this time next year, I should be only too pleased to let you know. Unfortunately, I don't have a crystal ball.' The refrence is to the crystal ball used by fortune-tellers.

8. **a roller-coaster life** – a life packed with non-stop action and excitement, periods of great happiness and excitement alternating with periods of sadness and boredom. 'The film star decided to give up her roller-coaster life in order to settle down quietly with her family.' Also: **one's life has more ups and downs than a roller-coaster ride; a roller-coaster five (etc.) years of doing something**.

9. **an emotional roller-coaster** – suffering from great mood swings, being happy one day and gloomy the next.

10. **a roller-coaster relationship** – a relationship between two people, periods of joy and bliss alternating rapidly with periods of quarrelling and strife; an on-and-off partnership. 'The famous pop star and his wife are never long out of the news headlines, due to their roller-coaster relationship.' cf. **'a love–hate relationship' 126/7**.

Music-making

1. **music to one's ears** – the pleasure one feels on receiving a piece of good news, especially news of the discomfiture of an old enemy. 'I hear Matthew has had to resign from the ministry. That must be music to your ears, Tom!' cf. **'meat and drink' 180/10**.

2. **to face the music** – to answer for the consequences of one's actions. 'We have just received a complaint about you from the dean of your college, Jack; you will have to face the music next term.'

3. **to blow one's own trumpet** – to praise oneself publicly, to boast about one's achievements. 'You have to blow your own trumpet in business. If you don't, no one else will.'

4. **to trumpet something** – to proclaim something in a celebratory fashion. 'The new business school is proudly trumpeting its pupils' latest achievements in the local newspaper.'

5. **to beat the drum for someone** – to campaign noisily on somebody's behalf, to advertise his or her services energetically. 'While I'm in Hong Kong, I'll beat the drum for you; so you'll get plenty of publicity.'

6. **to drum something into someone** – to impress an idea forcefully on someone. 'It's been drummed into them ever since they were small that their country is the best in the world.'

7. **to be drummed out** – to be dismissed in a humiliating manner. 'It is shameful the way John cheats his customers. He would have been drummed out of any

decent company years ago.' The reference is to the dismissal of an officer from his regiment for dishonourable conduct; the dismissal takes effect in front of the soldiers with the drums beating.

8. **to fiddle / to be on the fiddle / to fiddle accounts** – to swindle, often by falsifying the accounts. 'I'm sure that Robert is on the fiddle; otherwise he couldn't afford all those holidays on the Riviera on his salary.'

9. **as fit as a fiddle** – to be in excellent health. 'I've worked for 20 years without a holiday and I'm as fit as a fiddle!' cf. **'as sound as a bell' 160/13**.

10. **to harp on the same string** – to make the same point over and over again. 'I wish you wouldn't harp on the same string every time I light a cigarette. I know smoking is bad for the health, but I won't give it up!'

11. **to whistle in the dark** – to talk optimistically in order to keep up one's courage. 'Have you got any evidence, Frank, for believing things are going to improve, or are you just whistling in the dark?'

12. **to whistle for it** – to ask in vain for the repayment of one's money. 'I'm afraid you've seen the last of your money, Paul. You can whistle for it as far as Richard is concerned.'

13. **to pull out all the stops** – to make a tremendous effort. 'When the airport told us Mary's luggage had been lost, Father pulled out all the stops to get it back to her.' The stops refer to organ stops. When the organist pulls out all the stops, the organ is being played at full volume. The

church organ is the most powerful of all musical instruments.

1. **to soft-pedal** – to understate the importance of, to moderate. 'The workers are soft-pedalling their demands in case the company goes bankrupt and they lose their jobs.' When the soft pedal is down, the piano plays more quietly.

2. **to strike the right note** – to behave in a manner that is suited to the occasion. 'In his address to the men, the army chaplain struck just the right note; he was serious without being grim and friendly without being familiar.' The reference is to a musical note.

3. **to strike a chord** – (1) to remind one of something. 'This book I am reading strikes a chord; I must have read it before, many years ago.' (2) a feeling of instant rapport with others. ' "We must prevent battery farming," Marion exclaimed. "We know our action will strike a chord with all those who love birds and animals." '

4. **to compare notes** – to exchange ideas and opinions. The reference is to musical notation.

5. **to be in tune with someone** – to have a good understanding with someone. 'I have always been in tune with my children, even when they were teenagers.'

6. **out of tune with** – out of sympathy with, having nothing in common with. 'I don't think Paul enjoyed the African tour; he was out of tune with his companions.'

7. **to call the tune** – to impose one's will. 'You must do what your uncle asks. He is paying for your training so he has a right to call the tune.' From the proverb 'He who pays the piper calls the tune'.

8. **to the tune of** – the excessive amount of . . . 'Martin was charged by the hotel to the tune of £650 a week.'

9. **to be/not to be tuned in to** – to be/not to be in sympathy with. 'The teacher was not tuned in to the feelings of her pupils.' The reference is to the tuning in of a radio to a frequency.

10. **canned music** – pre-recorded music. 'You can always tell whether it is canned music or live music.'

canned laughter – pre-recorded laughter.

Vocal and Dance Music

11. **to change one's tune** – to change one's manner, usually after being disappointed or humiliated; but it can also be used when one has been proved wrong. 'Mother said I would never make a painter, but she'll have to change her tune now that I've won first prize at the County Exhibition.'

12. **to sing someone's praises** – to speak very highly of someone, to praise him or her enthusiastically. 'Julie was singing your praises this afternoon. You must have made a very good impression on her.'

13. **to sing (to the police)** (slang) – to inform on one's criminal associates. The larger part of police evidence is supplied by the criminals themselves in the hope of getting lighter sentences.

14. **to sing for one's supper** – to do some unaccustomed work to pay one's keep. 'If Jackie wants to stay on with us after she has finished here, she will have to sing for her supper. I'm not giving her free board and lodging.'

15. **to go for a song** – to be sold for a very small sum. 'The house went for a song because the owner had to raise money quickly.'

16. **to make a song and dance about** – to make an unnecessary fuss about. 'I don't know why Mrs Scott should have made such a song and dance about her daughter coming home at three o'clock in the morning. Angela is 19 years old and not a little girl any longer.'

17. **to dance attendance on someone** – to be over-anxious to please and assist someone. 'I don't know why Lady Miriam should expect me to dance attendance on her all day. I'm only a friend of the family, not her servant.'

18. **to lead someone a (pretty) dance** – to put someone to a great deal of trouble before agreeing to what he or she wants. 'I must say Mr Vincent led me a pretty

dance. I've never worked so hard in my life to win a customer.'

1. **to waltz home** – to win easily. 'With two of Fulham's team off the field with injuries, Rangers should have waltzed home.'

Show

2. **to steal the show** – to capture all the attention. 'At the garden party, the innocent charm of her beautiful teenage daughter stole the show from the hostess.'

3. **the show must go on** – one must fulfil one's obligations whatever the cost to one's own feelings. 'I am so sorry that your husband has lost his job, but you cannot cancel your campaign now; the show must go on.' There is a tradition in the theatre that the show must go on, whatever happens, except in the case of accident or illness.

4. **to give the show away** – to tell everyone what is going to happen. 'Father will be making an announcement after dinner to the guests, but I won't tell you what about; that would be giving the show away.'

5. **to run the show** – to organize a protest or riot. 'Country dwellers in favour of fox-hunting are accusing professional anarchists of running the show to ban fox-hunting.'

6. **good show** – well done, splendid. 'So you will be able to come to the party. Good show!' (rather dated but still in use).
   it's a bad show – disappointing news, very wrong. 'It's a bad show Alan wasn't given leave to come; what a mean way to treat him.'

7. **to get the show on the road** – to put an idea into effect, to get something organized. 'You deserve the credit for getting the show on the road.' The 'show' was originally the theatrical company on tour.

8. **only a side-show** – an activity of only incidental importance. 'The company's work in Australia is only a side-show; the bulk of the business is in London.' In a circus, there used to be side-shows like the 'strong man', the bearded lady and the freaks who were on display in the intervals of the performance but were not part of it.

9. **a show-down** – a show of strength to settle a dispute and force a person to withdraw or apologize. 'If that lout doesn't stop annoying my sister, I'll have a show-down with him.' The reference is to poker when the players lay down their cards on the table face upwards to show the strength of their hands.

Scene

10. **behind the scenes** – out of the public view. 'There is always a lot of manoeuvring behind the scenes before a new government is formed.' A theatrical term for all the work done behind the stage by the electricians, make-up artists, costume designers and so on (which the audience does not see).

11. **to make a scene** – to give way to one's emotions, especially anger or grief, in a dramatic manner. 'The bill is much too high, but for goodness sake let's pay it rather than make a scene.'

12. **to set the scene for** – to describe the background to an event (historic, literary, sporting, etc.). 'Before he began his lecture on the Battle of Jutland, Mr Walker set the scene for the naval cadets by describing the background to the action.'

13. **to come on the scene** – to appear, to make one's presence felt. 'Until Marx and Engels came on the scene, no one had attached any importance to the class war.'

Stage

14. **stage-fright** – the fear experienced when speaking in front of an audience. 'Although John prepared his sermons with great care, he always had a moment or two of stage-fright when he addressed the congregation.' A theatrical term for the nervousness of actors on the stage, especially when they are appearing for the first time. cf. **'first-night nerves' 319/ 12**.

15. **a stage-whisper** – a whisper that is

intended to be heard by others, as a whisper on the stage is intended to be heard by the audience. 'During the headmaster's end-of-term speech, his wife would entertain the boys with her stage whispers which could be heard all over the assembly room.'

1. **to stage-manage** – to plan in detail an operation or important event. 'At the annual conference of the party, one delegate complained that the speeches had been stage-managed.' In the theatre, every detail of the production is stage-managed.

2. **to stage a recovery/a come-back** – to repeat one's earlier success, after retirement or failure. 'The majority of athletes who try to stage a come-back are unsuccessful.'

3. **to set the stage** – to set something in motion, to prepare. 'The admission by the largest cigarette-maker that smoking can cause disease, sets the stage for legislation to ban tobacco advertising.'

4. **to hold the stage** – to be able to engage an audience's attention. 'As young as he is, he can still hold the stage with his beautiful voice.'

5. **to upstage a rival** – to divert attention from a rival, to put him or her at a disadvantage. 'The managing director resented the way Forbes was trying to upstage him at the board meeting.' An actor is upstaged when he is obliged to turn his back on the audience in order to speak to his colleague upstage, i.e. at the back of the stage. When this happens, the attention of the audience is centred on the rival upstage, and the actor at the front of the stage is at a disadvantage.

Part

6. **to throw oneself into a part** – to accept with enthusiasm a duty that has been laid on one. 'Having been unexpectedly appointed to the Chair of the housing committee on the local council, Jill threw herself into the part with all her energy.'

7. **to look the part** – to resemble a particular type of person in manner and appearance. 'You may hate being a captain in

the Royal Artillery, but you certainly look the part.'

8. **to play a part** – (1) to assist in an activity or project, to cooperate in. 'Tom played an important part in starting the local youth club.' (2) to assume a false role, to pretend to be somebody one is not. 'Jeremy plays the part of the caring nephew to perfection, but don't let him fool you; it's her money he's after.'

Play, Piece, Role

9. **as good as a play** – as entertaining as a performance at the theatre. 'It was most amusing to watch Hobson wriggling under your cross-examination – as good as a play.' A comment allegedly made by Charles II on a debate in the House of Lords.

10. **the villain of the piece** – the real cause of the evil. 'There is no doubt that inflation is the villain of the piece; it has bankrupted thousands of small businesses and even put state industries in danger.' A theatrical phrase for the wicked character in a drama.

11. **to play a role** – to take a part in, or to be of some importance to. 'Although the couple had been married for many years, the husband's mother still played an important role in their lives.'

12. **to take over the role of** – to accept responsibility from someone else. 'In a government reshuffle, one minister might take over the role of another as decreed by the prime minister.'

13. **a role model** – a good example to follow. 'A child's role model is often his or her mother, father or a favourite teacher.'

14. **to cast someone in the role of the villain** – to fix blame on someone, to hold him or her responsible for a wrong. 'Since you have cast me in the role of the villain, I hope you will give me the opportunity to reply to your accusations.' The reference is to the distribution of roles among the actors in a theatre company.

Image, Mask

1. **to change one's image** – to create a different impression of oneself, mostly in public life. 'You really must change your image, John, if you want to achieve something in your Party.'

2. **to dent an image** – to inflict damage on a reputation. 'The drunken reputation of the famous pop star severely dented his image in the eyes of his teenage fans'. cf. **'a fallen idol' 41/10**.

3. **the spitting image** – an exact lookalike. 'Have you met Clive? He is the spitting image of his father.'

4. **to let the mask slip** – to show one's true feelings for a moment. 'Everyone thought she adored her uncle but when he was taken into custody, she let the mask slip and gave a little smile.'

5. **to be unmasked** – to be named, found out. 'A conman working with a foreign syndicate for fixing football matches was finally unmasked.'

Act

6. **to put on an act** – to dissimulate, to act in a way that is deliberately misleading. 'That boy is putting on an act; I don't believe he has hurt himself at all.'

7. **to get in on the act** – to imitate someone else in the hope of obtaining the same advantages. 'I have been making a good living from my mushroom growing, and now I see that my neighbour is getting in on the act, too.'

8. **to get/put one's act together** – to get oneself organized. 'You had better get your act together before you lose any more customers.' This phrase comes from the circus when the members of a troupe get their act ready for the performance.

9. **a hard/tough act to follow** – the perfect execution of a task which is hard for others to imitate. 'His long experience in the money market makes it a tough act for young stockbrokers to follow.'

10. **to clean up one's act** – to make an effort to improve oneself. 'If you really want that job, you will have to clean up your act.'

11. **to act on a whim** – to do something impulsively, without careful thought. 'Marion bought that strange-looking antique on a whim, and now she is stuck with it.'

Some More from the Theatre

12. **first-night nerves** – an attack of nerves that some people experience when taking part in a public event, especially when it is for the first time. 'Winston Churchill often suffered from first-night nerves on the eve of an important debate in the House of Commons.' 'First-night nerves' refers to the nervousness felt by the actors the first night a play is performed in public. cf. **'stage-fright' 317/14**.

13. **to take the lead** – to be in control. 'The man just released from prison took the lead in the latest spate of burglaries.'

14. **to take one's cue from** – to follow someone else's example. 'When we were staying with the Garners, we noticed that the children took their cue from the eldest boy; when he began to laugh, they would all laugh, too.' In the theatre, the cue is a gesture or word spoken by one actor which serves as a warning signal for another to say his or her words.

15. **to fluff one's lines** – to fail to perform well. 'Can you imagine speaking to a television audience of 150 million, Eddie? I'm sure you'd fluff your lines sometimes.'

16. **a dress-rehearsal** – a final preparation. 'In the early part of the 20th century, five years at a public school was a dress-rehearsal for military service on the Western Front.' A dress-rehearsal is the final rehearsal when actors wear the costumes in which they will appear at the performance.

17. **to be in the limelight** – to be the centre of public attention. Limelight usually has the meaning of an intense but passing attention. 'My daughter was in the limelight for a few days for challenging the school bully, but the excitement soon died down.' The limelight was used in the 19th century for lighting the stage.

It would focus on one actor on the stage, leaving the others in the dark. Limelight is produced by heating lime in a hot flame.

1. **to be in the spotlight** – to be the focus of attention. 'After the writer had published her feelings about her unfaithful husband, she was in the spotlight for some time.'

2. **to come into the spotlight** – to come to the attention of the public. 'The spy's treachery came into the spotlight when he showed off about it in his sensational autobiography.'

3. **to put someone/something under the spotlight** – to draw public attention to someone/something. 'The shortcomings of the NHS have been put under the spotlight time and time again and yet there still is no improvement.'

4. **to play to the gallery** – to court the applause of the uneducated by showing off in front of them. 'Although Borotra was one of the most brilliant tennis players of all time, he sometimes played to the gallery.' The cheapest seats in the theatre are in the gallery.

5. **to ring the curtain down** – to put an end to; used in connection with life, marriage, career, happiness, business, plans, etc. 'The scandal rang the curtain down on a promising career.' In former times, a bell was rung at the end of each act as a signal for the curtain to be lowered.

6. **resting** – a euphemistic phrase used by actors for being unemployed until they are offered another acting part. The duration of this 'resting' time is very unpredictable and may vary from a few weeks to several years. 'Poor Christine! She never seems to be offered exciting roles any more, and is still resting.'

The Opera

7. **it/the opera isn't over till the fat lady/someone sings** – there is still time for things to change. ' "I haven't come across anyone interesting yet at this party," Richard moaned. "But it's still quite early and more people are arriving," said his friend. "The opera isn't over till the fat lady sings!" '

Puppet Theatre

8. **a puppet** – someone who is under the control of someone else. 'It is feared that some officials in the government are the puppets of spin doctors.'

9. **a puppet government** – a government whose actions are under someone else's control. 'The rebels met secretly and discussed ways in which they could overthrow their puppet government.'

10. **to pull strings** – to make use of private influence to obtain favours. 'I've had no promotion, although I've been 10 years in the service. Can't you pull some strings for me?' From puppeteering, i.e. the manipulation of puppets by pulling the strings.

11. **with strings attached** – certain conditions have to be met. 'Margaret accepted the job, although there were strings attached – like starting at eight and working on Saturdays.'

12. **no strings attached** – without conditions. 'If you don't like the job, you can leave any time – no strings attached.'

13. **to have someone on a string** – to have someone under one's control. 'She won't do a thing without asking him first. He's got her on a string.'

Magic, Spells, Tricks

14. **like magic / to work like magic** – to have an astonishing effect. 'Your honey-and-onion drink worked like magic. My cough has completely gone!' cf. '**to work like a charm**' 43/9.

15. **if I had a magic wand . . .** – a picturesque way of expressing a vain wish. 'If I had a magic wand, I would do away with unemployment this very moment.' In fairy stories and in pantomime, the fairy godmother accomplishes good by waving her magic wand and making a wish which is immediately realized.

16. **to be/fall under someone's spell** – to be fascinated by someone. 'Mr Hancock is

far too old for her, but she seems to have fallen under his spell.'

1. **to break a spell** – to escape from the influence of someone. 'Ned's indifferent reaction to her tears had broken the spell he had over her.'

2. **a bag of tricks / the whole bag of tricks** – all of a person's tools or equipment. 'I've no idea where the plumber has gone, but I'm sure he'll be back; he has left his whole bag of tricks in the bathroom.' The term comes from the conjuror's bag in which he carries his equipment for the performance of his tricks.

3. **to do a vanishing trick/one of his vanishing tricks** – to disappear suddenly when it suits someone's purpose. 'The day before the rent was due, Andy did one of his vanishing tricks.' The allusion is to the magician's art of causing a person to disappear and reappear again.

4. **that should do the trick** – that should serve our purpose. 'I've stopped the bleeding and bandaged the wound; that should do the trick until you get him to hospital.'

5. **to fail to do the trick** – to take certain measures which then do not work. 'If Antony doesn't do his homework, don't allow him to go out today. If that fails to do the trick, withdraw his pocket money for a week.'

6. **to try/use every trick in the book** – to try every device one can think of, to go to any length to get the desired result. 'Frank so wanted to appear on the television programme and he tried every trick in the book, but it was all for nothing.'

7. **to have a trick** – to have a habit or mannerism. 'It sounds as if the man you were talking to was Paul, because Paul has the same trick of repeating himself.'

8. **to be/get up to one's old tricks again** – to use a device (generally dishonest) that one has used successfully in the past. 'So Philip has been up to his old tricks again. It's extraordinary how many people fall for his hard-luck story.'

9. **to know a trick or two/a thing or two** – to acquire a certain cunning in the course of one's experience. 'You learn a trick or two after 30 years in business.'

10. **to play a confidence trick on someone** – to tell someone a falsehood to get money out of him or her. So called because the success of the trick depends on winning the confidence of the victim.

/11. **dirty tricks** – deceitful and dishonourable acts.
    a dirty-tricks campaign – a campaign aimed at harming the integrity of a political opponent. 'During the election process for the new leader of the Party, several dirty-tricks campaigns were launched against the participating candidates.' Frequent usage: **a dirty-tricks campaign is in full swing**.

The Circus

12. **to walk a tight-rope** – to act with the greatest possible caution in an extremely delicate situation. 'The two teenage girls are always quarrelling with each other, so their mother has to walk a tight-rope between them.'

13. **to go/put through the hoop / to jump through hoops** – to subject someone to a harsh discipline or procedure. 'The lieutenant really put us through the hoop when we joined the ship.' 'Jenny had to jump through hoops to open her environmental awareness centre, but she managed it at last.' At circuses, lions, tigers and leopards are put through the hoop for the entertainment of the audience. cf. '**to go through the mill**' 281/3.

14. **juggling / a juggling act** – to try to balance several different tasks at the same time. Frequently used when one parent, usually a woman, has to try to apportion time fairly for housework, children, career and husband/partner. Frequent usage: **single parents trying to juggle complicated lives; four (etc.) children under the age of 10 are a juggling act; we are always juggling with too many tasks; we have to juggle child-care and work.**

15. **as thin as a whip / whip-thin** – lean and slender but still powerful. 'Rachel

didn't like the look of the new sports teacher. She was as thin as a whip and looked very grim.' cf. **'as thin/skinny as a rake'** 252/9; **'to look like a stick insect'** 78/12.

1. **a tongue like a whip** – to make cutting and rather cruel remarks; to be very sharp-witted. 'I do feel sorry for you, Polly, having a mother-in-law like that. She's got a tongue like a whip, and no sense of humour.'

   one's voice cracks like a whip – the sound of one's voice cuts through other noise, demanding attention. ' "Answer me now, Joshua!" The teacher's clear voice cracked like a whip and a deathly hush descended on the classroom.'

2. **to have/hold the whip hand** – to have someone in one's power. cf. **'to gain the upper hand'** 98/5.

3. **a crackdown** – putting a stop to certain activities, etc. 'Hotels have been threatened with a crackdown on prices, as they are often not making clear how much guests are paying and for what.'

Word

1. **a man of his word** – a trustworthy man who will do what he promises.

2. **a word to the wise** – one word of advice or even a hint is enough for an intelligent man or woman. The derivation is from the Latin '*verbum sat sapienti*' (a word is enough to the wise).

3. **as good as one's word** – to do exactly what one has promised. Often said when the promise is unlikely to be kept. 'I didn't think for one moment Bob would keep his promise but he was as good as his word.'

4. **from the word go** – right from the very beginning. 'From the word go Smithers has made trouble for us.'

5. **to give one's word** – to pledge one's honour on the truth of one's word. cf. '**word of honour' 325/1**.

6. **to give the word to** – (of officers in the armed services and the police) to command. 'The major gave his men the word to open fire on the enemy.'

7. **to break one's word** – to fail to do what one has promised.

8. **to go back on one's word** – to change one's mind about keeping a promise in a way which causes great indignation. 'You can't go back on your word now; without the loan you promised us, we shall lose all our savings.'

9. **to have a word with someone** – to have a brief conversation with someone.

10. **to have the last word** – (1) to insist one is in the right in an argument. 'Denise is so argumentative; she will always have the last word.' (2) to take the final decision. 'I like your cost-cutting idea but you had better talk it over with the manager; he has the last word.' (3) the most authoritative source of information on a subject. 'Gilbert has the last word on the life of Winston Churchill, having written many volumes on his chosen subject.'

11. **his word is law** – he must be obeyed. 'When we were children, our father expected us to do what he told us without questioning his orders. His word was law.'

12. **I don't believe a word of it** – the whole story is a lie from start to finish.

13. **in a word** – very briefly. 'Our son is bored with the office work, he dislikes his colleagues and he quarrels with the boss. In a word, he hates the job.'

14. **to keep one's word** – to do what one has promised.

15. **to leave word** – to leave a message. 'They left word for Anne at the hospital to come back later.'

16. **mum's the word** – don't talk about it to anyone. This is a secret between the two of us; 'mum' is used here to describe the expressive sound made by a person when his lips are closed. The word 'mum' is related to the verb 'mumble' (to speak weakly), and to 'mummers', who, in earlier times, entertained at Christmas parties in dumb shows.

17. **my word!** – an exclamation of surprise. 'My word! This is the second time you've had a rise in your wages this year. Aren't you doing well!'

1. **my word is my bond** – my word is as good as a signed contract. 'You can rely on my promise, even though it is not in writing. My word is my bond.'

2. **not the word for it** – an inadequate or insufficiently strong description. 'Impolite is not the word for it; he was downright insulting!'

3. **not to get in a word edgeways** – to find it impossible to take part in a conversation because the other person is talking continuously.

4. **to spread/preach the word** – to preach the gospel of Jesus Christ. 'We often see Jehovah's Witnesses going from door to door spreading the word.'

5. **to put in a good word for someone** – to praise or recommend someone to a third party, who is in a position to help him or her. 'I would like the job Mrs Hornby is advertising. When you see her tomorrow, can you put in a good word for me.'

6. **say the word** – you only need to ask, and your wishes will be carried out. 'Say the word, and I'll marry you tomorrow.'

7. **send word** – send a message. 'As soon as you arrive, send word that you are safe.'

8. **spread the word** – inform as many people as possible. 'Jack Dickson will be speaking at the town hall at eight o'clock on Saturday. Spread the word.'

9. **word spreads / to spread the (good) word** – to pass on good news or praise of something to many people. 'Last January, only two children had read the latest Harry Potter book. But word spread and, by March, everyone in the class had read it.' 'Anyone paying his gas bill within a few days will get a reduction of several pounds. Do spread the good word!'

10. **to take someone at his word** – to act on the literal meaning of someone's words without making sure that he or she means to be taken seriously. 'I told Stephen to be sure to visit us if ever he came to Spain. Two weeks later, he arrived at our villa with six suitcases. He had taken me at my word.'

11. **to stand by one's word** – to honour one's promise. 'I shall stand by my word and buy shares in your company, even though their value has fallen.'

12. **to take someone's word for it** – to believe that he or she is speaking the truth without making further inquiries. 'Don't take my word for it – you can see for yourself.'

13. **the buzz word** – the fashionable word. A 'buzz word' might be 'community', e.g. 'community services', 'community care', 'community health', the 'Chinese community', the 'community centre', and 'community singing'. 'Stress' is the buzz word of modern times.

14. **a dirty word** – (1) a word that is frowned upon, e.g. a swear-word. ' "Don't use such dirty words!" said the mother to her young son.' (2) an idea that is not favoured. 'Is marriage such a dirty word? In my view, stable marriages families are the foundation of a good society.'

15. **the last word in** – the very best and most up-to-date. 'The hotel is the last word in luxury and elegance.'

16. **the operative word** – the most important word. 'You can take any route you like but please drive carefully. The operative word is carefully.'

17. **a kettle word** – a word pronounced in exactly the same way as another but which has a different spelling and a different meaning, e.g. hair/hare; stair/stare; mail/male; hole/whole; bear/bare. The term (also known as a homophone) is derived from the image of water boiling in a kettle and coming out as steam in two different places (through the spout and through the hole in the lid).

18. **upon my word** – an exclamation expressing surprise (usually unpleasant) or impatience. 'Upon my word, what is the matter with our managing clerk? He is always ill – he must be a hypochondriac!'

19. **the word is** – a rumour, usually well founded, that something will happen. 'The word is that next month we shall be ordered overseas.'

1. **word came** – information was received.

2. **word for word** – literally. 'I translated the passage word for word from German into English.'

3. **word of honour** – (first person) I pledge my honour that I am telling the truth. cf. **'to give one's word' 323/5**.

4. **word perfect** – able to recite every word of a poem, part, etc., without a mistake.

5. **word splitting** (derogatory) – making subtle distinctions, e.g. distinguishing between 'governance' and 'government', 'gentlemanly' and 'gentlemanlike', 'preciseness' and 'precision'. cf. **'to split hairs' 84/1**.

Words

6. **a war of words** – quarrelling and arguments between two parties, a hostile exchange of opinions. 'Dave and Amanda had completely different ideas about where to spend their summer holiday, and what started as an amicable discussion soon degenerated into a war of words.'

7. **a man of few words** – someone who avoids conversation whenever he can. Sometimes used as a euphemism for an unsociable person.
    a man of many words – a garrulous person, one who prefers three words when one would have done.

8. **actions speak louder than words** – 'The clergyman had often preached against the sin of drunkenness. One day, he was arrested for being drunk and disorderly. Actions speak louder than words.'

9. **to bandy words** – to enter into an argument with someone. 'Don't bandy words with that man. He is a violent character.'

10. **big words** – boastful words. ' "We shall beat the champions easily." "Big words!" '

11. **empty words** – meaningless words. ' "Sam telephoned this morning to apologize for his behaviour last night." "Empty words!" '

12. **famous last words** – a humorous comment predicting disaster for an impractical undertaking. ' "With modern technology, we can climb Everest in half the time it took Hillary and Tenzing in 1953." "Famous last words!" '

13. **hang upon someone's words** – to pay slavish attention to what someone is saying. 'Sharon is full of admiration for Paul and hangs upon his words.' 'Words' may be replaced by 'lips' with the same meaning.

14. **to have words with** – to quarrel with. 'Ever since my sister had words with our neighbour, he hasn't spoken to us.'

15. **in other words** – put in another way in order to summarize what the speaker/writer has said or to deduce his true intention from the words he has used. ' "Kate is sorry she can't come with us to France but the crossing always makes her feel sick and the trip would be too expensive." "In other words, she doesn't want to come with us!" '

16. **let the words stand** – make no change. 'The editor is satisfied with the original wording of your article. Let the words stand.'

17. **mark my words** – listen carefully to what I am telling you. 'Mark my words, the boy will ruin himself before he is 40.' Said by George V about his son, Edward Prince of Wales, shortly before the death of the king.

18. **not in so many words** – not actually said, although it was clearly meant. ' "Did Margaret refuse your offer of help?" "Not in so many words, but it was obvious from her manner that she did not want any help from me." '

19. **not to mince one's words** – to speak bluntly without troubling to be tactful. 'I won't mince my words: you are rude to the staff and insolent to the manager; you will have to go.'

20. **too (adjective) for words** – too (adjective) to be expressed in words. 'Because of the epidemic we can't leave the hospital. It is too sickening for words.' Many adjectives can be used with this idiom, most of which express the speaker's feelings, e.g. beautiful, ugly, frightful, boring,

annoying, exasperating, sickening, disgusting and disappointing.

1. **waste words on someone** – waste time and effort speaking to someone. 'Don't waste words on that man; he isn't interested in our complaint.'

2. **to weigh one's words** – to choose one's words with the greatest care. 'When you are being interviewed for a job, you must weigh your words before answering the questions they put to you.'

3. **be lost for words / to be at a loss for words** – to be so astonished or shocked that one is unable to put one's feelings into words. 'Julia was so shocked by Philip's behaviour that she was at a loss for words.'

4. **words fail me** – I cannot express my feelings in words. 'When I try to describe my experience in the prison camp, words fail me.'

Possessives and plurals of nouns follow immediately after the singular unless there is a spelling change within the word. Thus **day's** *and* **days** *follow* **day** *and precede* **daylight***; but* **men** *follows* **memory***, not* **man** *and* **man's***, and* **ladies** *precedes* **lady***.*

A

A, A.1. 256/13

ABC, as easy/simple as ABC **265/4**

ability, Houdini-like ability **230/4**

above-board 311/4

abyss, look into the abyss, an **a.** of despair/loneliness/misery/ignorance **16/13**

accent, a cut-glass accent **169/17**; a lady-like **a. 235/4**; an a. you could cut with a knife **170/7**

accident, a happy accident **138/2**; look like an **a.** waiting to happen **138/3**

account, square an account **267/5**

accounts, doctor the accounts **278/6**; square **a. 267/4**

ace, trump someone's ace **310/12**

Achilles', Achilles' heel **225/13**

acid, an acid test **268/12**

acne, acne Majorca **134/13**

act, an act of God **42/12**; act on a whim **319/11**; a hard/tough **a.** to follow **319/9**; a juggling **a. 321/14**; clean up one's **a. 319/10**; get in on the **a. 319/7**; get/put one's **a.** together **319/8**; put on an **a. 319/6**; read the riot **a. 277/11**

action, an action spearheaded by **249/1**

actions, actions feel like a sword through one's heart **245/1**

Adam, not to know someone from Adam **223/12**; the old **A.**, as old as **A. 223/11**

Adonis, an Adonis, an **A.** complex **224/15**

advocate, the devil's advocate **276/14**

affair, a Heath Robinson affair **229/4**; a hole-and-corner **a. 158/15**

Aga, an Aga saga **172/4**

Agag, walk like Agag **224/1**

age, a green old age **4/16**; an **a. 33/13**; a ripe old **a. 33/12**; be/act one's **a. 33/15**; come of **a. 33/9**; feel one's **a. 33/16**; look/

looking good for one's **a. 33/17**; New **A. 33/20**; show one's **a. 33/18**; the **A.** of Aquarius **33/19**; the **a.** of consent **33/10**; the awkward **a. 33/11**; the electronic **a. 34/1**; the Golden **A. 10/8**; the third **a. 259/13**

ages, it's ages since . . . **33/14**

agony, an agony aunt/uncle, **a.** column **136/4**; pile on the agony **136/3**

agreement, a gentleman's agreement **276/17**; a one-sided **a. 256/18**

air, air rage **126/17**; an **a.** kiss **12/3**; as free as (the) **a. 12/7**; clear the **a. 11/12**; cut the **a. 11/4**; go up in the **a. 12/4**; crystal **a. 169/16**; hot **a. 11/11**; in the **a. 12/5**; into thin **a. 11/3**; make the **a.** turn blue **3/10**; on/off the **a. 11/14**; out of thin **a. 11/3**; sniff the **a.** like an old war-horse **56/11**; something in the **a. 12/6**; walk/dance on **a. 12/2**

airs, airs and graces **11/7**; put on **a.**/give oneself **a. 11/6**

airing, give public airing to something **11/13**

air-kissing 12/3

airlines, cowboy airlines **281/7**

airy-fairy 11/8

aisle, head down the aisle **150/9**

alabaster, an alabaster face/**a.** skin **85/23**

Aladdin's, an Aladdin's cave **227/3**

alarm, set alarm bells ringing **160/16**; sound **a.** bells **160/15**

albatross, have an albatross round one's neck **71/2**

Alec, a smart Alec **222/16**

Alice, like Alice in Wonderland **228/7**

Alice-like, 228/7

alive, alive and kicking **37/10**

all-time, an all-time high/low **27/4**

alpha, alpha and omega **265/5**

also-ran, an also-ran **308/8**

background, a good background/no **b.** 104/
12; have a silver-spoon **b.** 295/6
backhander 97/23
backing, give one's (full) backing 103/13
backlash 103/14
back-pedal 303/16
backroom, backroom boys 285/15
backscratching 104/14
backseat, a backseat driver 153/11
backstairs 161/16
backtrack 148/16
back-up, a back-up service 103/12
bacon, bring home the bacon 181/3; go
together like **b.** and eggs 181/5; save someone's **b.** 181/4
badger, to badger 62/1
bag, a bag of bones 198/13; a **b.** of nerves
109/17; a **b.** of tricks/the whole **b.** of tricks
321/2; a mixed **b.** 198/16; **b.** and baggage
198/12; growing **b.** 198/17; it's in the **b.**
198/14; look like an old **b.**, an old **b.** 199/
2
bags, pack one's bags 198/15
bag-lady, look like a bag-lady 199/3
bag-people 199/4
bait, rise to the bait 303/9
baker's, a baker's dozen 261/7
bald-headed, go bald-headed at 82/10
ball, a fancy-dress ball 191/11; be a **b.** and
chain on someone 251/8; have/not to have
a crystal **b.** 314/7; have the **b.** at one's feet
300/10; keep the **b.** rolling 300/12; on the
b. 300/11; play **b.** 300/8; the **b.** is in your
court 300/6
ballgame, a completely/whole new ballgame
298/2
balloon, go down like a lead balloon 313/8;
swell like a **b.** 313/10; to **b.** 313/9; when
the **b.** goes up 279/7
ball-park, in the ball-park, a **b.** figure 300/
7
balm, like balm to one's soul 43/8
ban, a blanket ban 165/4
banana, a banana republic 183/13; **b.** fingers
183/15; a **b.** skin 183/12
bananas, go bananas 183/14
band, a one-man band 257/5; be/feel like an
elastic **b.** about to snap 200/7
bandbox, bandbox fresh / **b.** neat 198/11
bandit, a one-armed bandit 257/4
bandwagon, climb/jump on the bandwagon
237/3
bank, break the bank, without breaking the **b.**
292/12
baptism, a baptism of fire 274/13
bar, colour bar 2/4
barbed-wire, barbed-wire defences 240/5

Barbour, the Barbour brigade 231/8
bare-faced 84/8
bare-knuckle, a bare-knuckle fighter 239/20
bargain, drive a hard bargain 151/16
barge-pole, not to touch with a barge-pole
205/15
bark, his bark is worse than his bite 54/6
barrack-room, a barrack-room lawyer 276/
12
barrel, over a barrel 151/2; scrape the **b.**/the
bottom of the **b.** 151/3
bat, as blind as a bat 62/8; off one's own **b.**
301/6; play a straight **b.** 301/5; run like a
b. out of hell 62/9
bats, bats in the belfry 62/10
batteries, recharge one's batteries 254/5
battle, a battle of wits 120/12; a **b.** royal 235/
8; a pitched **b.** 239/2; a running **b.** 239/9;
be locked in **b.** 239/6; fight a losing **b.**
239/5; half the **b.** 239/3; mark out the **b.**
lines 239/8; the **b.** of the bulge 239/4; win
a **b.** 239/1
battle-axe 248/11
bay, at bay 303/5; keep at **b.** 303/5
beam, broad in the beam 204/9; focus like a
laser **b.** on something 168/8; on one's **b.**
ends 204/10
bean, not to have a bean 184/17; not worth a
b. 184/18
beans, full of beans 184/15; know how many
b. make five 184/19; spill the **b.** 184/16
bear, give someone a bear hug/a friendly **b.**
hug 65/4; like a **b.** with a sore head, as
cross/savage as a **b.** with a sore head 65/3
bears, bears and bulls on the Stock Exchange
65/5
beard, a beard peppered with grey 182/4;
sport a **b.** 298/12; a goatee **b.** / a goat-like
b. 59/4
bearish, bearish of a share 65/5
beast, nail the beast 52/9
beat, off someone's beat 279/15
beauty, Beauty and the Beast 52/10; **b.** food
174/5; drop-dead **b.** 39/4
beaver, beaver away 61/17
bed, a bed of nails 164/7; a **b.** of roses 46/9; a
b. of thorns 47/15; a Procrustean **b.** 226/
8; get out of **b.** on the wrong side 164/3;
have made one's **b.** and have to lie on it
164/4; it isn't a **b.** of roses 46/10
bedfellows, make good/bad bedfellows 164/5
bedlam, bedlam/absolute **b.** 209/15
bedrock 17/4
bedside, a good bedside manner 164/2
bee, a bee in one's bonnet 196/6; as busy as a
b. 77/7; take to something like a **b.** to
honey 77/10

bullish, bullish of a share **65/5**
bullshit, talk bullshit **217/9**
bully-boy, bully-boy tactics **271/11**
bum-bag 199/1
bunch, a bunch of fives **260/2**
burglar, a cat burglar **55/8**
burn-out, career burn-out, **b.** syndrome **285/13**
bus, miss the bus **153/6**
bush, beat about the bush **50/8**; spread like a **b.** fire **15/8**; take to the **b. 50/9**
bush-telegraph 50/10
business, a bad business **284/12**; have no **b.** in a place **284/7**; make something one's **b. 284/5**; mean **b. 284/6**; mind your own **b. 284/8**; monkey **b. 64/7**; not to be in the **b.** of **284/11**; put **b.** someone's way **148/10**; send someone about his **b. 284/9**; unfinished **b. 284/10**
busman's, a busman's holiday **280/13**
bus-stop-queue, bus-stop-queue rage **126/16**
busybody 80/3
butcher 280/7
butter, a butter mountain **176/4**; as if **b.** wouldn't melt in one's mouth **176/3**; as soft as **b. 175/17**; **b.** up **175/18**; spread the **b.** too thick **176/1**
butter-fingers 176/2
butterflies, butterflies in one's stomach/ tummy **77/4**
butterfly, a butterfly mind, like a **b.**, as elusive as a **b. 77/2**; break a **b.** on a wheel **77/3**
butterfly-like 77/2
button, as bright as a button/as cute as a **b. 196/15**; on the **b. 196/14**; press the **b. 197/2**
buttoned, have something buttoned up **197/3**
button-hole, button-hole someone **197/1**
by-gones, let **b.** be by-gones **34/11**

C

cabinet, kitchen cabinet **163/4**
Caesarean a Caesarean operation/a **C. 225/11**
Caesar's, like Caesar's wife **225/12**
Cain, raise Cain **223/14**
cake, a cake walk **179/4**; over-egg the **c. 175/15**; that takes the **c.! 179/14**; you can't have your **c.** and eat it **179/2**
cakes, go like hot cakes **179/7**
calf, kill the fatted calf **58/8**; the golden **c. 295/4**
calf-love 58/9
calibre 244/5
call, a cold call **283/7**
calm, the calm before the storm **23/13**
calorie, a calorie bomb **247/11**

camel, swallow a camel and strain at a gnat **63/14**
cameo a cameo role/part **296/1**
campaign, a campaign spearheaded by **249/1**; a press **c. 286/3**
can, carry the can **169/3**; open/open up a **c.** of worms **76/7**
canary, sing like a canary **71/6**
cancer, the cancer at the heart of it all **135/4**; spread/grow/invade like **c. 135/3**
candidate, a squeaky-clean candidate **236/11**
candle, burn the candle at both ends **168/11**; not fit to hold a **c.** to/cannot hold a **c.** to **168/10**
candle-end, candle-end economies **169/1**
candy, an arm candy **96/7**
cannon, a loose cannon **244/7**
cannon-fodder 244/8
canoe, paddle one's own canoe **205/14**
canter, win in a canter/an easy **c. 305/6**
Canute, like King Canute **229/7**
Canute-like 229/7
canvassing, cold canvassing **283/7**
cap, go cap in hand **196/3**; if the **c.** fits, wear it **196/1**; put on one's thinking **c. 195/16**; set one's **c.** at **196/4**; throw up one's **c.**/ throw one's **c.** in the air **196/2**; wear a dunce's **c. 195/17**
caps, that caps it all/to cap it all **195/15**
captive, a captive market **151/4**
car, hot-wire a car **254/2**
carbuncle, like a monstrous carbuncle **134/14**
card, a card/quite a **c. 309/11**; have a **c.** up one's sleeve **310/6**; one's leading/trump **c. 309/12**; play one's best **c. 310/1**; the red **c. 3/3**; the yellow **c. 5/9**
cards, hold all the cards in one's hands **310/3**; on the **c. 310/5**; play one's **c.** close to one's chest **103/1**; play one's **c.** well **310/2**; put one's **c.** on the table **310/8**; show one's **c. 310/4**; stack the **c. 310/7**
career, career burn-out **285/13**
Carey Street, be/end up in Carey Street **209/14**
carpet, bite the carpet **167/10**; like a magic **c. 167/12**; roll out the red **c. 167/9**; sweep something under the **c. 167/7**
carpet-bagger 167/11
carpeted 167/8
carrot, like a carrot to a donkey **57/21**; more **c.** and less stick **185/7**
cart, put the cart before the horse **57/7**; upset the apple **c. 183/8**
cartload, as clever as a cartload of monkeys **64/6**
Casanova, he's a real Casanova! **229/10**

case, a case of history repeating itself **268/5**; a cast-iron **c. 18/8**; a ground-breaking **c. 17/14**; an open-and-shut **c. 276/9**; it's a **c.** of stick and carrot **185/7**

cash, cash in on **290/14**; hard **c. 290/16**; be strapped for **c. 290/17**

cash-in-hand 290/15

cashstrapped 290/17

cast-iron, a cast-iron case, a **c.** defence/guarantee/pledge, a **c.** constitution **18/8**

castles, castles in Spain **211/3**; **c.** in the air **12/1**

cat, a cat burglar **55/8**; a **c.** may look at a king **55/20**; a **c.** nap **55/6**; a fat **c. 56/3**; bell the **c. 55/17**; grin/smile like a Cheshire **C.**/like the Cheshire **C. 228/8**; has the **c.** got your tongue? **55/18**; lead a **c.** and dog life **55/1**; let the **c.** out of the bag **55/9**; like a **c.** on hot bricks **55/10**; like the **c.** that swallowed the cream **56/1**; not a **c.** in hell's chance **55/13**; play **c.** and mouse **55/2**; put/set the **c.** among the pigeons **55/3**

cat's, be made a cat's paw of **55/19**; **c.** pyjamas **56/2**; **c.** whiskers **56/2**; like the Cheshire **C.** smile **228/8**

cats, rain cats and dogs **19/11**

cat-call 55/7

catch, a Catch-22 situation **261/15**; **c.** out **301/4**; have a **c.** in it **304/10**

Catholic, in Catholic circles **266/12**

catty, be catty **55/4**

cauliflower, a cauliflower ear **185/11**

caution, throw caution to the winds **23/4**

cavalry, charge in like the 7th Cavalry **241/10**

cave, an Aladdin's cave **227/3**

caviare, caviare to the general **74/10**

ceiling, a glass ceiling **161/14**

cellar, have a good cellar **163/5**

ceremony, stand on ceremony **236/5**

certainty, a moral certainty **122/4**

chain, a chain **251/6**; a **c.** gang **251/7**; a **c.** letter **251/5**

chair, address the Chair **165/18**; appeal to the **C. 165/19**; take the **C. 165/17**

chairs, playing musical chairs **165/20**

chalice, a poisoned chalice **169/6**

chalk, as different as chalk and cheese **175/1**; as white as **c. 269/12**, not by a long **c. 269/11**; not to know **c.** from cheese **175/2**

chalk-white 269/12

challenge, duck a challenge **70/4**

chameleon-like 62/11

champagne, a champagne lifestyle **186/20**; a **c.** socialist **187/1**

chance, a chance in a million, not one **c.** in a million **262/11**; a dog's **c. 53/6**; a golden

c. 10/2; an earthly **c. 16/7**; a fighting **c. 239/15**; a sporting **c. 298/11**; jump at the **c. 306/7**

chancery, put someone in Chancery **209/10**

change, a change of heart **116/3**; a sea **c. 205/11**; get no **c.** out of **290/18**

chapter, a chapter of accidents **287/7**; give/quote **c.** and verse **274/12**; the final **c. 287/6**

character, an anaemic character **134/15**; blacken someone's **c. 7/7**; in **c. 122/12**; out of **c. 122/12**; (quite) a **c. 122/13**

charge, trump up a charge **310/13**

Charlie, a proper Charlie/make a **C.** of someone **222/14**

charm, work like a charm **43/9**

chase, a wild goose chase **70/9**

chaser, an ambulance chaser **138/4**; a storm **c. 24/3**

chasm, a yawning chasm **125/2**

checkmate 309/2

cheek, cheek by jowl with **94/12**; have a **c. 94/8**; none of your **c. 94/10**; the **c.** of the devil **94/9**; turn the other **c. 94/11**

cheeks, petal-soft cheeks **46/6**

cheerleader 301/2

cheese, a big cheese **175/4**; hard **c.! 174/6**; mousetrap **c. 60/3**

cheesed, cheesed off **175/5**

cheese-paring, be cheese-paring **175/3**

cheese-parings 175/3

chemistry, a special/strange chemistry **268/10**

cheque, a blank cheque **291/8**

Cheshire, grin/smile like a Cheshire Cat/like the **C.** Cat/like the **C.** Cat's smile **228/8**

chest, a war chest **238/5**; get something off one's **c. 103/2**; one's **c.** is as flat as a pancake **179/10**; open something up like a treasure **c. 296/6**

chestnut, an old chestnut **49/24**

chestnuts, pull the chestnuts out of the fire **15/7**

chicken, as tender as a chicken **69/8**; **c.** feed, make something look like **c.** feed **69/14**; **c.**/**c.** hearted **69/5**; **c.** out **69/6**; look like a plucked **c. 69/12**; look like a trussed **c. 69/13**; run around like a headless **c.**, run something like a headless **c. 69/11**; she's no (spring) **c. 69/7**; that's like asking which came first, the **c.** or the egg **69/10**

chickens, don't count your chickens **69/9**

chiefs, there are too many chiefs and not enough Indians **219/4**

child, a child wife **142/7**; a sandwich **c. 177/5**; **c.** of nature **142/4**; latch-key **c. 159/17**; like a **c. 142/1**; love **c. 142/5**; the **c.** is

spoil for a **f. 239/13**; take the **f.** out of someone **239/14**

fighter, a bare-knuckle fighter, a dirty **f. 239/ 20**

fighting, fighting fit **239/18**; hand-to-hand **f. 98/20**

figure, a father figure **140/16**; a **f.** of fun **80/9**; cut a poor **f. 80/8**; have a stick-insect **f. 78/12**

film, a blue film **4/11**

finances, finances are tight **289/4**

finger, a finger in every pie **180/2**; have a **f.** on the pulse **102/10**; have more (of something) in one's little **f.** than someone else has in his whole body **102/13**; I can't put my **f.** on it but . . . **102/1**; lay a **f.** on **102/ 7**; not to lift a **f. 102/11**; point the **f.** at **102/5**; pull/take your **f.** out **102/12**; put a **f.** to one's lips **91/15**; put the **f.** on **102/9**; twist someone round one's little **f. 101/15**

fingers, all fingers and thumbs **101/11**; be able to count on the **f.**/on the **f.** of one hand **102/6**; be caught with one's **f.** in the till **99/20**; burn one's **f. 101/14**; **f.** like bananas/banana **f. 183/15**; green **f. 4/15**; have itching **f. 134/11**; keep one's **f.** crossed **101/18**; put two **f.** up to something **102/8**; slip through one's **f. 102/3**; snap one's **f.** at **102/4**; work one's **f.** to the bone **102/2**

fingertips, at one's fingertips **101/16**; to one's **f. 101/17**

fire, as quick as fire/quick **f. 15/5**; as red as **f. 2/6**; as sure as **f. 15/6**; catch **f. 15/2**; come under **f. 14/17**; **f.** and brimstone **15/10**; **f.** away! **14/9**; fight **f.** with **f. 14/16**; friendly **f. 15/1**; hang **f. 14/12**; play with **f. 15/4**; spread like wild **f.**/like a bush **f.**/like prairie **f. 15/8**; through **f.** and water **14/8**; where's the **f.? 14/10**

fired, be fired **14/13**

fire-bug 78/2

fire-eater 14/7

fireguard, as useless as a chocolate fireguard **178/15**

firestorm, trigger a firestorm **15/9**

first, first and last **257/7**; **f.** come, **f.** served **257/6**; get a **f. 257/13**

first-night, first-night nerves **319/12**

fish, a big fish **73/1**; a big **f.** in a small pond **73/2**; a cold **f. 73/4**; a queer **f. 73/3**; cry stinking **f. 73/10**; drink like a **f. 73/9**; have other **f.** to fry **73/12**; land a **f. 73/5**; like a **f.** out of water **73/6**; like being in a **f.** bowl **74/3**; need something like a **f.** needs a bicycle **74/4**; neither **f.**, flesh, fowl nor good red herring, neither **f.**, flesh nor fowl

73/11; only a small **f. 73/1**; there are plenty more **f.** in the sea **73/13**

fishes, feed the fishes **73/14**

fishcake, the fishcake syndrome **179/11**

fish-wife 141/12

fit, a fit of nerves **110/2**; throw a **f. 137/1**

fits, by fits and starts **137/2**

five, give someone five/high **f. 260/2**

fix, a quick fix **137/9**

flag, hang out or show the white flag **6/6**; the **f.** at half-mast **256/11**

flame, an old flame **15/11**

flames, fan the flames **15/12**

flash, a flash in the pan **171/15**

flea, with a flea in his ear **78/8**; a (mere) **f.**-bite **78/7**

flea-market 78/9

flesh, flesh and blood **110/9**; **f.** out **110/11**; goose **f. 70/11**; in the **f. 110/8**; make one's **f.** creep **110/13**; one's own **f.** and blood **110/10**; press the **f. 110/15**; put on **f. 110/12**

flexitime, work flexitime **32/22**

flies, descend/be like flies on or around someone **76/15**; die/dying off/killed/drop/shoot down like **f. 76/14**; no **f.** on him **76/13**; swarm like **f.** around someone/something **76/16**

flight, flight of fancy **125/9**

fling, have a **f.**/embark on a **f. 139/9**

flint-hearted 18/9

flit, a moonlight flit **25/2**

flock, like a flock of sheep **58/11**; shepherd his **f. 280/2**

flood, before the Flood **14/3**; stem the **f. 14/4**

floods, be in floods of tears **14/5**

floodgates, open the floodgates **14/6**

floor, cross the floor of the House **161/7**; fall through the **f. 161/10**; **f.** show **161/13**; get in on the ground **f. 161/12**; have/take the **f. 161/9**; shop **f. 283/1**; sink through the **f. 161/11**; wipe the **f.** with **161/8**

flow, go with the flow **14/1**

flower, flower people **46/1**; **f.** power, **46/1**.

flowers, flowers in May **46/2**; say it with **f.! 46/3**

flu, spread like flu in winter **132/17**

flush, in the first flush of, the first **f.** of love, courtship **257/10**

fly, a fly in the ointment **76/10**; a **f.** on the wall **76/12**; he/she couldn't hurt/harm a **f. 76/11**; trap/catch/capture something like a **f.** in amber **77/1**

fly-by-night, a fly-by-night operator **32/8**

focus, a focus group **236/17**

fog, in a fog **21/6**

hellbent, hellbent on **44/14**
hellhole **44/15**
hello, a golden hello **294/16**
helm, be at the helm **204/15**
hen, hen party/night **68/16**; like a **h.** with one chicken **68/18**; look like a plucked **h. 69/12**
Henry, Hooray Henry **222/17**
Herod, out-herod Herod **224/10**
herring, a red herring across the path **74/6**
hey-day **31/9**
hiccup, only a hiccup/a mere **h. 135/1**
high, an all-time high **27/4**
high-brow **88/6**
high-flyer **285/10**
high-handed **96/21**
high-profile, a high-profile life **36/9**
high-street, high-street Titans **225/2**
highway, the information highway **146/2**
hill, be over the hill **152/4**; up **h.** and down dale **152/2**
hills, as old as the hills **152/3**
hilt, up to the hilt **245/11**
hinge, hinge on **159/15**
hip, shoot from the hip **246/9**
hire, hire and fire **14/14**
history, airbrush someone out of history **268/3**; ancient/past **h. 268/4**; go down in **h. 268/2**; **h.** repeats itself, **h.** teaches us . . . **268/5**; make **h. 267/18**
hit-and-run **307/13**
hobbled, be doubly hobbled **259/5**
hobby, a rich man's hobby **285/4**; ride a **h.** horse (to death) **57/2**
Hobson's, Hobson's choice **231/1**
hog, go the whole hog **59/18**; to **h. 59/17**
hole, go into a black hole **7/17**; like the Black **H.** of Calcutta **7/18**; make a **h.** in one's purse, something is set to blow a big **h.** in one's purse/wallet **197/12**; make a **h.** in the water **13/6**; need/want something like a **h.** in the head **82/15**; the nineteenth **h. 261/12**
holes, pick holes in **202/4**
hole-and-corner, a hole-and-corner affair **158/15**
hole-in-the-wall **156/14**
holiday, a busman's holiday **280/13**; make a Roman **h. 218/5**
Hollywood, in Hollywood circles **266/12**
holy, the holy of holies **274/3**
Holy Grail **41/6**
home, a broken home **155/19**; a green **h. 5/1**; a **h.** from **h. 155/15**; a **h.** truth, close to **h.**; **156/4**; an 'at **h.**', be 'at **h.**' to people **155/13**; be/feel at **h.** with **155/11**; bring **h.** the bacon **181/3**; bring something **h. 156/3**;

come **h.** to roost **67/16**; feel like **h. 155/12**; **h.** and dry **156/1**; **h.** in on **156/7**; not at **h. 155/14**; nothing to write **h.** about **156/5**; one's **h.** becomes a battleground **239/7**; romp **h. 156/6**; the last **h. 155/18**; waltz **h. 317/1**
Homer, Homer sometimes nods **225/8**
home-shopping **155/16**
homesick **155/17**
homework, do one's homework **156/2**
honey, a honey trap **177/13**; be as sweet as **h. 177/12**
honeymoon, the honeymoon is over **177/16**
honey-pot, a honey-pot town **177/14**; **h.** areas **177/15**
honour, no honour among thieves **281/14**
hoof, show the cloven hoof **59/5**
hook, by hook or by crook **253/4**; let someone off the **h. 303/12**; swallow **h.** line and sinker/anchor **303/10**
hooked, be hooked on **303/11**
hoop, go/put through the hoop **321/13**
hoops, jump through hoops **321/13**
hooray, Hooray Henry **222/17**
hoots, not to care two hoots **258/2**
hop, catch someone on the hop **306/15**
hope a fond hope **129/13**; **h.** against **h. 129/12**
hopes, build up someone's hopes **129/15**; pin one's **h.** on **129/14**
hopping, hopping mad **306/16**
horizon, room (large) on the horizon **24/14**
horizons, broaden one's horizons **24/13**
hornets', bring a hornets' nest about one's ears **77/12**
horror, a horror scenario **128/4**; have a **h.** of the knife **170/10**
horse, a dark horse **56/9**; a **h.** of another colour **57/13**; a **h.** whisperer **57/15**; an old war **h. 56/11**; a stalking **h. 56/10**; a Trojan **h. 218/20**; a willing **h. 56/15**; back the wrong **h. 56/12**; eat like a **h. 56/13**; flog a dead **h. 57/1**; give the **h.** its head **81/10**; **h.** sense **56/18**; on one's high **h.**, don't get on your high **h.** with me **57/4**; ride a hobby **h.** (to death) **57/2**; work like a **h. 56/14**
horse's, straight from the horse's mouth **57/5**
horses, frighten the horses **57/12**; hold your **h.! 157/13**; **h.** for courses **57/14**; swop **h.** in mid-stream/halfway across the stream **57/10**; white **h. 6/10**; wild **h.** would not drag it out of me **57/11**
horse-laugh **56/16**
horseplay **56/17**
horse-trading **56/19**
host, reckon without one's host **265/10**

item, to be an item **139/6**
It Girls 143/3
ivory, an ivory tower **150/10**
ivory-tower, an ivory-tower existence **150/10**
ivy, 'The ivy can grow no higher than its host' **47/6**

J

jack, a cheap jack **221/6**; a **j.** in office **221/5**; before one could say **J.** Robinson **221/13**; every **J.** has his Jill **221/12**; every man **j.** of them **221/7**; I'm all right, **J. 221/4**; **J.** is as good as his master **221/9**; **j.** of all trades **221/10**; **J.** Sprat **221/11**; **J.** Tar **221/14**; **j.** up **221/17**
jack-in-the-box 221/15
jacket, an Eton jacket **193/1**
jackpot, hit the jackpot **221/16**
Jacob's, Jacob's ladder **223/15**
jail-bird 66/8
jam, a jam sandwich **177/7**; do you want **j.** on it? **178/7**; in a **j. 178/4**; it's **j.** tomorrow, **j.** yesterday, but never **j.** today! **178/8**
jam-packed 178/5
Jane, a dear Jane letter **223/5**; plain **J 223/4**
Janus, Janus, **J.**-like **225/3**
jaw, jaw away **91/9**; sock on the **j. 191/7**
jaws, out of the jaws of death **91/10**
jay-walker 68/5
jealousy, eaten up with jealousy **188/9**
Jehu, drive like Jehu **224/4**
Jekyll, a Jekyll and Hyde personality **227/12**
jelly, shake/tremble/quiver like a jelly, turn someone to **j.**, laugh like a **j. 178/16**
Jeremiah 224/6
jerry-built 222/22
Jerusalem, the Jerusalem syndrome **133/11**
jet, the jet set **153/1**
jewel, like a jewel **295/10**; shine/twinkle like a **j. 295/9**; the **j.** in the crown **295/8**
jewels, like jewels **295/10**
jigsaw, like a jigsaw puzzle **312/9**
jitters, have the jitters, give someone the **j. 128/9**
job, a dead-end job **146/8**; a hatchet **j.** 248/10; an inside **j. 272/12**; a nine-to-five **j. 34/7**; a nose **j. 89/12**; a plum **j. 184/2**; land/be offered a plum **j. 184/3**; a put-up **j. 272/13**; axe a **j. 253/2**; boot out of a **j. 190/9**; give something up as a bad **j. 273/2**; have a **j. 272/11**; it's a good **j. 272/15**; just the **j. 272/14**; the devil's own **j. 44/17**
Job's, a Job's comforter **224/9**
jobs, jobs for the boys **273/3**
Joe, Joe Public/**J.** Bloggs **222/18**

John, a dear John letter **223/5**; go to the **j. 222/2**
johns, long johns **222/1**
John Bull 221/18
joint, case the joint/casing the **j. 150/5**
joke, a blue joke **4/11**; a black **j. 7/20**; a corny **j. 47/18**; a sick **j. 135/5**
jokes, quick-fire jokes **15/5**
Jolly Roger 222/3
jolt, a severe jolt **241/17**
Joneses, keeping up with the Joneses **232/2**
joy, get no joy from **129/11**; wish someone **j. 129/10**
joyrider 281/16
joyriding, go joyriding **281/16**
jubilee, a Golden Jubilee **10/10**; a Silver **J. 10/12**
Judas, play Judas **224/12**
judge, as sober as a judge **276/10**
judgement, against one's better judgement **277/5**; a snap **j. 277/4**; cloud one's **j. 277/7**; sit in **j.** on **277/6**
juggling, juggling/a **j.** act **321/14**
jugular, go for the jugular **240/7**
juice, stew in one's own juice **181/2**
jump, for/due for the high jump **306/6**; **j.** before being pushed **306/7**; one **j.** ahead **306/12**
jump-start 304/2
junction, spaghetti junction **180/8**
jungle, the blackboard jungle, the concrete **j. 269/10**
junk, junk food **174/2**; **j.** mail, **j.** e-mail **286/18**
junkie, a Net junkie **137/8**
justice, do oneself justice, do someone/something **j. 277/8**; poetic **j. 277/9**

K

Kafka-like/Kafka-esque 229/2
kaleidoscope, like a kaleidoscope **312/10**
kangaroo, a kangaroo court **64/1**; to **k. 63/15**
keel, be on an even keel **204/14**
keep, keep someone sweet **189/3**; **k.** something low-key **160/2**; **k.** to the straight and narrow (path) **149/7**
keeper, am I my brother's keeper? **143/12**
kettle, a kettle word **324/17**; a pretty **k.** of fish **73/7**
key, a key industry **160/8**; a **k.** player **160/9**; a **k.** speech **160/7**; a skeleton **k. 112/4**; have the **k.** of the door **159/16**; the **k.** position **160/4**; the **k.** to the problem **160/3**; the **k.** word **160/6**; they can throw away the **k. 159/18**
keyed, keyed up **160/1**

measure, take someone's measure **265/11**
measures, draconian measures **226/3**
meat, it must have been meat and drink to you **180/10**; one's man **m.** is another man's poison **180/11**; the **m.** or filling in the sandwich **177/3**; there's a lot of **m.** in it **180/9**
Mecca 212/4
media, a media queen **234/9**
medicine, the medicine could be worse than the illness **137/13**
medium, a happy medium **124/11**
meltdown, a financial meltdown, a stock-market **m. 293/13**
memory, an elephant's memory **63/12**; go down **m.** lane **148/12**; have a **m.** like a sieve **171/4**
men, faceless men **86/1**; grey **m. 9/4**; **m.** in blue **4/3**
mend, be on the mend **138/9**
mental, mental **120/3**; **m.** block **120/4**
mentality, the Mandarin mentality **219/8**
mercies, leave a person to someone's tender mercies **124/2**; thankful for small **m. 275/1**
mess, a mess of potage **181/10**
message, get the message **284/18**
method, method in his madness **136/16**; socratic **m. 225/10**
methods, topsy-turvy teaching methods **213/1**
Methuselah, as old as Methuselah **225/7**
Micawber, like a Micawber/Micawberish **228/2**
micky, take the micky out of **222/15**
microscope, be put under the microscope **268/9**
Midas, the Midas touch **226/5**
middle-age, middle-age spread **189/9**
midnight, burn the midnight oil **32/7**
midsummer, midsummer madness **136/15**
Mikado, the Mikado syndrome **309/9**
milch, a milch cow **58/3**
mile, run a mile **267/14**; spot something a **m.** off **267/13**; stand/stick out a **m. 267/11**; win by a **m. 267/12**
miles, not a hundred miles away **262/8**
milestone 267/15
milk, imbibe with one's mother's milk **174/11**; it's no use crying over spilt **m. 174/8**; to **m. 174/6**; **m.** and water **174/9**; **m.** teeth **92/7**; mother's **m. 174/11**; the **m.** of human kindness **174/7**
mill, go through the mill, put somebody through the **m. 281/3**
millions, the dumb millions **132/2**

millstone, carry a millstone round one's neck **95/6**
mincemeat, make mincemeat of someone **180/12**
mind, a butterfly mind **77/2**; a grasshopper **m. 77/2**; a closed **m. 118/8**; an open **m. 118/8**; a Rolls-Royce **m. 231/6**; be driven out of one's **m. 118/5**; be easy in **m. 119/14**; be in one's right **m. 118/4**; bear/keep in **m. 119/8**; broaden the **m. 119/23**; call to **m. 118/10**; cast one's **m.** back **118/11**; change one's **m. 119/2**; cross one's **m. 119/9**; get something out of one's **m. 119/16**; have a good **m. 118/3**; have a **m.** as sharp as a razor/a razor-sharp **m. 120/1**; have a **m.** like a cesspool/cesspit/sewer **120/2**; have a **m.** like a steel trap **119/24**; have a **m.** of one's own **118/13**; have a one-track **m. 256/17**; have in **m. 118/7**; have something on one's **m. 119/11**; have something imprinted on one's **m. 119/18**; know one's (own) **m. 118/12**; leap to **m. 308/13**; make the **m.** boggle, the **m.** boggles **119/22**; make up one's **m. 118/2**; **m.** over matter **118/1**; **m.** you **119/3**; not to know one's own **m. 118/12**; of one **m. 119/5**; one's **m.** goes blank **118/6**; out of one's **m. 118/5**; prey/weigh on one's **m. 119/11**; put/give one's **m.** to **119/7**; put someone's **m.** at rest/at ease **119/13**; set one's **m.** on **119/4**; slip one's **m. 119/10**; speak one's **m. 119/19**; take one's **m.** off something **119/17**; to my **m. 119/6**
mind's, in one's mind's eye **87/23**
minds, be in two minds **119/1**
minefield, a minefield, **m.** of emotion, legal **m.**, like walking through a **m. 247/16**
mint, in mint condition **291/7**
miracle, nothing short of a miracle **41/5**
mirrors, mirrors of the universe, natural/man-made **m.** of the universe **168/6**
misery, put someone out of his misery **128/17**
mist, shrouded in mist **40/1**
model, a role model **318/13**
mole 62/6
moment, a red-letter moment **2/16**; the **m.** of truth **33/6**; the psychological **m. 33/7**; unguarded **m. 33/4**
moments, have its moments **33/5**
Monday, Black Monday **30/10**; **M.** morning feeling **30/9**
Mondeo, Mondeo man **141/11**
money, a money spinner **289/5**; be after the big **m. 289/17**; black **m. 289/8**; blow one's **m.** on something **290/2**; blue one's **m. 3/6**; coin **m. 291/1**; conscience **m. 122/3**;

easy **m. 289/11**; electronic/hard/paper **m. 289/14**; fork out **m. 290/11**; for my **m. 290/12**; funny **m. 289/7**; have **m.** stick to one's fingers **101/13**; in the **m.**/be rolling in **m.**, be made of/awash in **m. 289/2**; knock some **m.** off **289/15**; launder **m./m.** laundering **290/4**; like taking **m.** from blind beggars **290/13**; **m.** burns a hole in one's pocket **197/13**; **m.** down the drain **289/1**; **m.** for jam **178/6**; **m.** for old rope **290/6**; **m.** is no object **290/5**; **m.** is tight **289/4**; put one's **m.** on something/someone **290/8**; put one's **m.** where one's mouth is **290/7**; rake in the **m. 252/11**; ready **m. 289/10**; serious **m. 289/13**; smart **m. 289/12**; spend **m.** like water **289/16**; throw good **m.** after bad **290/1**; throw **m.** at something **290/3**

monkey, get one's monkey up **64/5**; have a **m.** on one's back **64/8**; make a **m.** of **64/4**; **m.** business **64/7**; **m.** tricks **64/3**; **m.** with **64/2**

monkeys, the three wise monkeys **259/10**

monster, a Frankenstein monster **229/1**

month, a month of Sundays **30/13**

Montezuma's, Montezuma's revenge **231/4**

Monty, go the full Monty **223/3**

mood, a black mood **7/6**; **m.** food **174/5**

moon, be over the moon **24/16**; live on the **m. 25/1**; once in a blue **m. 3/8**

moonlight, do a moonlight/a **m.** flit **25/2**

moonlighting 25/3

moral, a moral certainty **122/4**; a **m.** victory **122/6**; **m.** support **122/5**

morals, have the morals of an alley-cat **55/11**

morning, Monday morning feeling **30/9**; **m.** breath **32/10**

moth, like a moth (that flies) round a light **77/5**

moth-eaten, moth-eaten ideas **77/6**

mother, mother and father of **141/20**; **m.** tongue **141/15**; the **M.** of Parliaments **236/8**

mother's, darling **141/17**; imbibe with one's **m.** milk **174/11**; on the **m.** side **141/2**

mother-complex 141/16

motherhood, like motherhood, we are all for it **141/14**

motion, table a motion **165/13**

mountain, a butter mountain **176/4**; a **m.** of red tape **2/15**; make a **m.** out of a molehill **62/7**

mouse, a little mouse, as quiet/timid as a **m. 60/1**; a **m.** potato **185/6**

mousetrap, mousetrap cheese **60/3**

moustache, a toothbrush moustache **172/14**; sport a **m. 298/12**

mouth, a big mouth **90/18**; a loose **m. 90/23**; down in the **m. 90/17**; foam at the **m. 91/5**; make one's **m.** water **91/4**; open one's **m.** too wide **91/3**; rosebud **m. 46/6**; shoot off one's **m. 90/19**; stand convicted out of one's own **m. 90/24**; the horse's **m. 57/5**

mouths, out of the mouths of babes and sucklings **91/6**

mouthful 90/20

movement, a pincer movement **240/17**

movers, movers and shakers **285/7**

MP, lobby an MP **236/12**

muck, to rake up the muck **17/18**

muck-raking 17/18

mud, fling/sling mud at someone **18/3**

mudslinger 18/3

mudslinging 18/3

mug, mug up **169/5**

mug's, a mug's game **297/17**

mule, as stubborn as a mule **57/18**

multitude, cover a multitude of sins **274/15**

mum, a gymslip mum **192/2**

mumbo jumbo 217/1

murder, shout blue murder **3/11**

muscle, carry a lot of muscle **113/2**; **m.** in **113/3**; not to move a **m. 113/1**; use one's **m. 113/2**

muscle-bound 113/4

museum, museum piece **150/14**

mushroom, to mushroom **185/9**

music, canned music **316/10**; face the **m. 315/2**; **m.** to one's ears **315/1**

mustard, as keen as mustard **182/6**; cut the **m.**/not cut the **m. 182/7**

muster, pass muster **279/9**

mutton, as dead as mutton **180/14**; **m.** dressed as lamb **180/15**

myopia, intellectual myopia **134/1**

mystery, shrouded in mystery **40/1**

N

nail, as dead as the nail in a coffin **250/11**; drive a **n.**/another **n.**/a final **n.** into someone's coffin **250/10**; hit the **n.** on the head **251/2**; pay on the **n. 250/9**

nails, as hard as nails **250/8**

name, a bad name, give someone a bad **n. 220/2**; a double-barrelled **n. 259/3**; a household **n. 220/18**; clear one's **n. 220/8**; drag someone's **n.** through the mud, one's **n.** is mud **220/19**; have a **n.** for **220/3**; in heaven's **n. 42/3**; in the **n.** of **220/12**; know by **n. 220/6**; lend one's **n.** to **220/11**; live on one's **n. 36/21**; maiden **n. 220/16**; make a **n.** for oneself **220/5**; one's good

n. 255/1; a **n.** cruncher 255/2; one's **n.** is up 255/4; take care of **n.** one 255/5
numbers, in round numbers 255/8
nut, a hard nut to crack 186/7; off one's **n.** 186/5
nuts, be nuts 186/5; be **n.** about someone 186/2; drive someone **n.** 186/4; the **n.** and bolts 251/4
nut-case 186/6
nutshell, put in a nutshell 186/8

O

oath, the Hippocratic Oath 227/2
oats, sow one's wild oats 47/19
object, an object lesson 263/9
observation, a razor-sharp observation 173/9
obvious, be blindingly obvious 131/9
Occam's, Occam's razor 231/2
occupation, a blind-alley occupation 131/7
odds, pay over the odds 293/10
odour, an odour of sanctity 273/16
Oedipus, the Oedipus complex 227/1
off-day 30/17
offensive, go on the offensive 240/2
offering, a peace offering 242/3
off-hand 98/15
office, office rage 126/16
official, a tin-pot official 171/13
ohnosecond, be struck by the ohnosecond 33/8
oil, midnight oil 32/7; no **o.** painting 269/7; palm **o.** 100/18; pour **o.** on troubled waters 12/17
old-maidish 280/5
olive, the olive branch 50/21
omelette, you can't make an omelette without breaking eggs 175/14
once, once and for all 257/15
once-over, give someone/something the once-over 257/16
one, back to square one 257/3; be at **o.** 257/14; be the last **o.** to 256/16; from day **o.** 257/2; go **o.** better 256/19; it's all **o.** to him 257/1; **o.** in a thousand 262/9; **o.** over the eight 260/13; **o.** too many for someone 256/15; take **o.** with another 256/22
one-man, a one-man band 257/5
one-night, a one-night stand 32/9
one-off 256/21
one-sided 256/18
one-track, have a one-track mind 256/17
onions, know one's onions 185/8
open-air, open-air planning 12/8
opera, it/the opera isn't over till the fat lady/someone sings 320/7; soap **o.** 173/6

operation, a Caesarean operation 225/11; a cloak and dagger **o.** 194/2; a domino-type of **o.** 309/7; like a military **o.** 241/5
operator, a fly-by-night operator 32/8
opinions, golden opinions 10/6
opportunity, a golden opportunity 10/2; jump at an **o.** 306/7
Oprah, the Oprah effect 231/10
orange, a sucked orange 183/1; squeeze the **o.** until the pips squeak 182/13
oratory, soap-box oratory 173/7
order, in apple-pie order 183/10; the **o.** of the day 31/16; the pecking **o.** 69/15
orders, give someone his/her marching orders 240/14; take holy **o.** 274/5
organization, a penny-farthing organization 292/3
ostrich, like an ostrich (with its head in the sand), **o.**-like 72/5; **o.** belief. **o.** policy 72/5
Othello's, Othello's syndrome 227/10
out at elbows 96/13
out-of-body, an out-of-body experience 80/7
out-of-pocket, out-of-pocket expenses 197/5
outskirts, on the outskirts 191/22
oven, as hot as an oven 172/3
overboard, go overboard 204/11
owl, a night owl 71/12; a solemn **o.** 71/11; as wise as an **o.**/a wise old **o.** 71/10
oyster, as close as an oyster, as close as a Kentish **o.** 74/11
Ozymandias, remember Ozymandias 226/10

P

pace, at a snail/s pace/at a snail-like **p.** 78/13
pack, a pack of lies 122/11; a rat **p.** 60/9
packet, make a packet/cost a **p.** 293/1
pages, thumb through the pages of a book 101/9
pain, a pain in the neck, be the biggest **p.** in the backside 136/1; no **p.**, no gain 135/12; **p.** hits someone like a sledgehammer 252/5; spare someone **p.** 135/16
pains, at pains/take **p.** to 135/15; growing **p.** 136/2
paint, as interesting as/like watching paint dry 269/6
painted, not as black as one is painted 7/8
painting, no oil painting 269/7
pair, have only one pair of hands 97/5; like a **p.** of bellows 253/14; not to touch someone/something with a **p.** of tongs 252/6; show a clean **p.** of heels 108/9
Pale, beyond the Pale 210/7
pall, hang over something like a pall, **p.** of dust/darkness/smoke hangs over something, throw a **p.** of gloom over something 40/2

period 265/6

person, a person of family 140/6; step into another p.'s shoes 190/3

personality, a Jekyll and Hyde personality 227/12

pest, a squeegee pest 79/1

pet, a pet hate/aversion 126/10; p. name 52/11

petard, hoist with his own petard 248/8

Peter, rob Peter to pay Paul 222/4

Peter Pan 222/5

petrel, a stormy petrel 70/19

petticoat, petticoat government 192/3

pew, take a pew 273/9

Philadelphia, a Philadelphia lawyer 276/11

Philistine 219/2

phoenix, like a phoenix from the ashes, emerge like a p., reappear like a p. 71/8

phoenix-like 71/8

phone, be glued to the phone 270/4

phrase, coin a phrase 291/6; a stock p. 217/3

pick, the pick of the bunch 47/11

pickle, in a pickle, in a nice/fine p. 182/8

picnic, it's a picnic, no p. 187/11

pickpocket, a pickpocket government 197/9

picture, a perfect picture, as pretty as a p. 168/2; paint a gloomy/sad/bleak/worrying p. 269/5; put someone in the p., do you get the p.? 167/15; see/look at the whole p. 167/14; the p. of health 168/3

picture-perfect 168/2

picture-pretty 168/2

pie, as sweet as pie 180/3; eat humble p. 180/1; p. in the sky 179/16

piece, a museum piece 150/14; a nasty p. of work 272/8; a p. of cake 179/3; a p. of Jesuitry 224/14; a p. of skirt 191/18; give someone a p. of one's mind 119/20; like holding a p. of history 267/19; like making contact with a p. of history 267/19

pieces, fall/go to pieces 128/7; pick up the p. 128/8; thirty p. of silver 295/7

pig, a male chauvinist pig 59/8; a p. in a poke/buy a p. in a poke 59/12; eat like a p., as greedy as a p. 59/9; like a stuck p. 59/6; p. it 59/10

pigs, pigs in clover 59/11

pigeon-hole, to pigeon-hole, put someone into a p. 68/12

pig-headed 59/7

pikestaff, as plain as a pikestaff 248/12

pile, a pile of junk 169/2

pill, a bitter pill to swallow 137/15; a p. popper 137/10; sugar the p. 178/9

pillar, a pillar of society 158/9; a p. of strength 158/10; from p. to post 158/8

pillow, pillow talk 164/10

pillow-talk, fish for pillow-talk information 164/10

pilot, a sky pilot 278/16; a p. scheme 279/1; drop the p. 278/17

pimples, goose pimples 70/11

pin, as neat/clean as a new pin 200/11; like pulling the p. from a grenade 247/15

pins, for two pins 258/3; not to give two p. for someone 258/3; p. and needles 200/12

pincer, a pincer movement 240/17

pinch, feel the pinch 130/6; take with a p. of salt 181/16

pincher, a penny pincher 292/1

pink, pink of condition/in the p. 9/14; p. of perfection 9/13

pink-pounder 9/20

pipe-line, in the pipe-line 158/8

pips, squeeze until the pips squeak 182/13

Pipsqueak 222/24

pistol, hold a pistol to someone's head 244/1

pitch, at fever pitch 132/10; carve out a p. 152/9

pity, more's the pity 124/3

place, all over the place 208/17; a p. in the sun 209/4; be in the right/wrong p. at the right/wrong time 29/9; come to the right p. 209/9; fall into p. 209/6; in p., out of p. 208/16; keep someone in his p. 208/18; know a p. like the back/palm of one's hand 100/9; know one's p. 209/3; not to be one's p. to 209/2; one's p. of work becomes a battle-ground 239/7; put a p. on the map 268/6; put someone in his p. 208/19

places, go places 209/8; in high p. 209/7

plague, a plague on both your houses 132/18; avoid like the p. 132/16; p. someone 132/15; sweep across like a p./spread like the p. 132/17

plan, shelve a plan 167/1

planning, open-air planning 11/14

plans, go cool on plans 20/16; sell p. to the voters 283/5; unveil p. 196/8

plaster, use as a sticking plaster 137/16

plate, be handed something on a plate 170/2; enough on one's p. 170/1

play, a cloak and dagger play 194/1; as good as a p. 318/9; child's p. 142/2; foul p. 299/12; p. along with 299/3; p. down 298/17; p. fast and loose 299/5; p. hard to get 298/18; p. havoc with 299/8; p. it cool 299/7; p. one person off against another 299/10; p. oneself in 298/15; p. safe 299/1; p. someone up 298/16; p. upon someone's feelings, sympathy, etc. 299/11; p. up to 299/2

played, played out 299/4

player, a key player **160/9**; an unseeded **p. 48/18**

players, seeded players **48/18**

pleading, special pleading **276/8**

plot, lose the plot **287/12**; the **p.** thickens **287/13**

plug, pull the plug on someone, pull the **p. 254/3**; pull the **p.** on something **254/4**

plum, a plum role/job/post, land/be offered a **p.** job **184/2**

plunge, take the plunge **305/18**

poacher, the poacher turned gamekeeper **280/3**

pocket, dig into one's pocket, dig deep into one's **p. 197/10**; have someone in one's **p. 198/2**; hit the **p. 197/6**; in **p.**/out of **p. 197/5**; in one another's **p. 198/1**; line one's **p. 197/7**; pick someone's **p. 197/8**; **p.** something **197/14**

po-faced 85/17

point, a Blimpish point of view **230/9**; a brownie **p. 8/14**; a sore **p. 136/11**; be close to breaking **p. 128/6**; hammer a **p.** home **251/13**; make one's **p. 265/8**; reaching breaking **p. 128/6**

points, win on points **302/8**

point-blank, a point-blank refusal **244/2**; tell someone **p. 244/2**

poison, look like poison at someone **189/12**; name your **p. 189/14**; spit **p. 189/13**

poison-pen, a poison-pen letter **269/14**

poker, a poker face **311/2**; as stiff as a **p. 252/13**

policeman, a sleeping policeman **125/5**

policemen, burnt-out policemen **47/13**

politician, a budding politician **47/13**

policies, blood and iron policies **114/4**; go cool on **p. 20/16**; Robin Hood **p. 228/3**

policy, a scorched-earth policy **16/9**; a zero-tolerance **p. 255/11**; ostrich **p. 72/5**; the **p.** of the big stick **51/2**; the stick and carrot **p. 185/7**

politics, parish pump politics **273/13**; shop-floor **p. 283/1**

poll, a straw poll **48/7**; rig the **p. 237/2**

poodle, nobody's poodle **54/10**

popper, a pill popper **137/10**

porridge, like swimming through porridge **180/7**

portrait, chocolate-box portrait **178/14**

position, jockey for position **281/6**; the key **p. 160/4**

possession, possession is nine-points of the law **261/1**

possum, play possum **62/4**

post, a plum post **184/2**

postcard-blue 3/5

postcode, the postcode lottery **311/10**

pot, a **p.** of money **171/11**; a **p.** shot **171/12**; a/the **p.** of gold at the end of the rainbow **294/15**; go to **p. 171/5**; in the melting **p. 171/9**; keep the **p.** boiling **171/7**; **p. 171/14**; take **p.** luck **171/6**; the **p.** calling the kettle black **171/10**

pots, have pots of money **171/11**

potato, a couch potato **185/5**; drop something like a hot **p.**, be handed a hot **p.**, a political hot **p.**, be thrown like a hot **p. 185/4**

pot-belly 103/6

pot-boiler 171/8

pound, have one's pound of flesh **110/14**; make a quick **p. 292/10**; the grey **p. 9/7**

pounds, pile on the pounds, shed **p. 189/5**

poverty, a poverty trap **248/6**

powder, keep one's powder dry **244/10**

power, a power house **233/8**; a **p.** nap, **p.** breakfast, lunch, etc. **233/3**; a **p.** partnership/a **p.** couple **233/2**; a second-class **p. 233/5**; do one the **p.** of good **233/7**; flower **p. 46/1**; grey **p. 9/6**; **p.** dressing **233/6**; pester **p. 233/1**; the **p.** behind the throne **235/13**; the **p.** of the pink pound **9/19**; thirst for **p. 233/4**; trade on the trappings of **p. 233/4**

powers, draconian powers **226/3**

power-hungry 233/4

power-mad 233/4

prairie, spread like a prairie fire **15/8**

praises, sing someone's praises **316/12**

pregnancy, gymslip pregnancy **192/2**

prejudice, prejudice has no sell-by date **283/6**; without **p. 278/2**

presence, presence of mind **119/21**; round-the-clock **p. 34/5**

president, run for president **308/6**

press, a good/bad press **286/1**; a **p.** campaign **286/3**; the gutter **p. 286/2**

pressure, like a pressure cooker **172/1**; peer **p.**/peer-group **p. 271/13**; snap under **p. 128/5**

price, a price war **238/7**; pay the **p.**/a heavy **p. 293/2**

prices, prices have gone through the roof **157/20**; **p.** shoot up like a rocket **314/4**; sky-high **p. 24/10**; slash **p. 293/3**

pride, be someone's pride and joy **129/9**; pocket one's **p. 197/16**; **p.** of place **209/5**; swallow one's **p. 123/14**

priest, high priest **273/8**; unfrock a **p. 192/1**

prime, the prime of life **35/2**

primrose, the primrose path **46/12**

prince, the prince of liars **234/11**
princess, feel like a princess **234/14**; the People's **P. 234/15**
print, the small print **277/12**
prison, like a prison, like being in a **p. 150/13**
problem, the Patsy problem **232/1**; the revolving-door **p. 159/13**; wrestle with a **p. 302/10**
problems, have teething problems **134/2**
profession, the oldest profession **273/4**
profile, keep a low profile **269/2**; raise one's **p. 269/3**
progress, snail-like progress **78/3**
proof, the proof of the pudding is in the eating **180/5**
prophets, prophets of doom **43/11**
proposal, put a proposal on the table **165/12**; shelve a **p. 167/1**
prose, purple prose **9/11**
prostitute, an InterCity prostitute **282/7**
prune, to prune **184/10**
prunes, prunes and prisms **184/11**
p's, mind one's p's and q's **286/16**
psychobabble 216/11
public, give public airing to something **11/13**; in the **p.** eye **87/22**; Joe **P. 222/18**; out of the **p.** purse **198/8**; sell something to the **p. 283/5**
pudding, over-egg the pudding **175/15**
puff, disappear in a puff of smoke **15/13**
pulp, pulp fiction, a **p.** magazine, a **p.** novel **287/10**
pump, the parish pump/parish-**p.** politics **273/13**
pumpkin, the pumpkin has not turned into a coach **186/2**
Punch, as pleased as Punch **228/9**; play **P.** and Judy over something **228/10**
punch, beat someone to the punch **302/6**; pack a **p. 302/5**
punches, pull one's punches **302/4**
punishments, draconian punishments **226/3**
pup, sell someone a pup **54/12**
puppet, a puppet **320/8**
puppy, a puppy, a young **p. 54/13**; **p.** love **54/15**
puppy-fat 54/14
purdah, be/live/keep someone in purdah **167/6**
purple, born in the purple, marry into the **p.**, raised to the **p. 9/10**
purposes, at cross purposes **122/15**
purse, dig (deep) into one's purse **198/6**; out of the public **p. 198/8**; put up a **p. 198/7**; you cannot make a silk **p.** out of a sow's ear **59/14**

purse-proud 198/3
purse-strings, hold the purse-strings **198/4**; loosen one's **p. 198/5**
pussy-foot 56/8
put, put someone wise to **123/4**
putty, as soft as putty, like **p. 253/10**; be **p.** in someone's hands **253/9**
puzzle, like a puzzle/like a jigsaw **p.**/like piecing together a **p. 312/9**
pyjamas, the cat's pyjamas **56/2**

Q

quack, a cyber quack **278/9**
quarrel, patch up a quarrel **200/8**
quarter, have a bad quarter of an hour **256/1**; no **q.** was given **256/2**
queen, a drag queen **234/10**; a media **q. 234/9**; **q.** it **234/8**; to feel like **q. 234/7**
Queen Anne, as dead as Queen Anne/**Q. A.** is dead **229/11**
Queen's, Queen's English **215/5**
question, a question of time **29/1**; be open to **q.**, an open **q. 264/11**; call into **q. 264/8**; beg the **q. 281/11**; out of the **q. 264/10** place a **q.** mark over something, a big **q.** mark is hanging over something **264/9**; pop the **q. 264/12**; the big **q. 264/6**; the million/64 million dollar **q. 292/8**; the **q.** of the hour **32/19**; the West Lothian **Q. 210/5**
questions, ask me no questions and I'll tell you no lies **264/4**; fire off **q. 14/11**; hard/searching **q. 264/7**; with no **q.** asked **264/5**
queue, jump the queue **153/5**
quick, cut to the quick **102/14**
quick-fire, quick-fire gags/jokes/verses **15/5**
quick-witted 120/9
quirk, a quirk of fate **41/3**

R

rabbit, produce/pull the rabbit out of the hat **60/15**
rabbits, breed like rabbits **60/16**
race, a race against time **28/17**; an elephant **r. 63/13**; **r.** relations **139/2**; the rat **r. 60/8**
rag, a red rag to a bull, like a red **r.** to someone **2/11**; as limp as a **r.** doll/like a **r.** doll **312/6**; feel like a wet **r.**/like a washed-out **r. 201/16**; the local **r. 201/10**
rags, from rags to riches **202/2**; glad **r. 202/1**
ragbag 201/12
rage, air rage **126/17**; all the **r. 126/14**; road **r.**, office **r.**, supermarket-trolley **r.**, bus-stop-queue **r.**, cigarette-smoke **r. 126/16**;

shame, a crying shame **127/8**; put (someone) to s. **127/9**; s. on you! **127/7**

Shangri-la, like Shangri-la **212/12**

share, bullish/bearish of a share **65/5**; the lion's s. **64/16**

shares, shares shoot up like a rocket **314/4**

shark, a shark, circle around someone like a s. smelling blood/like a s. with its prey **75/5**

sheep, as silly as a sheep **58/10**; count s. **58/12**; like being savaged by a dead s. **58/15**; separate the s. from the goats **58/13**; the black s. (of the family) **7/12**

sheet, as white as a sheet **6/3**; the s. anchor **205/4**

shelf, be on the shelf **166/17**

shelf-life 166/18

shell, come out of one's shell **63/1**; hit like a s. **246/18**; withdraw into one's s. **63/1**

shell-shocked 247/2

shelve, shelve (a plan or proposal) **167/1**

shepherd, to shepherd **280/1**; s. one's flock **280/2**

shift, a graveyard shift **39/19**

shilling, cut off with the shilling **292/5**

ship, go down with the ship **203/5**; jump s. **306/10**; run a tight s. **203/6**; the s. of the desert **203/7**; when my s. comes home **203/2**

ships, ships in the night/s. that pass in the night **203/3**

shipshape, all shipshape **203/1**

shirt, a stuffed shirt **192/13**; keep one's s. on **192/9**; put one's s. on something **192/10**; without a s. to one's back **192/12**

shirty 192/14

shivers, give one the shivers **21/5**; send s. down one's spine **104/20**

shock, brace yourself for a shock **193/11**

shockwaves, send shockwaves through something **13/18**

shoe, where the shoe pinches **190/1**

shoes, a dead man's shoes **190/4**; in another's s. **190/5**; shake in one's s. **190/6**; step into another person's s. **190/3**

shoe-string, on a shoe-string **190/2**

shoot, a fashion shoot **246/4**; s. down **246/7**; s. off **246/11**

shooting, a shooting gallery **246/5**

shop, a bucket shop **282/18**; all over the s. **282/17**; a tuck s. **282/19**; come to the wrong s. **282/15**; mind the s. **282/13**; to s. **282/11**; s. around **283/2**; s. floor, s.-floor politics **283/1**; shut up s. **282/16**; talk s. **282/12**; the other s. **282/14**

shoplifting 282/20

short, short and curlies **83/20**

short-handed 97/2

shot, a long shot **245/15**; a Parthian s. **219/1**; a pot s. **171/12**; a s. across the bows **204/16**; a s. in the arm **246/1**; a s. in the dark **245/16**; be s. of someone **246/3**; have a s. **246/2**; like a s. **245/14**

shots, call the shots **245/18**; no more s. in the locker **245/17**

shot-gun, a shot-gun marriage **139/11**

shoulder, a shoulder to cry on **95/16**; give it to someone straight from the s. **95/10**; give someone the cold s. **95/11**; put one's s. to the wheel **95/15**; s. out **95/8**; stand s. to s. with someone **95/17**; straight from the s. **95/10**

shoulders, carry/have on one's shoulders **95/7**; have broad s. **95/13**; rub s. with **95/12**

shouting, be all over bar the shouting **127/6**

show, a show of hands **100/7**; floor s. **161/13**; get the s. on the road **317/7**; give the s. away **317/4**; good s. **317/6**; it's a bad s. **317/6**; run the s. **317/5**; s. willing **123/1**; steal the s. **317/2**; the s. must go on **317/3**

show-down 317/9

shrift, give someone short shrift **273/14**

shutters, put up the shutters, this is where the s. come down **161/6**

shuttle, shuttle diplomacy **280/15**

Shylock, a Shylock **227/9**

sick, be sick and tired **135/6**

sick-building, sick-building syndrome **133/8**

sickies, serial sickies **135/7**

side, bat on that side of the wicket **301/8**; born the wrong s. of the blanket **165/2**; brush to one s. **172/10**; come down on the right/wrong s. of the fence **162/9**; err on the right s. **122/7**; know which s. one's bread is buttered **176/16**; laugh on the other s. of one's face **85/15**; like the dark s. of the moon **25/4**; look on the black s. **7/6**; on the father's/mother's s. **141/2**; on the right s. of the law **275/6**; on the s. of the angels **43/3**; on the wrong s. of the law **275/6**; sunny s. up **24/15**; the other s. of the coin **291/3**; the wrong/right s. of fifty **262/2**

sides, two sides of the same coin **291/4**

side-show, only a side-show **317/8**

sight, a sight for sore eyes **136/12**; at first s. **43/3**; second s. **258/14**

sights, set one's sights on something **244/3**

sign, a tell-tale sign **287/11**

signature, a signature dish **170/3**

silence, a deafening silence, the s. was deafening **131/14**; buy someone's s. **283/3**

silhouette, have a stick-insect silhouette **78/12**

silk, as soft/smooth as silk **199/11**; take s.